HOUSE OF COMMONS SESSIONAL PAPERS OF THE EIGHTEENTH CENTURY

We wish to express our thanks and appreciation for the kind permission of the **Librarian of the Department of Industry** *to reproduce the documents contained in this volume.*

HOUSE OF COMMONS SESSIONAL PAPERS of the EIGHTEENTH CENTURY

Edited by SHEILA LAMBERT

Volume 134

George III

Public Records 1799-1800 part 2

SR Scholarly Resources Inc.
1508 Pennsylvania Avenue · Wilmington, Delaware 19806

Library of Congress Catalog Card Number: 74-33160
House of Commons Sessional Papers of the Eighteenth Century

Publisher's Note

Every effort has been made to locate the best preserved and most legible copy of the original documents, some of which have suffered severely from the ravages of time. The facsimiles faithfully reflect the condition of the originals. New and precise technology has been employed in the reproduction process to enhance readability yet preserve the flavor of the original to the best of our ability.

The papers are reproduced exactly including leaves carrying the license to print and blank pages where they occur. Printing in color has been avoided and certain oversized originals have been reduced to facilitate reproduction and uniformity in binding. Pages that have been so reduced are marked with an asterisk adjoining the page number.

International Standard Book Numbers

Complete set George I 0-8420-2014-4
Complete set George II 0-8420-2015-2
Complete set George III 0-8420-2016-0
List Volume I, 1715-1760 0-8420-1911-1
List Volume II, 1761-1800 . . . . 0-8420-1912-X
THIS VOLUME 0-8420-2031-4

Scholarly Resources, Inc.
Wilmington, Delaware
Printed in the United States of America
by McGregor & Werner, Inc.

HOUSE OF COMMONS PAPERS
GEORGE III

Volume 134

Contents

A

OTLAND.

finished.

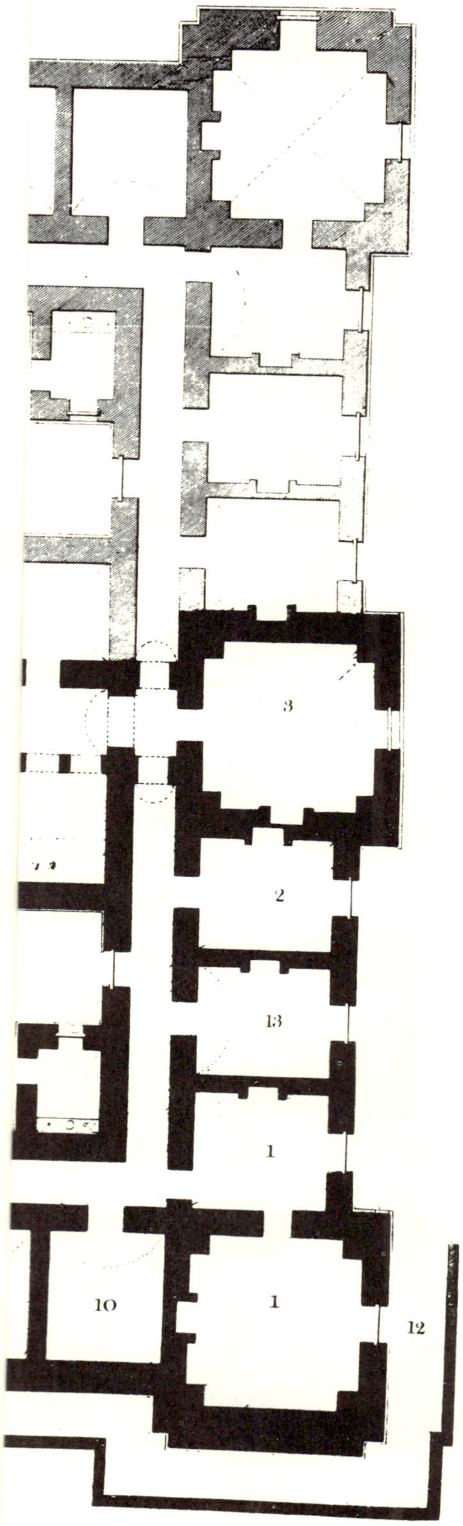

Engraved by James Basire

1*

B

SCOTLAND.

be finished.

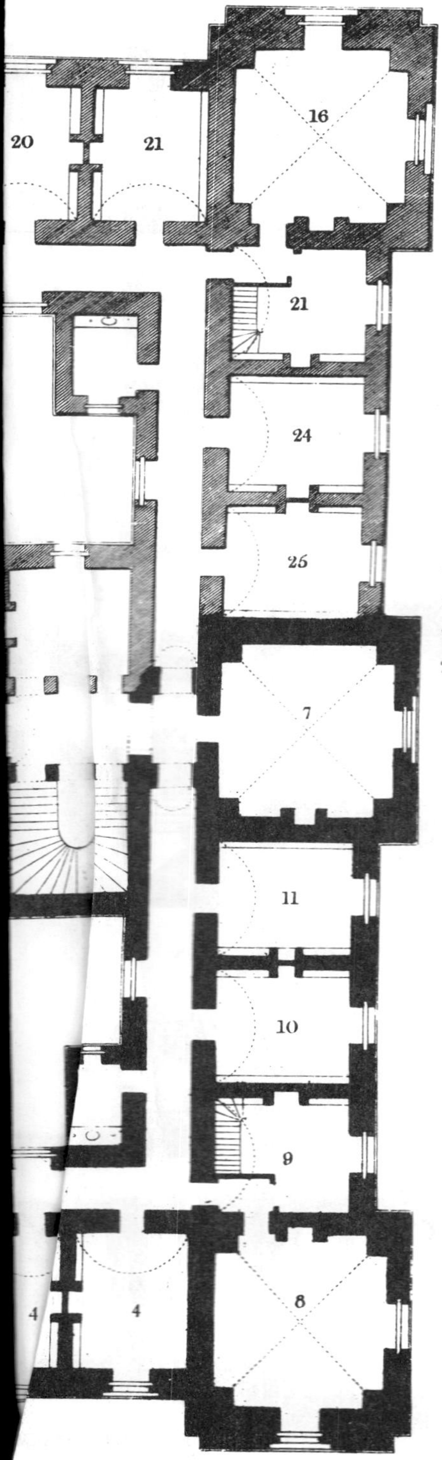

REFERENCES

to the unfinished Part of the Building.

16 *Extractors Office.*
17 *Writers Hall.*
18 *Offices for Principal Clerks of Session.*
19 *D^o......for Under D^o....................*
20 *D^o......for Registration.*
21 *D^o......for Extractors.*
22 *Commissary.*
23 *Sealing Office.*
24 *Office for Principal Clerk of Sasines.*
25 *D^o......for Under D^o....................*

Engraved by James Basire.

APPEND

SCOTLAND

Order

Engraved by James Basire.

SCOTLAND.

GENERAL REPOSITORY.

Appendix (V. a.)

Return by the Lord Clerk Regifter's Deputies for keeping the Records of SCOTLAND, to an Order of the Select Committee on the Public Records, &c. of this Kingdom; dated Martis 25° die Februarij 1800; Charles Abbot, Efq; in the Chair.

Introductory Obfervations concerning the Records of Scotland—their Foundation—Nature—and Arrangement.

Of the FOUNDATION of the Records of Scotland:

THE more antient Records of Scotland have difappeared fince the Time of Edw. I. of England; hence we are ignorant of the precife Nature of the Original Inftitution of thofe Records, as well as of the Period when that Original Inftitution took place. It is proved however, by incontrovertible Documents ftill exifting, that as early as the Year 1282 the Records of Scotland were numerous and multifarious; that they were then under the Charge of a Public Officer of eminent Rank; and that they were kept in the Royal Treafury *. We may therefore fairly conclude, that their Original Inftitution had taken place many Years antecedent to that Period.

Regarding them in their prefent State, we muft fpeak of them as eftablifhed partly by Ufage and partly by Statute. Under the former Clafs we rank thofe which have in fact been originally introduced by particular Clerks from Motives of Expediency, without any direct Legiflative Authority, as well as thofe which have been appointed by Statutes of the Legiflature now loft: Under the latter are comprehended thofe which have been eftablifhed by Acts of Parliament, that ftill appear upon our Statute Book. At prefent it feems unneceffary to enter into a particular Enumeration of the different Records which fall under each of thofe Two Claffes.

SCOTLAND. Appendix (V. a.)

The Public Officer to whom was intrufted the Keeping, and Formation too, of the Records of Scotland, deemed antiently of Public Importance, was ftiled, "Cuftos Rotulorum Regni Scotiæ †," or "Clerk "of Regifter."

In the Year 1567, we find this Officer ftiled in his Commiffion "Clerke of his Heinefs Regiftre Seffiorum "Privie Counfall and Checker Rollis." He is afterwards named ftill more minutely, "Clericus noftrorum "Regiftrorum et Rotulorum, atque Concilii et Sef-"fionis Scaccarii omniumque Generalium Conciliorum "Parliamentorumque et Ordinum Conventuum Regni."

In Terms of his Commiffion he acted as prefiding Clerk in the High Court of Parliament, in the Privy Council, in the Supreme Civil Courts of Seffion, and of Exchequer, and in the Courts of every Commiffion iffued under the Authority of the Parliament, or of the Crown; of courfe the Proceedings of thofe Courts were digefted, written out, and afterwards recorded under his Infpection; and the Original Minutes and other Documents, together with the Records of the Proceedings, were confided to his Care, and depofited in an Office of which he had the exclufive Cuftody.

To render his Controul ftill more effectual, he had the Power of appointing all the Principal Clerks employed in thofe various Departments, who were his immediate Deputies, and in that Character attended him in the Courts to which they refpectively belonged, where they officiated under his Direction.

Befides the Powers conferred on the Clerk Regifter by the Tenor of his Commiffion, other Powers were from Time to Time fuperadded by different Acts of Parliament.

On the Whole, his Office was accounted fo highly important to the Public, that it conftituted him an Officer of State, and entitled him to a feat in Parliament. Hence the Clerk Regifter, like the Privy Seal, and the other Officers of State, bears, by Courtefy, the Title of Lord.

On this Point perhaps we may feem to have faid more than the prefent Object required. Our Motive is to

* The Documents here alluded to are, 1. An Inventory printed in Mr. Rymer's Fœdera, Vol. I. Page 227. made up in the Year 1282, of many Inftruments among the Archives of Scotland relating to Tranfactions with Foreign States; to which are annexed the Titles of a few Charters. A fhort Note fubjoined to that Inventory fhews, that the other Archives of Scotland, which probably regarded the internal Polity of the Community, were even then very numerous. The Note is thus expreffed; viz. "Aliæ multæ literæ funt in Thefauraria Domini Regis "tam in pixidis cophinis, quam in facculis de quibus nihil eft hic fpecificatum." 2. Two Inventories, now in the Chapter Houfe at Weftminfter, of the Records of Scotland, drawn up Ten Years after the former, namely, in the Year 1292, under the Authority of King Edward I. of England, on Occafion of the Competition for the Crown of Scotland. The Note juft tranfcribed is in fome Degree elucidated by thofe Inventories, efpecially the laft of them, which though conceived in very general Terms, mentions no fewer than Eleven Hundred and Seventy-one Rolls, befides Four larger Rolls, confifting of One Hundred and Ten Pieces together with Thirteen Papal Bulls, Thirty Letters from Cardinals, and various detached Inftruments.

† See in Prynne's Collections, Vol. III. p. 548. a Writ by King Edward I. directed to the Bifhop of St. Andrew's, to the Conftable of Edinburgh Caftle, et "Willielmo de Dunfres Cuftodi Rotulorum Regni Scotiæ." In the Inventory of the Inftruments conveyed to Berwick on Tweed, in Obedience to that Writ of King Edward, the fame Gentleman is again named, "Cuftodi Rotulorum Regni Scotiæ." Calendars of Ancient Charters, p. 327. and Index, Anno 1629, of many Records of Charters, p. 10 of the Introduction. This Latin Defignation (Defcription) is tranflated "Clerk of Regifter."—See that Index, Page 61, N° 31. Page 67, N° 3. Page 68, N° 13. Page 74, N° 65. Page 85, N° 198. and Page 119, N° 28.

SCOTLAND.

Appendix (V. a.)

to ſhew, that by thus uniting in the Perſon of an Officer, ſo highly reſpectable, the Formation, the Superintendance, and the Cuſtody of the Records, Experience, that only ſure Guide in every Political Inſtitution, had the faireſt and fulleſt Scope, and the moſt powerful Operation; Errors and Abuſes were quickly diſcovered and corrected, Defects were perceived, and adequate Remedies provided; and the Clerk Regiſter's eminent Station in the State, muſt have given every Propoſal and Remonſtrance of his, relative to the Records, its proper Weight.

Under theſe Circumſtances the Records of Scotland were gradually brought to a regular Syſtem ſignally admirable in its Deſign.

Nature of the Records of Scotland:

A Record in Scotland ought to contain "a full and "exact Literatim Copy of the Original Deed or Inſtru- "ment recorded."

All Deeds or Inſtruments of every Kind may, if the Poſſeſſors of them chooſe, be recorded for Preſervation *. And every Deed conſtituting a Perſonal Claim of Debt, or an Obligation to perform ſome lawful Preſtation, if intended to be made the Foundation of Perſonal Diligence (Execution) either for Payment of that Debt, or Performance of that Obligation, muſt be put upon Record previouſly to Execution being iſſued on it.

But of this Syſtem the Branch of the higheſt Importance to the Kingdom regards our Real or Immoveable Property. That important Branch indeed may be conſidered as conſtituting a diſtinct and ſeparate Syſtem of itſelf, which has now ſubſiſted 182 Years. All Inſtruments requiſite to the final Conſtitution, and to the Tranſmiſſion of Real Property of every Kind, and to the Conſtitution, Tranſmiſſion, and Extinction of every voluntary Incumbrance (Mortgage) †, and every Step of legal Diligence, directed againſt ſuch Property, muſt neceſſarily be put upon Record, within certain preſcribed Periods, elſe they become invalid, ineffectual, and no better than waſte Paper.

From this particular Branch of our Syſtem, Conſequences the moſt ſalutary and beneficial, both to Individuals and to the Community, have reſulted. The Title Deeds reſpecting Real Property are connected with Certainty and Preciſion; and may, if neceſſary, be at a moderate Expenſe traced back nearly Two Centuries. The Credit of Proprietors of Real Eſtates is ſtrengthened and confirmed; becauſe though ſuch Proprietors ſhould be incumbered with Debt, yet, as the Extent of their Mortgages is exactly aſcertained, no Room is left for Exaggeration.

The ſame Syſtem is no leſs favourable to the Security of Creditors, who can never be expoſed to Hazard, unleſs through their own Inattention; and who have it in their Power to ſecure on their Debtors Real Property, and Perſonal Debts of every Denomination ‡.

From the Inventories of the Records of Scotland, to which Reference has been made above, they appear to have been antiently written in the Form of Rolls—than which a Form more inconvenient for Conſultation or Inſpection could ſcarcely be deviſed. It appears therefore, that as early as the Reign of David II. at leaſt, a Practice began to prevail of writing the Records in Books. By a Public Statute in the Year 1469, the King's Rolls and Regiſters were appointed to be put in Books; but the Accounts in Exchequer continued, this Statute notwithſtanding, to be kept in Rolls till the Year 1672, when another Act was paſſed appointing them to be likewiſe written in Books. Since that Period therefore, all the Records of Scotland have been written in the Form of Books.

The Books, in which are recorded the Inſtruments relative to the Conſtitution of the Rights to Real Property, and to Mortgages, and to their Tranſmiſſion and Extinction, and the Books of Record formed in the different Shires, which ſtill continue tranſmiſſible to the General Repoſitory, are authenticated in a Manner ſingularly peculiar, which merits particular Attention.

Thoſe Books are iſſued Blank from the Lord Regiſter's Office to the different Clerks by whom thoſe Records are to be formed; and previouſly to their being ſo iſſued, they undergo an Operation called Marking. It is performed thus: Every Folio of the Book is numbered 1, 2, 3, &c. by one of the Lord Regiſter's Deputies for keeping the Records. The Deputy, at the ſame Time, ſuperſcribes every Tenth Folio with his Name at full Length, and every intermediate Folio with the Initial Letters of his Name. A Docket is prefixed, mentioning the Diſtrict and the particular Species of Record for which the Book is intended, and containing ſome general Directions about the Manner in which the Inſtruments ought to be ingroſſed. Another Docket is ſubjoined at the End of the Book, mentioning the Number of Folios of which the Book conſiſts. Both theſe Dockets are ſubſcribed by the Deputy, and likewiſe by the Lord Regiſter's Ordinary Man of Buſineſs at Edinburgh.

The original Intention of this Operation appears to have been to prevent Interpolation and Cancellation, for by that Means a ſingle Leaf can neither be added nor abſtracted without Detection.

But it has been productive of another Effect ſingularly beneficial. It forces a regular Tranſmiſſion to the General Repoſitory of the Records ſubjected to that Operation, becauſe the preceding Book muſt, when fully written, be brought in before a new Book can be delivered out. Hence the Tranſmiſſion of thoſe Records is regular and certain; whereas without ſuch a compulſory Check, there is Reaſon to believe that many Inſtruments would never be recorded at all; that of the Books, although fairly written out, ſome ſhould be withheld, and probably altogether loſt; and that the Lord Regiſter ſhould be involved in perpetual Expenſe and Trouble, in order to furniſh the Negligent, and to force the Books of Record, that ſhould be actually ingroſſed, out of the Hands of thoſe to whom their Formation is intruſted.

The Advantage of this Solemnity becomes more ſtriking, and is more ſenſibly felt when contraſted with the Rules by which the Tranſmiſſion of the Records, not ſubjected to the Formality of Marking, is regulated, and with the Conſequences thence reſulting.

Reſpecting

---

* Although a Deed or Inſtrument ſhould not contain the uſual Clauſe of Regiſtration, it may nevertheleſs be recorded as a Probative Writ.

† We include not the Warrants of thoſe Inſtruments, viz. Charters, Diſpoſitions, and Heritable Bonds. If however any Alteration in this important Branch ſhould be deemed by any Means admiſſible, theſe Two perhaps ought likewiſe to be recorded.

‡ By the Law of Scotland a Creditor can, by a Step of Diligence, or Writ called an Inhibition, ſo attach his Debtor's Real Eſtate, even for a Claim or Debt before being finally eſtabliſhed in a Cavil of Law, as to prevent the Debtor from ſelling or mortgaging his Real Eſtate in Prejudice of the Debt ſo claimed, by any voluntary Tranſaction poſterior to the Execution of that Writ; and the Effect of this Diligence reaches to the Real Property not only belonging to the Debtor at the Time when it is executed, but likewiſe to his future Acquiſitions of ſuch Property. It is neceſſary however that the Creditor, by the uſual Form of Citation, inſtitute an Action for eſtabliſhing his Claim previouſly to his obtaining the Writ of Inhibition. By another Step of Diligence called an Adjudication, which is a Decree in Foro of the ſupreme Civil Court, a Creditor can directly ſubject his Debtor's Real Eſtate to a Perſonal Debt, even though contrary to the Debtor's Inclination; and on Proof of the Bankruptcy of the Proprietor of a Real Eſtate, ſuch Eſtate, if not entailed, will be ſold under the Authority of the Court of Seſſion, without the Proprietor's Conſent.

Respecting the Decrees of the Court of Session, and the Deeds recorded under the Authority of that Court *, it merits Observation, that in the former the various written Pleadings and Steps of Procedure; and in the latter, the Original Deeds presented for Registration, are kept and deposited in the General Register House, as well as the Books in which they are respectively recorded; and that a Copy, authenticated by the Subscription of one of the Principal Clerks of the Court, is delivered to the Party. Of those Decrees therefore, and Registered Instruments, not only the Originals themselves, but likewise the Records of those Originals, being thus preserved in Public Custody, we become possessed of Two Duplicates of the same Thing: a Formality apparently unnecessary, and attended with some Inconveniency †.

Each Book of Record has its corresponding Minute Book or Index.

Every Deed, presented in order to be recorded, ought to be immediately entered in the Minute Book, which therefore regulates the Order in which the Deeds must be recorded. Hence the Deeds necessarily enter the Record in Chronological Order, according to the Dates of their being respectively presented.

In the Minute Books of the Records of such of those Deeds as are ordained to be recorded within a certain Period posterior to their Dates, every Entry must bear its true Date prefixed, and ought to be subscribed by the Person who presents the Deed, and by him who has the forming of the Record.

On the Original Deed, after it has been recorded, a short Docket or Attestation is written and subscribed by him who forms the Record, bearing that the Deed has been recorded in such and such a Register; and the Number of the Book, and the Folios of the Book, are likewise added on all Deeds that enter the Register of Sasines.

ARRANGEMENT of the Records of Scotland:

The General Register House is admirably constructed for the Reception and Arrangement, not only of the Records still existing, but likewise of those of the same Kinds which, computing by what we now have, shall probably become transmissible for some Centuries to come. Had the original Plan been carried into complete Execution, this large, elegant, and most useful Edifice, should have consisted of Two great Divisions; viz. a circular Building inclosed in a Square one, touching each other in Four Points.

See Elevation, Plans, and Section annexed.

Of the Square Building only One Half has been finished, namely, the South Front, and a Trifle more than Half of the East and West Wings; viz. a few Feet beyond their Points of Junction with the Circular Building.

The whole Circular Building is completed.

Both Buildings consist of a sunk Story and of Two upper Stories. The Rooms in the sunk Story are paved.

The Two upper Stories are arched, and the Rooms are divided from each other by Thick Stone Walls, and are paved above those Arches. Hence no Building can be less exposed to Hazard from Fire.

No Person sleeps in any Part of the Building. The Whole is allotted for Public Purposes only.

All the Square Building, except the Front Centre Room in each Story, is possessed by the various Clerks resident in Edinburgh, connected with the different Courts of Law, and with the Formation of the various Records, made up in the Metropolis.

The whole Circular Building, together with those Two Rooms in the Centre of the Square Building, is appropriated for the ultimate Reception and Arrangement of all the Records transmissible to the General Repository.

The Circular Building consists of a large Dome separated into Two Divisions, an upper and a lower, by a Gallery paved with Stone, to which we arrive by a Stone Stair: This Gallery renders the upper Part of the Dome accessible.

In the Sunk Story, directly under the Centre of the Dome, Four different Furnaces have been constructed, from each of which proceeds a Flue running in a Spiral Direction, under the Pavement of the Dome. In those Furnaces constant Fires are burnt during Summer as well as Winter: And as the Arches, Pavements, and Division Walls of Stone, secure the Records from Fire, so those Furnaces and Flues secure them from Damp: Hence those Two capital Enemies of Books and Papers seem to be effectually excluded.

The Circular Building again consists of Two Parts, namely, the Dome just mentioned, and a Range of smaller Apartments surrounding the Dome. The Number of those smaller Apartments is Twenty-three, exclusive of the whole sunk Story, of the Space occupied by the Stairs within the Circular Building leading to the sunk Story, and to the Gallery of the Two Centre Rooms of the Square Building; and of Three Passages on the First Floor, and as many on the Second (at the Points of Contact of the Square and Circular Buildings) leading to those Two Rooms, and to Two Stairs, the one in the East, and the other in the West Wing of the Square Building, which Stairs conduct to both the great Divisions of the Edifice.

Those Three and Twenty Circular Apartments have, by Means of the Walls separating them from one another, nearly trebled the Space which, without those Walls, they could have comprehended; and it is obvious how admirably well they are adapted for the Purposes of methodical Arrangement.

The Two Centre Rooms of the Square Building, the Passages leading to them, and to the Two Stairs on the Wings, and the whole of the sunk Story may, when additional Accommodation shall become requisite, be rendered highly useful, without producing any Inconveniency or Deformity.

Without speaking at this Time of the Records of Parliament, of those of the Court of Exchequer, and of other antient Records, now not likely to increase, the Registers at present transmissible to the General Repository, are, 1. The Records of the Privy Seal—and 2. Those of the Great Seal, which Two Classes contain all Royal Charters of Lands, and other Grants by the Sovereign, authenticated by his Privy Seal and Great Seal.—3. The Records General, and Particular of Sasines.—4. The Records General, and Particular of Hornings and Inhibitions.—5. The Records of the Abbreviates of Adjudications.—6. The Records of Registrations in the Books of Council and Session - and 7. The Records of the extracted Decrees of the Court of Session; together with the Minute Books, and Indexes of the Books of Record of all those different Branches, the Records of the Great Seal excepted; and it has been already remarked, that besides

* The Registration of such Deeds is formally a Decree as much as Decrees in Foro Contentioso, with this Distinction, that the Decree of Registration proceeds on the voluntary Consent of the Party or Parties by whom the Deed is granted, expressed in the Clause of Registration; and therefore that Decree neither requires previous Citation nor admits any Opposition, and the Records of Registration have always been kept separate and distinct from those of the Decrees. By the Clause of Registration, which is now inserted in almost every Deed or Instrument of Importance executed in Scotland (Bills of Exchange, Promissory Notes, Instruments of Sasine, some Charters, and a few other Deeds excepted) the Party or Parties "Consent to the Registration hereof in the Books of Council and Session, or others competent therein to remain for Preservation;" and if necessary, that Letters of Horning on Six Days Charge and other Executorials needful, may pass and be directed hereon in due Form as Efficies; and for that Effect they constitute .... their Procurators.

† The Records of Decrees and their Warrants (that is, the original written Pleadings and Steps of Procedure) occupy alone as large a Space as that occupied by all the other Records together.

SCOTLAND.
Appendix (V. 2.)

besides the Books of Record of the Two last Branches, the Original Deeds registered, and the Warrants of the extracted Decrees of the Court of Session, are likewise deposited in the General Register House.

Of all the Records here enumerated, the Arrangement like the Recording, is perfectly Chronological, Day by Day, Month by Month, and Year by Year.

The Records of the same Nature, and for the same District, are placed together separately from the other Records; and large vacant Spaces are left after each Class, sufficient for receiving the Records of the same Class, that may be sent in during many future Years.

Having premised these introductory Observations, we proceed to answer the several Questions referred to us:

(1.) The Records of Parliament from the Year 1210 to the Year 1707, 37 Volumes; many of the Original Papers, Minutes, &c. or Warrants.

2. The Records of the Privy Seal, from 1499 to 1774, about 170 Vols.

3. The Records of the Great Seal, from about 1318 to 1788; Twelve Rolls, and more than 150 extremely large Volumes.

4. Some Records of Privy Council, from 1545 to 1644.

5. The Books of Record of the General Register of Sasines, from 1617 to 1800; more than 700 Volumes.

6. The Books of Record of the Particular Registers of Sasines, a few of which commence in 1600, but by far the greater Part in 1617, most of them have been transmitted as late as the present Month, some Two or Three Years back. They consist of about 1200 Volumes, many of which are of a large Size.

7. The Books of Record of the General Register of Hornings and Inhibitions, from 1602 to 1780; more than 1200 Volumes.

8. The Books of Record of the Particular Register of Hornings and Inhibitions, from about 1580 to different Periods (like those of the Particular Registers of Sasines); more than 600 Volumes.

9. The Books of Record of the Allowances of Apprisings, and Abbreviates of Adjudications, from 1636 till 1785; 128 Volumes.

10. The Record Books of Deeds registered in the Books of Session, from 1554 to 1789, consisting of 1390 Volumes, some of which are exceedingly large.

11. The Books of Record of the extracted Decrees of the Old Session, and of the Lords of Council and Session, from 1478 to 1789; about 2660 Volumes, many of which are very large.

The Warrants of those extracted Decrees.

12. Some antient Record Books of Exchequer, viz.

Responde Books;
Signatures;
Decrees of Exchequer;
General Account Books of Exchequer;
Accounts of Treasurers, Comptrollers, &c.;
Rentals of the King's Property;
Rentals of Feu Duties, Tax Ward Duties, &c.;
Accounts of the Thirds of Benefices;
Books of Rates;
Books relative to the Customs;
Books relative to Taxations;
Artillery and Army Accounts;
Household Accounts;
Books of the Expense of the King's Works;

These different Books relative to Exchequer Business, commence and end at very different Periods; the most antient begin in the Year 1449, the latest end in 1659; about [illegible] Volumes in all.

13. Warrants of the Elections of the Representatives of the Peers of Scotland to sit in the House of Lords of the Parliament of Great Britain, from 1707 to 1798.

Records of those Elections, from the 5th of May 1761.

14. Many Papers relative to Visitations of Universities, apparently incomplete.

15. Records of Conventions of Estates.

16. Various Papers relative to Teinds (Tythes.)

17. Records of Cautionaries in confirming Testaments.

18. Record of Cautionaries for keeping Lawburrows.

19. Record of Cautionaries for looking Arrestments.

20. Records of several Sheriffs Courts.

21. Records of a few Burrows.

22. About Fifty Protocol Books of Notaries.

23. Registers of Forfeitures.

24. A few Records relative to Ecclesiastical Business.

25. Many detached Original Charters, Royal Proclamations, &c.

(2.) The Building is situated at Edinburgh, and, as has been stated more particularly in the introductory Observations, it consists of a Dome about 50 Feet in Diameter, and of Twenty-five Apartments surrounding the Dome. See Elevation, Plans, and Section annexed.

The Dome and all those Apartments are arched; all the Apartments but One are paved above the Arches, and they are all divided from one another by thick Stone Walls; hence they are considered secure from Fire.

In the sunk Story under the Centre of the Dome are Four Furnaces, from each of which proceeds a Flue in a spiral Direction under the Pavement of the Dome. In these Furnaces large Fires are kept constantly burning. This is supposed to secure the Records from Damp.

The Building affords admirably excellent Accommodation, not only for the Records at present in the General Repository, but for those likewise which shall probably be transmitted thither for Centuries to come. It is Public Property.

(3.) Before proceeding to answer this Question, we humbly take the Liberty to premise, that the Room in the Castle of Edinburgh, where the Records of Scotland were more antiently kept, was extremely improper for that Purpose, both on account of its very confined Dimensions, and of its local Situation, within a Fortress inaccessible during all those intestine Commotions with which Scotland was formerly so often and so grievously afflicted, and exposed from the same Cause to the utmost Hazard of Fire; and that the Two Cellars below the Inner Session House, whither the Records were carried from the Castle, were not only too small, but having on one Side been sunk more than Eighteen Feet below the Level of the Ground, and a Common Sewer having past under One of the Rooms, the Records were unavoidably subjected to a great Degree of Damp, of which the bad Consequences are to be immediately stated; while at the same Time they were very far indeed from being exempted from the Hazard of Fire. The Smallness of those Apartments seems to have induced the Gentlemen who filled the Office of Clerk Register, to allow several of their Deputies to retain in their Private Custody, the Records belonging to the particular Departments in which those Deputies officiated: hence some of those Records were abstracted, some mislaid, and some lost. And in the Year 1700, all the Records then in the Private Custody of the Clerk to the Commission of Teinds, by Virtue of one of those Grants, were destroyed by Fire.

In Answer therefore to this Question, we must say, A few are totally destroyed by Damp; a few more are considerably damaged by the same Cause; the Writing in several Instances is much decayed, and some of the Books (of the Records of Parliament especially) having been frequently consulted, and handled with little Care, have been in various Parts mutilated, torn, and defaced; the greater Part by far are, speaking generally, in good Preservation.

The Records are arranged in Chronological Order; and those of each Branch are placed together; vacant Places being left after each Class of those that are likely

4 to

SCOTLAND.

Appendix (V. a.)

to increase, sufficient in general for receiving those of the same Class, that shall probably be sent in during many future Years.

(4.) In the Year 1676 an Inventory of the Records then in the Custody of the Lord Clerk Register, appears to have been made under the Authority of the Court of Session. That Inventory is inserted in the Books of Sederunt of the Court of Session; and there is a Duplicate of it in the General Register House. Not only have 124 Years elapsed since that Inventory was made, but it is found to be extremely defective; for without mentioning other material Omissions, not a single Book of the Exchequer Records is to be found in it; although of that Branch, which consists of more than 500 Volumes, the latest bears date Seventeen Years before the Inventory was made.

All the most important of our Records (those of the Great Seal excepted) and by far the greater Part of the less important, have particular Minute Books or Indexes.

To form a General Repertory of the Whole, would be a proper and important Measure. The preceding State will shew, that such a Work must be tedious and laborious, and of course expensive. With the Assistance of Two young Men, whom the present Deputy Keepers are educating in this Department with unusual Care, they conjecture that such a Repertory might be accomplished in Eighteen or Twenty Months.

Nothing is more wanted than an Index to the Records of the Great Seal. The Deputy Keepers are willing to convey to the Public, on receiving a suitable Recompence, a Manuscript Index which is their Private Property *; but they do by no Means think it such an Index as those Books require. In many Instances, the Contents of the Charters ought to be more particularly stated, and it will never be so useful as it ought to be, till accurate Alphabetical Indexes, both of Persons and Places, are formed.

To form Indexes to the Books of Record, which have never had Minute Books, would prove a most laborious Work, and of course must be attended with very great Expense indeed; and from long Experience, it can be said, that such a Work would be attended with little, if any Utility.

(5.) Two Deputies have been from Time immemorial employed under the Lord Clerk Register for taking Care of the General Repository; the General Duties of those Deputies embrace every Circumstance connected with the Preservation, the Arrangement, and the Utility of the Records.

They mark and issue the Books in which some of the most important Branches of the Records are ingrossed; they receive back the Books (after they are written out) from the different Offices to which they were issued; they exhibit the Minute Books or Indexes of the different Records, as well as the Books of Record themselves, to all who desire to consult them; they assist the Perusal of those who consult the more antient; and they discharge a variety of other Duties, which it would not be easy to enumerate.

As the Custody of the Records, and the Business thence resulting, constitutes the sole Occupation of those Deputies, their Attention to their Charge is undeviating, and their Attendance uninterrupted. As their Emoluments are commensurated by their Labours, their Diligence will not be doubted. They disregard Holidays, and their Hours of Attendance are regulated by their Work.

Each of the Deputies receives from the Public, a Net Annual Salary of £.50. sterling.

Their Fees are as follow:

Table of FEES exigible at the General Register-House:

For every Deed or Instrument inspected, 5*s*.

For marking Books of Record, at the Rate of ½*d*. for each Page, and a trifling Fraction more, or 47*s*. for a Book of 1060 Pages.

For Extracts of Deeds recorded in the Books of Session, 1*s*. each Sheet.

For Extracts of Decrees, Charters, Sasines, &c. 1*s*. 6*d*. each Sheet.

For the Use of the Minute Books of the General Register of Sasines, in order to search for Incumbrances or Titles, 10*s*.

For the Use of the Minute Books of the Particular Registers of Sasines, for the same Purpose, 10*s*.

For the Minute Books of the General Register of Inhibitions, for the same Purpose, 10*s*.

For those of the Particular Registers of Inhibitions, for the same Purpose, 10*s*.—and

For those of the Abbreviates of Adjudications, for the same Purpose, 10*s*.

For each Book, carried to the Courts of Session or Exchequer, &c. 7*s*. 6*d*.

For every certified Copy of any Deed, recorded, at the Rate of 5*s*. each Sheet (rarely called for—not a single Sheet perhaps in a whole Year.)

For Trouble preceding and at the Election of a Peer, £.5. 5*s*.—and

For making the Return, £.5. 5*s*. more—in all £.10. 10*s*.

For giving a Deed out of the Register, by Warrant of the Court of Session, 10*s*. 6*d*.

Marking on the Minute-Book, a Discharge of an Inhibition, &c. 2*s*. 6*d*. †

When employed to make Searches of Incumbrances, the Deputy Keepers charge 1*s*. for each Year of the Particular Registers of Sasines for the Shires of Edinburgh and Renfrew (because those Shires contain not only the Suburbs of the Cities of Edinburgh and Glasgow, but several large Towns and Villages besides) and 6*d*. for each Year of the other Registers of Sasines, Inhibitions, and Abbreviates of Adjudications.

For other Researches, the Deputy Keepers charge in Proportion to the Time and Labour attending them.

The Deputy Keepers regret their Inability to answer the concluding Part of this Question, with the minute Accuracy they would wish; but they will state the Amount of their Emoluments as Deputy Keepers of the Records, at the very highest Sum to which they believe they ever arose, viz. at £.200. a Year each, exclusive of their Salary, and of the Profits of their Personal Industry.

(6.) The Deputy Keepers conceive this Question to be fully answered already, under the Answer to the Question immediately preceding.

(7.) It is impossible for the Deputies to answer this Question; for many Searches and Inspections are made in their Office, with the Object and Extent of which they are totally unacquainted; they exhibit the Minute Books and Records called for, and afterwards replace them in their proper Situations, without asking any Questions, or requiring any Explanation. In ascertaining their Fees, they are satisfied with the general Affirmation of the Party.

The Amount of Emoluments mentioned above, renders, perhaps, the Impossibility of answering this Question the less material.

(8.) 1st. The more early Books of the Records of the Parliament of Scotland, are much torn, mutilated, and

* It consists of nearly 1,800 Pages closely written.

† Instances of giving out Deeds, and marking Discharges of Inhibitions, &c. occur very seldom.

and decayed: To print thofe may be faid to be a Work of Neceffity, becaufe otherwife they will foon become, in many Parts, illegible and ufelefs. To print the Whole would be a Work proper in itfelf, and of National Importance; they might perhaps extend to Twelve or Fifteen Volumes of the Size of thofe of the Rotuli Parliamentorum of England.

2d. It would be highly proper too to print the Twelve exifting Rolls, and the Firft Book of Royal Charters, becaufe the Writing of thofe Rolls, and of that Book, is much decayed.

3d. It feems right likewife to make a full and particular Inventory or Repertory at leaft, if not a Book of Record, of the detached Charters, &c. mentioned above (N° 25, under the Anfwer to Queftion 1.)

On this Head various other Objects prefent themfelves; thofe however which have been ftated are the moft neceffary and urgent, and are therefore at prefent judged fufficient.

Willm Robertfon,
Alexr Robertfon.

Edinburgh, General Regifter-Houfe,
Friday the 7th of March 1800.

Appendix (V. b.)

Return of WILLIAM ROBERTSON, Efquire, One of the Deputies of the Lord Clerk Regifter of Scotland, to certain Queftions of the Select Committee on the Public Records, &c. of the Kingdom.

Queftion 1.

" In what State are the Parliamentary Records of Scotland ?"

Anfwer:

The more early Books of the Parliamentary Records of Scotland, are in a deplorable perifhing State; the Writing in general is much decayed, and in various Parts the Books are mutilated, torn, and defaced: Thefe Obfervations apply in fome Meafure to the firft Twenty-one Volumes (now bound in Eleven) but more ftrongly to the firft Nine: the laft Fifteen Volumes, which are by much the largeft, are in no bad Condition.

Queftion 2.

" From what Period do they commence, and to what Time are they continued ?"

Anfwer:

The Firft Volume is marked on the Back "1210—1424—1474," and the Date, 1210, appears to be founded on a Paffage in the Manufcript *, the laft Volume ends abruptly, the 27th of November 1706; the Reft of the Proceedings of the Union Parliament, viz. from 27th November 1706, to 25th of March 1707, remaining to this Day unrecorded; but the Original Authenticated Minutes are preferved in the General Regifter Houfe.

Queftion 3.

" Are they complete? If not, are any Materials known of, by which they might be made fo?"

Anfwer:

They are not complete, nor is it at prefent known that there are any Materials by which they might be made complete. If any fuch do exift, they are moft likely to be difcovered by the Exertions of the Honourable Committee, which, at the fame Time that they muft infallibly be productive of other effential Advantages to the Public, will in all Probability be the Means of refcuing from Oblivion, and from Deftruction, many of the venerable Remains of the written Antiquities of this Kingdom.

Queftion 4.

" Has any Plan been thought of for printing the Parliamentary Records of Scotland ?"

Anfwer:

The prefent Lord Clerk Regifter, Lord Frederick Campbell, has long entertained Thoughts of getting thofe Records printed for the Public Benefit, as the Journals of both Houfes, and the Parliamentary Rolls had been printed in England: Lord Frederick has had this great Work in view ever fince the Year 1787, and in Compliance with his Lordfhip's earneft and repeated Injunctions, the Work was in the Year 1792 actually begun. The Perfon whom the Committee has honoured with thefe Queftions, tranfcribed with his own Hand as much of that Part of thofe Records which is moft decayed as may probably extend in print to nearly Two Folio Volumes of 600 Pages each, viz. the Firft Five Original Books, and about One Eighth Part of the Sixth; at the fame Time he caufed Three different Specimens of Print to be thrown off, that Lord Frederick, and any Gentlemen whom he might confult on the Subject, might be enabled to fix on the Specimen they fhould judge the moft proper to be adopted.

Queftion 5.

" To what Number of Volumes would fuch a Work extend, and what would be the Expenfe of printing the fame ?"

Anfwer:

Both Branches of this Queftion depend fo very much on Conjecture, that the Refpondent ventures with extreme Diffidence to anfwer it. On the firft Branch, judging it beft that the Expenfe (if the Work fhall be executed at the Public Charge) fhould fall fhort of the Eftimate rather than exceed it, he will give his Opinion on the largeft probable Scale: He therefore humbly takes the Liberty to fay, that all the Parliamentary Records of Scotland, printed with a Type as large as that of the Rotuli Parliamentorum of England, and on a Page fomewhat lefs crowded, would not exceed 15 Volumes Folio, of 600 Pages each.

The Expenfe of Printing depends on the Number of Copies, on the Quality of the Paper, and on the Size of the Type.

---

* This Date however is undoubtedly erroneous. But the Error feems to be too immaterial to merit the Attention of the Committee. In fact, on the 4th Page of Volume I. we read the following Words, written by the fame Hand which has written the reft of the Manufcript, viz.

" Heir begynnis ye Lawyis maid be King Alexr King Wilzamis Sone In the firft
" Alexandyr,
" Of the Selling of Landys.
" The Zeir of Grace Im CC and X ye Day of the Incarnatione yt is to fay Sanct Mary in lenteryne At Scone Alexr King of Scottis
" throu Common Counfale for the Profet of the Lande," &c.

Now as it is an agreed Point that King William died in the Year 1214, it is impoffible that thofe Laws of his Son King Alexander could have been enacted in the Year 1210. Some Numerical Letter therefore muft in the tranfcribing have been omitted by the Clerk after the *X*, perhaps an *L*, which would make the Year 1240, inftead of 1210.

	£.	s.	d.
If the Records of the Parliament of Scotland be printed with a Type and Page the Size of that of the "Petitiones in Parliamento," in Two Columns, with Marginal Notes, it will cost, for 500 Copies, per Sheet - - - - - - -	1	14	—
Paper for 500 Copies, 22 Quires, at 27s. per Ream, say - -	1	10	—
Per Sheet, or 4 Pages - - - - - - - - - - - -	3	4	—
Two Volumes of 600 Pages each, being together 300 Sheets, at £. 3. 4s. per Sheet, will cost, for 500 Copies - - -	960	—	—
To throwing off 500 Copies more, 300 Sheets, at 6s. - - - - - - - - - - - - £.90 — —			
To Paper for Ditto, at 30s. per Sheet, as above 450 — —			
	540	—	—
	£.1,500	—	—

Edinburgh, General Register-House,
the 17th of April, 1800.

Willm Robertson.

Appendix (V. c.)

GENERAL ACCOUNT of the Expense of the Repository for the Records in Scotland:

	£.	s.	d.
1. Price paid for the Ground on which the Building is erected, and for the adjoining Area - - - - - - - - -	3,925	17	2
2. Expense of levelling the Area, inclosing it with Wood, digging Foundations, removing Earth, building Drains, bringing in Water, and various other Incidental Expenses, previous to the Commencement, and during the Progress of the Building - - - - - - - -	1,509	12	10
3. Payments to Mr. Adam the Architect, 2½ per Cent. of the Expense of the Building, and an Allowance of £. 50. for every Journey to Scotland - - - - - - -	1,245	16	6
4. Salary to James Salisbury, Clerk to the Works for 1772 and 1789, and intermediate Years, at £. 100. Yearly -	1,800	—	—
5. Expense of Mason Work, including Brick Arches and Stone Pavement - - - - - - - - - - - - -	16,810	8	4½
6. Wood and Wright Work, including Windows, Glazing, Roofing, Slating, &c. - - - - - - - - - - - -	8,367	8	2½
7. Plumber's Accounts - - - - - - - - - - - - -	1,620	18	6
8. Plaisterer's Account - - - - - - - - - - - -	976	10	8
9. Iron Rails, Gates, and Lamp Posts - - - - - - - -	979	15	10
10. Painter's Account - - - - - - - - - - - - - -	407	3	6
Amount of the Expense - - - - - - £.	37,643	11	7

Attested by
George Home.

30th May 1800.

It was begun and finished out of Grants of Money arising from the Sale of Forfeited Estates in that Part of the Kingdom, which was paid into the Two Public Banks here, and drawn from thence, from Time to Time, as it was wanted. In the Beginning of the Work, the Money passed from the Banks to the Tradesmen, through the Hands of the late Mr. Alexander Tait; after his Death I undertook the Charge of that Part of the Business, and by that Means had an Opportunity of becoming acquainted with the Particulars of the Expense: The Accounts from which the above Abstract is made out, are lodged in the General Repository.

George Home.

Appendix (W. 1. to W. 5.)

OFFICES OF STATE.

SCOTLAND.
Great Seal Office.

Appendix (W. 1)

Appendix (W. 1.)

Report from the GREAT SEAL OFFICE of Scotland, to the several Questions contained in an Order of the Select Committee on the Public Records, &c. of this Kingdom; dated 28th February 1800.

BEFORE answering the particular Queries, I have to premise, that the Duke of Gordon was appointed Lord Keeper of the Great Seal for Scotland in July 1794; and I was then named, and have ever since acted as his Grace's Deputy. From that Period, I have humbly to report, in answer to the several Queries in their Order:

To the First:

There are no Records attached to this Office; but the Writs passing the Great Seal of Scotland, which consist of Charters from the Crown, Patents of Invention, Commissions of Public Appointments, and Remissions of Crimes, are expede as follows.

They are all previously prepared by the Director of Chancery in Scotland; after which His Majesty's Warrants, authorizing them to be so prepared and sealed, are brought to and left with the Deputy Keeper of the Great Seal, as his Authority for affixing the Seal.

To the Second:

These Warrands have hitherto been deposited in Repositories, kept by the Deputy Keeper, in his own House at Edinburgh.

To the Third:

The Warrands above mentioned, are put up Annually, according to their Dates.

To the Fourth:

They are all as yet in perfect Preservation, correct and complete, since the Period of the Duke of Gordon's Appointment; and an Index or Inventory, put up with the Warrands of each Year, periodically arranged.

To the Fifth:

Instead of His Majesty's Warrands remaining in the Private Custody of the Lord Keeper, or his Deputy, and being exposed to Accident, by the Death of either, it is humbly suggested, that it would be an Improvement to have an Apartment for this Office, in the General Register House at Edinburgh, as allotted to the other Public Departments; it would also be an Additional Security to the Public, if the Warrants above mentioned were deposited at the End of every Year, by Authority of the Legislature, in the General Repository, kept under the Direction of the Lord Clerk Register, with Periodical Inventories applicable thereto.

2. Another and very material Improvement would be, to have the same Authority for directing full and correct Duplicates of all Deeds, which pass the Great Seal of Scotland, to be authenticated by the Lord Keeper's Deputy, signing a Docket, subjoined to each Charter or other Writ, declaring the Principal to have been signed and sealed of that Date; and those certified Duplicates to be regularly bound up, at the End of every Year, as a Record, with an Index annexed thereto.

The Legislature ought also to sanction the Authority of Extracts to be taken from such Record, and certified by the Lord Keeper's Deputy, or his Successors in Office, in order to supply the Want of any Charters, or other Writs so recorded, when lost.

Because Instances have occurred, where from the Want of such authentic Record, the Parties have been put to the tedious and expensive Circuit of an Action of proving the Tenor, before the Court of Session, to supply the Loss of Charters; and in Political Competitions, that Remedy, by its Delay, may prove inadequate to the Inconvenience.

All which is humbly submitted to the Consideration of the Committee, by

Cha. Gordon,
Deputy Keeper of the Great Seal of Scotland.

22d March 1800.

Appendix (W. 2.)

Return from the PRIVY SEAL OFFICE in Scotland, to the Questions of the Committee

(1.) THERE is in the Custody of the Clerk or Writer to the Privy Seal, and his Deputy, and lodged in the Privy Seal Office, within the General Register House of Edinburgh, a regular Record of all Grants which have passed the Privy Seal of Scotland, from February 1795 to the Date of this Return. There are Two Sorts of Registers in the Privy Seal Office, One in the Latin Language, and the other in English. In the Latin Register is recorded all Precepts directed to the Keeper of the Great Seal, for expeding Charters or Grants of Land holding of the Crown in Scotland. And in the English Register is recorded all Grants of Pension, Presentations to Churches and Professorship, Commissions to inferior Officers, and Tacks of Tiends belonging to the Crown. There is also lodged in the Privy Seal Office, in the Custody of the Deputy Keeper of the Privy Seal, all the Warrants of the several Grants which have passed the Privy Seal, during the Period the present Lord Keeper has been in Office.

(2.) The Privy Seal Office, in which the Records and Warrants mentioned are deposited, is within the General Register House of Edinburgh, and in Condition, of perfect Security and Accommodation for keeping Records.

(3.) The Registers above-mentioned are regularly bound up and arranged, and are in a State of perfect Preservation and good Order.

(4.) There is a complete Index to the Registers, and a Book (called a Minute Book) containing a List of the Warrants above mentioned.

(5.) No

(5.) No Improvement occurs by which the above Records or Warrants could be made more commodious or accessible to the Public.

Alex^r Menzies,
Deputy Keeper of the Privy Seal of Scotland.

Rob. Menzies,
Deputy Writer to the Privy Seal.

Privy Seal Office, Edinburgh,
26th March 1800.

Appendix (W. 3.)

Return from the SIGNET OFFICE in Scotland, to the Questions of the Committee.

(1.) ALL Writes, which by the Law of Scotland are issued in the King's Name, pass through this Office, and are stamped with the Signet.

They consist of,

1. Summonses to Defendants in Suits before the Court of Session.

2. Writes issued incidentally by the Court of Session, in the Course of legal Proceedings before that Court.

3. Writes for attaching the Persons and Effects of Debtors, proceeding on Authority of the Court of Session.

4. Precepts proceeding on Signatures or Warrants issued by the Court of Exchequer, for expeding Charters of Lands holding of the Crown.

Excepting those of Class 2, the whole Writes must be signed by a Writer or Clerk to the Signet. Those of Class 2, are signed by the Clerks of the Court of Session.

All of the Writes, after being stamped, are entered in a Register or Minute Book before they are delivered from the Office, a Series of which Books is, with some few Exceptions, extant from the Year 1649.

Some of the Writes of the First Class do not require any Warrant for being signeted; others of that Class require a previous Order of the Court of Session, which remains at the Signet Office, as the Warrant of the Write.

The Writes of Class 2 being issued in consequence of Orders of the Court of Session, in the Course of Suits depending in that Court, and being signed by a Clerk of the Court, require no other Warrant for being signeted.

The Writes in the 3d Class, which are the most numerous, are issued, either in pursuance of Decreets or Judgments of the Court of Session, or in consequence of Bills or previous Applications to that Court for having such Writes issued; when they proceed on Decreets or Judgments, these are returned to the Party along with the Write after it is signeted; when upon Bills, the latter remain in the Signet Office as the Warrant, and from which, Extracts of the Writes subscribed by one of the Clerks of the Signet, can afterwards be given out, if requisite.

The Writes of the 4th Class, viz. Precepts proceeding on Signatures issued by the Exchequer, and directed to the Keeper of the Privy Seal, are made out in the Latin Language, prepared and subscribed by Clerks to the Signet, and when the Precept is signeted, the Signature remains at the Signet Office as the Warrant.

The Signatures on which Precepts have been issued, are extant from 1607, with some Deficiency, till 1650, from which Period they are completely extant. They are kept separate from the Warrants of the other Two Classes, and are arranged in Alphabetical Bundles, till 8th July 1779; from which Period, in consequence of a Regulation of the Society of Clerks to the Signet, they have all been written on Paper of the same Size, and are bound up in Annual Volumes; and there is a complete Catalogue or Index of the whole Signatures that are extant.

Besides the Warrants of the Writes detailed in the preceding Classes, there are not in the Signet Office, any Original Records, Rolls, Instruments, Registers, or Manuscript Books or Papers, containing any Acts or Proceedings by Royal, Parliamentary, Judicial, or any other Public Authority.

(2.) The Signet and the Warrants are kept in Apartments of a House belonging to the Society of Clerks to the Signet, and where they have their Hall and Library. It is in a centrical Situation, near to the Courts of Session and Exchequer, but the Accommodation is not good, though considerably improved by some additional Apartments fitted up about Fifteen Years ago. The House is connected with other Buildings, and the Inconvenience arising from this Situation having been much felt, there is at present a Treaty going on and nearly concluded, for the Purchase of a House quite detached from other Buildings, and not much farther distant from the Courts, where it is supposed there will be ample Accommodation.

(3.) The Warrants extant are all in a State of Preservation; and, as already noticed, those of the 1st and 3d Class are put up in Daily Files, and thereafter in Monthly Bundles, in regular Order. The Signatures composing the 4th Class are in Alphabetical Bundles, previous to the Year 1779, and thereafter bound in Annual Volumes.

(4.) Every Write passing the Signet is regularly entered in a Daily Register or Minute Book, from Perusal of which, and looking into the Monthly corresponding Roll, any particular Warrant can easily be found; and as to the Signatures, besides the above Minute Book, there is a complete Catalogue or Index of the Whole that are extant.

(5.) Nothing farther at present occurs as necessary or expedient for rendering the Use of the Records at the Signet Office more convenient to the Public.

All which is humbly reported by,

Hugh Warrender,
Deputy Keeper.

Signet Office, Edinburgh,
10th April 1800.

SCOTLAND.
Lyon Office.

Appendix (W.4.)

Appendix (W. 4.)

Return from the LYON OFFICE in SCOTLAND, to the Select Committee of the House of Commons on the Public Records, &c. of this Kingdom; in obedience to their Order, bearing Date 30th April 1800.

(1.) IN a former Return made from this Office, to an Order of the Select Committee on Finance, bearing Date 1st March 1798, it was stated to be the particular Duty of the Lord Lyon King at Arms, and his Depute, to examine into the Characters, Knowledge, and general Abilities of Heralds, Pursuivants, and Messengers at Arms; and that upon finding them qualified, he has the sole Right of admitting them to their respective Offices. It was also stated, that there is express Power given by Statute, to the Lord Lyon and the Heralds of Scotland, to visit the Arms of all Noblemen, Barons, and Gentlemen, borne and used in that Kingdom, to distinguish them by congruent Differences, and thereafter to matriculate them in the Books and Registers of the Lyon Office. That by the same Statute, 1672, Cap. 21. the Lord Lyon is invested with the sole Power of giving Armorial Bearings to virtuous and well-deserving Persons; and with the Power of judging in all Complaints brought against Heralds, Pursuivants, and Messengers, before the Lyon Court; and of suspending, depriving, or otherwise punishing them for Delinquency or Negligence in their Offices.

To these Powers, with which Lord Lyon is so invested, the Public Records, Rolls, Instruments, and Manuscript Books and Papers, in the Custody of the Lyon Office in Scotland, do chiefly relate. There are indeed said to be other Manuscript Books and printed Treatises upon Heraldry, in the Custody of the Lyon Clerk, who was also Deputy to the late Lord Lyon; but he insists that they are the Private Property of his former Constituent, as having been purchased by him. The proper Records of the Office were therefore pointed out by him to be,

1. A large Folio Volume, written on Vellum, containing the Record of the Matriculations (in so far as they have taken place) of the Armorial Bearings of the Kings of Scotland and Great Britain, of James Duke of Albany, and of the Archbishops, Bishops, Nobility, and Gentry, and Royal Burghs of Scotland, commencing in 1678, and not yet quite finished, with a complete Index thereto.

2. A large Folio Book, intituled "The Lyon Register of Processions, Letters of Precedency, Testificates, and Forefaulters," commencing with the Order of Procession at opening the Parliament of Scotland by his Royal Highness James Duke of York, upon 25th July 1681.

N. B. This Book contains in the other End of it, an Ordinance of Sir Alexander Erskine, of Camno, Lord Lyon, relative to Funeral Paintings, dated 27th July 1697; with a few Memorandums of the Funeral Escutcheons of different Persons deceased; but upon the Whole, it appears to be very imperfect.

3. A Book, intituled "Birth Brief Register," begun 3d December 1728, apparently very distinct, and almost finished.

4. A Book, containing the Proceedings of the Lyon Court, commencing 13th February 1629, and ending 5th January 1650.

5. A Book, containing the Proceedings of the Lyon Court, commencing 8th August 1663, and ending 6th November 1694; not completed to the End.

6. Register of Decrees of the Lyon Court against Messengers, commencing 6th November 1700, and ending 16th February 1703; written upon Twenty-two Pages, but consisting of several Hundred Pages still Blank.

7. A Book, containing the Proceedings of the Lyon Court, commencing in 1728, ending 1770.

8. A Book, containing the Proceedings of the Lyon Court, commencing in 1770, which is still current.

9. Record of Messengers Admissions, begun 1630, ending 1650.

10. Record of Messengers Admissions, begun 1660, ending 1663; containing also the Record of the Admission of Heralds and Pursuivants, from December 1660, to February 1661.

11. A Book, stated to contain the Record of Admissions of Heralds and Pursuivants, from June 1663, to July 1687; and of Messengers, from June 1663, to 11th November 1693.

12. A Book, stated to contain the Admission of Heralds and Pursuivants, from 1692 to 1726; and of Messengers, from 1693 to 1722.

13. Register of Admission of Messengers, from 7th October 1754, to 14th November 1777.

14. Register of Admissions of Messengers, commencing 9th January 1778, brought down to 14th June 1800, the Date of the last Admission; not yet finished.

15. A small Quarto Book, containing the Register of Commissions to Heralds and Pursuivants, commencing 9th March 1729, and ending 21st April 1796.

16. Responde Book of the Lyon Office, commencing 4th October 1754, ending 29th April 1770; after which there is an Entry in Mr. Boswell's Hand-writing, in the following Words: "The Entries in this Book discontinued; a large Register Book or Journal, being provided for Entry of Receipts of Money, and all other Matters respecting the Lyon Office, after a new Form."

17. The large Folio Book above referred to, apparently intended to contain Minutes of the whole Proceedings in the Office; begun 1st November 1770, and ending 10th April 1775. After this Period, no Minutes of the Proceedings are entered; it consists of many Hundred Pages, but only Fifty of them are written upon.

Besides the above Books, there are a Number of Old Processes and Old and Current Bonds of Cautionry for Messengers in the Lyon Office.

(2.) The Building in which the above Books and other Records and Papers, which do or are supposed to belong to the Lyon Office, are lodged, is the Private House of Mr. Boswell, the Lyon Clerk, in Saint Andrew's Square, Edinburgh; it is admitted by him, that he was offered an Apartment in the General Register House at Edinburgh, which he refused, because it was not to his Taste. The House in which these Records now are, is believed to be the Private Property of Mr. Boswell. He has hitherto claimed no Rent for the Room in which these Records are deposited. There is indeed a Question at present under Submission to the Lord Advocate of Scotland, between him and the Lord Lyon, who maintains from former Practice, that he or his Deputy are entitled

SCOTLAND. Lyon Office.

Appendix (W. 4.)

entitled to the Custody of Records. The Room in which these Records are kept, is on the Ground Floor of Mr. Boswell's House, is low, inconvenient, and by no Means secure, it being the Common Office kept by him as a Writer to the Signet, and of Course subject to the Intrusion of many Persons who have no Business to transact with the Lyon Office.

(3.) The Books and Papers before mentioned are in proper Preservation, and tolerably well arranged. The Papers are arranged in Alphabetical Order.

(4.) There appear to be no General Catalogues, Calendars, Schedules, or Repertories; neither is there any Particular Index to any of the Books, except to Nos. 1, 2, and 3.

There would no great Utility result from these Records being completed, at least in comparison of the immense Time and Trouble which it would cost to complete them. Several of the Volumes of the Proceedings of the Lyon Court are lost or missing from the Office, and it is believed are irrecoverable. The most antient Volume of Records of Arms known to exist, is in the Library of the Faculty of Advocates in Edinburgh. How it came there is not known; but they allow the Officers of the Lyon Court Inspection of it whenever they please, although they are said to be very unwilling to part it to the Office.

(5.) Until within these Thirty Years, the only Officers belonging to or connected with the Lyon Court were, 1st. The Lord Lyon.—2d. His Depute.—3d. The Six Heralds and Six Pursuivants.—4th. The Lyon Clerk, who had occasionally a Depute when Old Age or Infirmities disabled him from acting.—5th. A Herald Painter, who was generally, as his Name bears, one of the Heralds.—6th. A Fiscal.—and 7th. A Macer of Court.

But at or soon after Mr. Boswell's Appointment in 1770, to the Joint Offices of Lyon Depute and Lyon Clerk, he thought proper to add, 8th. An Officer under the Name of "Keeper of the Records;" which Office was formerly discharged by the Lyon Depute.—9th. Four Solicitors or Attorneys of Court.—And 10th. To class His Majesty's Six Household Trumpeters for Scotland, under the Office; although it is not known or believed that Lord Lyon has any Jurisdiction over these Persons.

The Duties of the Lord Lyon, the Lyon Depute, Heralds, Pursuivants, Clerk, and other proper Officers of the Lyon Court, their Days and Hours of Attendance, the general Amount of their Net Annual Salaries, Allowances, and Emoluments, are all mentioned in the Return already made, and in Two Appendixes thereto by this Office, to the Order of the Select Committee of the House of Commons, bearing Date 1st March 1798.

The Salary of the Lord Lyon is therein stated to be Six Hundred Pounds per Annum, subject to the usual Tax upon Salaries, and to the Payment of a Salary to his Depute.

THE Allowances and Emoluments payable to Lord Lyon, and his Depute, by the Public in Scotland, are,

			£.	s.	d.
For matriculating in, the Arms of- -	A Duke - - -	Lord Lyon - - - - -	26	5	—
		His Depute - - - - -	4	4	—
	A Marquis - - -	Lord Lyon - - - - -	24	3	—
		His Depute - - - - -	3	13	6
	An Earl - - - -	Lord Lyon - - - - -	24	—	—
		His Depute - - - - -	3	3	—
	A Viscount - - -	Lord Lyon - - - - -	19	—	—
		His Depute - - - - -	2	2	—
	A Baron - - -	Lord Lyon - - - - -	16	—	—
		His Depute - - - - -	2	2	—
	Knights and Gentlemen - -	Lord Lyon - - - - -	6	13	4
		His Depute - - - - -	1	6	8

But if any of the Family were formerly matriculated, the Charge is only One Half of the above Fees; viz.

	£.	s.	d.
Lord Lyon - - - - - - - -	3	6	8
His Depute - - - - - - - -	—	13	4

When any Knights or Gentlemen instruct that they are entitled to, and obtain Supporters, the Fees are, - - - - - -

	£.	s.	d.
Lord Lyon - - - - - - - -	21	—	—
His Depute - - - - - - - -	3	3	—

The Lord Lyon has also a Fee of £. 8. 6s. 8d. upon the Admission of every Messenger at Arms.

SCOTLAND.
Lyon Office.
Appendix (W. 4.)

Table of FEES paid into the Lyon Office, of the Shares paid into the Lord Lyon, and Heralds, and Purſuivants of Scotland, and of the Proportion paid to each Herald and Purſuivant, being the ſame Fees as are received by the Herald Office, in England, from all thoſe on whom His Majeſty, his Heirs, &c. &c. ſhall confer any Honour or Dignity, conform to His Majeſty's Warrant under the Great Seal of Scotland; bearing Date the 9th of June 1731.

FEES PAID INTO	Lyon Office.	Lord Lyon.	Six Heralds.	Six Purſuivants.	Share of a Herald.	Share of a Purſuivant.
Sterling Money.	£. s. d.	£. s. d.	£. s. d.	£. s. d.	£. s. d.	£. s. d.
Creation of a Prince of Wales -	106 13 4	53 6 8	32 — —	21 6 8	5 6 8	3 11 $1\frac{1}{2}$
A Duke or Ducheſs - - -	53 6 8	26 13 4	16 — —	10 13 4	2 13 4	1 15 $6\frac{2}{3}$
A Marquis or Marchioneſs - -	40 — —	20 — —	12 — —	8 — —	2 — —	1 6 8
An Earl or Counteſs - - -	26 13 4	13 6 8	8 — —	5 6 8	1 6 8	— 17 $9\frac{1}{3}$
A Viſcount or Viſcounteſs - -	20 — —	10 — —	6 — —	4 — —	1 — —	— 13 4
A Baron or Baroneſs - - -	16 — —	8 — —	4 16 —	3 4 —	— 16 —	— 10 8
A Knight Baronet - - - -	9 3 4	2 10 —	4 — —	2 13 4	— 13 4	— 8 $10\frac{1}{3}$
A Knight Batchelor - - - -	8 10 —	2 10 —	3 12 —	2 8 —	— 12 —	— 8 —

The Lord Lyon's Net Receipts from Salary and Fees of Office, after Deduction of Taxes, &c. amount upon an Average of the laſt Three Years, to little more than £.800. Sterling per Annum.

The Fees and Emoluments to the Lyon Depute, excluſive of the Salary from Lord Lyon, amount upon the ſame Average to about £. 20. Sterling per Annum.

The Average of the Fees to Heralds and Purſuivants, excluſive of their Salaries, is to the former about £. 20. a Year; and to the latter about £. 13. Sterling.

Mr. Boſwell, the Clerk, declines to give any Average of his Fees, until the Queſtions between him and Lord Lyon are ſettled, by the Deciſion of the Lord Advocate of Scotland; but from an Old Table of Fees, found in the Office, and ſaid to be made up in 1760, the Fees of the Lyon Clerk, of his Depute, and of the Herald Painter, are ſtated to be as follow; viz.

			£.	s.	d.
For Matriculating in the Lyon Regiſter the Arms of - -	A Duke - - - - -	Lyon Clerk - - - -	3	3	—
		Depute Clerk - - - -	1	1	—
		Seal and Ribbons - - -	—	10	6
		Painting - - - - -	1	1	—
	A Marquis - - - -	Lyon Clerk - - - -	2	12	6
		Depute Clerk - - - -	1	1	—
		Seal and Ribbons - - -	—	10	6
		Painting - - - - -	1	1	—
	An Earl, a Viſcount, and a Baron - - - - -	Lyon Clerk - - - -	2	2	—
		Depute Clerk - - - -	1	1	—
		Seal and Ribbons - - -	—	10	6
		Painting - - - - -	1	1	—
	Knights and Gentlemen -	Lyon Clerk - - - -	1	—	—
		Depute Clerk - - - -	—	5	—
		Seal and Ribbons - - -	—	2	6
		Painting - - - - -	—	10	6
But when theſe laſt are found entitled to Supporters, the Fees are		To Lyon Clerk - - -	2	2	—
		Depute Clerk - - -	1	1	—
		Seal and Ribbons - -	—	5	—
		Painting - - - -	1	1	—

A trifling Advantage has taken place upon the Charge for Seals, &c. and the Fees for Painting are now charged at leaſt Double.

The Lyon Clerk is alſo entitled to the following Fees; viz.

		£.	s.	d.
Upon the Admiſſion of every - - - -	Herald - - - - - - - - - - - - -	8	6	8
	Purſuivant - - - - - - - - - - -	5	11	$1\frac{4}{12}$
	Meſſenger at Arms - - - - - - - - -	2	1	8

His

SCOTLAND. Lyon Office.

Appendix (W. 5.)

His Fees upon Judicial Proceedings before the Lyon Court are,

	£.	s.	d.
For drawing a Messenger's Bond of Cautionry	—	5	—
every Extract thereof	—	5	—
every Complaint at Head Courts	—	2	6
every Precept, including 2 s. 6 d. to Fiscal	—	10	6
Defences, Answers, Replies, &c.	—	2	6
Officer at calling every Precept	—	—	6
Clerk at every calling of the Cause	—	2	6
every Sheet of an Act or Warrant	—	1	8
every full Sheet of a Decreet	—	1	8
every repeated Sheet and Bill Sheets	—	1	2
every Petition to Court	—	2	6

(6.) The Lyon Depute, in Absence of the Lord Lyon, is the Person understood and believed to have the Special Care of the Records, Books and Papers, belonging to the Office. But this is disputed by Mr. Boswell, who maintains, that it is the peculiar Province of the Clerk to have the Custody of these Papers. If the Office of Keeper of Records shall be continued, it will be certainly his Duty, by whomsoever he is appointed, to discharge the Duties specified in this Question.

(7.) There are no other Matters, not comprized in the preceding Questions, which it is necessary or expedient to observe for rendering the Use of the Records more convenient to the Public, which are not already specified in the former Return made in consequence of the Order of the Select Committee of the House of Commons, dated 1st March 1798.

All which is humbly reported, by

James Home,
Lyon Depute.

Appendix (W. 5.)

Edinburgh General Register House,
30th June 1800.

SIR,

I AM very sorry, that on Saturday last, when your Letter of the 25th of June reached Edinburgh, I was in the Country.

It was my first Care this Morning to make Inquiry about the Setts of Burghs mentioned in that Letter.

The Two Principal City Clerks of Edinburgh are Clerks to the Convention of Royal Burghs, and are the Keepers of the Records of the Convention.

On the Authority of one of those Gentlemen, John Dundas, Esquire, I can now inform you, that in consequence of an Order of the Convention, of Date, as Mr. Dundas says, the 15th of July 1708, the Setts * of all the Royal Burghs of Scotland are recorded in the Books of the Convention.

I have the Honour to be, with high and very respectful Regard,

Sir,
Your very humble and
very obedient Servant,
Willm Robertson.

Charles Abbot, Esq;

* [Note added by the Committee.]—Setts, are the Corporate Constitutions for the Government of these Burghs, on which the Rights of Election to Parliament entirely depend.

Appendix (X. 1. to X. 9.)

COURTS OF JUSTICE.

Appendix (X. 1. a.)

SCOTLAND. Court of Seſſion. Appendix (X. 1. a.)

Return tranſmitted by the COURT OF SESSION in SCOTLAND, to the Order of the Select Committee of the Houſe of Commons on the Public Records, &c. of this Kingdom.

(1.) THE Records belonging to the Court of Seſſion are, Firſt, The Books of Sederunt, in which are entered the Names of the Judges preſent at each Meeting of the Court; the Excuſes from thoſe that are abſent; the Admiſſion of the Judges, Advocates, Clerks of Seſſion, &c.; the Cenſures paſſed, or Puniſhments inflicted on Practitioners, Litigants, or Witneſſes, for Miſconduct in any Suits or Cauſes depending in Court; the Acts and Orders of Court in all Matters which do not fall within the Ordinary Exerciſe of their Juriſdiction, particularly the Acts and Orders made from Time to Time for correcting Abuſes in the Forms of Proceeding, and eſtabliſhing new Regulations for improving them; the Communications between the Sovereigns and the Court in more antient Times, and ſince the Union of the Two Kingdoms, between Parliament and the Court, in Matters relating to the Improvement of the Police, or the Laws of the Country.

The Court was eſtabliſhed in its preſent Form in 1532, but the earlieſt of the Books of Sederunt that are extant commences 15th January 1553, and ends 24th July 1555. The Second Volume extant commences 27th June 1560, and ends 13th of November 1567. The Third Volume extant commences 20th of October 1575, and ends 7th of November 1587. The Fourth Volume extant commences 1ſt of January 1587, and ends 21ſt of May 1608; but there is a Blank in it, from 24th of February 1604, to 19th of June 1605. The Fifth Volume extant commences 2d of November 1626, and from that Time to the preſent Date, the Volumes are regularly preſerved.

Secondly, There is a Public Record, called "the Books of Council and Seſſion," in which Deeds and Obligations of every Kind may be recorded, if they contain a Clauſe of Regiſtration, and almoſt every Deed of Importance in Scotland contains ſuch a Clauſe, by which the Grantor conſents that it may be regiſtered in the Books of Council and Seſſion, or in the Books of any other competent Court, not only for the Purpoſe of Preſervation, but that a Decree of the Court may be interpoſed to compel Performance. When theſe are recorded in the Books of Seſſion, the principal Deed is left with the Keeper of the Record, a Copy of it is inſerted in the Books kept for that Purpoſe, and an Office Copy, called an Extract, is given out to the Party, ſigned by One of the Principal Clerks of Seſſion, and containing a Warrant for all neceſſary Execution againſt the Grantor of the Deed. The Proteſts of Bills and Promiſſory Notes, though they contain no Clauſe of Regiſtration, are authorized by Statute to be recorded in this Regiſter, and to have the ſame Privilege of ſummary Execution upon them as takes place upon Deeds recorded by Conſent of the Grantor.

Thirdly, Another Branch of this Record is called the "Record of Probative Writs," in which every Probative Writing may be recorded, with or without a Clauſe of Regiſtration; but the Original Deeds recorded in this Regiſter, are returned to the Party, and the Extract contains no Warrant for Execution.

Fourthly, A Record of all the Decrees pronounced by the Court, that are extracted. Theſe Extracts contain a full Copy of all the Proceedings in the Cauſe. The Copy given out to the Party, in whoſe Favour the Decree is pronounced, is authenticated by the Subſcription of a Principal Clerk of Seſſion, and another Copy is entered in the Record.

All theſe Records are under the immediate Charge and Inſpection of the Principal Clerks of Seſſion, and Officers named by them; but they never have more in their Cuſtody than the Records of the laſt Ten Years, the Reſt are regularly tranſmitted to the General Repoſitory, under the Care of the Lord Regiſter and his Deputies, ſo that all the Books containing the Deeds recorded and Decrees extracted, that are extant previous to 1790, with the Deeds themſelves, are now in the General Regiſter. Thoſe for the Year 1790 will be placed there in February or March 1801, and ſo on in Succeſſion from Year to Year.

(2.) The Books of Sederunt are kept in a Preſs in the Wall of the Room where the Court meets, and where they are perfectly free from Damp, and in little or no Hazard from Fire. The Offices of the Clerks of Seſſion, where the other Records are kept, are in a Part of the Building erected for the General Repoſitory.

(3.) Some of the Books of Sederunt, particularly the older ones, have many looſe Leaves in them; in other Reſpects they are in good Preſervation. The other Records being in ſo late a Period, are clean and in perfect good Order, as well as their Warrants, except the Warrants of ſome of the Decrees, which paſſing frequently through the Hands of Agents, Lawyers, and their Clerks, during the Dependence of the Cauſe in Court, many of the Papers are much ſullied, chaffed, and torn, before they are placed in the Regiſter; but after that they can ſuffer no further Damage. The Deeds are arranged in the Order in which they are preſented for Regiſtration, and the Decrees in the Order in which they are extracted.

(4.) The principal Articles in the Books of Sederunt are printed and publiſhed in a large Folio Volume in 1790, and to that Volume there is an accurate Index. There are complete Manuſcript Indexes to the other Records, which are compared with the Books, and with the Deeds recorded, when they are tranſmitted by the Clerks of Seſſion to the Lord Regiſter, or his Deputies, who receive no Record without an Index or Minute Book being delivered along with it, and without comparing that Index with the Record.

(5.) The Clerks of Seſſion and Officers appointed by them, have the Care of theſe Records, as a Part of their Official Duty. They have no Salaries from the Public, and the Fees received by them for the Regiſtration of Deeds, and Extracts of Decrees, are particularly mentioned in a former Report upon that Subject; to which it may here be added, that the Perſons appointed by them to take the immediate Charge of the Regiſtration of Deeds, have certain Fees excluſive of what is paid to the

See 1685. c. 38.

See Proceedings on the Finance Reports; ordered to be printed, 18th June 1799.

2

the Clerks: there are Three Offices, and a Superintendant or Keeper of the Registrations in each Office; the Fees paid to the Six Clerks are only One Shilling and a Penny, and One Third of a Penny, for the First Sheet of every Deed registered, and Ten Pence for the Second Sheet; but they receive nothing for the other Sheets. The Average Amount of these small Fees to the Principal Clerks, for the last Three Years, is £. 356. 14*s*. 6*d*. being £. 59. 9*s*. 1/11 *d*. to each. The Person who has the Care of the Registrations under the Clerks has Six Pence and Two Thirds of a Penny for the First Sheet, Ten Pence for the Second Sheet, and One Shilling One Penny, and One Third of a Penny, for each of the other Sheets. The Emoluments of the Three, on an Average of Three Years, amount to the Sum of £. 57. 14*s*. 6*d*. The Hours of Attendance are from Nine in the Morning to Eight at Night, in the Time of Session, allowing an Hour for Dinner, and from Ten to Three in Time of Vacation.

(6.) Is already answered.

(7.) It would certainly contribute to the better Preservation of the Books of Sederunt, and of every other material Record in the Kingdom, if they were transmitted from Time to Time to the General Repository; of this no Man can doubt who has an Opportunity of seeing the State of the Records there, and in the Hands of less Public Custodiers.

It would be an Improvement in the Register of Probative Writs, if the Writings themselves were left in the Record; it has been alledged that forged and fictitious Writings have been recorded there, with a View no Doubt to destroy them immediately after recording. This Record seems to have been intended for the Preservation of useful Writings that had all the Solemnities of formal Deeds probative in a Court of Law; but the Term Probative Writing is too indefinite for the Keeper of a Record to judge of; and it is his Interest to admit every Thing, however frivolous or incorrect, that is offered for recording.

The Record of Decrees before the Court is unnecessarily voluminous. The whole Written Pleadings given into Court during the Progress of the Litigation, are entered in the Extract, and in the Record, though many of them are mere Repetitions; nor can this be avoided unless some Rule is adopted for confining the Extract to certain Original and essential Parts of the Procedure, which form the Ground Work of all the Rest. If the Decrees were shorter, every Decree pronounced might be extracted, and the Record would by this Means be more useful and more complete.

Alex^r Menzies,
Senr Princ^l Clerk of Session.

Register Office, Edinburgh,
9th April 1800.

Appendix (X. 1. b.)

Return of the Keeper of the General Minute Book.

UNDERSTANDING that the Record of the General Minute Book of the Court of Session in Scotland, of which I was appointed Keeper in January last, by Commission under the Great Seal, has not been taken Notice of in any of the late Reports, in consequence of your circular Letters, I shall state what occurs relating to that Record, for your Information.

(1.) The Nature of my Office, is Keeper of the General Minute Book of the Court of Session, wherein is transcribed, from the different Minute Books kept by the Six Inner and Six Outer House Clerks of Court, the Names and Designations of the Parties in all Acts and Decrees pronounced, with their Dates, &c. a Copy of which, in Place of being read from the MS. as was formerly done, is now printed and distributed Twice a Week during the Sitting of each Session, for the Information of the Practitioners of Court, who subscribe for the same, and the Annual General Minute Book is kept as a Record, to which the Leiges resort for Searches.

(2. 3. & 4.) This Record, in which there appear some small Chasms, has been under the Charge of the Keepers since the End of the Sixteenth Century, and is at present kept in One of the Apartments of the sunk Ground Floor of the General Register House, a Room by no Means adapted for such a Record, as from its low Situation the Records are actually injured, while the Keeper, his Clerk, and those making Searches, cannot, owing to its Dampness, continue in it for any Length of Time.

(5.) I have One Clerk, who is pretty constantly employed for the Six Months the Sessions continue; his Allowance from Perquisites is about £. 30. per Annum, and I give him the like Sum for extra Trouble, which consists chiefly in transcribing for the Press, distributing the printed Copies to Practitioners, and framing an Index to the Annual printed Volumes.

(6.) I have the Charge of these Records as Keeper, as my Predecessors had; and as any Fees to me arise from small Perquisites, that depend on the Business before the Court, and the printed Copies, subject to Printing, Paper, &c. and as my Appointment only took place in January last, I cannot say what these may Annually amount to, though I am told Mr. Gordon, the late Keeper, made a Return of them in his Life-time.

(7.) As the Records are by no Means in so proper an Arrangement and State of Preservation as I could wish, and as they are resorted to for Searches, I humbly submit, that it would be necessary and highly expedient, for rendering them more useful and convenient to the Public, that they were deposited in a more comfortable Room up Stairs, which I have been endeavouring to procure, hitherto without Effect.

Will. Mac Farlane.

Edinburgh, No. 14, North Frederick Street,
7th June 1800.

Appendix (X. 1. c.)

BILL CHAMBER,
July 4th, 1800.

Answers to the Questions of the Select Committee on the Public Records, &c. of this Kingdom, relative to the Record of Abbreviates of Adjudication, and Hornings against Superiors, kept at Edinburgh.

ADJUDICATION*, formerly called Apprising, was a legal Mode of attaching Heritable Property known in Scotland,

* It is believed that there is no Action authorized by the Law of England, similar to our Process of Adjudication, whereby a Creditor can attach the Heritable Estate of his Debtor, and thereby get a legal Transfer of the Property in Payment of his Debt.

SCOTLAND.
Court of Session.
Appendix (X. 1. c.)

Scotland, prior to the Year 1636, and has been practised downwards.

A Record wherein these legal Transfers of Property should be entered and kept, for the Information of the Leiges, was thought of so early as An. 1661, C. 31, when a Public Statute was made, authorizing and regulating it.

The Record was ordained by Act of Parliament to be kept by the Clerks of the Bills; and we find in the Statute 17 Charles II. Parl. 2, Sec. 30, several Regulations as to the Fees of this Register. Other Ordinances respecting it were made by the Acts of additional Regulations in 1695, and Acts of Sederunt of the Lords of Session, 18th January 1715, unnecessary to be detailed.

As a very considerable Part of the Landed Property in Scotland is acquired, or in some Measure affected by the Process of Adjudication, it may be proper to mention, that in all the late Bankrupt Statutes relating to Scotland, particular Attention has been paid to recording Adjudications.

By the last of these Acts, 33 George III. Sec. 11, an Abstract of the Signature of Adjudication presented in Exchequer, where the Lands hold of the Crown, and of a Charge on Letters of Horning, where they are held of a Subject superior, are appointed to be recorded in the Register of Abbreviates of Adjudication.

Having stated so much regarding the Institution and Object of this Record, the Method of keeping it shall now be detailed, which is the chief Object of the Questions.

(1.) That there is an Index or Minute Book, in which is entered, immediately upon being presented at the Office, the Title of the Writ or Paper, the Party's Name in whose Favour it is made, and the Party's Name against whom it is issued, with the Date, both Day of the Month and Hour of the Day of presenting, with the Person's Name and Designation who presents it, and this he subscribes. For the more easily consulting this Index or Minute Book (as it is called) the Defendant's Name is put upon the Margin. All which is done in the following Form:

Copy of the Entry of an Abbreviate of Adjudication from the Minute Book:

" Vigesimo Septimo Junij 1800mo.

" Two Abbreviates of Adjudication. Lieutenant Colonel Alexander Graham Sterling, of Duchray and Auchyle, Heir in General, served and retoured to the deceast Dame Jean Sterling, of Auchyle, designed in the Disposition therein mentioned, Widow of Sir James Stirling, of Glorat, Baronet, conform to retour of his General Service, expede before the Magistrates of Edinburgh, the Eight Day of June last, duly retoured to Chancery against Gavin Ralston, of Ralston, Esquire, now Captain in the Elgin Regiment of Fencibles, as lawfully charged to enter Heir in Special, to the deceast Gavin Ralston, of Ralston, Esquire, in Manner mentioned in the said Decreet of Adjudication.

" Presented betwixt the Hours of Ten and Twelve Forenoon, by Thomas Baird, Writer in Edinburgh.

(Signed) " *Thomas Baird.*"

N. B. The following is the Form of entering a Signature of Adjudication in the Minute Book:

" Vigesimo Septimo Junij 1800mo.

" Signature of Adjudication. Thomas Sommers, Vintner in Edinburgh, for himself, and in Trust for the Creditors of the deceast John Carr, Lord Ballenden of Broughton, of all and whole the Office of Usher of His Majesty's Court of Exchequer, in that Part of Great Britain called Scotland, adjudged by the said Thomas Sommers, from the said Lord Ballenden.

" Presented at the Bill Chamber, betwixt the Hours of One and Two Afternoon, by Thomas Millar, Writer in Edinburgh.

(Signed) " *Thomas Millar.*"

Form of entering Horning against Superiors in the Minute Book:

" Vigesimo Octavo Junij 1800mo.

" Horning with the Executions. David Christie, Writer in Edinburgh, Trustee for Anderson Horseburgh and Company, Merchants in Glasgow, against the Superiors of the Lands, and others adjudged by him, from Charles Kelburn, Shipmaster in Greenock.

" Presented betwixt Eleven and Twelve o'Clock Forenoon, by David Christie, Writer in Edinburgh.

(See Sub.) " *David Christie.*"

Docket upon the Adjudication subscribed by the Keeper:

The Act of Parliament requires that Two Abbreviates of every Adjudication be made, One to be left for the Record, the other to be returned to the Party, along with the Principal Adjudication, having the following Docket written upon the last Page:

" Apud Edinburgum Decimo Nono Die Junij
" Anno Domini Millesimo Octingentesimo:

" Which Day the Abbreviate of the Decreet of Ad-
" judication above mentioned was presented at the Bill
" Chamber, with said Decreet; and the said Abbreviate
" was duly recorded in the Register of Abbreviates of
" Adjudications, conform to Act of Parliament: Ano-
" ther Abbreviate of said Decreet being left conform
" to Act of Sederunt anent depositing Abbreviates in
" said Office.

" *John Watson.*"

Docket upon the Abbreviate subscribed by the Keeper:

And upon the Abbreviate, the following Docket is written:

" Apud Edinburgum Decimo Nono Die Mensis
" Junij Anno Domini Millesimo Octingen-
" tesimo:

" The Decreet of Adjucation, of which this is an
" Abbreviate, is extracted, and was this Day presented
" with the said Abbreviate; and the Abbreviate was
" duly recorded in the Record of Abbreviates of Adju-
" dications, conform to Act of Parliament.

" *John Watson.*"

Similar Dockets (mutatis mutandis) are written upon the Signatures of Adjudications and Hornings against Superiors.

After all the foregoing Entries and Dockets are made, the Abbreviates, Signatures, and Hornings, with the Charges, are copied over Verbatim into a Book, in the Order of their being presented. These Books are every 10 Years lodged with the Lord Registrar and his Deputies, i. e. the Reporters keep only the last 10 Years. The Abbreviates, &c. themselves, lie in this Office.

(2.) The Room or Office where these Records are kept, is the same in which the other Departments of the Bill Chamber are carried on. It is a small Room in the West Wing of the General Register Office.

It is much too small for a Record of this Consequence, in Conjunction with the other Branches of the Bill Chamber. It is also inconvenient in many other Respects, so much so, that the present Reporters have taken the Liberty of applying to the Lord President of the Court of Session, begging his Interposition with the Lord Register * to procure a fitter Apartment.

It is perhaps enough at present to state, that from Want of proper Accommodation, the Reporters can say with Truth, that for many Years back the Office has suffered an Annual Loss of about £.14. Sterling, out of a Revenue of not more than £.120. Sterling, arising from this Branch of their Department, and which is the principal Branch.

(3.) The Records of this Office, for at least 60 Years back, are in good Order, and properly arranged according to their Dates. Many of the Records, prior to the above Period, were in Confusion when transported to the present Register Office. They were at that Time thrown into One of the Damp Rooms in the sunk Floor of the Register House, where they have been allowed to lie ever since. One Object of an Application for a proper Apartment is to rescue these from perishing, and to put them in proper Order.

(4.) This Question is already answered; for at least 60 Years back, full and complete Indexes or Minute Books, as described in Answer to Question the First, are in the Office, or have been transmitted to the General Repository, along with the Record Books. Were a separate Office procured for this Record, the present Keepers think, that with an Assistant for Six or Eight Months, they could arrange and inventory the Whole from the earliest Period.

(5.) The present Reporters are the only Officers employed in this Office, so far as it regards the Records. The Hours of Attendance are, during the Sitting of the Court of Session, from Eight to Nine o'Clock in the Morning, and from Two to Four o'Clock in the Afternoon, in the Office. But they are understood to be in the Parliament House, or at a Call, during the other Hours of the Forenoon. During the Recess or Vacation of the Court of Session, the Hours of Attendance are from Ten to Twelve in the Forenoon, and from One to Two in the Afternoon.

The Depute Clerks (the Reporters) have no Salary. The Fees or Emoluments of this Office, are £.4. Scots (or 6*s.* 8*d.* Sterling) for recording the First Sheet of the Abbreviate of Adjudication; and £.1. Scots (or 1*s.* 8*d.* Sterling) for every after Sheet. They do not average above Two Sheets each. This is the whole Charge that is made for keeping the Minute Book, for Writing the Certificates or Dockets, for recording the Abbreviates, and for furnishing all the necessary Books, Paper, Pens, &c. They are further entitled to a Fee of 5*s.* Sterling, for a Search of 10 Years in the Minute Book; and if for a shorter Period, 2*s.* 6*d.* And when an Extract of an Abbreviate is given, the same Charge is made as for recording.

These Fees have been the same for more than 50 Years back; for obvious Reasons, the Reporters intend to make Application for some Addition to the present Allowance.

(6.) One or other of the Keepers attend in the Office during the Hours specified in the immediately foregoing Answer; and no Search is made but under their Eye, or by themselves when required. If the Search is made by themselves, they charge 6*d.* per Annum for Trouble, i. e. if the Search is for Five Years, they charge 2*s.* 6*d.*; if for Ten Years, 5*s.* and so on.

(7.) This Record is accurately and regularly kept. The Inconvenience of the Office, however, from the Bustle and Noise attendant on what is properly the Bill Chamber Branch, and which is unavoidable, obliges the Deputes (the Reporters) to give out the Records to another Office to be copied or booked, for which they pay from £.12. to £.14. Sterling, per Annum; whereas, were the Office suitable, they would bring up and book the Records themselves.

There is only One other Improvement upon this Record occurs to the Reporters, and that is, to keep a Particular Book wherein the first effectual Adjudication should be entered. The Plan of this would not readily be understood by the Committee, as it is believed there is nothing in the Law of England similar to our Process of Adjudication; but they mean soon to lay some Proposals regarding this before the Lord President of the Court of Session.

The Reporters are further the Clerks to Loosings of Arrestments and Lawborrows. The Bonds given by the Parties in these Cases are presented to them, and they are responsible to a certain Degree for the Sufficiency of the Caution offered, i. e. that the Persons who subscribe these Bonds, are at the Time habite and repute responsible for the Sums therein contained. The Reporters pass the Warrants for these, and are the Custodiers of all the Bonds. These Bonds are also kept in this Office, already too much crouded and confused with other Matters. The Fees of these are,

	Sterling. *s.*	*d.*
For Writing and receiving the Bond of Caution in loosing Arrestment - - - - -	7	6
For Writing and receiving the Bond of Caution in Lawborrows - - - - - - - -	5	10
For Extracts of either of the above Bonds - -	3	—

Table of FEES for Recording, &c. Abbreviates of Adjudication:

N. B. They have been always calculated in Scots Money.

	Sterling. *s.*	*d.*
For entering the Abbreviate in the Minute Book, for Writing the Two Dockets for recording the Abbreviate, furnishing all the necessary Books, Paper, &c. for the first Sheet, £ 4. Scots, or - - - - - - - -	6	8
For the 2d, and every after Sheet, 1 Scots, or -	1	8
For a Search of the Books for 10 Years - -	5	—
For a Search of One or Two Books, being less than 10 Years - - - - - - - -	2	6
For Trouble in Searching, when done by the Keeper, each Year - - - - - - - - -	—	6
For an Extract of an Abbreviate, same Dues as above for recording.		

In further Obedience to the Queries, the Reporters have only to add, that the Total Amount of the Fees of this Office from all the Branches, as Keepers of the Records, Clerks to Loosings of Arrestments and Lawborrows, and to the Single Bills, is at an Average of the last Three Years, £.184. Sterling, or £.92. per Annum, to each of the Depute Clerks.

All which is humbly reported by

John Watson,
James Merser, } Joint Keepers.

* [Note of a Letter from the Lord Register.]—" I have upon the Spot examined the Office of Mr. John Watson, Keeper of the Record " of Abbreviates of Adjudication, and find that he has no good Ground of Complaint.

" Edinburgh, July 1800. " *Fred. Campbell.*"

SCOTLAND.
Court of Justiciary.
Appendix (X. 2.)

Appendix (X. 2.)

COURT OF JUSTICIARY.

Return by the Deputy Clerk of the High Court of JUSTICIARY in Scotland, to Two Orders made by the Honourable Committee of the House of Commons on the Public Records.

March 11, 1800.—Of this Date there was delivered by the Right Honourable the Lord Justice Clerk, to the Clerks of Justiciary, an Order of the Select Committee of the House of Commons on the Public Records, &c. dated 26th February, 1800, which had been received by his Lordship, requiring Answers by the proper Officer of Court, to certain Questions therein stated; and the High Court of Justiciary having met, ordered that the Principal Clerk of Justiciary, or his Deputy, being the proper Officer of the Court to whom it belongs, do forthwith prepare a full and accurate Return accordingly; and after the same has been perused and approved of by the Lord Justice Clerk, and such of the other Lords Commissioners of Justiciary as may be in Edinburgh at the Time, that he subscribe such Return, and transmit it to the Honourable Committee; and also send a Copy thereof, together with a Copy of the said Order and Questions, to the Lord Advocate, who it is informed is a Member of that Committee.

In obedience to these Orders, the Deputy Clerk of Justiciary humbly reports the following Answers:

(1.) The Principal Clerk of Justiciary, and his Deputies, have always had the Custody of the Records of that Court. The most antient Record extant begins in 1536. They have not been regularly preserved from that Time down to the 1672, as a good many Blanks occur in that early Period; the whole Record extant consists of Seventy four Volumes, Folio.

From the Year 1672, when the Parliamentary Regulations respecting the Judicatories in Scotland took place, this Record is perfectly complete.

The Record of this Court consists of First, The Scroll Book or Minute Book, which is used in Court for writing down the sundry Steps or Minutes of the Proceedings, Depositions of Witnesses, Admissions of Parties, Confessions of Pannels, and the Sentences and other Judgments of the Court, with the original Subscriptions thereto of the Judges, &c. &c.; and Secondly, What are called the Warrants of this Minute Book, such as Indictments, Petitions, &c. These are not ingrossed or copied into the Minute Book, but there referred to as to be taken in, when the Record is extended or made full and complete. Thereafter the Clerks have ever since the 1685, been in Use to make out a full and correct Copy, in large Folio Volumes, commonly called the Books of Adjournal, wherein the Whole of the above Particulars are in their due Order inserted at Length, for the Inspection of the Leiges, so that there is in fact, from 1685 downwards, a Double Record, viz. the Scroll or Minute Book, and Warrants, and the large Register just mentioned.

There are likewise in the Custody of the Principal Clerk of Justiciary, and his Deputies, the Records of the Three Circuit Courts of Justiciary in Scotland, from the Union in 1707, when the same were established, down to the present Time entire. The North consists of 44 Folio Volumes, the South of 23 Folio Volumes, and the West of 31 Folio Volumes of the Original Minute Books of those Courts, together with the separate Warrants therein referred to; but these have never been extended or wrote up together, in other Volumes, in the Manner of the Record of the High Court of Justiciary at Edinburgh.

There is likewise, in the Custody of the Principal Clerk of Justiciary and his Deputies, the Proceedings upon a Commission of Oyer and Terminer in the Year 1746, for trying certain Traitors, as being concerned in the Rebellion 1745-6, consisting of One Folio Volume, and the sundry Bills then found *.

There is likewise, in the Custody of the Principal Clerk of Justiciary and his Deputies, a considerable Part of the Records of the Privy Council of Scotland, previous to the Union of the Two Kingdoms, consisting of Forty-six Volumes Folio, which will be taken Notice of in a subsequent Part of this Report.

(2.) In answering this Question, it is hoped it will not be improper to give some Account of the Manner in which these Records have been preserved. The Justiciary Office, or Office of the Clerks of Justiciary, has always been kept in the House of the Principal Clerk or his Deputy, in a proper Apartment of which the Books of Record were kept; and in an Apartment adjoining to the old Justiciary Court House, where the Judges formerly sat, and the Courts were in Use to be held, were deposited, the Warrants or Papers relative to the said Records; but when the General Register House, erected by Parliamentary Authority, for the Safety of the Public Records of the Kingdom, was built, Two Apartments or Chambers in it were allotted to the Use of the Court of Justiciary, which were taken Possession of accordingly, and the whole Papers, Warrants, &c. deposited in the old Justiciary Court House, were carried thither, yet the Justiciary Office afterwards remained in the House of the Principal Clerk, where the Books of Records were still kept for the Inspection of the Public, and where all the Justiciary Business public and private, done out of Court, was and is carried on.

It may here too be observed, that the Justiciary Clerk's Office cannot be kept in the Register House, or any uninhabited Place, because it cannot conform to any Office Hours or Rules. The Clerks are liable to be called on at all the Hours of the Day or Night; nay, sometimes they are obliged, from the Nature of the Business, to call up the Judges themselves (or some of them) in the Middle of the Night; the Office therefore cannot be shut; and further it frequently happens, that in the course of Trials of the First Importance, Articles, in the Way of Evidence, are lodged in the Hands of the Clerk, which if deposited in an Office kept in an uninhabited Building, the Office might be broke into, these Articles carried off, and public Justice defeated. The Public Justiciary Office therefore, where the Extrajudicial Business is done, is and must be in the House of the Principal Clerk or his Deputy.

The Lord Justice Clerk and Lords Commissioners of Justiciary, with the Lord Advocate of Scotland, lately visited and carefully inspected the Two Apartments already mentioned, in the Register House, and the whole Records and Warrants therein deposited; and a Court having been soon after held, and their Lordships having duly considered the Situation of all Matters, made an Act or Order of Court, that the Clerks should immediately lodge in the said Apartments appropriated to the Court, in the General Register House, the whole Books of Records then in the Justiciary Office, and before particularly mentioned: and which Order, so far as hitherto practicable, has been complied with.

This General Register House is the Property of the Public, and is a Place of perfect Security against Fire; but

* There was another Commission of Oyer and Terminer held at Edinburgh, so late as the Year 1794, but the whole Proceedings thereon were carried off by Mr. Knapp, who came down from London as Clerk to that Court; and none of these Proceedings have ever been returned to the Clerk of Justiciary.

but unless the Apartments are particularly attended to, with proper Fires, and proper Ventilation, it must prove destructive to every Paper or Article therein deposited; for the Building is constructed completely of Stone, and the different Stories arched; not one Bit of Timber, in short, is in the whole Fabrick, excepting the Doors and Windows, and the Floor of One Room for the Lord Clerk Register. The Inside Accommodations for the Justiciary Records and Papers, are at present extremely bad and defective, so that a new and more complete Set of Presses, Shelves, Desks, and also Window Shutters, are absolutely necessary.

(3.) In general these Records are in a good State of Preservation, though some of the oldest Volumes are indeed frail, and require to be tenderly handled; they are all arranged in the Order of Time.

(4.) There are no General Catalogues or Calendars, nor Particular Indexes to these Records. When any Book of Record is called for, the Date is the only Thing to point out what is wanted, and latterly a running Margin has been added when writing up the Record, for the greater Facility in finding out the Case wanted. Were an Index made to the Record of the High Court of Justiciary at Edinburgh, from the Regulations in 1672, and of the Three Circuits Court, from 1707 down to the present Time, it would be of great Use to the Public, by shortening the Researches of Council and Agents, or Solicitors, into these Records; but it would be a Work of considerable Magnitude, even supposing it were to consist only of a List, arranged Alphabetically, of the Names of Parties, with the general Nature of the Crimes or Criminal Matters in which they were concerned, the Dates of the Proceedings thereon, and the particular Volumes or Repositories where such Proceedings may be found; and it is impossible to say with Precision what Time or Labour it might take; the Reporter supposes that it might be the chief Employment of One Clerk and an Assistant for Three Years or thereby; and as it would be considered as an extra Work, beyond what had been hitherto performed by or incumbent on the established Clerks, it is submitted, that during the Time of its going on, some Payments by Interim Warrants might be made to account of the Trouble, and when the Whole is compleated, it might be committed to the Court of Justiciary, to consider the Extent and Performance of the Work, and to give their Opinion of what Reward ought to be given for it.

(5.) The Business of the Justiciary Office, including the keeping of the Records, is discharged by the Principal Clerk and his Deputy, and constantly One, but commonly Two Assistants, who are paid by them. In a former Report the Salaries of the whole Judges and Officers of the Court were particularized. It may now be repeated so far, that the Salaries of the Principal and Deputy Clerk on the Establishment, are for the former £. 200. per Annum, and the latter £. 150. subject to a Deduction of 7½ per Cent. of these Sums; that the Fees for the Three Years then reported, averaged Annually, at the Rate of £. 106. 13*s*. 8*d*. to the Principal, being Two-thirds, and to the Deputy £. 53. 6*s*. 10*d*. being One-third. The Clerks, as has been said, cannot conform to any stated Hours of Attendance, and the Office must always be open.

The particular Fee of shewing One Volume of Record is Five Shillings; and for Searches, Certificates, &c. it is arbitrary, and suited agreeable to the Time and Labour it takes.

There is no Person specially intrusted with the Care of the Records; the same were shewn to Persons calling for Inspection of any of them, by whoever was attending in the Office, and who took back the Book when perused, and replaced it in its former Situation; but now that the Whole of these Records have, by Order of Court, been removed from the Justiciary Office, to the Chambers in the General Register House, a Person must necessarily be employed to attend there for that Special Purpose.

(7.) To this Question the Reporter begs leave to submit a few Observations:

1. The making an Index as before mentioned, would be of great Utility to the Practitioners in the Court, and the Litigants; much Time and Labour would be saved in Searches, as the Cases, Arguments, and Decisions, could immediately be resorted to.

2 It has been mentioned by the Judges, that it might be expedient, that in future the Minute Books and Warrants of the Circuit Courts should be wrote up or extended into a large Register in the same Way as the Proceedings of the High Court of Justiciary at Edinburgh. If this Measure should be adopted, such Allowance might be made therefore, as the Court, upon seeing the Work advance, might think proper to sanction and recommend as reasonable and adequate.

3. It is hoped it will not be deemed improper in the Reporter humbly to observe, that the Principal and Deputy Clerk of Justiciary having obtained their Offices in reliance on the Nature and Extent of the Duties and Burthens incumbered on them, being ascertained by former Usage, it would be extremely hard to lay upon them other new and heavy Burthens for the Security of the Records of Court, and the Accommodation of the Public, when no additional Emolument can be derived to them therefrom, but on the contrary, a very great deal of additional Trouble and Expence, through their being obliged to keep Two Offices instead of One; for as Matters are now situated, they must be under the Necessity of employing an Additional Assistant to attend at the Chamber in the General Register House, who cannot reasonably be paid with less than Sixty Pounds a Year; and also the Expense of Two Fires for these Apartments, and Coal and Candle, cannot be less than Ten Pounds a Year, besides fitting up the Chambers with proper Shelves, Presses, Desks; and the securing the Windows with strong Shutters, considering the present high Price of Wood and Workmanship, cannot be estimated at much less than £. 100.

These Matters were mentioned when the Judges and the Lord Advocate inspected the Apartments, and it is believed, they considered an adequate Provision for them to be reasonable. The Reporter has taken the Liberty of bringing this in view, not doubting that the Honourable Committee will consider it to be just and proper, that the Clerks should not be made Sufferers by the Arrangements which have been or may be made for the Benefit of the Public.

Additional Return by the Deputy Clerk of the High Court of Justiciary, respecting the Privy Council Records.

March 12, 1800.—This Day there was received at the Justiciary Office, under a cover, addressed "The "Privy Council Office, Edinburgh," an Order of the Select Committee on the Public Records, dated 28th February last, requiring an Answer to certain Questions therein specified: And in obedience to that Order, the following Answers are humbly made:

(1.) There is now no Privy Council Office in Scotland. There is in the Custody of the Clerks of Justiciary, as has been said, a considerable Part of the Records of the Privy Council of Scotland, consisting of 46 Volumes Folio; these Records from the Union had been lying (it is believed) in the Signet Office, but by

SCOTLAND.
Court of Justiciary.
Appendix (X. 2)

an Order of his late Majesty King George the Second, of Date the 7th of May, 1746, directed to the then Keeper of the Signet in Scotland, the said Records were ordered to be lodged with the Court of Justiciary, which was done accordingly, and they remained in the Justiciary Office, till removed by the Order of Court above recited, along with the other Records in the Justiciary Office, to the Chambers in the Register House. These Records consist of Thirty-four Volumes of what are called Acts and Decrees of Privy Council, beginning in 1571, and ending in 1705, not however in an uninterrupted Order (but subject to many Defects) nor can it be otherwise from the scattered Situation of that Record, and of Twelve Volumes of what is called the State Record, being the Proceedings of the Privy Council, in the Business relating to the State; they begin in 1661, and end about 1703, but these are likewise deficient.

There are likewise in the Possession of the Lord Clerk Register, in the General Register Office, many Volumes of the Privy Council Record, and One Volume said to be in the Hands of the Clerk of the Lord Lyon's Court. The Court of Justiciary have empowered and requested the Lord Justice Clerk to write to the Lord Clerk Register, in Name of the Court, to remove the Part of this Record in his Custody, into the Repository of the Court of Justiciary in the Register House, and deposit it in the same Place with the other Volumes, and likewise to take the most proper Methods for recovering and depositing, in the same Place, the Volume above mentioned in the Lyon Office, and all other Parts of the said Records which may be found elsewhere.

(2.) These Records, as before noticed, are in the Chambers allotted to the Justiciary in the General Register House before described.

(3.) The Records are in pretty good Preservation; they are arranged in Order of Time.

(4.) There are neither General Catalogues nor Particular Indexes to these Records.

(5.) Nothing occurs to the Reporter that could render these Records of greater Use to the Public; they are not much resorted to, but were they all placed together, a better and more satisfactory Account could be given of them, and the Public would be accommodated with readier Access to the Whole.

Jas Norris,
Deputy Clerk of Justiciary.

The foregoing Return has been perused and approved of by the Right Honourable the Lord Justice Clerk, and Lords Commissioners of Justiciary.

Dav. Rae.
Wm Nairne.
Will. Craig.

Edinburgh,
March 28, 1800.

Appendix (X. 3.)

Return from the Court of EXCHEQUER, in SCOTLAND, to certain Queftions of the Committee on the Public Records, &c. of the Kingdom.

The PUBLIC RECORDS of the COURT of EXCHEQUER:

Appendix (X. 3.)

1. PUBLIC RECORDS in the Office of

	RECORD.	NATURE and USE.	PERIOD.	CONDITION.		ARRANGEMENT, CATALOGUES,			
Number of the Record.	RECORD, ROLL, INSTRUMENT, MANUSCRIPT BOOK or PAPER, &c.	N.B. The RECORDS, of which an Account is given in this Part of the Report, are those which belonged to the antient Scottish Treasury and Exchequer, as these Establishments subsisted previously to the Constitution of the present Court of Exchequer in Scotland, in 1708, by Stat. 6 Ann. cap. 26.	PERIOD of TIME to which the Record relates.	The Record COMPLETE or DEFECTIVE.	State of PRESERVATION of the Records.	ORDER of ARRANGEMENT.	General CATALOGUES or Particular INDEXES, &c.	COMPLETE or DEFECTIVE.	Utility of COMPLETING Defective Catalogues.
1. 2. 3. 4.	EXCHEQUER MINUTES. - - - - ORDERS. TREASURY MINUTES. - - - - ORDERS.	THE Time at which an Exchequer was established in Scotland has not been accurately ascertained. It is certain however that an Exchequer existed in Scotland in the Reign of David II. about the Middle of the 14th Century; and it is probable that it had been established in the Century preceding. The Scottish Exchequer, like that of England, was the Revenue Court of the Sovereign; by which Means it was intimately connected with the Treasury. In Scotland this Court appears at all Times to have been composed of the Chief Officers of the Treasury, the High Treasurer, Treasurer Depute, or Commissioners of the Treasury, and of certain Officers associated with them, called Lords Auditors, or simply Lords of Exchequer. The Number of these Lords of Exchequer was not limited, but depended entirely on the Pleasure of the Sovereign by whom they were appointed. The Officers of the Treasury, though constituent Members of the Court of Exchequer, executed the Business of the Treasury Department by themselves, and the Treasury and Exchequer were entirely distinct and independent of each other. A separate Record was accordingly kept of the Pro-	From the Restoration in 1661, to the Constitution of the present Court of Exchequer at the Union, in 1708.	Several Volumes are wanting.	These Records are in a State of good Preservation.	These Minutes and Orders are all regularly ingrossed in the Order of their Dates, in Volumes.	There are no Catalogues or Indexes to these Records in the Custody of this Officer.		No Utility or Advantage could arise to the Public from making up Catalogues or Indexes to these Records.
5.	PUBLIC ACCOUNTS; viz. Army, Militia, Mint, &c.	ceedings of each. Of these Records of Treasury and Exchequer, the greater Part has been lost or destroyed; and those which now exist, are deposited, partly in the Exchequer Chambers, under the Custody of the King's Remembrancer; partly in the General Register Office.	From the Revolution in 1688, to the Union in 1707.	The Accounts of prior Payments for the like Service, so far as extant, are in the General Register Office.	Same as above.	These Accounts are tied up in separate Parcels.	Same as above.		Same as above.
6.	SIGNATURES.	SIGNATURES are of Two Kinds; viz. 1st, Signatures for new Infeftment, or Investiture; and, 2d, Signatures for Gifts. 1st. All Lands in Scotland, according to the Policy of the Feudal System, are holden by the respective Proprietors, by Feudal Tenure of the Sovereign as Superior or Lord Paramount, either immediately, or by the Intervention of one or more Subject-superiors, the first or highest of whom is an immediate Vassal of the Crown. The Charter by which a Crown Vassal holds his Lands, (like that granted by a Subject-superior to his Sub-vassal) contains certain Limitations and Restrictions affecting his Rights and Powers of Property in the Fee, and in particular prohibiting the Alienation of it to any Person not comprehended in the Order of Inheritance prescribed by the Investiture. These Limitations and Restrictions cannot be extinguished or defeated, but by obtaining from the Sovereign a new Investiture. Antiently, when Application was made to the Sovereign for a new Investiture of Lands or other Subjects, or Rights holden feudally of the Crown, the Person who made the Application employed a Clerk in the Office of the Secretary of State, called a Clerk to the Signet, to prepare a Letter to be presented by the Secretary to the Sovereign, containing a Draft of the Investiture demanded. The Sovereign expressed his Approbation of the Contents of the Letter, when presented to him, by prefixing to it his Royal Sign Manual or Signature; and the Letter being framed purposely for receiving the Royal Signature, and deriving thence its subsequent Use and Authority, was itself called a SIGNATURE.—The Signature after being passed (approved and signed) by the Sovereign, became a Warrant to the proper Officers for expediting, under the Great Seal of Scotland, a Charter from the Crown in Terms of the Signature; and the new Investiture was completed by the Charter passing under the Great Seal accordingly, and by the Infeftment being taken upon it. 2d. When Lands or other Subjects, Rights, Honours, Offices, or Privileges enjoyed by Subjects, reverted to the Crown, Jure Coronæ, or as Feudal Superior of the Kingdom, it was customary for the Kings of Scotland to bestow them by Gift on those Persons, who by their Attachment to the Sovereign, by their Services to the State, by their Qualifications to hold them, or by some natural Claim or Title, appeared to merit such Favours. In this Manner, in particular, were Gifted Single and Life Rent Escheats, and all other Casualties incident to the Feudal Tenures; whatever accrued to the Crown by Forfeiture, by Succession, as Ultimus Hæres, or by Bastardy; the Right to Tutories-Dative—to Ecclesiastical Benefices—Rights, Honours, Offices, and Privileges of various Kinds. All such Gifts were obtained upon Signatures, which, after being passed by the Sovereign, became Warrants to the proper Officers for expediting and completing the Gifts to which they referred, by passing them under the proper Seals. *(continued)*	Of Date prior to the Restoration in 1661.	Of these Signatures there are only sundry Volumes extant.	Same as above.	These Signatures are recorded in Volumes, in the Order of their respective Dates.			

the KING'S REMEMBRANCER. Appendix (X. 3.)

and REGULATIONS.			OFFICERS employed in Cuſtody and Arrangement.						PLACE of DEPOSIT.				
TIME and EXPENSE required for ſo doing.	Regulation for RESTORING Records to their proper Places.	New Regulations requiſite for rendering Uſe of the Record more convenient.	OFFICERS.	Their general DUTIES in reſpect of Cuſtody or Arrangement.	Attendance.	NET SALARY paid by the Public.	FEES demandable for Searches or Certificates.	Net Annual Amount of FEES on an Average of the laſt Three Years.	BUILDING.	Condition as to SECURITY.	Condition as to ACCOMMODATION.	PUBLIC or PRIVATE Property.	TENURE and TERM by and for which holden.
The Time and Expenſe would be very great of making up Catalogues or Indexes.	When Inſpection of theſe Records is demanded (which hardly ever occurs) the Remembrancer and his Clerks attend, and reſtore the Record to its proper Place.	No new Regulation is neceſſary for rendering the Uſe of theſe Records more convenient to the Public. The Officers and Clerks in whoſe Cuſtody they are, have by Experience ſuch perfect Knowledge of them, that they point out with Readineſs whatever is wanted.	Theſe Records are under the Cuſtody of the King's Remembrancer, and the Clerks in his Office.	The Duties are limited by the Nature of theſe Records to their Cuſtody only.	No Attendance is required on Account of theſe Records, they are ſo ſeldom wanted.	None.			Theſe Records are lodged in Apartments and Cloſets in the Building where the Court of Exchequer ſits, which is ſituated in the Parliament Square, Edinburgh.	Tolerably ſecure.	Rather incommodious.	This Building is the Property of the Corporation of the City of Edinburgh.	This Building has been long poſſeſſed by the Public, Rent free, for the Accommodation of the Court; and there is Reaſon to believe that Poſſeſſion will continue to be granted for the ſame Purpoſe in Perpetuity.
Same as above.	Same as above.	Same as above.	Same as above.	Same as above.	Same as above.	Same as above.			Same as above.	Same as above.	Same as above.	Same as above.	Same as above.
	Same as above.	Same as above.	Same as above.	Same as above.	Same as above.	Same as above.			Same as above.	Same as above.	Same as above.	Same as above.	Same as above.

Appendix (X. 3.)

1. PUBLIC RECORDS in the Office of

Number.	RECORD, ROLL, INSTRUMENT, MANUSCRIPT BOOK or PAPER, &c.	NATURE and USE.	PERIOD. Period of Time to which the Record relates.	CONDITION. The Record complete or defective.	State of Preservation of the Records.	ARRANGEMENT, CATALOGUES, Order of Arrangement.	General Catalogue or Particular Indexes, &c.	Complete or Defective	Utility of completing Defective Catalogues.
6.	SIGNATURES, *(continued.)*	Originally, all Signatures received the Royal Sign Manual; but when the Kings of Scotland, after the Accession of James VI. to the Crown of England in 1603, took up their Residence in England, a Power of passing certain Signatures without the Royal Superscription, and in the Absence of the Sovereign, was by Commission from the Crown delegated to the Scottish Exchequer; and as antient Forms required the King's Name to be prefixed to all Signatures, a Cachet or Seal, having a Fac-Simile of the Sign Manual of the Reigning Sovereign engraven upon it, was appointed by an Act of Privy Council, 4th April 1603, to be made and kept in Scotland, with which all Signatures passed in Exchequer should be sealed. An Officer in Exchequer, called Presenter of Signatures, was afterwards appointed, whose Duty it was to present to the Lords of Treasury and Exchequer all Signatures which they were empowered to pass. All Signatures not comprehended in the Commission to the Exchequer, continued to require and to receive the Royal Sign Manual. Signatures, after being passed by the Sovereign, or in Exchequer, were recorded in the Treasurer's Register in Exchequer before passing the Seals. Signatures appear to have been introduced into Practice, as the Form of obtaining the Sovereign's Consent to the Matters contained in them, and his Authority for completing, by passing under the Seals, the Charters or Gifts whereof they were the Warrants. They were useful as affording to the Sovereign and the Officers of the Crown an Opportunity of duly considering the Propriety and Expediency of all Royal Grants; and in Grants of new Investiture, it was the particular Duty of the Lords of Treasury and Exchequer to take Care that nothing was comprehended in the Signatures which the former Charters and Title Deeds did not authorize, or which was prejudicial to the Dignity, Honour, or Interests of the Crown, or to the Interests of Subjects deriving Right from the Crown. The Use of Signatures however was limited to that Stage of the Proceedings in the Execution of Grants from the Crown, which preceded the passing them under the Seals; for, by the sealing, all such Grants are completed; and from that Date accordingly the Charters or Gifts themselves, and not the Signatures on which they proceeded, afford the only legal Evidence of their Nature and Extent.	From the Restoration in 1661 to the Constitution of the present Court of Exchequer in 1708.	Complete.	These Records are in a State of good Preservation.	These Signatures are recorded in Volumes kept for that Purpose, in the Order of their respective Dates.	Subjoined to each Volume of the Record is a List of the Signatures, which List serves the Purpose of an Index.	These Lists are complete.	
7.	RESIGNATIONS.	RESIGNATION is the Form of Law by which a Vassal symbolically resigns his Fee to his Superior for a new Investiture. The proper Symbol of Resignation of Lands in Scotland is a Staff or Baton, which the Vassal, on his Knee, presents to the Superior, by whom it is immediately re-delivered to the Person in whose Favour the new Investiture is demanded. Upon the fact of Resignation being made, an Instrument is immediately extended by a Notary Public; and thereby the Resignation is completed. But the Resigner is not divested of the Fee by the Act of Resignation, until the Person in whose Favour it is made, complete his Right by Infeftment. Hence the Law of Scotland does not require Resignations to be registered: But for the better ordering the Proceedings in Exchequer, and to prevent the Trouble and Litigation which might be occasioned by different Resignations of the same Subject in favour of different Persons, a Register of Resignations made by Crown Vassals was appointed to be kept in the Exchequer, by an Officer, to whom a Salary was allowed, in Order that the Registration might not occasion Expense to the Persons concerned. The Form of the Register is a short Note or Entry of the Lands resigned, the Name of the Resigner, of the Person or Persons in whose Favour Resignation is made, and of the Notary Public and Witnesses by whom the Resignation is attested. The Signature of Resignation itself is recorded in the Register of Signatures. This Record serves as an Index to the Record of Signatures of Resignation, but is of no Use in ascertaining the Validity or Preference of Right founded on Resignations, which are completed by the Infeftment following thereon, and are accordingly preferred by the Priority of the respective Dates of Infeftment. The Ceremony of Resignation is performed either by the Superior and Vassal in Person, or by Procurators empowered to act for them. The Kings of Scotland seldom received Resignations in Person, but appointed Commissioners for that Purpose. When Power was given in 1603 by the Sovereign to the Lords of Treasury and Exchequer in Scotland, to pass certain Signatures, they were also appointed Commissioners for receiving Resignations in his Majesty's Name.	From A. D. 1636 to 1703.		Same as above.	These Resignations are recorded in the Order of their Dates in Volumes.	The Record itself is in the Nature of an Index, the Resignations recorded being entered in the Order of their Dates, and classed by Years and Terms.		

the KING'S REMEMBRANCER—(continued.) Appendix (X. 3.)

and REGULATIONS.			OFFICERS employed in Custody and Arrangement.						PLACE of DEPOSIT.				
TIME and EXPENSE required for so doing.	Regulation for RESTORING Records to their proper Places.	New Regulations requisite for rendering Use of the Record more convenient.	OFFICERS.	Their general DUTIES in respect of Custody or Arrangement.	Attendance.	NET SALARY paid by the Public.	FEES demandable for Searches or Certificates.	Net Annual Amount of FEES on an Average of the last Three Years.	BUILDING.	Condition as to SECURITY.	Condition as to ACCOMMODATION.	PUBLIC or PRIVATE Property.	TENURE and TERM by and for which holden
	When Inspection of these Records is demanded (which hardly ever occurs) the Remembrancer and his Clerks attend, and restore the Record to its proper Place.	No new Regulation is necessary for rendering the Use of these Records more convenient to the Public. The Officer and Clerks in whose Custody they are, have by Experience such perfect Knowledge of them, that they point out with Readiness whatever is wanted.	These Records are in the Custody of the King's Remembrancer and the Clerks in his Office.	The Duties are limited by the Nature of these Records to their Custody only.	No Attendance is required on account of these Records, they are so seldom wanted.	None.			These Records are lodged in Apartments and Closets in the Building where the Court of Exchequer sits, which is situated in the Parliament Square, Edinburgh.	Tolerably secure.	Rather incommodious.	This Building is the Property of the Corporation of the City of Edinburgh.	This Building has been long possessed by the Public, Rent free, for the Accommodation of the Court; and there is Reason to believe, that Possession will continue to be granted for the same Purpose in Perpetuity.
	Same as above.	Same as above.	Same as above.	Same as above.	Same as above.	Same as above.			Same as above.	Same as above.	Same as above.	Same as above.	Same as above.

Appendix (X. 3.)

1. PUBLIC RECORDS in the Court of

Number.	RECORD, ROLL, INSTRUMENT, MANUSCRIPT BOOK or PAPER, &c.	NATURE and USE.	PERIOD.	CONDITION.		ARRANGEMENT, CATALOGUES,			
			Period of Time to which the Record relates.	The Records complete or defective.	State of Preservation of the Records.	Order of Arrangement.	General Catalogues or Particular Indexes, &c.	Complete or Defective.	Utility of completing Defective Catalogues.
8.	BURROW, or BOROUGH ROLLS.	BOROUGHS ROYAL were erected or created by the Sovereign, who, by a Charter, called a Charter of Erection, granted in Feu a Portion of Lands, with certain Privileges annexed to it, to the Persons forming the Community or Incorporation of the Borough, and their Successors, to be holden by them as Vassals of the Crown, by the Feudal Tenure called Burgage-Holding, for the Yearly Performance of certain Services, and Payment of the Mails or Duties specified in the Reddendo Clauses of their respective Charters. These Duties or Borough Mails, as constituting a Part of the Public Revenue of the Crown, were accounted for Annually in Exchequer, where a Roll or Account was kept of all the Royal Boroughs, and of the Duties payable by each Borough; according to which Roll the Magistrates, who had the Collection of them within their respective Boroughs, were charged in rendering their Accounts. The Method of accounting was called "Fitting Æque's in Exchequer;" that is, balancing the Charge and Discharge of the Account. The Number of the Royal Boroughs in Scotland, at the Union of the Two Kingdoms, was 68; and the Amount of the Duties payable by them to the Crown was £.75. 4s. 7½d.	From the Year 1300 till the Union.	The Rolls of many Years are wanting.	These Records are in a State of good Preservation.	The Rolls are made up Annually.	None.		
9.	RENT ROLLS of the Estates of the Archbishops and Bishops, annexed to the Crown in 1690.	UPON the final Abolition of Episcopacy in Scotland, by the Acts of the Scottish Parliament passed in 1689, c. 3. and 1690, c. 5. immediately after the Revolution, the Landed Estates of the Archbishops and Bishops were annexed to the Crown; and a Return was delivered into Exchequer, by the Prelates or their Factors, of the Rents and Revenues arising from their Estates at the Date of the Annexation. See Page 436, Record No. 3.	1689 and 1690.	Several of these Rent Rolls are wanting.	Same as above.		Same as above.		
10.	ACCOUNTS of Payments made to the Army in Scotland.	THESE Accounts belonged to the Scottish Treasury.	From the Revolution in 1688 to the Union in 1707.	There are only some of the Accounts in this Office. The Accounts of prior Payments for the like Service, so far as they are extant, are in the Register Office.	Same as above.		Same as above.		

the KING'S REMEMBRANCER—(continued.) Appendix (X. 3.)

and REGULATIONS.			OFFICERS employed in Cuſtody and Arrangement.						PLACE of DEPOSIT.					
TIME and EXPENSE required for ſo doing.	Regulations for RESTORING Records to their proper Places.	New Regulations requiſite for rendering Uſe of the Records more convenient.	OFFICERS.	Their general DUTIES in reſpect of Cuſtody or Arrangement.	Attendance.	NET SALARY paid by the Public.	FEES demandable for Searches or Certificates.	Net Annual Amount of FEES on an Average of the laſt Three Years.	BUILDING.	Condition as to SECURITY.	Condition as to ACCOMMODATION.	PUBLIC or PRIVATE Property.	TENURE and TERM by and for which holden
	When Inſpection of theſe Records is demanded (which hardly ever occurs) the Remembrancer and his Clerks attend, and reſtore the Record to its proper Place.	No new Regulation is neceſſary for rendering the Uſe of theſe Records more convenient to the Public. The Officer and Clerks in whoſe Cuſtody they are, have by Experience ſuch perfect Knowledge of them, that they point out with Readineſs whatever is wanted.	Theſe Records are under the Cuſtody of the King's Remembrancer and the Clerks in his Office.	The Duties are limited by the Nature of theſe Records to their Cuſtody only.	No Attendance on account of theſe Records, they are ſo ſeldom wanted.	None.			Theſe Records are lodged in Apartments and Cloſets in the Building where the Court of Exchequer ſits, which is ſituated in the Parliament Square, Edinburgh.	Tolerably ſecure.	Rather incommodious.	The Building is the Property of the Corporation of the City of Edinburgh.	The Building has been long poſſeſſed by the Public Rent-free, for the Accommodation of the Court; and there is Reaſon to believe that Poſſeſſion will continue to be granted for the ſame Purpoſe in Perpetuity.
	Same as above.	Same as above.	Same as above.	Same as above.	Same as above.	Same as above.			Same as above.	Same as above.	Same as above.	Same as above.	Same as above.
	Same as above.	Same as above.	Same as above.	Same as above.	Same as above.	Same as above.			Same as above.	Same as above.	Same as above.	Same as above.	Same as above.

Appendix (X. 3.)

1. PUBLIC RECORDS [illegible]

RECORDS of Date subsequent to the Con[illegible]

<table>
<tr><th rowspan="2">Number.</th><th rowspan="2">RECORD, ROLL, INSTRUMENT, MANUSCRIPT BOOK or PAPER, &c.</th><th rowspan="2">NATURE and USE.</th><th>PERIOD.</th><th colspan="2">CONDITION.</th><th colspan="4">ARRANGEMENT, CATA[illegible]</th></tr>
<tr><th>PERIOD of TIME to which the Record relates.</th><th>The Records COMPLETE or DEFECTIVE.</th><th>State of PRESERVATION of the Records.</th><th>ORDER of ARRANGEMENT.</th><th>General CATALOGUES or Particular INDEXES, &c.</th><th>Completeness or Defectiveness.</th><th>Utility of COMPLETING Defective Catalogues.</th></tr>
<tr><td>1.</td><td>MINUTE BOOK.</td><td>I.—RECORDS belonging to the Court of EXCHEQUER as a Court of JUDICATURE.

1st. RECORDS in the REMEMBRANCER's own Custody.

THE MINUTE BOOK is made up in Court by the Remembrancer, and contains a short Note or Entry of the Names of the Plaintiff and Defendant, the Nature of the Action or Proceeding, the Motions made in Court thereupon, with the Order of Court, and the finding of Juries. The Judicial Procedure had upon these Motions, Orders, or Verdicts, is conducted in the Remembrancer's Office by the Sworn Clerks of Court under him; and all the Records thereof are under the immediate Custody of one of these Clerks, as "Keeper of the Records and Register of Orders," and form the Subject of a separate Report from him, which is hereto subjoined.</td><td>From the Constitution of the present Court of Exchequer to the present Time.</td><td>Complete.</td><td>In good Preservation.</td><td>The Entries which compose this Record are made regularly as the Proceeding to which they relate occur, in each Term, in a Volume.</td><td>None.</td><td></td><td>There would be no material Utility in making up Catalogues or Indexes to this Record.</td></tr>
<tr><td>2.</td><td>BOOK of RULES.</td><td>THESE RULES are Regulations, which were established by the present Court of Exchequer soon after its Constitution, for regulating the Forms of proceeding in all Actions and Matters brought into Court, and were framed by the first Barons of Exchequer in Scotland, after similar Regulations observed in the Court of Exchequer in England. A few additional Rules, which Experience had shewn to be requisite, have at different Periods since been added; and the Whole of these Rules are now in Observance.</td><td>Same as above.</td><td>Same as above.</td><td>Same as above.</td><td>These Rules are written in a Paper Book, in the Order of their Dates.</td><td>None requisite.</td><td></td><td>Same as above.</td></tr>
<tr><td>3.</td><td>ROLLS of Judicial Proceedings in Court.</td><td>2d. RECORDS in the Custody of "THE KEEPER OF RECORDS AND REGISTER OF ORDERS," an Officer in the King's Remembrancer's Office.

THESE ROLLS (which are on Parchment) form the Record in each particular Case, of the Judicial Proceedings between Plaintiff and Defendant in all Actions, Bills, Informations, &c. which come before the Court of Exchequer.</td><td rowspan="5">From the Constitution of the Court in 1708 to the Year 1791 inclusive.</td><td rowspan="5">Complete, with the Exception of a few Bundles of Rolls which are wanting, but which will probably be recovered in the Course of arranging the Records belonging to this Office. The Rolls subsequent to 1791 are still in the Hands of the Attornies.</td><td rowspan="5">In good Preservation; with the Exception of a few Rolls, relating to the Years 1723 and 1724, which were damaged by Water, while they were lodged in the King's Remembrancer's Office in the Building where the Court of Exchequer sits.</td><td>Each Roll is labelled, and the Whole are arranged by Terms and Years.</td><td rowspan="5">There is no Catalogue or Index to these Records. But prior to the Year 1767, there had been an Index to the Judicial Records, which was carried out of the Office by the then Keeper. Measures were taken by Order of the Court for its Recovery, but ineffectually; and it is not known whether it now exists.</td><td rowspan="5"></td><td rowspan="5">An Index to the Records (at least to the Books of Decrees and Orders) would be of Use to the Court and Officers belonging to it.</td></tr>
<tr><td>4.</td><td>FILES of WRITS.</td><td>ALL WRITS issuing from the Exchequer, in Judicial Matters, are issued from the Office of King's Remembrancer, and are filed there. They are issued in Behalf either of the King or of other Suitors in Court.</td><td>These Writs are filed in the Order in which they are issued.</td></tr>
<tr><td>5.</td><td>REGISTER of DECREES and ORDERS.</td><td>ALL ORDERS, DECREES, or JUDGMENTS of the Court of Exchequer, in Matters Judicial, are recorded in this Office in Volumes kept for that special Purpose.</td><td>Entered in Volumes in the Order of their Dates.</td></tr>
<tr><td>6.</td><td>INROLMENTS of LETTERS PATENT.</td><td>ALL LETTERS PATENT, after being first registered in a Record kept by the Remembrancer, are again recorded by one of the Sworn Clerks, by inrolling them upon Parchment Rolls.</td><td>Each Roll is labelled.</td></tr>
<tr><td>7.</td><td>COMMISSIONS for setting out the Limits of the different Ports in Scotland, WITH The RETURNS AND INROLMENTS thereof.</td><td>BY the Act of Parliament constituting the present Court of Exchequer, 6 Anne, cap. 26. sec. 18. "For the better "and more effectual ascertaining the Ports, Members, "Creeks, and Havens in Scotland, where Goods and Mer- "chandizes have been or may be exported or imported, and "the several Keys, Wharfs, and other Places where the "same may be put on Board any Ship or Vessel for Trans- "portation, or be unshipt or unladed for Importation;" it is enacted, "That the Queen's Majesty, her Heirs and Suc- "cessors, shall and may from Time to Time, by Commis- "sion or Commissions out of the Court of Exchequer in "Scotland, assign and appoint all such farther Places, Ports, "Members, and Creeks in Scotland, as shall be lawful for "the landing and discharging, lading or shipping of any "Goods, Wares, or Merchandizes in Scotland, and to "what antient and Head Ports respectively such Places, "Members, or Creeks shall respectively appertain, &c." Such Commissions are accordingly issued from the Remembrancer's Office, and the Commissions, with the Returns thereon, are inrolled on Rolls of Parchment by one of the Sworn Clerks.</td><td>The Commissions and Returns are upon the same File. The Inrolments are upon another File.</td></tr>
</table>

the KING'S REMEMBRANCER—(*continued*). Appendix ([illegible])

present Court of EXCHEQUER in SCOTLAND, by Stat. 6 Anne, Cap. 26.

and REGULATIONS.			OFFICERS employed in Custody and Arrangement.						PLACE of DEPOSIT.				
TIME and EXPENSE required for so doing.	Regulation for RESTORING Records to their proper Places.	New Regulations requisite for rendering Use of the Records more convenient.	OFFICERS.	Their general DUTIES in respect of Custody or Arrangement.	Attendance.	NET SALARY paid by the Public.	FEES demandable for Searches or Certificates.	Net Annual Amount of FEES on an Average of the last Three Years.	BUILDING.	Condition as to SECURITY.	Condition as to ACCOMMODATION.	PUBLIC or PRIVATE Property.	TENURE and TERM by and for which holden.
Time and Expense would be great.	This Record is never removed from its Place except by the Clerks in the Remembrancer's Office, when they have Occasion for it, by whom it is again restored to its proper Place.	Ready and immediate Access is had by those concerned to this and all other Public Records in this Office; and the Officers and Clerks in whose Custody they are, have by Experience such perfect Knowledge of them, that they point out at once, and without Trouble, whatever is wanted.	The King's Remembrancer and Clerks in his Office.	These Duties are, by the Nature of the Record, limited to the Custody alone.	Attendance is given in the King's Remembrancer's Office by himself, his Deputy or Attornies, on account of the general Business of the Office, every lawful Day (Holidays excepted, which are 14 in Number in the Year) from 9 o'Clock A. M. to 4 o'Clock P. M.	None.			In the Treasury Chambers and King's Remembrancer's Office, in the Building where the Court of Exchequer sits, in the Parliament Square in the City of Edinburgh.	Tolerably secure.	Sufficiently commodious.	This Building is the Property of the Incorporation of the City of Edinburgh.	It has been long possessed by the Public Rent-free for the Accommodation of the Court, and there is Reason to believe that Possession will continue to be granted for the same Purpose in Perpetuity.
Same as above.	Same as above.	Same as above.	Same as above.	Same as above.	Same as above.	Same as above.			Same as above.	Same as above.	Same as above.	Same as above.	Same as above.
An Index to the Whole of these Records could not be completed by the Keeper and an able Assistant in less Time than Eighteen Months or Two Years, and at an Expense of between £. 300 or £. 400.—An Index to the Orders and Decrees might be completed by the Keeper at a moderate Expense.	Same as above.	Same as above.	Keeper of the Records and Register of Orders.	The Duties of the Keeper, as to these Records, is limited in a great Measure to their Custody only.—He affords Inspection, and Certificates when wanted. The Keeper, after receiving the Rolls from the Clerks or Attornies, who make them up, lodges them in the proper Repositories.	Same as above.	£. 10 per Annum. Paid by the Barons out of the Sum allowed by the Public for the Support of the Court.	8 d. per Folio for Copies of Records. 3 s. 4 d. for certifying. 10 s. 6 d. when subpœna'd as a Witness upon Trials to produce Records.	Ten Shillings.	General Register Office in the City of Edinburgh.	Perfectly secure.	Perfectly commodious.	Public Property.	
									Same as Record No. 3.	Same as No. 3.	Same as No. 3.	Same as No. 3.	
									Same as No. 1.	Same as No. 1.	Same as No. 1.	Same as No. 1.	Same as No. 1.
									Same as No. 3.	Same as No. 3.	Same as No. 3.	Same as No. 3.	
									Same as Record No. 1.	Same as Record No. 1.	Same as Record No. 1.	Same as Record No. 1.	Same as Record No. 1.

Appendix (X. 3.) 1. PUBLIC RECORDS in the Office of the KING'S REMEMBRANCER,

Number.	RECORD, ROLL, INSTRUMENT, MANUSCRIPT BOOK or PAPER, &c.	NATURE and USE.	PERIOD.	CONDITION.		ARRANGEMENT, CATALOGUES;			
			Period of Time to which the Records relate.	The Records complete or defective.	State of Preservation of the Records.	Order of Arrangement.	General Catalogues or Particular Indexes, &c.	Complete or Defective.	Utility of completing Defective Catalogues.
		II.—RECORDS belonging to the Court of Exchequer, as a Board of Treasury and Revenue. 1. TREASURY.							
8.	MINUTE BOOK.	IN this Record a short Entry is made of the Substance of all Petitions addressed or read to the Barons, with the Orders made thereon; and in general of all Matters passing under the Deliberation and Order of the Court, relating to Treasury and Revenue Business.	From the Constitution of the present Court of Exchequer to the present Time.	Complete.	In good Preservation.	The Entries which compose this Record are made regularly as the Proceeding to which they relate occur in each Term, in a Volume.	None.		There would be no material Utility in making up Catalogues or Indexes to this Record.
9.	BOOK of ORDERS.	IN this Record are entered, in the Order of their Dates, and at full Length, all Orders of Court, in relation to Treasury and Revenue Business.	Same as above.	Same as above.	Same as above.	Same as above.	None.		Same as above.
10.	PETITIONS, MEMORIALS, BRIEVES, &c. with REPORTS thereon, presented and read to the Barons.	THE Business in this Department is carried on chiefly by Petitions, Memorials, &c. addressed to the Barons, and read in Court (i. e. in the Treasury Chambers) by the King's Remembrancer; on which Petitions, Memorials, &c. the Barons order Reports from the Remembrancer, from the Solicitor, or from the Tax Office, Customs, or Excise; and on the Petitions being again read in Court, with the Reports thereon, the Barons give their Order; and the Substance of the Petition, Report, and Order, is minuted by the Remembrancer.	Same as above.	Same as above.	Same as above.	The Original Petitions, &c. and Reports, are tied up in Parcels at the End of each Year for the last 10 Years, and kept in Clerks.	Till within these last 10 Years these Petitions, &c. and Reports, are arranged in Alphabetical Order.	Complete.	Same as above.
11.	RECORD of PETITIONS, MEMORIALS, &c. &c. REPORTS thereon.	THE Petitions, Memorials, &c. which are copied into this Record, are those which, having been presented to the King, or the Lords Commissioners of the Treasury in London, are referred to the Lord Chief Baron and Barons of Exchequer in Scotland, for their Opinion and Report. These Reports are drawn up by the King's Remembrancer or his Deputy, and when approved by the Barons are returned to the Treasury. The Petitions, &c. Reference and Reports, are thereafter recorded in this Book by the Remembrancer or his Clerks. The Original Petitions, &c. are returned with the Reports.	Same as above.	Same as above.	Same as above.	The Record is regularly kept in the Order of the Dates and Occurrences.	Particular Index.	Complete.	
12.	REGISTER of SIGNATURES.	THE Nature of Signatures has already been explained (Page 414, No. 6). By the Act constituting the present Court, Stat. 6 Anne, cap. 26. sec. 19. upon the Preamble, That whereas by the Treaty of Union it is provided, "That the Court of Exchequer in Scotland have Power of "passing Signatures, Gifts, Tutories, and in other Things "as the Court of Exchequer in Scotland, at the Time of the "said Treaty, had;"—It is enacted, "That Signatures, "Gifts, Tutories, and other Things, which were presented, "revised, and compounded, or which were passed or given "by the Lord High Treasurer or Commissioners of the "Treasury, or Court of Exchequer there, at the Time of "the said Treaty, which shall be given in, resigned, pre-"sented, revised, compounded, and expedited, as formerly; "with the Alteration only, that the Presenter of Signatures "shall present the said Signatures, Gifts, Tutories, and "other Things, to the Chief Baron and Barons of Exche-"quer in Scotland, who are hereby authorized and em-"powered to revise and compound the same, in the same "Manner, and with the same Powers, as the said Lord High Treasurer or Commissioners of "the Treasury of Scotland might have done; and thereafter in a Court of Exchequer to hear "Parties concerned, and to pass all such Signatures, Gifts, Tutores, and other Things aforesaid, "and especially to declare and appoint Fines, as the Court of Exchequer might have done at the "Time of the said Treaty: And such Signatures, Gifts, Tutores, and other Things aforesaid, "being passed in Exchequer, shall be recorded by the proper Clerks, and thereafter be expedited "at the proper Seals, as at the Time of the said Treaty, by the Law and Practice of Scotland, "was required."—These Signatures, &c. have accordingly been passed in Manner above directed, and after being passed have been recorded in the Treasury Register of Signatures in Exchequer, by the King's Remembrancer, by whom that Record has been kept since the Constitution of the present Court. This Record is not received in Court, even for the Purpose of revising subsequent Signatures of the same Lands, as legal Evidence of the Matters contained in the Charters or Gifts founded on the Signatures therein recorded; which Matters must be proved by the Charters or Gifts themselves after they have passed the Seals. Hence this Record is of very little Use as to those Charters or Gifts which have passed the Seals, except for the Purpose of shewing what Charters or Gifts have been granted by the Crown, and that these have been granted in a regular and legal Manner.—Besides Signatures of Lands, Gifts, [illegible], Leases of Tythes, &c. this Record also contains Commissions and Warrants of certain Kinds which pass under the Privy Seal of Scotland.	Same as above.	Same as above.	Same as above.	These Signatures are entered in the Order of their Dates, in Volumes kept for that Purpose.	There is a complete Particular Index to the Register of Signatures, called the Minute Book of Signatures.	Complete.	

of Date subsequent to the CONSTITUTION of the present Court of EXCHEQUER in SCOTLAND—(continued.) Appendix (X. 3.)

and REGULATIONS.			OFFICERS employed in Custody and Arrangement.						PLACE of DEPOSIT.				
TIME and EXPENSE required for so doing.	Regulation for RESTORING Records to their proper Places.	New Regulations requisite for rendering Use of the Record more convenient.	OFFICERS.	Their general DUTIES in respect of Custody or Arrangement.	Attendance.	NET SALARY paid by the Public.	FEES demandable for Searches or Certificates.	Net Annual Amount of FEES on an Average of the last Three Years.	BUILDING.	Condition as to SECURITY.	Condition as to ACCOMMODATION.	PUBLIC or PRIVATE Property.	TENURE and TERMS by and for which holden.
Time and Expense would be great.	This Record is at all Times in the Custody of the King's Remembrancer, by whom it is always restored to its proper Place.	None.	King's Remembrancer and Deputy.	These Duties are, by the Nature of the Record, limited to the Custody alone.	Attendance is given by the King's Remembrancer or his Deputy, on account of the general Business of the Office every lawful Day (Holidays excepted, which are 14 in Number in the Year) from Nine o'Clock A. M. till Four o'Clock P. M.	None.	None.		In the Treasury Chambers and King's Remembrancer's Office, in the Building where the Court of Exchequer sits in the Parliament Square, Edinburgh.	Tolerably secure.	Sufficiently commodious.	The Building is the Property of the Corporation of the City of Edinburgh.	It has been possessed by the Public, Rent-free, for the Accommodation of the Courts; and there is Reason to believe that Possession will continue to be granted for the same Purpose in Perpetuity.
Same as above.	Same as above.	None.	Same as above.	Same as above.	Same as above.	None.	None.		Same as above.	Tolerably secure.	Same as above.	Same as above.	Same as above.
Same as above.	Same as above.	None.	Same as above.	Same as above.	Same as above.	None.	Inspection of a Report, 2s. 6d.		Same as above.	Same as above.	Same as above.	Same as above.	Same as above.
	Same as above.	None.	Same as above.	Same as above.	Same as above.	None.	Inspection of a Volume, 1s. Report, } 2s. 6d. Order, }		Same as above.	Same as above.	Same as above.	Same as above.	Same as above.
	Same as above.	None.	Same as above.	The Remembrancer and his Deputy have this Record constantly in their Custody. The Record is made up by them, and arranged in Presses, &c	Same as above.	None.	Inspection of a Signature, 2s. 6d. Certificate or Exemplification, 6s. 8d.		In Presses or Closets in the Room where the Court sits.	Same as above.	Same as above.	Same as above.	Same as above.

Appendix (X. 3.)

1. PUBLIC RECORDS in the Office of the KING'S REMEMBRANCER.

Number.	RECORD, ROLL, INSTRUMENT, MANUSCRIPT BOOK or PAPER, &c.	NATURE and USE.	PERIOD. Period of Time to which the Records relate.	CONDITION. The Records Complete or Defective.	CONDITION. State of Preservation of the Records.	ARRANGEMENT, CATALOGUES, &c. Order of Arrangement.	General Catalogues or Particular Indexes, &c.	Complete or Defective.	Utility of completing Defective Catalogues.
13.	REGISTER of RESIGNATIONS.	THE Nature of Resignations, and the Use of this Record, have already been explained (Page 416, No. 7.) By St. 6 Anne, cap. 26. sec. 19. it is Enacted, " That the Court " of Exchequer in Scotland shall have Power to receive Re- " signations in her Majesty's Name of all Baronies, Lands, " Lordships, Tythes, Jurisdictions, Offices, and all other " Rights which were in Use to be resigned and received in " her Majesty's Name in the Exchequer at the Time of the " Treaty of Union:"—" Reserving nevertheless full Power " to her Majesty, her Heirs, and Successors, to receive Re- " signations immediately in her or their Royal Hands, &c." In 1794, the present Keeper of this Record made a consi- derable Improvement in the Manner of making it up, by comprehending in it, in so far as applicable, the like Parti- culars of all Signatures for new Investiture, as by Confirma- tion, Sale, Adjudication, &c. whereby this Record has been rendered more general and comprehensive, and more useful and convenient for the Public; and it is now as perfect as the Nature of the Case seems to require.	From the Re-establishment of this Record in 1726 to the present Time.	Complete.	In good Preservation.	The Entries in this Record are made in Volumes kep for the Purpose, in the Order of Dates.	The Record itself is in the Nature of an Index being arranged in Yearly and Termly Order, and exhibit- ing at one View " Names and Matter."	Complete.	
14.	BOROUGH ROLL.	THE Nature and Use of this Record has already been explained (Page 418, No. 8.)	As it stood at the Con- stitution of the Court in 1708.	Complete.	In good Pre- servation.				Same as No. 1.
15.	RECORDS of LETTERS PATENT, COMMISSIONS, and WARRANTS.	THE Letters Patent which are recorded in this Register are afterwards inrolled upon Rolls of Parchment by the Keeper of the Records in the Remembrancer's Office. This Record also contains Commissions of all Kinds granted to Judges, Officers, and others enjoying Salaries or Allowances on the Civil List Establishment of Scotland; as also Letters of Privy Seal; Royal Signs Manual; Treasury Warrants, &c. for Payments out of His Majesty's Civil List Revenues: Also sundry Instruments executed by the Barons in virtue of Letters under the Privy Seal, such as Warrants for Deeds passing under the Exchequer Seal, Grants of vacant Stipend, Bursaries, and the like.	From the Constitution of the pre- sent Court of Exchequer to the present Time.	Complete.	In good Preservation.	Order of Dates.			
16.	Signed PARTICULARS (*i. e.* General Fitted Accounts) of Accountants of the Public Revenues and Re- venues of the Crown; WITH The VOUCHERS thereof.	2. REVENUE. BY the Act constituting the present Court of Exchequer, Stat. 6 Anne, cap. 26. sec. 11. all Officers and Persons em- ployed in collecting, receiving, managing, paying, answering, or accounting for the Revenues of Customs, or Excise, or other Crown Revenues or Duties in Scotland, are placed under and subjected to the Rules, Orders, Directions, Au- thority, Power, and Jurisdiction of this Court, in all Things touching the said Revenues, Debts, Duties, or Accounts, and touching the collecting, ordering, and Management thereof, and the paying and answering the same, &c.—As to the Manner of accounting, it is provided, " That the " Auditor of these Revenues shall have the taking and mak- " ing up of all the said Accounts, which being sworn to by " the respective Accountants as to the Truth thereof, and " allowed and declared by the Court of Exchequer, the " same shall be examined, entered, and inrolled in the " Office of King's Remembrancer; and Particulars and " Vouchers of each Account, contained in a Bag for that " Purpose, shall be there left: And such Account shall be " also entered in the Office of Lord Treasurer's Remem- " brancer, in such Manner as is done in England in the like " Offices, and then shall be delivered into the Pipe Office; " and the Clerk of the Pipe shall cause the said Accounts to " be examined, and, if found true, to be entered and in- " rolled in said Office, and shall give a Quietus or Dis- " charge to the Accountant thereupon, which shall be a Dis- " charge to said Accountant to and for such Account as to " all the Revenues, Duties, Matters, and Things therein, " and thereby accounted for, paid, and answered, &c."—All the Accounts of the Public Revenues (whereof a parti- cular Account is given in the Auditor's Report) are made up according to these Directions, by the Auditor of Exche- quer (excepting the Accounts of the Revenues of Excise, which are made up by the Auditor of Excise); and after being sworn to and declared, are examined and recorded in the King's Remembrancer's Office, where the Vouchers are lodged. The different Revenues thus accounted for are, the Customs and Excise, Land Tax, Land Rents and Casu- alties, Bishoprick Rents, Chamberlainries, Affessed Taxes, &c. Impressed Monies.—By signed Particulars is here meant Ge- neral Fitted Accounts, made up by the Public Accountants.	From the Constitution of the present Court of Exchequer to the present Time.	Complete.	In good Preservation.	The Vouchers of each particular Year are put up in a Chest by themselves.			There would be no material Utility in making up Catalogues or Indexes to these Records.
17.	RECORD of the said several ACCOUNTS, after they have been declared.								

of Date subsequent to the CONSTITUTION of the present Court of EXCHEQUER in SCOTLAND—*(continued.)* **Appendix (X. 3.)**

and REGULATIONS.			OFFICERS employed in Custody and Arrangement.						PLACE of DEPOSIT.				
TIME and EXPENSE required for so doing.	Regulation for RESTORING Records to their proper Places.	New Regulations requisite for rendering Use of the Record more convenient.	OFFICERS.	Their general Duties in respect of Custody or Arrangement	Attendance.	NET SALARY paid by the Public.	FEES demandable for Searches or Certificates.	Net Annual Amount of FEES on an Average of the last Three Years.	BUILDING.	Condition as to SECURITY.	Condition as to ACCOMMODATION.	PUBLIC or PRIVATE Property.	TENURE and TERM by and for which holden.
	The Keeper of this Record attends in Person when Inspection of it is wanted, and restores it to its proper Place.	None.	The Clerk or Keeper of the Register of Resignations.	This is the only Record under the Custody of this Officer. The Volumes, being few in Number, require little Attention in their Arrangement.	Attendance is given by this Officer, on Account of the general Business of the Office, every lawful Day (Holidays excepted, which are 14 in Number in the Year) from Nine o'Clock A.M. till Four o'Clock P.M.	£.40 per Ann. in respect of making up and keeping the Record, and for performing all the Duties of the Office.	None.		In the Building where the Court of Exchequer sits, in the Parliament Square, in the City of Edinburgh.	Tolerably secure.	Sufficiently commodious.	This Building is the Property of the Corporation of the City of Edinburgh.	It has been long possessed by the Public, Rent-free, for the Accommodation of the Court; and there is Reason to believe, that Possession will continue to be granted for the same Purpose in Perpetuity.
	Same as No. 1.	None.	Same as No. 1.	Same as No. 1.	Same as No. 1.	None.			General Register Office in the City of Edinburgh.	Perfectly secure.	Perfectly commodious.	Public Property.	
	Same as No. 1.	None.	Same as No. 1.	Same as No. 1.	Same as No. 1.	None.	Inspection of a Commission, 2*s.* 6*d.* Exemplification - - - 6*s.* 8*d.*		Same as No. 1.	Same as No. 1.	Same as No. 1.	Same as No. 1.	Same as No. 1.
Time and Expense would be great.	When Inspection of these Records is demanded, the King's Remembrancer and his Clerks attend, and restore the Record to its proper Place.	None.	The King's Remembrancer, and Clerks in his Office.	The Remembrancer and his Deputy are charged with the Custody and Arrangement.	Attendance is given by the King's Remembrancer, by himself, his Deputy, and Clerks, on Account of the general Business of the Office, every lawful Day (Holidays excepted, which are 14 in Number in the Year) from Nine o'Clock A.M. till Four o'Clock P.M.	None.			General Register Office in the City of Edinburgh.	Perfectly secure.	Perfectly commodious.	Public Property.	

Appendix (X. 3.) PUBLIC RECORDS in the Office of the KING'S REMEMBRANCER,

Number.	RECORD, ROLL, INSTRUMENT, MANUSCRIPT BOOK or PAPER, &c.	NATURE and USE.	PERIOD. Period of Time to which the Records relate.	CONDITION. The Records complete or defective.	State of Preservation of the Records.	ARRANGEMENT, CATALOGUES, Order of Arrangement.	General Catalogues or Particular Indexes, &c.	Complete or Defective.	Utility of completing Defective Catalogues.
18.	LETTER BOOK.	IN this Book is inserted a Copy of all Letters of Correspondence with the Boards of Customs and Excise, with Sheriffs and Stewarts-Depute, Public Accountants, and others, relating to the Procedure of the Court.	From the Constitution of the present Court of Exchequer to the present Time.	Complete.	In good Preservation.	Order of Dates.			
19.	RECORD of All Sums of Money paid to the Receiver General of Customs, on account of Seizures of Uncustomed and Prohibited Goods condemned in Exchequer, or before the Justices of the Peace; and "the Comptroll-"ment Roll of Sei-"zures."	GOODS or Merchandizes are liable to be condemned on account either of Non-payment of Duties, or of unlawful Importation; that is, when imported notwithstanding their absolute Prohibition, or in a Manner contrary to the Laws for regulating Trade and Navigation. By the Laws imposing these Duties and Prohibitions, a certain Proportion (One Moiety, for Instance) of the Goods or Merchandize so condemned, is declared to belong to the Revenue Officer by whom they are seized; and the Remainder must be recovered for the Crown, and accounted for in Exchequer, by the Receiver General of Customs, to whom the King's Share is paid. This Record is made up and kept for the Purpose of a Check on the Receiver General; and from it is made up a Record, called THE COMPTROLMENT ROLL OF SEIZURES, which is transmitted to the Auditor of Exchequer when he audits the Receiver General's Account.	Same as above.	Complete.	In good Preservation.				
20.	DUPLICATES of All Surveys and Assessments of Duties on Houses, Windows, or Lights, Servants, Carriages, Horses, &c. and of Duties imposed upon Income.	BY Stat. 20 Geo. II. cap. 3. sec. 10 by which Act the First Assessed Taxes levied in Scotland were imposed, Duplicates of all the Assessments made by virtue thereof are ordered to be transmitted into the Office of King's Remembrancer in Exchequer; and in consequence of said Statute, and of subsequent uniform Practice, such Duplicates of the Assessments, both under said Statute and under every subsequent Tax Act, have accordingly been transmitted, received, and kept in said Office. This Regulation is of very great Use and Importance, as these Duplicates furnish the necessary Checks and Charges, both upon the Collectors of these Duties in the several Counties, Stewartries, Cities, and Boroughs throughout Scotland; and also upon the Receiver General thereof at Edinburgh. It is upon the Duplicates lodged in the Remembrancer's Office that all Prosecutions on account of said Duties, by the Solicitor thereof, are founded.—It is the Duty of the Remembrancer, on receiving the Duplicates so transmitted to him, to examine and see that the Assessments or Charges are made in strict Conformity to the several Acts of Parliament whereby these Duties are imposed.—The very great Increase and Extension of this Branch of the Public Revenue has rendered this Regulation, and the Duties performed by the Remembrancer, extremely important and essential. The Amount of these Duties in Scotland, in the first Year in which they were levied, viz. 1753, was £. 5,958. 15 s. 3 d. Their Amount for the Year 1792, the Year preceding the Commencement of the War, was £. 69,717. 14 s. 4 7/10 d. Their Amount under the Aid and Contribution Act in 1798 was £. 353,095. 10 s. 6 3/10 d.; and in 1799, in Conjunction with the Income Tax, they amounted to £. 482,635. 7 s. 6 1/4 d. The Salary of £. 50. per Annum, which the Remembrancer enjoys for his Trouble in this Department, was granted by the Treasury in 1765, when the Amount of these Duties was £. 8,954. 11 s. 6 d. and has not since been increased, although the Amount of the Duties, and consequently this Officer's Trouble, and the Importance of the Duty performed by him, have been very greatly augmented.	From 20 Geo. II. cap. 3. to the present Time.	Complete.	In good Preservation.	Arranged in Chests by the Year to which they relate.	None.		None.
21.	RECORD of APPEALS.	THIS is a Record of all Cases appealed from the Commissioners of the Assessed Taxes, and of all Orders and Judgments of the Barons of Exchequer, in regard to said Appeals.	From 20 Geo. II. to the present Time.	Complete.	In good Preservation.	Order of Dates.			

of Date ſubſequent to the CONSTITUTION of the preſent Court of EXCHEQUER in SCOTLAND—(*continued.*) Appendix (X. 5.)

and REGULATIONS.			OFFICERS employed in Cuſtody and Arrangement.						PLACE of DEPOSIT.				
TIME and EXPENSE required for ſo doing.	Regulation for RESTORING Records to their proper Places.	New Regulations requiſite for rendering Uſe of the Record more convenient.	OFFICERS.	Their general Duties in reſpect of Cuſtody or Arrangement.	Attendance.	NET SALARY paid by the Public.	FEES demandable for Searches or Certificates.	Net Annual Amount of FEES on an Average of the laſt Three Years.	BUILDING.	Condition as to SECURITY.	Condition as to ACCOMMODATION.	PUBLIC or PRIVATE Property.	TENURE and TERM by and for which holden.
	Same as No. 8.	None.	King's Remembrancer, his Deputy and Clerks.	Have the Cuſtody and making up the Record.	Attendance is given by the King's Remembrancer, by himſelf, his Deputy, and Clerks, on Account of the general Buſineſs of the Office, every lawful Day (Holidays excepted, which are 14 in Number in the Year) from Nine o'Clock A.M. till Four o'Clock P.M.	None.			Same as No. 1.	Same as No. 1.	Same as No. 1.	Same as No. 1.	Same as No. 1.
			Same as above.	Same as above.	Same as above.	£. 20.							
Great.			King's Remembrancer, by virtue of 20 Geo. II. cap. 3. ſec. 10.		Same as above.	£. 50.			General Regiſter Office in the City of Edinburgh.	Perfectly ſecure.	Perfectly commodious.	Public Property.	
			King's Remembrancer, Deputy, and Clerks.	Making up and Cuſtody.	Same as above.	None.			Same as No. 1.	Same as No. 1.	Same as No. 1.	Same as No. 1.	Same as No. 1.

Appendix (X. 3.) 1. PUBLIC RECORDS in the Office of the KING'S REMEMBRANCER,

Number.	RECORD, ROLL, INSTRUMENT, MANUSCRIPT BOOK or PAPER, &c.	NATURE and USE.	Period.	Condition.		Arrangement, Catalogues,			
			Period of Time to which the Records relate.	The Records complete or defective.	State of Preservation of the Records.	Order of Arrangement.	General Catalogues or Particular Indexes, &c.	Complete or Defective.	Utility of completing Defective Catalogues.
22.	RECORD of OPINIONS of the CROWN COUNCIL.	THESE Opinions are delivered by the Lord Advocate and Solicitor General for Scotland, upon Public Matters referred to them for their Opinion, by Order of the Court of Exchequer.	From the Constitution of the Court to the present Time.	Complete.	In good Preservation.	Order of Dates.			
23.	RECORD of BONDS and RECOGNIZANCES.	THIS is a Record of all Recognizances granted or entered into in Judicial Procedure in the Court of Exchequer, and of all Bonds, Securities, &c. exacted from Accountants of the Crown in Exchequer (the Commissioners of Excise excepted) and in Gifts of Tutory, Dative, &c.	From the Constitution of the Court to the present Time.	Complete.	In good Preservation.	Same as above.			
24.	- - - - - -	3. FORFEITED ESTATES. Sundry BOOKS, ACCOUNTS, RENT ROLLS, and Procedure of various Kinds of the Commissioners of Inquiry, relating to the Management and Sale of the Estates forfeited for Rebellion in the Year 1715.			In good Preservation.				
25.	- - - - - -	Sundry BOOKS, RENT ROLLS, and other Procedure, relating to the Management of the Estates forfeited for Rebellion in the Year 1745, during the Period when these Estates were under the Management of the Barons of Exchequer, viz. the Year 1746, until sundry of the Estates were annexed to the Crown, and placed under the Management of Commissioners, by Statute 25 Geo. II. cap. 41. in the Year 1752.	From 1746 to 1752.		In good Preservation.				
26.	- - - - - -	All BOOKS, RENT ROLLS, ACCOUNTS, and other Procedure of the Commissioners for Management of the Estates forfeited to the Crown for Rebellion in 1745, appointed by Statute 25 Geo. II. cap. 41. from the Appointment of said Commissioners in 1752, until said Estates were restored to the Heirs of the forfeited Persons in the Year 1784, by Statute 24 Geo. III. cap. 57. 2d Sess.	From 1752 to 1784.		In good Preservation.				
27.	- - - - - -	PROCEDURE of the Barons of Exchequer relative to the Estates forfeited for Rebellion in 1745, since the Statute 24 Geo. III. cap. 57. whereby these Estates were restored to the Heirs of the forfeited Persons.	From 1784 to		In good Preservation.				

END OF THE REPORT OF RECORDS IN

of Date ſubſequent to the CONSTITUTION of the preſent Court of EXCHEQUER in SCOTLAND—(continued.) Appendix (X. 3.)

and REGULATIONS.			OFFICERS employed in Cuſtody and Arrangement.						PLACE of DEPOSIT.				
TIME and EXPENSE required for ſo doing.	Regulation for RESTORING Records to their proper Places.	New Regulations requiſite for rendering Uſe of the Record more convenient.	OFFICERS.	Their general Duties in reſpect of Cuſtody or Arrangement.	Attendance.	NET SALARY paid by the Public.	FEES demandable for Searches or Certificates.	Net Annual Amount of FEES on an Average of the laſt Three Years.	BUILDING.	Condition as to SECURITY.	Condition as to ACCOMMODATION.	PUBLIC or PRIVATE Property.	TENURE and TERM by and for which holden.
			King's Remembrancer, Deputy, and Clerks.	Making up and Cuſtody.	Attendance is given by the King's Remembrancer, or his Deputy, on Account of the General Buſineſs of the Office, every lawful Day (Holidays excepted, which are 14 in Number in the Year) from Nine o'Clock A. M. till Four o'Clock P. M.	None.			Same as No. 1.	Same as No. 1.	Same as No. 1.	Same as No. 1.	Same as No. 1.
			Same as above.	Same as above.	Same as above.	Same as above.			Same as above.	Same as above.	Same as above.	Same as above.	Same as above.
			Same as above.	Theſe Duties are, by the Nature of the Records, limited to the Cuſtody alone.	Same as No. 1.	None.			In the Building where the Court of Exchequer ſits, in the Parliament Square, Edinburgh.	Tolerably ſecure.	Sufficiently commodious.	The Building is the Property of the Corporation of the City of Edinburgh.	Same as No. 1.
			Same as above.	Same as above.	Same as above.	Same as above.			Same as above.	Same as above.	Same as above.	Same as above.	Same as above.
			Same as above.	Same as above.	Same as above.	Same as above.			Same as above.	Same as above.	Same as above.	Same as above.	Same as above.
			Same as above.	Same as above.	Same as above.	Same as above.			Same as above.	Same as above.	Same as above.	Same as above.	Same as above.

THE OFFICE OF KING'S REMEMBRANCER.

Appendix (X. 3.)

2. PUBLIC RECORDS in the Office of

Number of the Record.	RECORD. RECORD, ROLL, INSTRUMENT, MANUSCRIPT BOOK or PAPER, &c.	NATURE and USE. N. B. The RECORD, No. 1. is the only Record in this Office which relates to a Period prior to the Conſtitution of the Court of Exchequer in 1708, by 6 Anne, cap. 26.	PERIOD. Period of Time to which the Records relate.	CONDITION. The Records Complete or Defective.	State of Preservation of the Records.	ARRANGEMENT, CATALOGUES, Order of Arrangement.	General Catalogues or Particular Indexes, &c.	Complete or Defective	Utility of completing Defective Catalogues.
1.	ROLLS of SHERIFFS ACCOUNTS.	SHERIFFS, Stewarts, Chamberlains, and Baillies, were charged by ſeveral antient Scottiſh Acts of Parliament with levying or Collection of all the feudal Caſualties or Duties accruing to the Sovereign, as Superior of the Lands ſituated within their reſpective Territories or Juriſdictions: And they were obliged to appear Yearly in Exchequer, there to render an Account and make Payment of the Duties received or collected by them on Account of the Crown. Rolls or Accounts of the King's Property, and of the Feudal Duties payable to the Crown, were kept in Exchequer, according to which theſe Officers were charged in rendering their Accounts; and they were required by the Statutes to which Alluſion is above made, "to make full Payment Æque with the Rolls;" whence the Manner of accounting was called, "Making or fitting Æques in Exchequer." Of theſe Rolls, the Principal was that which was Annually tranſmitted to Exchequer from the Chancery, and which was called the Reſponde Book; becauſe, according to the Charge contained in it, the Sheriffs were bound to "anſwer" or account for the Duties received by them for Behoof of the Crown. The Reſponde Book was a Record made up Yearly in Chancery of all feudal Caſualties, as Ward, Marriage, Non-entry, Relief, which became due or payable to the Crown upon the Inveſtiture of a Crown Vaſſal, the Precept or Warrant for which iſſued from Chancery, and was executed by the Sheriff of the Territory where the Lands were ſituated, who was required in the Precept to take Security for the Payment of theſe Duties, and to account for them in Exchequer.—By the Scottiſh Statute 16[illegible]2, cap. 16. Sheriffs were charged alſo with the Collection of all Feu and Blanch Duties payable Annually by the Crown Vaſſals, which did not amount to £. 10. Scots Money; as to which, it was by that Act enacted, "That Liſts of the Vaſſals, and of the Blanch and "Feu Duties payable by them, be ſubſcribed by the Com-"miſſioners of the Treaſury, and ſent to the Sheriffs of "the ſeveral Shires, who, or their Deputies, ſhall charge "the Vaſſals for Payment of theſe Duties, and ſhall be "countable for them to the Exchequer."—Laſtly, Sheriffs were bound to account in Exchequer for Behoof of the Crown for certain Fines or Portions of Fines levied in their reſpective Courts, and for Waifs and Strays.	Commencing about the Year 1400, and continued down to the Union of the Two Kingdoms.	Tolerably complete.	In good Preſervation.	Regularly arranged, or lodged in Preſſes or Cloſets. Same as above.	No General Catalogue, but Particular Index. Same as above.		
2.	ROLLS of SHERIFFS ACCOUNTS.	BY the Statute 6 Anne, cap. 26. eſtabliſhing the preſent Court of Exchequer, it is enacted, "That the Barons of "the Court of Exchequer in Scotland ſhall have full Power "and Authority to take and paſs the Accounts of all "Sheriffs and other Officers in Scotland having the Execu-"tion of any Proceſs iſſuing out of and returnable in Ex-"chequer, for the levying of any Revenue or Money for the "Crown; and to charge and diſcharge them according to "Right and Juſtice, and in ſuch Manner and Form as the "ſaid Sheriffs and Officers before the Union were uſed to "be charged and diſcharged, and to have their Accounts "paſſed, or as the Barons ſhall order, direct, or appoint."—Since the paſſing of this Act, Sheriffs Accounts have been made up in Exchequer by the Lord Treaſurer's Remembrancer, who makes up the Charge againſt them from the Reſponde Books tranſmitted from the Chancery, and from the Property Roll kept in Exchequer.—The Sheriffs are credited for certain public Services ſtated in the Diſcharge.—The Accounts, after being ſworn to and ſigned by the Barons, are recorded in this Office, and alſo in the Office of the Clerk of the Pipe, who makes out a Quietus upon each particular Account.	From the Union of the Two Kingdoms to the Term of Whitſunday 1799.	Complete.	In good Preſervation.	Same as above.	Same as above.		
3	BOOK, Containing a Rental of Petty Feu and Blanch Duties, under £. 10. Scots Money, payable Annually by the Vaſſals of the Crown, in the ſeveral Counties in Scotland.	THESE are the Feu or Blanch Duties, with the Collection and Account of which Sheriffs are Annually charged in Exchequer.—(See above, Records Nos. 1. and 2.) Feu and Blanch Duties are the proper Annual Payments or Reddenda payable by Crown Vaſſals, who hold their Lands by the Feudal Tenures of Feu-holding or Blanch-holding. The former Duty was originally an adequate Rent of the Lands, and conſiſts in Money, Grain, or Perſonal Services connected with Huſbandry, paid Nomine Feudi-firmæ.—Blanch Duties are an eluſory Rent, paid in Acknowledgment of Vaſſalage to the Superior, Nomine Albæ-firmæ, and conſiſting of a Penny Money, a Roſe, a Pair of Spurs, &c.	From the Conſtitution of the Court in 1708 to the preſent Time.	Complete.	In good Preſervation	Same as above.	Same as above.		

the LORD TREASURER'S REMEMBRANCER. Appendix (X. 3.)

and REGULATIONS.			OFFICERS employed in Custody and Arrangement.						PLACE of DEPOSIT.				
TIME and EXPENSE required for so doing.	Regulation for RESTORING Records to their proper Places.	New Regulations requisite for rendering Use of the Record more convenient.	OFFICERS.	Their general DUTIES in respect of Custody or Arrangement.	Attendance.	NET SALARY paid by the Public.	FEES demandable for Searches or Certificates.	Net Annual Amount of FEES on an Average of the last Three Years.	BUILDING.	Condition as to SECURITY.	Condition as to ACCOMMODATION.	PUBLIC or PRIVATE Property.	TENURE and TERM by and for which holden.
	The Lord Treasurer's Remembrancer, who has the Custody of these Records, attends when any Search is made or Inspection given of the Records, and takes Care that they be regularly and carefully returned to their proper Places. Ready and immediate Access is had by the Public to the Records at all Times.	It does not occur at present that any Improvements could be made in the Mode of keeping the Records for rendering the Use of them more convenient for the Public.—The Room in Court in which they are deposited, though not large, is well adapted for Business; and although the Books and Papers belonging to the Office have of late become rather too numerous and bulky for the Accommodation which it affords, yet this Inconvenience has been guarded against, and will speedily be remedied, by removing all the Records (except those of a recent Date) to an Apartment in the General Register Office, which has been allotted to the Lord Treasurer's Remembrancer and Clerk of the Pipe jointly; which Removal it is proposed to effect at the Close of the present Year.	The Deputy Lord Treasurer's Remembrancer, by whom the general Business of the Office is carried on.		Every lawful Day, for more than Eight Hours, Holidays excepted, which in the Course of the Year are 14 in Number.	None.	There is a fixed Fee for giving Inspection of certain Records, exigible from those who may desire the same, viz. 2 s. 6 d. for Inspection of a Book or other Record, or for a Certificate or Exemplification.	£ 2. 10 s.	Court of Exchequer.	Moderately secure.	Moderately commodious.	Belongs to the Corporation of the City of Edinburgh.	Has been for a long Time enjoyed by the Public Rent-free, for the Accommodation of the Court; and there is Reason to believe that Possession of it will continue to be granted for this Purpose in Perpetuity.
			Same as above.		Same as above.	None.			Same as above.	Same as above.	Same as above.	Same as above.	Same as above.
			Same as above.		Same as above.	None.			Same as above.	Same as above.	Same as above.	Same as above.	Same as above.
			Same as above.		Same as above.	None.			Same as above.	Same as above.	Same as above.	Same as above.	Same as above.

Appendix (X. 3.)

2. PUBLIC RECORDS in the Office of

Number.	RECORD, ROLL, INSTRUMENT, MANUSCRIPT BOOK or PAPER, &c.	NATURE and USE.	PERIOD.	CONDITION.		ARRANGEMENT, CATALOGUES,			
			PERIOD or TIME to which the Records relate.	The Records COMPLETE or DEFECTIVE.	State of PRESERVATION of the Records.	ORDER of ARRANGEMENT.	General CATALOGUES or Particular INDEXES, &c.	COMPLETE or DEFECTIVE.	Utility of COMPLETING Defective Catalogues.
4.	ORDERS of COURT, for allowing to Sheriffs and Stewarts Depute, Sums disbursed by them in the Public Service.	IN making up Annually the Accounts of Sheriffs and Stewarts Depute for the different Shires and Stewartries in Scotland, these Officers take Credit in their Discharge for Sums of Money disbursed by them in the Public Service; and upon their making Oath to the Truth of said Accounts, and producing Vouchers for the Particulars of their Expenditure, the Accounts are then declared, and the Total Amount of the Surplusages due to the Sheriffs are laid before the Barons, who make Application to the Lords of the Treasury for a Sign Manual for the Total Amount of said Surplusages.	From the Constitution of the Court in 1708 to the present Time.	Complete.	In good Preservation.	Regularly arranged, and lodged in Presses or Closets.	No General Catalogue, but a Particular Index.		
5.	ACCOUNT of PAYMENTS to the Receiver General of the Crown Revenues, by Sheriffs and Stewarts Depute.	THESE Payments consist of the Casualties, Feu and Blanch Duties under £. 10. Scots, Fines, Waifs, Strays, &c. received and collected on account of the Crown by Sheriffs and Stewarts Depute, and by them accounted for in Exchequer, and paid over to the Receiver General of His Majesty's Crown Rents and Casualties.—This Record forms a Charge against said Receiver General in rendering his Account in Exchequer.	Same as above.	Complete.	In good Preservation.	Entered Annually in a Book. Same as No. 1.	Same as above.		
6.	ROLL of CROWN VASSALS, and Other Accountants, Who are bound to account in Exchequer either for Crown Rents or for Public Money received by them.	THE Crown Vassals, who are bound to account or to make Æques in Exchequer for the Crown Rents due by them for their respective Lands, are those whose Feu or Blanch Duties exceed in Amount the Sum of £. 10. Scots Money. (See Record, No. 1.)—This Roll is corrected Annually, made up, and transmitted to Chancery, with Directions to issue Precepts for summoning the Persons contained in said Roll, to come and account and make Payment in Exchequer.—The other Accountants here mentioned are, the Receiver General of Land Rents and Casualties, Land Tax, and Assessed Taxes, Commissioners of Excise, Receiver and Comptroller General of Customs, Chamberlains, Sheriffs and Stewarts Depute, Accountants for Imprest Money, Receivers of Bishoprick Rents, Receiver of One Shilling Tax on Pensions, Salaries, &c. Petty Feuars, and Magistrates of Beroughs.	This Roll is made up Annually since the Constitution of the Court in 1708 to the present Time.	Complete.	In good Preservation.	This Roll is made up Annually. Same as No. 1.	Same as above.		
7.	BOOK of FIARS.	IT is a Branch of the Ministerial Duties of Sheriffs and Stewarts Depute, in all the Shires and Stewartries in Scotland, Yearly to strike the Sheriff-Fiars, in the Month of February; that is, to settle by a Sentence, proceeding on a Report of a Jury, the Average Price or Rate of the different Kinds of Grain, the Growth of the County of the preceding Year. The Forms of proceeding in striking the Fiars are prescribed by an Act of Sederunt of the Court of Session, dated the 21st December 1723. These Fiars serve as a Rule for settling private Contracts relative to the Purchase and Sale of Grain, where the Prices either are not or cannot be otherwise ascertained; and for determining the Money Composition to be paid to the Crown by Crown Vassals, whose Land Rents or Duties are payable in Grain; and for the latter Purpose a Return is made into Exchequer Annually, and a Record is there kept of the Fiars of those Counties in which His Majesty's Land Rents are payable in Grain.	Same as above.	Complete.	In good Preservation.	This Record is made up Annually in Books kept for the Purpose, and lodged in Presses or Closets.	Same as above.		
8.	PETITIONS of CROWN VASSALS, REPORTS, and ORDERS of COURT thereon.	THESE Petitions are addressed to the Court, and upon being read in Court by the King's Remembrancer or his Deputy, are referred by the Barons to the Lord Treasurer's Remembrancer for his Report. The Petitions and Reports being again read in Court, the Barons make their Order or Judgment thereon. The Petitions, Reports, and Orders are then recorded by the Lord Treasurer's Remembrancer, in a Book kept by him for that Purpose.	Same as above.	Complete.	In good Preservation.	In the Order of Dates. Same as No. 1.	Same as above.		
9.	RECORD of PUBLIC ACCOUNTS.	AS to the Authority on which this Record is founded, see Statute 6 Anne, cap. 26. sec. 11. and Page 424 of this Report, Nos. 16 and 17.—The Public Accounts recorded by the Lord Treasurer's Remembrancer are the following; viz. Land Rents and Casualties, Land Tax, Chamberlains, Customs, Excise, Bishoprick Rents, Accounts of Sheriffs and Stewarts Depute, Assessed Taxes, Imprest Monies, One Shilling Tax on Salaries, and Pensions.	Same as above.	Complete.	In good Preservation.	These Accounts are recorded in Books kept for that Purpose.	Same as above.		

the LORD TREASURER'S REMEMBRANCER—*(continued.)* Appendix (X. 3.)

and REGULATIONS.			OFFICERS employed in Custody and Arrangement.						PLACE of DEPOSIT.				
TIME and EXPENSE required for so doing.	Regulation for RESTORING Records to their proper Places.	New Regulations requisite for rendering Use of the Records more convenient.	OFFICERS.	Their general DUTIES in respect of Custody or Arrangement.	Attendance.	NET SALARY paid by the Public.	FEES demandable for Searches or Certificates.	Net Annual Amount of FEES on an Average of the last Three Years.	BUILDING.	Condition as to SECURITY.	Condition as to ACCOMMODATION.	PUBLIC or PRIVATE Property.	TENURE and TERM by and for which holden.
	Same as in Page 431.	Same as in Page 431.	The Deputy Lord Treasurer's Remembrancer, by whom the general Business of the Office is carried on		Every lawful Day, for more than Eight Hours, Holidays excepted, which in the Course of the Year are 14 in Number.	None.	Same as in Page 431.	Same as in Page 431.	Court of Exchequer.	Moderately secure.	Moderately commodious.	Belongs to the Corporation of the City of Edinburgh.	Same as No. 1.
			Same as above.		Same as above.	None.			Same as above.	Same as above.	Same as above.	Same as above.	Same as above.
			Same as above.		Same as above.	None.			Same as above.	Same as above.	Same as above.	Same as above.	Same as above.
			Same as above.		Same as above.	None.			Same as above.	Same as above.	Same as above.	Same as above.	Same as above.
			Same as above.		Same as above.	None.			Same as above.	Same as above.	Same as above.	Same as above.	Same as above.
			Same as above.		Same as above.	None.			Same as above.	Same as above.	Same as above.	Same as above.	Same as above.

Appendix (X. 3.)

2. PUBLIC RECORDS in the Office of

Numbers.	RECORD, ROLL, INSTRUMENT, MANUSCRIPT BOOK or PAPER, &c.	NATURE and USE.	PERIOD.	CONDITION.		ARRANGEMENT, CATALOGUES,			
			Period of Time to which the Records relate.	The Records complete or defective.	State of Preservation of the Records.	Order of Arrangement.	General Catalogues or Particular Indexes, &c.	Complete or Defective.	Utility of completing Defective Catalogues.
10.	RECORD of LETTERS PATENT and COMMISSIONS, and of IMPREST WARRANTS for Surplusages paid to Sheriffs and Stewarts Depute.	THE Commissions granted by Letters Patent, which are entered in this Record, are those to the Barons and Officers of Exchequer, to the Lord Advocate and Solicitor General, to Sheriffs and Stewarts Depute, to the Receiver General of Crown Rents and Casualties, &c. When, in the Accounts which are Annually rendered in Exchequer by Sheriffs and Stewarts Depute, there is a Surplus on the Discharge credited to these Accountants, arising from Monies disbursed by them in the Public Service, a Warrant is obtained, on Application to the Treasury, under the Royal Sign Manual, countersigned by the Commissioners of the Treasury, directing the Payment of these Surplusages; under Authority of which Warrant the Barons of Exchequer issue their Warrants on the Receiver General of the Land Rents, for paying to each Sheriff and Stewarts Depute the Amount of the Surplusage appearing due to him on the Foot of his Account.	From the Constitution of the Court in 1708 to the present Time.	Complete.	In good Preservation.	This Record is in the Form of a Book, and in the Order of the Dates. Same as No. 1.	No General Catalogue, but a Particular Index.		
11.	INROLMENTS of LETTERS PATENT.	THE Letters Patent entered in this Record are those granted to the Commissioners of the Customs and of the Excise, and the Officers of said Revenues who hold Patent Offices.	Same as above.	Complete.	In good Preservation.	Same as No. 1.	Same as above.		
12.	ROLL of VALUATION for the Shire of Argyle.	THIS Roll was made up by certain Commissioners under Authority of a Public Statute, 22 Geo. II. cap. 29. intituled, "An Act for making an authentic Roll of Valuation for the Shire of Argyle, A. D. 1749."	Made up in the Year 1750.	Complete.	In good Preservation.	This Valuation is recorded in a Book.	Same as above.		

END OF THE REPORT OF THE RECORDS IN THE

the LORD TREASURER'S REMEMBRANCER—(*continued.*) Appendix. (X. 3.)

and REGULATIONS.			OFFICERS employed in Custody and Arrangement.						PLACE of DEPOSIT.				
TIME and EXPENSE required for so doing.	Regulation for RESTORING Records to their proper Places.	New Regulations requisite for rendering Use of the Records more convenient.	OFFICERS.	Their general DUTIES in respect of Custody or Arrangement.	Attendance.	NET SALARY paid by the Public.	FEES demandable for Searches or Certificates.	Net Annual Amount of FEES on an Average of the last Three Years.	BUILDING.	Condition as to SECURITY.	Condition as to ACCOMMODATION.	PUBLIC or PRIVATE Property.	TENURE and TERM by and for which holden.
	Same as in Page 431.	Same as in Page 431.	The Deputy Lord Treasurer's Remembrancer, by whom the general Business of the Office is carried on.		Every lawful Day, for more than Eight Hours, Holidays excepted, which in the Course of the Year are 14 in Number.	None.	Same as in Page 431.	Same as in Page 431.	Court of Exchequer.	Moderately secure.	Moderately commodious.	Belongs to the Corporation of the City of Edinburgh.	Has been for a long Time enjoyed by the Public, Rent-free, for the Accommodation of the Court; and there is Reason to believe that Possession of it will continue to be granted for this Purpose in Perpetuity.
			Same as above.		Same as above.	None.			Same as above.	Same as above.	Same as above.	Same as above.	Same as above.
			Same as above.		Same as above.	None.			Same as above.	Same as above.	Same as above.	Same as above.	Same as above.

OFFICE OF THE LORD TREASURER'S REMEMBRANCER.

Appendix (X. 3.)

3. PUBLIC RECORDS in the

Number.	RECORD. RECORD, ROLL, INSTRUMENT, MANUSCRIPT BOOK or PAPER, &c.	NATURE and USE. N. B. RECORD, No. 1, is the only Record in this Office which relates to a Period prior to the Constitution of the present Court of Exchequer in 1708, by 6 Anne, cap. 26.	PERIOD. Period of Time to which the Records relate.	CONDITION. The Records complete or defective.	CONDITION. State of Preservation of the Records.	ARRANGEMENT, CATALOGUES. Order of Arrangement.	ARRANGEMENT, CATALOGUES. General Catalogues or Particular Indexes, &c.	ARRANGEMENT, CATALOGUES. Complete or Defective.	ARRANGEMENT, CATALOGUES. Utility of completing Defective Catalogues.
1.	CHAMBERLAIN'S ROLLS.	CHAMBERLAINS were Officers charged with the Collection of the Feudal Duties Annually payable to the Crown by the Crown Vassals, within certain Districts, called Chamberlainries, over which these Officers were placed. Chamberlains held their Offices, either Heritably, for Life, or during the Pleasure of those by whom they were appointed. They were appointed by the Sovereign, the Great Chamberlain, the Comptroller, or the Lord Treasurer; and they were accountable to their Constituent in Exchequer Annually for the Feu and Blanch Duties, or other Crown Rents or Revenues received by them, in the same Manner with Sheriffs, Stewarts, and Baillies.—(See Page 430 of this Report, Record No. 1.)	From 1326 to 1549.	Incomplete.—The Rolls of many Years are wanting. There are in Existence 222.		These Rolls are in no regular Order, farther than they are labelled with the Year or Years to which they relate, and are arranged in Presses.	None.		No Utility would arise either from putting these Records into better Order, or from making Catalogues or Indexes to them, never being called for but by the Antiquarian.
2.	PROPERTY ROLL.	1. RECORDS relating to CROWN RENTS and CASUALTIES, and PUBLIC ACCOUNTS. THIS is a Record of all Feu and Blanch Duties, exceeding in their Amount the Sum of £. 10. Scots Money, which, by the Provision of the Act of the Scottish Parliament, 1672, cap. 16. are accounted for and paid in Exchequer; while those which do not exceed or amount to that Sum are collected in the several Shires and Stewartries, by the Sheriffs, Stewarts, or Chamberlains.—(See Pages 430 and 432 of this Report, Nos. 1, 2, 3, and 6.)—The Record contains the Names of the Lands for which these Duties are paid, the Names of the Proprietors thereof, and the Amount of the Duties payable by each. These Duties are payable Annually.	Commencing 31st July 1709, and continued down Yearly to the present Time.	Complete.	Good.		No General Catalogues belong to the Records, but each Record has its own Particular Index at the Beginning or End of each Volume.	These Indexes are complete.	
3.	RENTALS of the ARCHBISHOPRICKS and BISHOPRICKS.	UPON the final Abolition of Episcopacy in Scotland, by the Acts of the Scottish Parliament passed in 1689, cap. 3. and 1690, cap. 5. at the Revolution, the Landed Estates of the Archbishops and Bishops were annexed to the Crown, and Rentals or Rent Rolls thereof were returned into Treasury by the dignified Clergy themselves, or by their Factors or Stewards. The Archbishopricks in Scotland were, 1. of St. Andrews; and, 2. Glasgow.—The Bishopricks were those of—1. Aberdeen; 2. Brechin; 3. Caithness; 4. Dumblane; 5. Dunkeld; 6. Edinburgh; 7. Moray; 8. Orkney; 9. Ross; 10. Argyle; 11. Galloway; and, 12. The Isles.		Complete.	Good.				
4.	RECORD of COMPOSITIONS on SIGNATURES.	BY the genuine Principles of the Feudal System (founded on the originally gratuitous Nature of Feus) no Vassal could transfer his Right in the Feu to another Person, who was not entitled to succeed to it according to the Order of Inheritance prescribed by the Charter or Investiture granted by the Superior, of whom the Feu was holden; and agreeably to these Principles the Superior was not obliged to receive any such Person, as his Vassal, in his Lands, contrary to his Pleasure and Consent, upon any Conditions whatsoever. This Right of Refusal on the Part of the Superior, and the Restrictions imposed thereby on the free Transmission and Commerce of Land, was first abridged by Statute (1469, cap. 37. confirmed and extended by Stat. 1672, cap. 19. 1681, cap. 17. and 1690, cap. 20.) in favour of Creditors, whom Superiors were compelled to receive as Vassals in the Lands of their Debtors, on Payment of a Fine or Composition of a Year's Rent of the Lands; and afterwards in favour of Heirs of Entail, by consequence of the Statute 1685, cap. 22. authorizing Entails. These Statutes were directed chiefly against Subject-Superiors.—The Sovereigns had, by several Acts of Privy Council, mentioned in Statute 1578, cap. 66. given up the Right of Refusal, for the Public Utility; so that Purchasers of Lands holden of the Crown were from that Period secure of being received as Vassals by the King, upon paying a Fine or Composition to the Treasury, which by Practice had been fixed at One-sixth Part of the valued Rent of the Lands, according to a general Valuation of all the Lands in Scotland, made in 1649. The Right of Refusal competent to Subject-Superiors, which had been abridged in Manner above-mentioned, was absolutely taken away by Statute 20 Geo. II. cap. 50. with Reservation however of the Fee or Casualty of a Year's Rent of the Lands, as allowed by the Act 1469, cap. 37.—From the Period above	Commencing 25th May 1708, and continued down to the present Time.	Complete.	Good.				

Office of the AUDITOR. Appendix (X. 3.)

and REGULATIONS.			OFFICERS employed in Cuſtody and Arrangement.						PLACE of DEPOSIT.				
TIME and EXPENSE required for ſo doing.	Regulation for RESTORING Records to their proper Places.	New Regulations requiſite for rendering Uſe of the Record more convenient.	OFFICERS.	Their general DUTIES in reſpect of Cuſtody or Arrangement.	Attendance.	NET SALARY paid by the Public.	FEES demandable for Searches or Certificates.	Net Annual Amount of FEES on an Average of the laſt Three Years.	BUILDING.	Condition as to SECURITY.	Condition as to ACCOMMODATION.	PUBLIC or PRIVATE Property.	TENURE and TERM by and for which holden.
Much Time, and ſome Expenſe.									General Regiſter Office for Scotland.	Perfectly ſecure.	Perfectly commodious.	Public Property.	
	No Officer or Perſon is ſpecially intruſted with the Care of reſtoring the Records to their proper Place, upon a Search or Certificate being granted; but this Duty is performed by the Auditor's Clerks, who attend upon theſe Occaſions.	The Public ſeldom call for Inſpection of any of the Records of this Office, and therefore no new Regulation appears requiſite for rendering the Uſe of them more convenient for the Public.	The Auditor, his Deputy, and Clerks, have the Cuſtody and Arrangement of all the Records in his Office.		Attendance the ſame as in the Return of the King's Remembrancer.	There is no Salary paid by the Public, ſolely in reſpect of the Cuſtody and Arrangement of theſe Records, excluſively of the Salary paid on Account of the general Duties of the Office.	2 *s.* 6 *d.* for ſhewing each Record. 6 *s.* 8 *d.* for a Certificate.	£. 2.	In the Building occupied by the Court of Exchequer, ſituated in the Parliament Square, in the City of Edinburgh.	Moderately ſecure.	Not commodious.	The Property of the Corporation of the City of Edinburgh.	By Grant from the Corporation of the City of Edinburgh. This Building has for a long Time been occupied by the Court, Rent-free; and there is every Reaſon to believe that it will be continued in the Poſſeſſion of the Public, on the ſame Terms, in Perpetuity.

Appendix (X. 3.) 3. PUBLIC RECORDS in the

Number.	RECORD, ROLL, INSTRUMENT, MANUSCRIPT BOOK or PAPER, &c.	NATURE and USE.	PERIOD. PERIOD of TIME to which the Records relate.	CONDITION. The Records COMPLETE or DEFECTIVE.	State of PRESERVATION of the Records.	ARRANGEMENT, CATALOGUES, ORDER of ARRANGEMENT.	General CATALOGUES or Particular INDEXES, &c.	COMPLETE or DEFECTIVE.	Utility of COMPLETING Defective Catalogues.
4.	RECORD of COMPOSITIONS on SIGNATURES, *(continued.)*	above mentioned; viz. 1578, the Crown has continued to receive all Purchasers (called Singular Successors) as Vassals in Lands holden of the Crown, on Payment in Exchequer of a Fine or Composition of One-sixth Part of the valued Rent, as above-mentioned.—By the Act 6 Anne, cap. 26. sec. 19. constituting the present Court of Exchequer in Scotland, the Barons are authorized to settle the Compositions payable to the Crown on the passing of Signatures for new Infeftment or Investiture, in the same Manner as had been practised in the Scottish Court of Exchequer; and upon the Accession of each Sovereign to the Throne of Great Britain, since the Union of the Two Kingdoms, a Letter has been issued under the Privy Seal of Scotland, directing and authorizing the Barons, in all Cases where Compositions are due to the Crown, at passing Signatures in favour of Purchasers, called Singular Successors, to take One-sixth Part of the valued Rent from all Sorts of People, without any Distinction or Alteration whatever; and to cause the same to be paid to His Majesty's Use accordingly. These Compositions are struck by the Auditor and Presenter of Signatures, and are paid to the Receiver General of Crown Rents and Casualties. The Amount of the Composition payable to the Crown by the Heir of a Crown Vassal, upon obtaining Infeftment, is Eleven Shillings and One Penny $\frac{4}{12}$ Sterling Money; and it is paid and accounted for in like Manner in Exchequer.—This Record specifies the Amount of each Composition paid to said Receiver General.—(See Page 432, No. 6, and Page 434, Record No. 12.)	Commencing 25th May 1708, and continued down to the present Time.	Complete.	Good.		No General Catalogues belong to the Records; but each Record has its own Particular Index at the Beginning or End of each Volume.	These Indexes are complete.	
5.	RECORD of COMPOSITIONS on Leases of BISHOPS' TEINDS.	WHEN the Landed Estates of the Archbishops and Bishops in Scotland were annexed to the Crown, upon the final Abolition of Episcopacy at the Revolution, a similar Annexation took place of the Teinds or Tythes to which the dignified Clergy had Right. From that Period the Crown has been in the Practice of granting Tacks or Leases of these Teinds, either to the Proprietors of the Lands out of which they are payable, or to other Persons or Incorporations who had originally obtained such Tacks: These Tacks are obtained in Exchequer; and the Power of the Barons to grant them, is founded both on Statute 6 Anne, cap. 26. and on Letter under the Privy Seal of Scotland, issued by the Sovereign at his Accession, authorizing them to grant such Tacks for a Term not exceeding Nineteen Years, and on Payment of a Fine or Composition of Three Years Value to the Receiver of the Crown Rents and Casualties.	Commencing at Lammas Term in 1710, and continued to the present Time.	Complete.	Good.				
6.	RECORDS of PUBLIC ACCOUNTS.	BY Statute 6 Anne, cap. 26. whereby the present Court of Exchequer in Scotland is established, it is enacted, sec. 11. That the Person or Persons appointed by His Majesty (under the Seal ordered to be kept in Scotland by the Treaty of Union, in place of the Great Seal thereof) to be Auditor or Auditors of the Revenues or Duties of Customs or Excise, or other Crown Revenues, Debts, or Duties in Scotland, shall have the taking and making up of all Accounts relative thereto. Under the Authority of this Statute, the Accounts of every Branch of the Public or Crown Revenues (the Excise excepted, for which a particular Auditor is appointed) with the Vouchers thereof, are duly delivered into the Auditor of Exchequer, in order to be examined, audited, and made up by him, previously to their being sworn to and declared before the Barons. The Accounts thus presented to the Auditor are called Signed Particulars; and from these, Two Copies are made up by him in the proper Forms of Exchequer; the one upon Paper, which is lodged in the Auditor's Office; and the other upon Parchment, which, after being sworn to and declared, is recorded successively in the Offices of King's Remembrancer, Lord Treasurer's Remembrancer, and of the Pipe, as mentioned Page 424 of this Report, Records Nos. 16 and 17. The Public Accounts thus audited are the following; viz. Customs, Land Tax, Land Rents and Casualties, Bishoprick Rents, Chamberlainries, Assessed Taxes, &c. Imprest Monies.	Commencing 1st May 1707, and continued down to the present Time.	Complete.	Good.				

Office of the AUDITOR—(continued.) Appendix (X. 3.)

and REGULATIONS.			OFFICERS employed in Custody and Arrangement.						PLACE OF DEPOSIT.				
TIME and EXPENSE required for so doing.	Regulation for RESTORING Records to their proper Places.	New Regulations requisite for rendering Use of the Record more convenient.	OFFICERS.	Their general Duties in respect of Custody or Arrangement.	Attendance.	NET SALARY paid by the Public.	FEES demandable for Searches or Certificates.	Net Annual Amount of FEES on an Average of the last Three Years.	BUILDING.	Condition as to SECURITY.	Condition as to ACCOMMODATION.	PUBLIC or PRIVATE Property.	TENURE and TERMS by and for which holden.
	No Officer or Person is specially intrusted with the Care of restoring the Records to their proper Place, upon a Search or Certificate being granted; but this Duty is performed by the Auditor's Clerks, who attend upon these Occasions.	The Public seldom call for Inspection of any of the Records of this Office, and therefore no new Regulation appears requisite for rendering the Use of them more convenient for the Public.	The Auditor, his Deputy, and Clerks, have the Custody and Arrangement of all the Records in his Office.		Attendance the same as in the Return of the King's Remembrancer.	There is no Salary paid by the Public, solely in respect of the Custody and Arrangement of these Records, exclusively of the Salary paid on Account of the general Duties of the Office.	2 s. 6 d. for shewing each Record. 6 s. 8 d. for a Certificate.	£. 2.	In the Building occupied by the Court of Exchequer, situated in the Parliament Square, in the City of Edinburgh.	Moderately secure.	Not commodious.	The Property of the Corporation of the City of Edinburgh.	By Grant from the Corporation of the City of Edinburgh. This Building has for a long Time been occupied by the Court, Rent-free; and there is every Reason to believe, that it will be continued in the Possession of the Public, on the same Terms, in Perpetuity.

Appendix (X. 3.)

3. PUBLIC RECORDS in

Number.	RECORD, ROLL, INSTRUMENT, MANUSCRIPT BOOK or PAPER, &c.	NATURE and USE.	PERIOD.	CONDITION.		ARRANGEMENT, CATALOGUES,			
			PERIOD of TIME to which the Records relate.	The Records COMPLETE or DEFECTIVE.	State of PRESERVATION of the Records.	ORDER of ARRANGEMENT.	General CATALOGUES or Particular INDEXES, &c.	COMPLETE or DEFECTIVE.	Utility of COMPLETING Defective Catalogues.
7.	RECORD of the CIVIL LIST ESTABLISHMENT for SCOTLAND, and of Inſtrument Warrants, Precepts, Certificates, &c. thereunto relating.	2. RECORDS of the CIVIL LIST ESTABLISHMENT of SCOTLAND. AT the Commencement of every Reign ſince the Union of the Two Kingdoms, there has been iſſued, under the Royal Superſcription and Counterſign of the Lords Commiſſioners of the Treaſury, an Eſtabliſhment or Liſt of Payments for Civil Affairs in Scotland, accompanied by a Letter or Inſtrument under the Privy Seal of Scotland, ſigned and counterſigned in the ſame Manner, addreſſed to the ſaid Commiſſioners at London, and to the Lord Chief Baron and remanent Barons of Exchequer in Scotland, and to all others to whom the ſame ſhall appertain, containing Inſtructions, Directions, and Authority for making ſaid Payments. The Eſtabliſhment and Inſtrument of Privy Seal of His preſent Majeſty are dated 19th June 1761; and the Directions therein contained are ſtrictly obſerved in the Manner of making up and of paying the Scottiſh Civil Liſt Eſtabliſhment. In Compliance with theſe Directions, the Chief Baron, or Two of the Barons of Exchequer, cauſe to be made out by the Auditor, Quarterly, a Liſt or Certificate (called a Quarterly Eſtabliſhment) of all ſuch Sum or Sums of Money as are due to any Officers or other Perſons for Fees, Salaries, or any other Allowances, according to the ſaid Eſtabliſhment of His Majeſty, and purſuant to ſuch Warrants under the Royal Sign Manual or Privy Seal of Scotland, counterſigned by the Commiſſioners of the Treaſury, as are tranſmitted to them. This Quarterly Eſtabliſhment, after being examined and ſubſcribed by the Chief Baron, or Two Barons of Exchequer, is on the Quarter Day (5th January, 5th April, 5th July, and 10th October) or on the firſt lawful Day thereafter, tranſmitted to the Lords Commiſſioners of the Treaſury at London for their Lordſhips Approbation, and in order to receive their Authority to pay the ſame; and a Duplicate is ſent along with it to be lodged in the Treaſury. On receiving the Quarterly Eſtabliſhment, the Lords Commiſſioners of the Treaſury (if they have no Objection thereunto) ſignify their Approbation thereof, by ſubjoining and ſubſcribing a ſhort Docket to that Effect; and then return it to the Exchequer in Scotland, "to the End that the Chief Baron and Barons may direct "Payment of the ſame, according to His Majeſty's Letter "of Privy Seal in that Behalf."—At the ſame Time that the Eſtabliſhment is ſent to London, a Letter is written by the King's Remembrancer, by Order of the Barons, to the Receiver General of the Cuſtoms and Caſhier of Exciſe, intimating to them the Amount of the Sums which will be required to pay the Eſtabliſhment, and which it will be neceſſary for them to retain in their Hands for that Purpoſe; and requiring them to make a Return into Exchequer of the Caſh then in their Poſſeſſion. On receiving back the Eſtabliſhment from London, with the Approbation of the Lords of the Treaſury, and Directions for paying it, the Lord Chief Baron, or Two of the Barons of Exchequer, iſſue Warrants on the Receiver General of the Cuſtoms and Caſhier of Exciſe, for impreſting into the Hands of the Receiver General of His Majeſty's Crown Rents and Caſualties (who is at preſent Paymaſter of the Eſtabliſhment) out of ſuch Part of the Revenues of Cuſtoms and Exciſe, as by Law is applicable to the Payment of the Fees, Salaries, and other Charges for keeping up the Courts of Seſſion, Juſticiary, Exchequer, Admiralty, and Commiſſaries, and for paying the Keepers of the Great and Privy Seals, and the Sheriffs Depute and Subſtitute, ſo much upon Account as ſhall be ſufficient to ſatisfy what is due on the Eſtabliſhment for ſaid Purpoſes; which Sums ſo impreſted the Receiver General is directed to apply and pay accordingly.—The ſaid Receiver General (as Paymaſter of the Eſtabliſhment) is alſo authorized and commanded by the Inſtrument of Privy Seal, out of the Money received by him for His Majeſty's Crown Rents and Caſualties, or out of ſuch Parts of the Revenues of Cuſtoms (viz. the Duty of Tonnage and Poundage, and Compoſitions in Exchequer upon Seizures of Prohibited and Uncuſtomed Goods) or of Exciſe (viz. the Hereditary and Temporary Exciſe, and a Proportion of Fines and Forfeitures) as are at His Majeſty's Diſpoſal, and as ſhall be received by him or impreſted into his Hands by Barons Warrants, to pay and ſatisfy all ſuch other Fees, Salaries, and Allowances contained in the Civil Liſt Eſtabliſhment, or in Warrants under the Privy Seal or Sign Manual, as have no Relation to the ſaid Courts. Precepts ſigned by the Chief Baron and Barons, or any Two of them are then iſſued upon the	Commencing with the firſt Eſtabliſhment of her Majeſty Queen Anne, of Date 13th June 1708, and continued down Quarterly to the Quarter ending 5th April 1800.	Complete.	Good.		No General Catalogues belong to the Records, but each Record has its own Particular Index at the Beginning or End of each Volume.	Theſe Indexes are complete.	

Office of the AUDITOR—(continued.) Appendix (X. 3.)

and REGULATIONS.			OFFICERS employed in Custody and Arrangement.						PLACE of DEPOSIT.				
TIME and EXPENSE required for so doing.	Regulation for RESTORING Records to their proper Places.	New Regulations requisite for rendering Use of the Record more convenient.	OFFICERS.	Their general Duties in respect of Custody or Arrangement.	Attendance.	NET SALARY paid by the Public.	FEES demandable for Searches or Certificates.	Net Annual Amount of FEES on an Average of the last Three Years.	BUILDING.	Condition as to SECURITY.	Condition as to ACCOMMODATION.	PUBLIC or PRIVATE Property.	TENURE and TERM by and for which holden.
	No Officer or Person is specially intrusted with the Care of restoring the Records to their proper Place, upon a Search or Certificate being granted; but this Duty is performed by the Auditor's Clerks, who attend upon these Occasions.	The Public seldom call for Inspection of any of the Records of this Office, and therefore no new Regulation appears requisite for rendering the Use of them more convenient for the Public.	The Auditor, his Deputy, and Clerks, have the Custody and Arrangement of all the Records in his Office.		Attendance the same as in the Return of the King's Remembrancer.	There is no Salary paid by the Public, solely in respect of the Custody and Arrangement of these Records, exclusively of the Salary paid on Account of the general Duties of the Office.	2 s. 6 d. for shewing each Record. 6 s. 8 d. for a Certificate.		In the Building occupied by the Court of Exchequer, situated in the Parliament Square, in the City of Edinburgh.	Moderately secure.	Not commodious.	The Property of the Corporation of the City of Edinburgh.	By Grant from the Corporation of the City of Edinburgh. This Building has for a long Time been occupied by the Court, Rent-free; and there is every Reason to believe, that it will be continued in the Possession of the Public, on the same Terms, in Perpetuity.

5 T

Appendix (X. 3.)

3. PUBLIC RECORDS in the

Number.	RECORD, ROLL, INSTRUMENT, MANUSCRIPT BOOK or PAPER, &c.	NATURE and USE.	PERIOD. Period of Time to which the Records relate.	CONDITION. The Records complete or defective.	CONDITION. State of Preservation of the Records.	ARRANGEMENT, CATALOGUES, Order of Arrangement.	ARRANGEMENT, CATALOGUES, General Catalogues or Particular Indexes, &c.	ARRANGEMENT, CATALOGUES, Complete or Defective	ARRANGEMENT, CATALOGUES, Utility of completing Defective Catalogues.
7.	RECORD of the CIVIL LIST ESTABLISHMENT for SCOTLAND, &c. (continued.)	the said Receiver General (as Paymaster) in Favour of each individual Person to whom any Sum or Sums of Money is due, either by virtue of the Establishment or of Warrants as aforesaid; and such Persons, upon presenting these Precepts to the Receiver General, receive instant Payment in Cash of the Money due to them, without any Discount or Charge whatever. These Imprest Warrants and Precepts are all framed in the Auditor's Office.—Certificates of all Sums of Money imprested as above into the Hands of the Receiver General, are transmitted from the Boards of Customs and Excise to the Offices of the Auditor and King's Remembrancer in Exchequer, in order that he may be duly and regularly charged with the same in rendering his Accounts in Exchequer.—All of the Establishments, Lists, Certificates, Precepts, &c. are recorded in the Auditor's Office.					No General Catalogues belong to these Records; but each Record has its own Particular Index at the Beginning or End of each Volume.	These Indexes are complete.	
8	RECORD of SIGNS MANUAL, &c.	IN this Record are entered all Royal Signs Manual, Patents, Grants under the Great and Privy Seals, and Warrants from the Lords Commissioners of the Treasury for Pensions, &c.	From 5th May 1709 to the present Time.	Complete.	Good.				
9.	RECORD of COMMISSIONS, &c.	IN this Record are entered all Commissions granted by His Majesty to the Lord President and Lords of Session, Lord Justice General, Lord Justice Clerk, and Lords Commissioners of Justiciary, Lord Chief Baron and Barons of Exchequer, Sheriffs and Stewarts Depute, and their Substitutes; and to all other Officers on His Majesty's Establishment, or Persons holding Commissions from His Majesty, or receiving Salaries paid out of the Public or Crown Revenues.	From 16th May 1709 to the present Time.	Complete.	Good.				

END OF THE REPORT OF THE RECORDS

Appendix (X. 3.)

4. PUBLIC RECORDS in the

Number.	RECORD. RECORD, ROLL, INSTRUMENT, MANUSCRIPT BOOK or PAPER, &c.	NATURE and USE.	PERIOD. Period of Time to which the Records relate.	CONDITION. The Records complete or defective.	CONDITION. State of Preservation of the Records:	ARRANGEMENT, CATALOGUES, Order of Arrangement.	ARRANGEMENT, CATALOGUES, General Catalogues or Particular Indexes, &c.	ARRANGEMENT, CATALOGUES, Complete or Defective.	ARRANGEMENT, CATALOGUES, Utility of completing Defective Catalogues.
1.	GREAT ROLL of PUBLIC ACCOUNTS.	AN Account has already been given (Page 424, Nos. 16 and 17; Page 432, No. 9; and Page 438, No. 6.) of the Public Revenues, which are accounted for in Exchequer, and of the Manner in which they are accounted for. By Statute 6 Anne, cap. 26. constituting the present Court of Exchequer in Scotland, it is enacted, Sec. 11. That the Public Accounts, after being made up and sworn to, shall be recorded in the Office of the King's Remembrancer and Lord Treasurer's Remembrancer, and finally "shall be delivered "into the Pipe Office, in the Court of Exchequer, in Scot-"land; and that the Clerk of the Pipe, or Chief Officer in "that Office, or his Deputy, (in case that Office shall be "executed by Deputy) shall cause the said Accounts to be "examined, and if found true, to be entered and inrolled "in said Office, and shall make and give a Quietus or Dis-"charge to the Accountant thereupon; which shall be a "Discharge to and for such Accountant as to all the Re-"venues, Duties, Matters, and Things therein and thereby "accounted for, paid, and answered."—The Rolls of the Public Accountants are thus finally lodged in this Office; and the Record is there kept also, in which are entered the Quietuses of these Accounts.	There are a few Accounts of Date prior to the Union of the Two Kingdoms, but the regular Series of these Records commences with the Institution of the present Court of Exchequer in 1708, by Stat. 6 Anne, cap. 26.	Before the Register House was built, the Records of this Office were in the private Custody of the Clerk of the Pipe for the Time, or his Deputy, in which Situation some of them were lost; but these are not numerous, and it is not known where they are.—Some Blanks in the Records appear to have proceeded from the Irregularity of the Public Accountants in making up and passing their Accounts.	Good.	In the Order of Dates, according to the Subject to which they relate.	The Books of Record have Indexes of the Accounts which they contain, which correspond with the Rolls.—There is also a Catalogue or Schedule made out some Years ago of the Records belonging to this Office, which are missing.		
2.	RECORD BOOKS of QUIETUSES.								

Edinburgh,
Exchequer Chambers,
3d June 1800.

Office of the AUDITOR—(*continued.*) Appendix (X. 3.)

and REGULATIONS. — OFFICERS employed in Cuſtody and Arrangement. — PLACE of DEPOSIT.

TIME and EXPENSE required for ſo doing.	Regulation for RESTORING Records to their proper Places.	New Regulations requiſite for rendering Uſe of the Record more convenient.	OFFICERS.	Their general DUTIES in reſpect of Cuſtody or Arrangement.	Attendance.	NET SALARY paid by the Public.	FEES demandable for Searches or Certificates.	Net Annual Amount of FEES on an Average of the laſt Three Years.	BUILDING.	Condition as to SECURITY.	Condition as to ACCOMMODATION.	PUBLIC or PRIVATE Property.	TENURE and TERM by and for which holden.
	No Officer or Perſon is ſpecially intruſted with the Care of reſtoring the Records to their proper Place, upon a Search or Certificate being granted; but this Duty is performed by the Auditor's Clerks, who attend upon theſe Occaſions.	The Public ſeldom call for Inſpection of any of the Records of this Office, and therefore no new Regulation appears requiſite for rendering the Uſe of them more convenient for the Public.	The Auditor, his Deputy, and Clerks, have the Cuſtody and Arrangement of all the Records in his Office.		Attendance the ſame as in the Return of the King's Remembrancer.	There is no Salary paid by the Public, ſolely in reſpect of the Cuſtody and Arrangement of theſe Records, excluſively of the Salary paid on Account of the general Duties of the Office.	2 *s.* 6 *d.* for ſhewing each Record. 6 *s.* 8 *d.* for a Certificate.	£. 2.	In the Building occupied by the Court of Exchequer, ſituated in the Parliament Square, in the City of Edinburgh.	Moderately ſecure.	Not commodious.	The Property of the Corporation of the City of Edinburgh.	By Grant from the Corporation of the City of Edinburgh. This Building has for a long Time been occupied by the Court, Rent-free; and there is every Reaſon to believe, that it will be continued in the Poſſeſſion of the Public, on the ſame Terms, in Perpetuity.

IN THE AUDITOR'S OFFICE.

Office of CLERK of the PIPE. Appendix (X. 3.)

and REGULATIONS. — OFFICERS employed in Cuſtody and Arrangement. — PLACE of DEPOSIT.

TIME and EXPENSE required for ſo doing.	Regulations for RESTORING Records to their proper Places.	New Regulations requiſite for rendering Uſe of the Records more convenient.	OFFICERS.	Their general DUTIES in reſpect of Cuſtody or Arrangement.	Attendance.	NET SALARY paid by the Public.	FEES demandable for Searches or Certificates.	Net Annual Amount of FEES on an Average of the laſt Three Years.	BUILDING.	Condition as to SECURITY.	Condition as to ACCOMMODATION.	PUBLIC or PRIVATE Property.	TENURE and TERM by and for which holden.
		The Records of the Pipe, as they relate only to the Public Revenue of the Country, are not conſidered as open for public Inſpection.	The Records are in the Cuſtody of one of the Joint Clerks of the Pipe.				Theſe Records are ſhewn only to Officers of the Crown, who have Occaſion to inſpect them; but no Fees are ever demanded on ſuch Occaſions.		General Regiſter Office, in an Apartment allotted jointly to the Clerk of the Pipe and Lord Treaſurer's Remembrancer.	Perfectly ſecure.	Perfectly commodious.	Public Property.	

Framed by
Pat. Murray,
King's Remembrancer.

SCOTLAND.
Chancery Office.

Appendix (X. 4.)

Appendix (X. 4.)

CHANCERY OFFICE.

Report by the Deputy Director of Chancery in Scotland, in obedience to the Order of the Select Committee on the Public Records, &c. of the Kingdom; dated 26th February 1800.

TO the Questions contained in the Order of the Select Committee, the following Answers are submitted:

(1.) The Records kept in the Chancery Office, are,

1. Record of the Charters of Lands and other Heretages in Scotland, holding of the Crown. These Charters are all written by the Clerks in the Chancery Office, and it is their Duty to record them in proper Books.

The Whole of the Records of the Crown Charters were formerly kept in the Chancery Office; but by a Decree of the Court of Session in Scotland, 9th December 1773, upon a Representation of the Lord Clerk Register, they were ordered to be lodged in the General Register House of Scotland; and accordingly all these Records, down to 6th August 1788, have been lodged in the General Register House.

By the before mentioned Decree, these Records are allowed to remain in the Chancery Office for Ten Years after the Date of the last Charter recorded in each Book. There are now Five Books or Volumes of these Charters in the Chancery, besides a Volume going on, not yet filled up. The First of these Volumes, commencing at 6th August 1788, and ending on 2d June 1790, will be delivered into the Register House in June next.

2. Record of the Charters of Lands and other Heretages holding of the Prince or Stewart of Scotland.

This Record commences in 1620, and is regularly continued to the present Period, in Five Volumes.

3. Record of Commissions under the Great Seal, Remissions or Pardons of Crimes, Patents for Discoveries, and Exemplifications thereof.

There is One Volume of this Record commencing in 1766, and ending in 1798, remaining in the Chancery Office; and another Volume begun at the last Period, not yet filled up. The former Volumes have, under the Authority of the before mentioned Decree, been lodged in the General Register House.

4. Record of Retours of General and Special Services of Heirs to their Ancestors, and of other Services, upon Brieves issued from Chancery.

This Record commences in 1547, and is continued down to the present Period, consisting of Ninety-two Volumes, besides the Volume now going on, and not yet filled up. The Fifth Volume, however, comprehending the Period from 1610 to 1614, is missing. The first Twenty-one Volumes of these Records were, during the Protectorship of Oliver Cromwell, carried from Scotland to the Tower of London, and after the Restoration of King Charles II. were returned to Scotland; but having been sent back by Sea, some of the Volumes have been damaged by Water, and it is supposed that the Fifth Volume, which is missing, may have been lost or mislaid in the Carriage of these Records to or from London.

It may be proper to notice that there must be many Retours of Lands in Scotland, which have not been recorded. This however occasions no Loss to the Public, although Individuals may at Times feel Inconvenience from the Want of the Evidence of such Retours upon Record; but when any old Retours are discovered, they are brought to the Chancery Office and recorded.

5. Record of Precepts upon Special Services, or Retours of Lands and other Heretages in Scotland.

This Record commences only in 1750, and is continued in Three Volumes down to 1751, when it stops, probably from its having been considered unnecessary, as it is fully supplied by the following.

6. Record of Respondes, or of the Sums payable by the Vassals of Lands holding of the Crown, or Prince and Stewart of Scotland, for which Sums the Sheriffs or Stewarts are answerable to the Exchequer; and which Sums or Respondes are specially mentioned in the Precepts flowing from the Chancery, upon the Special Services of Heirs to their Ancestors.

This Record commences in 1588, and is continued down to the present Time, in Twenty-one Volumes.

(2.) The Chancery Records are kept in a Room in the North East Corner of the General Register House in Edinburgh, on the Second Floor. This Room, like the others in this Building, is well adapted for the Security of the Records, the Walls being all of Stone, and the Floor and Roof likewise arched with Stone. The Register House is Public Property.

(3.) All the before mentioned Records are in general in good Preservation. The Record of Retours is in several Instances considerably damaged, as before mentioned, by Water; and some of the early Volumes of the Record of Respondes are not in good Condition. These Records are arranged in different Presses in the Order of their Dates.

(4.) There are complete and correct Indexes to the Records of the Charters and Retours. The Retours, or the Indexes thereof, serve sufficiently for Indexes to the Record of Respondes. There are no Indexes to the Record of Commissions, &c. but when that Record is carried to the General Register, an Index to it is made by the Clerks in that Office.

(5.) There are always Two Clerks officiating in the Office, whose Duty it is to take Care of the Records kept there. They attend every lawful Day in the Year, from Ten in the Forenoon until Eight in the Afternoon. They are allowed Forty Five Pounds per Annum from the Exchequer, for making out the Precepts from the Chancery to the Vassals of the Crown, for Payment of the Crown Duties, and for their Trouble in attending occasionally at the Exchequer, with such Records as may be necessary for revising the Signatures of Lands holding of the Crown or Prince. From the Circumstance of the Record of Charters being now lodged in the General Register House, the Fees for Searches in this Office are very few and inconsiderable. Some Searches are made in the Record of Retours, and the Fees are in Proportion to the Length of the Search. If only One Retour is searched for, the Fee paid is Half a Crown if it is not found, and Five Shillings if found. The Clerks have not received above Seven Pounds Ten Shillings per Annum, upon an Average of the Amount of the Fees of Searches in this Office, for the last Three Years.

(6.) The Clerks in the Office have the Custody of the Records; upon a Search of any particular Book of Records being made, the Book is regularly returned to its proper Place. The Books are never carried out of the Office, excepting when they are taken to the Exchequer, upon the Revisal of Signatures, as already mentioned, or produced at a Service before the Sheriff of Edinburgh, or the Macers of the Court of Session; and in all such Cases, One of the Clerks always attends with the Books, and brings them back to the Office.

(7.) The Records kept in the Chancery Office being now reduced to so small a Compass, and the Convenience of the Public being as much attended to as the Nature of the Business requires, or can admit of, no further

further Obſervations appear neceſſary to be offered upon the Subject.

James Dundas,
Deputy Director of Chancery in Scotland.

Edinburgh,
12th March 1800.

Appendix (X. 5.)
COMMISSARY COURT.

Return from the Principal and Under Clerks of the COMMISSARY COURT at EDINBURGH, to the Requiſition made by the Committee on the Public Records, &c. of the Kingdom.

THE Juriſdiction of the Commiſſary Court conſiſts of ſeveral different Branches, which it may be neceſſary briefly to enumerate.

Each Dioceſe or antient Biſhoprick in Scotland, has its particular Commiſſary, to which Number Two or Three more have been added ſince the Reformation; the Dioceſe of Edinburgh has a Commiſſary Court conſiſting of Four Judges, and this Court may, on Account of its more extenſive and more important Juriſdiction, be termed Superior, the others Inferior Commiſſariots.

Each Inferior Commiſſary has a Power of granting Adminiſtration of the Effects of thoſe who die within the Territory to which his Juriſdiction is limited; and alſo of deciding, in the firſt Inſtance, in all Actions of ſimple Adherence, that is, in Actions at the Inſtance of one married Perſon againſt the other, complaining of wilful Separation, and concluding that the Defendant ſhould by Order of Court be ordained to return and adhere to the Plaintiff; in all Actions of Scandal or Defamation, and in petty Actions for Sums not exceeding in Value Forty Pounds Scots.

The Commiſſaries of Edinburgh exerciſe the ſame Juriſdiction in all Cauſes of the ſame Nature, ariſing within the Bounds of their peculiar Territory, comprehending the Counties of Edinburgh, Haddington, and Linlithgow, commonly called the Three Lothians; and beſides, in Caſes of Adherence, it extends over Scotland.

As a Superior Court, the Commiſſaries of Edinburgh have a Power of reviewing, as a Court of Appeal, the Sentences of all Inferior Commiſſaries in Scotland; this Power, however, has of late Years been ſo ſeldom reſorted to, that it may be ſaid to be almoſt in deſuetude.

They have alſo a Privative Juriſdiction extending all over Scotland, in the following Caſes.

They only, can grant Letters of Adminiſtration to the Executors of Perſons dying in England, or Abroad, and having Sums of Money or Effects due or belonging to them in Scotland.

They, to the Excluſion of all other Courts whatever, take Cognizance of all Cauſes properly Conſiſtorial; ſuch as Declarators of Marriage, including all Queſtions whatever relating to the Conſtitution of that important Contract; Actions of Separation, a Menſa et Thoro, with or without Concluſions for ſeparate Alimony, on Account of Maltreatment, Declarators of Nullity of Marriage, on Account of Pre-Contract, Conſanguinity, Impotency, &c.; Declarators of Baſtardy, in which they take Cognizance of all Cauſes in which the reputed Legitimacy of any Individual is called in Queſtion; in all Actions of Divorce, on Account of Adultery or wilful Deſertion; in all which Caſes their Sentences completely diſſolve the Matrimonial Connection, and empower the Parties to marry again; theſe Actions, with ſome others of leſſer Importance, are only competent before the Commiſſaries of Edinburgh, whoſe Juriſdiction therein extends all over Scotland. In all theſe Caſes, the Witneſſes adduced by either Party muſt be examined by One or other of the Four Commiſſaries of Edinburgh, and the Whole of the Evidence muſt be dictated by the Judge Examinator, to one or other of the Clerks of Court, and by him committed to Writing, on Paper duly ſtamped, in order that the Depoſitions duly authenticated by the Signatures of the Deponents, and of the Judge, may be duly preſerved until Sentence, and ever after make Part of the Record of Court.

SCOTLAND.
Commiſſary Court.
Appendix (X. 5.)

As theſe ſeveral Functions of the Court require regular Records to be kept, it is competent, and has alſo become uſual to record in this Court for Preſervation, and for Execution, all ſuch Private Deeds, Conveyances, Bonds, Obligations, Wills, &c. as are brought in and preſented for that Purpoſe, by any Perſon having a legal Intereſt in the Deeds to be recorded, to whom is returned a Copy thereof, called an Extract, authenticated by the Clerk, which is entitled to the ſame Credit as the Original Writing, in all Tranſactions in Scotland, and in the Courts of Juſtice there.

And alſo to record for Preſervation, only the Schedules or Inventories of the Eſtates, Heretable and Perſonal, of Pupils and Minors, &c. made up in Terms of the Scots Act of Parliament, 1672, c. 2.

The Records of this Court thus come to conſiſt of ſeveral different Branches, which ſhall be enumerated below.

(1.) The Court was inſtituted in its preſent Form, in the Year 1560, and the Clerks of the Commiſſary Court have the Cuſtody of no Records previous to that Period.

From that Period, the Duty of the Clerks, ſo far as connected with the Subject of the Report, conſiſted—1. In preſerving and arranging all the Original Rolls, Deeds, Pleadings, Judgments, and Decrees, which they were required either by their Public Duty or Private Requiſition to record, ſo as that Acceſs to theſe Original Documents might readily be had at all Times.—2. In giving forth certified Copies of theſe Records, to the Party obtaining the Decree, or regiſtering the Deed, which having the Form of an Original, might be the Foundation of the Execution competent by Law.—3. In making out and preſerving in bound Books, full and accurate Copies of all Deeds, Teſtaments (that is, Letters of Adminiſtration) and Decrees, including the whole Evidence adduced by the Parties, and the Pleadings and Arguments thereon, ſo as Recourſe may at any Time be more readily and more ſafely had to theſe Office Copies, than to the Original Documents themſelves.—4. In ſearching for and pointing out to any Party duly authorized to inquire, any Deed, Teſtament, or Decree, which may be ſpecified if recorded in their Regiſter.—5. In making out and delivering to any Perſon duly authorized to demand the ſame, an authenticated Office Copy, having the Force and Effect of an Original, of any Deed, Teſtament, or Decree, &c. regiſtered in or pronounced by the Court at any Time ſince its Inſtitution.

The Record itſelf conſiſts at preſent of Five ſeveral Branches.

The Firſt contains the Regiſter of all Cauſes properly Conſiſtorial, which were formerly enumerated in the Introduction to this Report; alſo the Record of all Actions of Defamation and Slander.

The Warrants, as they are called, or Originals of this Branch of the Record, conſiſt of the Original Writs or Summonſes by which the Action is brought into Court; the Pleadings of the Parties both in Fact and Law; the Original Deeds, Writings, and other Vouchers produced by either Party to ſubſtantiate their Aſſertions; the Evidence of all Witneſſes cited and examined before the Court, ſigned by the Witneſſes and the Judge who examined them, and reduced into Writing by One of the Clerks of Court; the written Arguments of the Parties, Solicitors, or Counſel, the various Interlocutory Sentences, and Occaſional Orders pronounced by the Court, and the Definitive Sentence in the Cauſe. Theſe Original Papers are all put up in Bundles, each Bundle

SCOTLAND.
Commissary Court.
Appendix (X. 5.)

containing the Papers belonging to one Cause; these Bundles are again tied up in larger Parcels, each Parcel containing the Causes which have been decided within a certain specific Period; these Parcels are covered with strong Paper, and the Period to which each relates legibly marked on the Outside of the Parcels, which are then arranged according to Order of Time, on Shelves, in the Apartments in the Register Office, to be afterwards mentioned.

A full Copy of each Cause is made out and delivered to the prevailing Party, called an Extracted Decree; and another is also made out and inserted according to the Date of the Decree in the Record.

2. A Record is kept for registering Edicts or Applications, praying for Letters of Administration, with all the Proceedings thereon; for the Insertion of Tutorial and Curatorial Inventories; for Actions concluding for Constitution of Debts due by Persons deceased, and against their Executors; for Payment of these Debts; and for Civil Actions for Sums under £.40. Scots.

The Warrants of this Record are preserved in a similar Manner, and they also are copied out in Books for more ready Consultation, like the Consistorial Decrees.

3. The Record for Testaments, that is, for Letters of Administration, granted by the Court to the Executors of deceased Persons named in their Wills, and, where there is no Will, to the nearest in Kin, Widow, or Creditors of the deceased.

The Warrants of this Record are, the Wills and Testaments made by the Deceased, and the Inventories of their Personal Estates and Effects produced by the Executors, who obtain the Administration thereof; and also the Inventories given in by Executors, decreed by the Court, to deceased Persons who have made no Will, called Executors Dative, to whom Special Administration has been granted, with a Reference to the Date of the Decree, on the Edict by which, the relative Proceedings may be readily found in the Record last mentioned.

4. A separate Record is kept for the Insertion of the Bonds granted by the Executors, with their Sureties or Cautioners, binding themselves to the Extent of the Sums contained in the respective Inventories, that they shall faithfully administer the same, and render an Account and Payment thereof to all concerned.

Lastly, the Register of Deeds of Conveyance, Wills, Bonds, Obligations, Contracts, and other Writings brought in by the Owners thereof, and recorded for Preservation or Execution.

The Originals of these Deeds are carefully preserved and arranged; Copies are inserted in Books kept for that Purpose; authenticated Office Copies, called Extracts, are delivered to the Persons bringing the same to be recorded; future Extracts of these, as well as of every other Part of the Record, are at any after Time made out and delivered to any Person having a legal Title to demand the same, on paying the Fees to the Clerks for making out such Second Extract.

All the Warrants are preserved and arranged, from the Institution of the Court in 1560, down to the present Time.

The Copies inserted in the bound Books, are brought forward to a Period which, in none of them, reach actually down to the present Year, but all of which are in the Course of being completed; they have fallen behind, principally owing to the great Numbers of important Causes brought before the Court, which have increased so much of late Years, as to occupy much Time, and to render the Fund usually set apart for that Purpose inadequate to the Purpose of speedily making up the Deficiency; and also the confined Space occupied by the Clerks of Court, which will not admit of so many Hands being employed at once, as would be requisite to write out the Records in Arrear within a very limited Time.

[A particular Report on this Subject would occupy much Room, but it shall be made out if required.]

(2.) The Records are lodged in Two low Rooms in the Public Register Office in Edinburgh, where they are perfectly safe from all Fear of Accident. The Keys of these Rooms are kept by the Clerks of Court, and as the Business requisite to be done in arranging and searching these Records, does not require constant Attendance, none is given at these Rooms excepting when required by any Individual having Occasion to consult any Part of their Contents; the Clerks of Court give constant Attendance at an Office adjoining the Parliament House in Edinburgh, where all the Official Business (Searches alone excepted) is carried on, and where all depending Actions, and very recent Records are kept, for the Conveniency of ready Consultation by Parties, Clerks, or Judges; this Office being also the Place where the Judges sit for the Purpose of taking Proofs, deliberating on, and deciding Causes, &c.; this Office is Private Property, and held by Lease from Year to Year, the Rent being paid out of the Official Emoluments of the Clerks of Court.

(3.) The Records, as may be gathered from what has been already said, are in good Preservation, and are so arranged, that they may be consulted with little Trouble, and any Part of their Contents readily found.

(4.) There are Indexes called Minute and Responde Books to each Record, in which are respectively entered the Date of each Decree, with the Names of the Parties; the Names of the deceased Persons to whose Executors Administration has been granted in regular Order of Time; the Deeds of Conveyance, Wills, &c. recorded; and the Names of the Parties, in the same Way, by Means of which Minute Books or Indexes the Clerks can easily find out any Decreet, Testament, Deed, &c. which any Person wishes to see.

(5.) In this Office there is a Principal Clerk, who holds his Commission from the King, with a Power of naming a Deputy for Life; there is also a Deputy Clerk, holding his Commission from the Principal, with a Power of naming Substitutes to act, and to authenticate Extracts in his Absence; there are also Two Under Clerks who constantly attend the Official Business in the Office, and the Courts, one or other of them having always a Commission as Substitute to subscribe and authenticate Extracts or Writs issued from the Office; and a Writing Clerk, and sometimes Two, as Business requires, also attend in the Office. All these Officers are in their subordinate Capacities responsible for the proper Care of the Records, and have the Custody of them. The Public Court is held on Friday in each Week of the Year, but Proofs and Evidence are taken, and other Procedure and Official Business carried on by the Judges and Clerks, every lawful Day, at the Clerks Office; the stated Hours of Attendance for the Under Clerks above mentioned, being from Ten in the Morning until Three in the Afternoon, and from Four to Six in the Evening, excepting on Saturday, when the Office is not kept open later than Two in the Afternoon. None of the Clerks have any Annual Salaries, Allowances, or Emoluments paid to them by the Public, that is, paid out of the Public Revenue; but the Emoluments of Office to them, and their Under Clerks, arise solely from certain settled Fees payable on Extracts or Copies of the aforesaid Decrees, Testaments, or Letters of Administration, &c. which are authenticated by the Clerk (commonly with the Seal of Office appended) and given to the Parties about the Time Judgment is given or pronounced in them by the Court, and from the Proofs and Procedure in the above mentioned Causes, which while pending demand much Attention.

The principal Part of the Emoluments of the Clerks, as

as already mentioned, arises from their proper Duty as Clerks of Court; a small Part, however, of their Emolument is connected with the Custody of the Records, and this arises in the following Manner:

After the first Extract has been delivered out to the Person obtaining a Decree or Letters of Administration, or recording a Deed, it sometimes happens, that Persons having Interest, search the Records for old-Deeds, Letters of Administration, or Decrees, and these Persons, when successful in their Search, also sometimes demand certified Office Copies of such Decrees, &c.

For these Searches and Second Extracts, are paid as follow: For the Searches, from 2*s.* 6*d.* to Half a Guinea, according to the Period during which the Inaccuracy or Ignorance of the Party applying may oblige the Clerks to examine the Books before finding the Deed, Decree, &c.

	s.	*d.*
For each Sheet of a Second Extract, or authenticated Copy from the Record of Deeds of Conveyance, Bonds, Wills, &c. each Sheet consisting of 2 Pages of 30 Lines, 7 Words in each Line	1	6
For each Sheet of a Second Extract, from the Record of Testaments	2	6
For each Sheet of a Second Extract or authenticated Copy, from all other Records mentioned above	3	8½
For a Copy of any Part of a Record unauthenticated, 6*d.* per Page, besides the Fees for the Search.		

The Emoluments, however, arising from these Searches and Second Extracts, are in general so trifling, that no separate Account has ever been kept of their Amount, from which an Average can be made out; they may, however, be estimated nearly as follow:

Emoluments from Searches, one Year with another about £.5. per Annum.

Emoluments from Second Extracts, extremely various, from the different Lengths of Decrees or Deeds so extracted, but one Year with another not exceeding £.20.

The Clerks do on no Occasion suffer any Part of the Record to be removed out of their Custody; Searches are always made by themselves; Second Extracts are written out under their immediate Inspection in the Office, and the Records again immediately replaced.

(6.) Is already answered.

(7.) It does not occur to the Reporters, that any Arrangement of the Business, or Keeping of the Records of the Office, can be anyways rendered more convenient or more advantageous to the Public, than by the present Practice.

All which is humbly reported by

Jo. Coldstream, Sub. Clerk.
Patrick Murray, Sub. Clerk.

Appendix (X. 6.)

ADMIRALTY COURT.

Return to the Questions put to the proper Officer of the Court of ADMIRALTY in Scotland, by Order of the Select Committee on the Public Records, &c. of the Kingdom; dated 26th February 1800.

(1.) THE several Sorts of Public Records, Rolls, Instruments, and Manuscript Books and Papers, in the Custody of the said Court of Admiralty, are the following; viz.

First, The Record, wherein are ingrossed, 1st. Commissions from the Crown to the several Judge Admirals of Scotland, and by them to their Deputes, Clerks, Procurators, and Macers of the Court. 2d. Commissions from the Crown to the several Vice Admirals of Scotland, and from them to their Deputes. 3d. Bonds of Caution or Surety in Judicial Proceedings before the said Court of Admiralty in Maritime Cases, Indentures between Seamen and Seamen, &c. The First of these Records commences and ends in 1674; but there is a Chasm from that Period until 1702; and from that Date to the present Time this Record is complete.

Second, The Diet Books or Rolls of Court, in which are ingrossed the several Steps of Procedure in all Actions that come before the Judge of the said Court of Admiralty, relative to Maritime and Mercantile Transactions or Questions, and the Condemnation of Prizes which fall under his Cognizance; and the Judicial Proceedings, when finally determined by his Lordship, are tied up in Bundles, according to their Dates, with a Schedule of the Proceedings in each Cause, and deposited agreeably to the Answer to the Second Question.

Third, A Book, intituled "Receipt Book," wherein a Receipt is given by a Procurator of Court or his Clerk, for the Steps of Procedure in every Action borrowed by him or them from Time to Time, in course of the Judicial Proceedings in such Causes, which serves as an obligatory Document against both, for the faithful Return thereof to the Clerk of Court; and in case of Neglect or Refusal, is the Ground of Diligence issuing against them to compel the Return thereof.

(2.) The Building in which these Records are kept, is a Room set apart for that Purpose in the General Register House, built by Government, for all the Public Records of Scotland, except those in Daily Use, which are kept in the Admiralty Office in the Lawn Market of Edinburgh, in which the Depute Clerk of Court resides, which is Private Property, and held by him in Lease from Year to Year.

(3.) These Records are all in good Order and Preservation, and are arranged in the Order of their Dates.

(4.) The Records above mentioned are, complete and correct General Catalogues, Calendars, Schedules, and Repertories of the several Particulars before specified; but there are no Particular Indexes except as to the First Record of Commissions, &c. No other Utility or Advantage would result from Indexes being made of the Diet and Receipt Books, or of the Warrants and Judicial Proceedings themselves, further than pointing out more easily and readily the several Particulars ingrossed in these Books, and a progressive Alphabetical List of the Plaintiffs and Defendants Names, or Parties in the several Causes. The shortest Time necessary for completing such Indexes, by the ordinary Diligence of the Depute Clerk of Admiralty and his Clerks, the Persons usually employed in the said Court of Admiralty, is Six Months. No Indexes belonging to the High Court of Admiralty in Scotland are known to exist elsewhere.

(5.) The Officer employed for the Custody and Arrangement of these Records, is the Depute Clerk of Admiralty, whose Duty it is to have the Custody and Arrangement of the Records above specified, and who gives Attendance in the Office every lawful Day, from Ten in the Morning until Seven in the Evening. Neither the Principal nor Depute Clerks have any Annual Salaries, and only certain Emoluments and Allowances paid to them for each Search, certified Copy, and

SCOTLAND.
Teind Office.
Appendix (X. 7.)

and Attendance, and for Inspection of said Records, which are arbitrary, and according to the Trouble they have had relative thereto; no specific Account has ever been kept by them of these Fees; but upon an Average of Three Years, they cannot exceed £. 40. per Annum.

(6.) The Person specially intrusted with the aforesaid Records is the said Depute Clerk of Admiralty, whose Duty it is to attend upon every Search, to authenticate every certified Copy, and to take Care that every Record be duly and safely restored to its proper Place.

(7.) The only Matter not comprized in the Questions referred to, which it might be necessary and expedient to observe, for rendering the Use of the said Records and the Proceedings more convenient to the Public, would be to bind up the aforesaid Schedules of the Judicial Proceedings in all Causes which have been finally determined by the Judge Admiral, according to their Dates, with an Alphabetical Index, as before specified in the Order of these Dates.

James Dickson,
Deputy Clerk of Admiralty.

Appendix (X. 7.)

TEIND OFFICE.

Return to the SELECT COMMITTEE on the Public Records, &c. of the Kingdom.

(1.) THE Records in this Office relate to Valuations of Tythes, the Establishment of Churches and Stipends to the Clergy. Of the more antient Records there is a Book, in which are bound up the Reports of the Sub-Commissioners of sundry Presbyteries, made in the Years 1629, 1630, and 1631. There are Two Reports by the Sub-Commissioners of Two other Presbyteries, made up of the same Period. There is also a Book, containing the Procedure of the High Commission, from March 1630 to June 1633, in regular Progression. In the Year 1700, the House in which the Office was kept, was consumed by Fire, and it is said that the other Records and Documents belonging to and then in the Office were burnt. By an Act of Parliament in 1707, vesting the Powers of former Commissioners in the Lords of Council and Session, it was appointed for supplying the lost Registers, that Extracts from authentic Records being presented to the Lords Commissioners, the same should be recorded in a particular Register; and Extracts from this Record are declared to be valid. A considerable Number of these authentic Extracts have accordingly been given in and recorded in this Register, according to the Date of their being presented. The Procedure of the Court of Commission, since its Establishment in 1707, is regularly entered in a Register, and the Decreets are from Time to Time recorded in Books, according to their Dates; and the Warrants of these Decreets (i. e. Rolls, Instruments, and Documents) are wrapped up in Bundles Annually. The Whole of these are Manuscript Books and Papers.

(2.) The Teind Office, in which these are kept, is a Room in the General Register House in Edinburgh; the Condition of which, as to Security and Accommodation for the keeping thereof, is said to be well planned and executed, and Public Property.

(3.) The Book first mentioned, viz. that containing Reports of various Sub-Commissioners, is in some Places illegible, from the Substance of the Ink being wasted or destroyed by Wet or Damp, probably in some Degree before being bound up; some few other Places are lacerated and torn, but the greatest Part of it is very legible and entire. All the other Records are distinct and entire, and the Arrangement and Order of them have been described under Answer 1.

(4.) There are complete Indexes to the particular Matters contained in each of the Records, carried on progressively, according to their Dates. It is not known that any Indexes, &c. belonging to the Teind Office, exist any where else. There are a few partial Extracts and Excerpts of Proceedings by the Commission in the Years 1629, 1630, &c. in the Custody of the Keepers of the General Register Office, of which they have a complete Index.

(5.) The Officers or Clerks belonging to this Office are, a Principal Clerk, Two Deputy Clerks, and an Extractor. The Principal and Deputies have the Custody of the Records and Papers, and the Deputies take the more particular Charge of them and their Arrangement. The Deputies attend to do the Business of the Office every lawful Day during the Sitting of the Court, from Nine o'Clock in the Morning, until Three o'Clock in the Afternoon; and from Five o'Clock to Eight o'Clock in the Evening; and in Time of Vacation, from Ten o'Clock in the Forenoon to Three o'Clock in the Afternoon; and in general also until Eight o'Clock in the Evening. There are no Annual Salaries, Allowances, or Emoluments paid to the Clerks by the Public (if by the Word Public is meant the Government) in respect of such Custody, &c. and no Table of Fees is fixed as demandable for a Search, Certificate, Copy of or Attendance with Records. Practice has indeed established a Perquisite of 2*s.* 6*d.* as due to the Deputies for a Search, and taking a Note of any Matter in the Records; and if a Copy or Certificate is wanted, it is paid for according to the Length or Trouble attending it; and these Searches, Certificates, &c. are so few, and produce so small Sums, that it is impossible to state any Average Annual Amount of them.

(6.) The Deputy Clerks take the particular Charge of the Records, and attend upon every Search, which is always made in the Office, and under the Eye of one or other of them; and upon its being finished, they restore the Book or Record to its proper Place. The Records are never allowed to be carried out of the Office, unless when a Book is necessary in the Court, whither it is carried and brought back by one or other of the Deputies.

(7.) There do not occur any further Matters necessary for rendering the Use of the Records more convenient to the Public.

Teind Office, Edinburgh,
9th May 1800.

James Miller, Deputy,
Chas Bowman, Deputy,
In Absence of the
Principal Clerk.

Appendix (X. 8.)

TAILZIES AND INVENTORIES.

Return of the Register of TAILZIES in Scotland, to the Select Committee on the Public Records of the Kingdom.

BEFORE answering the Questions contained in the Order, it is proper to mention that the Keeper of the

the Regifter of Tailzies is likewife Keeper of the Regifter of Inventories, given up by Heirs entering to their Predeceffors "cum beneficio Inventorii." It is only the Firft of thefe that is mentioned in the Order; but the following Anfwers apply to both.

(1.) The Public Records in the Cuftody of the Regifter of Tailzies and Inventories are: The entire Record of Tailzies, from its Eftablifhment in 1685, down to this Day, confifting of 31 Folio Volumes, and a 32d begun.—The Record of Inventories, from December 1721, down to this Day, confifting of Five Folio Volumes, and a Sixth nearly completed. Thefe Volumes begin with N° III. The Firft and Second Volumes never were in the Poffeffion of the prefent Keeper, nor did he know where they were to be found, until within thefe few Days that he learned they were in the General Regifter. They contain the Inventories recorded, from the Inftitution of the Regifter in 1695 to December 1721, when the Third Volume begins.

He has no other Rolls, Inftruments, or Papers, in his Cuftody, than thofe he has mentioned.

(2.) As the Keeper of the Regifter of Tailzies and Inventories is always One of the Principal Clerks of Seffion, each of whom have a Room in the General Regifter Houfe, thefe Records are depofited in the Room poffeffed by the Clerk of Seffion, who is the Keeper of them for the Time.

(3.) Both Records are complete, and in perfect Prefervation, except Volume IV. of the Record of Tailzies, from which one Sheet was torn out, as mentioned in the Books of Sederunt of the Court of Seffion, 17 December 1761, and was afterwards fupplied by a Decree of the Court of Seffion proving the Tenor thereof, which is inferted in a fubfequent Volume.

(4.) There are correct and complete Catalogues of both Records.

(5.) The Principal Keeper of the Record names a Deputy, who has the immediate Cuftody of the Records, and gives conftant Attendance every Day, except Sundays, from Ten in the Morning to Three in the Afternoon, and from Half an Hour after Four until Eight in the Evening, during the Sittings of the Court of Seffion; and from Ten in the Morning until Two in the Afternoon during the Vacations.

Neither the Keeper of the Regifter nor his Deputies have any Salaries, Allowances, or Emoluments of any Kind paid to them by the Public; each of them has ftated Fees paid by thofe who make ufe of the Record, conformable to the following Table.

FEES paid to the Keeper of the Regifter:

	£.	s.	d.
For Recording each Sheet of a Tailzie - -	—	3	9½
For Writing a Certificate or Docket on the principal Deed of Entail, certifying the Date, the Volume, and the Pages in the Volume in which it is recorded - -	1	1	—
For every Sheet of a Tailzie extracted from the Record, and attefted by the Keeper of the Regifter - - - - - - - -	—	3	9½
For every Sheet of an Inventory recorded or extracted - - - - - - - - -	—	6	2

Fees paid to the Deputy Keeper:

	£.	s.	d.
For recording a Tailzie, each Sheet - -	—	1	2
For authenticated Extracts of Tailzies, each Sheet - - - - - - - - - - - -	—	1	2
For Copies or Excerpts from the Record, not authenticated by the Subfcription of the Keeper, each Sheet - - - - - -	—	1	2
For Infpecting or Searching in the Record of Tailzies, each Volume - - - -	—	2	6
Befides the above Fees, the Deputy generally receives an additional Gratuity of 10*d.* upon each Sheet, for recording a Tailzie.			
For recording or extracting each Sheet of Inventories - - - - - - - - - -	—	1	2
The Record of Inventories is feldom looked at, but when it is, the Fee for infpecting each Volume is - - - - - - -	—	2	6
The Average of the Fees received by the Keeper of the Regifter for the laft Three Years is - - - - - - - - - -	78	12	—
The Average of the Fees received by the Deputy in the fame Time is - - - -	39	9	—

(6.) The Keeper of the Regifter being obliged to attend his Duty in the Court of Seffion during the greateft Part of the Day, the Cuftody of the Record falls chiefly upon the Deputy. No Part of the Records are permitted to be taken out of the Room in which they are lodged. The Searches are made either by the Deputy himfelf, or in his Prefence; and when the Search of One Volume is finifhed, it is put up in its Place before another is taken down.

(7.) It would, in the Opinion of the prefent Keeper of the above Regifters, render them more fecure, if the Volumes, as they were completed, were from Time to Time tranfmitted to the General Repofitory, under the Care of the Lord Regifter and his Deputies; this would no doubt leffen the Emoluments of the Office, but it would increafe the Security of the Record, for Reafons too obvious to require to be particularly mentioned. The regular Tranfmiffion of many of the other principal Records, is exprefsly provided for by Statute, which is one Caufe of their being kept and preferved with fo much Regularity. And there feems no good Reafon why the Record of Tailzies or Inventories, or indeed any other Record, fhould be excepted from this general Rule, now that there is a Building fit to receive and preferve them.

All which is humbly fubmitted by

George Home.

Edinburgh,
20th March 1800.

Appendix (X. 9.)

INTERRUPTION OR HORNING OFFICE.

Return from the INTERRUPTION OR HORNING OFFICE, to the Queftions of the Select Committee on the Public Records of the Kingdom.

(1.) THE Records in this Office confift of Three feveral Sorts: 1ft, a Record, containing Interruptions, Summonfes, and other Writs for preventing the Prefcription of real Rights; 2dly, a Record, containing Inhibitions, Interdictions, and Petitions for Sequeftrations; 3dly, a Record, containing Letters of Hornings; thefe different Letters, Diligences, or Papers, are prefented at this Office within the Time prefcribed by Law, and ingroffed in the Record to which they belong, and the Letters returned to the Ingiver, within 24 Hours from the Date of prefenting the fame, with a Certificate written thereon, and figned by the Keeper of the faid Regifter or his Deputy, certifying that the fame is duly

 recorded

SCOTLAND.
Interruption or Horning Office.

Appendix (X. 9.)

recorded conformable to the Act of Parliament. To each of these Records there is an Index or Minute Book kept, in which is ingrossed the Year, Month, Day, and Hour of presenting the Letters, the Names of the Parties and Ingiver, or Presenter of the same; which last signs the said Minute Book, by Way of Receipt for the Letters, and exonerating the Keeper that the same were recorded and returned.

(2.) The Horning or Interruption Office, in which the above are kept, is a Room in the General Register House, Edinburgh; the Condition of which, as to Security and Accommodation for the keeping thereof, is well planned and executed, and is Public Property.

(3.) The whole Records are distinct and entire, arranged in proper Order, and filed up to the present Time. There are only Ten Years Records preceding the present, allowed to be in this Office; all former Records being lodged in the General Repository in the Register House, and kept by the Lord Clerk Register and his Deputies.

(4.) There are no Records, Indexes, &c. belonging to this Office any where else than above described.

(5.) The Officers belonging to this Office are a Principal Keeper, who appoints a Deputy and a Clerk for ingrossing the Letters or Papers into the Record. The Principal or his Deputy and Clerk must attend every lawful Day, from Eight in the Morning until Eight at Night, during the Sitting of the Court; and from Nine in the Morning until Eight at Night during the Vacation. The Keeper has an Annual Salary of £.20. from Government; there is no Table of Fees for a Search, Certificate or Copy from the Registers; Practice has established a Perquisite of 1 *s.* or 2 *s.* 6 *d.* as due for a Search, and if a Note or Copy is wanted, it is paid for, according to its Length or Trouble attending it; these are so few, it is impossible to state an Average Annual Amount of them. The Keeper pays his Deputy and Clerk.

(6.) Searches are always made in this Office, and the Records never allowed to be carried out of it, until they are removed, as in N° 3.

(7.) There do not occur any further Matters necessary for rendering the Use of the Records more convenient for the Public.

Ja. Newbigging,
Keeper.

Edinburgh, Horning Office,
May 17, 1800.

Appendix (Y. 1. to Y. 33.)

COUNTY REGISTRIES.

SCOTLAND.
Sheriffs Courts.
Appendix (Y. 1.)

SHERIFFS COURTS.

Appendix (Y. 1.)

Return of the Sheriff Substitute, of the County of ABERDEEN, to certain Questions contained in an Order of the Select Committee on the Public Records of the Kingdom.

SIR,

I HAVE received from you the Order of a Committee of the House of Commons, of date 28th February last, signed by Charles Abbot, Esquire, and addressed "to the Sheriff of Aberdeenshire." In obedience thereto, and to your Directions, I beg leave to answer to the several Queries of the Order, as follows:

Answer to Query I.

The Records of the Freeholders; the Register of Services of Heirs, of Tutorial and Curatorial Inventories, of all Judicial Proceedings carried on before the Sheriff, of all Deeds recorded in the Sheriff's Books, either for Preservation, Publication, or Execution; the Record of Letters of Horning, and of Inhibitions, used within the County, are lodged and kept in my Custody, as Sheriff Clerk: The other Public Records of the County, are those of the Justices of the Peace, and Commissioners of Supply, the Register of Sasines, and the Court Books of the Commissary of the Diocese; of these, the Two first are kept by the respective Clerks of the Peace, and of Supply; the Register of Sasines by the proper Keeper thereof; and the Commissary Books by the Commissary Clerk; which last Record (as well as the Sheriff's) is competent for the Registration of Deeds, whether directed to Preservation or Execution, and is frequently (I believe) used for that Purpose.

Court Records. In further Answer to this Query, regular Books are kept by me of the different Steps of Judicial Procedure held before the Sheriff, in which every individual Step or Motion is entered of its proper Date. Minute or Index Books are also kept, for leading to the immediate Discovery of Writings inquired after; in the same Manner, Receipt Books are kept for the Security of Steps of Process or Writs lent out to Parties, in the Progress of Litigation. The Date of the oldest Record of this Kind in this Office, is October 1697; and they are regularly preserved since, with the Exception of the Court Books, from March 1718 to June 1721, and from July 1744 to June 1747.

Freeholders Records. 2. The Freeholder's Record consists of a progressive Series of the Minutes of their Meetings and Resolves, under the Signature of the Preses for the Time being; it is bound up in Folio Volumes: The most antient of these Records bears Date only in September 1727; the Minutes, from October 1739, to September 1740, are missing.

Record of Services. 3. The Register of Services of Heirs, consists of the Claims of the respective Persons desiring Service to their Ancestors (with the Instructions or Warrants of their Claims); when the Services are completed, Extracts are issued under the Clerk's Hand; the Claims are occasionally bound up in regular Parcels, the Minute Books whereof reach back to 1649, and are complete.

Of Tutorial and Curatorial Inventories. 4. With regard to Tutorial and Curatorial Inventories, the Record is kept in the precise same Way with the last Article, the principal Inventories being retained, and Extracts issued. The Minute Book appears to commence of the same Date with the Books of Services.

Of Deeds and Probative Writs. 5. In the very same Way, with regard to Deeds registered for Preservation or Publication, excepting those recorded merely as probative, which are returned to the Parties, and the recorded Copy only kept. The Register of Probative Writs begins in 1630, and is wanting from August 1643 to September 1649, inclusive.

Records of Hornings, &c. 6. As to Hornings and Inhibitions, a Book is transmitted from Time to Time, from the proper Office at Edinburgh, into which, Copies of these Writs are entered here, and the Principal Writs returned to the Parties. The Volumes, when completed, are transmitted to Edinburgh; of course I am ignorant of the earliest Date of this Record.

Of Fiars, &c. Corn Laws. 7. It is finally to be stated, that the Sheriff Clerk is Custodiar of the Record of Fiars, or Annual medium Prices of Victuals, as ascertained by a Jury, before the Sheriff; this Record commences in 1705, and is entire: He is also Keeper of the Record of Monthly Returns of Victual Prices, as ascertained under the Authority of the late Statute of His present Majesty; and which Record, attended with considerable additional Trouble, is regularly kept.

It will not be expected that I should say any thing of the other County Records, which are under the Charge of different and distinct Officers.

Answer to Query II.

1. The Records under my Custody are kept in a Building called the "Record-Office," situated at the East End of the Castle Street of Aberdeen. This Building was erected about the Year 1780, by Public and Individual Subscription, principally by the Exertions of John Gordon of Craig, then Sheriff Clerk, and of Alexander Innes of Breda, then Commissary of this Shire; upon whose Security, Money was borrowed for supplying Deficiences.

2. The Condition of this Building is very tolerable as to Accommodation, and very sufficient as to Security, being particularly constructed to resist Fire.

3. The Property of the House stands, by Deed of Settlement, vested "in the President of the Society of "Procurators in Aberdeen, and his Successors in Office, "and their Assignees, for the Use of the County and City "of Aberdeen." Dated and recorded in Sheriffs Court Books, 5th May 1783.

4. It is provided by this Deed, that the Building shall never be disposed of without "the unanimous Consent "of said President, &c. and of the Sheriff and Commissary Clerks for the Time being."

Answer to Query III.

The Records (in as far as I can discover) are in good Condition, and in the most accurate Order. It has not been

SCOTLAND.
Sheriffs Courts.
Appendix (Y. 1.)

been in my Power, minutely and personally to investigate them all, on account of my Father's Death (who was also my Predecessor in Office) within a Fortnight past; but my Brother, who has been Deputy Clerk for Ten Years, enables me confidently to say, that the Accuracy, which was my Father's constant Study, has carefully been observed. The Order in which the Records are arranged, is that of Dates.

Answer to Query IV.

1. This Query has been to a certain Extent answered: The Indexes, or Minute Books, are very distinct, and (unless as before excepted) are complete.

2. I am humbly of Opinion that no farther Catalogues are requisite for this Office, as the present lead with precision to the principal Records and Warrants.

3. In the Instance where the Record is deficient, it applies to antient Dates; and I cannot give any Explanation of the Cause or Manner of the Omission, nor point out a Mode of Recovery; it happened, in all the Instances, long before my Father obtained the Office of Sheriff Clerk, in 1764.

Answer to Query V.

1. The Business of this Office is performed by the Principal Clerk, one or more Deputies, and such Number of Writing Clerks (generally Four) as Circumstances require. The Deputies for the most Part (under the Inspection of the Principal) attend to the Arrangement of the several Records. Attendance is given, every lawful Day of the Year, from Eight in the Morning to Eight in the Evening.

2. The Fees payable to the Principal Clerk will best appear from a Copy of the "Table of Fees" (herewith transmitted) regulated by Act of Sederunt of the Court of Session in 1748; to this must be added, that there are certain other Allowances by the Freeholders for Inrolments, and Inspection of their Records (which are in the Whole very inconsiderable) and that the Sheriff has this Year allowed Three Pounds of the Twelve Pounds per Annum, granted by the above mentioned Corn Law of His present Majesty. As to the Deputy Clerks and Writers, the Principal Clerk generally makes such Agreement with them as he can: The Allowance made by my Father, for many Years past, to the Deputies, has been One Fourth of the greater Part of the Fees, and a Salary besides (they paying the Writers.)

3. I perceive from my Father's Books, that the Average Free Balance of his Profits for the Three last Years, including the whole Emoluments of the Sheriff Clerk's Office, is One Hundred and Sixty-one Pounds Two Shillings and One Penny Sterling.

Answer to Query VI.

1. The Records are under the constant personal Care of the Deputy, and other Clerks, the Principal being always responsible: One or other attends upon every Search, and restores with his own Hand every Book and Paper to its own Place.

2. There are no other Denominations of Officers a Principal and Deputy Sheriff Clerks, Writers, and sometimes indentured Apprentices.

3. In depending Suits before the Sheriff, Principal Papers are given up, pro tempore, to the Parties upon Receipt; in no other Cases is any Principal Paper ever suffered to leave the Record, having been once lodged there; but an Extract (or certified Copy) is furnished whenever required, on Payment of the regulated Fees.

Answer to Query VII.

It does not occur to me that any new Regulations are requisite for rendering the Use of the Records kept within this Office more convenient to the Public, unless I might presume to suggest the Expediency of some Extension of the Fees established more than Half a Century ago, and which I well know from my Father's Information, and that of a Succession of Deputies, are really inadequate to the present Duties of constant Labour and Risk, and to the Means of procuring and paying respectable Deputies, and the necessary Writing Clerks in these Times; and to the Means of defraying the attendant Expenses of Servants, Fire, Candles, &c. &c. and, above all, Stationary.

Application was made by the whole Sheriff Clerks in Scotland, for this Purpose, a few Years ago (1783) to the Court of Session; but that Court, "in respect the "Act of Sederunt in 1748, was declared by the Ju- "risdiction Act (20th George II.) to be binding on all "Parties, unless and until the same shall be altered by "Act of Parliament, found that this Court had no Pow- "er to alter, vary, or make Addition to the Fees then "established," and therefore refused, &c. All which is respectively reported by

James Gordon,
Sheriff Clerk of Aberdeenshire.

19th March 1800.

To David Morice, Esq; Sheriff Substitute of the County of Aberdeen.

I, David Morice, Sheriff Substitute of Aberdeenshire, do, in Compliance with the Order of the Select Committee of the House of Commons on the Public Records, &c. of the Kingdom; dated 28th February last, transmitted to me; certify, That the Sheriff of Aberdeenshire has no Custody or Charge of any of the Public Records, Rolls, Instruments, Manuscript Books or Public Papers of the Shire; that they are all kept by the Sheriff Clerk of the Shire, whose Appointment is totally Independant of the Sheriff; that James Gordon, Esq; who signs the before-written Letter to me, is present Sheriff Clerk of this Shire; and that, to the best of my Knowledge and Belief, his Report on the State of the Records under his Charge, is a just one.

D. Morice.

Aberdeen,
20th March 1800.

THIS is the Table of Fees to which my Report to the Sheriff, for the Committee of the House of Commons, of this Date, refers.

James Gordon,
Sheriff Clerk, Aberdeenshire.

March 1800.

The Fees and Dues of Clerks, and other Officers, in Sheriff and Steward Courts, in Civil Cases, as regulated by Act of Sederunt, 16th March 1748.

Sterling.	£.	s.	d.
For registrating each Sheet of Hornings, Interdictions, Inhibitions, and Lawburrows, with their Executions, to Clerk and Servants - - - - -	—	1	4½
For an Extract of a Horning, Inhibition, Interdiction, or Lawburrows, with the Execution, for the First Sheet, to Clerk and Servants - - - - -	—	1	2
Every other Sheet - - - - -	—	1	—
For registrating every Sheet of Bonds, Instruments of Protest, Tacks, Dispositions, and Inventories of Heirs entering "cum beneficio," and for any other Writings given in to be registrated, to Clerk and Servants - - - - - - -	—	1	2½

For

	£.	s.	d.
For an Extract of Fiars, to Clerk and Servants	—	—	8
For every Libel or Summons, where the Sum is under Forty Pounds Scots	—	—	6
For a Libel or Summons, where the Sum is above Forty Pounds Scots	—	1	—
For every Precept for summoning Witnesses and Parties, pro confesso	—	—	2
Letters of Arrestment, or loosing thereof	—	—	10
For a Petition or Answer	—	—	6
For Writing a Bond of Cautionry	—	1	—
For receiving thereof	—	—	6
For producing an Advocation	—	1	—

For Writing Depositions of Parties and Witnesses:

	£.	s.	d.
For every Deposition of a Party	—	1	—
For each of the First Six Witnesses	—	1	—
For every other Witness	—	—	6
To the Clerk, for extracting every Decreet not exceeding Twenty-five Pounds Scots	—	1	—
To the Clerk, for extracting every Decreet exceeding Twenty-five Pounds, and not exceeding Forty Pounds Scots	—	1	8
To the Clerk, for extracting every Decreet exceeding Forty Pounds, and not exceeding Sixty Pounds Scots	—	3	—
For writing and recording each Sheet of these Decreets	—	—	6
To Clerks and Servants, for extracting all Decreets, Acts, or Commissions, in Causes exceeding Sixty Pounds Scots in Value, for the First Sheet	—	2	6
For every other Sheet	—	1	6
But for every repeated Sheet of a Decreet, where any Acts or Commissions have been extracted, only	—	—	8
For every Sheet of Decreets of transumpt	—	1	2½

That each Sheet of an Extract, written Sheet-ways, consist of Forty-nine Lines, at the Rate of Thirteen Words in each Line; and if written Book ways, that it consist of Two Pages, and of Thirty-six Lines in each Page, and after the Rate of Nine Words in the Line.

	£.	s.	d.
That for every Appeal entered against any Decreet, Sentence, or Judgment, there be paid to the Clerk, by the Appellant, for recording the Appeal, and taking the Bond of Caution	—	1	—

And that the Clerk insert the said Appeal in every Extract to be thereafter given out by him, of such Decreet, for which his Dues are to be paid after the same Rate as the Rest of the Extract.

For Services of Heirs:

	£.	s.	d.
For a general Service, to Clerks and Servants' drawing the Claim, and expeding the Service, and to Officers and Witnesses for executing the Brieve at the Market-cross	—	15	—
For Acts of Curatory, and Process for making up Tutorial or Curatorial Inventories, each Sheet	—	5	—

For Special Services as follows:

	£.	s.	d.
To drawing the Claim, expeding the Service, and giving the Retour or Extract of the Service, including Officers and Witnesses Fees for executing the Brieves, for the First Sheet	—	15	—
For every other Sheet	—	5	—

For Seisins to be paid as follows:

	£.	s.	d.
1. The Current Price of the Vellum or Parchment for the Time.			
2. For the First Sheet that it fills up of the Clerk's Protocoll as Notary	—	6	8
And for every other Sheet	—	5	—

That the Clerk receive for his Pains, for taking the Infeftment, as follows:

	£.	s.	d.
If it is taken at the Distance from the Clerk's Office of Three Miles, or under, that he be paid for an Estate not exceeding Two Thousand Merks of Yearly Rent	1	1	—
If exceeding Two Thousand Merks, and not exceeding Five Thousand Merks	2	2	—
If exceeding Five Thousand Merks, and not exceeding Ten Thousand Merks	3	3	—
If exceeding Ten Thousand Merks, and not exceeding Twenty Thousand Merks	4	4	—
And for any Estate exceeding Twenty Thousand Merks	5	5	—
And no more whatever the Estate be.			
If it exceeds Three Miles, that for every other Mile that the Clerk taking the Seisin shall be obliged to travel to the Place where Seisin is given, until it amounts to Ten Miles, there be paid	—	5	—
And if it exceed Ten Miles, for every other Mile	—	2	6
For Sequestration of a Bankrupt Tenant's Effects, such a Sum as shall be judged reasonable by the Sheriff, the highest not exceeding	1	—	—
The lowest not under	—	5	—
And for each Person qualifying in Terms of Law, and for the Certificate thereof	—	2	6

For transacted Processes and Decreets, the One Half of what they would have amounted to, if extracted.

And that Services of Relicts to their Terce pay One Half of Special Services; Services of Tutory to pay as general Services, and Services of Idiotry and Furiosity to pay as general Services, and the Witnesses to be paid for as in other Processes.

	£.	s.	d.
To the Officer for summoning a Party or Witness, or charging to make Payment on Decreet or Precept, to himself, and Two Witnesses to the Execution	—	—	8
But if the Parties or Witnesses cited or charged, exceed Three in Number, and are within One Mile of one another, in that Case only for each	—	—	6

Item, For each Mile the Officer and his Two Witnesses travel, from the Place of his Residence, there shall be paid to him a further Sum of Six Pence, provided always that the whole Sum paid the Officer, for himself and his Two Witnesses, does not exceed Half a Crown for One Day, whatever be the Number of Miles, or Number of Parties or Witnesses to be summoned.

	£.	s.	d.
To the Bar-Officers that attend the Court, for the Oath of each Party or Witness	—	—	1
For executing of a Caption for Reproduction of a Process	—	—	6

The Officer for himself, Witnesses, and Apprisers, &c. to be paid for Poindings at the Discretion of the Party Employer, for which the Officer assigns him to the Sheriffee.

Extracted forth of the Books of Sederunt by

Tho. Gibson.

SCOTLAND.
Sheriffs Courts.
Appendix (Y. 1.)

Fees and Dues of the Clerks and other Officers, in Sheriff and Stewart Courts, in Criminal Cases, as regulated by Act of Adjournal, 21st March 1748.

	Sterling. £.	s.	d.
When a Private Pursuer, to the Procurator Fiscal for his Concurrence	—	1	2½
For every Complaint, and Warrant to cite, to the Clerk	—	1	—
Every Oath of a Party, to the Clerk	—	1	—
To the Clerk, for an Oath of a Witness, for the First Six each	—	1	—
Every Oath above that Number	—	—	6
To the Clerk, for every Petition or Answer	—	1	—
To the Clerk, for Letters of Intimation or Liberation, besides Dues of the Petition	—	1	6
To the Clerk, for Petition and Information, and Warrant of Commitment	—	2	6
For Criminal Letters to Ditto, for the First Sheet	—	2	6
Every other Sheet	—	1	6
To Bill, and Letters of Diligence on Indictment	—	2	6
To the Clerk, for Bill, and Letters of Exculpation	—	2	6
For a Bail Bond from a Defender for Appearance	—	2	6
To the Clerk, from the Defender, at deserting the Diet	—	2	6
For recording every Sheet of Information, either for Pursuer or Defender	—	1	8
For every Appeal entered against any Decreet, Sentence, or Judgment, there be paid to the Clerk, by the Appellant, for recording the Appeal, and taking the Bond of Caution	—	1	—
To the Clerks and Servants, for extracting Decreets, Acts, or Commissions, for the First Sheet	—	2	6
For every other Sheet	—	1	6
That the Clerk insert the said Appeal in every Extract to be thereafter given out by him of such Decreet, for which his Dues are to be paid after the same Rate as the Rest of the Extract.			
To the Officer for summoning a Party or Witness, to himself, and Two Witnesses to the Execution, his Employer furnishing the Copy	—	—	8
But if the Parties or Witnesses cited exceed Three in Number, and are within One Mile of one another, in that Case only for each	—	—	6
Item, For each Mile the Officer and his Two Witnesses travel from the Place of his Residence, there shall be paid to him a further Sum of Six Shillings (provided always that the whole Sum paid the Officer, for himself and his Two Witnesses, does not exceed Half a Crown for One Day, whatever be the Number of Miles, or Number of Parties or Witnesses to be summoned, and that the Employer furnish Copies)	—	—	6
To the Bar Officers that attend the Court, for the Oath of each Party or Witness	—	—	1
To the Officer and Witnesses, for summoning a whole Assize of Forty-five Persons in Town, or a Mile round, the Employer furnishing the Copies	—	3	9

Extracted forth of the Books of Adjournal, by
Jo. Davidson.

By Act of Adjournal of the High Court of Justiciary, of Date the 21st of July 1749, all Parties who enter Appeals in Terms of an Act of Parliament, of the 20th of His Majesty's Reign, intituled, "An Act for taking away and abolishing Heretable Jurisdictions," &c. are ordained, on or before the First Day appointed for holding the Circuit Courts in the several Stations respective, to lodge the said Appeals in the Hand of the Clerk of Court, in order to having the same inrolled; with Certification, that if Parties shall not comply with the Directions of the said Act of Adjournal, such Appeals shall not be received, but shall be held as not entered, leaving to the Appellant to take such other Remedy as accords of Law. And it is further declared, that in these Cases, the Judges will award such Expenses to the Respondent as they shall see Cause.

J. G.
S. C.

Appendix (Y. 2.)

Return by the Sheriff Depute of Ayrshire, to the Questions of the Committee.

THE Records of this County are under the Charge of the Sheriff Clerk thereof, an Officer appointed for Life by the Keeper of His Majesty's Signet; but as the Sheriff has the Superintendance of that Officer, he shall proceed to answer the different Questions contained in the Order of the Committee.

The Records of the County of Ayr may be enumerated under the following Classes:

Answer to Queries First and Third:

Class I.—The Records of all Processes extracted, unextracted, and compromised, or Processes in which no final Decrees have been pronounced. The extracted and unextracted Processes of each Month are bundled up; and afterwards those of a whole Year put into large Presses, and Minute Books and Rolls of them are regularly kept. The compromised Actions, and those in which no final Decrees have been pronounced, are bundled up by the Year, and Minute Books thereof are likewise regularly kept. The Members and Procurators, before the Sheriff Court, have Liberty to borrow any of these Processes upon their Receipts, and regular Receipt Books are kept. The Decreets and extracted Decreets are preserved in good Order from the Year 1717; and the compromised Processes, or those in which no final Decrees have been pronounced, from the Year 1740 down to the present Time.

Class II.—The Record of all Deeds, such as Bonds, Bills, Dispositions of Heretable Property, Assignations, Tacks, Subtacks, Submissions, and Decreets Arbitral, Latter Wills, &c. which are inserted in Books properly bound; and distinct Catalogues thereof, under the Denomination of Minute Books, are kept of each Paper, &c. recorded, whereby the Papers can be easily found. This Record commences in the Year 1682, but is only filled up, or the above Writings copied into the said Books, down to the 27th February 1767. The Principal Papers themselves, however, are all preserved in good Order, those of each Month tied up in separate Bundles, and afterwards arranged in large Presses, in which those of each Year are separately kept.

Class III.—Record of Hornings, Inhibitions, Interdictions, Relaxations, &c. The Book in which these Writings are ingrossed is sent by the Keeper of the General Register at Edinburgh to the Sheriff Clerk, each Leaf is marked with the Keeper's Initials, and every Tenth Leaf

Leaf with his Name; so soon as the Book is filled up, it is returned to the General Register Office at Edinburgh, and a new one sent out; the present Book commences 10th September 1792.

Class IV.—Register of Intimations by Heirs of Entail, to the next Heirs of Entail, and Improvements made in consequence thereof on entailed Estates, in Terms of an Act of Parliament passed in the Eighth Year of His present Majesty's Reign, intituled, "An "Act to encourage the Improvement of Lands, Te-"nements, and Hereditaments, in that Part of Great "Britain called Scotland, held under Settlements of "strict Entail." This Record commences 6th March 1771.

Class V.—Record of General and Special Services. This Record commences in the Year 1717, and is brought down to the present Time.

Class VI.—Record of the Yearly Fiars or Prices of Grain in the County. This Record commences in the Year 1658, and is brought forward to the present Period. Record of the Monthly Prices of Grain, in Terms of an Act of Parliament, passed in the First Session of the Seventeenth Parliament of Great Britain, which is also completely brought up.

Class VII.—Record of the Court of Freeholders of the County of Ayr, containing their Claims of Inrolment, Minutes of their Meetings, and Elections, &c. This Record begins in the Year 1702.

Class VIII.—The Record of Probative Writs. This Record commences in the Year 1735, and is regularly carried on to the present Period.

Answer to Query Second:

The Place where the Records are kept, is Two small Rooms or Apartments in the Dwelling House of the Sheriff Clerk Depute, which is situated in the Centre of the Town of Ayr, with contiguous Dwelling Houses above, below, and on either Side; it is possessed from Year to Year for Payment of a Yearly Rent. From the above Description, it will be obvious that the Records are at present much exposed to Danger from Fire; and as there is no safe Place for depositing them in Ayr, the Chief Burgh of the County, a House erected for this Purpose would be highly beneficial to the County, and to the Public at large.

Answer to Query Fourth:

It has been above noticed, that complete Minute Books are kept of all the Processes and Decrees pronounced, as well as of all the Bonds, Bills, &c. recorded, by which any of these can be found upon the shortest Search. The great Utility which would result from bringing down this Record to the present Time, and afterwards carrying it on regularly, is too obvious to admit of any particular Observations. To bring down the Record to this Time would occupy One Clerk for Six Years, with a Salary not under £.40. nor exceeding £.50. per Annum. There are no Catalogues, &c. or Minute Books missing at this Office; these being in full Preservation.

Answer to Query Fifth:

The Sheriff Clerk, in virtue of the Powers granted to him by his Commission, appoints a Depute; to these Officers belong the Custody and Arrangement of the Records of this County. The Clerk Depute employs Three Clerks under him, who attend every lawful Day from Eight o'Clock in the Morning to Eight o'Clock at Night.

Neither the Sheriff Clerk nor his Depute have any Salaries from the Public, their Emoluments consisting of Fees conformable to a Table fixed by the Court of Session in the Year 1748, in consequence of a Special Act of Parliament.

The Depute Clerk receives a Salary from his Constituent, and the inferior Clerks have small Allowances for their Writings. The Fees of each Search and Certificate are from 1 s. to 2 s. which upon an Average for the last Three Years amounts to about £. 4. per Annum. The whole Free Emoluments of the Sheriff Clerk, after deducting all Expenses necessarily attending upon his Office, amount to about £. 130. at an Average of Three Years past.

Answer to Query Sixth:

The Sheriff Clerk, and in his Absence his Depute, is specially intrusted with the Care of the Records, &c. One of them attends upon every Search, &c. and takes Care that the Records, &c. be duly and safely restored to their proper Places.

Answer to Query Seventh:

Great Advantage would result from proper Offices being built and vaulted, so as to secure the Records from Fire; and it would be also highly beneficial that the Records were completely brought up and ingrossed in bound Books; but the present Allowances to the Sheriff Clerk for this and other Services, from the Alteration of Circumstances, and particularly the Diminution of the Value of Money since these were fixed, more than Half a Century ago, are now extremely inadequate.

Their Fees have not been raised since the Year 1748; some Years ago the whole Sheriff Clerks of Scotland made Application to the Court of Session to get their Fees augmented; but although the Court were of Opinion, that the present Fees and Perquisites were too small, yet they were also of Opinion, that without new Powers granted to them by Parliament for that Purpose, they had no Authority to give any Addition to them.

Ed. McCormick,
S. D.

Ayr,
25th April 1800.

Appendix (Y. 3.)

Return of the Sheriff Clerk of ARGYLLSHIRE, to the Questions of the Committee.

(1.) THERE are belonging to the Sheriff's Court of Argyle, the following Public Records, or Manuscript Books and Papers; viz.

1. Diet Book of Court:

In this Book are entered all the Actions that on each Court Day are called before the Sheriff; and the Diet Book is the proper Authority for ascertaining in whose Hands any Action lies, as well as the Dates of whatever Decreets or Interlocutors are pronounced by the Sheriff; which Decreets are always understood to be in the Clerk's Hands, and form Part of the Records of Court. In this Book are also recorded the Commissions, Admissions, and Appointments of all the Members and Officers of Court.

It is here also that are ingrossed the whole Minutes of Procedure in Criminal Trials before the Sheriff. This Record commences upon the 8th of June 1709, and is carried down to the present Date.

2. Register of Letters of Horning, Inhibition, and Interdiction:

In this Record are ingrossed Letters of Horning, Inhibition, and Interdiction, with their Executions; and as relative to it, there is kept a Minute Book, containing an Entry of the Date of recording the Letters, with the Names and Designations both of Pursuers and Defenders, with

SCOTLAND.
Sheriffs Courts.
Appendix (Y. 3.)

with the Folio of the Book in which the same is recorded; and prior to recording, this Minute is subscribed by the Producer of the Letters, and by the Sheriff Clerk as Keeper of the Record; to this Book there are two Indexes, one of the Pursuers and another of the Defenders.

By the Law of Scotland, this Record is not allowed to remain in the Hands of any Provincial Clerk, longer than until the Volume is filled up; after which it is always sent to be joined to the General Records of the Kingdom, kept at Edinburgh, under the Custody of the Lord Register or his Servants. Of this Record, it may be observed, that for the greater Security of the Lieges, the different Sheriff Clerks in Scotland must receive the Volume from the Lord Register's Office, and that each Folio is subscribed by One of the Lord Register's Clerks, who likewise writes and subscribes Dockets to its beginning and concluding Pages, mentioning the Number of Folios contained in the whole Book, for which the Sheriff Clerks pay a very high Fee, between Six and Seven Pounds. In this County, this Record is filled up to the present Day.

3. Register of Deeds, Bonds, and Bills:

In this Record are ingrossed, both for Preservation and Execution, all Deeds and Bonds when regularly executed, regarding either Heretage or Moveables; as also Notarial Instruments, or Protests upon Inland Bills, or Bills of Exchange; with Discharges or Extinctions of Debt; and for the Ease of searching into it, there is likewise kept a Minute Book, which serves as an Index. This Record is justly considered as of great Authority and Utility, and in this County commences so far back as the 18th Day of November 1665; from which Period it has been, at a considerable Expense to the Sheriff Clerk, regularly filled up, down to the Year 1795, and is still going on; a Clerk being kept for the Special Purpose of filling up this Record, and that of Hornings, &c. above mentioned; although the Fees of Office are by much too small for defraying the Expense. The Original Papers ingrossed in this Record, are regularly bundled up according to their respective Dates of recording; are in the Hands of the Sheriff Clerk, and in good Preservation.

4. Register of Services, &c.

In this Record are ingrossed the Procedure before the Sheriff, upon Brieves issued from the Chancery, for serving and cognoscing of Heirs, Curators, &c. It commences upon the 11th Day of October 1700, and is regularly carried down to 1742.

The following Causes are assigned for this Record's not being carried down to a later Period.

The present Clerk, upon receiving his Commission, found 25 Years unfilled up, and he understood that the original Reason of this Stop was, that some particular Services had been called up to the Court of Session, from which they had not been returned for a long Time. And fully conscious of the Importance of this Record, he had every Inclination to fill it up equally with the Register of Bonds, Deeds, &c. but from the Smallness of the Fees allowed, found it impossible to do both, and he gave the Preference to the Register of Bonds and Deeds; for this Reason, that the Retours of Services are all recorded in Chancery, being the Court to which Recourse is usually had for searching into Matters of this Nature, so that there is in a Manner a double Security; but there being no other Security for the Preservation of Bonds and Deeds, but the Care bestowed upon them in the Sheriff Court, the Clerk thought that this last deserved the utmost Attention: but particular Care has been taken to preserve the Original Processes upon those Brieves, with Schedules for filling up the Record, if the Clerk should be at any Time enabled to do so. As nearly as can be computed, the Expense of filling up this Record since the Year 1742, would not be less than £.100. and would require the constant Labour of a Clerk for about Two Years.

5. Register of Decreets:

As far back as the End of the last Century, and for a few Years in the Beginning of the present One, the Decreets of the Sheriff were all minuted, and ingrossed in a Record; this was during a Period when the Decreets were few in Number; but for these Sixty or Seventy Years, when Business increased, there has been no Attempt made to book any of them, from a certainty that the Fees of Office could not afford it, as well as from a consciousness that the Booking of them was not very material. However, they are regularly bundled up according to their different Months and Years; and "in gremio" of each Decreet is a Scroll of the Extract, which was given out so as to preserve an Uniformity to a Second Extract, if it should be called for, which is scarcely ever the Case. They are in good Preservation; but to book them would be a very great Labour, and it would be difficult to form an Estimate of the Expense of doing it; but there can be no doubt that it would amount to many Hundred Pounds, at the same Time that any Advantage to be derived from it is scarcely conceivable.

6. Register of the Minutes of the Freeholders of ARGYLLSHIRE:

In this Record are ingrossed the Minutes of the Freeholders of the County, at their Michaelmas Head Courts, for receiving of Claims, making up the Roll of Freeholders, and Assessment of Rogue Money, as well as the Election of Members of Parliament.

This Book could be of no earlier Date than the Union of the Two Kingdoms of England and Scotland, in the Year 1707; it begins with the Election of a Member to the First British Parliament, and is regularly carried down to the present Day.

7. Register of Probative Writs:

In this Register are ingrossed Missive Letters on Business, fitted Accounts and such other Papers, as might afterwards be used as Adminicles in Proof of any Thing alledged, either in Prosecution or Defence. The Original Writing, after being given in and booked, is allowed to be taken up again upon Receipt, by the Person who gave it in. In short it is a Record for Preservation of the Tenor of such Writings as are without legal Formalities, which have no Clause of Registration, and therefore not entitled to have the Decreet of a Judge interponed for summary Execution. This Record is filled up to the present Day, and is in good Preservation.

8. Register of Accounts of Improvements on Entailed Estates:

This Record is kept in consequence of an Act of Parliament, passed in the Reign of His present Majesty, for ingrossing in it the Accounts and Vouchers of Ameliorations, made by the Proprietors of entailed Estates on their Properties. All the Accounts and Vouchers given in to this Record, after being ingrossed, are taken up, upon Receipt, by the Producers. The Record is regularly kept in Terms of the Act of Parliament, and is carried down to the present Date.

(2.) The Records of the Sheriff Court of Argyll, have been for these Thirty Years and upwards kept in a small Chamber of the Room where the Sheriff Court ordinarily sits, in the Town House of Inverary, Head Burgh of the County. The House was built by the County of Argyll, upon Ground the Property of his Grace the Duke of Argyll, and in all Probability by Sufferance from his Grace.

This Chamber can neither be called safe nor commodious, being just over the Common Gaol. It is the Place in which the Sheriff Clerk carries on his Business.

(3. & 4.) The different Answers to the 1st Question, render superfluous any Answer to the 3d and 4th Questions

(5.) The Sheriff Clerk, who is an Officer appointed by the Crown, is the Person employed for the Custody and

and Arrangement of the Records above-mentioned; he is Clerk to all the Judicial Proceedings before the Sheriff, and is entitled to the Custody of all his Sentences and Decreets; he also receives and fills up in the said Records the Writs given in to be recorded; and all Extracts of the Sheriff's Decreets, and of Papers ingrossed in the Records, are compared by him with the Originals, and authenticated with his Subscription. There is regular Attendance given in his Office on all lawful Days, from Nine o'Clock in the Morning, until Eight o'Clock at Night; and he is obliged to shew any Record or Paper in his Custody, to any Person who may call for a Sight of it; and who can condescend upon the Date, without Fee or Reward. He has no Annual Salary or Allowance paid to him by the Public, for the Custody of the said Records. His Emoluments arise from Fees upon the Judicial Proceedings before the Sheriff; from Fees on the Extracts of Decreets, and other Extracts from the said Record; which Fees were regulated and ascertained by an Act of Sederunt, of the Court of Session, in the Year 1748. The Annual Emoluments arising from the Whole of the Sheriff Clerk's Business in this County, taking an Average of the Three last Years, amounted to the Sum of £.161. Sterling; and the Expense paid to Clerks and Servants, and the other necessary Disbursements of his Office, amounted to the Sum of £.60. which being deducted from the Emoluments, left him for his own Pains, and Trouble and Attendance, the Sum of £.101. And for this Office he paid £.600.

(6.) The Answer to this Question is contained in the immediate preceding Answer.

(7.) From these Answers given to the Questions, it will appear, that some of the Records are left unfilled up, owing to the Inadequacy of the Fees of Office to accomplish that End. The Clerk's Income, as above stated, is evidently burthened to as great a Degree as it can bear. The Public Confidence placed in him, either for the Preservation of Papers, or authenticating of Extracts, is likewise apparent; and whether or not there is any Room for applying to him the common Axiom, "that every Man ought to be paid according to the Trust placed in him," it belongs to others to determine.

About Ten Years ago, a Joint Application was made to the Court of Session by all the Sheriff Clerks in Scotland, for an Augmentation of their Fees; the Desire of which was refused by the Court of Session, not for Want of good Grounds on the Part of the Applicants, but because the Act of Parliament, which empowered that Court to make a Table of Fees in the Year 1748, had limited their Powers to that particular Period; and without a new Act, they could give no Relief.

Arch. Campbell.

Appendix (Y. 4.)

Return from the Sheriff of BAMFFSHIRE, to the Questions of the Committee.

IN obedience to the Order of the said Committee, the Sheriff reports, that there are no Public Records, Rolls, Instruments, Manuscript Books or Papers in his Custody, as Sheriff of Bamffshire; all such Matters being under the peculiar Charge of the Sheriff Clerk of the County; but by a Communication from that Gentleman, the Sheriff is enabled to report the Situation of the Records of the County.

(1.) The Record (which commences nearly 200 Years ago) is composed chiefly of the Proceedings, Acts, and Decrees made and had in the Sheriff or County Court; and of registered Protests upon Bills, in order to obtain compulsory Diligence against the Debtors; and lastly, of principal Deeds or Writings, recorded for Preservation or Diligence, by the Parties interested therein.

The Sheriff Clerk, as Deputy of the Lord Clerk Register of Scotland, also keeps a separate Record of Hornings, Inhibitions, and such like Diligence of the Law of Scotland; which Record is rather of a temporary Nature, because whenever one Book is filled up, it is transmitted to the General Register at Edinburgh, and replaced by another clean Book.

The present Sheriff Clerk is also Keeper of the Provincial Record of Sasines or Infeofments in Land, which indeed is the most material Record of the Whole; and like the One immediately above described, is transmitted from Time to Time, as the Volume is filled up, to the General Register at Edinburgh; and the keeping of this Record is no Part of the Duty of the Sheriff Clerk as such, but is a separate and distinct Office in the Gift of the Lord Clerk Register.

(2.) All the above-mentioned Records are at present kept in the House of the Sheriff Clerk in the Town of Bamff; a Building in good Repair, but not Proof against Fire, yet is sufficiently commodious. It is the Property of the Sheriff Clerk himself; but there is now a perfectly commodious Fire-proof Place, erected by the County, for the keeping of their Records, into which it is intended speedily to remove them; and this Building is Public Property.

(3.) The Records above mentioned are in general in good Preservation; and they are arranged progressively from the Commencement down to the present Time, conformably to the Nature of the Record.

(4.) There are complete Catalogues or Inventories of the whole Records, conformable to their different Names, by Means of which any Paper or other Matter sought for, can be found with great Ease, and in a very short Time.

(5.) In this small County, the only Officers employed about the Records are, the Sheriff Clerk himself, and One Clerk who acts as his Deputy; and their Duties are to record all Writings given in, and to issue certified Extracts of Copies thereof, and of the Proceedings of the County Court. They attend every Day from Eight o'Clock in the Morning until Eight o'Clock at Night. They have no Salary or Allowance paid to them by the Public, in respect to the Custody of the Records; but their Emoluments arise from stated Fees for Searches, or certified Copies of all Papers issued by them; which upon an Average of the last Three Years amounts in gross to about £.100. Sterling, for all the Offices held by the Sheriff Clerk; and these Emoluments are composed of various Items, difficult to be stated; but the Principal are, a Fee of One Shilling and Two Pence Halfpenny, for recording each Protest on a Bill, or Sheet of any Deed; and from Six Pence to One Shilling and Six Pence, for certified Copies of the Procedure in the Sheriff Court, conformably to the Sum contained in the Summons or Foundation of the Action; for subscribing of which the Sheriff Clerk has also a Fee of Six Pence or a Shilling, conformably to the Sum; and he has a Fee of One Shilling for every Oath of a Party or Witness in the Sheriff Court; but these Fees are included in the above general Average of his Emolument.

(6.) It is the peculiar Duty of the Sheriff Clerk to take Care of the Records, to attend upon every Search, and to take Care that every Record, &c. be duly and safely restored and kept in its proper Place.

(7.) It does not appear that any Thing could be done by which the Use of the said Records, &c. could be rendered more convenient to the Public than at present; and no Complaint exists against the present Practice.

All which is humbly reported to the Honourable Select Committee, by

May 17, 1800. *Geo. Forbes,*
Sheriff Substitute of Bamffshire, N. B.

Appendix (Y. 5.)

Return by the Sheriff of BERWICKSHIRE, to the Questions of the Committee.

(1.) THE Sheriff of Berwickshire has no Custody of Public Records or Papers belonging to the County or the Public: The Sheriff Clerk (who is not appointed by the Sheriff) has the Custody of the Sentences and Records of the

SCOTLAND.
Sheriff Courts.
Appendix (Y. 5.)

the Sheriff Court; of Deeds and Obligations given in by Persons to be recorded, for Preservation or for Execution of Law; of Persons entitled to elect and be elected Members of Parliament; and of the Elections for Members of Parliament for the County. These Papers and Records are from the Time of the Union, and some of them are older.

(2.) The Sheriff Court-House is in Greenlaw, a small Village in the Western Part of the County, and there is a Room in it where the Sheriff Clerk places the above Papers and Records, after they are filled up by him: This House belongs to the County, but is not commodious nor secure; the Room in which the Papers and Records are kept, is locked up without Fire, and immediately above a Room used for incarcerating Insolvent Debtors.

(3.) The above Papers and Records are distinctly arranged from the Time of the Union, and in good Preservation and Order, so far as completed.

(4.) There are distinct Minute Books or Indexes of the Sentences and Writs recorded, which easily and distinctly lead to the Writ itself, or to the Record of it.

The Record of Elections is complete: The Record of the Sheriff Court may be behind from Twenty to Thirty Years, and of Deeds and Obligations about Ten Years back. One Person employed constantly in that Employment would complete the Whole in Two or Three Years.

Besides these Records of the Sheriff Court, the Commissary Court has a Record of Testaments; i. e. of Persons who claim or make up Titles to the Moveable or Personal Estates of deceased Persons; and a Record of Deeds and Obligations, which are kept by the Commissary Clerk, in his own House, now in Dunse.

The Clerk to the Justices of Peace keeps Records of their Meetings, chiefly relative to the Highways and Bridges of the County, and the Recovery of small Debts; and the Clerk to the Commissioners of Supply, a Record of the Transfer, or Division of the Cess or Land Tax.

There are also a Record of Sasines, and a Record of Inhibitions, affecting Landed Property; but these Two last do not remain in the County, but are sent into the General Register House at Edinburgh, so soon as filled up.

(5.) The Sheriff Clerk employs Sub-Clerks, or Persons to write for him, sometimes more and sometimes less, as he thinks fit, or the Business requires, and pays them as he pleases. He has no Salary, but he is paid by the Individuals or Persons interested in the Business, according to Fees fixed by Act of Sederunt of the Lords of the Council and Session, Anno 1748; which, although then reasonable, are certainly now too small, and not adequate to the Importance and Trouble of the Office.

(6.) It belongs to the Office of Clerk to take Care of the Records, and to do what is required in this Question.

(7.) If a proper House was built in the Town of Dunse, a considerable Town in the Middle of the County, and where the Sheriff Clerk and Professional Men reside, the Public Records and Papers would be better kept there, under their immediate Care and Inspection, and more convenient for the Public at large.

There was a Town House in Dunse, which became ruinous, and was lately taken down; the County, sensible of its Utility, have agreed to give Three Hundred Pounds towards building a new one; but this is so inadequate for the Purpose that it has not yet been set about: It would require One Thousand Five Hundred or Two Thousand Pounds, to build a proper House; and it has been proposed to raise the Money by Subscription; but People in general have so many other Occasions for their Money at present, that a sufficient Fund cannot be raised in that Way. If One Thousand Pounds could be gotten from Government for the Purpose, the Remainder might certainly be procured by Subscription. It is proposed that the House should contain Lodging for a Gaoler, a Guard Room for Soldiers and their Baggage, Rooms for the Justices of Peace, &c. Rooms for Records, &c. Prisons, and Clock and Bell: If Government is inclined to give any thing to this Work, the Sheriff of the County will be glad to be informed of it.

Dunse, 21st April, 1800. *Ab. Christie,* Sh. Sub.

72*

Appendix (Y. 6.)

Return from the Sheriff of the County of BUTE, to the Questions of the Committee.

THAT as Sheriff he has not in his Custody any Public Records, Rolls, Instruments, Manuscript Books or Papers, falling under the Description of Public Records, it not belonging to the Office of Sheriff to keep any of the Records: That the Sheriff Clerk is charged with and has the Privilege of keeping them, and derives the whole Emolument which from thence accrues.

But in order that the Select Committee may receive Answers to the several Queries, the Sheriff has procured from the Clerk the following Return to them: viz.

(1.) The Public Records of the Sheriff Court consist, 1st. Of the Proceedings in all Suits which have been prosecuted therein, with the Interlocutory Judgments and final Decrees pronounced in such Suits: 2d. Original Bonds, Instruments of Protest on Bills, Leases of Lands and other Real Property, Contracts, Dispositions of Heritage, Family Settlements, and Deeds of various other Kinds, which have been given in from Time to Time to be registered, and must remain in the Custody of the Clerk, who is not permitted to return the Originals: 3d. A Series of Register Books whereinto those several Deeds have been transcribed, commencing with the Month of April 1761: 4th. A Book for the recording of Hornings, Interdictions, Inhibitions, and Lawburrows, with their Executions; the Books of this Sort falling to be sent to the General Register Office at Edinburgh, whenever a Volume is filled up: 5th. A Book, containing Copies of the Rolls of Freeholders entitled to vote in the Election of Members to Parliament, for the County, as made up at their Michaelmas Meetings, or Meetings for Election, together with Minutes of the Proceedings at all such Meetings; of which Rolls and Minutes the Sheriff Clerk is to give Extracts, and at all Michaelmas and Election Meetings to produce the Book itself to the Freeholders: 6th. A Book of Record for Notices, by the Proprietors of Entailed Estates, of their Intention to lay out Money on Improvements, with an Intent of being Creditors in respect thereof to the succeeding Heirs, and for recording the Accounts of the Money so laid out periodically, and Vouchers thereof: 7th. A Book, wherein Commissions to Sheriffs, or their Substitutes, and the Admissions of Clerks, Procurators, and Officers, are recorded, and all Ministerial Acts and Regulations by the Sheriff, in Matters falling under his Power, are entered: 8th. A Book, containing the Prices of Grain and Oatmeal, as proven Monthly before the Sheriff, pursuant to the Act 31st Geo. III. Cap. 30: 9th. Books containing the Lists of Persons who have been returned by the Sheriff to serve on Juries, and of those obtaining Game Certificates, or Armorial Bearing Certificates: 10th. Rolls of Persons qualifying to Government before the Sheriff of the County: There is also a Variety of Miscellaneous Writings and Papers, which cannot be reduced under General Heads.

(2.) There is not any Building appropriated to the keeping of the Records of this County. The Sheriff Clerk happens to be also Town Clerk of the Borough of Rothesay; hence an Opportunity is afforded of lodging the Sheriff Court Records in the same Apartment of the Town-House where the Borough Records are kept: There is no Cause for Complaint on the Head of its being either insecure or incommodious; but the other Parts of the Town House being insufficient, a Plan is in contemplation for allocating the same and Appendages thereof to other Purposes, and building a new one in another Situation. Whether the Town will provide Accommodation for the Sheriff Court Records, and the Sheriff Clerk, in the New Building, is not known; at any Rate there would be little Chance that these Records last mentioned would be allowed to remain in the Town House, should the Offices of Sheriff Clerk and Town Clerk be enjoyed by different Persons, unless the County secure the Privileges of Accommodation there, by contributing a Proportion of the Expense which behoved necessarily to be incurred.

(3.) The Records, since March 1761, are in perfect Preservation, and all the Court Proceedings and loose Deeds are made up in Bundles, answering to the

4 Years

Years in which the Suits were determined, or the Deeds were given in to be recorded. There are very few Records extant here, antecedent to the Protectorate of Cromwell, his Governor of the Castle of Rothesay having, it is said, carried off the Records then in the County; and, owing to those subsequent to that Time, and prior to 1761, having been kept in Private Houses, and other Causes, they are found to be very defective. Some have been lost, and are understood to be now irrecoverable.

(4.) Since 1761 there are complete and correct General Indexes to each Book; and the Journal of the Court, called the Diet Book, points out the Law Suits of each Year: It does not occur at present, that any thing is wanting to complete the Indexes.

(5.) As has been already remarked, the Sheriff Clerk is charged with the Custody and Arrangement of the Records; he gives what Attendance is found necessary, without Restriction to particular Hours; he has no Salary paid him by the Public, in respect of such Custody and Attendance; nor can he, without being guilty of a Transgression, demand any Fee for making or allowing a Search to be made, or for Attendance with the Records, whilst any one is examining Deeds or Writings therein. The whole Emoluments of his Office arise on certain Articles of Business, almost wholly enumerated in Tables of Fees authorized by the Courts of Session and Justiciary in the Year 1748, which, considering the Decrease in the Value of Money since that Period, are become now very inadequate; besides which several Articles of Business, which ought to have been therein provided for, are entirely omitted.

(6.) From what has been already stated, an Answer may be gathered, namely, that here there is not any other than the Sheriff Clerk specially intrusted with the Care of the Records, or whose Duty it is to attend upon every Search, and to take Care that every Record and Paper be duly and safely restored to its proper Place.

(7.) On this it occurs that it would be desirable to have a fixed and safe Repository in every County for the Custody and Preservation of the Records, the Want of which appears to have been productive of very bad Consequences here; and that the Tables of Fees payable to the Sheriff Clerks should undergo a Revisal, and be augmented where necessary; and where there have been Omissions formerly, that these be now supplied, which it appears can be done only by Parliamentary Authority.

All which is humbly submitted,

Arch[d] Moore, S. S.

SCOTLAND. Sheriff Courts.

Appendix (Y. 7.)

Appendix (Y. 7.)

Return of the Sheriff Clerk of CAITHNESS, to the Questions of the Committee.

(1.) THE Public Records in the Respondent's Custody, as Sheriff Clerk of Caithness, are, 1st. The Records of all Deeds and Conveyances, Bonds and other Securities, Contracts, Discharges, and Public Instruments, commencing in the Year 1677: 2dly. The Records of Processes, Decreets, and Judicial Proceedings and Sentences, in Cases Civil and Criminal, from the Year 1748: 3dly. The Records of Hornings and Inhibitions since the Year 1719: and, 4thly. The Record of the Proceedings for ascertaining the Yearly and Monthly Prices of Corn and Grain within the Shire, commencing in the Year 1783.

(2.) The aforesaid Records are kept in a House rented by the Respondent in the Town of Thurso, sufficient in Point of Accommodation for the keeping thereof, but not Proof against Fire, nor is there any such House in Thurso. The present House is Private Property, and the Respondent holds it by a Lease from the Proprietor, of which there are Six Years to run.

(3.) The [illegible] Records were not all in a State of the best Preservation, when the Respondent came to the Possession of them, in the Year 1768. He had to collect them in different Parts of the Shire, where former Sheriff Clerks had resided, and found that they had been but indifferently cared for. He has, however, since endeavoured to preserve them in pretty good Order, though not without considerable Trouble, arising in a great Measure from his being sometimes obliged to remove them from one House to another, for want of a Public permanent Repository for these Records.

(4.) There are no General Catalogues, Calendars, or Schedules kept. The Books wherein Copies of the Deeds are ingrossed, have Marginal Indexes, denoting the Title of the Deed or other Writing, and the Names of the Parties to the same; and the Principal Writings, called the Warrants of the Record, are bundled up by the Years of their being given in to be recorded, and so arranged as that the Deeds recorded within any given Period may soon be found out. The Record Books are not completely filled up, but One Extra Clerk, by diligent Application, would be sufficient to complete them in the Course of Six or Eight Months.

(5.) The Respondent always has One, and sometimes Two or Three Assistants in his Office; but these are only occasionally employed in the Arrangement of the Records in his Custody. It is more particularly the Duty of his Principal Clerk to receive the Writings brought to the Office to be recorded, to write and give out Extracts, and to deposit the Principal Deeds in their proper Places. But when Searches are to be made, and Certificates are required regarding Deeds recorded for any distant Period, the Respondent always takes that Part of the Duty upon himself. The Office is open at all Times from Eight in the Morning until Eight at Night, Sundays excepted; and the Salary and Emoluments which the Respondent pays his First Clerk amount generally to from £. 40. to £. 50. per Annum. But his Duty is not altogether confined to the Custody of the Records, and he does not receive any Emoluments from the Public in respect of the Custody of the Records.

The Fees demandable for recording Deeds, &c. and giving Extracts, are the same as are contained in the Table of Fees regulated by Act of Sederunt of the Lords of Council and Session, Anno 1748, a Copy of which Table the Respondent begs leave to annex, and to refer to the same *. Besides these he is entitled to a Fee for Searches of 6*d*. for each Year of the Period for which the Search is made. Although the Trust is great and the Trouble considerable, yet the Fees are paltry indeed; and if the Committee will but glance at the abovementioned Table, they will perceive that the Allowances to Sheriff Clerks are in no Respect adequate to their Trouble in any Instance; and surely they bear no Proportion to the advanced Prices of all the Necessaries of Life, since the Period at which these Fees were established. It would be becoming the Wisdom and Justice of the Legislature to increase the Fees of the Sheriff Clerks, as well as they have augmented the Salaries of the Sheriffs in Scotland. As Matters stand at present, so very trifling are the Fees arising to the Respondent from the Custody of the Records of the County of Caithness, that he cannot state the Gross Annual Amount thereof, upon an Average of the last Three Years, beyond the Sum of £. 15. per Annum.

* See Page 452.

(6.) This Question seems to be fully answered, by what has been stated under the former Questions.

(7.) It occurs, in answer to this Question, that it would contribute to the Security and Convenience of the Public, if in every Shire there was a House provided at the Public Expense for the Reception and Custody of the Records of the Shire; in which House there ought to be at least One Apartment vaulted and Proof against Fire, besides a Suite of Chambers for the Sheriff Clerk and his Assistants to write in. And it may not be improper here to notice, that although the Sheriff of Caithness constantly holds his Courts in Thurso, it being the most centrical Place in the County, yet there is no proper Court House, nor indeed any Gaol in the Town, by which Means the Lieges, as well as the Members of Court, experience much Inconvenience. Here too the Respondent will beg leave to revert to what he formerly observed, regarding the extreme Smallness of the Fees of Sheriff Clerks; and to add, that it would be highly expedient for the Interest of the Public, that a Public Officer of so much Trust were suitably compensated for his Trouble, which at present is clearly not the Case.

Thurso, July 12th, 1800.

John Rose, Sheriff Clerk of Caithnesshire.

SCOTLAND.
Sheriff Courts.
Appendix (Y. 8.)

Appendix (Y. 8.)

Return of the Sheriff Clerk of Clackmannan, to the Questions of the Committee.

(1.) THE Public Records, Rolls, Instruments, and Manuscript Books and Papers, in the Custody of the Sheriff Clerk, are,

1st. The Sheriff Court Books, or Sederunt Books of the Sheriff Court, in which the Acts and Decrees of the Sheriff in all Processes and Judicial Proceedings before him are minuted; these Books are Sixteen in Number; the first or oldest of these Books in the Custody of the Sheriff Clerk begins the penult Day of September, 1698, and they are continued regularly down to the present Time, besides the ordinary Actions or Processes for Debts, &c. to which these Books have a special Reference, the Services of Brieves from the Chancery, directed to the Sheriff of Clackmannan, Acts of Curatory, and the Minutes of the Freeholders of the County, and the Verdicts of the Jury, by which the Annual Fiar Prices of the several Sorts of Grain, the Produce of the County, are ascertained in the Month of February Yearly, are all ingrossed in the said Court Books: The Reporter observes, in examining these Books, that the Clerk had discontinued to enter the Acts and Minutes of Court in Processes before the Sheriff, from 10th February 1748, to 9th August 1764, when the keeping of these Books having come under the Charge of the Reporter; he then began and has continued to enter the Minutes, Acts, and Interlocutors in the different Processes in the said Books.

2d. The principal Processes and Causes to which these Books relate, which are kept in separate Bundles or Rolls, Annually, as they come to be determined, and are deposited in Presses made for that Purpose.

3d. Register of Writes and Securities given in to the Sheriff Clerk's Office for Registration. It has not been the Practice in the County of Clackmannan to record these Writings in any particular Book; when such Writings are given in to the Clerk's Chamber for Registration, there are noted upon the Back, the Date of presenting, the Name of the Sheriff in Office for the Time, and of the Person who presents the same; and the Extract being written out is signed by the Clerk, and delivered to the Party requiring the same; these principal Writes are then put up in a Press, called the Register Press, where they remain, and every Person having Interest, is intitled to demand from the Clerk, Extracts of such Writings on Payment of the regulated Fees: The Writes in the said Register, are as far back as the 26th of November 1707; when the present Sheriff Clerk entered upon Office, he made out a complete Inventory of these Writes, which is deposited in the Register Press along with them, and which he is continuing forward.

4th. Registration of Hornings, Inhibitions, &c. This Register Book the Sheriff Clerk purchases from the Lord Clerk Register, and in it are ingrossed the Hornings, Inhibitions, Interdictions, &c. with their Executions given in for Registration; a Minute Book whereof is also kept by the Clerk, in which such Hornings, Inhibitions, &c. are minuted at the Time of their being presented at the Office, and the Presenter signs the said Minute Book; when the said Register is filled up, it must be returned back to the Lord Clerk Register, to be kept amongst the Public Records for the Use of the Leiges. The present Sheriff Clerk took out a new Register Book from the Lord Clerk Register upon the 7th February 1769, which is not yet near filled up, but must, when filled up, be returned to the Lord Clerk Register along with its Minute Book.

5th. Two Court Books, in which are entered the Minutes, Proof, and Verdict of the Jury, ascertaining the Monthly Prices of Grain within the County, in Terms of the Act of Parliament, intituled, "An Act for regu-"lating the Importation and Exportation of Corn and "Grain, &c." and the Returns made by the Sheriff, Monthly, to the Receiver of Corn Returns, London; the First of these Books beginning 3d August 1774.

(2.) The Buildings in which these Books and Records are kept, are situated in the Town of Alloa, and are a Part of the House which the Sheriff Clerk possesses, and are in tolerable good Condition, as to Security and Accommodation: The House is Private Property, possessed by the Sheriff Clerk from Year to Year, without any written Lease. The present Sheriff Clerk has lived and kept these Records there, these Twenty-four Years past.

(3.) The Court Books and Records in general are in a tolerable good Condition, and also the Processes, except those of the early Period, which are much worn and defaced, but are in no worse State than when he first knew them.

(4.) There have never been any General Catalogues, Calendars, Schedules, or Repertories of any of the foregoing Records, nor any Particular Indexes to any of them, as far as the present Sheriff Clerk ever knew. The Sheriff Court Book, in which the Rolls of Processes are recorded every Court Day, and the "Res Gestæ" minuted, answers the Purpose of an Index to the Processes. It does not appear that much Utility could result from such Catalogues, &c. being made; the Reporter has held the Office of Sheriff Clerk of Clackmannanshire for Thirty-two Years, and never found any Inconvenience from the Want of Catalogues or Indexes. Most Part of the Processes pursued before the Sheriff Court are for Payment of Small Debts; and when Decrees are obtained, they are extracted, and the Original Warrants are no longer inquired after.

Were it thought necessary to inventory these Processes, or to make Indexes to them, it would require a considerable Time to do it, even with extra Assistance; but the Reporter cannot condescend upon the Time it would require, without knowing what might be intended, or thought necessary to be done; he humbly suggests that little Advantage could arise from it.

(5.) There are no Officers or Clerks employed for the Custody and Arrangement of the Records, &c. in the Office of the Sheriff Clerk of Clackmannanshire, except the Reporter himself, and One Clerk, whom he engages at a small Salary; their Attendance in the Office is every Day from Nine in the Morning until Six at Night, and sometimes later. Neither the Sheriff Clerk nor his Servant have any Annual Salary or Allowances, except the Fees payable to them for their Labours by the Leiges, conformable to a Table thereof hereto annexed*, as regulated and fixed by the Court of Session, 16th March 1748.

The Reporter has not been in the Practice of keeping any Account of the Annual Amount of the Fees arising from his Office; he always considered them worth from £. 40. to £ 50. per Annum; but in order to come at the Fact, he, upon the 22d of November 1798, prepared a Cash Box, in which he kept the whole Fees and Emoluments of his Office for One Year, to 22d November 1799, when he found that the Whole amounted only to £. 42. 8*s*. 4*d*. Sterling; he has kept the like Account from the 22d November 1799 to this Date, near Seven Months, and the Whole in that Period amounts to £. 21. 17*s*. 8*d*.; from these Fees of Office, the Reporter pays £. 17. Sterling Yearly to a Clerk, who assists him in the Business of keeping the Records, extracting the Acts and Decrees of the Court, &c.

(6.) There is no Person specially intrusted with the Care of the said Records, &c. except the Sheriff Clerk himself, and the Clerk whom he employs, and for whom he is answerable: Persons requiring any Search to be made in any of the Records, are allowed to examine the Books and Records in the Office themselves, if they desire it, and obtain from the Clerk such Certificates as the Records warrant, after which the Records are restored to their proper Places.

(7.) It may be expedient to observe, that it would be of obvious Advantage, and would render the Use of the Records, &c. more convenient to the Public, that a Public Office was provided for the Security and Keeping of the Records; such Records would be more detached from other Business, and examined with greater Facility; but the Reporter does not understand that any of the Sheriff

* This being an Act of Sederunt of the Court of Session, is not transmitted or annexed.

riff Clerks in Scotland have any Public Office or Repository for keeping and preserving the Record, except such as they have provided themselves without any Allowance from the Public, nor that there are any Funds provided for erecting and establishing such Public Offices.

In Scotland the Sheriffs are not Custodiers of Records, these are committed to the Custody of the Sheriff Clerks.

June 12th, 1800. *John Jameson.*

Appendix (Y. 9.)

Return from the Sheriff Clerk of CROMARTY, to the Questions of the Committee.

THIS County is one of the smallest in Scotland, although the Harbour of which this Place can boast, is perhaps among the First in it. The greatest Part of this County is locally situated in the County of Ross, and under the same Sheriff, who acts occasionally here by a Substitute. The only Record kept, is a Minute Book for Infertion of small Causes, chiefly removing of Tenants, of course the Clerk's Fees of this Office are not worth 40*s.* a Year, except when a General Election takes place, which happens only occasionally with the neighbouring County of Nairn; and upon that Occasion the Sheriff Clerk may get from £. 10. to £. 20. as the successful Candidate pleases. There is a Record kept for the Minutes of the Freeholders of the County, which goes as far back as the Year 1768; before that Period it does not seem to be so accurately kept. There is a very good Court House, which was built some Years ago, chiefly at the Expense of the County, and the Two Books above mentioned lie there in safety, but they are seldom used. The Law authorizing Justices of the Peace to take Cognizance of small Causes, makes the Attendance of the Sheriff less necessary; besides the Inhabitants are peaceably disposed.

16th June 1800. *Walter Ross.*

Appendix (Y. 10.)

Return by the Sheriff of DUMBARTONSHIRE, to the Questions of the Committee.

BEFORE answering the Questions put by the Select Committee, which the Sheriff will endeavour to do in their Order, he begs leave to premise, that the Records and other Matters referred to, are kept by the Sheriff Clerk, who is appointed by the Keeper of the Signet in Scotland, an Office held at present by the Right Honourable Henry Dundas, One of His Majesty's Principal Secretaries of State, who receives his Appointment from the Crown.

(1.) The Public Records, mentioned in this Question, are various, such as the Horning and Inhibition Record; the Records of Principal and Probative Writs; the Record of the Minutes and Proceedings of the County Freeholders; the Record of the Expense disbursed by Heirs of Entail on the Improvement of Entailed Estates; the Principal Processes and Minute Book of the Sheriff Court, of which no Particular Record is kept, except the Minute Books and Processes themselves, which last are very numerous; and the Record of Protests taken on Bills on which further Diligence is meant to be raised.

(2.) The Building wherein these Records are just now lodged, is Private Property, situated in the Town of Dumbarton, Head Burgh of the County, and in a Room of that Building tolerably secure and commodious at present; but the removing of these Records from Place to Place, which must always be done on the Change of the Sheriff Clerk, or of his removing from House to House, is of Necessity attended with much Injury and Inconvenience to the Records, and to their proper Arrangement.

(3.) The Records, &c. here, are in tolerably good Preservation, and are arranged according to their different Years.

(4.) There are not at present, nor has there ever been any Catalogues, &c. of the said Records, except Minute Books of the Two Principal Records of Hornings and Inhibitions, and of Principal Writings given in to be recorded either for Execution or Preservation.

(5.) The Attendance of the Sheriff Clerk himself, and of a Person employed by him, are in general absolutely necessary here for the Dispatch of the various Branches of Duty and Business required in this Office, where Attendance is given all the Days of the Week (Sundays excepted) from Eight o'Clock A. M. to Eight at Night, except the Breakfast and Dinner Hours; but the Clerk has no fixed Salary for himself, or those employed by him, nor any other Fee, except those contained in Two Tables made by the Courts of Session and Justiciary in Scotland, on the 16th and 21st of March 1748, under the Authority of an Act of Parliament for that Purpose; and the Sheriff understands, that in the Way the Fees are paid, the Sheriff Clerk, for himself and Servant, has not, for the last Three Years, averaged more than from £. 50. to £. 60. Sterling, Yearly, out of which he pays the Rent of his Office and other Expenses attending the conducting of the Public Business. The Reasons assigned for the Emoluments of Office being so small, are the following: 1. The low and incomplete Tables of Fees, established as above in the Year 1748.—2. The Impossibility of the Clerks being able to make some of the Fees fixed in the said Tables effectual, owing to his having no hold of the Persons liable, whereby the same is completely lost; and although the Sheriff Clerks in Scotland, several Years ago, complained for Redress to the Court of Session, and craved a Review of the said Tables, yet the Court found they could do nothing without a new Act of Parliament, their Powers under the former Act being exhausted.

(6.) The Sheriff Clerk, and Person deputed by him, are the only Persons intrusted with the Care of the Records, who attend Searches, and restore the Registers to their proper Place.

Edinburgh,
3d May 1800. *J. Colquhoun.*

Appendix (Y. 11.)

Return from the Sheriff of DUMFRIESSHIRE, to the Questions of the Committee.

(1.) IT cannot be said that there are "any "Public Records, Rolls, Instruments, or Manuscript "Books or Papers, in the Custody of the Sheriff of "Dumfriesshire," or of any other Sheriff in Scotland. None are intrusted to the Sheriff officially. And the Person who acts as the Clerk of the Sheriff Court is not appointed by the Sheriff, but by One of the Officers of State in Scotland; viz. the Keeper of the King's Signet.

What follows is humbly submitted, respecting the Records and other Writings in the Custody of the Sheriff Clerk of Dumfriesshire; these are,

1. Processes extracted; i. e. Actions in which an authentic Copy of the Pleadings and Proceedings has been given out by the Clerk. Processes not extracted, being either where a Decree has not been pronounced, or where, although a Decree has been pronounced, the Parties have not demanded a Copy. Under the same Head may also be included the Proceedings in the Services of Heirs, when held in the Sheriff Court.

2. Deeds or Writings; such as Bonds, Dispositions, Leases, Latter Wills, &c. bearing "a Clause of Registration," which has an Effect somewhat similar to that of a Recognizance in England; also Instruments of Protest, which in certain Cases, may, by Special Statute, be recorded to the same Effect as if they had contained a Clause of Registration.

3. Probative Deeds or Writings, which, although they do not bear a Clause of Registration, may by vir-

SCOTLAND.
Sheriffs Courts.
Appendix (Y. 11.)

tue of particular Statutes be registered, not to the Effect of warranting Execution as those mentioned above, but for the Purpose of preserving Copies of the Writings, which are in general held to be authentic.

4. Denunciations, Hornings, Inhibitions, and other Writings of the same Kind, also recorded in virtue of particular Statutes.

5. Contracts of Excambion, and other Transactions relative to Entailed Estates, recorded in virtue of 10 Geo. III. cap. 51.

6. The Proceedings in the Meetings of Freeholders called by the Sheriff.

7. The Proceedings relative to the Fiars, or Prices of particular Sorts of Grain, which are ascertained by the Sheriff, each Year, for the levying of the Crown Rents, so far as payable in Kind; also those held for making the Monthly Returns of the Prices of Grain, as directed by an Act passed in 1791.

8. The Inventories of the Lands and Estates of deceased Persons, to whom their Heirs do enter, and serve themselves "cum beneficio Inventarij," as directed by 1695, cap. 24. —And the State of those Records is as follows:

1. When the present Sheriff Clerk was appointed in the End of the Year 1776, (it is informed) he received, according to an Inventory or Minute Book, which was found at that Time in the Office, the whole Papers therein specified (a few only excepted) being Decrees extracted, or not extracted, and bearing Date from 1674 to 1738. The Sheriff Clerk also received in 1776, according to another Inventory or Minute Book, the Decrees then in the Office, in which Extracts had been given out from 1738 down to the Time of his Appointment. The Sheriff Clerk also, at the same Time, received, according to an Inventory or Minute Book, certain Decrees extracted, the First of them dated in 1748; and that Book, with a subsequent One, comprehends the whole unextracted Decrees down to the present Time, so that these Decrees may easily be discovered at any Time. Since the Year 1776 too, the Decrees which have been extracted appear to be in regular Order, Minute Books or Inventories being kept, by which any Decree may easily be found.

Besides the Minute Books or Inventories already mentioned, the Sheriff Clerk of Dumfriesshire has regularly, since the Year 1715, kept what is called a Diet Book, containing the Names of the Parties whose Causes are called on each Court Day or Diet, and a short Note of the Proceedings then held.

2. The present Sheriff Clerk, it would appear, received on his Appointment the whole Deeds and Instruments of Protest, then in the Office, as specified in Inventories or Minute Books delivered to him, with the Exception of some Writings then missing. These Inventories or Minute Books were from 1715 to 1776, and from this Period regular Inventories have been kept.

3. What are called Probative Writings or Deeds, are recorded in a Book kept for that Purpose, and the Originals returned to the Persons presenting them. The First Record of this Kind now extant in the County of Dumfries begins 14th June 1716; and it has been regularly carried on to the present Time.

4. The Writings in this Class are recorded in a Book, and afterwards returned to the Parties presenting them. The Book kept for the Purpose, as soon as it is filled up, is transmitted to Edinburgh, where it remains with the other Records of the same Kind. The Book now used commences on 14th August 1794, and a regular Inventory or Minute Book is kept, as required by the Statute.

5. This Record (i. e. the Contracts of Excambion, &c.) begins in November 1771, and has been regularly carried on ever since. The Original Papers, after being copied into the Record, are returned.

6. The Proceedings of the Freeholders have been regularly recorded in a Book kept for the Purpose, since 1733 down to the present Time.

7. The Proceedings relating to the Fiars are extant since the Year 1626, with the Exception of a few Years; and those relating to the Monthly Returns of the Price of Grain are also extant since September 1791, when the Statute introduced that Form.

8. The Record of Inventories begins in October 1715, and has been regularly carried on until now.

These are the Particulars which seem to be included in the First Question proposed by the Committee.

(2.) The Building, within which the Records in the Custody of the Sheriff Clerk of Dumfriesshire are lodged, is in the Principal Street of the County Town, and is possessed by the Sheriff Clerk in virtue of a Lease from the Owner; and it cannot be said to be secure, there being Dwelling Houses and Shops under the same Roof with it; neither the Sheriff Clerk nor his Deputy reside near it; and the Place or Room where the Records are kept, being exceedingly Damp, and Two or Three Feet below the Level of the Street, the Papers in it, it is supposed from these Causes, are in a very decayed State, insomuch that many of them cannot be handled without being injured, and in many Parts they appear to be illegible; and there is a Hazard of their being entirely lost, if they are allowed to remain much longer in the same Situation.

(3.) The Answer appears from what has been already stated.

(4.) This also has been answered in Part. It does not appear that such Defects, as have been noticed, can be supplied at this Time.

(5. & 6.) The Sheriff Clerk has a Deputy, who attends to the Business of the Office, and in general Two Clerks or Apprentices, who are in the Office from Nine in the Morning until Nine at Night, during every lawful Day of the Week. No Annual Salaries or Allowances are paid by the Public, the whole Emoluments arising from the Fees of Office, which, upon an Average taken from the last Three Years, may amount to £. 250. Yearly. The Amount of these Fees is in general fixed by an Act of Sedurunt, or Regulation of the Court of Session in 1748.

(7.) A proper Place for keeping the Records equally secure from Damp and from Fire, and separated from other Buildings, and also more under the immediate Care of the Sheriff Clerk, and his Deputy, appears to be necessary. And as often as a new Sheriff Clerk is appointed, it would be proper that some Person, authorized by the Keeper of the Signet, or by the Sheriff of the County, should be called upon to see that the Records are properly delivered over to the Sheriff Clerk by the Representatives of his Predecessor, or the Defects made up as far as possible.

It may be proper farther to notice, that Records, nearly of the same Nature with those above mentioned, are kept by the different Town Clerks in each of the Four Royal Burghs within the County of Dumfries. These Clerks are appointed generally for Life, by the Magistrates; other Records are kept by the Commissary or Judge in Consistorial Matters, who will give in a separate Report.

It may also be mentioned, that there is a Record of Sasines or Infestments kept, in the Town of Dumfries, for

for the County of Dumfries, and Stewartry of Kirkcudbright; a particular Clerk is named by the Crown for the Purpose. These Writings are recorded in a Book given out by the Clerk of the General Register at Edinburgh; and as soon as it is full, it is transmitted to Edinburgh, and a new one obtained, and a regular Minute Book is kept, as the Law directs.

All which is humbly submitted,

Ro. Craigie.

Edinburgh,
20th May 1800.

Appendix (Y. 12.)

Return of the Sheriff Depute of the County of EDINBURGH, to the Questions of the Committee.

I HAVE to inform the Committee, that there are no Records whatever under my Custody, as Sheriff of Edinburghshire; but that the Public Records of the County are under the Charge and Custody of the Sheriff Clerk; an Officer appointed in this and every other County in Scotland by the Keeper of His Majesty's Signet. As the Records, however, are under my Cognizance as Sheriff Depute, I have made particular Inquiry into their State, and am enabled to return an Answer to the Questions of the Honourable Committee.

In Answer to Question 1:—I have to report, that the several Sorts of Records are as follow:

Class 1. Extracted Processes or Actions which have been in dependance before the Sheriff, and Extracts of the Sentences given out by the Clerk, so as to be carried into final Execution. These Processes are regularly arranged in Months and Years; and an Index or Minute Book kept of the Whole, in a regular Manner, since the Year 1710. There are different Years of the Processes, and also Minute Books in Existence, previous to that Period, but neither of them in proper Order or complete Preservation.

2. Unextracted Processes or Actions which have depended before the Sheriff, but which either never became final, or in which the Sentences were not extracted. Along with these are bundled up the more trifling Criminal Records of the Office, such as, Complaints for Assaults, Sentences of Banishment from the County for Petty Thefts, and Summary Applications of different Kinds. These are also put up in different Months and Years, and Indexes or Minute Books kept nearly as far back as the preceding.

3. The Record of Deeds kept for the County, in which are registered, Dispositions, Bonds, Indentures, and Protests for Non-payment of Bills, and in short any Deed containing a Clause of Registration. This Register is not peculiar to this Office; similar ones being kept at the same Fees by the City and Commissary Clerks, so that the Employers may take their Deeds to any of these Records they may chuse to prefer.

In this Office, the Deeds recorded are not only bundled up by Months and Years, but complete Copies of the Whole made, which are bound up in a Volume at the End of every Twelve Months. The Papers themselves are in Existence since about the Year 1700, and the Volumes Two or Three Years earlier, and are uniformly continued down to this Date, excepting a Chasm of Three Years in 1769, 70, and 71; during which the Papers seem either not to have been recorded, or the Record Copies to have been lost. The Principal Papers, however, are in Existence and good Order.

4. The Record of Hornings; a Species of Diligence in the Law of Scotland for Recovery of Debts; respecting which nothing further is necessary to be said than that the Book in which this Record is kept, is, when finished, transmitted to the Office of the Lord Clerk Register for Scotland, with its Index or Minute Book.

5. The Register of Inhibitions, which is also transmitted to the Register Office in the same Manner as the last Article.

6. The Register of Improvements on Entailed Estates; A Record opened and kept in Terms of the Statute 10 Geo. III. cap. 51. in which Contracts of Excambion of Entailed Lands, and Accounts of Improvements on Entailed Estates, within the County, are recorded for the Purposes mentioned in the Statute; of these there are Two Volumes.

7. The Criminal Records; the Principal of which, being the Examination of Criminals, and Precognitions relative thereto, are transmitted to the Office of the Crown Agent, for the Purpose of bringing the Criminals to Trial before the Court of Justiciary; besides which, however, there are kept in this Office, a Manuscript Volume, containing the Trials by Jury before the Sheriff of the County, commencing in 1746; and a List of Vagrants or Petty Thieves and Criminals, with their Descriptions, as they appear when examined.

8. A Book, in which the Procedures, relative to striking the Fiar Prices of Victual for the County, are ingrossed. This Book commences Anno 1786; before which Time the said Procedures were kept on loose Sheets, which are still in Existence.

9. The Procedures relative to the Corn Laws, consisting of Three Volumes, Two relative to the Monthly Prices of Grain, and One under the former Statute, when these Prices were taken once a Quarter.

10. The Record of Services of Heirs, &c. which are regularly ingrossed in Volumes since the Year 1750, and the Warrants also bundled up according to their Years; the Volume serving as an Index to the Warrants; and

Lastly, The Minute Books of the Meetings of the Freeholders of the County, which are complete since the Union of the Kingdoms in 1707.

Besides these, several other MS. Books are kept in the Office for the Accommodation of the Public during the Dependance of Processes; such as, Receipt Books for borrowing Processes; Books, for inserting Acts of Caution; and Books, in which the Names of the Processes are entered, when advised or judged in by the Sheriff.

(2.) The Building or Office, in which these Records are lodged, is situated in Brodie's Close, Lawnmarket, City of Edinburgh. It is by no Means secure from Fire, being under the same Roof, and connected with Private Dwelling Houses; and it is very deficient indeed with respect to Accommodation. It is let from Year to Year (being Private Property) to the Sheriff Clerk, at a Rent of £. 25. per Annum.

(3.) The Records are in general in a good State of Preservation; only some of the earlier Volumes of Class 3 have suffered a little from Damp. They are as well arranged as the Accommodation in the Office will permit; but when another Office can be obtained, it is intended to have each Class regularly arranged by itself, which cannot at present conveniently be done. They are, however, in such a State of Order, that the Clerks can in a very short Time lay their Hands upon any Paper wanted within the Periods before specified.

(4.) As already mentioned, there are complete and correct Catalogues, or Indexes of the Three First Classes of

SCOTLAND.
Sheriffs Courts.

Appendix (Y. 12.)

of Records which only need them; and these also are kept separate and distinct from each other.

(5.) The Sheriff Clerk has at present in this Office Six Clerks under him, Two of whom also officiate for the Clerk of the Peace, and a Third attends as Clerk to the Sheriff in the Criminal Department; all of whom are neither paid by the Public, nor by Annual Salary, but by certain Allowances from the Principal Clerks' Fees, which Fees are chiefly in Terms of a Table fixed by Act of Sederunt of the Lords of Council and Session, Anno 1748, in consequence of the Enactment of the 20th Geo. II. cap. 43; and these Fees have undergone very little Variations since. The Amount of the Fees paid to the Principal Sheriff Clerk, after deducting Payment of the Under Clerks, is about £. 500. per Annum. The Charge for Searches is from 1 *s.* to 2 *s.* 6 *d.* according to the Distance of Time at which the Paper asked for has been recorded. The Annual Amount of these Searches is so very trifling as not to be worth mentioning, not exceeding at most Five Pounds a Year.

(6.) There is no Office for the Purpose stated in the Interrogatory. But it is the Duty of the Clerks to restore the Papers to their proper Place. The Principal Extractor in the Office has the Charge of this being done; and no new Regulation in this Respect seems to be necessary.

(7.) Nothing material occurs to me necessary or expedient for rendering the Records of the Office more useful or convenient to the Public, further than as already mentioned, an Office with more Apartments and larger Rooms, which is much wanted; and it would be desirable to have a Building solely appropriated for that Purpose, unconnected with private Buildings.

James Clerk,
Sheriff Depute of Edinburghshire.

Appendix (Y. 13.)

Return of the Sheriff of the County of Elgin, to the Questions of the Committee.

(1.) THE only Records kept in the said Office have been Records of Probative Writs, and of Actions and Processes brought before the Sheriff. The oldest Record of Deeds found in the Office, commences in the Year 1654, and ends 8th April 1656. From the above Period, no Record appears to have been kept until March 1668, when it commences again and ends in December 1674, from which last Period to June 1687, there seems to be a Want of the Records; when in June 1687, the Record again commences, and terminates in August 1696; which Record appears to be considerably mutilated, and several Leaves wanting. Item, another Record commencing in September 1696, and ending October 1704. Item, Register of Contracts, Bonds, &c. commencing 3d November 1704, and ending October 1706; in which Record many Leaves are wanting. Item, Inventory of principal Papers and other Writings given in to record, and found in the Custody of James Fraser, then Sheriff Clerk, commencing in the Year 1700, and ending 22d December in the Year 1756; from that Period, no Records appear to have been kept, but the Original Deeds tied up and placed in the Office until 15th June 1790, when regular Records were again kept, and proper Indexes thereof, until the present Period. Item, Inventory of Processes and Actions, the First whereof commences June 1700, and ends 2d November 1756; during the above Period, the Records themselves are wanting; there then appears no Record until the 15th July 1757, when it again commences, and terminates on the 7th of August 1761; from that Date until the 11th February 1774, the Record is again wanting; and from 11th Februrary 1774 until the present Period, it is complete. But although the Records are themselves missing, the chief Part of the Original Writings remain in the Office.

(2.) The Sheriff Clerk's Office has hitherto been my Private Property, and is in general kept in the House where the Sheriff Clerk resides.

(3.) The present Sheriff Clerk has been at every possible Pains to preserve the Records, and to render them as complete as their State would admit of.

(4.) Answered by Question 1st, in so far as relates to Catalogues, &c.; and with regard to the State of the Records, from what is mentioned under Question 1, it would be altogether impossible to make these complete, from the Defects already mentioned; and from the present State of the Sheriff Clerk's Office, the Records and Writings therein, are in as regular and good Order as it is possible to have them.

(5.) There is one Principal Sheriff Clerk, and a Deputy Clerk, employed for the Custody and Arrangement of the Records, &c. who sometimes have under them One or Two Clerks, as they find Occasion for them; and the Office is in general attended from Morning until Night; these Clerks have no Annual Salaries, and are rewarded by the Public; the Fees payable to them, are fixed by an Act of the Court of Session, dated 16th March 1748; and upon the Whole, the Emoluments arising from the Office, for some Years past, have not exceeded the Annual Sum of £. 100. being considerably diminished, in consequence of the late Act of Parliament authorizing the Justices of the Peace to judge in Causes under £. 3. 6 *s.* 8 *d.* in value. It is at present the Business of the Deputy Clerk to keep the Records, and attend the Searches made therein; and the Name of the Office is well known by that of the Sheriff Clerk's Office.

(7.) The only Thing that occurs to the Sheriff in relation to this Article, is, that the Sheriff Clerk in Office should be deemed accountable for all the Records; that they should be complete and carefully kept, under such Penalties as the Committee may in their Wisdom adopt, to enforce Regularity; as the Sheriff has not the Custody and keeping of the Records, and of course is not answerable for them; and whereby the Clerk or Clerks succeeding to the Office, will, on account of their Responsibility, be attentive in future that the Records are complete before they enter on the Management and Charge of the Office.

The County Record for Instruments of Infeftment respecting Heritable Property, is kept in a separate Office; the Keeper of that Record is Mr. Alexander Grant, Writer to the Signet, Edinburgh; and his Depute is Mr. Patrick Duff, Writer, in Elgin.

Geo. Fenton,
Sheriff Substitute.

Elgin,
26th March, 1800.

Appendix (Y. 14.)

Return of the Sheriff of Fifeshire, to the Questions of the Committee.

THERE are no Records, Rolls, Instruments, Manuscript Books or Papers, in the Custody of any Sheriff in Scotland.

Every

Every Thing of that Nature is under the Charge of an Officer, who is appointed by the Keeper of His Majesty's Signet.

This Officer is called the Sheriff Clerk, because he officiates in the Capacity of Clerk to the Sheriff Court; but is in no Ways dependent upon the Sheriff, nor accountable to him, except for a faithful and regular Record of the Proceedings which take place in the Sheriff Court.

(1.) The Records in the Possession, and under the Charge of the Sheriff Clerk of Fife, are:

1. A Record of Dispositions, Conveyances, and Leases of Land; Assignations to Moveables; Destinations of a Testamentary Nature; Contracts and Agreements; Arbitrations, and the Awards proceeding upon them; Protests of Bills; with many other Deeds of a similar Nature, which the Parties think proper to record.

These Deeds are recorded for Preservation; and the Originals remain in the Custody of the Sheriff Clerk, who gives out a Copy of the Deed subscribed by him, and bearing that the recording of it was sanctioned by the Sheriff. For this Copy a small Fee is paid, which is fixed and regulated by proper Authority.

This Record commences in the Year 1700, and is regularly kept; for the first Years it is not in the best State of Preservation, but still it is legible.

The Gentleman who is at present Sheriff Clerk, though extremely attentive to his Duty, has not found it practicable to bring forward this Record regularly to the present Time; but the Deficiency would be supplied by the additional Assistance of Two Clerks, for Two Years; an Accommodation which could not fail to be of great Utility to the Public.

2. A Record of Inhibitions (Injunctions) Hornings, Denunciations, and other Diligences of that Nature, with the Discharges of them when they are recalled, and no longer in Force; all of which, by the Law of Scotland, must be entered into a Public Record.

These are all recorded in a Book, issued from the General Register Office for Scotland, kept at Edinburgh.

This Book is regularly subscribed by the Lord Clerk Register, or his Deputies; and is returned to the General Register Office at Edinburgh as soon as it is completed, together with an Abridgment of the Matters contained in it, and a regular Index.

When delivered to the Sheriff Clerk, it contains about 530 blank Leaves; and will be filled up in the course of Six or Eight Years, according to the Number of Deeds which are presented to be recorded.

3. Record of the Proceedings of the Freeholders of the County, both at their Annual Meetings held at Michaelmas; and in the Case of Elections for chusing a Representative for the County.

This Record is ordained to be kept by an Act of the Scots Parliament 1681, c. 21. which appoints "The "Freeholders to meet and convene at the Head Burghs "of the respective Shires, at the Michaelmas Head "Courts Yearly, to revise the Roll of Election, and "make such Alterations therein as have occurred since "their last Meeting, from Time to Time; which Roll "for Election shall be insert in the Sheriff's Books par-"ticularly appointed for that End."

This Record does not appear to have been kept in the County of Fife, until the Year 1733; since that Period it has been regularly kept, and is in a perfect State of Preservation.

4. A Record of the whole Processes or Actions of Debt, Injury, or Trespass, which are brought before the Sheriff of the County in his Judicial Capacity; in which every Step of Procedure is regularly entered in his Presence, by the Clerk; and every Cause called, and some Progress made in it, Twice every Week during the Year, with the Exception of a few Weeks in Seed Time, and a few Weeks in Harvest. This laborious Duty is generally performed in Court, by a Person appointed by the Sheriff, who must have a Knowledge of Law, and support a respectable State in the County. Notwithstanding this, he receives a very inadequate Return. In the extensive County of Fife, in which a vast Number of Questions necessarily occur, the Sheriff Substitute's Salary from the Public, is only £. 60. a Year, without Fees or Perquisites of any Kind; and though he is prohibited from practising as an Attorney or Steward within the County, the Judgments of the Substitute are received by the Sheriff, in every Case that the Parties apply for it.

5. There is also a Record of the Procedure of the Sheriff, in striking the Fiars or Prices of Grain. This is done by a Jury upon a Proof laid before them, in the Month of February in every Year; and a Record, containing a regular Detail of every Step of Procedure in this Matter, commences in the Year 1700, and is in very good Preservation for the last 50 Years; but previous to that Period has suffered by not having been kept in a proper Place.

6. There is also a Record kept in consequence of an Act of Parliament, 10 Geo. III. c. 51. by which the Proprietors of Entailed Estates are made Creditors to the succeeding Heirs of Entail, for Three-fourth Parts of the Money laid out in making improvements, to the Extent of Four Years Free Rent of the Entailed Estate; provided such Proprietor of an Entailed Estate, "shall "Annually, during the making of such Improvements, "within Four Months after the Term of Martinmas, "lodge with the Sheriff or Stewart Clerk of the County, "an Account of the Money expended during Twelve "Months preceding that Term, subscribed by him, with "the Vouchers."

These are the only Records which are under the Charge of the Sheriff Clerk, or with which the Sheriff has any Concern; or any Opportunity to know their State and Situation; and even with respect to these, excepting the Sederunt Book of his own Court, he has no Superintendance or Controul.

But it may not be improper to mention, that besides Two Ecclesiastical Courts of Record, (Presbyteries and Synods) there is a Commissary Court for Consistorial Matters, and Thirteen Royal Burghs, in this County; all of them having Jurisdiction, holding Courts within their respective Burghs, and having regular Records.

It is also proper to mention, that there is at Cupar, the County Town of Fife, a Record for the Registration of all Sasines, Infeftments, and other Instruments, which relate to Heritable Property. The Person who holds this important Trust is called the Keeper of the Register of Sasines; and is appointed by the Crown. He has no Salary; his whole Emoluments being derived from a regulated Fee, upon each Page of the Deed that is recorded, and vary according to the Extent of the County, and other Circumstances.

One of these Circumstances is, that it is in the Option of the Person who wishes to record a Sasine, to do so either in the particular Register of the County, or in the general Register of Sasines at Edinburgh. The same is the Case with respect to the Deeds which are to be recorded for Preservation, which may be done in the Books of the Lords of Council and Session, in place of the Sheriff Court Books, when the Party thinks proper to prefer that Record.

A Book is delivered from the General Register in Edinburgh, to the Keepers of the particular Registers of Sasines, in the different Counties in Scotland, for the Purpose of recording in it all the Deeds that are presented to them; and when it is completed, it is returned to the Register Office at Edinburgh, and a new Book obtained.

When an Instrument is recorded in the Register of Sasines, the principal Deed is returned, docketed on the Back by the Keeper, specifying the Volume, the Pages of the Volume, and the Date of Registration; and in order to facilitate the Diſcovery of every Deed that is ſearched for, a Minute Book is kept of all the Deeds which are entered, bearing a Reference to the Record.

A Search into the Records for Forty Years, is attended with a very conſiderable Expenſe; and yet without it there can be no Security, as Forty Years is required by the Law of Scotland, as the Term of Preſcription, in all Queſtions reſpecting Heritable Property.

Place where the Records are depoſited:

(2.) Theſe Records have uſually been kept by the Sheriff Clerk of Fife, in the Houſe where he reſides. But the Gentleman who has the Office at preſent, has lately erected, at a conſiderable Expenſe, a proper Office adjoining to his own Houſe, and detached from the Street.

In this Office he has One Room vaulted, and proof againſt Fire, where the principal Deeds and Records are depoſited; and another Room likewiſe proof againſt Fire, in which the current Records are kept and carried on.

(3.) Already anſwered.

(4.) There are complete and correct General Catalogues, Calendars, or Repertories of all the different Records, under the Charge of the Sheriff Clerk of Fife; and alſo of the Record of Saſines, in the Form of a Minute Book, containing a ſhort Abridgment, or rather the Titles of the Deeds recorded, are inſerted Seriatim. Without this, a Search of the Records would be a moſt laborious and almoſt inextricable Work, if the whole Deeds that have been inſerted for 40 Years muſt be attentively peruſed "ad longum" upon every Occaſion that the Record was to be examined.

Of the Deeds which are recorded for Preſervation, there is no Index of the Names of the Grantors, which would be of great Utility, as it would diminiſh very conſiderably the Expenſe of a Search, and might very eaſily be accompliſhed without much Expenſe. But ſuch an Index could be of no Uſe in the Deeds affecting Heritable Property, as it is not the Name of the Proprietor but of the Eſtate, and of every Farm or Parcel of that Eſtate that muſt be attended to; and many of theſe are known by different Names, which might give Occaſion to Deception and Fraud.

(5.) The Clerks employed are the Principal Sheriff Clerk, his Deputy, and Two Writing Clerks, whoſe Duty it is to regiſter and arrange all the Writings or Deeds given in to them, which are received at all Times in every lawful Day, without Regard to or Limitation of the Hours of Attendance.

There are no Salaries, Allowances, or Emoluments paid to them by the Public in reſpect of ſuch Cuſtody. The only Fees which they receive are paid by ſuch Individuals as have Deeds to record, and the Amount of them is aſcertained by a Table which was fixed by the Court of Seſſion ſo far back as the Year 1748*. Since that Period, theſe Fees have remained the ſame, and are by no Means adequate to the Labour of the Clerks, who are conſtantly employed in the Inſertion of Deeds in the Record.

* See Page 452.

The Net Annual Amount of the Income of the Sheriff Clerk of Fife, upon an Average of Three Years of the Whole of his Emoluments as Sheriff Clerk, may be eſtimated at £. 200. according to the beſt Information that the Sheriff has been able to obtain, having never received an explicit Anſwer to that Queſtion, which has occaſioned the Delay in forwarding the preſent Report.

(6.) The Sheriff Clerk has the immediate Charge and Care of all theſe Records; and when any Search is deſired it is made by himſelf or his Deputy, who give the proper Extract or Certificate, and attend and take out the Deed or Record, and ſee it replaced in its proper Situation.

(7.) This Query embraces ſuch an Extent of Matter, that it is not very eaſy to make an Anſwer to it. Such Circumſtances however as occur to the Reporter to be of the Nature to which the Inquiries of the Honourable Committee apply, he conſiders it his Duty to ſtate.

The firſt Object which naturally attracts the Attention of Perſons who are employed in making the Uſe of the Public Records more convenient to the Public, is, a Place where they can be depoſited with Safety, and where eaſy Acceſs to them can be obtained for the Accommodation of the Public.

Although ſomething of this Kind has been recently built by the Sheriff Clerk of Fife, yet it is neither of that Extent nor in that Situation in which ſuch an Office ought to be; and in moſt Counties of Scotland the Records of every Deſcription are kept in the Houſes of the Perſons who have the Charge of them, expoſed to all that Danger from Fire which Public Records ought to be ſecured againſt at almoſt any Expenſe.

It would be highly expedient to have in every County Town a handſome and convenient Court Houſe, for the Sheriff to hold his Courts and adminiſter Juſtice in; and the Building ought to be of ſuch an Extent as to contain proper and convenient Apartments for all the Records, where they may be depoſited in a perfect State of Security from any Danger from Fire, and where they may be properly taken Care of in every Reſpect, and eaſy Acceſs to them had when Occaſion requires it.

It might be an Inſtruction to the Sheriff of the County, and conſidered as a Part of his Duty, to beſtow particular Attention to the State of the different Records, and to the Manner in which they are kept, and particularly that they are regularly brought forward, and not permitted to fall into Arrear.

The Sheriff ought to be made reſponſible for the Accuracy and Regularity of the Records within his County, in the ſame Manner as he is reſponſible for the Diſcharge of the other Parts of his Duty in the Circuit Courts, which are held by Two of the Lords of Juſticiary all over Scotland Twice every Year.

The important Truſt confided in the Sheriffs by this new Arrangement would naturally lead their Attention to many Improvements, by making Indexes and other Alterations, that would be of great Utility to the Public; and completely ſecure Regularity, Preciſion, and Diſpatch in the preſent eſtabliſhed Records of every Deſcription within the County, over which any Controul was committed to them.

If any Meaſure of this Kind is conſidered as worthy of Conſideration, and after mature Conſideration is to be adopted, it would ſeem to be proper that the Sheriff Clerks, in place of being independent of the Sheriff Deputes, ſhould be appointed by the Sheriffs, in the ſame Manner as they appoint their Subſtitutes; that they ſhould be accountable like them for their Conduct to the Sheriff; and that they ſhould have the ſame Power of removing the Sheriff Clerk, as they have at preſent of removing the Sheriff Subſtitute.

But before any Meaſure of this Kind can be adopted, whatever may be its Utility to the Public, full Compenſation ought to be made to the Keeper of His Majeſty's Signet, for the very conſiderable Diminution which the Emoluments of his Office would ſuffer by this Alteration.

If this Plan of a new Court Houſe and Record Office in every County Town of Scotland were to be adopted, it might be accompliſhed without much Aid from the Public, by an Aſſeſſment upon the Counties, which might be rendered ſo light that they would neither feel nor complain of it, and at the ſame Time the Object, in the Courſe of Two or Three Years, obtained in a very complete Manner.

The Report of

Neil Ferguſſon,
Sheriff Depute of Fifeſhire.

Appendix (Y. 15.)

Return from the Sheriff of FORFARSHIRE, to the Queſtions of the Committeee.

AS the Records connected with the Office of Sheriff, are in my Cuſtody as Sheriff Clerk, I beg leave to anſwer the Queries of the Committee as follows:

(1.) The whole Actions or Proceſſes for Debt, Injury, or Treſpaſs; the Proceſſes for Service of Heirs to their Predeceſſors, and making up Tutorial and Curatorial Inventories, with the whole Judicial Proceedings before the Sheriff; the Record of Letters of Horning and Inhibition; the Record of the Proceedings of the Meetings of Freeholders; the Original Deeds lodged for recording in the Sheriff Court Books, and the Records applicable thereto, are in my Cuſtody as Sheriff Clerk.

The other Public Records within the County, not connected with the Sheriff's Office, are, the Record of Saſines or Infeftments upon Landed Eſtates, kept by a ſeparate Clerk (who has no Connection with the Sheriff Clerk) in the Town of Dundee; the Records of the Commiſſary Court, Juſtices of Peace, Magiſtrates of Royal Burghs, and Commiſſioners of Supply, in their particular Lines of Duty, kept by their reſpective Clerks.

Of the Judicial Procedure in all Queſtions and Matters before the Sheriff, regular Index or Minute Books are kept, for aſcertaining the Steps, and how and when the Buſineſs is concluded. The Minute Books here commence in January 1705, and, excepting a Deficiency from the 1ſt June 1710 to the 10th Auguſt 1717, are complete to this Date. A few of the Original Proceſſes, prior to 1700, and the Proceſſes for the laſt Hundred Years, are in Preſervation.

The Record of Hornings and Inhibitions is ſuperſcribed by the proper Officer at Edinburgh; and when a Volume is completely filled up, it is from Time to Time returned there. The Volume we are preſently uſing here, commences on the 28th Day of May 1787, and continues perfectly regular to the preſent Date.

The Procedures at the different Meetings of Freeholders are entered in regular extended Minutes ſubſcribed by the Preſes. These Original Minutes commence in the Year 1727. There are ſeveral Years deficient ſoon after Commencement. In the Year 1740, a Practice was introduced of tranſcribing theſe Minutes into a proper Record, appropriated ſolely for the Buſineſs of the Freeholders, and this Practice has continued to the preſent Time, the Record being completely filled up to the Minutes of the laſt Meeting incluſive.

The Fiars Prices of Victual are Annually ſtruck by a Jury before the Sheriff. The Minutes or full Narration of the whole Procedure, are regularly made up, and (excepting for the Year 1735) fully in Preſervation from the Year 1728 to this Time. The Prices of Grain are alſo aſcertained Monthly, by a Jury before the Sheriff, agreeably to an Act of Parliament in the 31ſt Year of His preſent Majeſty. The Original Minutes, with a Record applicable thereto, are complete from that Time to this Date.

(2.) The Records connected with the Office of Sheriff, are kept under my Charge as Sheriff Clerk, in Apartments, which are Part of a Public Building within the Town of Forfar, called the County and Town Houſe. The Accommodation and Safety of the Papers, are both of them reaſonably ſufficient. The Building is not inſured.

(3.) The Original Papers, Records, and Minute or Index Books are arranged, each Kind (as they regard different Matters) by themſelves, and according to their Order of Time; and excepting thoſe of antient Date, are in good Condition.

(4.) I beg leave to refer to what is already ſtated, as to the Original Papers, Records, and Minute Books. The Catalogue or Minute Books of Deeds, commence in January 1693; are wanting from 12th February 1709, to 2d November 1714, and are complete from that Date to the preſent. The Books in which the Deeds are copied at length, are defective in ſome particular Periods, prior to my entering upon the Office of Sheriff Clerk, particularly for Years preceding the Year 1753, and for ſome few Years ſince; but no Inconvenience ariſes, the Deeds themſelves, and the Entry of them in the Minute Books, being complete; and ever ſince my Entry to the Charge of the Office of Sheriff Clerk, I have kept an Extra Writing Clerk employed in bringing up the deficient Copyings in theſe Books.

(5.) The Officers employed here are the Principal Sheriff Clerk and a Deputy, and ſuch Number of Writing Clerks (generally Three) as are neceſſary. The Principal Clerk and Deputy attend to the Arrangement of the Papers and Records. They have no Salary from the Public for keeping them. The Hours of Attendance, and during which the Office is open every Day (Sunday excepted) throughout the Year, are from Eight in the Morning to Eight in the Evening. The Fees paid to the Principal Sheriff Clerk are aſcertained by a Table, regulated by Act of Sederunt of the Court of Seſſions, in virtue of an Act of Parliament Anno 1748. The Principal Sheriff Clerk makes an Agreement with the Deputy and Writing Clerks, according to Circumſtances. There is no Rule of Fees demandable "for "each Search, Certificate, Copy of or Attendance "with the Records, &c. whereof the Sheriff Clerk has "the Cuſtody." Where a Search and Certificate from the Regiſter of Inhibitions is called for, the uſual Payment is Six Pence for each Year. There is no Payment for a Search from the other Records; but merely the common extracting Dues, when an Extract is taken out. It being only ſomething more than One Year ſince the former Sheriff Clerk died, the preſent Sheriff Clerk cannot give an Account of the Average of theſe Dues for the Three laſt Years.

(6.) The Principal Sheriff Clerk and his Deputy are alone intruſted with the Care of the Original Papers and Records. One of them always attends a Search; and every Original Paper, with the Record and Minute Books, are reſtored to their proper Places, immediately after the Buſineſs of the Search is accompliſhed. There is no Denomination of Officers, other than the Principal and Depute Clerks, Writers, and Indentured Apprentices.

(7.) Upon this Query I beg leave to obſerve, that a Practice has crept in, and now very generally prevails, in this and many other Counties, of recording Papers in various Offices, and in many Inſtances improper Offices, to the great Inconvenience of, and often entirely to diſappoint the Lieges in their Inquiries after them. Deeds and Writings of various Kinds, where the Parties concerned do not reſide in Royal Burghs, and where the Subject Matter of the Deed has no Relation whatever to Borough Concerns, are frequently recorded, not in the Sheriff Court Books of the County, where alone they ought to be, but in the Commiſſary Court Books, and very often in the Town Court Books, ſometimes of One Burgh, and ſometimes of another, which, from the Uncertainty where to find them, frequently fruſtrates the Lieges and the Parties concerned in their Search. This is a Loſs and Inconvenience much complained of, but the Remedy is eaſy. All Deeds regarding Heritable Property, within Royal Burghs, ought to be recorded in the Town Court Books of

SCOTLAND.
Sheriffs Courts.
Appendix (Y. 15.)

of that Burgh. In Matters of Personal Concern within Burghs, as the Sheriff and Magistrates have a cumulative Jurisdiction, Deeds regarding these Matters, such as Dispositions, Contracts, Leases, Assignations, &c. may (at the Pleasure of Parties) be recorded either in the Sheriff Court Books or Town Court Books; and all Deeds of every Kind regarding Personal or other Concerns, where the Parties reside in the Country, and not within the Jurisdiction of Royal Burghs, ought solely and exclusively to be recorded in the Sheriff Court Books of the County, in and under whose Jurisdiction they are, or (in like Manner at the Pleasure of Parties) in the Books of Council and Session, as having a general cumulative Jurisdiction over Scotland.

The Act of Sederunt and Table of Dues, regulating the Fees of Sheriff Clerks, were settled upwards of Half a Century ago. These Fees being found in many Particulars very inadequate, as well as the Table defective, the Sheriff Clerks, about Seventeen Years since, applied to the Court of Session for an Alteration, which (from the Nature of, and the Duties they have to discharge) was on all Hands thought reasonable; but the Court of Session found, that having once executed the Powers vested in them by the Act of Parliament 1748, they could not resume the Business without a new Act of Parliament. I beg leave to submit whether the present does not afford a proper Opportunity for renewing the Powers of the Court of Session, or otherwise rendering some more equitable Compensation to Sheriff Clerks, whose Office requires Public Confidence, as well as unremitted Labour and Application.

All which is respectfully reported to the Sheriff of Forfarshire by

Patrick Orr,
Sheriff Clerk.

This is the Letter and Report of the Sheriff Clerk of Forfarshire; and after examining the same, respectfully reported to the Chairman and Committee, by

Pa. Chalmers,
Sheriff of Forfarshire.

Forfar,
27th March 1800.

Appendix (Y. 16.)

Return of the Sheriff Depute of the County of HADDINGTON, to the Questions of the Committee.

(1.) THE Records kept in the Sheriff Clerk's Office of the County of Haddington, are as follow; viz.

1. Record of the Prices of Grain, commonly called Fiars, commencing in 1627.

2. Record of the Elections of Representatives for the County in Parliament, commencing in 1708, being the First Election after the Union.

3. Freeholders Record, which was not very regularly kept prior to the Year 1743, but which has been distinctly so from that Time.

4. Record of Bonds, Obligations, and other Deeds of that Kind, which is traced back for a considerable Period of Time, brought forward to August 1798, and will be still carried on.

5. Minute or Index Book of Bonds, Obligations, &c. brought down to 1st January 1800. (Nos. 4 and 5 at the Expense of the Sheriff Clerk, without any Allowance therefore.)

6. The Record containing the Rolls of all the Causes, depending at one Time before the Sheriff; which Rolls are called over every Day the Sheriff holds a Court; and what is determined by the Sheriff in each Cause or Suit, is shortly totted in the said Roll Book.

7. Record, commonly called the Diet Book of the Sheriff Court, in which are regularly ingrossed all the Interlocutors or Sentences pronounced in each Cause by the Sheriff, either upon the Court Days, or upon any other Days.

No Allowance is made to the Sheriff Clerk for Numbers 6 and 7.

8. Not in Use. To Ingross Extracted Decreets in a Register since some time in the Year 1755. The general Practice from that Time has been to make out, in the First Place, Draughts of such Decreets, which serve as a Direction for making out the Principal Extracts thereof.

These Draughts are put up with the Grounds and Warrants of the Decreets, and the whole are afterwards kept and preserved.

The present Sheriff Clerk has made a very material Improvement upon the said former Practice.

The Grounds and Warrants, and full Draughts of the Decreets, are put up in separate Bundles for each Month, and a distinct Monthly Index is kept thereof, and the Whole kept and preserved.

The Court of Session made Regulations about 50 Years ago, injoining that Decreets should be registered. This seems in general to have been observed for Three or Four Years to the Period already mentioned, when it was discontinued.

The greatest Part of these Decreets were passed for Payment of small Debts, and being therefore soon at an End by obtaining Payment, it seems to have been considered as not a Matter of any Public Utility to record Decreets of that or any similar temporary Description; besides, the Fees appointed by the Regulations of the Court of Session, Anno 1748, for Decreets for small Sums of Money, are so extremely moderate, that the Sheriff Clerks could not then, and far less can now, afford to bear that Extra Expense.

A great Proportion of these Decreets are passed for Sums under £. 3. 6*s.* 8*d.* Sterling; yet by the aforesaid Regulations, the Sheriff Clerk is only allowed 6*d.* per Sheet for writing and recording each Sheet of such Decreets, after the First Sheet.

It occurs to be observed under this Head, that in addition to a copious Index, it may be attended with some Degree of Public Benefit to ingross in a Register or Book all such Decreets as regard permanent Objects, such as Excambions of Lands; also settling the Marches or Boundaries of Landed Properties, and the like; but it is humbly suggested, that a reasonable Allowance ought to be made to the Sheriff Clerks on this Account.

9. Record of Criminal Trials, commences about 70 Years ago.

10. The Register of Hornings, Inhibitions, &c. and Minute or Index Book thereof, are most regularly kept and carried forward to the Date hereof.

11. The Register of Vouchers of Improvements upon Entailed Estates, in virtue of the Act of the 10th of George III. is also regularly carried on.

12. The Register of the Reports of the Corn Laws is also Monthly carried on.

There is no Register of Infestments kept in this County for the County, that Register is kept in the County of Edinburgh; but there are Registers of Infestments kept within the Royal Burghs of Haddington, Dunbar, and North Berwick, for recording Infestments within these respective Royalties. These Burghs are situated within the County of Haddington.

(2.) The Building or Repository for the County Records is situated below the great County Room. It is is Fire Proof. A confiderable Time elapfed after Building it, before the Records were removed to it. It was then thought to be perfectly dry, but it was found by Experience, that it ftill retained fome Dampnefs; and therefore the greateft Attention was obferved to have it properly aired in dry Weather, and now it is perfectly dry, and the Records will receive no Injury from it. It was built at the Expenfe of the County; and is therefore confidered as Public Property: But it is not a commodious Apartment for Daily Bufinefs; and therefore the Sheriff Clerk occupies a convenient Apartment in a Houfe which is his own Private Property, for that Purpofe, in which however he only keeps fuch Parts of the Public Papers and Records, as are in Ufe for the Time; and fo foon as that ceafes, they are lodged in the above Repofitory.

(3.) The Records and Papers before mentioned, excepting the old Parts thereof, are in good Prefervation; and for the Arrangement of them, Reference is made to Anfwer Firft.

(4.) Reference is partly made to Anfwer Firft; and in regard to a Retrofpect to bring forward thefe Matters, it has as yet been found impoffible to form any fair Eftimate of the Expenfe of doing the fame, and it will require fome confiderable Time to do it, as well as to condefcend upon the Affiftance neceffary for completing it, and the Time within which the fame might be fo completed with any Degree of Accuracy and Correctnefs.

The Sheriff never heard of any other Catalogues or Indexes, except thofe in the Public Office.

(5.) The Sheriff Clerk has the Cuftody and Arrangement of the faid Public Records, and attends, by himfelf or his Clerks, at all proper and reafonable Hours, to execute every Part of the Duty of the Office. He has not One Shilling of Salary allowed to him from the Public. He is indeed allowed certain Fees and Emoluments eftablifhed by a Table thereof, Anno 1748; but there is no Allowance therein made to him, for being Cuftodier of the Public Records.

The Sheriff has not had any Opportunity to know, or Concern with, the Amount of the Fees and Emoluments of the Sheriff Clerk. He has however enquired of that Officer about the fame; and the Anfwer he received was, that for many Years prior to the 1ft July 1798, he kept no Particular Account of the faid Fees and Emoluments, but that he can, after 1ft July 1800, give the Average Amount for the Two Years preceding that Date.

(6.) Reference is made to Anfwer the Fifth.

(7.) No other Matters occur to the Sheriff refpecting the faid Records, except what he has above ftated.

But it appears to the Sheriff to be but fair to add this general Obfervation, that in his Opinion the Sheriff Clerk is upon the Whole rather under paid, than over paid, for executing the Bufinefs of his Office.

Will. Law.

Appendix (Y. 17.)

Return of the Sheriff Depute of INVERNESS-SHIRE, to the Queftions of the Committee.

(1.) THE Sheriff is not Cuftodier of any Public Records, Rolls, or Inftruments, Manufcript Books or Papers, belonging to the County. The Sheriff Clerk, who is not appointed by the Sheriff, but by the Keeper of His Majefty's Signet, is by Law, Cuftodier of all the Records and Papers connected with the Office of Sheriff. Thefe Records and Papers confift of, the whole Proceffes and Judicial Procedures, both Civil and Criminal, carried on before the Sheriff Court; of all Deeds and Inftruments given in to be recorded, either for Prefervation, or that the Diligence of the Law may follow on them; and, the Proceedings of the Freeholders at their Michaelmas Head Courts and Meetings for electing Members of Parliament. The Proceffes or Judicial Proceedings are extant as far back as the Year 1720; the Record of Deeds and Inftruments, as far back as the Year 1708; the Record of Freeholders, as far back as the Year 1727.

(2.) The Place where thefe Records and Papers are kept, is a Houfe or Apartment in the Town of Invernefs, rented by the Sheriff Clerk for the Time being, or his Depute, in fuch Part of the Town as he finds moft convenient. There is no fixed Place within the County for this Purpofe, other than any Apartment that the Sheriff Clerk can find moft commodious, and on the eafieft Terms, the Yearly Rent of which is paid by him. The Places thus rented are far from affording Security for the Safety of the Records, or proper Accommodation for having them kept in a regular Manner. The Records are expofed to the Accident of Fire, which was fatal to them in the Year 1710; and the Places where they are kept may be liable to be broken into, and the Records and Papers abftracted.

(3.) The Records are in a tolerable State of Prefervation. The Proceffes, or Judicial Proceedings, are no other Ways arranged than by being tied up in Bundles by the Year, and locked up in Wooden Preffes which lie in the Sheriff Clerk's Office. The Books of Records, Deeds, and Inftruments, are progreffively carried on in order, as is alfo the Record of Freeholders and Elections, and thefe Records, duly marked on the Back, are alfo depofited in locked Preffes, in the faid Office, along with the Warrants.

(4.) There are no Catalogues or Inventories of Proceffes, or Judicial Proceedings, prior to the Year 1781; but fince that Period, regular Catalogues or Schedules have been kept. There is alfo a particular Index to each Book of Records fince 1781; but no regular Index was made of thefe Records prior to that Period. It would certainly be of much Public Utility to have thefe Catalogues and Indexes completed, as it would not only promote Difpatch in fearching for any Paper or Record that is wanted, but it would alfo operate as a Check on the Cuftodier of the Records, and prevent any Abftraction thereof by him or others, in the courfe of fearching or removing them from one Apartment to another, or otherwife. It is thought that thefe might be completed in the courfe of Four Months, by a proper Perfon appointed to affift the Sheriff Clerk. It is not believed that any fuch Catalogues, &c. as are wanting in this Office, exift any where elfe, or that any fuch were ever made.

(5.) There are no Officers or Clerks employed for the Cuftody and Arrangement of the Records, &c. That Duty being performed by the Sheriff Clerk alone, or thofe employed by him, who attend in the Office during ordinary Hours of Bufinefs, being from Eight in the Morning until Nine at Night. There is no Annual Allowance or Salary paid to the Sheriff Clerk by the Public in refpect of fuch Cuftody, nor has he any Emolument for any Search, Certificate, or Copy, &c. other than what is regulated by the Table of Fees eftablifhed by the Court of Seffion in the Year 1748.

(6.) There is no Perfon, other than the Sheriff Clerk, fpecially intrufted with the Care of the faid Records, whofe Duty it is to attend upon every Search, and

SCOTLAND.
Sheriffs Courts.
Appendix (Y. 17.)

and to take Care that every Record, &c. be safely restored to its proper Place; neither do I know any Regulation observed for effecting these Purposes.

(7.) There is no Suggestion not comprized in the preceding Questions, which occurs as necessary or expedient to observe for rendering the Use of the Records, &c. more convenient to the Public; other than, in the First Place, that a proper Public Apartment should be established, where the Records of the County should be deposited without being liable to be removed; and that such Place should be so built and constructed, as to secure the Records from the Risk of Fire; and that some reasonable Allowance should be made to the Sheriff Clerk for his Trouble as Custodier of them, either by an Annual Salary to be paid by the Public, or by establishing certain Fees for his Trouble in searching, giving out Certificates and Copies, and the Attendance in taking and replacing the Records, and by tying him down to carry on regular Inventories of all Processes and Papers deposited in his Office, and an Index of the Books of Record; all of which ought to be Patent to the Public upon Payment of a reasonable Fee for his Trouble.

Simon Fraser,
Sheriff Depute of Inverness-Shire.

20th March 1800.

Appendix (Y. 18.)

Return of the Sheriff Depute of KINCARDINESHIRE, to the Questions of the Committee.

I BEG leave to submit the following Answers to each Query contained in the Committee's Order.

(1.) The Custody of the Records of the Sheriff Court of Kincardineshire, is committed to the Sheriff Clerk of the County; an Officer not named by the Sheriff, but who holds his Office immediately from the Crown. The Records under his Charge are as follow:

1st. The different Papers composing (or produced in) Processes or Actions at Law, carried on and pursued before the Sheriff of the County, whether Civil or Criminal, Ordinary or Summary, commencing from 1697.

2d. What is strictly called Registrations, comprizing Bonds, Testaments, Settlements, Contracts, Dispositions, Tacks, and other Deeds, containing Clauses of Registration, for Diligence, or for Preservation; also Protests upon Bills and Promissory Notes, for Non-acceptance, or for Non-payment: Of all these there is a regular Series since the Commencement of the Eighteenth Century: There are also some previous to that Period, but chiefly without Arrangement, or being in a good State of Preservation, or complete. It was formerly the Practice to engross Copies of all such Registrations in a Book or Register, which still exists from the Year 1697 to 1747, but since that Period it does not appear to have been the Practice to ingross the Registrations in any Book, but merely to quote them and put them up in Masses, in the Order of their Dates, retaining the principal Writings, and giving out Extracts when required.

3d. Register of Probative Writs, containing true Copies inserted in a Book, of all such Writings, of whatever Kind, as any Person may give in, whether containing a Clause of Registration or not, the principal Papers being returned with a Certificate of their being thus registered. This Register commences in the Year 1715, and is still regularly carried on.

4th. Register of Hornings, Inhibitions, and Interdictions, being Diligences well known in the Law of Scotland. These are ingrossed in a particular Book purchased from the Clerk Register; each Sheet of which is previously subscribed by him, or some Person having Authority from him. As soon as a Volume is completed, it is returned to the Register at Edinburgh, where it is retained; and a new Volume transmitted to the Sheriff Clerk; by this Means there is never more than One Volume in the Custody of the Sheriff Clerk. The one at present in his Custody commences 22d December 1787.

5th. Freeholders Records, partly inserted in Books, and some of them on Papers apart; consisting of Claims of Inrolment, and Minutes of the Annual Michaelmas Meetings of Freeholders and Head Courts; also Minutes of Elections of Members of Parliament for the County, and the Accounts between the Freeholders and their Collectors of Cess and Rogue Money. The earliest Records of this Description are contained in Sederunt Books, and commence in the Year 1698; from which Time there appears to be a regular Series.

6th. Services General and Special of Heirs to their Ancestors, commencing in the Year 1664.

7th. Tutorial and Curatorial Inventories of the Means and Estates of Minors under the Charge of their Guardians, commencing 1638.

8th. Fiars and Prices of Victual, as ascertained Yearly by a Jury under the Direction of the Sheriff, in Terms of the Act of Sederunt of the Court of Session of 21st December 1723; commencing 1752.

9th. Register of the Prices of Victual, as ascertained Monthly by the Sheriff and a Jury, in Terms of the Corn Law; beginning in September 1791.

10th. Register of the Names of Persons to whom Game Certificates or Shooting Licences have been granted under the Game Laws; beginning 1786.

11th. The Public General Acts passed in the British Parliament, in Terms of the Resolutions or Standing Orders of the House of Commons; commencing with 38th Geo. III.

There is also a Register of Commissions granted to the Members of the Sheriff Court of Kincardineshire.

It was formerly the Practice, besides retaining the principal Papers composing the Processes or Actions at Law before the Sheriff Court, also, when the Judgments in them were extracted, to record these Extracts in Books; and there are several Volumes of that Kind in my Custody; but this Practice has long been in disuse, and seems unnecessary, the Original Papers being kept.

(2.) Previous to the Year 1786, the Records were kept in the Private House of the Sheriff Clerk, but about that Period, the Freeholders and Heritors of the County erected a commodious Building, containing the Court Room, where the Sheriff and other Courts sit, and the County Meetings are held, another Apartment used as a Committee Room, a writing Office for the Sheriff Clerk, an Apartment for keeping the Records, and a Gaol for Criminals, &c. This Building is situated in or close by the Town of Stonehaven, and in point of Security is advantageous for the Records; but the Accommodation in this Respect is not so good as could be wished for, and the Situation of the Building is also very Damp; the Effects of that upon the Papers, can only be prevented by carefully airing the Record Room, and frequently keeping Fires in it. The Property of the Building appears to belong to the Freeholders and Heritors of the County.

(3.) The Records of the first Description are in a State of perfect Preservation, from the Year 1732, and arranged according to their Dates; previous to that Period, they are neither in good Preservation nor regular Order.

Those

Those of the second Description are also in perfect Order and Arrangement, according to their Dates, from the Commencement of the Eighteenth Century; previous to that Period, they are neither in good Preservation nor arranged.

The Third and Fourth Descriptions are in perfect Preservation and Arrangement.

The Fifth, Sixth, Seventh, Eighth, Ninth, and Tenth Sorts of Records, are also in a State of good Peservation, and being all kept distinct and separate, appear to have all the Arrangement necessary.

The Eleventh Description is in a State of perfect Preservation, but by no means complete; probably owing to the great Number of Copies of the Acts, which require to be dispatched throughout the Kingdom. It frequently happens that no Copies of some Acts are sent to the Sheriff Clerk, and at present there are several wanting of those specified in the printed Index or Table sent. Owing to this, the Acts have not hitherto been bound up in Volumes as was intended, and it is much to be wished that a Measure so useful as sending and preserving these Acts in the Custody of the Sheriff Clerk, might be fully attended to, and the Sets made complete.

(4.) Applicable to the First Sort of Records, there is kept what is called a Diet Book, in which there are shortly minuted, the different Steps taken in Processes, as the giving in Defences, Answers, Replies, Term of proving, &c. A regular Series of these, commences in 1743, and they are complete from that Period, but there are none before that Time. When there is a Judgment or Decision in any Process, it is also minuted in what is called the Minute Book, by inserting the Names of the Pursuer (Plaintiff) and the Defender (Defendant;) which Minute Book thus contains a List or Catalogue of all Decrees pronounced by the Sheriff, according to the Order of the Time of pronouncing. There are such Minute Books in my Custody from 1697 to 1715, from 1718 to 1737, from 1743 to 1776, when another Hiatus occurs till 1791, since which they have been regularly kept.

Applicable to the Second Sort of Records, there is a similar Minute Book, which has lately been completed by me, where defective, with considerable Labour, from the Year 1700; previous to that Period there are no Minute Books, but these Records lie together without Arrangement.

The Third, Eighth, and Tenth Sorts, being kept in separate Books, have no Index or Minute Book annexed to them, and do not appear to require such, unless the Third Sort, which would be more complete with a proper Index or Table of Contents.

To the Fourth Sort there is a regular Minute Book, according to the Date of Registration.

To the Fifth, Sixth, Seventh, and Ninth Sorts, there appears no Minute Book or Index, but as the Papers belonging to each Kind are separately put up, and are comparatively few in Number, there does not seem to be much Occasion for any Minute Book.

To the Eleventh Sort, there are sent down Indexes or Tables of Contents, at the End of each Session of Parliament.

From what is already noticed, it is apparent in what Respect the Minute Books, &c. are defective, but it is not easy to ascertain what Degree of Utility would result from their Completion; no Doubt it might be advantageous for the Public to have all the early Registrations (Second Sort) inventoried and arranged, because some valuable Deeds may be among them, which it is next to impossible to find out in their present State. In the same Manner it might be also advantageous to procure a regular Minute Book of Decrees (First Sort) made out where defective, but this would be a Work of considerable Labour and irksome Toil, and could not be completed without additional Assistance, or at least extraordinary Diligence of the Persons usually employed in the Office, and suitable Reward, during Six Months, comprizing however the Months of August, September, and October, when there is in common less of Ordinary Business to be executed in the Office.

With regard to the last Part of the Query, it has been already noticed that the County Register of Hornings is transmitted to the General Register at Edinburgh, where it remains with the Minute Books; and it may also be noticed, that the Register of Sasines or Infeftments of Persons in Heritable Property, in Kincardineshire, is kept at Aberdeen by a Public Officer there, appointed for that Purpose.

(5.) The Officers employed here are, besides the Principal Sheriff Clerk, a Deputy, and such Number of Writing Clerks (generally Three) as are found necessary; whose Duties chiefly consist in making out the Writings issued from the Office, and signed by the Principal Clerk or his Deputy; they also, with the Deputy, have the immediate Charge of the Records, or keeping them in a proper State of Arrangement, and taking Care that all Papers be put up in their proper Places, after being minuted and brought back from those who are intitled to borrow them on Receipt. The Hours of Attendance are from Eight o'Clock in the Morning to Eight at Night. For the Custody and Arrangement of the Records, neither the Principal Clerk, his Deputy or Apprentices, have any Allowance whatever. The Emoluments of the Sheriff Clerk consist in what he is paid for certain Writings which he makes out, signs, and issues, according to a Rate fixed in the Year 1748, by the Lords of Council and Session; in so far as regards Civil Matters, by Act of Sederunt dated 16th March that Year; and by the Lords Commissioners of Justiciary, so far as regards Criminal Cases, by Act of Adjournment 21st March 1748: No Addition has been made to them since that Period. The Annual Emoluments arising to me from the Office, upon an Average of the Three last Years, for which I can make up an Account, amount to £. 140. Sterling.

No Fees are payable on Account of a Search of the Records, unless a written Certificate is required and given.

(6.) The Care of the Records is intrusted to me as Sheriff Clerk, and those employed under me; whose Duty it is to attend in the Manner specified in the Answer to the preceding Question. When any Record is borrowed, by those intitled to it, a Receipt is given in a Book kept for that Purpose, which is examined at the End of every Session; and any Records, which may then be outstanding, are called in and replaced in their proper Situation. The Receipt given is Ground for Application for a Summary Caption (Personal Arrest) against any Person refusing to return the Record borrowed.

(7.) Nothing additional occurs to me, which it would be necessary to observe, besides what is contained in the Answers already given in.

Al. Burnett,
Sheriff Depute.

10th April 1800.

Appendix (Y. 19.)

Return from the Sheriff Substitute of KINROSS-SHIRE, to the Questions of the Committee.

(1.) FOR Kinross-shire: In Kinross there is a Keeper of the Register of Sasines, who puts upon Record Sasines and other Instruments which relate to Heritable Property only. The Volume or Book of Record when written or filled up, is returned to the General Register Office

SCOTLAND.
Sheriffs Courts.
Appendix (Y. 19.)

Office at Edinburgh, and another Volume got from thence in its place, to be filled up in writing as the former, which generally requires some Years in this Shire to do, and to this Record a Minute Book or Index is kept, also returned with the Volume to Edinburgh.

The Sheriff keeps no Record, nor has he any Charge of Books or Papers of any Kind of a Public Nature, farther than the Sederunt Court Book, where, in Court Days, all Processes are regularly entered in his Presence, by the Clerk.

The Sheriff Clerk keeps an Office, in which he not only bundles up the Processes of Court by the Year (Yearly) but also records Tacks of Heritable Property, Contracts, and Dismertions of a Testamentary Nature, and Protests of Bills, &c.; the Original is retained, and an Extract given out.

This Registration consists merely of depositing the Principal and giving out a Registrate Copy under the Subscription of the Clerk, and expressed as sanctioned by the Sheriff.

The Sheriff Clerk is also Clerk to the Freeholders, and keeps their Record of Inrolments.

(2.) The Keeper of the Record of Sasines has his Office in his own Dwelling-House.

The Prison or County-House is situate in the Middle of the Town of Kinross, which was rebuilt by the Crown in 1771. One of the upper Rooms was allotted for the Sheriff Clerk's Chamber and Record Office; but it has never been occupied as such, farther than soon after 1771, the Court Papers, and Papers put on Record, at least the greatest Part of them, appear to have been deposited in that Room, where they are still lying upon the Floor, not in the best Order. Previous to 1771, the Sheriff Clerk had his Office in a Room any where in the Town where he could find most convenient, which he rented.

The present Sheriff Clerk, and his Two Predecessors in Office, have since some Time after 1771, kept their Office in their Dwelling-House. At present, and since 1789, the Sheriff Court Papers, and those put on Record, are in a safe and dry State; but if the Room in the County House was properly fitted up, and Fires kept when needful, it would be the best and safest Repository of any in this Shire.

Previous to 17[illegible], the County House was said to belong to the Barony of Kinross, as the Superior (then the Bruces) were Sheriffs Principal until the Jurisdiction Act took place; whether it is now Public or Private Property I am not certain, but I should think it is Public, for no Annual Rent is asked or paid for it, or Rent of any Kind.

The Keeper of the Record of Sasines holds his Office by a Commission from the Crown.

(3.) Question answered in the above.

(4.) All Papers and Instruments are recorded in the Register of Sasines, the Principal is returned to the Holder, docketed on the back by the Keeper, specifying the Volume, the Pages where it is recorded, and the Date when done, and for the Use of Search the Minute Book is kept. As the Sheriff Clerk deposits the Principal, the Copy he gives out is the only Index by which it can be found, except by a Search; the Sederunt Book of the Sheriff Court is the Index or Catalogue of Court Processes.

The Utility to the Public in this Shire, if the Sheriff Clerk's Record Office was properly fitted up, and put on a proper Footing, would be great; for I have known many old Papers of consequence could not be found on a Search, which had been deposited, and perhaps again given out in a vague Manner.

If this Office was properly shelfed and divided so as to receive Papers, by the Year in which they were deposited, they could be arranged and put in their Place perhaps in less than Six Months.

To get this accomplished, some Years ago I volunteered my Services to several of the Gentlemen, to superintend the Business along with the Clerk and Procurators of Court, who were equally willing to allot for the Purpose a given Time Weekly.

If all Papers found in a State of Preservation, are to be put on Record by way of Catalogue or Index, it is impossible for me to say the Time or the Assistance that would be necessary to complete the same, at least until they are first properly arranged by the Year.

I know of no Catalogues or Indexes existing any where else; only it may be proper here to observe, That every Proprietor has it in his Choice to record his Writs and Evidences of Heritable Property either here or in the Register of Sasines in Edinburgh; also of other Papers which should properly come into the Sheriff Clerk's Record, some are sent to Edinburgh, and recorded in the Books of Council and Session; this Practice is still kept up in Part.

There is no Record of Inhibitions in this Shire, all these are recorded in Edinburgh.

(5.) The Keeper of the Register of Sasines, and the Sheriff Clerk, are the only Officers employed in keeping and arranging these Records; and their respective Duties are to register and arrange such Writs or Deeds as are given in, which are received at all Times in every lawful Day, without regard to Hours.

The Keeper of the Record of Sasines has no Salary from Government or the Public; his Emoluments arise wholly from the Dues paid for recording, which are always charged as near the Edinburgh Prices as possible, which I am told are about 3*s.* 4*d.* Sterling per Page in the Book or Register, and which come to from 1[illegible]*s.* 6*d.* to £. 1. Sterling for each Sasine in common Cases, according to the Number of Leaves. There is no Table of Fees; a Search is 5*s.* Sterling for each Year through the Record.

Our present Keeper has not held his Situation much above a Year and a Half, therefore he cannot give his Average Income for Three Years; in the former Keeper's Time (now dead) I always understood the Register brought him from £.20. to £.26. Sterling per Annum.

The Sheriff Clerk has no Salary from Government or the Public; his Income wholly arises from Dues or Fees, according to Act of Sederunt of the Court of Session, 16th March 1748, and Table thereto annexed. This Yearly Income from his Office, in this small Shire, runs, upon an Average of Three Years, to about £. 36. Sterling; he has no Payment for Attendance.

(6.) The Persons entrusted are the Keeper of the Register of Sasines, and the Sheriff Clerk Depute, they officially bear these Designations, and are responsible in their respective Offices.

(7.) A Minute Book begun and carried on by way of Catalogue or Index, by the Sheriff Clerk, is not only necessary, but it would be very convenient to find all Papers deposited for Preservation, and have them marked in the same Way that is done in the Minute Book for the Registers of Sasines, at a small Expense.

James Stedman,
Sheriff Substitute.

5th April, 1800.

Appendix (Y. 20.)

Return from the Steward Substitute of the Stewartry of KIRKCUDBRIGHT, to the Questions of the Committee.

(1.) THE Public Records in the Hands of the Steward Depute of said Stewartry and his Substitute, are

1st. Record of Decreets in Civil Causes, commencing in the Year 1698.

2d. Record of Criminal Causes, commencing 31st May, 1750.

3d. Record of Bonds, Bills, Deeds, &c. registered for Preservation and Execution, commencing in the Year 1667.

4th. Record of Probative Writs, commencing 20th November 1746.

5th. Record of the Proceedings of the Freeholders of the County, at their Annual Michaelmas Meetings and Meetings for Elections, commencing 9th October 1739.

6th. Record of the Accounts of Improvements of Entailed Estates, and of the Vouchers thereof, commencing 4th December 1773.

7th. Record of Hornings and Inhibitions, &c. commencing 20th March 1782.

8th. Record of Inventories of Heirs entering "cum beneficio Inventarij," commencing 30th June 1744.

(2.) The Steward Clerk's Office, in which the Records are kept, is situated in the Borough of Kirkcudbright, and is a small uncomfortable House, neither safe nor commodious for the Dispository of the Records of the County. This House was the Property of Alexander Gordon, Esquire, of Campbellton, the late Steward Clerk, who died in the Month of December last; no new Clerk is yet appointed by the Keeper of the Signet, in whose Gift the Appointment is; and this House is held by the Person who acts as Interim Clerk, upon no other Tenure than the tacit Permission of Mr. Gordon's Heirs.

(3.) The Records are in a tolerable State of Preservation, and arranged by the Year.

(4.) There are Inventories of the Records, but they are not complete. Formerly the Stewartry was divided into Two Districts, and One Court was held at Bridgend of Dumfries, for the Inhabitants of the Ten Parishes East of the River Urr; and another Court at Kirkcudbright for the Eighteen Parishes West of Urr: The Inventory of the Records kept at Bridgend of Dumfries is complete, but that kept at Kirkcudbright is not so, for the Inventory of Decreets, &c. goes no further back than 1733, and that of Bonds, Bills, Deeds, &c. no further back than 16th March 1744; no Inventories or Indexes of the Records are known to be in the Hands of any other Person. Although the early Part of the Records in the Steward Clerk's Office is not often resorted to, yet it would be very useful to have them inventoried and arranged, for they are sometimes of Importance in Questions concerning Heritable Property. Were the Clerks in the Office to devote their Time to making Inventories of these antient Records, they could perhaps complete them in the course of Four or Five Months; and any Two Persons, versant in such Business, could complete them within the same Period.

(5.) The Steward Clerk and his Deputy have the Custody of the Records, and it is their Duty to arrange them by the Year, and keep proper Indexes or Inventories of them: The Clerk or his Deputy generally gives Attendance in the Office from Nine o'Clock in the Morning to Eight in the Evening. The Fees of a Search for any Process or Registered Paper, are understood to be 1*s.* for each Year of the Search. The Fees of a Copy, or Extract of any Part of the Records, are fixed by Act of Sederunt, 16th March 1748, and are as follow:

	s.	*d.*
For an Extract or Copy of a Horning, Inhibition, Interdiction, or Lawburrow, for the First Sheet - - - - - -	1	2
And for every other Sheet - - -	1	0
For an Extract or Copy of any Bond, Bill, or Deed, for each Sheet - - - - - -	1	2½
And for an Extract or Copy of any Decreet or Process, for the First Sheet - - -	2	6
And for every other Sheet - - - - -	1	6

N. B. Where the Sums contained in these Decreets do not amount to £. 5. the Fees of Extract are considerably less.

The net Annual Amount of the Steward Clerk's Fees (for all his Trouble in attending the Steward Courts, keeping a Journal of the Proceedings, arranging, inventorying, and taking Care of the Records, making Extracts or Copies, &c. &c.) upon the Average of the last Three Years, is £. 90; and of this Sum there may be from £. 5 to £. 6. for Searches. These Fees are in many Instances too small, and very inadequate to the Trouble of doing the Business.

(6.) The Steward Clerk or his Depute are the only Persons intrusted with the Care of the Records, and they generally attend upon every Search, and take Care that the Records be restored to their proper Place.

(7.) To render the Records more safe, and the Use of them more convenient to the Public, the following Matters seem principally to be wanting:

1st. A proper House, vaulted to guard against Accidents by Fire.

2d. A Set of Presses, with a separate Division for the Records of each Year.

3d. A certain Number of Copies of the Indexes in Inventories of each Year should be printed, bound, and deposited in the Steward Clerk's Office, to be at all Times ready to have Recourse to; for in the present State of Things, the Manuscript Inventories, unbound, soon get worn and spoiled by handling and tossing about, so as to be almost illegible.

James Gordon.

6th June, 1800.

Appendix (Y. 21. a.)

Return from the Sheriff Substitute of LANARKSHIRE, to the Questions of the Committee.

(1.) THE Sheriffs in Scotland are not the Custodiers of any Public Records, nor of the Records of the Sheriff Courts, nor of any Rolls, Instruments, Manuscript Books, or Papers: The Sheriff Clerks are the Custodiers of these.

The Shire of Lanark is divided into Three Wards or Districts, called, The Upper, Middle, and Lower Wards. A Sheriff Court is kept at Lanark for the Upper, at Hamilton for the Middle, and at Glasgow for the Lower Wards; and at each of these Places separate Records are kept for their several Districts, all of which are of the same Nature. I judged it proper to premise these Observations; but the following Answers

SCOTLAND.
Sheriffs Courts.

Appendix (Y. 24. a.)

are intended to relate particularly to the State and Nature of the Records kept at Glasgow.

Those in the Sheriff Court here consist of,

1. Record of Hornings, Inhibitions, Interdictions, Discharges, and Renunciations of Mortgages and Heritable Bonds, for the Lower or Under Ward or District.—These Writings are all ingrossed in One Book; and as each Volume is filled up, it is transmitted to the General Register at Edinburgh, where it is there laid up among the Public Records. A new Volume is sent to the Sheriff Clerk, for which he pays a Sum greatly beyond its intrinsic Value, to be filled up, and when finished it is returned as the former, and so on, so that the Whole of this Record is deposited in the General Register (except the Volume in use) which of course when finished will be also returned to the General Register.

2. Record of Probative Writes:—which is complete to this Period, from January 1773, being the Commencement of the First Volume in the Possession of the Clerk. This Record contains Papers, Extracts of which are Probative, although the Principal Papers themselves should be lost. The Principal Papers, when recorded, are always returned to the Presenter of them.

3. Record of Deeds:—Which Deeds are retained by the Clerk, and Extracts thereof given out, which are Probative in Courts of Law. This Record consists of Dispositions, Assignments, Bonds, Leases, Settlements, Protests upon Bills, &c. There are Deeds in the Office as far back as the Year 1666, but no Book of Record appears until the Year 1748. This Record is filled up, from the Year last mentioned, until the 10th Day of August 1775, and consists of Fifteen Folio Volumes; and from that Time to 1785, the Record has not been bound up, but is upon loose Sheets, which are in proper Order for binding. Since the last Period however the Record has not been kept up, even in loose Sheets; but the Papers are carefully tied up in Monthly Bundles, and kept in progressive Order, and upon the Back of each Paper the Day, Month, and Year of the Presentation for recording, together with the Name of the Person who presented it, is indorsed. A Minute Book is likewise kept of these Particulars, with a short Description of the Papers, from which they can be much easier discovered if wanted than from the Record.

4. Record of Decrees of the Court in Processes:—This Record commences in June 1748, of which only Two Folio Volumes can be discovered; the First commencing of the above Date, and ending in December 1752; and the Second begins in August 1774 and ends in December 1775, and from that Time until April 1786 the Record has been carried up, but not bound up in Volumes. This Record has been however continued since, in a more abridged Way, and so far as I can judge equally effectual, and of course at a much less Expense to the Lieges. In place of inserting verbatim every Word of a Process in the Record, which is the Practice, and which often requires many Hundreds of Pages, a Copy of the essential Parts of the Decree is made, and the proper Places for copying in the Pleadings, is referred to thus [Here take in such and such Papers] describing them, and so on; and these Copies are put in the Process itself, and answer every Purpose that a full Copy in the Record could do, in case a Second Extract was required. During the Progress of the Processes, the different Stages of Procedure which take place are marked down in a Book, called The Act Book.

This Record commences in May 1748, is brought down to this Period, and consists of Sixteen Folio Volumes, besides the one in use. This Record ought, in natural Order, to have been inserted before the last.

5. Record, which contains the Services of Heirs to their Predecessors, and the Cognoscing of Lunatics and furious Persons, in order to have Guardians appointed to them.—The Record in the Office commences in December 1754, and consists of Five Volumes, besides the one in the Progress of being filled up, and has been regularly carried down to this Period.

6. Record respecting the Business of the Corn Act, 31 Geo. III. which has been regularly carried down since its Commencement.

(2.) The Building in which the Sheriff Clerk's Office and Records, &c. are kept, is situated in the New Town of Glasgow, in a Street called Wilson's Street, between Two and Three Hundred Yards from the Cross, the most centrical Part of the City. The Clerks Office, so far back as I can remember, which is upwards of 30 Years past, has (with an Exception of short Duration) been in Rented Houses, frequently removed from one Part of the City to another. The present Office is Private Property, rented by the Clerk, and which, in consequence of a Lease, he is to possess until Whitsunday 1801. At that Term he will have been there for Seven Years. The Building in which it is situated consists of Three Flats, occupied above the Office, by different Tenants, as Dwelling Houses, where Fires are constantly kept. I have often known the Records, in a much more insecure Situation from Fire, where Tenants possessed both the Flats above and below the Office as Dwelling Places, in which Fires were constantly used. Places like these are certainly very insecure for the invaluable Depositaries of the Deeds of the Public.

(3.) The Records and Papers about the Office are in a very good State of Preservation, except some of a very old Date, that have obviously suffered very considerably from Fire. The Arrangement has been already described in Answer to Questions (3) and (4.)

These Answers serve also as an Answer to the First Paragraph of Question (4.)

In answer to the remaining Parts of that Question, it appears that the principal Utility which would attend having the Records completed, would be, that in Case of an Accident by Fire, the one might be saved while the other might be destroyed, and in this Case the Public have a double Security for the Preservation of their important Papers, I mean Principal Deeds, such as Dispositions, Leases, &c. With regard to the Records of Decreets and Protests, they do not occur precisely in that point of View, because the Extracts of them are in general put into immediate Execution, and the Debts for which they are issued, made good or bad, and of consequence, second Extracts are rarely applied for, as if Payments are recovered, their Use is at an end, and the cumbrous Load and Expense of recording are totally lost; and where Payments cannot be recovered, they are in general very much in the same Situation; besides, Creditors are at particular Pains in the last Case to preserve them to avoid a Second Expense; at any Rate, in case the Processes or Protests are not lost or destroyed by Fire, they can be as easily resorted to as though a Record existed.

The ordinary Business of the Clerk's Office, including the keeping of the Records, engages the Time of sometimes Three and sometimes Four Clerks; and at the Time when the Record was discontinued to be filled up, the whole Time of One Clerk was necessary to carry them forward. The Business of the Office has so increased since that Time, owing to the Consequences of the Increase of Commercial Intercourse and Population, that it is supposed it would now require Three or Four Additional Clerks to carry it on, and it is difficult even to conjecture what Space of Time it would require to complete them.

The whole Catalogues, Indexes, &c. (which it is believed) are in the Office, are condescended upon, and nothing

nothing can be said with regard to those that may be wanting, if any are.

(5.) The Sheriff Clerk is, as already noticed, the Custodier of the Records, and he or his Depute and Subaltern Clerks are always at hand to search for and shew any Record or Paper wanted during the Hours of their Attendance, which is from Ten o'Clock of the Morning until Eight o'Clock at Night, and later as Business requires. The Time occupied in Searching the Records do not, it is believed, require Twelve Hours in a Year. The Emoluments for these Searches, Certified Copies, and Second Extracts of Deeds, &c. upon an Average of any Number of Years, so far as can be recollected, has not amounted to Forty or Fifty Shillings Annually; but as no particular Account of them has been kept, the precise Average cannot be condescended upon. Neither the Clerk, nor any Person about the Office, have any Salary from the Public, nor in any other Way, for keeping the Records. His Income arises from the Emoluments of his Office alone, for which very ample Compensation is given to the Public in Labour. His Fees of Office are the same they were 50 Years ago, and are in many Instances a great deal too low, more especially considering the great Change which has taken place in the Expense of Living.

The only Exception, if it can be called one, is, that by the Corn Act, before noticed, of 31 Geo. III. an Allowance is made to the Sheriff of 20*s.* for each Monthly Report of the Prices of Corn, to the Receiver of Corn Returns, to defray the Expense of citing Juries and Witnesses, and paying the Clerk for keeping the Record. In this Instance, the Clerk may be said to be paid by the Public. This leads me naturally to mention how Matters stand with regard to his legal Charge in this Respect, in which I will be obliged necessarily to intrude myself as Sheriff Substitute, and as this is the Case I hope I shall be pardoned for making a few short Remarks relative to my Official Situation.

By a posterior Act of 33 Geo. III. for amending the former, it is Enacted, That the aforesaid Sum of 20*s.* shall be allowed to the Sheriff, over and above all the necessary Charges for carrying the First Act into Execution, and that these Charges shall be allowed in the Sheriff's Accounts with the Exchequer.

The Enactment appeared so very clear to me, and I believe to all the Sheriff Substitutes in Scotland, that the above 20*s.* was intended and allowed by the Legislature as a Recompense to the Acting Sheriff, for his great additional Trouble in taking the Proofs and making the Returns, and that the other Charges were to be paid by the Exchequer, that I and all the Sheriff Substitutes within the Circle of my Acquaintance, have uplifted and applied that Monthly Allowance to our own Use, not doubting that the other Charges would be paid in Manner before stated; and indeed it was considered that Government, by making that Allowance, meant it as a small Increase to the very inadequate Salaries of the Sheriff Substitutes.

It is true, that Sheriff Deputes are only mentioned, but it never can be conceived that it was intended for any other Person than the Resident Sheriff, who does the actual Labour; and to prevent even Ambiguity here, the Intention, if so, might have been so defined. Although this trifling Allowance had been given to the Sheriff Substitutes, in addition to their Salaries, and particularly with regard to myself, I can say that my Public Services are by no Means overpaid.

I have for 16 Years bypast discharged the arduous and laborious Business of Sheriff Substitute or Resident Sheriff, for the great commercial and populous City of Glasgow and surrounding Country. Since I undertook that Office, I have been almost a Slave to the Duties of it, which in point of Magnitude and Importance are perhaps inferior to few judicial Situations in Scotland. I foolishly hoped, at my entering upon the Office, that my Private Business, as a Law Practitioner, which was then considerable, would increase and become still more respectable from the Name of Sheriff; but in this I found myself disappointed. What I had, I almost totally, from a mistaken Idea of the Public, lost, as it was conceived a Judge would not demean himself to execute Private Business; and from a considerable Income, arising from my former Practice, I have been under the Necessity, on account of a very large Family, to adhere to a Public Office, of which the Salary and Perquisites have never been able to defray the One-Half of my Family Expense. I hope, however, I have supported the Character of a Sheriff Substitute with that Respectability which the Office requires; and although the Income is small, and I am to a Certainty a very great Loser, while others are gaining by their Professions; yet it has become an Object in my advanced Years, and in the State of my Property otherways, to abide by it, as the Business which I have lost never could be regained. The Annual Salary is, after paying Exchequer Fees, between £.67. and £.68. a very inadequate Salary, I have no Hesitation in saying, to the Rank and Importance of the Office which I have long had the Honour to fill. It is an unpleasant Situation indeed for a Person to be declining in his Circumstances every Day, and becoming every Year more rapid, by the immense Increase of the Expense of Living and Public Taxes, without any Prospect of ameliorating them. This can easily be conceived when it is stated that I have for a great Number of Years had a Family, consisting of Twelve Children, and Servants, to subsist, without the smallest Assistance from any of them. I hope I shall be forgiven for these few Remarks, as I have for many Years wished them to be known; and have embraced the Opportunity of stating them to the Honourable Committee, as what perhaps may be in some Measure connected with the Objects of their Researches, leaving to it's Consideration, whether some Provision ought to be made in favour of the Sheriff Substitutes. It might be easily done by imposing a small Duty in their Favour, upon each Process brought into Court, and the different Substitutes would in that Case be paid in Proportion to their Labour. It would at any rate be a small Matter to Government to make their Condition comfortable, and their Salaries at least equal to their necessary Expenditure. Not however to pursue these Observations farther, I have to remark, that the Barons of the Exchequer have positively refused to allow the Clerk any Fees for keeping the Corn Record, or any of the other Charges incurred in the Execution of the Act, alleging that the 20*s.* uplifted by the Sheriff Substitutes, for each Monthly Return, fall to be applied in the first Place towards Extinction of these Charges, and of course not a Farthing of the Clerk's Fees, or other Charges, have been paid since the Year 1791, when the Act commenced. It appears clear to me, as I have already mentioned, from the Act 33 Geo. III. that the Sum was intended for the Sheriff's Trouble. However, in the Circumstances of the Case, as a Misapprehension subsists, it would be a most desirable Matter that the Legislature would ascertain the Point, in some Act of Parliament, that the Creditors on this Branch of Public Business, who have been long clamorous for Payment, should be paid either by the Exchequer, or by the Sheriff Substitutes.

(6.) Is already in great Part answered. The Records and Papers are always duly restored to their proper Places, so soon as the Purpose for which they are wanted is answered. No particular Person about the Office is appointed to this Charge.

(7.) In answer to the last Question, nothing occurs in particular to state as necessary or expedient to observe for rendering the Use of the said Records, &c. more convenient

SCOTLAND.
Sheriffs Courts.

Appendix (Y. 21. b.)

convenient to the Public, than what may be gathered from the foregoing Observations. In general it may be remarked, it would be a most important Matter that the Records and Deeds, under the Charge of the Clerk, should be kept in a Place of Security against Fire, and in some stationary Place, to prevent their being lost, or put in a State of Confusion by removing.

The Report of

Robert Græme,
Sheriff Substitute.

Glasgow,
9th April 1800.

Appendix (Y. 21. b.)

Return from the Sheriff Depute of Lanarkshire, to the Questions of the Committee.

AS I conceive it to be the Object of the Committee to obtain Information, not only as to the particular Records which belong to the Sheriff's Court, but as to every Matter of that Description, situated within the respective Counties in Scotland; and as the Report, formerly sent by the Sheriff Substitute at Glasgow, is, in that Point of View and in other Respects, defective, I think it proper to furnish the Committee with a Statement of the following additional Particulars.

Referring to the former Answer for this County, it will be remembered, that the Sheriff Clerk and his Deputes, not the Sheriff, is the proper Custodier of the Records of that Department.

As formerly mentioned also, the County of Lanark is divided into Three Districts, at each of which a Sheriff's Court is held; viz. at Glasgow, at Lanark, and Hamilton. The State of that Record, in the District of Glasgow, being already fully answered, it is only required to take Notice of the other Two, of Lanark and Hamilton.

District of Lanark:

(1.) The Records belonging to the Sheriff's Court are, in this District, in the Custody of the Sheriff's Clerk's Depute, and consist of,

1. Decreets of Processes before the Sheriff Court,—which are Annually bundled up, and those extracted, entered in a Register; which however has been only partially done until about the Year 1748, and is from that Period continued down until within these Seven Years past; when little or no Utility being derived from the Practice, as the Decreets are always extracted from the Warrants or original Papers, it has been discontinued.
2. Act Books, being the Proceedings of the Sheriffs Court in every Cause, marked every Court Day, and which are pretty regular from the beginning of last Century.
3. Register of Bonds, Contracts, Protested Bills, and other Deeds; the Warrants and Originals being preserved.
4. Record of Fiars or Prices of Grain, Annually, fixed by a Jury summoned for that Purpose.
5. Record of Services of Heirs, from 1696 to the present Time.
6. Records of Probative Writs of Deeds, from 1770 to the present Time.
7. Record of Hornings and Inhibitions, &c. from 1773 to the present Time. The Books of this Record, when filled up, are transmitted to the General Register House at Edinburgh.
8. Records of Certificates of Licenses for killing Game, from September 1784 to the present Time.

(2.) These Records are lodged in the Sheriff's Clerk's Office, being a Room hired from Year to Year, by the Principal Clerk for the County, and which is Private Property.

(3.) These Records are partly in Books, and in general in a tolerable State of Preservation, except some of the Originals or Warrants prior to 1748, which from Damp have been somewhat injured.

(4.) There are complete Minute Books, or Abbreviations of the Register of Bonds and Decreets, from 1696 to the present Time. There is also a Minute Book of Hornings and Inhibitions regularly kept. The other Records in general have sufficient Indexes.

(5.) The Sheriff Clerk's Depute is the only Person employed in this District, to arrange and take Charge of all the Records mentioned. His Duty is to attend the Sheriff's Court, and give out Extracts to those who require them, &c. The Hour of Attendance is from Ten in the Morning until Six in the Evening. The Sheriff Clerk's Depute has no Salary paid by the Public, but receives a Salary from the Principal Sheriff Clerk, and accounts to him for the Fees of Office.

These are fixed at a small Sum per Sheet for Registration of Deeds, Extracts of Decreets, &c.; and a proportional Fee for Searches and other Trouble and Labour incident to these Records.

(6.) It has been already mentioned, that the Sheriff Clerk and his Depute have the exclusive Charge of these Records.

District of Hamilton:

(1.) The Records in this District are likewise in the Possession of the Sheriff Clerk's Depute, and consist of,

1. The Record or Register of Probative Writs or Deeds, such as Dispositions, Tacks, Bonds, Protested Bills, &c. &c.
2. The Record of Judicial Proceedings, as, Extracted Decreets obtained before the Sheriff's Court.
3. The Record of Inhibitions and Hornings.
4. Records of Minutes of the Proceedings of the Court of Freeholders of the County.

(2.) These Records are kept in a Dwelling House, occupied by the Sheriff Clerk's Depute, which is Private Property.

(3. & 4.) The principal Deeds to which these Records relate are put up in Bundles, and marked of the Year in which they are recorded. The Decreets of the Court are also put up in the same Manner, and so marked. There is besides, a Minute Book, and an Act Book, kept by the Clerk; in which all the Acts of Court and Judicial Proceedings are briefly recorded by their particular Dates; all of which are pretty regularly brought down to the present Period. The whole of these Records are deposited in Cases and Boxes, and are in general in good Preservation. At the same Time, it must be admitted that these Minute Books and Act Books are not adequate in Point of Utility to a regular and complete Index; and though it would be a Matter of very considerable Labour, there is no Doubt, if Means were furnished, but that it would be accomplished.

(5. & 6.) The only Officer employed in this Department is the Sheriff Clerk's Depute, whose Duty it is to record all Deeds, &c. given in for that Purpose; as also to attend to the Business of the Sheriff's Court, to write the Minutes and Acts of Court, to extract all the Sentences and Slips of Procedure that may be required; for this Business regular Fees are charged, but for his Individual Trouble the Sheriff Clerk's Depute is paid by his Constituent.

(7.) It

(7.) It has been already mentioned, that in all the Three Diftricts of this County, the Records under the Charge of the Sheriff Clerk are kept merely in Apartments that are Private Property, and by no Means either convenient or fecure. It would certainly, therefore, be a great Improvement upon this Eftablifhment, if in each of the Three Towns of Glafgow, Hamilton, and Lanark, a proper Building was acquired by the Public for containing the Records, and in fome of them, particularly in the Town of Hamilton, for holding the Sheriff's Court. This Building might be fitted up in fuch a Manner as to be fecure from Fire, which in none of the Three Diftricts is the Cafe at prefent; and it might alfo internally be fo arranged, as to render Accefs to the Records depofited infinitely more eafy and convenient to the Public. An Office of this Nature is peculiarly required in Glafgow, the Bufinefs carried on before the Sheriff Court, in that populous Commercial City, being exceedingly great and important, and which for feveral Years paft has very much increafed.

It is alfo proper to obferve, that the Sheriff's Subftitutes, particularly thofe at Hamilton and Glafgow, are, confidering the Importance of their Duty and Situation, very inadequately paid; the Salary of the Firft being only £.30 Sterling, and that of the Second no more than £.70 Sterling per Annum.

Befides thefe Matters of Record, which relate to the Jurifdiction of the Sheriff Depute, or are in the Cuftody of the Sheriff Clerk, the following may alfo, it is conceived with Propriety, be mentioned, in order that they may be known, and if thought expedient, more particularly be enquired into.

1. Particular Regifter of Safines, Reverfions, &c. for the County of Lanark, kept at Hamilton. There is a particular Clerk, the Keeper of this Record, who receives from the General Regifter Houfe at Edinburgh a large Folio Book, wherein are recorded all the Infeftments and other competent Deeds; whenever this Book is filled up, he tranfmits it to the General Regifter, accompanied with a Minute Book, narrating fhortly the Contents, both of which are then prefented for the Ufe of the Public.

2. Records of the Commiffary or Confiftorial Court of Glafgow, kept in that City.

3. Record of the Commiffary Court of Hamilton and Corn Price, kept alfo at Glafgow.

4. Record of the Commiffary Court of Lanark, kept there.

5. The Royal Burgh of Glafgow, which poffeffes a Jurifdiction, Court, and Correfpondent Records.

6. The Royal Burgh of Lanark, which has a Jurifdiction, Court, and Correfpondent Records.

7. The Royal Burgh of Rutherglen, in the fame Situation.

8. Record of the Commiffioners of Supply; confifting of the Minutes of the Proceedings of the Commiffioners of Supply, the Valuation of the Lands in the County, the fubdivifions thereof which occafionally happen, and other Matters incident to that Department.

9. Records of fuch Towns as were prior to the Jurifdiction Act in 1748, Burghs of Regality; viz. the Town of Hamilton and fome others, which ftill poffefs a certain limited Jurifdiction, a Court, and Correfpondent Records.

10. Records of the Church Courts; confifting of,
 1. Seffion Record in each Parifh, wherein are inferted Births, Baptifms, Deaths, &c.
 2. Prefbytery Record, containing Minutes of the Proceedings kept by their own Clerk, who is a Clergyman.
 3. Synod Record.—The Synod of Glafgow is held within this County, and the Records thereof kept in the fame Manner as the former.

R. Hamilton,
Sheriff Depute of Lanarkfhire.

Edinburgh,
June 15th, 1800.

SCOTLAND.
Sheriffs Courts.
Appendix (Y. 22.)

Appendix (Y. 22.)

Return from the Sheriff of the County of LINLITHGOW, to the Queftions of the Committee.

THE only Records in the Cuftody of the Sheriff of the County of Linlithgow, are as follow:

(1.) The Record of Contracts, Obligations, and Deeds of Individuals, prefented for Regiftration; which Prefentment is made for Two feveral Purpofes:—Either for the Keeping only and Prefervation of the Deed, or towards the obtaining of lawful Execution againft the Party Debtor in fuch Contract, Deed, &c.; for which Purpofe the previous Entry of the written Deed upon Record, is, by the Law of Scotland, a neceffary Circumftance.

The Original Writings, given in to be recorded, are retained in the Office, in a regular Series, as the Warrants of Regiftration; and are in a State of Order and Prefervation; and they are tranfcribed into Books of Record; to each of which there is an Index, bearing the Titles and Defcriptions of the feveral Deeds entered therein, and the Dates of Regiftration. The Dues of Regiftration are One Shilling and Two Pence per Sheet, each Sheet confifting of Two Pages, each Page of Thirty-fix Lines, and each Line of Nine Words.

This Record commences in the Year 1701, and is continued down to the prefent Time. It is in the immediate Cuftody of the Sheriff Clerk, and is kept in his Private Houfe; there being no Public Building appointed for that Purpofe.

The Record is acceffible, to be confulted at all ordinary Hours for doing Bufinefs. The Sheriff Clerk, for this and the other various Duties of his Office, has generally under him Two Clerks or Apprentices. An Extract, or Official Copy of any fuch recorded Writing, may be obtained from him by any Perfon, on Payment of the like Fee as on the Original Regiftration The Sheriff Clerk has no Salary or Allowance whatfoever from the Public, and his Fees have not received any Increafe fince the Year 1748, and only a trifling Increafe for more than a Century. The Annual Emoluments of his Office in all its Branches of Duty, which are multifarious and extenfive, do not exceed £.150.

But as no feparate Account has ever been kept of the Produce of the Fees of particular Branches, no more Special Return can be made on that Head.

(2.) The only other Record under the immediate Care of the Sheriff, is the Record of the Judicial Proceedings and Decrees of the Sheriff's Court of Law; which is the Ordinary Court in Scotland for all fuch Suits and Actions as are not appropriated exclufively to the Supreme Courts of Seffions and Jufticiary. The original Proceedings in all fuch Actions are carefully preferved and arranged, according to their Dates, in the Office of the Sheriff Clerk, which is kept, attended, and managed in this Branch as in that above mentioned. He is obliged, on Demand, to give out to any One demanding it, an Extract or Official Copy of each Sentence or Decree; which Extracts contain, by Cuftom, the whole previous Proceedings leading to that Decree; and for which he is paid at the Rate of 1*s.* 6*d.* per Sheet, computed as above mentioned. When a Decree has thus been extracted, a Copy of it ought regularly to be entered, at the fame Time, in a Book of Record, to be kept with the Sheriff Clerk; but, owing to the Infufficiency of the Fees for that Purpofe, no fuch Book has ever been kept, (as I underftand) in the County of Linlithgow. To fupply this Deficiency, a very long Time, a Number of additional Clerks, and a great Expenfe, would of courfe be requifite, much greater, indeed, as it appeareth to me, than the Benefit or Ufe of fuch Record warrants or requires; becaufe the Original Proceedings

SCOTLAND.
Sheriffs Courts.
Appendix (Y. 23.)

ceedings themselves always remain in the Office, under the Care of the Clerk, who can give out a new Extract of them to any one who requires it.

(3.) The only other Records, of which the Sheriff Clerk has the Official Custody, are that of the Election of Members of Parliament, which extends from 1685 to the present Day, and is contained in Three Books; and that of the Michaelmas Head Court of Freeholders, which extends from 1733 to the present Time, and is contained in Four several Books. I do not know that there are any Means of supplying these Minutes prior to 1733; neither has any Inconvenience been experienced, so far as I know, from the Want of them.

The Valuation Rolls of the County, which serve to regulate the Payment of the Land Tax, and the Qualifications of Freeholders, are also in the Hands of the Sheriff Clerk—One in 1667, and the other in 1687.

The Sheriff Clerk is often, but not necessarily, a "Jure Officii" Clerk also to the Justices of Peace, and to the Commissioners of Supply.

1. The Minutes of the Meetings of Justices of Peace are preserved in Five several Books, from 1689 to 1719; and from 1726 to the present Time, they are also preserved in Six several Books.

2. Those of the Commissioners of Supply, from 1689 to 1719, and from 1720 to the present Time, are also preserved in Six several Books.

It does not consist with my Knowledge, that any material Inconvenience has resulted from the Want of the Proceedings in earlier Times, nor do I know that the Means are extant of supplying the Deficiency.

All which is humbly reported by

David Hume,
Sheriff Depute.

Appendix (Y. 23.)

Return from the Sheriff of Nairn, to the Questions of the Committee.

TO the First Question stated in the Order, the Sheriff answers, That in this County, and he supposes in all the Counties of Scotland, a Variety of Records are kept and preserved; 1. A Record or Minute Book of all the Proceedings which take place before him, as Judge Ordinary of the Bounds: 2. A Record, wherein are ingrossed the Proceedings upon the Corn Laws: 3. One in which all Inhibitions, Hornings, and other Deeds, are ingrossed: 4. A Record in which the Proceedings of the Justices of the Peace and Commissioners of Supply are minuted: 5. A Record in which the whole Proceedings of the Freeholders are ingrossed, either at Elections for Members to Parliament, or at the Annual Michaelmas Meetings: 6. A Record in which are ingrossed the Proceedings of the Court of Lieutenancy, upon the Militia and other Acts, under the Direction of him and his Deputies: 7. A Record in which Sasines of Burgage Lands and Tenements are ingrossed; and, lastly, a Register in which Sasines upon the County Lands are ingrossed: But this last Record is kept in the Neighbouring County of Elgin, which answers for both.

(2.) These Records are uniformly kept by the Clerks, in Offices appointed by them for that Purpose, generally in their own Lodgings, Private Property, and for which they have no Allowance whatever from the Public. Great Care is taken for their Preservation, as being considered highly interesting to the Public and Individuals.

(3.) These Records are kept in the best possible State of Preservation, and arranged in such Order, that any Paper may be got upon Information at what Time it was delivered for Registration.

(4.) There are Minute Books kept along with these Records, upon looking at which the Deeds themselves can be almost immediately recovered, and Extracts of them given out. The remaining Part of this Question requires no Answer, as the Records are complete and not detached.

(5.) This Question is in Effect answered by the First, as the Clerks are the Custodiers and only Officers employed in the Arrangement of these Records. Attendance is at all Times given by them or their Servants for Searching them, in order to satisfy every Inquiry which may be made regarding them. The Clerks have no Salary, or other Allowance whatever from Government. Their Fees are regulated by an Act of Sederunt of the Court of Session, and however adequate to the Trouble they might have been considered many Years ago, when fixed, they are now of the most trifling and insignificant Nature, and very inadequate to the Trouble of Gentlemen, who must be bred to Business before their Admission as Clerks. In this County the Fees are casual, precarious, and uncertain, and do not upon an Average exceed £.30.

(6.) This Question is also in Effect answered. The Clerks, or their Servants, are the only Persons employed in the Care or Search of the Public Records, and in their Arrangement when the Search is finished. The usual Allowance made for a Search is extremely trifling, and do not here exceed 5*s.* for a Search of many Years; very often not rewarded at all.

(7.) It does not occur, that any Improvement in the Case of the Records in this County is necessary. They are of the first Public Utility, well attended to, and if some additional Encouragement was given to the Clerks for their Trouble, more Regularity might be expected.

Geo. Abercromby,
Sheriff Depute.

Appendix (Y. 24.)

RETURN by the Sheriff Subftitute of ORKNEY, to the Queftions of the Committee.

(1.) THE following is a Particular Lift of the Records of the Sheriff Court of Orkney, and the Periods to which each Sort relates.

N° 1. REGISTER of BONDS, DISPOSITIONS, &c.

VOLS.	COMMENCING.	ENDING.
1.	4 September - - 1611.	10 September - - 1632.
2.	21 Auguft - - - 1612.	4 October - - - 1615.
3.	15 October - - - 1615.	4 February - - - 1643.
4.	20 July - - - - 1638.	22 Auguft - - - 1662.
5.	25 February - - - 1647.	13 February - - - 1656.
6.	16 July - - - - 1655.	24 January - - - 1660.
7.	4 June - - - - 1661.	18 February - - - 1664.
8.	18 February - - - 1664.	11 June - - - - 1667.
9.	20 January - - - 1665.	5 October - - - 1673.
10.	15 June - - - - 1665.	4 May - - - - 1675.
11.	11 June - - - - 1667.	23 February - - - 1669.
12.	23 February - - - 1669.	4 October - - - 1672.
13.	4 Auguft - - - 1675.	1 February - - - 1681.
14.	11 Auguft - - - 1707.	9 February - - - 1720.
15.	1 June - - - - 1732.	17 November - - 1738.
16.	20 November - - 1738.	30 June - - - - 1746.
17.	22 May - - - - 1751.	21 May - - - - 1761.
18.	1 June - - - - 1761.	4 December - - 1767.
19.	4 December - - 1767.	25 September - - 1775.

N° 2. REGISTER of HORNINGS, INHIBITIONS, &c.

VOLS.	COMMENCING.	ENDING.
1.	5 March - - - 1610.	31 October - - - 1613.
2.	12 December - - 1612.	29 May - - - - 1628.
3.	12 July - - - - 1615.	9 Auguft - - - 1658.
4.	5 September - - 1628.	10 June - - - - 1636.
5.	2 July - - - - 1636.	27 July - - - - 1642.
6.	23 October - - - 1646.	25 July - - - - 1658.
7.	9 Auguft - - - 1661.	6 July - - - - 1663.
8.	8 July - - - - 1663.	16 December - - 1666.
9.	16 November - - 1665.	4 June - - - - 1674.
10.	14 December - - 1666.	1 December - - 1669.
11.	4 Auguft - - - 1675.	10 Auguft - - - 1680.
12.	11 Auguft - - - 1680.	19 December - - 1693.
13.	16 January - - - 1694.	12 January - - - 1706.
14.	6 March - - - 1706.	15 Auguft - - - 1727.
15.	22 December - - 1727.	6 February - - - 1752.
16.	4 October - - - 1752.	18 October - - - 1793.
17.	23 October - - - 1793.	20 June - - - - 1796.
18.	20 June - - - - 1796.	4 February - - - 1800.

N° 3. REGISTER of PROCESSES, DECREETS, SERVICES, &c.

VOLS.	COMMENCING.	ENDING.
1.	7 November - - 1612.	2 March - - - 1630.
2.	5 November - - 1614.	21 July - - - - 1638.
3.	22 January - - - 1615.	11 December - - 1628.
4.	2 March - - - 1630.	18 April - - - - 1648.
5.	25 March - - - 1656.	15 November - - 1659.
6.	9 July - - - - 1661.	10 January - - - 1665.
7.	6 December - - 1663.	22 July - - - - 1675.
8.	11 January - - - 1665.	18 November - - 1665.
9.	8 June - - - - 1665.	16 January - - - 1674.
10.	17 November - - 1675.	2 October - - - 1686.
11.	25 July - - - - 1676.	26 February - - - 1684.
12.	29 June - - - - 1732.	23 February - - - 1748.

N° 4. REGISTER

SCOTLAND.
Sheriff's Courts.
Appendix (Y. 24.)

N° 4. REGISTER of the PROCEEDINGS of the FREEHOLDERS of ORKNEY, and ELECTION of MEMBERS to PARLIAMENT.

VOLS.	COMMENCING.	ENDING.
1.	23 May - - - - 1734.	14 November - - 1780.
2.	29 March - - - 1781.	13 November - - 1792.
3.	12 November - - 1793.	12 November - - 1799.

N° 5. REGISTER of the FIAR PRICES of the COUNTY.

VOLS.	COMMENCING.	ENDING.
1.	19 February - - - 1785.	4 March - - - 1800.

It appears, at some Periods, Two Sets of Registers were kept, one for the Earldom, and the other for the Bishoprick of Orkney. It also appears, that the Decrees of the Commissary and Admiral Courts were sometimes inserted in these Records, and some Proceedings at Shetland.

All Bonds and other Writs, given in to be recorded in the Register N° 1, as above, since the Year 1775, lie with the Clerk of the Court, each marked on the Back as recorded of the Date given in; but no Book of Record has been kept for that Purpose since that Period. The Register N° 2, as above, is carried down to the present Period; but the Register N° 3, has been discontinued since the Year 1748. All the Processes, however, since that Period, which are very numerous, have been preserved, and also lie with the Clerk of Court.

(2.) There is no Public Building or Office allotted for these Records. They are kept by the Sheriff Clerk or his Depute for the Time being; and lodged in his Private House; which cannot be considered as a Place either of Security or Accommodation.

(3.) The Records are in a tolerable State of Preservation, and arranged according to their respective Dates.

(4.) On the Margins of each Record, and opposite to each Deed or Writing, is marked its Title or Superscription; but there are no General or Particular Catalogues, Calendars, Schedules, Repertories, or Indexes, to any of the Records, and it is supposed none were ever made up or kept in the Office. Much Time, Trouble, and Expense, would be saved to the Lieges, were there Particular Indexes to each Record, arranged in Alphabetical Order, in the Form annexed. Immediately on looking into these Indexes, any Writing wanted might be found. From the Want of such Indexes, Days, Weeks, and Months are often spent in the Search of the Records, and frequently without Success. The Sheriff Clerk Depute, the Person usually employed in the Office, by his ordinary Diligence, with the Assistance of the Sheriff Substitute, might, in the Space of Six Months, make up complete Indexes to all the Records; and the more useful Part might be accomplished in Three Months.

(5.) The Sheriff Clerk Depute is the only Person employed for the Custody and Arrangement of the Records, &c. He receives all the Papers given in to be recorded, and marks and arranges them accordingly; and gives out Extracts or attested Copies thereof when demanded. He gives Access to and Inspection of the Records at all Times; but none of the Records are given out of the Office on any Pretence whatever. He has no Salary allowed him, but he is intitled to and draws all the Fees of Office, as established by the Acts of Sederunt of the Lords of Council and Session in Scotland, 16th and 18th March 1748; Copies of which accompany this Return *. He is generally allowed Half-a-Guinea for a whole Day's Attendance on a Search of the Records, and in proportion for a longer or shorter Time. This Allowance, taken at a Medium of Three Years, amounts to £. 15 per Year; and the whole Allowances, Emoluments, and Fees of this Office, including the £. 15, are equal to £. 60 a Year.

* See Page 452.

(6.) The principal Sheriff Clerk and his Depute, are specially intrusted with the Care of the Records; and it is the Duty of both, or one or other of them, to attend upon every Search, and to take Care that every Record be duly and safely returned to its proper Place.

(7.) As Property in general, both Real and Personal, in a great Measure depends on the Safety and Preservation of these Records, they certainly ought not to be left in the Hands or Lodgings of any Clerk or his Depute; they ought to be deposited in a Public Office, situated in the most centrical and safe Part of the Town of Kirkwall, the only Royal Burgh in the County, and at some Distance from every other Building, in case of Fire. The Sheriff Clerk, or his Depute, ought to give constant Attendance at this Office, from Eight o'Clock in the Morning until Eight at Night in the Summer Months, and from Ten in the Forenoon until Four in the Afternoon the rest of the Year. A proper Room ought also to be fitted up in this Office for holding the Sheriff Courts, and for transacting the other Business of the County, from which easy Access might be had to the Records without removing them. It is supposed Eight Hundred Pounds would purchase the Ground and execute an Office of sufficient Size and Accommodation.

Sheriff Clerk's Office,
Kirkwall, 16th May 1800.

Robert Nicolson,
Sheriff Substitute of Orkney.

N° 1. INDEX

N° 1. INDEX to the Regifter of Bond, &c. of the Sheriff Court of Orkney.

	Title of Superfcription.	PARTIES.	Date of Regiftration.	N° of Regifter.	N° of Page.
A.	Bond - - -	Adams, John, to James Stiles -	24 March 1800	- 20 -	- 8
	Difpofition - -	Anderfon, James, to Adam White	25 D° D°	- D° -	- 16
B.	Affignation - -	Boll, Thomas, to William Scott	26 D° D°	- D° -	- 24
	Obligation - -	Burges, James, to Thomas Wilks	28 D° D°	- D° -	- 32

N° 2. INDEX to the Regifter of Hornings, &c. of the Sheriff Court of Orkney.

	TITLE.	PARTIES.	Date of Regiftration.	N° of Regifter.	N° of Page.
A.	Horning - - -	Adams, John, ag^t James Stiles -	24 March 1800	- 19 -	- 10
	Inhibition - -	Anderfon, John, ag^t Adam White	25 D° D°	- D° -	- 15
B.	Horning - - -	Boll, Thomas, ag^t William Scott	26 D° D°	- D° -	- 22
	Inhibition - -	Burges, James, ag^t Thomas Wilks	28 D° D°	- D° -	- 29

N° 3. INDEX to the Regifter of Proceffes, &c. of the Sheriff Court of Orkney.

	TITLE.	PARTIES.	YEAR.	N°.	
A.	Removing - -	Adams, John, ag^t James Stiles -	- 1799. -	- 2,040.	
	Wackening - -	Anderfon, James, ag^t Adam White	- 1800. -	- 2,050.	
B.	Criminal Action	Boll, Thomas, ag^t William Scott	- - D° - -	- 2,051.	
	Forthcoming -	Burges, James, ag^t Adam White	- - D° - -	- 2,052.	

Appendix (Y. 24. b.)

Return by the Sheriff Subftitute of SHETLAND, to the Queftions of the Committee.

(1.) THE Public Records kept in Shetland confift of the Sheriff and Commiffary Court Books and Regifter of Safines. The Sheriff Court Books appear to have been kept as far back as the Year 1687, but from that Period to the Year 1766 the Books have been kept irregularly, and feveral of them unfilled up; but from 1766 to the prefent Period they have been regularly filled up and attended to.

For this Part of the County there is a particular Regifter of Safines kept, commencing in the Year 1744, and up to the prefent Date, accompanied by regular Minute Books.

(2.) There is no Building appropriated for the keeping of Records. They always follow the Sheriff and Commiffary Clerks, and the Keeper of the Regifter of Safines, and are depofited by them in their Private Lodgings, without any Fee or Reward.

(3.) The Records in the prefent Poffeffion of the Sheriff Clerk are in a good State of Prefervation. The Proceffes are all numbered, and the Regifter of Safines can at any Time be had Recourfe to by the Minute Books.

(4.) The greateft Part of this Queftion is anfwered in the preceding. The Proceffes can always be had Recourfe to by the Numbers, and the Safines by the Minute Book, and that within a very fhort Space of Time, perhaps not more than Half an Hour. It does not appear that any other Indexes or Catalogues are wanting; but it muft be here obferved, that the Sheriff Court Records and Proceffes, as well as the Commiffary Court Records and Proceffes, always remain with the Clerks of thofe Courts. The Book which contains the Record of Safines, when filled up, is always fent to the General Regifter of Safines at Edinburgh, and a new Book fent to the Depute Keeper of Safines here.

(5.) There are neither Officers nor Clerks employed for the Cuftody of Records and Proceffes, other than the Sheriff Clerk, who is always appointed by Government. The Commiffary Clerk, who is appointed by the Commiffary, and the Depute Keeper of the Record of Safines, who is appointed by the Keeper of the Record, and who is again appointed by Government. The Duties of all thefe Offices are executed by thefe Clerks, and in this County Admiffion to the Records may be had at all Times of the Day. No Salaries are affixed to any of thefe Offices, and the Dues of the Clerks are fixed by Act of Sederunt, fo that the Amount of their Emoluments is perfectly uncertain, and varies every Year. They are at the utmoft but very trifling. Nothing is charged by the prefent Clerk for fearching the Records.

(6.) The Clerk of the Sheriff Court, it has been already obferved, has the Charge of the Sheriff Court Records, and it is his Duty to attend upon every Search. The Record Books he never gives out of his Hands. If a Procefs is borrowed by any of the Parties Litigants, every Paper is numbered, and a Receipt granted for the Re-delivery.

(7.) It appears highly neceffary that a Houfe fhould be built for keeping the Records and Proceffes, containing Three Apartments, One for the Sheriff Clerk, and the Records and Proceffes of that Court; a Second for the Commiffary Clerk and his Records; and

SCOTLAND.
Sheriffs Courts.

Appendix (Y. 25.)

a Third for the Keeper of the Register of Sasines. That Coal and Candle should be allowed for these Offices. That the Reason for proposing this will perhaps not be deemed insufficient, when it is stated, that until the present Sheriff Clerk, who is also Commissary Depute and Keeper of the Record of Sasines (Mr. Francis Heddell) got Possession of these Records and Processes, and removed them to his own House a few Years ago, the Public Records were by no Means kept in a regular Manner and good Condition. That upon the Demise of the Clerks or Keepers, the Processes and Records were often thrown in among the Private Papers of the deceased, from which much Trouble and Confusion ensued, and not unfrequently Loss to the Public. In particular several Years ago One of the Commissary Records was long missing, and was at last discovered upon the Top of a Bed, with many of the Leaves torn out, by which several Individuals suffered in their Interest.

Wal. Scott,
Sheriff Substitute of Shetland.

Sheriff Clerk's Office,
Leuvick, 4th June 1800.

Appendix (Y. 25.)

Return from the Sheriff of Peebleshire, to the Questions of the Committee.

AS Sheriff of Peebles I have no Custody of any Sorts of Public Records, Rolls, Instruments, Manuscript Books, or Papers.

The Records of the County are in the Custody of and kept by the Sheriff Clerk, an Officer whom the Sheriff cannot appoint, and whose Office is commonly at the Disposal of the Person holding the Office of Keeper of the Signet of Scotland.

Wishing however to communicate every Information upon this Subject to the Select Committee, I have obtained from the Sheriff Clerk the following Report upon the Records in his Custody.

J. Wolfe Murray,
Sheriff Depute of Peebles.

(1.) The several Sorts of Public Records, Rolls, Instruments, Manuscript Books and Papers, kept in the Sheriff Clerk's Office of Peebles, may be classed under the Thirteen following Heads; viz.

1. The Record of Bonds, Bills, and other Deeds, relating both to Real and Personal Property.

2. What are called the Sheriff Head Court Books, in which are contained the Services of Heirs expede before the Sheriff; and also the Minutes of the Freeholders at their Annual Meetings on Michaelmas Day, which is called the Michaelmas Head Court; as also the Minutes of the Freeholders assembled for the Purpose of electing a Representative in Parliament for the County, besides several other Things not strictly connected with the Sheriff Court.

3. The Sheriff Court Books, which appear to be kept solely for the Purpose of inserting the Decrees and Sentences pronounced by the Sheriff.

4. The Records of these Decrees and Sentences.

5. The Diet Books of the Sheriff Court, in which are ingrossed all the different Steps of Procedure that take place every Court Day in the various Causes before the Court.

6. Register of Hornings, Inhibitions, &c.

7. The Criminal Sederunt Book before the Sheriff Court.

8. The Records of Services of Heirs.

9. The Minutes and Records of the Proceedings of the Barons and Freeholders of Peebleshire.

10. The Minutes of the Commissioners of Supply of the said County.

11. The Minutes of the Justices of Peace of the said County.

12. The Sederunt Book relating to the Corn Act, 31 Geo. III.: and,

13. The Warrants and Principal Minutes from which most of the preceding Books are made up. The Periods of Time to which each Sort relate are as under:

1. Record of Bonds, Bills, &c.:

Book 1 commences 15th November 1617, and ends 9th July 1623, subjoined to a Book, intituled, "Sheriff Court Book, from 6th October 1607, to 15th November 1617."—Wants an Index. The Ink and Writing are much defaced, and obliterated.

Book 2 commences 17th July 1623, and ends 17th May 1641.—Without an Index, but on the Whole appears to be in good Condition.

Book 3 commences . . . . . May 1641, and ends 16th March 1658.—Wants an Index; and from the Faintness and Discolouring of the Ink, is scarcely legible.

Book 4 commences 20th . . . . 1658, and ends 15th January 1667.—Wants an Index; and from the Badness of the Ink, is almost illegible.

Book 5 commences 1st March 1667, and ends 16th November 1670; subjoined to a Book, intituled, "Commissary's Register of Bonds," from 1st July 1624, to 1st March 1667.—Wants an Index, and is scarcely legible.

Book 6 commences 16th November 1670, and ends 17th August 1681.—Has an Index, and is in good Order; but there seems a Chasm in the Records from this last mentioned Period to 30th June 1691, though a great many of the Deeds put upon Record during that intermediate Space appear to be extant, though but in bad Order and Condition. The next Book in the Sheriff Clerks Office, viz.

Book 7, commences 30th June 1691, and ends 3d October 1699.—Has an Index, and is in good Order.

Book 8 commences 10th October 1699, and ends 12th September 1706.—Has an Index, and is in good Order.

Book 9 commences 24th September 1706, and ends 10th June 1715.—Without an Index, but is in good Order.

Book 10 commences 20th June 1715, and ends 19th December 1742.—Without an Index, and in many Places is illegible, from the Hand-writing.

From this Period the Records do not seem to have been properly kept until the 21st June 1757, but which might be supplied, as the greater Part of the Warrants appear to be extant.

Book 11 commences 21st June 1757, and ends 31st August 1769.—Has an Index, and is in good Order.

Book 12 commences 8th September 1769, and ends 6th January 1780.—Has an Index, and is in good Order.

Book 13 commences 19th January 1780, and ends 1st February 1790.—Has an Index, and is in good Order.

Book 14 commences 1st February 1790, continues down to the present Period, and is not yet completed.

2. The Sheriff Head Court Books:

Book 1 commences 6th October 1607, and ends 15th November 1617.—Is annexed to the Register of Bonds, marked N° 1. is without an Index, and in bad Order.

Book 2 commences 1636, and ends 1652.—Without an Index, and is much defaced.

6 Book

Book 3 commences 1667, and ends 1672.—Without an Index, and in many Places is quite illegible.

Book 4 commences 28th December 1674, and ends 24th April 1683.—Without an Index, but in other Refpects is in tolerable good Order.

Book 5 commences 25th May 1683, and ends 8th September 1696.—Without an Index, but otherwife is in good Order.

Book 6 commences 6th October 1696, and ends 25th December 1716.—Without an Index, but in other Refpects is in good Order.

Book 7 commences 14th January 1690, and ends 24th June 1735.—Without an Index, but in other Refpects is in good Order.

Book 8 commences 1ft July 1735, and ends 4th October 1757.—Without an Index, but is in tolerable good Order.

As before obferved, thefe Books, though intituled "Sheriffs Books," are appropriated not folely to recording the Decrees and Sentences of the Sheriff, but have been alfo ufed for recording the Minutes of the Freeholders at their Michaelmas Head Court, and other occafional Meetings, and for the Services of Heirs, expeded during the aforefaid Periods; for each of which Purpofes the prefent Sheriff Clerk, fince his Entry to Office, has been in the Ufe of keeping feparate Books, as will be afterwards noticed.

3. Sheriff Court Books:

Book 1 commences 18th January 1717, and ends 15th November 1753.—Without an Index, and is fcarcely legible in many Places, owing to the Badnefs of the Hand-writing.

4. Records of the Decrees and Sentences of the Sheriff:

Book 1 commences 26th April 1757, and ends 17th April 1764.—With an Index, and is in good Order.

Book 2 commences 30th September 1764, and ends 18th December 1770.—Has an Index, and is in good Order.

Book 3 commences 29th January 1771, and ends 14th November 1775.—With an Index, and is in good Order.

Book 4 commences 27th February 1776, and ends 30th November 1779.—With an Index, and is in good Order.

Book 5 commences 18th January 1780, and ends 31ft October 1786.—With an Index, and is in good Order.

Book 6 commences 9th January 1787, and ends 9th November 1790.—With an Index, and is in good Order.

When a full Copy of the Proceedings in an Action is given to any of the Parties, it is called an Extract. There are Record Copies of all thefe Extracts fince the laft-mentioned Period, and when they are bound up in a Book will make a Seventh Volume.

Only fuch Proceffes as the Parties get extracted are put upon Record, for which the Sheriff Clerk receives for his Trouble in fcrolling out the Decree, making a fair Copy for the Party wanting it, and another Copy for the Record only, at the Rate of 2*s.* 6*d.* for the Firft Sheet, which contains Two Pages, and each Page muft contain 36 Lines, and each Line Nine Words, and 1*s.* 6*d.* per Sheet for every other Sheet.

5. Diet Books of the Sheriff Court:

Book 1 commences 28th November 1738, and ends 27th November 1753.

Book 2 commences 25th March 1755, and ends 14th Auguft 1759.

Book 3 commences 28th Auguft 1759, and ends 7th May 1765.

Book 4 commences 11th February 1766, and ends 26th December 1775.

Book 5 commences 23d January 1776, and ends 18th June 1782.

Book 6 commences 25th June 1782, and ends 18th December 1787.

Book 7 commences 8th January 1788, and ends 24th December 1793.

Book 8 commences 14th January 1794, and ends 15th Auguft 1797.

Book 9 commences 22d Auguft 1797, and ends 24th December 1799.

Book 10 commences 7th January 1800, and is not yet completed.

None of thefe have an Index, nor is there perhaps any Ufe for it.

6. Regifter of Hornings, Inhibitions, &c.:

Book 1 commences 1623, and ends 1628.—Without an Index, is much torn and defaced, and generally illegible.

Book 2 commences 6th Auguft 1683, and ends 27th January 1770.—With an Index, and is in tolerable good Order.

Since that Period no Hornings have been regularly recorded; but as the Warrants are preferved, and in good Order, they could in a few Months be all properly booked.

7. Criminal Sederunt Book:

Book 1 commences 5th September 1758, and ends 24th May 1792.—Has no Index, but is in good Order.

Book 2 commences 14th Auguft 1792, continues down to this Period, and is not yet completed.

8. Records of Services of Heirs:

The only Book kept for the fole Purpofe commences 16th June 1763, and comes down to this Period, and is not yet completed.

9. Records of the Minutes of the Freeholders:

Book 1 commences 5th October 1757, and ends 1ft October 1783.

Book 2 commences 4th May 1784, and comes down to the prefent Period.—Not completed.

Some of the Minutes of the Freeholders, previous to the Year 1757, do not feem to be upon Record; but there are ftill extant loofe Scraps of Paper, on which for fome Time the original Minutes feem to have been written; and the reft, being the greater Part, are contained in the older Books above noticed, intituled, "Sheriff Court Books."

10. Minutes of the Commiffioners of Supply:

Book 1 commences 18th November 1680, and ends 23d July 1695.—Stitched in a Piece of Blue Paper, feems to be very defective at the Beginning, but in other Refpects is in good Order.

Book 2 commences 9th March 1696, and ends 2d June 1730.—Stitched in Blue Paper, but in good Order.

Book 3 commences June 1731, and ends 6th May 1747.—It confifts of a few Sheets of Paper ftitched together, of which feveral Leaves feem to be wanting, and the reft is in bad Order.

Book 4 commences 14th May 1747, and ends 14th Auguft 1753.—Confifts of a few Sheets of Paper, ftitched together, but is in good Order.

Book

SCOTLAND.
Sheriffs Courts.
Appendix (Y. 25.)

Book 5 commences 1st May 175., and ends 30th April 1768, and is in good Order.

Book 6 commences 29th April 1769, and ends 30th April 1784, and is in good Order.

Book 7 commences 1st June 1784, and ends 16th October 1798, and is in good Order.

Book 8 commences 30th April 1799, and comes down to this Period.—Not completed.

None of these Eight Volumes have an Index.

11. Proceedings of the Justices of Peace:

Book 1 commences 1656, ends 1727, and is very imperfect.

Book 2 commences 24th October 1758, and continues down to this Period, and is not completed.

These last-mentioned Sets of Books, viz. for the Commissioners of Supply, and the Justices of the Peace, are not any Part of the proper Records of the Sheriff Court; but the Sheriff Clerk being also Clerk to the Commissioners of Supply, and the Justices of Peace, keeps the Record of these Proceedings.

12. Sederunt Book relating to the Corn Act:

Commences 15th September 1791, and continues down to this Period.—Not completed.

Though the present Sheriff Clerk succeeded to the Office in the Year 1758, and though he did every Thing in his Power to get Possession of the old Records and Papers connected with the Sheriff Court, and even raised an Action for that Purpose against his Predecessor and his Depute, still he did not get Possession of them until after the Death of the Clerk Depute, which happened in the Year 1783, when his Family being about to remove from the House wherein he resided, and deeming these Records and Papers to be useless Lumber, sent them in an open Cart to the Sheriff Clerk's House in a State of the utmost Confusion, and which accounts for the Records and Papers being so much defaced and defective prior to the Year 1758.

(2.) The Building where the Records are kept is situated in the Town of Peebles. The Room in which they are so kept makes Part of the Dwelling House of the Sheriff Clerk, which though small is commodious enough for the Purpose, and the Records are in the same State of Security as the Furniture and Property in the said Dwelling House. The House is Private Property, and holds Burgage of the Town of Peebles.

(3. & 4.) The Sheriff Clerk begs leave to refer the Committee to his Answer to the First Question, which he trusts will prove so far satisfactory. In that Answer he has specified in what State of Preservation the said Records are: he has also therein pointed out such of them as have Indexes, and such of them as are defective in that Respect. As to the Second Part of Question Third, the Sheriff Clerk reports, that the Records are arranged in the same Order as mentioned before, and that the Warrants and Principal Papers being the Groundwork of Part of the said Records, are bundled up Year by Year, as they are recorded.

The completing of such of the Records as may be defective would certainly be attended with Utility, but to what Degree the Sheriff Clerk cannot presume to take upon him to say. However he is of Opinion, that it is next to an Impossibility that the said Records can be put into such a complete State as could be wished; for though in some Instances they might be made up from the Warrants which are extant, yet in general it would be impracticable, owing to the Antiquity of the Hand-writing, and the defaced and torn State of many of these Warrants. But should it appear to the Select Committee to be attended with any Utility to have such of them as are still legible, transcribed in a fair Hand, the Sheriff Clerk will most cheerfully and readily undertake to get it done with the quickest Dispatch, though he cannot possibly with any Degree of Accuracy say how long Time it would require to do so, and of course cannot estimate the Expense.

The Writings or Warrants which appear to the Sheriff Clerk the most necessary and useful to be immediately put upon Record, are those of Hornings, Inhibitions, &c. and which, by the ordinary Diligence of the Person usually employed in the Sheriff Clerk's Office, might be completed in the course of Six Months from this Date.

There are no Records, Catalogues, nor Indexes, appertaining to the said Office, existing elsewhere, according to the best of the Sheriff Clerk's Knowledge. Since he came to Peebles he has been informed that several of the antient Records have been applied to culinary and other Purposes; but as to the Certainty of the Fact he cannot positively say, though it appears probable that such Things might have happened, from the various Chasms that appear in the Records.

(5.) The Emoluments arising from the Sheriff Clerkship being but inconsiderable, not exceeding, Communibus Annis, from £.50. to £.60. per Annum, and the Circumstances of the Sheriff Clerk by no Means opulent, the only Officer or Clerk he has employed for the Custody and Arrangement of the Records for many Years is his Son, whose general Duty is directed not only to that but to every other Branch connected with the Sheriff Clerk's Office. His Office is open every Day (Sundays excepted) and at all Hours of the Day: he has no Annual Salary, Allowance, nor Emolument paid him by the Public in respect of the Custody of the said Records, &c. except what arises from the Dues paid to him for recording the Deeds, Decrees, or other Writings. He is allowed by the Person demanding the same, for every Search of the Records, &c. whereof he has the Custody, at the Rate of 6*d.* for each Year contained in the Volume searched, and 5*s.* for every Certificate specifying the Result of such Search. The Searches demanded, and Certificates granted, are so trifling, that the Sheriff Clerk's Net Annual Profits therefrom, upon an Average of the Three last Years, do not amount to above 30*s.* or 40*s.*

(6.) This is already answered in the foregoing, with this Addition, that it is the Duty of the Sheriff Clerk and his Depute to attend upon every Search, and to take Care that every Record, &c. be duly and safely restored to its proper Place.

Appendix (Y. 26.)

Return from the Sheriff Substitute of PERTHSHIRE, to the Questions of the Committee.

THE Public Records in this County, and I believe in the several Counties in Scotland, are under the special Charge and keeping of the Clerks of the several Courts, such as the Sheriff Clerk, the Clerk to the Peace, the Clerks of Royal Burghs, and the Clerks to the Commissaries.

The Sheriff Clerks, before the Heritable Jurisdictions were abolished in the Year 1748, were named by the Sheriff's Principal, and since that Time they have been appointed either directly by Government, or by an Officer

Officer to whom the Nomination is delegated by Government. There is no Salary attached to the Office, the Emoluments arising solely from the Table of Fees, as regulated by an Act of Sederunt of the Court of Session, 16th March 1748 *. That Table is strictly adhered to by the Sheriff Clerks in this County; and from the Lapse of Time, and the Difference in the Value of Money now, some of those Fees, particularly what regards recording Deeds, &c. are by no Means adequate to the Trouble occasioned to the Clerk, and the Responsibility attaching to him. If I might be permitted to state my Opinion on this Point, it would be, that the Fees for recording and issuing the Extract or Certified Copy, in place of 1*s.* 2½*d.* should be 2*s.* 4*d.* per Law Sheet, being 36 Lines on each of Two Pages, and Nine Words in each Line.

* See Page 452.

From the great Extent of this County, Sheriff Courts are held at Perth and Dunblane, at each of which Places Public Records are kept by the Sheriff Clerks, or their Deputies. The State of these Records will appear by Two Reports herewith transmitted, marked by me of this Date, as relative hereto. In these I think the several Questions stated in the Order of the Committee have been answered; and it only remains for me, in answering the Seventh Question, to say, that in my humble Opinion the Records are not in Safety in Private Houses, and are liable to Accidents, particularly by Fire, notwithstanding the great Care and Attention of the Clerks to prevent them.

The Burgh of Perth have lately, at the Expense of the Incorporation, built a House for their Records, Fire-proof, and the Honourable Committee will judge how far it may not be necessary to oblige the County also to have a Record House, and to lodge the Records in one Part of it, and the Principal Deeds in a separate Part, by which, if any Accident should happen to the one, the other might be resorted to.

The Commissaries of Dunblane and Dunkeld (both in this County) keep Records of Deeds, &c. the same as the Sheriff Clerk. It were to be wished that One Record for the County were established, because when a Search becomes necessary, it often occasions much Trouble and Inconvenience to find out the Court where the Paper wanted has been given in to be recorded. Whereas, if One Record for the County was established, the Search would be easy and certain. If then the Committee should be of Opinion, that a Record House for the County is necessary, it will remain with them to judge whether the whole Records detached in the different Offices should not be directed to be lodged there, and to be put under the Charge of the Sheriff Clerk.

James Chalmers,
Sheriff Substitute of Perthshire.

SIR,

I would have acknowledged the Receipt of the Order of the Committee of the House of Commons, of the 28th of February last, and furnished you with Answers to the several Questions contained in it sooner, had I not found it necessary to apply for Information from the Deputy Sheriff Clerk of the Western District of this County, with regard to the State of the Records there, which having now received, I beg leave, agreeably to your Directions, to answer the Questions in their Order, as follows:

(1.) The Records of Judicial Proceedings carried on before the Sheriff, comprehending Actions for Debt, Injury, and Trespass. The Records of Services of Heirs; of the Minutes of Freeholders; of Tutorial and Curatorial Inventories; of Acts of Curatory; of Deeds recorded in the Sheriff Court Books for Execution, Publication, or Preservation. The Record of the Commissions of Sheriffs Principal and Substitute, and of their qualifying to Government upon their being admitted to Office, and of the Acts, Orders, and Regulations of Court; of the Yearly Fiar Prices of Grain and Oatmeal; of the Monthly Prices of Grain, fixed by a Jury, for regulating the Importation and Exportation of Grain; the Record of the Accounts of Improvements on Entailed Estates; and the Record of Letters of Horning, Inhibition, and Interdiction, are all kept by me and Mr. James Murray, Joint Sheriff Clerks of this County.

The other Public Records of this County consist of the Minutes of the Justices of the Peace, and Commissioners of Supply, and the Judicial Procedures before them; the particular Register of Sasines, Reversions, &c. for this County, kept by William Ross, Writer in Perth; the Record of the Commissary Courts of Dunblane and Dunkeld, and the Royal Burghs of Perth and Culross, kept by the Clerks of those Courts.

Of the Judicial Procedures before the Sheriff Court, regular Books are kept, in which each separate Act of Judicial Procedure, in the various Pleas and Processes brought before it, is regularly though shortly entered of its Date. The Books of this Kind commence in 1543; are deficient from 1550 to 1552; from 1587 to 1590; from 1594 to 1602; from 1610 to 1613; from 1620 to 1652; and from February 1770 to June 1772; but for all other Years are complete to the present Time.

Regular Index or Minute Books are also kept of the final Decrees pronounced in this Court; the oldest bears Date 1676, and, with the Exception of the Minute Book from 1688 to 1700, which is wanting, are complete to this Date.

The Principal Decreets themselves in my Custody commence in 1700, and are continued to the present Time. They are regularly and carefully massed up in the Order of their Dates, and are in a good State of Preservation.

Services of Heirs:—The Record of the Services of Heirs composes the Claims of Persons requiring to be served Heirs to their Ancestors, with the Proceedings of the Jury of 15 Men, who pass upon them, and their Verdict; besides the Claims, with the Procedures on them, which are massed up in the Order of their Dates, the Extracts given out are regularly entered in Books kept for that Purpose. The Claims are extant from 1695 downwards to this Date. The Records in which the Extracts are entered commence in 1596, and, excepting from 1602 to 1652, which are wanting, are carried down to the present Day. All of them are in a good State of Preservation.

Record of the Minutes of Freeholders:—Commences in 1724, and is complete to the present Time.

Record of Acts appointing Curators to Minors:—Commences in 1597, and, excepting from 1694 to 1700, is complete to the present Time.

The Principal Papers are only to be found from February 1696 downwards.

Record of Tutorial and Curatorial Inventories:—Is complete from its Commencement in 1673 to the present Time; the Act appointing Tutorial and Curatorial Inventories to be made up and recorded having passed in 1672.

The Principal Papers are only to be found from 1696 downwards.

Record of Deeds:—The Principal Deeds given in to be recorded in the Sheriff Court Books for Preservation, Execution, or Publication, are in our Custody from 1661 to the present Time, with the Exception only of the Year 1668, which is wanting. They are carefully massed up in the Order of their Dates, and are in a good State of Preservation. The Registers of Recorded Deeds however commence in 1570, and are continued

SCOTLAND.
Sheriffs Courts.

Appendix (Y. 26)

to 1575. They are wanting from 1575 to 1652; but they are extant from 1652 nearly to the present Time, and what is wanting to complete them will be speedily supplied.

Minute Books or Indexes to these Records are complete from 1652 to the present Time; but from 1673 to 1688, and from 1703 to 1719, the Indexes are in very bad Order. They might be supplied at an Expense of about £.20.

Record of Commissions to Sheriffs, and Acts, Orders, and Regulations of Court:—Commences the 6th April 1748, and is carried down to this Day.

Record of the Yearly Fiar Prices of Grain:—Commences with the Crop and Year 1630, and is complete to the present Time.

Record of the Monthly Prices of Grain:—Commences 15th September 1791, and is complete to this Day.

Record of Hornings, Inhibitions, &c.:—Is transmitted from Time to Time by the proper Officer at Edinburgh, and returned to the same Officer when completed. The present Record commenced the 6th March 1794, and with its Minute Book has been since regularly filled up.

Record of Accounts of Improvements on Entailed Estates:—Is complete from September 1770, when it commenced, to the present Time.

(2.) The Papers and Records before mentioned are kept in a House situated in the Watergate of Perth, belonging in Property to and occupied by me James Paton. The Places fitted up for them are as commodious as Circumstances can admit of; but no Private Dwelling House can be considered as a fit Repository for Deeds and Records of such Moment, particularly as they are in no State of Security from Fire. The House is held by me in absolute Property by the Tenure of Burgage, or, in other Words, holden of the King in Perpetuity.

(3.) The original Papers, Registers, and the Minute or Index Books, are separately arranged in Order of Time, and, excepting as already noticed, are in a good State of Preservation.

(4.) This Question has already been answered in part. I can give no Account of the Papers that appear in the Registers previous to 1661: they never were in my Custody; and I can only suppose that some of them may have been lost in the Troubles that took place in this Country about the Time of the Revolution, or during the Rebellions in the Year 1715 and 1745. Perhaps also some of them may have been lost in changing them from one Private House to another, upon a Change of Clerks, by Death or otherwise. I never knew the Records placed any where else than in the House I occupy.

(5.) The Business of this Office is performed by the Principal Clerks, Two or more Deputies, and such a Number of Writing Clerks or Apprentices (commonly Five, and sometimes Six,) as Circumstances require. The said James Paton, or One of the Deputies, attends to the Arrangement of the Records and Papers, though this is sometimes also attended to by the Writing Clerks or Apprentices under their Inspection. No Salary is annexed to the Office. The Hours of Attendance are every lawful Day from Eight o'Clock in the Morning until Eight in the Evening. The Fees payable to the Principal Clerks are ascertained by an Act of Sederunt of the Court of Session in 1748, &c. * The Allowance made to the Principal Deputy has gentrally been a Fourth of the Emoluments, and the Allowance to Clerks and Apprentices has been such as Circumstances made necessary. The Fees arising from the principal Record, that of Deeds, including the Fees arising from the Records of Hornings and Inhibitions, of Fiars, of Acts of Curatory, and of Tutorial and Curatorial Inventories, amount upon an Average of Three Years to £.63. 9*s.* 4*d.* Had it been deemed necessary to have stated the Average Amount of the Total Fees and Emoluments arising to the Sheriff Clerk, including those not properly connected with the Records, it would have been here mentioned.

* See One Table for all the Sheriffs Returns, Page 452.

9

(6.) The Records are under the constant Care of the said James Paton, and the Principal Deputy and Clerks in the Office. The said James Paton, or One of the Deputies or Clerks, attends upon every Search that is made, and great Care is taken to return every Paper and Book to its proper Place, after the Search is completed.

Excepting the Principal Clerks and the Deputies, and the Writing Clerks and Apprentices, there is no other Denomination of Officers. While Suits are in dependance, Papers are delivered to Practitioners upon Receipt; but after Decree is finally pronounced, and extracted, the Papers are never allowed to be taken from the Records. Extracts are however given out when desired, on Payment of the Fees established by the Act of Sederunt before mentioned.

(7.) Knowing that you mean to suggest some Things for rendering the Records more secure and useful than they have hitherto been, I find it altogether unnecessary to suggest any Thing upon that Subject myself. I shall conclude with observing, that the Fees payable to the Sheriff Clerks were established Half a Century ago, in the course of which Time Money has decreased more than a Half; that there are many Pieces of Service to which no Fee is attached by Authority; and that though in some Instances the Fees in the Table may be deemed even yet adequate, those relating to the Recording and Extracting of Deeds are certainly not so; more especially now that Writing Clerks must be better paid than formerly, and that the Expense of Stationary has been nearly doubled within these last Ten Years. No Injury could possibly arise from the Court of Session being authorized to regulate the Fees of Sheriff Clerks, from Time to Time, as Necessity required; and it appears to be expedient and proper that an Act of Parliament should be passed for giving them this Authority.

All which is respectfully reported to the Sheriff of the County of Perth, by

James Paton.

The Report from the Clerk of the Western District of this County accompanies this.

Perth,
9th April 1800.

Perth, 10th April 1800.

This is the Report of Mr. James Paton, Joint Sheriff Clerk of Perthshire, relative to the Records kept at Perth, referred to in my Letter of this Date, in Answer to the Questions contained in the Order of the Committee on the Public Records of the Kingdom, of 28th February last, transmitted to the Sheriff of Perthshire.

James Chalmers,
Sheriff Substitute of Perthshire.

Anſwers by John Rob, Sheriff and Commiſſary Clerk Depute at DUNBLANE, to the Queſtions of the Select Committee on the Public Records, &c. of the Kingdom.

(1.) THERE are kept at Dunblane the Commiſſary Court Records, from the Year 1661 to the preſent Period, conſiſting of 16 Volumes Folio, wherein are recorded Confirmed Teſtaments only; and the Records of the ſaid Court, from 1669 alſo to the preſent Period, conſiſting of 38 Volumes Folio, wherein Bonds, Bills, Decreets, and other Deeds are recorded. Alſo the Minute Books of the ſaid Commiſſary Court, conſiſting of 27 Volumes Folio, ſome whereof, prior to the Period firſt above mentioned, were laid aſide as uſeleſs by James Ruſſell, Clerk of the ſaid Commiſſariot, upon his Admiſſion to the ſaid Office in Anno 1729. They are however ſtill preſerved, but are not legible.

Item, The Regiſter of the Court of Regality of Dunblane, from the Year 1698 to the Year 1747, about which Time Heritable Juriſdictions were aboliſhed, and conſiſting of Three Folio Volumes. It does not appear that any Record was kept of the Proceedings of this Court prior to the Period above mentioned; if they were, they are not now extant. In the Volume in my Poſſeſſion there are ingroſſed, beſides the Proceedings of the Court, Tranſumpts of the Writes of ſeveral Heritable Subjects lying in and about Dunblane.

Item, The Records of the Sheriff Court, held at Dunblane, wherein are recorded Bonds, Bills, and other Deeds, from the Year 1749 to the preſent Period, and conſiſting of Three Volumes, together with the ſeveral Proceſſes which have depended before the Commiſſary Court for 100 Years, and before the Sheriff Court, from the Period of its Eſtabliſhment in Anno 1748; and the Minute Books of the Sheriff Court from that Period, Eleven in Number.

(2.) The Building in which the above mentioned Records and Papers are kept is ſituated within Dunblane, and within that Part thereof called The Miln Row. They are kept in a Room of the Houſe there, which is occupied by me as a Dwelling Houſe, which Houſe is covered with Slate, and is in every Reſpect a ſafe and commodious Place for the Keeping of theſe Records. It is my Private Property, and has been uſed for the ſame Purpoſe by my Predeceſſors in Office for more than a Century paſt. I would however beg leave humbly to ſuggeſt, that it might be ſtill more ſafe to have a Room fitted up in an uninhabited Houſe, for the Purpoſe of keeping theſe Records, &c. and that Part of the Public Priſon might be appropriated to that Purpoſe.

(3.) The Books above mentioned, together with the Deeds, &c. therein recorded, are in the beſt State of Preſervation. The Books are numbered according to their Dates, and the Title on the Back mentions the Date of their Commencement, and the Period to which they are brought up. The Deeds, &c. are folded, the Date of their being recorded, with the Name of the Judge preſiding at the Time, marked on the Back, tied up in Bundles, according to their Dates of Recording, each Bundle containing the Deeds, &c. recorded in One Year, and put into Preſſes; which Preſſes are numbered, divided into Shelves, and the Shelves alſo numbered, and marked with the Year wherein the Incloſures were recorded.

(4.) There are Indexes annexed to each Volume, mentioning the Titles of the Papers therein recorded, and the Page of the Book wherein they are ingroſſed. I have not diſcovered many Miſtakes in theſe Indexes, but found a Difficulty ſometimes in finding the Paper wanted; I therefore began, and have nearly completed a General Catalogue or Liſt of the whole Papers recorded, with Columns annexed to the Title of each, ſhewing the Date of Recording, the Number of the Preſs and Shelf wherein the Papers are to be found, and the Number of the Volume wherein they are recorded. I have alſo carried on, from the Year 1795 (the Period at which I came into Office) an Alphabetical Liſt of the Purſuer's and Defender's Names in each Proceſs before both Courts, with Two Columns annexed; the Firſt ſhewing the Date of Calling in Court, and the Second the Date of Diſcerning or Aſſoilzying. By theſe Means and Methods I can eaſily lay my Hands upon any Paper or Proceſs wanted in a very ſhort Time, and I do not know of any eaſier Method that could be deviſed. The Books, Indexes, Papers, and Catalogues, are wholly in my Office, and I do not know of any that are wanting.

(5.) The Records and Papers are entirely under my Charge, and there are Two Clerks employed in my Office, who write Extracts of ſuch Papers as are wanted. It is the Buſineſs of One of theſe to fill up the Record, that is, to inſert therein ſuch Papers as are given in for the Purpoſe of being recorded. They attend from Seven in the Morning until Eight in the Evening, allowing Two Hours for Breakfaſt and Dinner; but when Occaſion requires, they are employed at all Hours of the Night as well as the Day.

The Fees are 14½*d.* for each Law Sheet of Extracts, as ſettled by the Lords of Council and Seſſion, in Anno 1748, being 1*s.* each Sheet to me, and 2½*d.* to my Clerk for ingroſſing the ſame in the Record, and for writing out the Extract; and theſe Fees, beſides the Stamp Duty of 1*s.* for each Sheet of Paper whereon the Extracts are written, and beſides which Fees of 14½*d.* per Law Sheet, I, my Conſtituents, and Clerks, have no Salary or other Emolument. The Proportion above mentioned of 1*s.* for each Sheet of Extracts from the Records of the Sheriff Court, is divided equally betwixt my Conſtituent, the Sheriff Clerk at Perth, and me, and amount on an Average of the laſt Three Years to £.15. Sterling; and that of the Commiſſary Court is divided in the following Proportions; viz. Two-Third Parts thereof to the Commiſſary, and the other Third Part to the Principal Clerk; and from which Third Part I have an Allowance of Eight Guineas Yearly, and which, with One Half of the Sheriff Clerk's Fees above mentioned, is my Allowance for making Searches, having the Cuſtody of the Records, and all other Trouble attending that Buſineſs. The Commiſſary and Principal Clerk's Proportion of theſe Fees amount on an Average of the laſt Three Years to £.30. excluſive of the Fees of Court.

(6.) As mentioned above, the Books of Record, and Papers therein ingroſſed, are wholly under my Charge; and it is my Duty to attend upon any Search, and to take Care that every Record, &c. be duly and ſafely reſtored to its proper Place.

(7.) I am not ſenſible that there are any Matters, not comprized in the preceding Anſwers, which it might be neceſſary or expedient to obſerve for rendering the Uſe of theſe Records, &c. more convenient to the Public than they are at preſent. The Deeds recorded relate chiefly to Matters or Things pertaining to Perſons reſident in or connected with that Diſtrict of Country wherein they are ſituated; and it is more convenient for thoſe Perſons to have Recourſe to the Records where they are preſently kept, than if they were removed to any Place of greater Diſtance.

John Rob.

Dunblane,
2d April 1800.

Perth,

SCOTLAND.
Sheriffs Courts.
Appendix (Y. 27.)

Perth, 10th April 1800.

This is the Report of Mr. John Rob, Sheriff Clerk Depute at Dunblane, relative to the Records kept there, referred to in my Letter of this Date, in Answer to the Questions contained in the Order of the Committee on the Public Records of the Kingdom, of 28th February last, transmitted to the Sheriff of Perthshire.

James Chalmers,
Sheriff Substitute of Perthshire.

Appendix (Y. 27.)

Return by the Sheriff of RENFREWSHIRE, to the Questions of the Committee.

(1.) BY the Constitution of Sheriff Courts in Scotland, the Public Records of Court are kept in the Custody of the Sheriff Clerk, and the Place where they are kept is called "The Sheriff Clerk's Office." The Records in the Custody of the Sheriff Clerk of Renfrewshire are not entire, or in a regular State of Arrangement, farther back than the Year 1748. By the Act of that Year, abolishing the Heritable Sheriffships, and other Heritable Jurisdictions in Scotland, and vesting the Judicial and Ministerial Powers of the Office of Sheriff in Sheriffs Depute, named by the Crown, the Nomination of the Sheriff Clerks was likeways resumed by the Crown; and the former Sheriff Clerks, as well as the Clerks of the abolished Jurisdictions of Regality (to whom Compensation was made by Government) were directed to deliver over the Records in their Custody to the new Sheriff Clerks; but from some Cause, which cannot now be accounted for, probably owing to former Irregularity, and the Difficulty of giving and receiving them upon Inventory, it would appear that the old Records had not been fully or in any regular Order transferred into the Possession of the Sheriff Clerk appointed at that Time.

The Records since the Year 1748, are as follow:

1. The Judicial Proceedings of the Sheriff Court are composed of the written Warrants, Pleadings, Acts, and Decrees, relative to the different Suits brought before the Court. The Papers belonging to each Suit are called "A Process." These Processes are carefully tied up in Bundles, arranged regularly according to their Dates.

2. Certain Books, in which the various Judicial Steps in Civil Suits are shortly inserted at the Time in progressive Order. These Books, termed "Act Books," consist of 16 Volumes Folio, with One Volume previous to that Period, commencing in 1739, and ending in 1747.

3. The Record of Proceedings in Trials by Jury before the Sheriff in Criminal Causes, 3 Volumes.

4. Principal Deeds, Contracts, Bonds, and Instruments of Protest of Bills, given in to be registered in the Sheriff Court Books, as the Ground of legal Diligence, and for Preservation. A full certified Copy, called "An Extract," containing a Decree and Precept (by legal Fiction) authorizing Diligence and Distress of Goods in the Sheriff's Name, being given out under the Official Signature of the Sheriff Clerk, and the Principal Writing retained. These are carefully tied up in Bundles, according to the Date of presenting, and are arranged in regular Order.

5. The Record Copy of those Deeds, &c. complete from the Year 1785 (the Date of the Appointment of the present Sheriff Clerk) down to the last Year, but not yet bound up in Volumes. For the Period previous to the Appointment of the present Clerk, this Part of the Record is incomplete.

6. The Record of Probative Writs; that is, of such Writings as cannot be recorded for Diligence and Execution from Want of the Conventional Agreement and Consent of Parties, expressed in a particular Clause in the Deed, termed the Clause of "Registration," or from Want of legal Solemnities, but which, by Special Statute, admit of being recorded, and Extracts thereof to bear Faith, as the Means of Probation, the Principal Writing being returned to the Party, and docketed by the Sheriff Clerk.

7. The Record of the Proceedings of the Freeholders of the County in the Michaelmas Head Courts, and Meetings for Election of the County Representative in Parliament, 6 Volumes.

8. The Record Book of Hornings, Inhibitions, and Interdictions; that is, of Writs which are issued against the Lands, &c. of Debtors within the County. This Book is given out to the Clerk, blank, from the Lord Register's Office at Edinburgh, superscribed on the Leaves by One of his Lordship's Deputies, and again returned to that Office when filled up; a Fee being paid by the Sheriff Clerk to the Lord Register for every new Book.

9. The Record of the Fiar Prices of Grain of the County, between Christmas and Candlemas, struck Annually by the Sheriff and a Jury, 2 Volumes.

10. The Record of the Prices of Grain, struck formerly Quarterly, now Monthly, for regulating the Exportation and Importation of Corn, 2 Volumes, bound up. The Remainder goes on progressively, and is not yet bound.

11. The Record of Vouchers of Improvements on Entailed Estates, in Terms of the Act 10 George III. 1 Volume.

12. The Record of Certificates issued with respect to the killing of Game; of stamped Memorandums and Licenses; and Certificates of Practitioners before the Sheriff Court.

(2.) Until within these last Seven Years, those Records (as is still the Case in almost all the Counties in Scotland) were kept in the Sheriff Clerk's House, or in hired Apartments, at his Expense, subject to every contingent Risk, and to the destructive Consequences of frequent Removal, or of not being regularly transferred upon the Death of the Person in Possession. Now they are deposited in a handsome Stone Building, situated in the new Town of Paisley (the Seat of the Sheriff Court) erected about Seven Years ago by the County: it consists of Two Apartments allotted for the Office of the Sheriff Clerk, arched with Brick, and paved with Stone; two vaulted Apartments underneath intended for containing Records, but not yet finished, and which may probably be found too damp for the Purpose. Above the Sheriff Clerk's Office a Room is kept for the Meetings of County Committees; and above that another Room, at present occupied as an Office by the Collector of the Land Tax.

Much Praise is due to the Landholders of the County of Renfrew, at whose Expense this useful Edifice has been erected; but it is to be regretted that its Dimensions are much too small to answer long the Purposes of a Deposit of Public Records constantly increasing.

(3.) The Records in this Office, as above enumerated, are in a good State of Preservation, deposited in Presses and Recesses in the vaulted Apartments allotted to the Sheriff Clerk, and arranged in the Order above mentioned.

(4.) Separate Catalogues or Indexes are not in use. The Act Books of the Court serve as an Index to all the Judicial Processes and Decrees. The Books are titled and dated on the Back, and every Bundle of Writings is wrapped up in coarse Paper, and has a Label affixed, denoting the Period to which it belongs.

The

The only Part of the Records which it occurs there might be particular Utility in rendering more complete is, that which respects the Register of Bonds, Contracts, and Deeds. To complete these from the Year 1748, at which Date, as already stated, the regular Collection of Papers commences, down to the Year 1785, from which last Date the Record Copy is nearly brought up, it is estimated by the Sheriff Clerk, might cost from £.30. to £.40. Sterling.

The Utility would consist in the additional Security to the Public, by having a Duplicate of each Paper recorded in a Book, and by the superior Advantage of those Books, in point of Preservation, over the Writings themselves against the Decay of Time; but with regard to Accidents by Fire, if the Deeds and the Books are kept in an insecure Place, and in the same Apartment, the Danger must be the same.

The recording of the Extracts of Decrees; that is, the keeping a Duplicate of the whole Papers, Written Debate, Proof, Interlocutory Proceedings, and final Judgment in the Cause, has gone into disuse in this, and it is believed in all the other Courts in Scotland, excepting the Supreme Civil Court, owing to the Introduction of the Practice of giving out short Precepts, for the Purpose of Execution, in place of full Extracts, which has been found of superior Advantage to the Public, from the Dispatch and Facility thereby afforded in the recovering of Debts. To bring up this Part of the Records from the Year 1748, would be attended with incalculable Labour and Expense; while the Utility does not appear very obvious, the Decrees of the inferior Court not comprehending Declaratory Rights concerning Heritable Property, like those of the Supreme Court, but being confined chiefly to Matters of Debt, which in general are either recovered or found to be ultimately bad.

But whatever Utility might arise from bringing up the Records of the Sheriff Courts, the Remedy would be incomplete unless extended to the Records of the same Kind in the Commissary Courts, and in the Court of every Royal Burgh in Scotland, which in the Aggregate would be found to comprehend perhaps a more extensive Collection than that of the Sheriff Courts.

(5.) The Business of the Sheriff Clerk's Office is conducted by the Sheriff Clerk, or his Deputy, and Two young Men under him. The Principal Clerk is appointed by the Keeper of His Majesty's Signet. The Hours of Attendance are from Eight o'Clock in the Morning until Eight o'Clock at Night daily.

The Duty of the Sheriff Clerk is to write the Proceedings in the Sheriff's Court, and in all the other Departments of the Sheriff's Official Duty; to record and give out Extracts of recorded Writings, and of the Judicial Proceedings of the Court on Precepts upon these; to arrange and keep in due Order the Records of the Court, and to give Inspection of them to all Parties concerned.

The Fees of the Sheriff Clerks in Scotland are stated in the Tables fixed in consequence of the Act 20 Geo. III. c. 43. p. 40. by an Act of Sederunt of the Lords of Council and Session, 16th March 1748, with regard to Civil Causes and Matters; and by an Act of Adjournal of the Court of Justiciary with regard to Criminal Causes. A Copy of this Table of Fees is annexed to the Report of the Sheriff of Aberdeen *.

* See Page 452.

There is no Provision made by the Tables for Fees of searching and giving Inspection of Records. The Sheriff Clerk has no Salary or Emoluments from Government other than the regulated Fees arising from Proceedings in the Discovery or Prosecution of Public Delinquencies before the Sheriff.

(6. & 7.) Upon these nothing farther occurs than has been stated in the course of the preceding Answers.

The Return of

John Connell,
Sheriff of Renfrewshire.

Edinburgh,
19th May 1800.

Appendix to the above Return:

The Emoluments of the Sheriff Clerk, upon an Average of the Three last Years, are estimated by him at £.200. per Annum.

John Connell.

Edinburgh,
7th June 1800.

Appendix (Y. 28.)

Return by the Sheriffs Depute of ROSS-SHIRE, to the Questions of the Committee.

THE County Records in Scotland are not placed in the Custody, or under the Charge of the Sheriffs, but are in the Possession and Care of a Public Officer, denominated The Sheriff Clerk, whose Appointment does not rest with the Sheriffs, and who, in the general Discharge of his Duty (particularly that Part which respects the Records) is entirely independant of the Sheriffs, and, so far as understood, beyond his Controul. From this Statement, the Committee will perceive that the Sheriff could not, from his own proper Knowledge, give satisfactory Answers to the Questions proposed to him by them. He, however, to save them Time and Trouble, has made Application to the Person who holds the Office of Sheriff Clerk within the County of Ross, for the best Information he could give, and for that Purpose transmitted to him the Questions sent to himself, and now transmits his Letter to the Sheriff in answer, which he must acknowledge is neither so full, satisfactory, nor explicit, as he could have wished. He will, however, subjoin some Observations which may tend to elucidate the Subject, without pretending to be able to give explicit Answers to the several Questions proposed.

The great and General Record, wherein all Deeds, whereby Property is mortgaged or transferred, are inserted, whether by Heritable Bond, Disposition, or Charter, with the Sasines or Infeftments following thereon, is kept at Edinburgh, in a Building appropriated for the Purpose, called The Register Office. From thence Blank Books are issued to Deputy Keepers in the several Districts of Scotland, wherein all Infeftments within the District must be inscribed, within a Time limited by Law, from the passing such Infeftment; and when the Book is filled up, it is returned to Edinburgh, to be lodged in the General Register. The Deputy for the District to which this County is annexed, resides and has his Office at Inverness. There is no House appropriated for the Purpose of keeping and preserving the Records of the County within this Shire, nor is it common to have a House for the Purpose in any of the other Counties, so far as has come under the Sheriff of Ross's Observation; although it doubtless would be attended with much Public Benefit, that a Building for the Purpose should be erected in every County, and put under the Care and Management of a Person who has made the Custody and Arrangement of the various Records his chief Employment. Of the several Records which happen to be kept within the County, and are not transmitted to the General Register at Edinburgh, the most important, as stated in the Sheriff Clerk's Letter, are,

 1. The

SCOTLAND.
Sheriffs Courts.
Appendix (Y. 28.)

1. The Record of the Proceedings of the Freeholders, which enregisters the States of their Roll of Voters for a Member of Parliament, and of the Alterations which take place in it. The Proceedings on all Elections of Knights of the Shire, so far as the Freeholders are concerned, and upon all contested Votes, or whatever regards such Elections.

2. The Record of all Bonds, or Personal Securities for Debt, of all Deeds of Settlement within the County, of all Deeds on Bargains, or Transactions of Business, whether intended for the Purpose that Execution or the Diligence of the Law should follow on them, or recorded simply for Preservation.

3. The Record of the Proceedings for securing the Property of Minors, and ascertaining the Steps taken by their legal or appointed Guardians.

4. The Record of all Proceedings under the Acts of Parliament, which authorize the Improvement of Entailed Estates, under certain Regulations, Limitations, and Restrictions, which is enacted to be kept in the Sheriff Clerk's Office.

5. The Record of all Law Suits, whether instituted by Civil Action, or on Criminal Complaint in the Sheriff's Court, wherein nearly all Questions which occur within the County (excepting only such as respect the Property of Land) are heard and determined in the first Instance.

6. The Record of Submissions, and Decrees Arbitral, or Awards following on them, which may either be recorded in the County Registers, or transmitted to the General Register at Edinburgh.

In case it should occur to the Wisdom of Parliament, that a Building for the Preservation of the Public Records should be erected in each County, wherein they could be kept with Safety, and regularly arranged; such Building for the County of Ross should be erected within the Burgh of Tain, where the Sheriff Depute's Court meets, where the Principal Sheriff Clerk resides, where the Freeholders Court uniformly meets, and which is the Head Burgh of the County of Ross.

The Sheriff Clerk, as already stated, is the legal Custodier of all the County Records, for which he has no Salary or Allowance, other than some few Perquisites for Attendance on the Freeholders Court, and keeping their Record. The Dues of Extract, for such Papers as may be required to be extracted, and his Fees of Office as Clerk to the Sheriff Court, in all Cases which are brought there for Determination, must depend in the Business brought before the Court, or the Spirit of Litigation amongst the People.

It would certainly be attended with the most salutary and beneficial Effects, if there were a Public Building in each County, for the Preservation of their Records; and that some small Salary adequate to the Trouble should be annexed to the Office of Keeper of these Records, who should be obliged to arrange them in a regular and orderly Manner in such Building, so as that easy Access could be had for the Inspection of any Recorded Deed or Decree, and Extracts could be obtained at the shortest possible Notice. How this is to be accomplished, the Sheriff of Ross will not even presume to hint, satisfied that the Business is in the best possible Hands for experiencing its Utility and Necessity; and that it will finally appear to them, that the Execution of such a Measure would be attended with the most singular Advantages to the Kingdom in general, as well as to Individuals.

All which is humbly submitted to the Honourable Committee, with the Letter referred to, and herewith transmitted by

Don^d M. Leod,
Sheriff Depute of Ross and Cromarty.

Geanies House, near Tain,
29th March 1800.

Tain, 26th March 1800.

SIR,

Mr. Barclay delivered to me Yesterday the Order of the Select Committee on the Public Records, &c. of the Kingdom, transmitted to you by CHARLES ABBOT, Esq; Chairman, and intimating a Wish from you that I should this Day give you Answers, so far as I was able, to the several Questions it contains with which I am acquainted; and this I shall endeavour to do as far as the Time allowed will admit, without entering into the Propriety of having a proper Place for keeping the Records, of which you are the best Judge. One Thing I am pretty certain of, that few Counties in Scotland are so apt to suffer, and very likely many Individuals in it may suffer, from the Want of it. The Places where Records are kept are so many, and the different Gifts of the Office of Sheriff Clerk have for Years back been so numerous, and the Deputations and Substitutions falling of course into so many Hands, that I am apprehensive a Life of much longer Duration than I can expect mine to be, were I to live to a good old Age, would not be sufficient to collect them together, and put them in proper Order, were they all to be found; and the only Thing that occurs to me for their Preservation in Time to come is, the House of Commons directing the Measure, that the Deputes and Substitutes in all Parts of the Country, should be obliged, within a limited Time, to lodge in the Office of the Principal Clerk, all the Books and Records in their Possession, to be deposited in the Place appropriate for keeping them. I hope you will excuse my mentioning this, because I know, at least with respect to getting the Records together, and putting them in Order, that Measure is necessary.

(1.) The several Sorts of Public Records are, The Record of the Freeholders; the Record of all Deeds and Settlements, and of all Transactions in the Country where the Parties either wish Execution to follow, or to be kept for Preservation; the Record of the Effects of all Minors, and the Record of all Suits and Pleas before the Sheriff's Court.

N. B. The Register of Inhibitions belongs properly to the General Register at Edinburgh.

(2.) There is no Building where the Records are kept, but they are carried by the Sheriff Clerk, his Deputes, and Substitutes, as they happen to succeed into Office, into whatever House they reside, and removed from one to another without Order or Regularity, sometimes once a Year, the Tenure by which they hold their Houses generally for that Period, being Private Property.

(3.) From what has been already said, it will be understood that the Records are in no good State of Preservation; and that, except very late Occurrences, they are not and could not be arranged in any Order.

(4.) Except in the Record of Pleas before the Sheriff's Court, there are no Catalogues, Indexes, &c. for the Reasons already mentioned. For answering the Remainder of this Question, the Sheriff, from what has been already said, is the only Judge.

(5.) The Sheriff Clerk is the Keeper of the Records with his Assistance, and is obliged to attend every lawful Day, from Ten in the Morning until Eight at Night. The Fees attending this Part of the Duty cannot be ascertained at present, and their Amount depends intirely upon the Length of the Deed required, and the Distance of Time of its being recorded.

I would be more explicit were I writing to any other; and

and as far as is neceſſary for you, I have already hinted at the Sixth and Seventh Queſtions. And am,

SIR,

Your moſt obedient humble Servant,

Tho. Suter.

Appendix (Y. 29.)

Return by the Sheriff Clerk of the County of ROXBURGH, to the Queſtions of the Committee.

(1.) THE Records kept in the Sheriff Clerk's Office of the County of Roxburgh, are,

1. A Record of Hornings, Inhibitions, Relaxations, Interdictions, &c. The Book now on Hand commences the 1ſt Day of May 1795, and contains 529 Leaves, the firſt and laſt Leaf are ſigned by Mr. James Farrier, Clerk to the Signet, having Commiſſion for that Effect from the Lord Clerk Regiſter, and each Tenth Leaf by Alexander Robertſon, Keeper of the Records in His Majeſty's General Regiſter Houſe, and every other Leaf marked with the initial Letters of Mr. Robertſon's Name. That Record is at this Date full, from the Beginning to the Leaf 342, and when completed it will be returned to the General Regiſter Office at Edinburgh, where all thoſe of the ſame Kind for the County of Roxburgh, prior to the 1ſt of May 1795, are preſerved.

2. A Record of Diſpoſitions, Aſſignations, Laſt Wills and Teſtaments, Contracts, Submiſſions, and Decree Arbitrals, Articles, and Minutes of Sales, Bonds, Proteſts of Bills and Promiſſory Notes, Diſcharges, Renunciations, Factories, Commiſſions, &c.; of all which, Extracts or authenticated Copies are given out and ſubſcribed by the Clerk, and the Principal Deed or Writing preſerved as a Record, with a regular Marking on the Back of the Date, of its being recorded, and of the Name of the Procurator or Agent who preſents the ſame, and of the Sheriff Depute for the Time being.

3. A Record of all the Proceſſes, Actions, and Queſtions, which are ſued and determined before the Sheriff Court.

4. A Record in conſequence of the Act of Parliament, 10 George III. cap. 51. intituled, "An Act to "encourage the Improvement of Lands, Tenements, "Hereditaments, in that Part of Great Britain called "Scotland, held under Settlements of ſtrict Entail." Which Record contains the Notices given by the Perſon in Poſſeſſion to the next Heir of Entail of the intended Buildings and Improvements, and afterwards the Particulars of the Expenſe of ſuch Buildings and Improvements, as they occur.

5. A Record of the Freeholders of the County, containing all their Proceedings at the Michaelmas Head Courts on the Firſt Tueſday of October, every Year, for adjuſting the Election Roll; of all Claims for Inrolment; and of the Minutes of the ſeveral Meetings and Elections.

6. A Record of the Game Certificates of Qualification to kill Game, and of Deputations to Game Keepers Annually.

7. A Record of the Procurators, who take their Annual Licenſe to practiſe.

(2.) The Building where the before-mentioned Records are lodged and kept, is the Property in Fee Simple of James Potts, is ſituated in the Town of Jedburgh, in an Area behind, and detached from his Dwelling Houſe. It is covered with Tile, and the Proprietor intends to cover it with Blue Slate, in place of the Tile, in the courſe of this Summer. In point of Situation it is as ſecure from Fire and Flood as any Building of the Kind can be. The Proprietor receives no Rent or other Allowance on Account of the Office, neither does he receive any Allowance for Record Books.

(3.) Prior to the Month of January 1746, when the late Thomas Potts, Father of the aforeſaid James Potts, was appointed to the Office of Sheriff Clerk, the Five Records firſt mentioned were not kept in regular Order, but ſince that Time they are recorded in Books kept for the Purpoſe, and the Writings themſelves are bundled regularly, Monthly, and Annually, and continue to be kept ſo.

(4.) From January 1746 there are complete and correct Catalogues or Indexes of all the Writings recorded; and before that Period it would be impracticable to make them ſo complete, as many of them are loſt.

(5.) There is no Officer or Clerk employed ſpecially for the Cuſtody or Arrangement of the Records. The Sheriff Clerk receives no Salary, Allowance, or Emolument from the Public, for making up and keeping the Records, or any of them. He pays the Clerks whom he employs to aſſiſt him in carrying on the Buſineſs of his Office in general, and his own Fees are regulated and fixed by the Act of Sederunt, 16th March 1748, following, upon the Act 20 George II. cap. 50. and never have been increaſed. Attendance is always given in the Office from Nine in the Morning until Eight at Night, on all lawful Days, and, when neceſſary, at all Times. The Annual Amount of what ariſes from Searches and Certificates of the Records, is ſo inſignificant that no ſeparate Account is kept or can be given of it.

(6.) The foregoing Anſwer applies to it.

(7.) Regarding the Records, James Potts can point out no Method more expedient or advantageous to the Public than the Mode adopted in this Office ſince 1746. The Lord Clerk Regiſter, or his Deputes, are paid by the Sheriff Clerks for the Regiſters of Hornings, &c. at the Time they are iſſued. The preſent Record coſt £.6. 15*s.* 6*d.*

Ja. Potts.

Roxburghſhire,
Sheriff Clerk's Office, Jedburgh,
May 21, 1800.

Appendix (Y. 30.)

Return from the Sheriff Clerk of SELKIRKSHIRE, to the Queſtions of the Committee.

IN anſwer to the Letter addreſſed to our Sheriff, reſpecting the Public Records, I have ſubjoined a State of thoſe kept by me in this County as Sheriff Clerk:

(1.) Record of Hornings, Inhibitions, and Interdictions: this Record was begun upon the 10th of November 1729, and has ever ſince been regularly kept in a Book delivered to the Sheriff Clerk of the County, at that Time, by the Earl of Marchmont, Lord Clerk Regiſter. This Record is in perfect Preſervation: it conſiſts of 427 Leaves, 421 of which are filled up.

(2.) Record of Bonds, Teſtaments, and other Deeds of Conſequence, with Proteſts of Bills. This Record is

SCOTLAND. Sheriffs Courts.

Appendix (Y. 30.)

is partly kept in a Book; but upon Inſpection, it appears that the Record is not complete, from the Clerks in former Times having neglected to regiſter the different Papers at the Time they were preſented.

(3.) The Emoluments ariſing to me, as Sheriff Clerk, for keeping theſe Records, are merely trifling; there is no Salary annexed to the Office of Sheriff Clerk; and at an Average of Three Years laſt paſt, my Profits have not exceeded Two Pounds Sterling Annually, for the Deeds, Hornings, Inhibitions, &c. entered in the above Record. From the Smallneſs of this County, and the Clerk's Profits ariſing from trifling Fees only, the Office of Sheriff Clerk in Selkirkſhire, is not worth more than Eight or Ten Pounds Yearly.

(4.) There are no other Public Records, except the above, kept by me as Sheriff Clerk. They are kept in my Office in my Dwelling Houſe, ſituate in the Middle of the Town of Selkirk, a ſlated Building my own Property, but ſurrounded by thatched Buildings on every Side.

(5.) If any Explanation or further Information is wanted, it will be dutifully and reſpectfully given by

John Lang,
Sheriff Clerk.

Appendix (Y. 31.)

Return by the Sheriff Clerk Depute of Stirlingshire, to the Queſtions of the Committee.

(1.) THE ſeveral Sorts of Public Records of the ſaid Shire, lie in the Cuſtody of the Sheriff Clerk, and comprehend the Regiſters of Bonds, Diſpoſitions, Aſſignations, Tacks, Bills, Probative Writs, &c. together with the Court Books, which contain the Minutes and periodical Progreſs of Proceſſes, from their Commencement to their Concluſion. The principal Papers recorded and Proceſſes alſo remain with the Clerk, excepting the Probative Writs, which are returned to the Parties on their Receipt, and none of theſe Records is more antient than the Year 1633.

(2.) The Building in which theſe Records are lodged, is a Room ſituated in a Cloſe on the North Side of the High Street of Stirling, Head Burgh of the Shire, and belongs in Property to the Sheriff Clerk.

(3.) The ſaid Records are in a tolerable State of Preſervation, and arranged in pretty decent Order.

(4.) Every Record has its own Index.

(5.) The only Officers or Clerks employed for the Cuſtody and Arrangement of theſe Records are, the Sheriff Clerk, his Depute, and an Apprentice or Two, that may happen to be in the Office. Their Attendance is conſtant, for they are obliged to anſwer at all Hours; and their Fees are the ſame with the Fees of the other Sheriff Clerks in Scotland, as regulated by an Act of Sederunt of the Court of Seſſion; which Fees are paid by thoſe who get Extracts of Papers. There is no Salary annexed to the Office, and the whole Emoluments may amount to about One Hundred Pounds Sterling per Annum.

(6.) There is no Perſon ſpecially intruſted with the Care of the ſaid Records, except the Sheriff Clerk himſelf; but every Perſon in the Office is as careful of them as poſſible.

(7.) It is believed that the foregoing Facts contain Anſwers to the ſeveral Queſtions of the Select Committee; and nothing occurs for making the ſaid Records convenient to the Public.

Alex. Dow,
Sheriff Clerk Depute.

Appendix (Y. 32.)

Return from the Sheriff Subſtitute of Sutherlandshire, to the Queſtions of the Committee.

IN anſwer to the ſeveral Queſtions relative to the Public Records of the ſaid County, I have in general to obſerve, that as Sheriff, there are no Records, Rolls, or any other Manuſcript Books or Papers, in my Cuſtody. But as I have ſeen Letters directed to the Sheriff Clerk of the County, with a Reference to the Letter and Queries directed for and put to me, I would, for him, as in the Knowledge of every Particular in which he can anſwer theſe Queſtions, ſay,

In anſwer to the Firſt Queſtion—That the Records are ſuch only as are connected with the Sheriff Court; and which are compoſed of the ſeveral Proceſſes carried on before the Sheriff Court, of which he, the Clerk, gives Extracts; for which he is paid according to the Regulations laid down by the Court of Seſſion: and, added to this Proceſs Record, he has a Book of Records, wherein Hornings, Inhibitions, Interdicts, &c. are recorded, and from which he gives Extracts, when demanded.

(2.) Theſe Records are kept in a Room, ſeparate for the Purpoſe, in the Town or Court Houſe of the Burgh of Dornoch, Head Burgh of the County, within which Burgh the Clerk reſides; and which Houſe and Room are in good Condition, both as to Security, Safety, and Accommodation, and is the Public Property of the County and Burghs; the Sheriff and Commiſſary Courts being held in it as well as Burgh Courts.

(3.) The Records referred to are in a State of perfect Preſervation, and arranged in Parcels for each of the Years which they reſpect: and an Index kept of the Record of Hornings, &c. leading to the Period and Page of the Book on which the Hornings, &c. are written.

(4.) No Catalogues, Calendars, or Schedules kept; nor does it appear that any Degree of Utility would reſult from the ſame being kept.

(5.) The Sheriff and Commiſſary Clerks are the only Perſons employed for the Cuſtody and Arrangement of the Records alluded to; have no particular Days or Hours for Attendance, they being at Hand when officially called to perform any of the Branches of their Office; have no Salaries affixed to their Office, other than the Fee allowed by Special Regulation, as ſaid is, for each Search, Certificate, or Extract, they may make or give, and which will appear from a Copy of theſe Regulations*. * See Page 452.

(6.) There are no other Perſons whatever intruſted with the Care of the ſaid Records, &c. but thoſe already mentioned.

(7.) Hitherto nothing appears neceſſary or expedient to be obſerved for rendering the Uſe of the ſaid Records more

SCOTLAND. Sheriffs Courts. Appendix (Y. 33.)

more convenient for the Public, than what already applies to the Exercise and Duty of the Clerks.

I have the Honour to be, with all due Respect,

Hugh M'Culloch,
Sheriff Substitute of Sutherland, N. B.

Dornoch,
16 June 1800.

Appendix (Y. 33.)

Return by the Sheriff Substitute of WIGTOWNSHIRE, to the Questions of the Committee.

THE Sheriff has not the Custody of any of the Records of the County; these are intrusted to the Care of the Sheriff Clerk, an Officer appointed by the Keeper of His Majesty's Signet; and the Duties of the Office here are performed by a Deputy appointed by the Principal Clerk, who is paid by him for his Trouble.

(1.) The several Sorts of Public Records in his Custody are, of Processes or Actions for Debts, &c. commencing 1700: Minute Books, containing Roll of Causes moved each Court Day, and the Steps of Procedure in each of them, commencing 1769: Of Dispositions to Property, Contracts, Assignations, &c. commencing 1690: Of Services of Heirs, claiming the Property of their Predecessors, &c. commencing 1676: Books of Record and Minutes of the Freeholders of the County, relative to Returns of Members of Parliament, commencing 1702: And of Monthly Returns of the Prices of Corn, to the Receiver of Corn Returns, London, commencing 1791: Besides these, the same Person holds the Office of Register of Instruments of Sasine, Reversions, and Renunciations, and Discharges upon Heritable Property; and of Hornings, Inhibitions, and Lawburrows, for which he keeps Two Books, which are furnished by the Lord Clerk Register, to whom the old ones are returned so soon as filled up; the present one for Sasines, commences in November 1797, and that for Hornings, &c. in March 1794.

(2.) The Depute Clerk, in whose Custody these Records are, rents a House in the Burgh of Wigtown, from Year to Year, in which he lives, and where the Records are kept. The Accommodation is sufficient, but the House is not more secure than the other Houses in the Burgh.

(3.) All the Records appear to be in a good State of Preservation, and are arranged and bundled up in regular Order, agreeable to their Years.

(4.) It does not appear that there have been any Catalogues, Calendars, Schedules, Repertories, or Indexes, kept of the said Record, except the Minute Book of Processes above referred to, and Minute Books of the Sasines, &c. and of the Hornings, &c. shortly stating the Substance of the Instrument, its Date, and Date of recording. The Two last are transmitted to Edinburgh with the Books themselves. It certainly would be a Security and Advantage to the Leiges, were a regular Catalogue to be made out and kept of the Dispositions, Contracts, Assignations, and other Deeds, recorded since 1690; but it is judged that this could not be done in less Time than Three Months constant Employ of One Person; and the Depute Clerk, who is well qualified for the Task, would undertake it, but, with the Duties of the Office, would require Nine or Ten Months to complete it in.

(5.) No other Officer or Clerk is employed for the Custody and Arrangement of the Records of the County, except the Depute Sheriff Clerk. He attends in the Office every lawful Day, and at all Hours of the Day, for the Dispatch of Business; but complains of the constant Attendance, and that particular Hours are not allotted in that Office as in any other Public Office in the Kingdom. The Annual Average Amount of the Sheriff Clerk's Fees will be about £.110. and £.10 more as Keeper of the Records of Sasines, &c. and of Hornings, &c. out of which the Principal pays the Depute £.48. from which he furnishes an Office in his House for keeping the Records and transacting his Business in, Fireing, and Stationary Articles, and a Clerk to write when he requires Assistance. There is no Allowance from the Public for keeping the Records; and the Fees mentioned in the Table*, make up the whole Emoluments of the Offices.

* See Page 451.

(6.) As already mentioned, there is no Person intrusted with the Care of the Records but the Depute Clerk, who attends in the Office as above; and when a Search is required, he makes it himself, and does not allow any Person to interfere with the Record; and when he finds the Deed wanted, he gives out an Extract of it, if required, and restores the Original to its Place.

(7.) It does not occur as necessary or expedient, to suggest any Improvement as to the Records, further than what has been already mentioned, as to a Catalogue of the Deeds recorded, to be made out in a regular Book, which should be authenticated occasionally by the Sheriff or other Public Officer: and that the Records be kept in a Place of greater Security than in Presses in an ordinary Room in a House, subject to Fire and other Accidents.—All which is humbly submitted by

Will. W. Connell,
Sheriff Substitute.

Appendix (Z.)

PUBLIC LIBRARY.

SCOTLAND.
Public Library.

Appendix (Z.)

Report of the Curators of the Library of the Faculty of Advocates, in compliance with the Order of the Select Committee of the House of Commons on the Public Records, &c. of the Kingdom, 26th February 1800.

THE Library of the Faculty of Advocates has at no Period been considered as a Public Office, where Deeds or Papers might be deposited for Preservation and Security. The whole Books, Manuscripts, and Papers, which it contains, are the Property of the Faculty, and have been acquired partly by Donations, but chiefly by Purchases. Hence the particular Matters, which fall under the Description of those upon which the present Return is required, are comparatively but few in Number. It appears however to the Curators, that the best Mode of fulfilling the Design of the present Inquiry, and of answering the First Question of the Order of the Committee, fully and with Precision, will be to set down, according to their Importance and Authenticity, whatever Matters are contained in this Library, which are either directly comprehended in the Order, or have a Relation to what is understood to be the Object in View.

(1.) In answer accordingly to the First Question, the Curators give the following Report and Enumeration of what they conceive to be of Importance, either as properly and strictly Matter of Record, or as containing apparently authentic and original Information as to the History of the Times and Transactions to which the different Manuscripts and Papers particularly relate:

1. Original Record of Writs or Deeds, by James VI. of Scotland, with Advice of his Secret Council, from January 1586, to May 1588.

2. Original Record of Writs passing the Signet, with Advice of the Privy Council, from November 1630, to June 1642.

3. An Original Record of the Proceedings of certain Itinerant Justiciary Courts, in the Reign of James IV.

4. A Collection of Original Charters, from the Time of William the Lyon, to the Middle of the 16th Century.

5. Record of Charters and other Deeds, granted by Anne of Denmark, Queen of James VI. to different Vassals in the Lordship of Dunfermline, settled on her at her Marriage, about the Beginning of the 16th Century.

6. A Collection of Original Bulls, by Pope Adrian IV. 1155, and his Successors, down to Paul IV. 1555.

7. Chartulary, or Original Record of Charters and other Deeds respecting the Bishoprick of Aberdeen, from about the Year 1078, to the Middle of the 16th Century.

8. Chartulary, or Original Record of Charters, &c. relating to the Abbey of Arbroathe, from about the Middle of the 14th to the End of the 15th Century.

9. A Charter by James V. to the Abbey of Cambuskenneth, containing an Enumeration and Confirmation of all former Grants, dated 1535.

10. Chartulary, or Original Record of Charters and other Deeds, relating to the Abbey of Dunfermline, in the 13th and down to the 16th Century.

11. Chartulary, or Original Record of Charters, Bulls, and other Deeds relating to the Abbey of Scone, in the Reigns of King William, Malcolm IV. Alexander III. and Robert Bruce.

12. Chartulary, or Original Record of Charters, Bulls, and other Deeds, relating to the Abbey of Kelso, in the 12th, 13th, and 14th Centuries.

13. Chartulary, or Original Record of Charters and other Deeds relating to the Abbey of Balmerinoch, in the 13th and 14th Centuries.

14. Chartulary, or Original Record of Charters and other Deeds relating to the Abbey of Melross, from King David I. the Founder, 1140, down to Alexander II.

15. Chartulary, or Original Record of Charters and other Deeds to the Abbey and Convent of Dryburgh.

16. Chartulary, or Original Record of Charters, Bulls, and other Deeds, relating to the Abbey of Newbottle, from King David I. in 1140, down to the Reign of Robert Bruce.

17. Chartulary, or Original Record of Charters, Bulls, and other Deeds, relating to the Abbey of Saint Mary, and Saint Andrew's of Lundoris, from 1457 to 1530.

18. Records of Charters, Sasines, and other Deeds, in Favour of the Vassals of the Commendator of Saint Andrew, and the Prior of the Abbey of Pittenweem, about the Middle of the 16th Century.

19. Notarial Copy of Charters and other Deeds, granted to the Hospital of Sottra, in the 13th Century.

20. Notarial Copy of Charters and other Deeds in Favour of Maison de Dieu, near Elgin, from 1225 to 1546.

21. Protacole of Notaries, containing Entries of Deeds and Instruments, from December 1537 to November 1543; from 1548 to 1556; from 1590 to 1612; from 1608 to 1626; and from 1615 to 1629.

22. The Original Record of the Transactions of the Presbytery of Aberdeen, from October 1598, to June 1600.

23. Record of the Proceedings of the Synod of Lothian and Tweedale, from May 1657, to May 1661.

24. A Collection of Documents relating to the Exchequer, comprehending Rolls, Rentals, &c. of the Crown Lands and others, from 1264, and at other Periods, down to about the Middle of the last Century.

25. A Rental of the Bishoprick of Moray, from 1565 to 1569.

26. Original Record of State Letters, and Dispatches from King James IV. and from the Government of Scotland,

Scotland, during the Minority of James V. to the different Princes and Powers in Europe; the Anſwers to ſeveral of which being alſo ingroſſed, commencing October 1505, and ending December 1524.

27. Original Record of Letters, from James V. and the Earl of Arran, Governor of the Kingdom, in the Infancy of Queen Mary, to the Kings of England, France, Norway, and Portugal, to the Duke of Guiſe, Earl of Suffolk, &c. &c. from 1539 to 1542.

28. A Collection of Letters to and from James VI. and the King of France, &c. relative to the Complaints and Grievances of the Scots Guards at Paris, and other Matters.

29. A Collection of Original Letters, by Anne of Denmark, Queen of James VI.; by Prince Henry and Prince Charles, his Sons; by Princeſs Elizabeth, his Daughter; by the Elector Palatine and his Son, to King James VI. entirely of a familiar Nature.

30. Originals and Copies of State Papers and Letters, during the Reigns of Queen Elizabeth, James VI. and down to the 5th Year of Charles I.

31. A Collection of Correſpondence, and Negotiation with France, during the Reign of James VI.

32. A Collection of Original Letters, and Papers of a Public Nature, relative to Negotiations with Denmark and Norway, during the Reigns of James VI. and Charles I.

33. Record kept by Sir William Alexander, after wards Earl of Stirling, Principal Secretary of State, of original Letters by King Charles I. to the ſeveral conſtituted Authorities, Perſons in Office, and Corporate Bodies in Scotland, from July 1626 to July 1627.

34. A Collection of Correſpondence, and Negotiation with different Princes of Italy, in the Reign of James VI. and Charles I.

35. A Collection of Original Letters, and Negotiation with the Kings of Poland, Sweden, and different Princes of the German Empire, in the Reigns of James VI. and Charles I. from 1600 to 1626.

36. A Collection of Originals, and Copies of State Papers, relating to the Diſturbances in Great Britain and Ireland, during the Reign of Charles I.

37. Minutes of the Convention of Eſtates in the Kingdom of Scotland, held at Edinburgh on the 4th of March 1689, and continued to the 22d July 1690.

(2.) Theſe Records, Manuſcripts, &c are all lodged in the Library of the Faculty of Advocates, conſiſting of Six Rooms, ſituated immediately under the large Hall, called The Parliament Houſe, and ſome other Apartments, where the Courts of Juſtice are held. The whole Building is the Property of the City of Edinburgh, is entirely of Stone, with a leaden Roof, and by means of ſome recent Purchaſes of old Houſes and Areas, by the City and the Faculty of Advocates, is almoſt completely detached from any other, and is therefore not much in Danger of any Accident from Fire.

(3.) The above Records, &c. are in general in tolerable Preſervation, and are arranged in one particular Place of the Library, under different Letters and Numbers, ſo that eaſy and immediate Acceſs can be had to them, when required.

(4.) The Faculty of Advocates have lately ordered a complete Deſcriptive Catalogue of all the Manuſcripts in their Poſſeſſion, to be made out, diſtinct from the General Catalogue of the Library, in which they are included: This Work is far advanced, and when completed, will render the Acceſs to theſe Matters ſtill more eaſy and convenient to thoſe who may wiſh, with the Permiſſion of the Faculty, to examine them.

(5.) The above Enumeration comprehends all the Particulars upon which the Curators are enabled, at preſent, to make a Return. When the Catalogue of theſe Matters is finiſhed, ſome others deſerving of Notice may perhaps occur: But beſides theſe, there is in the Library a conſiderable Number of Manuſcripts of an Hiſtorical Nature, together with many Legal Treatiſes, and Reports of Adjudged Caſes, by eminent Lawyers of the Times.

By Order of the Curators,

Alexr Manners,
Librarian.

Edinburgh,
19th March 1800.

II. Other RETURNS to Special Orders of the Committee.

Concerning the different Modes heretofore used in WRITING and PRESERVING the Public Records and Papers of the Realm, and the MODES which may be most adviseable to use in future.

SPECIAL RETURNS.

Appendix (A. A.)

Appendix (A. A.)

Return of THOMAS ASTLE, Esq; Keeper of the Records in the Tower of London; with engraved Copies of ROYAL CHARTERS, from the Reign of William the Conqueror to Henry VIII. from Originals in his Possession.

To the Honourable the Select Committee on the Public Records of the Kingdom.

IN compliance with your Order of the 9th Instant, I communicate the following Observations which have occurred to me, concerning the different Modes heretofore used in Writing, and preserving the Records and Papers of the Realm, and those which it may be most adviseable to use in future.

1. The Characters which were introduced into this Country by King William the First, were at that Time called Lombardic, but soon afterwards they acquired the Appellation of Norman Characters, which were generally used in Grants, Charters, Public Instruments, and Law Proceedings, with very little Alteration from that Period until the Reign of King Edward III. In that of King Richard II. Variations took place in Hand-Writings, of Records and Law Proceedings; the Characters used from that Time to the Reign of King Henry VIII. are composed partly of Characters called Set Chancery and Common Chancery, and of some of the Letters called Court-Hand. The Chancery Letters were used for all Records which passed the Great Seal; the Court-Hand in the Courts of King's Bench and Common Pleas, for Fines, Placita, Adjudicata, &c. These latter Characters came into general Use about the Middle of the 16th Century, and were continued until the beginning of the late Reign, when they were entirely disused; they were originally the Lombardic or Norman, but corrupted and deformed to so great a degree, that they bore very little Resemblance to their Prototypes. In the 16th Century the English Lawyers ingrossed their Conveyances and Legal Instruments, in Characters called Secretary, which are still in Use.

Many Grants and Charters, especially those written by the Monks, were in Letters called Modern Gothic, which took place in England in the 12th Century.

From the latter End of the 13th to the 17th Century, our Lawyers, when they wrote in the English Language, made use of Characters which were derived from the modern Gothic; these were generally used by them for Conveyances, Wills, &c. until about the Middle of the 17th Century. I think the Set Chancery the most durable, and therefore the most proper to be used in future for Patents, Charters, &c.

2. The Ink to be used for our National Records, is of great Importance, but the Composition of this necessary Article has not been sufficiently attended to; and the making it improperly doth not arise from our Ignorance, or for want of Materials, but from Negligence Knavery, and Avarice. It is an Object of the utmost Importance that our Public Records, as also the Conveyances of Property, by Deeds, Wills, or otherwise, which affect the same, should be written with Ink of such durable Quality, as may best resist the destructive Powers of Time and the Elements. The Necessity of paying greater Attention to this Subject, will appear by comparing the Rolls and Records which have been written from the 15th Century to the End of the 17th, with the MSS. and Records now remaining from the 7th to the Middle of the 13th Century, which are, generally speaking, in excellent Preservation; but the former, though of more modern Date, are frequently found so much defaced that they are scarcely legible. The Ink which has been used at the Pell-Office in the Exchequer, for more than a Century past, is the best which I have seen, but how it is compounded I cannot set forth. There are a great Variety of Receipts for making Inks to be found in a Work by Peter Caneparius de Atramentis, London, 1660, 4to.; and in the Works of Lewis, and other Writers upon that Subject: but I recommend a Reference to the President and Council of the Royal Society, in which Body are many excellent Chymists, to point out the best Method of making Ink, to be used at the several Offices for Records: Instances of durable Ink in early Times, and of bad Ink in modern Times, may be seen at most of the Public Offices, particularly at the Tower and at the Rolls Chapel.

3. The most durable Materials for Records, are Parchment or Vellum, although strong Paper Volumes are very proper, admitting they are kept free from Damp and Dust; many of these may be seen in several of the Public Offices, particularly in that of the Auditor of the Land Revenue at Westminster, and in different Departments of the Exchequer.

4. I conceive Books to be as proper for Records as Rolls, provided they are carefully deposited; the Books of Domesday on Vellum, which are above 700 Years old, are still in admirable Preservation.

5. I entirely disapprove of placing Records in Bags or Chests, having observed too many Instances of their suffering by being so kept. This must have occurred to the Committee in the course of their View of the different Repositories of Records. The best Method, in my Opinion, to be used for their Preservation, is to deposit them in Presses, at a Distance of at least Three Inches from the Walls, with Holes in the Fronts and behind, to allow the Air to pass through. Wire Doors are sometimes used in Libraries, but these admit Dust and too much air. Racks will also answer the Purpose very well; but every Place where Records are intended to be deposited, should be kept perfectly free from Damp or Moisture, and the Windows and Doors of the Presses should be frequently opened in fair Weather, especially in the Summer Season. It may be, however, objected to Racks, that they admit too much Air.

6. The Buildings best adapted for the Preservation of Records, are those which are the most secure and most free

free from Damp. With respect to Security, I beg leave to refer this Honourable Committee to my Return concerning the Room called Wakefield Tower, in the Tower of London. I think one of the best Plans which I have seen for a Depôt of Records, is that of the General Register House at Edinburgh.

All which is humbly submitted by

Thos Astle.

Battersea Rise,
June 12, 1800.

Appendix (B. B.)

Return of JOHN TOPHAM, Esq; One of the Commissioners of the State Paper Office; with engraved Specimens of DOMESDAY[a], Account of an ALIEN PRIORY, 18 Edw. II[b]. and INQUISITIO NONÆ[c], 15 Edw. III.

[a] Chapter House.
[b] King's Rem. Off.
[c] Ibidem.

To the Honourable the Select Committee on the Public Records of the Kingdom.

IN pursuance of the Order of this Honourable Committee, dated the 9th Day of June, 1800, requesting me "To communicate to this Committee, without Delay, such Observations as may have occurred to me concerning the different Modes heretofore used in writing and preserving the Public Records and Papers of the Realm, and those Modes which it may be most adviseable to use in future, under the following Heads; viz. with regard to the Modes of writing: 1st. the Character; 2d. the Ink; 3d. the Materials written upon; viz. Paper, Parchment, Vellum, &c. And with regard to the Modes of preserving them:

"1st. The Use of Rolls or Books.

"2d. The putting them into Bags, or Chests, or Presses, or upon open Racks.

"3d. The Sorts of Buildings best adapted to the Purpose."

I beg leave most respectfully to state to this Committee, that the Modes heretofore used in Writing the Public Records have been various, with respect to the Character in which they are written: In the Times of the Saxons, the Character was strong, large, and plain; the Norman Character, which succeeded, was smaller, and became so minute in the Reigns of Richard I. and John, as to be scarcely legible; many Abbreviations were also used, which increased the Difficulty in reading the Character; the Court Hand and Chancery Hands, generally used for Law Proceedings, were full of Contractions: These Characters were calculated for Duration; but from their Form, and Number of Abbreviations used, were very difficult to the Generality of Readers, so that few but Professional Men were capable of decyphering them: The common Text Hand or Ingrossing Characters were founded on, and succeeded those last mentioned; these are still in general Use in the Profession of the Law, but they are become almost unintelligible to all but Practitioners.

1st. Character.—With respect to the Modes of writing, I will beg leave to offer my Opinion, that the Letter or Character to be used for the Public Records, should be strong, plain, and clear, free from Flourish or Abbreviation, as being the best adapted for general Use and Duration.

2d. Ink.—The Ink to be used should be Black, and of the best Kind that can be now procured; but the Ink now made is certainly not so lasting as what was used in former Times: There are Liquids prepared and used for the Restoration of decayed or damaged Writings; but these should be used with much Care and Circumspection, otherwise they will affect and damage the Parchment or Material on which they may be applied; having the Effect of turning the Parchment nearly Black, or of the Colour of Walnut-Pickle.

3d. Materials.—The Materials to be written upon, should be Parchment or Vellum, as being more lasting and better adapted for the Preservation of Public Records than Paper.

With regard to the Modes of preserving the Public Records:

1st. I think that Rolls are better calculated for their Preservation than Books; the latter I admit may be more convenient for Inspection and general Use, but I am convinced that Rolls will preserve the Writing longer than Books.

2d. I think that open Racks, where Air can have free Current and Circulation, are better adapted for the Preservation of Records, than putting them into Bags or Chests, or even into Presses, where Air cannot be readily and generally admitted; Doors of open Wire may be formed for such Racks for the greater Safety of the Records, and to prevent their being improperly moved, or their Situations changed.

3d. The Buildings appropriated for the Preservation of Records should be perfectly dry, where Air can be freely admitted, and not liable to the scorching Heat of the Sun: If Fire should be found necessary, it should be introduced with much Care and Caution, but I would recommend that no Fire should be admitted into the Record Room itself. These Observations are submitted with much Deference and Respect to the Consideration of this Honourable Committee.

John Topham.

Bedford Row,
19th June, 1800.

Appendix (C. C.)

Return of JOSEPH PLANTA, Esq; Principal Librarian of the British Museum; with engraved Copies of the CAPITULA MAGNÆ CHARTÆ, MAGNA CHARTA, and the BULL of Pope LEO X. conferring the Title of Defensor Fidei on Henry VIII. from the Originals there.

IN obedience to the Order of the Honourable the Select Committee of the House of Commons on the Public Records, &c. of the Kingdom, directing me to communicate such Observations as may have occurred to me concerning the best Mode of writing, and the most secure Manner of preserving Public Records, I have the Honour to report as follows on the Six Questions therein proposed:

1st. As to the Characters used in Public Records, every one acquainted with the Writing of different Periods must have observed how much those of the earlier Times are superior in Beauty and Distinctness to those of the Middle and more recent Ages *; and that not content with the Neglect of Neatness and Elegance, modern Writers have also at different Times introduced a Variety of Hands, equally obscure and unsightly, and moreover loaded with such an Abundance of Contractions and Abbreviations, as to render Public Instruments almost unintelligible. Being persuaded that the greatest Facility to those who have Occasion to peruse Public Documents

---

* Of the gradual Decline in the Manner of Writing from the Sixth to the Sixteenth Century, some Idea may be formed by inspecting the Specimens given in the Sixteen Plates at the End of Casley's Catalogue of the Royal Library of Manuscripts.

SPECIAL RETURNS.

Appendix (C. C.)

cuments ought to be provided for, I humbly conceive that it would be greatly conducive to this Purpose, if the Variety of Hand-writings still used in the Practice of the Law, and in some of the Public Offices, were totally abolished, and none but a plain Round Hand, without Ornaments or Abbreviations, were adopted for all Instruments of legal Authority.

2d. Concerning the Kinds of Ink best calculated for Distinctness and Permanency, it must be owned that the Sort used in the Tenth and the preceding Centuries, appears to have been of a much superior Quality to those now made: The former, which seems to have been a Body Colour greatly resembling Indian Ink, we are told, was composed of either Soot, Lamp-Black, or Ivory Black, and certain Kinds of Gums, without any Vitriol or Vegetable Astringent *. Whether it be possible to recover that Ink I cannot take upon me to say, but I think it would be adviseable to cause an Inquiry to be made for that Purpose: As to modern Inks, the Subject has been fully and ably treated by the late Dr. Lewis, who proceeding upon accurate Chemical Experiments, has given us not only the Composition of a Liquid, of as Black and durable a Colour as the Materials now used are likely to afford, but also a Mode of preparing Paper or Parchment, so as to render the Duration of Writings upon them more permanent than they would be without that Preparation †.

It is worthy of Notice however that Instances occur, where Paper written upon with Astringent Ink has been entirely corroded and destroyed wherever it has come in contact with the Liquid: This probably has been occasioned by the improper Use of Acids in the Preparation of the Ink, an Evil which must be carefully guarded against, and which would be wholly obviated if the Composition of the Antients could be recovered.

Concerning the Danger of Erasures, which perhaps was the principal Inducement of preferring the modern to the antient Ink, it is to be observed that the Application of certain Acids lately discovered, renders it as easy to discharge the Stain of the former, as it is to scrape away or wipe out the Body Colour of the Antients; an essential Difference however, which may determine the Preference, is, that it will be easier to detect the Erasures of the one than the other, it being scarce possible to efface the antient Ink, without in some Measure injuring the Surface of the Paper or Parchment; whereas, with the modern Liquid, if the Erasure is performed with Skill and Dexterity, the Injury will hardly be perceptible.

It may not be foreign to the present Purpose to mention the Fluids which are occasionally used for reviving Writings which are faded or nearly obliterated: An Infusion of Gall-nuts, and the successive Application of the Phlogisticated Alkali, and a dilute Mineral Acid, recommended by Sir Charles Blagden ‡, are the Two only Means with which I am at present acquainted; but I am informed that there are others used in some of the Public Offices, which are as yet kept secret; if so, and if they are actually as useful as they are reported to be, I humbly submit whether it would not be adviseable to secure the best of them for the Benefit of the Public? I must however observe, that all the Compositions I have as yet heard of for this Purpose (except that of Sir Charles Blagden) are liable to the Objection, that while they revive for a Time the Ink made of Vitriol and Astringents, they in general leave a fixed Stain on the Paper or Vellum, which increases by Time, and renders the Documents to which they have been applied perfectly illegible; great Caution must be used in this Respect.

3d. As to the Materials for writing upon, there can be no Doubt that Vellum or Parchment are much preferable to Paper, for all Manner of Instruments that are to be handed down to Posterity. But here likewise I must observe, that our Ancestors appear to have had a better Mode of preparing Parchment than we possess at present; the Skins used at and before the Eleventh Century being in general finer, whiter, and of a more even Texture than those of a later Date. The Makers of Parchment I think might be instructed to use their Endeavours to arrive at the same Degree of Perfection; and should in this, as in some other Manufactories, the Mode of collecting the Duties be an Obstacle to so desirable an Improvement, the Vellum or Parchment made for the Use of the Public, might be exempted from such Restraints; and proper Persons might be appointed for the sole making of those Articles, on condition of their being prepared in the most perfect Manner.

4th. As to the Preference to be given either to Rolls or Books, I cannot hesitate to decide in Favour of the latter, especially where the Articles are of such a Length as to take up many Skins: Where the Instrument consists of only One or a few Skins, it may be doubled in the Manner in which Deeds are usually folded, and thus by keeping the Articles separate, much Facility will be afforded towards their methodical Arrangement; but One of the chief Reasons that induces me to object to the Mode of entering a Series of Deeds on a large Roll, is the numerous Instances I have observed where both Ends of the Rolls are become quite illegible and mutilated, by having been sometimes folded inwards, and sometimes outwards. The Books should be strongly bound in Boards, and the Leaves held tight together by means of Metal Clasps: No Wood should be used in the Covers, as this Substance frequently harbours Insects, which, when in their perfect State, are able to cut with their Teeth through many Folds of Vellum or Paper.

5th. I cannot but object to the Mode of preserving Records in close Presses or Chests, where, for Want of a free Circulation of Air, they will be liable to contract Damp and Mouldiness.

The best Mode of guarding against these Inconveniencies, as well as against the Effects of Dust, is to put the Records into Linen Bags, and to place them on Frames, not in contact with the Walls, and of which, if not the Shelves, at least Uprights are composed of open Rack-work; and if it be thought necessary to have Doors to these Presses, they also should consist of open Lattice or Wire-work.

6th. The same Object of providing for the Dryness and Airiness of the Repository, induces me to recommend a Building exposed to the South, or (as Westerly Winds are, in this Part of the Kingdom, generally attended with Rain) some Points to the East of the South. The Rays of the Sun, when admitted into a close Room, cause Heat to accumulate to a considerable Degree; and this Accumulation, which will take place at Intervals throughout the Year, will effectually dispel the Damp which would otherwise deposit, and become very pernicious. As however the Rays of Light will gradually discharge the Colour of any Sort of Ink, it will be proper that all the Fronts of the Cases opposite to the Light, be constructed in the Manner of Venetian Blinds, so as to admit the free Circulation of Air, and at the same Time to exclude the direct Rays of the Sun.

It will perhaps be needless to recommend proper Cautions against Fire, such as having the Building raised upon Arches, admitting none but Iron Doors, excluding Fires and Candles, and various other Expedients which skilful Architects are best able to suggest.

J. Planta.

British Museum,
June 28, 1800.

* Vid. Caneparius de Atramentis, p. 256. Edit. Lond.
† Vide Lewis's Commercium Philosophico-Technicum, p. 377—401.
‡ Vide Phil. Trans. Vol. lxxvii. p. 451—457.

Appendix (D. D.)

Return of JOHN CALEY, Esq; Keeper of the Records in the Augmentation Office; with engraved Copies of PRIVATE DEEDS, from the Reign of Hen. II. to the Reign of Hen. VIII. from the Originals in that Office.

To the Honourable the Select Committee on the Public Records, &c. of the Kingdom.

IN answer to the Questions proposed to me with respect, 1st, to the Modes heretofore used in writing and preserving the Public Records and Papers of the Realm; and 2dly, those Modes which it may be most adviseable to use in future; I humbly beg leave to state:

1st. As to the Modes heretofore used, that the Character or Hand-writing of antient Records, as far as my Observation has extended, has gradually degenerated from Age to Age; thus the Records of the Saxon Æra, whether written in Saxon or Latin, are infinitely more plain and legible than those of subsequent Æras; they are also little obscured with Abbreviations, which have created much Doubt and Ambiguity in After-ages, particularly in that valuable Record Domesday Book.

From the Norman Conquest, until the Reign of Henry III. the Character is in general plain and perspicuous; of this latter Reign however, there are many Records which cannot be read with facility, on account of the Intricacy of the Character, and the Number of Abbreviations.

The same Observations may be applied to Records from this Reign until that of Edward III. inclusive.

From this Period downwards, I have experimentally found that less Difficulty occurs in reading and translating Records, and that the Hands used from the Reign of Richard II. to that of Philip and Mary, are such as may be read without much Trouble.

Hitherto each Reign appears to have had a set of uniform Character; but in the Reign of Elizabeth and her Successors, the Clerical Mode seems to have been in a great Measure abandoned, and each Transcriber to have written according to his own Fancy; and it is observable that the English Records of the 16th and 17th Centuries are in general more difficult to be read than the Latin Records of preceding Ages.

Ample and accurate Specimens of the Characters used in all the Periods of English History may be seen in Mr. Astle's valuable Work on the Origin and Progress of Writing, to which I therefore beg leave to refer, as also to Madox's Formulare Anglicanum, and Casley's Catalogue of the MSS. in the King's Library.

The latter Book contains some Observations on Ink and Vellum, which I will beg leave to quote.

Casley says in his Preface, P. xi. speaking of the Antients, " It is very observable that they generally took " great Care to have good Ink and Colours for their " MSS. such as perhaps now cannot be made, and which, " in Books a Thousand Years old, appear as fresh as " if they were under an Hundred."

He says also, " It is even wonderful also to observe " how durable Vellum is, some Books of a Thousand " Years Age having no Signs of Decay, which, abat- " ing Accidents, may last to the End of the World; " but they made better Vellum a Thousand Years ago " than ever was made either before or since, as may ap- " pear by comparing Books of different Ages."

Having never made any particular Observations as to Inks, I do not feel myself competent to discuss that Subject; but with respect to the Preference to be given to Paper, Parchment, or Vellum, as applicable to Records, I have not the smallest Hesitation in declaring that I conceive the last to be by far the most valuable and proper for the Purpose.

2. As to the Modes which it may be most adviseable to use in future for preserving the Public Records, I humbly beg leave to suggest, that the Buildings in which they are deposited, should be as spacious as Circumstances may permit, that the Records should not be placed too near to each other, and that occasionally a Circulation of Air should be admitted into the Rooms.

Damp and Dust are the great Evils to be avoided, particularly the former; for when once Vellum, Parchment, or Paper, have taken Damp, the Damage is irretrievable, the Ink becomes discoloured, and, in no great length of Time, sometimes wholly vanishes; and the Substance of the Parchment, Paper, or Vellum quickly decays. I have known Instances of important modern Deeds, which from being placed in a damp Situation, have become so glued together, as to defy all the Powers of Art to separate them.

I have always considered it an unfortunate Circumstance that our Ancestors have recorded so many Public Acts upon Rolls, instead of entering them into Books; besides the Inconveniency of unfolding a Roll upon every Occasion of Resort, I am convinced there are many other solid Objections to be made against the Use of them, viz. they cannot be placed with equal Convenience, and they are infinitely more liable to accumulation of Dust, which, in spite of all the Care that can be taken, will, where the Numbers are considerable, be found too frequently to adhere to them, and pervade their Bodies.

Of the several Ways in which Rolls may be placed, viz. in Bags, Chests, Presses, or open Racks, I prefer the last but one, viz. Presses, which should however be occasionally opened to admit Air: My Reason for preferring Presses is, as being less liable to admit Dust, which Racks that are open do in great Quantity.

Before I conclude, I would wish to instance, as a Proof of the Superiority of Books to Rolls, the Inrolments of Wills in the Prerogative Office, Doctors Commons; where, notwithstanding the constant, and indeed daily Reference to those Books, they are to be found perfect and unhurt, though continually handled, and each Entry can be referred to in a few Minutes.

These imperfect Observations are submitted to the consideration of the Honourable Committee.

John Caley.

Gray's Inn,
4th July, 1800.

Appendix (E. E.)

Return of Mr. THOMAS BRYAN RICHARDS; with engraved Copies from the GREAT PIPE ROLL of the Exchequer, Temp. Hen. I. Hen. II. & Joh. and of the HUNDRED ROLL OXON, 7 Edw. I. EXTENTA MANERIJ, de Upton Berk. 7 Edw. I. and FOREST PERAMBULATION of Exemore, 18 Edw. I.:—the Three latter at the Tower.

To the Honourable the Select Committee of the House of Commons on the Records, &c. of this Kingdom.

THE earliest Records and Deeds which I have met with, were written in the Time of Edward the Confessor, in those Characters, which Mr. Astle, in his valuable Publication, justly calls elegant Saxon.

These Records may be arranged under Two Heads, namely, Regal and Monastic; by the former, I mean Royal Charters of Foundation and Donation to Monasteries, &c. and by the latter, their Chartularies, Registers, and Conventual Deeds. I must confess the Monastic Records are the fairest and best written, and the Ink of the most permanent Colour: This Superiority or Excellence I ascribe to the Caution observed by the Monks,

Monks, in the Choice of their Vellum, and the great Pains taken by the Perſons employed as Penmen, whoſe ſole Time was dedicated to that Service, and who took infinite Pains in their Works, not being reſtricted in Point of Time in their Labours. The elegant Saxon Characters are certainly the beſt that could be uſed, either for ſimplicity or fullneſs; the firſt rendering the Writing more eaſy and expeditious, and the latter more legible.

The Vellum uſed was ſelected for its Fineneſs and cloſe Texture, and perfect Clearneſs, from every Cauſe that might prevent the cutting or Formation of the Character or Adheſion of the Ink.

The Ink then uſed, conſiſted more of an encauſtic Nature, than that uſed in ſubſequent Ages, as is evident from its Solidity and Blackneſs, and on that Account leſs liable to fade or decay: Whatever the Ingredients were, I cannot preſume to ſay, but it is manifeſt that ſomething was made uſe of to ſtrike the Tincture deeper into the Vellum than any Method known at the preſent Time: I cannot help again obſerving the neceſſary Precaution that was taken to free the Vellum from every unctuous Quality, which would have counteracted the ſtriking of the Tincture, or cauſed an Excoriation of the Compoſition or Ink, when dry. The Inattention of the Vellum and Parchment Makers of the preſent Day, to theſe very requiſite Precautions, is the Cauſe why the Law Stationers or Scriveners are frequently neceſſitated to uſe a Compoſition called Parchment Pounce, conſiſting chiefly of Whiting mixed with a ſmall Quantity of Borax or Roſin, to render the flowing of the Ink more eaſy over the greaſy Places; the dreadful Effects of which I have too often ſeen in Numbers of modern Deeds (which have paſſed through my Hands) that have been kept in ſome damp Place, where the Humidity or Dampneſs has been abſorbed by the Quality of the Whiting, which cauſed Excoriations of the Ink in various Parts, ſo as to leave no Trace whatever of the Writing, whereby the Deed was rendered almoſt uſeleſs.

In reſpect to the Modes adopted by the Saxons, to preſerve their Records, I find ſome Difficulty even to venture an Opinion, not having ſeen any others than thoſe mentioned above; but that they uſed Rolls I conceive may be inferred from the Title of the Survey ſaid to have been made by King Ælfred, and generally known by the Title of Mag. Rot. de Winton, from which it is highly probable that William the Conqueror formed the Idea of his invaluable Record now called Domeſday Book. The Uſe of Rolls I conceive was always attended to, where the Nature was Publicity and Reference frequently required, as may be inferred from the great Number of them now remaining in the Tower.

The common Brevity of Charters, &c. relating to Monaſtic or Private Property, clearly evinces the Reaſon of their having been preſerved in their Munimentaries, &c. in ſeparate Boxes, allotted for the ſeveral Articles; where, although kept from a free Currency of Air (which I believe is highly eſſential for the Preſervation of Records of every Deſcription) they have nevertheleſs, from the Nature of the encauſtic Compoſition or Ink, retained in a very great Degree their priſtine Fullneſs of Colour.

Their Chartularies I conceive were formed upon two very neceſſary Principles, viz. the Conſervation of the Titles to their Poſſeſſions, in caſe the Original Grants, &c. ſhould be loſt or deſtroyed, and alſo for the more ready Reference to any particular Deed, whenever a Peruſal might be neceſſary. This neceſſary Precaution, I have Reaſon to believe, was antiently obſerved by Private Perſons, whoſe Poſſeſſions were large, and conſequently the Deeds numerous. My Reaſon for this Opinion, ariſes from a late Opportunity I had of examining the Boital Chartulary, compiled in the Reign of Henry VI. wherein are complete Copies of all the Deeds of ſeveral Eſtates, regularly arranged from the Reign of Edward the Confeſſor, down to the Time of its Compilation.

I humbly beg leave to ſuggeſt to this Honourable Committee, the Conſequences and Advantages that would ariſe from adopting the above Plan of Precaution, in reſpect to the Public Records of this Realm, as well antient as modern, becauſe Spoliation would be prevented, and Preſervation effected. I have always, with infinite Satisfaction, obſerved the Method uſed in the Prerogative Office, Doctors Commons, where there are regular Calendars and Regiſters kept for Public Inſpection; but the Original Wills are carefully preſerved, that they may be produced, when required, in any Court of Judicature.

Character.—The Character which I would recommend, is the modern Full Round Hand, as the moſt eligible, on account of Expedition and general Uſe, independant of the Certainty of Expreſſion; which, in the Old Text Hand, was frequently rendered indefinite by the direct Aſſimilazion of various Conſonants, as alſo difficult from the Occurrence of ſeveral Letters, which formed an Appearance of Indentations, and could only be well underſtood by Profeſſional Perſons. If an Error ſhould be made in any Record, I would not have any Eraſure made, but the Word or Words to remain with a Line drawn through them to notify the Error; as an Eraſure being written on might create a Doubt whether it might not have been an Alteration made to anſwer ſome private or ſiniſter Purpoſe.

Ink.—There are many modern Methods of making Ink; the beſt I have hitherto found, for the Space of Forty Years, is that made of ſimple Ingredients, viz. a due Proportion of Galls and Copperas, and clear Gum Arabic, having the ſoft Water previouſly boiled, and when cold, carefully poured off, leaving every Particle of Sediment behind.

In an Italian Book on Writing, publiſhed in 1547, by M. Giovan Battiſta Palatino, a Citizen of Rome, an eminent Writing Maſter, the following Recipe occurs:

"Take 3 Ounces of Galls, which ſhould be ſmall "and heavy, bruiſe them, afterwards put them into "a Bottle of Wine, or Rain Water, which is better, "and let them ſtand in the Sun for a Day or Two to "infuſe; then take Two Ounces of Copperas or Roman "Vitriol of a good Colour, and having bruiſed it very "fine, mix them well together, ſtirring them well with "a Fig Stick, and leave them in the Sun for One or "Two more Days; then ſtir all the Ingredients well "together, put to them 1 Ounce of clear Gum Arabic "well pulverized, and let it ſtand all Day; afterwards, "to make it clear and fair, put therein a ſmall Piece of "Pomegranate Bark, and give it a gentle Simmer over "the Fire; afterwards ſtrain it carefully off, and keep it "in a Glaſs Bottle or Veſſel of Lead, cloſe covered; "which completes the Proceſs."

In the Britiſh Muſeum, No 1327, Art. 46, Fol. 57, B. of the Harleian Manuſcripts, there is the Receipt of Mr. Geething, an eminent Writing Maſter in London, about 1620, to make Black Ink; this Receipt is nearly the ſame as that given by Palatino.

Materials.—Vellum.

Rolls.—Rolls for the Records, becauſe Spoliation cannot well be committed, and alſo that lying horizontally, they are leſs liable to harbour the Duſt; and at each End there ſhould be a Paſteboard Circle, of the Diameter of the Roll, marked with the Deſcription of its Purport and Year. But Paper Books for the Copies.

Racks.—Racks with cancellated or latticed Fronts and Backs, with Locks, whereby a free Currency of Air will be admitted, and at the ſame Time the Records kept ſecure; theſe Racks to be placed in the central Part of the Room, and by no Means againſt the Walls.

Buildings.—The Buildings to have a free Currency of Air, by oppoſite Windows, &c. Stucco Walls and double Doors.

Thomas Bryan Richards.

3d July, 1800.

Appendix (F. F.)

Return by William and Alexander Robertsons, the Lord Clerk Regifter's Deputies for keeping the Records of Scotland, to an Order of the Select Committee on the Public Records, &c. of the Kingdom; with an engraved Copy of an Act of Settlement of the Crown of Scotland, 1371.

(1.) In relation to "the Modes of Writing heretofore used:"—In writing the Records of Scotland, an Uniformity of Character, such as what we call the Chancery Hand here, or such as that used in some Departments of the Courts of Law in England, has never been attempted.

Antiently the Records of Scotland appear to have been, in general, written in a better Character than that in which they have been written during the last Century.

In several Instances in the Course of that Period, the Character is not only very indifferent, but many of the Books of Record subjected to the Formality of marking *, are written in a Character extremely minute, and in Lines very much crowded †.

But the Incorrectness with which our Records are in general written, is still more reprehensible.

(2.) The Ink formerly used in Writing our Records has sometimes been bad, but most commonly very good.

(3.) The Records of irredeemable Rights ‡, passed under the Great Seal, have been from the earliest Period, of which we have Knowledge even to the present Day, with the Exception of but Two small Books, the Fourth and Fifth written on Parchment; all the rest of the Records of Scotland have ever been written on Paper, which on the Whole appears to have been of good Quality.

"As to those Modes of Writing the Records, which it "may be most adviseable to use in future."

(1.) The Formation of the Records of Scotland is intrusted to so many different Persons, and those so distant in Situation from one another, as well as from the Seat of Justice, that to introduce in the Writing of those Records such an Uniformity of Character, as that hinted above, however desireable, is hardly possible. Nor indeed is it absolutely necessary.

But it seems to be not only right, but even necessary, that all the Records should be both well written and correctly written.

As this is in the Power of every Person to whom the Formation of the Records is committed, the proper Discharge of a Duty of such Consequence to the Community ought undoubtedly to be enforced by the most effectual Means.

(2.) If the universal Use of the same Sort of Ink, and that of the best and most approved Quality, could be established, it would be attended with very good Consequences; but at present there seems to be in Scotland no Reason for Complaint on this Head.

(3.) As the Idea of a Record is inseparably connected with that of Preservation, and as the Texture of the best Paper is far less durable than that of Parchment, the Use of Parchment in all Books of Record would be very proper. But as that Measure would be attended with considerable additional Expense, it would be reprobated as an oppressive Innovation—in prudence therefore it ought not perhaps to be attempted. The Use therefore of good P ap emay continue.

In the next Place:

"With regard to the Modes of preserving the Re-"cords:—1st. The Use of Rolls or Books:—2d. The "putting them into Bags, or Chests, or upon open "Racks:—3d. The Sorts of Building best adapted to "the Purpose."

Answer First, as to the former Usage:

More antiently the Use of Rolls seems to have prevailed in Scotland. But Books began to be introduced as early at least as the Time of our King David II.; and in the Year 1469, the Use of Books for all the Royal Records was enjoined by Parliamentary Authority.

More antiently too the Records of Scotland seem to have been kept in Boxes and Chests, "Pixidis & Cophinis," and in Bags, "Sacculis."

The Records too seem, at the same early Period, to have been deposited principally in the Royal Treasury within the Castle of Edinburgh; but we are ignorant in what Manner that Room was fitted up.

From the Castle they were removed to Two Rooms, below that in which the Court of Session sits, subterraneous on one Side to the Depth of more than 18 Feet. Those Rooms were fitted up throughout, with close Shelves (not Racks) the under Parts of which, to the Height of about Seven Feet from the Floor, were inclosed with Wooden Doors, and by that Means became Presses. There were, besides, a Variety of detached Presses on the Floor; together with a few old Boxes, in a decayed and insufficient Condition.

All the Records, as well in those Boxes and Presses, as on the open Shelves, were covered with Dust; and some which were on the lower Shelves of some Presses, in the Neighbourhood of a Common Sewer, which passed under One of the Rooms, were very much hurt with Damp.

There is Reason to believe that the Smallness of these Rooms was attended with one very ruinous Consequence; for it seems to have induced different Lords Register to permit several of those Clerks, who had the Formation of some of the Records, to retain their Books in their private Custody, instead of sending them to the General Repository. Hence some were burnt, and some were mislaid, or stolen, or lost.

As to the "Modes most adviseable to be observed in future."

Under this Head, we with most humble Deference take the Liberty to say, that we are from much Experience

* The Books in which are written the Records relative to Heritable or immoveable Property, are issued Blank from the Lord Register's Office to the different Clerks by whom those Records are formed; and previously to their being so issued, they are marked by the Lord Register's Deputies for keeping the Records. This Operation is by Experience found highly beneficial, particularly in forcing a regular Transmission of those Books to the General Repository, a new Book never being issued until the preceding Book be sent in. This regular Transmission obviates many probable bad Consequences. For this Marking, a Fee in the Proportion of £. 3. 6s. 8d. to the Lord Register, and of £. 2. 7s. to the Deputies, is due for a Book of 1,060 Folio Pages, which is a Trifle more than 1¼d. for each Page. The Object of Writing those Books so improperly is to save as much as possible of that paltry Fee.

† We have at this Moment One of those Books before us, in One Page of which not quite 12½ Inches long, and (exclusive of the Margin) less than 7 Inches broad, we count 112 Lines, and in each Line 19 Words at an Average. This bears a striking Resemblance to a Paternoster written on a Bit of Paper not larger than a Half Crown Piece.

‡ Charters of Apprising, now called Adjudications, Commissions, Remissions, Legitimations, &c. have been recorded in Paper Books since about the Year 1608. Hence the Records of the Great Seal since that Period consist of Two different Series of Books, distinguished by the Names of the Parchment and the Paper Register.

SPECIAL RETURNS.
Appendix (F. F.)

rience inclined to give Books a decided Preference to Rolls; to reject Bags and Chests, and to think that close Shelves, placed at the Distance of an Inch or Two from the Wall, are better than Racks, because the latter admit at the Bottom much Dust, which close Shelves exclude.

As to Presses there is more Difficulty; for although we know perfectly that they are far from being exempted from Dust, yet they undoubtedly are much less exposed to Dust than open Shelves. But besides the great additional Expense of Presses, it is humbly submitted whether the greater Hazard, to which they are exposed from Fire, does not in a considerable Degree counterbalance the Consideration of their admitting less Dust.

The Advantages of having all the Public Records of a Country * kept in One General Repository are, by long Experience in Scotland, found to be very great.

It is unnecessary to say, that the Building appropriated for this Purpose in any Country, ought to consist of the most durable Materials, and to be secured by every Precaution that Genius can suggest against all Hazard from Fire and Damp, those Two mortal Enemies of Books, Parchments, and Papers.

Its Magnitude ought evidently to be proportioned to the Number of Records intended to be placed in it, still keeping in View a long Track of Futurity.

And it ought to consist of as many different Apartments as possible, because, 1. the Quantity of Space is greatly increased by Division Walls, and because, 2. different Apartments may by that Means be appropriated to the different Provinces of a Kingdom, such as the Shires, for Example, of this Kingdom, and to the different supreme Courts of Law, &c. of which the Records are to be preserved.

And each Apartment should, as far as possible, be made capable of admitting such internal Subdivisions as may receive, in distinct and separate Spaces, the different Classes of Record used in each Shire; or in each Court of Law, &c. with vacant Room after each Class proportioned to the Extent of Futurity in View.

It is evident too, that some Apartments ought to be considerably larger than others, according to the particular Purpose for which they are intended.

And finally, all superfluous Matter ought most carefully to be excluded from the Record, that the Repository may be as little as possible encumbered with unnecessary Lumber.

It will be easily perceived, that in giving Obedience to this Head of the Order of the Honourable Committee, the Respondents have had their Eyes closely fixed on the Repository with which they have been so long connected.

Willm Robertson.
Alexr Robertson.

Edinburgh General Register House,
20th June 1800.

* We speak not of such overgrown Kingdoms as Russia or France, or the extensive and detached Provinces of the House of Austria.

Appendix (G. G.)

ESTIMATES of Catalogues, Calendars, and Indexes, to be printed, according to the Size and Type of the Sessional Indexes to the Journals of the House of Commons.

THE TOWER.

Patent Rolls, with Indexes Nominum et Locorum:			
Four Volumes, marked I. II. III. and IV. - - - - -	about - - -		450 Pages.
Claus Rolls, with Indexes, &c.			
Nine Volumes - - - - - - - - - -	about - - -		1,500
Charter Rolls, from K. John to the end of Ed. IV.			
Three Volumes; viz.			
King John - - - - - - -	about - -	100	
Henry III. - - - - - - - - - -		150	
Edward I. and IV. - - - - - - - - -		100	
Index Locorum to these 3 Books - - - - - - - -		150	
			500
Inquisitions Post Mortem:			
Nine Volumes:			
1.—Henry III. - - - - - - -	about - - -	40	
2.—Edward I. - - - - - - - - -		180	
3.—Edward II. - - - - - - - - -		184	
4.—Edward III. - - - - - - - - -		342	
5.—Richard II. - - - - - - - - -		232	
6.—Henry IV. - - - - - - - - -		75	
7.—Henry V. - - - - - - - - -		70	
8.—Henry. VI. - - - - - - - - -		220	
9.—Edward IV. and Rich. III. - - - - - - - -		120	
			1,463
			3,913

The

The ROLLS CHAPEL.

Parliamentary Returns from 33 Henry VIII. - - about - - -		80 Page
Nine Books of Escheat Bundles - - - - - - - - - -		486
Cardinal's Bundles, a small Quarto Book - - - - - - -		10
Index to Liveries, 4 Books - - - - - - - - - - -		445
Fine Rolls, commencing 1 Rich. III. - - - - - - - - -		60
		1,081
Patent, Confirmation, and Charter Rolls; viz.		
Richard III. - - - - - - - - - -	8	
Henry VII. 2 Books - - - - - - - - - -	300	
Henry VIII. 3 Books - - - - - - - - - -	350	
Ed. VI. and Ph. and Mary 3 Books - - - - - - -	350	
Elizabeth, 11 Books, - - - - - - - - - -	1,000	
James, 9 Books - - - - - - - - - - -	1,150	
Charles I. 9 Books - - - - - - - - - -	1,250	
Charles II. 3 Books - - - - - - - - - -	500	
James, 1 Book and Index Nom' - - - - - - -	20	
William & Mary, and William - - - - - - - -	120	
Anne - - - - - - - - - - -	80	
George I. with Index Loc. and Alp' - - - - - - -	100	
George II. with Index Loc. et Nom. - - - - - - -	200	
George III. - 1 to 18 - - - - - - - - -	150	
George III. - 19 to 26 - - - - - - - - -	60	
Index to the Confirmation Rolls - - - - - - - -	20	
Charter Rolls, Ric. III.—Hen. VII.—to 8 Hen. VIII. - - -	2	
		5,660
		6,741

The CHAPTER HOUSE.

Court of Wards and Liveries:—Transcripts of Inquisitions Post Mortem, Indexes Locorum et Virorum:		
Henry VIII. 2 to 12—8 and 9 Ditto—14 to 19 Ditto—19 to 23 Ditto—30 to 33 Ditto—34 Ditto, and to 5th of Philip and Mary—1 Eliz. to 7 James—8 James to 15 Charles.—These Transcripts are 8 large Volumes; the Indexes Locorum et Virorum to which, I suppose, may make about - -		300 Pages.
Index to the Bundle of Transcrips of Inquisitions Post Mortem, James I. to King Charles I. - - - - - - - - - - -		4
Surveys—Indexes Virorum:		
Henry VIII. 5 to 30—Ditto 19 to 33—Ditto 35 to 38—Ditto 31 to 38—Ditto 22 to 29 - - - - - - - - - - -	9	
Edward VI. 1 to 7—Ditto, and 1 to 5 Phil. and Mary - - - -	7	
1 to 10—and 11 to 21 Elizabeth - - - - - - - -	4	
		20
Particulars for Leases and Indentures, Indexes Locorum & Virorum—from 14 to 27 Elizabeth - - - - - - - - - - -		10
Decrees—Index Virorum:		
Elizabeth—15 to 22—22 to 29—31 to 39—39 to 43—43 to 45, and 1 to 3 James—6 Vols. - - - - - - - -	20	
James—3 to 8—8 and 9—10 and 11—12 to 14—14 to 17—18 to 20—21 and 22 - - - - - - - - -	20	
Charles I.—4 and 5—6 and 7—8 and 9—10 and 11—11 to 13—14 and 15—16 to 21 - - - - - - - - - - -	27	
		67
Particulars for Liveries——Edward VI. 1 to 5—Ditto 6 and 7 and 1 Mary—Henry VIII. 1 to 33—36 to 38 Ditto—1 to 5 Mary - -		14
Calendar to Book of Evidences - - - - - - - - -		6
Court of Augmentations:		
Index to Particulars for Grants in the Reign of Edward VI. - - -	4	
Index to Bills and Answers in the Reign of Edward VI. - - -	6	
		10
		431

(Continued.)

SPECIAL RETURNS.
Appendix (G. G.)

THE CHAPTER HOUSE *(continued.)*

Brought over - - - - - 431 Pages.

CALENDARS and INDEXES to, and Abstracts of PLEAS before the KING, in the Times of,
Richard I.
King John,
Edward I. II. and III.
Henry IV. and V.
} both in the King's Bench and Common Pleas.

ABSTRACTS of ASSIZE ROLLS—
Quo Warranto and Pleas of the Crown, &c.

These consist of 55 large Volumes, with Indexes Locorum, Nominum, et Rerum, to most of them—but the Indexes form at most but One Tenth, perhaps not more than One Fifteenth of the Whole.—The specific Particulars of each I have furnished Mr. Ellis with—The Counties are taken Alphabetically—I compute these for - - - - - - - - - 2,500

There are besides, 14 Volumes of divers Counties and Miscellanies, with several Periodical Indexes—which altogether, I suppose may make - - 700

3,200

Index Locorum et Virorum to DOMESDAY Two BOOKS - - - - - 200

3,831

THE AUGMENTATION OFFICE.

CALENDARS to the Deeds of Purchase and Exchange made by the Crown in the Reign of King Henry VIII.;—with Indexes of Places and Names - - - - - 147
Ditto - - - - Ditto - - - - Edward VI. - - - - - - - 84

231

CONVENTUAL Leases granted by the respective Monasteries before their Dissolution - 84

PARTICULARS for LEASES in the Time of Elizabeth and James I. - - -
4 Books of all the Counties in Alphabetical Arrangement - - -
1 - - - - - of Wales and mixed Counties,—and - - - - -
1 - - - - - a Supplemental Calendar - - - - - -
With Indexes of Names and Places to each of them - - - - -
I compute for - - - - -
} 539

854

THE MUSEUM.

3 Volumes of Indexes to Records, &c.—which Mr. Ayscough shewed me—I compute for - - - - - - - - - - - - - - - - 800
6 Ditto Cotton. Library—which Mr. Planta shewed me - - - - - - 400

1200

DUCHY OF LANCASTER.

Inquisitions Post Mortem - - - - - - - - - - - 100

RECAPITULATION.

At the Tower - - - - - - - -	3,913	Pages,	or - - -	4 Volumes.
Rolls Chapel - - - - - -	6,741	- -	or - - -	7
Chapter House - - - - -	3,831	- -	or - - -	4
Augmentation Office - -	854	- -	or - - -	1
Museum - - - - - - -	1,200	- -	or - - -	1
Duchy of Lancaster - - -	100			
	16,639	- -	or - -	17 Volumes.

Luke Hansard,
Printer to the Honourable the House of Commons.

July 1, 1800.

Appendix (H. H.)

Return of THOMAS ASTLE, Esq; and JOHN TOPHAM, Esq; to the Order of the Select Committee on the Public Records of the Kingdom, respecting the Unpublished Records.

AT the Select Committee upon the Public Records of the Kingdom:

Veneris, 4° die Aprilis, 1800;

Charles Abbot, Esq; in the Chair;

Ordered, That Thomas Astle, Esq; and John Topham, Esq; be requested to consider and report their Opinion to this Committee, upon the best Selection to be made of the unpublished Records of the Kingdom, for illustrating the General History of its Civil and Ecclesiastical Government and Jurisprudence; and particularly to report their Opinion upon the Utility of publishing the following Records and Instruments, or any others of the like Nature; pointing out the most perfect Copy of each, and such Parts of each as may exhibit the most perfect Specimens of their several Contents, and of their comparative Value; viz.

POLITICAL SURVEYS:
- Hundred Rolls,
- Extenta Manerii,
- Testa de Nevil,
- Nomina Villarum,
- Knights Fees and Aids.

ECCLESIASTICAL SURVEYS:
- Pope Nicholas's Taxation,
- Nonæ Rolls,
- King Henry VIIIth's Survey,
- Parliamentary Surveys.

JUDICIAL PROCEEDINGS:
- Curia Regis,
- Placita Forestæ,
- Year Books, &c.
- Inquisitions Post Mortem,
  and
- Recorded Oaths of Office antient and modern.

STATUTES and STATE PAPERS.

RETURN to the preceding Order.

To the Honourable the Select Committee upon the Public Records of the Kingdom.

Pursuant to the Request contained in your Order of the 4th Day of April last, we crave leave to state as follows:

I. POLITICAL SURVEYS:

HUNDRED ROLLS, temp. Edw. I.—These Rolls contain a very full and minute Survey in the Nature of Domesday, taken under a Commission to inquire into the Demesne Lands of the Crown, Knights Fees, Liberties, Franchises, Services, and Subtraction of Services, Malversation of Sheriffs, Escheators, &c. &c. The Rolls for Four Counties are extant in the Tower, and for about 30 more are in the Chapter House.

We are of Opinion that a Catalogue of these Rolls, both in the Tower and Chapter House, should be printed, together with the Commissions for taking them, and Specimens of the Roll for some One of the Hundreds in each County.

See Appendix to this Report (A. 1.) and Appendix (A. 2.)

EXTENTA MANERII, 4 Edw. I. 1276.—These are Inquisitions taken under what has been usually termed the Stat. 4 Edw. I. 1276. And we think a Catalogue of these Records, together with a few Specimens, should be printed, selecting, as nearly as may be, the same Hundreds or Places as are described in the Hundred Rolls, so far as they can be found.

There are many Extents of Manors amongst the Bundles of Inquisitions Post Mortem at the Tower, which end with the Reign of Edw. IV.; at the Rolls Chapel to the Reign of Charles I.; at the King's Remembrancer's Office, and at the Chapter House, at Westminster, from Edw. I. to Charles I.

See Appendix (G. 6. b.)

TESTA DE NEVIL, temp. Hen. III. and Edw. I.—This is a Survey of Knights Fees, Escheats, and Services, &c. and we are of Opinion, that a Table of the Contents of this Survey should be printed, either from the Original Two Volumes in the King's Remembrancer's Office, or from that at the Chapter House, with a few Specimens; selecting, as nearly as may be, the same Hundreds or Places as are described in the Hundred Rolls and Extenta Manerii.

See Return, Appendix (G. 6. a.) and Return, Appendix (A. 1. e.)

NOMINA VILLARUM, 9 Edw. II. 1315, &c.—A Book so called is supposed to be kept in the Treasurer's Remembrancer's Office in the Exchequer, and to contain the Sheriffs Returns of the Names of the Hundreds, Villages, &c. and of the Possessors thereof in each County, 9 Edw. II. 1315. But the total Confusion of the Records in that Office renders it impossible to ascertain the Fact. There is also some Reason to apprehend that it may have been destroyed by Fire.

See Appendix (G. 7. a. b.)

In the Harleian Library, No. 6,281, there is also a Book which is said to contain the Names of the Villages, &c. from 1316 to 1559; and upon Examination it appears to be a Transcript of that above mentioned, with the following Title: "A Transcript of the Book "called Nomina Villarum, kept in the Office of the "Treasurer's Remembrancer in the Exchequer." But this MS. doth not contain the Names of the Possessors of Hundreds, Manors, &c. to the Year 1559, as is stated in the Harleian Catalogue.

There is also another Book, called Nomina Villarum, at the Pipe Office, which commences soon after the Restoration, and contains an Alphabetical List of the Claims of Liberties and Privileges by the Lords of Hundreds, Manors, &c. classed in Counties; wherein are entered the Names of the Bailiffs and other Officers who have made their Returns of the different Claims into the Court of Exchequer upon Oath. We conceive that it may be expedient to print these Books containing the Nomina Villarum, if the MS. in the Museum shall, on further Examination, be found to be complete.

See Museum Return, Appendix (U.) and Pipe Office Return, Appendix (G. 8.)

KNIGHTS FEES and AIDS, 20 Edw. III. 1346, and temp. Hen. VI. 1440.—We think it may be occasionally useful in Matters of History and Pedigree, to refer to these Books, which are kept in the King's Remembrancer's Office; but we do not think them of sufficient general Utility to require to be printed.

See Appendix (G. 6. a.)

II. ECCLESIASTICAL SURVEYS:

POPE NICHOLAS'S TAXATION, circa 20 Edw. I. 1291.—This Ecclesiastical Survey of the Benefices is a most important Record, because all the Taxes, as well to our Kings as to the Popes, were regulated by it until the Survey made in the 26th Year of the Reign of Henry VIII.; and because all the Statutes of Colleges in our

SPECIAL RETURNS.
Appendix (H. H.)

our Universities, which were founded before the Reformation, are also regulated by this Criterion, which exempts their Benefices to a certain Value, from the Restrictions in the Statute concerning Pluralities. The Nonæ Rolls refer to this Survey.

It may be proper to observe, that the Taxation made in the Reign of Henry III. in the Pontificate of Pope Innocent the Fourth, which was denominated the Norwich Taxation (called the "Vetus Valor") appeared to have been very partial and much below the real Value, which occasioned this Taxation (called the "Verus Valor") to be made. Commissioners were appointed for that Purpose, who returned the real Value of all Benefices, which raised the Amount of the Taxes, both to the State, and to the Popes, very considerably. The Commissioners returned their Valuation or Taxation into the Exchequer, where it now remains in the King's Remembrancer's Office (Appendix G. 6. a.) and is in Two large Volumes in Folio, the One for the Province of Canterbury, the other for that of York; from which a Transcript was made and returned into Chancery, by virtue of the King's Writ, under the Great Seal, directed to the Treasurer and Barons of the Exchequer, as appears by the Title of the Record still remaining in the Tower: "Transcriptum Rotulorum de Scaccario, "in quibus Ecclesiastica Beneficia infra Angliam et Walliam, continetur, per Breve Regis de Magno Sigillo "directum de Thesaurario et Baronibus de eisdem, in "Cancellario mittendum, estque inter Compota de Anno Vicesimo Primo Edwardi Primi."

A Transcript of this Taxation is in the Library of Mr. Astle, made from the MS. in the Bodleian Library, No. 3595, 129, which was written in 1291, and formerly belonged to Sir Henry Spelman. Mr. Astle's Copy was also collated with the Original Manuscript in September 1722, and is certified by Mr. Ecton to agree therewith. This Transcript has also been compared with another antient Copy in the Library of Corpus Christi College, Oxford; and with another in the Bodleian Library, No. 5,027, Vol. 86,4. It has also been collated with the Roll in the Tower, and contains several Districts, more than are to be found in the Tower Record. Ex' Gr.

In the Deanery of Briseley, in the Archdeaconry of Norwich, it has the Valor of 29 Places more than the Tower Record, which begins with Langham; whereas Mr. Astle's Copy begins with Swanton.

In the Tower Record, the Deaneries of Dunwich, South Lingham, and Orford, in the Archdeaconry of Suffolk, are wanting; but they are supplied in Mr. Astle's Copy.

In the Archdeaconry of Lincoln, the following Deaneries are wanting in the Tower Record, which are in Mr. Astle's Copy; viz.

Jerdeburgh,	Bolinbroke,
Grymesby,	Horncastle,
Luthesk,	Hill,
Lutheburgh,	Grafthow,
Candleshaw,	Langton Abby.
Calsewath,	

In Yorkshire (p. 1.) of Mr. Astle's Copy, the Names of Places are not exactly in the same Order as in the Tower Record, but the Valuations of the Benefices are the same.

In the MS. above referred to in the Bodleian Library (No. 5,027. 86,4) are the Taxations of several Districts, wherein is contained the true Value according to Pope Nicholas's Taxation, and the former Value according to the Norwich Valor, a Transcript of which is in Mr. Astle's Copy (after Page 398) which shews the Difference between the former and the latter. We must observe, that Mr. Astle's Copy doth not agree with the Record in the Exchequer, especially in the Arrangement.

There are also Copies of Pope Nicholas's Taxation in the Libraries of Lichfield and Lincoln Cathedrals; but we do not know how far they may be perfect; and there is another Copy in the Cottonian Library, which was greatly damaged by the Fire in the Year 1731, which is worthy of Attention, it being in many Particulars more full than the Record in the Exchequer.

We think that the Books in the Exchequer, collated with such of the original Rolls as remain there, and with the antient Manuscript in the Cottonian Library in the British Museum, should be printed.

NONÆ ROLLS, 15 Edw. III. 1341.—A Calendar to these very valuable Rolls, which contain Surveys of Benefices referring to the Taxation of Pope Nicholas, and shewing the Circumstances which had produced an intermediate Increase or Decrease of Value, should be printed, with Mr. Vanderzee's Explanatory Account of them, and Specimens of some One of the most complete in each Diocese.

See Appendix to this Report (G. 6. b.)

SURVEYS, 26 Henry VIII.—These Surveys of the Possessions of Religious Houses were taken a short Time before their Dissolution, by Commissioners appointed for that Purpose; some are very full and descriptive of the Estates; others are less so; it is to be lamented that more of them were not returned into the First Fruits Office. After Inquiry, we cannot discover where others may be found; but we do not think it would be of any great Public Utility to print these; inasmuch as they are very voluminous, and may always be referred to.

See Appendix (G. 18.)

PARLIAMENTARY SURVEYS.—These Surveys of Ecclesiastical Benefices were taken during the Usurpation; they are principally at Lambeth, although several of them have been delivered over to the different Ecclesiastical Persons whom they concerned.

See Mr. Topham's Report, Appendix (T.)

But for Reasons similar to those which are assigned under the preceding Article, we do not recommend them to be printed.

III. JUDICIAL PROCEEDINGS:

CURIA REGIS, 6 R. I.—These Proceedings are preserved in the Chapter House, at Westminster; some of them appear to us to be worthy of Attention (See Appendix A. 1.); but they are not sufficiently perfect for Publication, and many complete Specimens of them are contained in the Notes to Madox's History of the Exchequer.

PLACITA FORESTÆ, 10 John, A. D. 1208.—It may be useful to print One General Catalogue of these Placita, which are now kept in the different Repositories.

See Appendix (A. 1. and A. 2. &c.)

ORDINATIONES SCACCARII.—The Ordinances and Regulations concerning the Exchequer, of the 16th, 17th, and 19th Edw. II. contained in the Red Book of the Exchequer, may deserve Publication. They are divided into Three Parts, the First whereof is subdivided into 50 Chapters; the Second into 14 Chapters; and the Third into 29 Chapters. The Whole very fairly written.

See Appendix (G. 6. a.)

YEAR BOOKS, temp. R. II. 1377, &c.—We think it may be expedient to print the Year Books, and Law Treatises, &c. preserved in the Libraries of Lincoln's Inn, the Temple, and in the British Museum, resting our Opinion in favour of such a Measure principally upon the Grounds alledged in the able and learned Report upon Lincoln's Inn Library.

See Appendix (Q. 3.)

INQUISITIONS POST MORTEM, 1. Hen. III. 1216. unto 20 Car. I. 1644.—We are of Opinion that the Calendars to these Records in the Chapter House at Westminster, the Tower, the Chapel of the Rolls, the Office of the Duchy of Lancaster, and in the King's

6 Remem-

Remembrancer's Office, should be published, they being the most authentic Accounts of the Descents of Families and of Property; but it would not be expedient to print any of the Originals. Calendars to those in the Chapter House are in the Harleian MSS. at the British Museum, and are intituled "Cole's Escheats."

Appendix (A. 1.) (A. 2.) (D. 1. b.) (C. 6. b.) (G. 6. a. and b.)

RECORDED OATHS OF OFFICE.—These Recorded Oaths of Office may deserve Publication, as they elucidate the Nature of each Office, and the Duty of the respective Officers.

See Appendix, Crown Office in Chancery (D. 2. a.) King's Remembrancer's Office (G. 6. d.) Chapter House (A. 1.)

IV. STATUTES:

Many Statutes and Ordinances, recorded in the Rolls of Parliament, are not inserted in the printed Statute Books, which are only Compilations by private Hands. We think it highly expedient that a complete and authoritative Edition of all the Statutes should be published. Such a Measure we observe was proposed in a Report made by a Committee of this Honourable House in 1796; and we think the Copies preserved in the Chapter House, the Exchequer, British Museum, Lincoln's Inn, and other Public Libraries, should be consulted in the Publication of such a Work.

See Appendix (A. 1.) (G. 6. a.) (Q. 3.) (U.)

V. STATE PAPERS:

Rymer's Fœdera is the greatest and most valuable Collection of this Nature. The 20th Volume contains the last Twelve Years of the Reign of King Charles the First, and the first Six Years of that of Charles the Second. We think it may be proper to add another Volume, which will continue the Work to the Period of the Revolution; and perhaps it might be desirable to continue it down to the Accession of the House of Hanover. The 59 Volumes of Mr. Rymer's MS. Collections in the British Museum, are most of them printed in the Fœdera, except a few Instruments and Papers of little Importance in the last Volume.

It does not occur to us at present, that there are any other Records or MSS. relative to the Civil and Ecclesiastical Government and Jurisprudence of this Country, which it would be desirable to print for the Public Use, in addition to those above specified; but it would be unquestionably useful to print such of the Principal Calendars and Indexes to the Records in the Tower, Chapter House, Rolls Chapel, and Augmentation Office, as are pointed out by the Keepers of those several Repositories in their Returns which have been communicated to us.

And we beg leave very particularly to recommend the Printing of the Catalogue of the Cottonian MSS. in the British Museum, recently compiled by the Principal Librarian, under the Orders of the Trustees; as it will point out a very considerable Number of important Documents unnoticed in the former Catalogue of that Collection, and tending greatly to illustrate the History, Laws, Government, and Constitution of this Country.

All which is humbly submitted by,

Thos Astle,
John Topham.

20 June 1800.

To CHARLES ABBOT, *Esq*;
Chairman of the Select Committee on the Public Records, &c.

SECOND

Exemplar CHARTARUM *Regum Angliæ.*

Guil. 1.

IN NOMINE SCE & INDIVIDUE TRINITATIS

Ego Witt di gra rex anglorum notu facio omibz tam

posteris qm presentib Archepi. — Huic q eccle Sci MARTINI

de Bello hanc in pimis dignitate regali auctoritate concedo.

Guil. 2.

Willelmus Rex anglorum. Archiepis. — Notu uob omibs & uolo. qd ego

Willelmus di gra rex anglorum filius Willelmi regis anglorum concedo & dono in pura

& ppetua elemosinam eccle Roffii sci andree apli ad uictu monachorum maneriu qd uocat

Hedenham

Hen. 1.

H. rex angl Ric Basset. & A. de Ver. & Vic. & Baron. &

omib; fidelib; suis franc. & anglic. de Norfolc. sat. Sciatis

me dedisse — Ebrard Epo de Norwic. C. solidatas Ap. Westm

Steph.

S. Rex Angl Archiepis. Epis. Abbatib. Comitib. Justic. Vic. Baron. & Ministris & Omnib

fidelib suis tocius Anglie sat. Sciatis q concessi Deo & Abbi & Monachis Cisterciensis

ordinis de Rupe de Tama — T. Roberto de Calsio Archid. & Ric de Luci. Apd Oxen

Hen. 2.

H. Rex Angl. & Dux Norm. & Aquit. & Comes And. Archiepis — ministerium

meu de Cameria mea cu liberatione q pertinet — Ap Geineforddam;

Ric. 1.

Ric. di gra Rex Angl. Dux Norm. Aquit. & Com Andeg. Archiepis Epis Abbatib

Comit. Baronib Justic. Vic. & Omnib balliuis & fidelib suis sat. Sciatis nos concessisse

& hac carta confirmasse Gilleberto Talebot p servicio suo Manerium de Linton

1. Joh.

Johes dei gra Rex Angl. Dns Hibnie. Dux Norm. Aquitan. & Com

Andeg. — Test. Galfr fil petri Com Essex — apd Westm. xxj die Junij Anno Regni nostri primo

Engraved for the REPORT ON THE Public Records OF THE Kingdom, &c.

Ordered to be printed 4th July 1800. *Engraved by James Basire.*

EXPLANATIO TABULÆ I.

Exemplar Chartarum Regum Angliæ.

Guil. 1.

In Nomine Sanctæ et individuæ Trinitatis Ego Willelmus Dei Gratia Rex Anglorum notum facio omnibus tam posteris quam præsentibus—Archiepiscopis—Huic igitur Ecclesiæ Sancti Martini de Bello.—Hanc in primis dignitatem regali auctoritate concedo.

Guil. 2.

Willelmus Rex Anglorum Archiepiscopis.—Notum vobis omnibus esse volo quod Ego Willelmus Dei Gratia Rex Anglorum filius Willelmi Regis Anglorum concedo et dono in puram et perpetuam elemosinam Ecclesiæ Roffensi Sancti Andræe Apostoli ad victum Monachorum Manerium quod vocatur Hedrehan.

Hen. 1.

Henricus Rex Anglorum Ricardo Basset et Alberico de Ver et Vicecomitibus et Baronibus et omnibus fidelibus suis Francis et Anglicis de Nortfolc Salutem. Sciatis me dedisse—Ebrardo Episcopo de Nortwic Centum Solidatas—apud Westm.

Steph.

Stephanus Rex Anglorum Archiepiscopis Episcopis Abbatibus Comitibus Justiciarijs Vicecomitibus Baronibus et Ministris et omnibus fidelibus suis totius Angliæ Salutem. Sciatis quia concessi Deo et Abbati et Monachis Cistercienfis Ordinis de Parco de Tama. Teste Roberto de Caisñ, Archidiacono et Ricardo de Luci. apud Oxen.

Hen. 2.

Henricus Rex Angliæ et Dux Normanniæ Aquitaniæ et Comes Andegaviæ—Archiepiscopis—Ministerium meum de Esnecca mea cum liberatione quæ pertinet.—apud Oximefordam.

Ric. 1.

Ricardus Dei Gratia Rex Angliæ Dux Normanniæ Aquitaniæ, et Comes Andegaviæ Archiepiscopis Episcopis Abbatibus Comitibus Baronibus Justiciarijs Vicecomitibus et omnibus Ballivis ac fidelibus suis Salutem. Sciatis nos concessisse et hac Carta confirmasse Gilleberto Talebot pro Servicio suo Manerium de Linton.

1 *Joh.*

Johannes Dei Gratia Rex Angliæ Dominus Hiberniæ Dux Normanniæ Aquitaniæ et Comes Andegaviæ—Teste Galfrido filio Petri Comitis Essex'—apud Westm' xi die Junij Anno Regni nostri primo.

Exemplar CHARTARUM *Regum Angliæ*

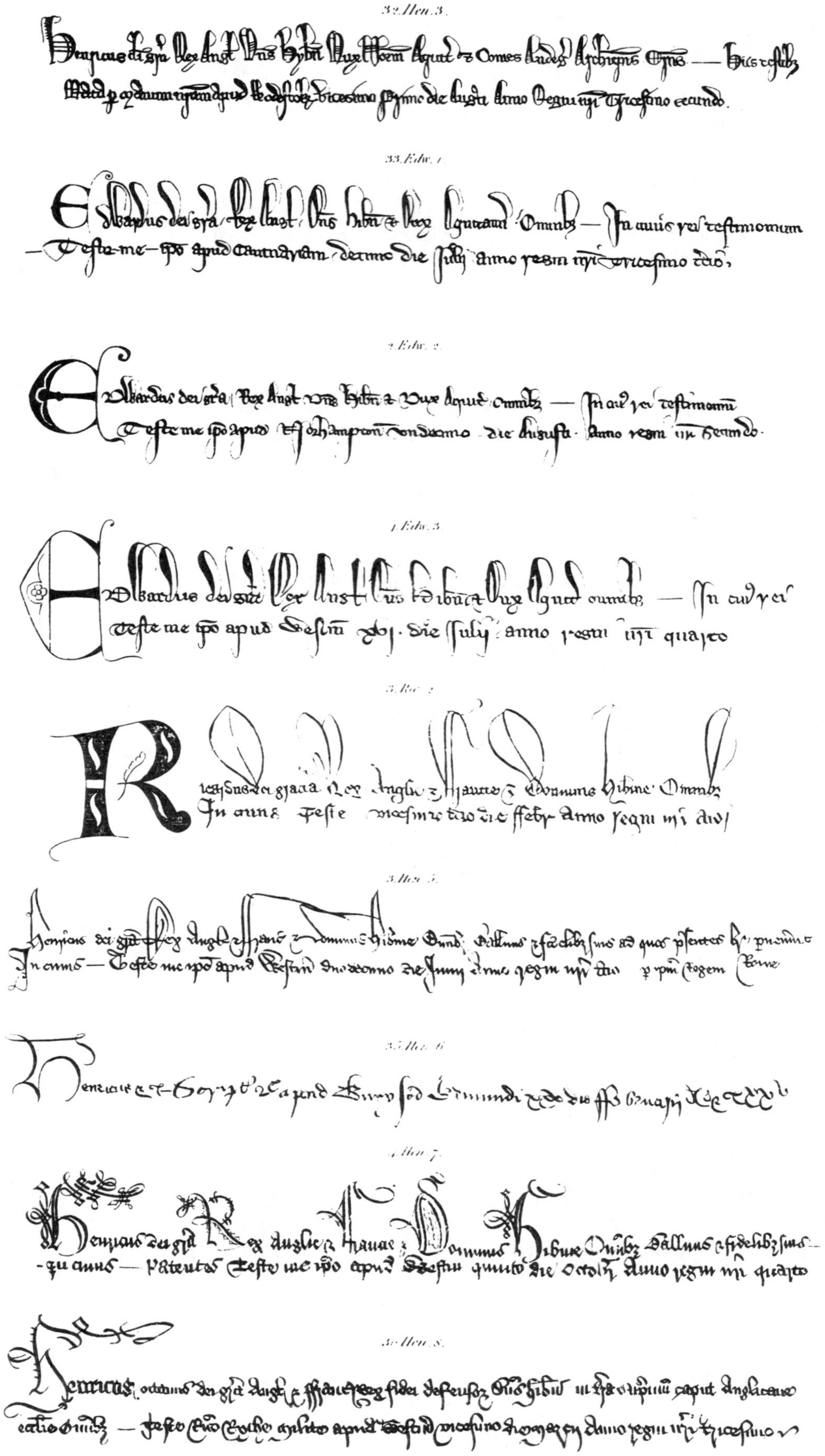

Engraved for the REPORT ON THE Public Records OF THE Kingdom, *&c.*

Ordered to be printed 4th July 1800

Engraved by James Basire

EXPLANATIO TABULÆ II.

Exemplar Chartarum Regum Angliæ.

32 *Hen.* 3.

Henricus Dei Gratia Rex Angliæ Dominus Hyberniæ Dux Normanniæ Aquitaniæ et Comes Andegaviæ Archiepiſcopis Epiſcopis Hijs Teſtibus Data per Manum noſtram apud Wodeſtok viceſimo primo die Auguſti Anno Regni noſtri triceſimo ſecundo.

33 *Edw.* 1.

Edwardus Dei Gratia Rex Angliæ Dominus Hiberniæ et Dux Aquitaniæ omnibus In cujus rei Teſtimonium Teſte me ipſo apud Cantuariam decimo die Julij Anno Regni noſtri triceſimo tercio.

2 *Edw.* 2.

Edwardus Dei Gratia Rex Angliæ Dominus Hiberniæ et Dux Aquitaniæ omnibus In cujus rei Teſtimonium Teſte me ipſo apud Norhampton undecimo die Auguſti Anno Regni noſtri ſecundo.

4 *Edw.* 3.

Edwardus Dei Gratia Rex Angliæ Dominus Hiberniæ et Dux Aquitaniæ omnibus In cujus rei Teſte me ipſo apud Weſtm' xvi die Julij Anno Regni noſtri quarto.

3 *Ric.* 2.

Ricardus Dei Gratia Rex Angliæ et Franciæ et Dominus Hiberniæ omnibus In cujus Teſte viceſimo tercio die Februarij Anno Regni noſtri tercio.

3 *Hen.* 5.

Henricus Dei Gratia Rex Angliæ et Franciæ et Dominus Hiberniæ omnibus Ballivis et fidelibus ſuis ad quos præſentes literæ pervenerint In cujus Teſte me ipſo apud Weſtm' duodecimo die Junij Anno Regni noſtri tercio Per ipſum Regem Romæ.

35 *Hen.* 6.

Henricus &c. Script' &c. Apud Bury Sancti Edmundi xxv die Februarij Anno &c. xxxv.

4 *Hen.* 7.

Henricus Dei Gratia Rex Angliæ et Franciæ et Dominus Hiberniæ omnibus Ballivis et fidelibus ſuis In cujus Patentes Teſte me ipſo apud Weſtm' quinto die Octobris Anni Regni noſtri quarto.

30 *Hen.* 8.

Henricus Octavus Dei Gratia Angliæ et Franciæ Rex Fidei Defenſor Dominus Hiberniæ in Terra ſupremum Caput Anglicanæ Eccleſiæ omnibus Teſte Ricardo Ryche Milite apud Weſtm' viceſimo die Marcij Anno Regni noſtri triceſimo.

Exemplar Libri Censualis

vocati

DOMESDAY BOOK.

SVDRIE.

30

HIC ANNOTANTVR TENENTES TRAS IN SVDRIE

.I. REX WILLELMVS.	.XX. Witts de Braiose.
.II. Archieps Cantuar.	.XXI. Witts filius Ansculfi.
.III. Eps Wintoniensis.	.XXII. Walterius filius Other.
.IIII. Eps Osbernus	.XXIII. Walterius de Douuai.
.V. Eps Baiocensis	.XXIIII. Gislebt fili Richeri.
.VI. Abb de Westmonast	.XXV. Goisfrid de Manneuile.
.VII. Abb de Wintonia	.XXVI. Goisfrid Orlateile.
.VIII. Abb de Certesy.	.XXVII. Eduuard Sarisberie.
.IX. Abb S Wandregisili.	.XXVIII. Robtus malet.
.X. Abb de Cruce S Leutfredi.	.XXIX. Milo crispin.
.XI. Abb de Labatailge.	.XXX. Haimo uicecomes.
.XII. Abbatissa de Berchinges.	.XXXI. Hunfrid camerarius.
.XIII. Canonici S pauli lundon.	.XXXII. Radulf de felgeres.
.XIIII. Eccla de Lanchei̇ge.	.XXXIII. Rainald fili Erchebaldi.
.XV. Comes Eustachius.	.XXXIIII. Albertus clericus.
.XVI. Comitissa Bononiensis.	.XXXV. Odard balistarius.
.XVII. Comes Moritoniensis.	.XXXVI. Osuuold Teodricus. 7 alii seruientes regis.
.XVIII. Comes Rogerius.	
.XIX. Ricard de Tonebrige.	

TERRA REGIS.

IN WOCHINGES HVND.

IN GILDEFORD habet Rex Willelmus .LXXV. hagas. in quib; manent .c.lxxv. homines.
T.R.E. reddeb .xviii. lib 7 iii. denar. Modo appciat .xxx. lib. 7 tam redd .xxx.ii. lib.
De supdictis hagis ht Rannulf clericus .iii. hagas ubi manent .vi. hoes. 7 inde ht isd Ranni saca 7 soca. nisi comune geldu in uilla uenerit unde nullus euadat. Si hō eius in uilla delinqt 7 diiudiat euadat. nil inde ht ppositus regis. Si u calumniat ibi fuerit 7 diiudicat. tc ht rex emenda. Sic tenuit eas Stigand archiep.
Rannulf uicecom ten .i. haga quā hucusq, tenuit de epo baiocsi. hoes u testificant qa n adiacet alicui manerio sed qui teneb ea T.R.E. concessit ei Tovi pposito uille. p emendatione uni sue forisfacture.
Altera dom e q ten ppositus epi baioc de co Bronlei. De hoc dnt hoes de comitatu. qd n ht aliā rectitudine. nisi qd quanda m dua cui erat dom accep ppositus uille. 7 ido misit eps domu ill in suo co. 7 hucusq; pdidit rex csuetudines. eps aut habet.
Dnt etiā hoes q uitauer de alia domo que iacet in Brunlei. ppt hoc tantu qd ppositus de ipsa uilla fuit amicus hois illius qui hanc domu habebat. 7 eo mortuo cuertit ea ad co.
Walerann qq; desaisiuit quendā homine de Bronlei. de una domo unde rex E. habeb csuetudine. Modo ten ea Otbtus cu csuetud sic dicit p rege W.
Robtus de Wateuile ten .i. domu. que reddeb omem csuetud T.R.E. modo nichil reddit.

REX W. ten in dnio WOCHINGES. De firma regis E. fuit. Tc se defd p. xv. hid 7 dim. Nunq; geldauer. Tra e .vi. car. In dnio e una. 7 xxxiii. uilli 7 ix. bord cu .xx. car. Ibi eccla. Osbn tenet. Ibi .i. molin de .xi. sol 7 iiii. den. Ibi xxxii. ac pti. Silua: de .c.xxxiii. porc.
De hac tra ten Walt fili otheri .iii. uirg. hanc qdā forestar tenuit. T.R.E. 7 ca fuit posita ext manerī p rege E. Ibi m nichil e.
T.R.E. 7 post. ualuit .xv. lib ad numer. Modo .xv. lib ad pensu 7 uicecomiti .xxv. sol.

REX ten in dnio STOCHAE. De firma regis E. fuit. Tc se defd p. xvii. hid. Nichil geldauer. Tra e .xvi. car. In dnio sunt ii. car. 7 xxiiii. uilli 7 x bord cu .xx. car. Ibi eccla. q. Witts ten de rege cu dimid hida in elemosina. Ibi .v. serui. 7 ii. molini de .xxv. sol 7 xvi ac pti. Silua: xl. porc. 7 ipsa e in parco regis.
T.R.E. 7 post: ualb .xii. lib. Modo: xv. lib. 7 tam qui ten redd .xv. lib ad pensu. Vicecom ht .xxv. solid

IN BRIXISTAN HVND.

REX ten BERMVNDESYE. Heraldus comes tenuit. Tc se defd p .xiii. hid. m p .xii. hid. Tra e .viii. car. In dnio e una car. 7 xxv. uilli 7 xxxiii. bord cu .iiii. car.
Ibi noua 7 pulchra eccla. 7 xx. ac pti. Silua: v. porc de pasnag. In Lundonia .xiii. burgses de .xliiii. den.
T.R.E. 7 m: ual .xv. lib 7 uicecom ht .xx. sol.
Comes morit ten .i. hidā que T.R.E. 7 post fuit in hoc co.

REX ten MERETONE. Heraldus comes tenuit. Tc se defd 7 m p .xx. hid. Tra e .xxi. car. In dnio sunt .ii. car. 7 lvi. uilli 7 xiii. bord cu .xviii. car. Ibi eccla. 7 ii. molini de .lx. sol. 7 x. ac pti. Silua: qt xx. porc.
T.R.E. ualb .xxv. lib. 7 post: xvi. lib. Modo: xxxv. lib. tam qui ten redd .xl.iii. lib. In Sudwerca .xvi. masure de .xviii. sol 7 ii. denar. huic co ptin.
Quidā Orcus ten .ii. hid que sep iacuer in isto co 7 sunt in alio hund. Ipse tenuit T.R.E. Tc se defd p .ii. hid. m p nichilo. Ibi .i. car in dnio. 7 ii. ac pti. Val sep .xx. sol.
Eps Lisoiensis ten in cherh .ii. solins qui huic co adiacuer T.R.E. 7 regis W. sic testant hoes de hund. Ipse reclamat aduocat epm baiocsen. 7 ppositus suus inde noluit placitare.

IN WALETON HVND.

REX ten in dnio WALETONE. T.R.E. 7 m se defd p .xi. hid. Tra e .xi. car. In dnio e una car. 7 xv. uilli 7 xiii. bord cu .x. car. Ibi .iii. serui 7 ii. molini de .xx. solid. 7 viii ac pti. Silua que e in chent:
Ricard de Tonebrige ten de hoc co unā uirgatā cu silua. unde abstulit rusticu qui ibi manebat. Nc reddit uicecomiti .x. sol. p annu.
Totu co T.R.E. ualb .xv. lib. Modo: x. lib.

IN CHEnchefelle HVND.

REX ten in dnio CHERCHEFELLE. Eddid regina tenuit. Tc se defd p .xxx.vii. hid 7 dim. Modo ad op regis p .xxxiiii. hid. Tra e In dnio sunt .iii. car. 7 lx vii. uilli 7 xi. bord cu .xxvi. car. Ibi .ii. molini de .xii. sol 7 ii. denar min. 7 xii. ac pti. Silua: c.xl. porc. de pasnag. 7 de herbagio: xl.iii. porc.
Modo appciat .xl. lib. 7 tam reddit.

Engraved for the REPORT ON THE Public Records OF THE Kingdom. &c.

Ordered to be printed 1st. July 1800.

Engraved by James Basire.

EXPLANATIO TABULÆ III.

EXEMPLAR LIBRI CENSUALIS

VOCATI

DOMESDAY BOOK.

SUDRIE.

Hic annotantur Tenentes Terras in Sudrie.

1. Rex Willelmus.
2. Archiepiſcopus Cantuarienſis.
3. Epiſcopus Wintonienſis.
4. Epiſcopus Oſbernus.
5. Epiſcopus Baiocenſis.
6. Abbas de Weſtmonaſterio.
7. Abbas de Wintonia.
8. Abbas de Certeſy.
9. Abbas Sancti Wandregeſilij.
10. Abbas de Cruce S. Leutfredi.
11. Abbas de Labatailge.
12. Abbatiſſa de Berchinges.
13. Canonici S. Pauli Lundoniæ.
14. Eccleſia de Lantheige.
15. Comes Euſtachius.
16. Comitiſſa Bononienſis.
17. Comes Moritonienſis.
18. Comes Rogerius.
19. Ricardus de Tonebrige.
20. Willelmus de Braioſe.
21. Willelmus filius Anſculfi.
22. Walterius filius Other.
23. Walterius de Douvai.
24. Giſlebertus filius Richerij.
25. Goisfridus de Mannevile.
26. Goisfridus Orlateile.
27. Eduvardus Sariſberie.
28. Robertus Malet.
29. Milo Criſpin.
30. Haimo Vicecomes.
31. Hunfridus Camerarius.
32. Radulfus de Felgeres.
33. Rainaldus filius Erchebaldi.
34. Albertus Clericus.
35. Odardus Baliſtarius.
36. Oſuvoldus Teodricus,
   et alij Servientes Regis.

TERRA REGIS. In WOCHINGES Hundred.

In Gildeford habet Rex Willelmus 75 Hagas in quibus manent 175 homines.

Tempore Regis Edwardi reddebant 18 lib. & 3 denar' Modo appreciantur 30 lib. & tamen reddunt 32 lib.

De ſupradictis Hagis habet Rannulfus Clericus 3 Hagas ubi manent 6 homines et inde habet iſdem Rannulfus ſacam & ſocam niſi commune geldum in villa venerit unde nullus evadat. Si homo ejus in Villa delinquit & divadiatus evadat nil inde habet præpoſitus Regis. Si vero calumniatus ibi fuerit & divadiatus tunc habet Rex emendam. Sic tenuit eas Arch' Stigandus.

Rannulfus Vicecomes tenet unam Hagam quam huculque tenuit de Epiſcopo Baiocenſi homines vero teſtificantur quia non adjacet alicui Manerio ſed qui tenebat eam T. R. E. conceſſit eam Tovi præpoſito Villæ pro emendatione unius ſuæ foriſfacturæ.

Altera Domus eſt quæ tenet præpoſitus Epiſcopi Baiocenſis de Manerio Bronlei. De hoc dicunt homines de Comitatu quod non habet ibi aliam rectitudinem, niſi quod quandam viduam cujus erat domus accepit præpoſitus Villæ, & idcirco miſit Epiſcopus Domum illam in ſuo Manerio & hucuſque perdidit Rex conſuetudines, Epiſcopus autem habet.

Dicunt etiam homines qui juraverunt de alia Domo quæ jacet in Brunlei propter hoc tantum quod præpoſitus de ipſa Villa fuit amicus hominis illius qui hanc Domum habebat & eo mortuo convertit eam ad Manerium de Bronlei.

Walerannus quoque deſaiſivit quendam hominem de una Domo unde Rex E. habebat conſuetudinem. Modo tenet eam Oſbertus cum conſuetudine ſicut dicit per Regem Willelmum. Robertus de Watevile tenet unam Domum quæ reddebat omnem conſuetudinem T. R. E. modo nichil reddit.

Rex Willelmus tenet in Dominio Wochinges. De Firma Regis E. fuit. Tunc ſe defendebat pro 15 Hidis & dimidia. Nunquam geldaverunt. Terra eſt 6 Carucatæ. In Dominio eſt una & 33 Villani & 9 Bordarij cum 20 Carucis Ibi Eccleſia. Oſbernus tenet & ibi Molendinum de 11 ſol. & 4 den. Ibi 32 Acræ Prati. Silva de 133 Porcis.

De hac Terra tenet Walterus Filius Otherij 3 Virgatas. Hanc quidam Foreſtarius tenuit T. R. E. & tunc fuit poſita extra Manerium per Regem. E. Ibi modo nichil eſt.

T. R. E. & poſt valuit 15 lib. ad numerum. Modo 15 lib. ad penſum & Vicecomiti 25 ſol.

Rex tenet in Dominio Stochæ. De firma Regis E. fuit. Tunc ſe defendebat pro 17 Hidis. Nichil geldaverunt. Terra eſt 16 Carucatæ. In Dominio ſunt 2æ Carucatæ & 24 Villani & 10 Bordarij cum 20 Carucis. Ibi Eccleſia quæ Willelmus tenet de Rege cum dimidia Hida in Elemoſina. Ibi 5 Servi & 2 Molini de 25 ſol. & 16 Acræ Prati. Silva 40 Porcorum & ipſa eſt in parco Regis.

T. R. E. & poſt valebat 12 lib. Modo 15 lib. Tamen qui tenet reddit 15 lib. ad penſum. Vicecomes habet 25 ſolid.

In BRIXISTAN Hundred.

Rex tenet Bermundeſye comes Heraldus tenuit. Tunc ſe defendebat pro 13 Hidis modo pro 12 Hidis. Terra eſt 8 Carucatæ. In Dominio eſt una Carucata & 25 Villani & 33 Bordarij cum 4 Carucis.

Ibi nova & pulchra Eccleſia & 20 Acræ Prati. Silva 5 Porcorum de Paſnagio. In Lundonia 13 Burgenſes de 44 Denarijs.

T. R. E. & modo valebat 15 lib. & Vicecomes habet 20 ſolidos.

Comes Moriton' tenet unam Hidam quæ T. R. E. & poſt fuit in hoc Manerio.

Rex tenet Meretone Comes Heraldus tenuit. Tunc ſe defendebat & modo pro 20ti Hidis. Terra eſt 21 Carucatæ. In Dominio ſunt 2 Carucatæ & 56 Villani & 13 Bordarij cum 18 Carucis. Ibi Eccleſia & 2 Molini de 60 ſol. & 10 Acræ Prati. Silva 80 Porcorum.

T. R. E. valebat 25 lib. & poſt 16 lib. Modo 35 lib. tamen qui tenent reddunt 43 lib. In Sudwerca 16 Maſuræ de 18 ſol' & 2 Denar' huic Manerio pertinebant.

Quidam Orcus tenet 2 Hidas quæ ſemper jacuerunt in iſto Manerio & ſunt in alio Hundredo. Ipſe tenuit T. R. E. Tunc ſe defendebat pro 2 Hidis modo pro nichilo. Ibi una Carucata in Dominio & 2 Acræ Prati. Valuit ſemper 20 ſol. Epiſcopus Liſoienſis tenet in Chent 2 Solins qui huic Manerio adjacuerunt T. R. E. & Regis Willelmi ſicut teſtantur homines de Hundredo. Ipſe reclamat Advocatum Epiſcopum Baiocenſem et præpoſitus ſuus inde noluit placitare.

In WALETON Hundred.

Rex tenet in Dominio Waletone. T. R. E. & modo ſe defendat pro 11 Hidis. Terra eſt 11 Carucatæ. In Dominio eſt una Carucata & 15 Villani & 14 Bordarij cum 10 Carucis. Ibi 3 Servi & 2 Molini de 30 ſolidis & 8 Acræ Prati. Silva quæ eſt in Chent.

Ricardus de Tonebridge tenet de hoc Manerio unam Virgatam cum Silva unde abſtulit ruſticum qui ibi manebat. Nunc reddit Vicecomiti 10 ſolidos per Annum.

Totum Manerium T. R. E. valebat 15 lib. Modo 10 lib.

In CHERCHEFELLE Hundred.

Rex tenet in Dominio Cherchefelle Eddid Regina tenuit. Tunc ſe defendebat pro 37 Hidis & dimidia. Modo ad opus Regis pro 34 Hidis. Terra eſt In Dominio ſunt 3 Carucatæ & 67 Villani & 11 Bordarij cum 26 Carucis. Ibi 2 Molini de 12 ſol. 2os Denar' minus & 12 Acræ Prati. Silva 140 Porcorum de Paſnagio & de Herbagio. 43 Porci. Modo appreciatur 40 lib. & tantum reddit.

Exemplar Computi de exit PRIOR ALIEN Com Sussex.

18 Edw. 2.

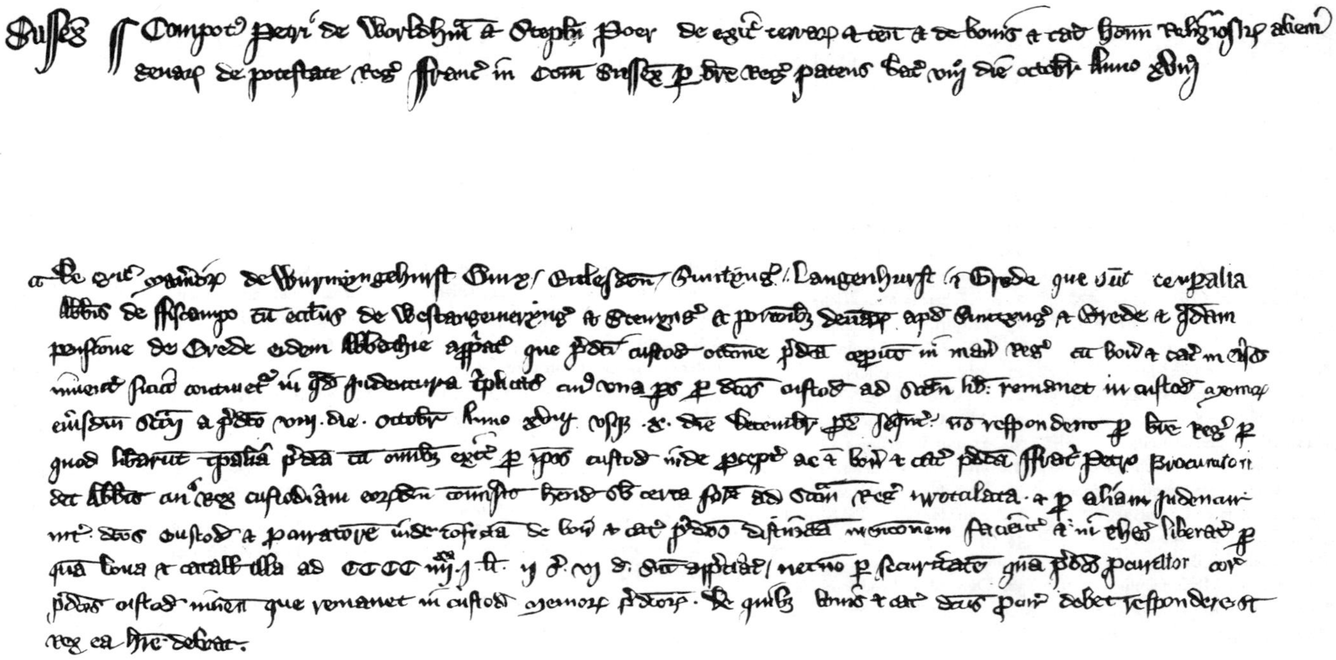

Exemplar Inquisitionis NONAE in Com Sussex.

15. Edw. 3.

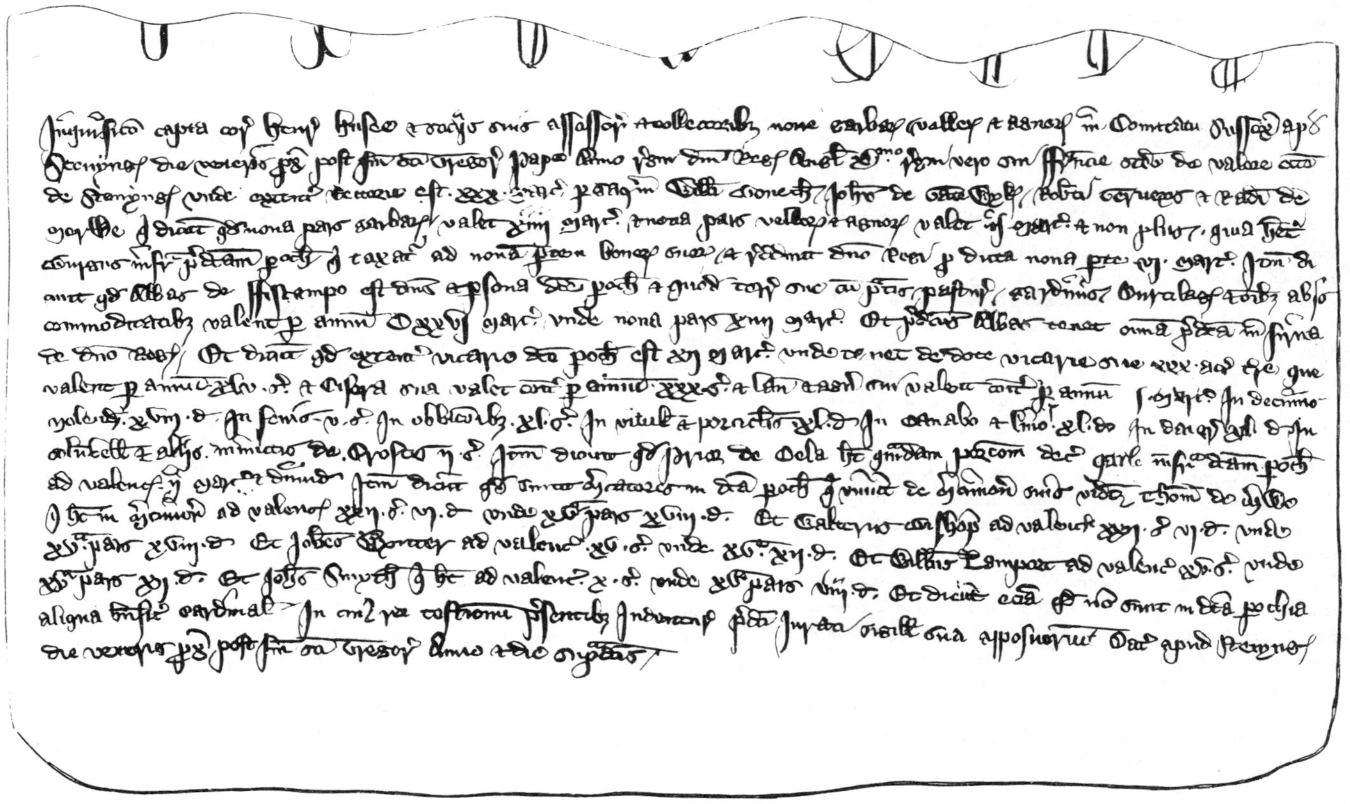

Engraved for the REPORT ON THE Public Records OF THE Kingdom, &c

Ordered to be Printed 4th July 1800. Engraved by James Basire.

EXPLANATIO TABULÆ IV.

Exemplar computi de exit' Prior' Alien' Com' Sussex'.

18 *Edw.* 2.

Sussex, ſs. **Compotus** Petri de Worldham & Stephani Poer de exitibus Terrarum et Tenementorum & de Bonis & Catallis Hominum Religioſorum alienigenarum de Poteſtate Regis Franciæ in Comitatu Suſſexiæ per Breve Regis patens datum 8vo die Octobris Anno 18vo.

De exitibus Maneriorum de Wurmyngehurſt Bury Eccleſdon Suntyng Langenhurſt & Brede quæ ſunt temporalia Abbatis de Fiſcampo cum Eccleſijs de Weſtangemeryng & Stenyng ac portionibus Decimarum apud Suntyng & Brede & quadam Penſione de Brede eidem Abbathiæ appropriata quæ prædicti Cuſtodes occaſione prædicta ceperint in Manus Regis cum Bonis & Catallis in eiſdem inventis ſicut continetur in quadam Indentura triplicata cujus una pars per dictos Cuſtodes ad Scaccarium liberata remanet in Cuſtodia Memorandorum ejuſdem Scaccarij a prædicto 8vo die Octobris Anno 18vo uſque 10 Diem Decembris proxime ſequentem non reſpondent per breve Regis per quod liberarunt temporalia prædicta cum omnibus exitibus per ipſos Cuſtodes inde perceptos acetiam Bona & Catalla prædicta Fratri Petro Procuratori dicti Abbatis cui Rex Cuſtodiam eorundem commiſit habendum ſub certa forma ad Scaccarium Regis irrotulata et per aliam Indenturam inter dictos Cuſtodes & Procuratorem inde confectam de Bonis & Catallis prædictis diſtinctam mentionem facientem et in Theſauraria liberatam per quam Bona & Catalla illa ad $48^{l}\ 2^{s}\ 6^{d}$ ſunt appreciata necnon per Securitatem quam prædictus Procurator coram prædictis Cuſtodibus invenit quæ remanet in Cuſtodia Memorandorum prædictorum de quibus Bonis & Catallis dictus Procurator debet reſpondere ut Rex ea habere debeat.

Exemplar Inquisitionis Nonæ in Com' Sussex'.

15 *Edw.* 3.

Inquisitio capta coram Henrico Huſee & Socijs ſuis Aſſeſſoribus et Collectoribus Nonæ Garbarum Vellerum et Agnorum in Comitatu Suſſexiæ apud Stenyng die Veneris proxime poſt feſtum Sancti Gregorij Papæ Anno Regni Domini Regis Angliæ 15mo Regni vero ſui Franciæ ſecundo de valore Eccleſiæ de Stenyng unde extenta Rectoriæ eſt 30 Marcæ per Sacramentum Willelmi Boneth Johannis de Gatewyk Roberti Gerveys & Radulphi de Merwe qui dicunt quod nona pars Garbarum valet 14 Marc' & nona pars Vellerum et Agnorum valet 2 Marc' et non plus quia habetur Burgus infra prædictam Parochiam qui taxatur ad nonam partem Bonorum ſuorum et reddit Domino Regi pro dicta nona parte 6 Marc'. Item dicunt quod Abbas de Fiſcampo eſt Dominus et Perſona dictæ Parochiæ et quod terræ ſuæ cum Pratis Paſturis Gardinis Curtilagijs et omnibus alijs Commoditatibus valent per Annum 126 Marcæ unde nona pars 14 Marcæ et prædictus Abbas tenet omnia prædicta in firma de Domino Rege et dicunt quod extenta Vicariæ dictæ Parochiæ eſt 12 Marcæ unde tenet de Dote Vicariæ ſuæ 30 Acras Terræ quæ valent per Annum 45^{s} et Ciſera ſua valet communiter per Annum 30^{s} et Lana & Agni ſui valent communiter per Annum 1 Marcam. In decimis Molendinorum 18^{d}. In Fænis 5^{s}. In Oblationibus 40^{s}. In Vitulis et Porcellis 40^{d}. In Canabo & Lino 40^{d}. In Daieria 40^{d}. In Columbellis & alijs Minutis de Croftis 2^{s}. Item dicunt quod Prior de Cela habet quandam portionem Decimarum Garbarum infra dictam Parochiam ad valentiam 2 Marcarum & dimidiam Item dicunt quod ſunt Mercatores in dicta Parochia qui vivunt de Mercimonijs ſuis videlicet Thomas de Merwe qui habet in Mercimonijs ad valentiam $22^{s}\ 6^{d}$ unde 15ma pars 18^{d} et Walterus Biſhop ad valentiam $22^{s}\ 6^{d}$ unde 15ma pars 18^{d} et Johannes Wynter ad valentiam 15^{s} unde $15^{ma}\ 12^{d}$ et Willelmus Lamport ad valentiam 15^{s} unde 15ma pars 12^{d} et Johannes Smyth qui habet ad valentiam 10^{s} unde 15ma pars 8^{d} et dicunt etiam quod non ſunt in dicta Parochia aliqua Beneficia cardinalia In cujus rei teſtimonium præſentibus Indenturis prædicti Jurati ſigilla ſua appoſuerunt Dat' apud Stenyng die Veneris proxima poſt feſtum Sancti Gregorij Anno et Die ſupradictis.

ARTIC[illegible]AGNE CARTE LIBERTATUM *sub Sigillo Regis* JOHANNIS.

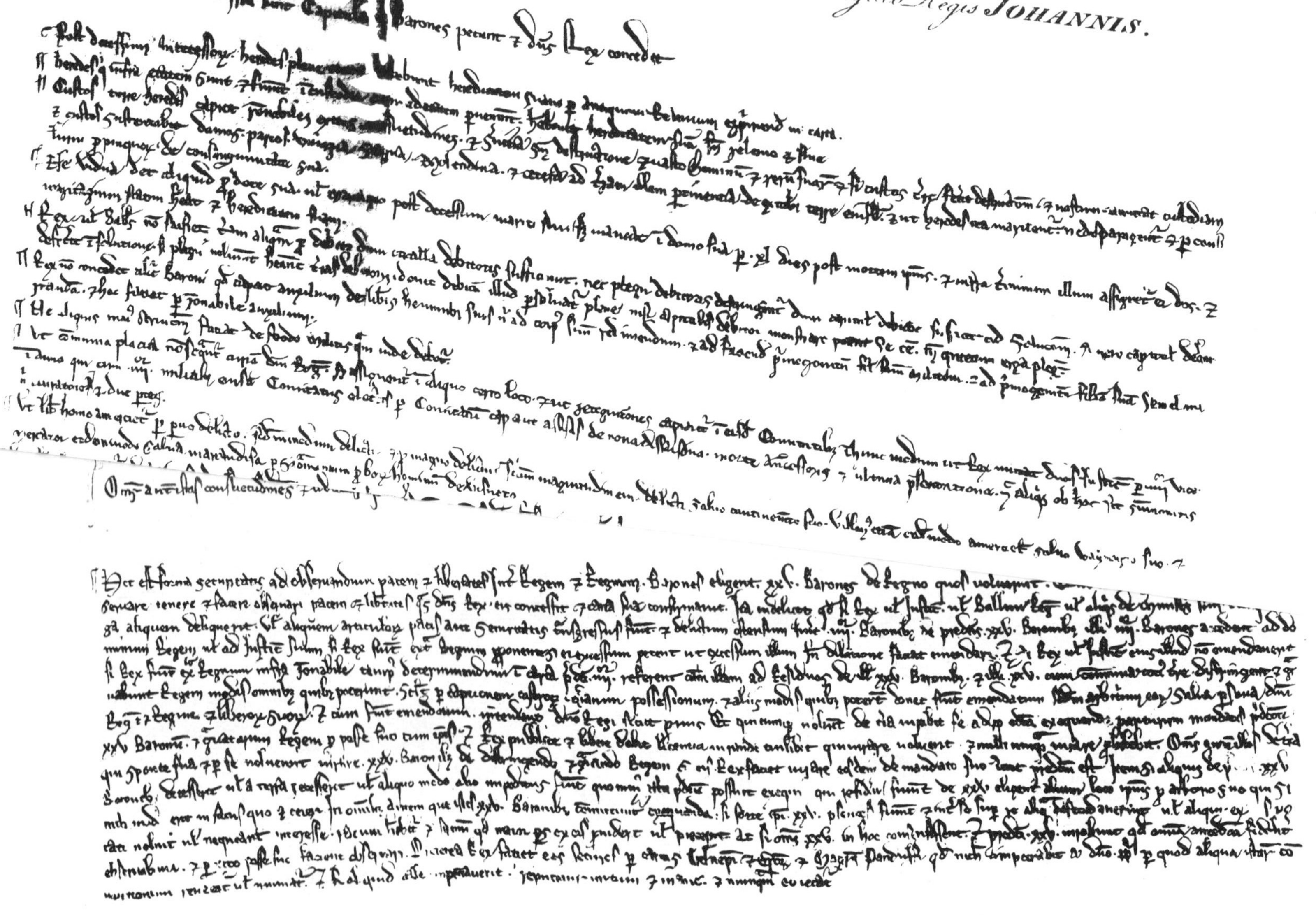

APPENDIX (CC)

Ordered to be printed 4

Engraved for the REPORT ON THE Public Records OF THE Kingdom *&c.*

Engraved by James

Articula Magne Carte Libertatum sub Sigillo Regis JOHANNIS.

ISTA SUNT CAPITULA QUE BARONES PETUNT ET DOMINUS REX CONCEDIT.

POST deceſſum anteceſſorum heredes plene etatis habebunt hereditatem ſuam per antiquum relevium exprimendum in carta

§. Heredes qui infra etatem ſunt et fuerint in cuſtodia cum ad etatem pervenerint 2
habebunt hereditatem ſuam ſine relevio et ſine

§. Cuſtos terre heredis capiat rationabiles exitus conſuetudines et ſervitia ſine deſtruc- 3
tione et vaſto hominum et rerum ſuarum et ſi cuſtos terre ſecerit deſtructionem et vaſtum amittat cuſtodiam et cuſtos ſuſtentabit domos parcos vivaria ſtagna molendina et cetera ad terram illam pertinentia de exitibus terre ejuſdem et ut heredes ita maritentur ne diſparagentur et per conſilium propinquorum de conſanguinitate ſuâ

§. Ne vidua det aliquid pro dote ſua vel maritagio poſt deceſſum mariti ſui ſed maneat 4
in domo ſua per xl dies poſt mortem ipſius et infra terminum illum aſſignetur ei dos et maritagium ſtatim habeat et hereditatem ſuam

§. Rex vel ballivus non ſaiſiet terram aliquam pro debito dum catalla debitoris ſufficiunt 5
nec plegii debitoris diſtringantur dum capitalis debitor ſufficit ad ſolutionem ſi vero capitalis debitor defecerit in ſolutione ſi plegii voluerint habeant terras debitoris donec debitum illud perſolvatur plene niſi capitalis debitor monſtrare poterit ſe eſſe inde quietum erga plegios

§. Rex non concedet alicui baroni quod capiat auxilium de liberis hominibus ſuis niſi 6
ad corpus ſuum redimendum et ad faciendum primogenitum filium ſuum militem et ad primogenitam filiam ſuam ſemel maritandam et hoc faciet per rationabile auxilium

§. Ne aliquis majus ſervitium faciat de feodo militis quam inde debetur 7

§. Ut communia placita non ſequantur curiam domini regis ſed aſſignentur in aliquo 8
certo loco et ut recognitiones capiantur in eiſdem comitatibus in hunc modum ut rex mittat duos juſticiarios per iiij^or^ vices in anno qui cum iiij^or^ militibus ejuſdem comitatus electis per comitatum capiant aſſiſas de nova diſſaiſina morte anteceſſoris et ultima preſentatione nec aliquis ob hoc ſit ſummonitus niſi juratores et due partes

§. Ut liber homo amercietur pro parvo delicto ſecundum modum delicti et pro magno 9
delicto ſecundum magnitudinem delicti ſalvo continemento ſuo villanus etiam eodem modo amercietur ſalvo waynagio ſuo et mercator eodem modo ſalva marcandiſa per ſacramentum proborum hominum de viſneto

§. Ut clericus amercietur de laico feodo ſuo ſecundum modum aliorum predictorum 10
et non ſecundum beneficium eccleſiaſticum

§. Ne aliqua villa amercietur pro pontibus faciendis ad riparias niſi ubi de jure 11
antiquitus eſſe ſolebant

§. Ut menſura vini bladi et latitudines pannorum et rerum aliarum emendetur et ita 12
de ponderibus

§. Ut aſſiſe de nova diſſaiſina et de morte anteceſſoris abbrevientur et ſimiliter de 13
aliis aſſiſis

§. Ut nullus vicecomes intromittat ſe de placitis ad coronam pertinentibus ſine corona- 14
toribus et ut comitatus et hundreda ſint ad antiquas firmas abſque nullo incremento exceptis dominicis maneriis regis

§. Si aliquis tenens de rege moriatur licebit vicecomiti vel alii ballivo regis ſeiſire et 15
imbreviare catallum ipſius per viſum legalium hominum ita tamen quod nichil inde amoveatur donec plenius ſciatur ſi debeat aliquod liquidum debitum domino regi et tunc debitum regis perſolvatur reſiduum vero relinquatur executoribus ad faciendum teſtamentum defuncti et ſi nichil regi debetur omnia catalla cedant defuncto

§. Si aliquis liber homo inteſtatus deceſſerit bona ſua per manum proximorum parentum 16
ſuorum et amicorum et per viſum eccleſie diſtribuantur

§. Ne vidue diſtringantur ad ſe maritandum dum voluerint ſine marito vivere ita tamen 17
quod ſecuritatem facient quod non maritabunt ſe ſine aſſenſu regis ſi de rege teneant vel dominorum ſuorum de quibus tenent

§. Ne

§. Ne conſtabularius vel alius ballivus capiat blada vel alia catalla niſi ſtatim denarios 18
inde reddat niſi reſpectum habere poſſit de voluntate venditoris

§. Ne conſtabularius poſſit diſtringere aliquem militem ad dandum denarios pro cuſtodia 19
caſtri ſi voluerit facere cuſtodiam illam in propria perſona vel per alium probum hominem
ſi ipſe eam facere non poſſit per rationabilem cauſam et ſi rex eum duxerit in excercitum
ſit quietus de cuſtodia ſecundum quantitatem temporis

§. Ne vicecomes vel ballivus regis vel aliquis alius capiat equos vel carettas alicujus 20
liberi hominis pro cariagio faciendo niſi ex voluntate ipſius

§. Ne rex vel ballivus ſuus capiat alienum boſcum ad caſtra vel ad alia agenda ſua niſi 21
per voluntatem ipſius cujus boſcus ille fuerit

§. Ne rex teneat terram eorum qui fuerint convicti de felonia niſi per unum annum et 22
unum diem ſed tunc reddatur domino feodi

§. Ut omnes kidelli de cetero penitus deponantur de Tamiſia et Medewaye et per 23
totam Angliam

§. Ne breve quod vocatur Precipe de cetero fiat alicui de aliquo tenemento unde liber 24
homo amittat curiam ſuam

§. Si quis fuerit diſſeiſitus vel prolongatus per regem ſine judicio de terris libertatibus et 25
jure ſuo ſtatim ei reſtituatur et ſi contentio ſuper hoc orta fuerit tunc inde diſponatur
per judicium xxv baronum et ut illi qui fuerint diſſaiſiti per patrem vel fratrem regis
rectum habeant ſine dilatione per judicium parium ſuorum in curia regis et ſi rex debeat
habere terminum aliorum cruce ſignatorum tunc archiepiſcopus et epiſcopi faciant inde
judicium ad certum diem appellatione remota

§. Ne aliquid detur pro brevi inquiſitionis de vita vel membris ſed libere concedatur 26
ſine precio et non negetur

§. Si aliquis tenet de rege per feodi firmam per ſokagium vel per burgagium et de 27
alio per ſervitium militis dominus rex non habebit cuſtodiam militum de feodo alterius
occaſione burgagii vel ſokagii nec debet habere cuſtodiam burgagii ſokagii vel feodi
firme et quod liber homo non amittat militiam ſuam occaſione parvarum ſergantiſarum
ſicuti de illis qui tenent aliquod tenementum reddendo inde cuttellos vel ſagittas
vel hujuſmodi

§. Ne aliquis ballivus poſſit ponere aliquem ad legem ſimplici loquela ſua ſine 28
teſtibus fidelibus

§. Ne corpus liberi hominis capiatur nec impriſonetur nec diſſaiſietur nec utlagetur 29
nec exuletur nec aliquo modo deſtruatur nec rex eat vel mittat ſuper eum vi niſi per
judicium parium ſuorum vel per legem terre

§. Ne jus vendatur vel differratur vel vetitum ſit 30

§. Quod mercatores habeant ſalvum ire et venire ad emendum vel vendendum ſine 31
omnibus malis toltis per antiquas et rectas conſuetudines

§. Ne ſcutagium vel auxilium ponatur in regno niſi per commune conſilium regni niſi ad 32
corpus regis redimendum et primogenitum filium ſuum militem faciendum et filiam ſuam
primogenitam ſemel maritandam et ad hoc fiat rationabile auxilium ſimili modo fiat de
taillagiis et auxiliis de civitate London' et de aliis civitatibus que inde habent libertates
et ut civitas London' plene habeat antiquas libertates et liberas conſuetudines ſuas tam
per aquas quam *per terras*

§. Ut liceat unicuique exire de regno et redire ſalva fide domini regis niſi tempore 33
werre per aliquod breve tempus propter communem utilitatem regni

§. Si quis mutuo aliquid acceperit a Judeis plus vel minus et moriatur antequam debitum 34
illud ſolvatur debitum non uſurabit quamdiu heres fuerit infra etatem de quocumque
teneat et ſi debitum illud inciderit in manum regis rex non capiet niſi catallum quod
continetur in carta

§. Si

§. Si quis moriatur et debitum debeat Judeis uxor ejus habeat dotem ſuam et ſi liberi remanſerint provideantur eis neceſſaria ſecundum tenementum et de reſiduo ſolvatur debitum ſalvo ſervitio dominorum ſimili modo fiat de aliis debitis et ut cuſtos terre reddat heredi cum ad plenam etatem pervenerit terram ſuam inſtauratam ſecundum quod rationabiliter poterit ſuſtinere de exitibus terre ejuſdem de carucis et wainnagiis 35

§. Si quis tenuerit de aliqua eſkaeta ſicut de honore Walingeford Notingeham Bonon' et Lankaſtr' et de aliis eſkaetis que ſunt in manu regis et ſunt baronie et obierit heres ejus non dabit aliud relevium vel faciet regi aliud ſervitium quam faceret baroni et ut rex eodem modo eam teneat quo baro eam tenuit 36

§. Ut fines qui facti ſunt pro dotibus maritagiis hereditatibus et amerciamentis injuſte et contra legem terre omnino condonentur vel fiat inde per judicium xxv baronum vel per judicium majoris partis eorumdem una cum archiepiſcopo et aliis quos ſecum vocare voluerit ita quod ſi aliquis vel aliqui de xxv fuerint in ſimili querela amoveantur et alii loco illorum per reſiduos de xxv ſubſtituantur 37

§. Quod obſides et carte reddantur que liberate fuerunt regi in ſecuritatem 38

§. Ut illi qui fuerint extra foreſtam non veniant coram juſticiariis de foreſta per communes ſummonitiones niſi ſunt in placito vel plegii fuerint et ut prave conſuetudines de foreſtis et de foreſtariis et warrenniis et vicecomitibus et rivariis emendentur per xii milites de quolibet comitatu qui debent eligi per probos homines ejuſdem comitatus 39

§. Ut rex amoveat penitus de balliva parentes et totam ſequelam Gerardi de Atyes quod de cetero balliam non habeant ſcilicet Engelardum Andream Petrum et Gyonem de Cancell' Gyonem de Cygon' Matheum de Martiny et fratres ejus et Galfridum nepotem ejus et Philippum Mark 40

§. Et ut rex amoveat alienigenas milites ſtipendiarios baliſtarios et ruttarios et ſervientes qui veniunt cum equis et armis ad nocumentum regni 41

§. Ut rex faciat juſticiarios conſtabularios vicecomites et ballivos de talibus qui ſciant legem terre et eam bene velint obſervare 42

§. Ut barones qui fundaverunt abbatias unde habent cartas regum vel antiquam tenuram habeant cuſtodiam earum cum vacaverint 43

§. Si rex Walenſes diſſaiſierit vel elongaverit de terris vel libertatibus vel de rebus aliis in Anglia vel in Wallia eis ſtatim ſine placito reddantur et ſi fuerint diſſaiſiti vel elongati de tenementis ſuis Anglie per patrem vel fratrem regis ſine judicio parium ſuorum rex eis ſine dilatione juſticiam exhibebit eo modo quo exhibet Anglicis juſticiam de tenementis ſuis Anglie ſecundum legem Anglie et de tenementis Wallie ſecundum legem Wallie et de tenementis marchie ſecundum legem marchie idem facient Walenſes regi et ſuis 44

<table>
<tr><td>§. Ut rex reddat filium Lewelini et preterea omnes obſides de Wallia et cartas que ei liberate fuerunt in ſecuritatem pacis - - - - - - - -</td><td rowspan="2">niſi aliter eſſe debeat per cartas quas rex habet per judicium archiepiſcopi et aliorum quos ſecum vocare voluerit</td><td>45</td></tr>
<tr><td>§. Ut rex faciat regi Scottorum de obſidibus reddendis et de libertatibus ſuis et jure ſuo ſecundum formam quam facit baronibus Anglie - -</td><td>46</td></tr>
</table>

§. Et omnes foreſte que ſunt aforeſtate per regem tempore ſuo deafforeſtentur et ita fiat de ripariis que per ipſum regem ſunt in defenſo 47

§. Omnes autem iſtas conſuetudines et libertates quas rex conceſſit regno tenendas quantum ad ſe pertinet erga ſuos omnes de regno tam clerici quam laici obſervabunt quantum ad ſe pertinet erga ſuos 48

§. Hec eſt forma ſecuritatis ad obſervandum pacem et libertates inter regem et regnum Barones eligent xxv barones de regno quos voluerint qui debent pro totis viribus ſuis obſervare tenere et facere obſervari pacem et libertates quas dominus rex eis conceſſit et carta ſua confirmavit ita videlicet quod ſi rex vel juſticiarius vel ballivi regis vel aliquis de 49

miniſtris

miniſtris ſuis in aliquo erga aliquem deliquerit vel aliquem articulorum pacis aut ſecuritatis tranſgreſſus fuerit et delictum oſtenſum fuerit iiij^or baronibus de predictis xxv baronibus illi iiij^or barones accedent ad dominum regem vel ad juſticiarium ſuum ſi rex fuerit extra regnum proponentes ei exceſſum petent ut exceſſum illum ſine dilatione faciat emendari et ſi rex vel juſticiarius ejus illud non emendaverit ſi rex fuerit extra regnum infra rationabile tempus determinandum in carta predicti iiij^or referent cauſam illam ad reſiduos de illis xxv baronibus et illi xxv cum communa totius terre diſtringent et gravabunt regem modis omnibus quibus poterunt ſcilicet per captionem caſtrorum terrarum poſſeſſionum et aliis modis quibus poterunt donec fuerit emendatum ſecundum arbitrium eorum ſalva perſona domini regis et regine et liberorum ſuorum et cum fuerit emendatum intendant domino regi ſicut prius et quicumque voluerit de terra jurabit ſe ad predicta exequenda pariturum mandatis predictorum xxv baronum et gravaturum regem pro poſſe ſuo cum ipſis et rex pubblice et libere dabit licentiam jurandi cuilibet qui jurare voluerit et nulli umquam jurare prohibebit omnes autem illos de terra qui ſponte ſua et per ſe noluerint jurare xxv baronibus de diſtringendo et gravando regem cum eis rex faciet jurare eoſdem de mandato ſuo ſicut predictum eſt Item ſi aliquis de predictis xxv baronibus deceſſerit vel a terra receſſerit vel aliquo modo alio impeditus fuerit quo minus iſta predicta poſſint exequi qui reſidui fuerint de xxv eligent alium loco ipſius pro arbitrio ſuo qui ſimili modo erit juratus quo et ceteri In omnibus autem que iſtis xxv baronibus committuntur exequenda ſi forte ipſi xxv preſentes fuerint et inter ſe ſuper re aliqua diſcordaverint vel aliqui ex eis vocati nolint vel nequeant intereſſe ratum habebitur et firmum quod major pars ex eis providerit vel preceperit ac ſi omnes xxv in hoc conſenſiſſent et predicti xxv jurabunt quod omnia antedicta fideliter obſervabunt et pro toto poſſe ſuo facient obſervari Preterea rex faciet eos ſecuros per cartas archiepiſcopi et epiſcoporum et magiſtri Pandulfi quod nichil impetrabit a domino papa per quod aliqua iſtarum conventionum revocetur vel minuatur et ſi aliquid tale impetraverit reputetur irritum et inane et nunquam eo utatur.

EXPLANATIO TABULÆ V^{a}.

Magna Carta Regis Johannis.

Johannes Dei gratia rex Anglie dominus Hybernie dux Normannie Aquitanie et comes Andegavie archiepiſcopis epiſcopis abbatibus comitibus baronibus juſticiariis foreſtariis vicecomitibus prepoſitis miniſtris et omnibus ballivis et fidelibus ſuis ſalutem Sciatis nos intuitu Dei et pro ſalute anime noſtre et omnium anteceſſorum et heredum noſtrorum ad honorem Dei et exaltationem ſancte eccleſie et emendationem regni noſtri per conſilium venerabilium patrum noſtrorum Stephani Cant' archiepiſcopi totius Anglie primatis et ſancte Romane eccleſie cardinalis Henrici Dublin' archiepiſcopi Willielmi London' Petri Winton' Joſcelini Bathon' et Glaſton' Hugonis Lincoln' Walteri Wygorn' Willielmi Coventr' et Benedicti Roff' epiſcoporum magiſtri Pandulfi domini pape ſubdiaconi et familiaris fratris Eymerici magiſtri militie templi in Anglia et nobilium virorum Willielmi Mariſcalli comitis Penbrok Willielmi comitis Sar' Willielmi comitis Warenn' Willielmi comitis Arundell' Alani de Galweya conſtabularii Scottie Warini filii Geroldi Petri filii Hereberti Huberti de Burgo ſeneſcalli Pictavie Hugonis de Nevill' Mathei filii Hereberti Thome Baſſet Alani Baſſet Philippi de Albin' Roberti de Roppel' Johannis Mariſcalli Johannis filii Hugonis et aliorum fidelium noſtrorum In primis conceſſiſſe Deo et hac preſenti carta noſtra confirmaſſe pro nobis et heredibus noſtris in perpetuum quod Anglicana eccleſia libera ſit et habeat jura ſua integra et libertates ſuas illeſas et ita volumus obſervari quod apparet ex eo quod libertatem electionum que maxima et magis neceſſaria reputatur eccleſie Anglicane mera et ſpontanea voluntate ante diſcordiam inter nos et barones noſtros motam conceſſimus et carta noſtra confirmavimus et eam optinuimus a domino papa Innocentio tertio confirmari quam et nos obſervabimus et ab heredibus noſtris in perpetuum bona fide volumus obſervari Conceſſimus etiam omnibus liberis hominibus regni noſtri pro nobis et heredibus noſtris in perpetuum omnes libertates ſubſcriptas habendas et tenendas eis et heredibus ſuis de nobis et heredibus noſtris Si quis comitum vel baronum noſtrorum ſive aliorum tenentium de nobis in capite per ſervitium militare mortuus fuerit et cum deceſſerit heres ſuus plene etatis fuerit et relevium debeat habeat hereditatem ſuam per antiquum relevium ſcilicet heres vel heredes comitis de baronia comitis integra per centum libras heres vel heredes baronis de baronia integra per centum libras heres vel heredes militis de feodo militis integro per centum ſolidos ad plus et qui minus debuerit minus det ſecundum antiquam conſuetudinem feodorum Si autem heres alicujus talium fuerit infra etatem et fuerit in cuſtodia cum ad etatem pervenerit habeat hereditatem ſuam ſine relevio et ſine fine Cuſtos terre hujuſmodi heredis qui infra etatem fuerit non capiat de terra heredis niſi rationabiles exitus et rationabiles conſuetudines et rationabilia ſervitia et hoc ſine deſtructione et vaſto hominum vel rerum et ſi nos commiſerimus cuſtodiam alicujus talis terre vicecomiti vel alicui alii qui de exitibus illius nobis reſpondere debeat et ille deſtructionem de cuſtodia fecerit vel vaſtum nos ab illo capiemus emendam et terra committatur duobus legalibus et diſcretis hominibus de feodo illo qui de exitibus reſpondeant nobis vel ei cui eos aſſignaverimus et ſi dederimus vel vendiderimus alicui cuſtodiam alicujus talis terre et ille deſtructionem inde fecerit vel vaſtum amittat ipſam cuſtodiam et tradatur duobus legalibus et diſcretis hominibus de feodo illo qui ſimiliter nobis reſpondeant ſicut predictum eſt Cuſtos autem quamdiu cuſtodiam terre habuerit ſuſtentet domos parcos vivaria ſtagna molendina et cetera ad terram illam pertinentia de exitibus terre ejuſdem et reddat heredi cum ad plenam etatem pervenerit terram ſuam totam inſtauratam de carrucis et wainnagiis ſecundum quod tempus wainnagii exiget et exitus terre rationabiliter poterunt ſuſtinere Heredes maritentur abſque diſparagatione ita tamen quod antequam contrahatur matrimonium oſtendatur propinquis de conſanguinitate ipſius heredis Vidua poſt mortem mariti ſui ſtatim et ſine difficultate habeat maritagium et hereditatem ſuam nec aliquid det pro dote ſua vel pro maritagio ſuo vel hereditate ſua quam hereditatem maritus ſuus et ipſa tenuerint die obitus ipſius mariti et maneat in domo mariti ſui per quadraginta dies poſt mortem ipſius infra quos aſſignetur ei dos ſua Nulla vidua diſtringatur ad ſe maritandum dum voluerit vivere ſine marito ita tamen quod ſecuritatem faciat quod ſe non maritabit ſine aſſenſu noſtro ſi de nobis tenuerit vel ſine aſſenſu domini ſui de quo tenuerit ſi de alio tenuerit Nec nos nec ballivi noſtri ſeiſiemus terram aliquam nec redditum pro debito aliquo quamdiu catalla debitoris ſufficiunt ad debitum reddendum nec plegii ipſius debitoris diſtringantur quamdiu ipſe capitalis debitor ſufficit ad ſolutionem debiti et ſi capitalis debitor defecerit in ſolutione debiti non habens unde ſolvat plegii reſpondeant de debito et ſi voluerint habeant terras et redditus debitoris donec ſit eis ſatiſfactum de debito quod ante pro eo ſolverint niſi capitalis debitor monſtraverit ſe eſſe quietum inde verſus eoſdem plegios Si quis mutuo ceperit aliquid a Judeis plus vel minus et moriatur antequam debitum illum ſolvatur debitum non uſuret quamdiu heres fuerit infra etatem de quocumque teneat et ſi debitum illud inciderit in manus noſtras nos non capiemus niſi catallum contentum in carta Et ſi quis moriatur et debitum debeat Judeis uxor ejus habeat dotem ſuam et nichil

nichil reddat de debito illo et ſi liberi ipſius defuncti qui fuerint infra etatem remanſerint provideantur eis neceſſaria ſecundum tenementum quod fuerit defuncti et de reſiduo ſolvatur debitum ſalvo ſervitio dominorum ſimili modo fiat de debitis que debentur aliis quam Judeis Nullum ſcutagium vel auxilium ponatur in regno noſtro niſi per commune conſilium regni noſtri niſi ad corpus noſtrum redimendum et primogenitum filium noſtrum militem faciendum et ad filiam noſtram primogenitam ſemel maritandam et ad hec non fiat niſi rationabile auxilium ſimili modo fiat de auxiliis de civitate London' Et civitas London' habeat omnes antiquas libertates et liberas conſuetudines ſuas tam per terras quam per aquas Preterea volumus et concedimus quod omnes alie civitates et burgi et ville et portus habeant omnes libertates et liberas conſuetudines ſuas Et ad habendum commune conſilium regni de auxilio aſſidendo aliter quam in tribus caſibus predictis vel de ſcutagio aſſidendo ſummoneri faciemus archiepiſcopos epiſcopos abbates comites et majores barones ſigillatim per litteras noſtras et preterea faciemus ſummoneri in generali per vicecomites et ballivos noſtros omnes illos qui de nobis tenent in capite ad certum diem ſcilicet ad terminum quadraginta dierum ad minus et ad certum locum et in omnibus litteris illius ſummonitionis cauſam ſummonitionis exprimemus et ſic facta ſummonitione negotium ad diem aſſignatum procedat ſecundum conſilium illorum qui preſentes fuerint quamvis non omnes ſummoniti venerint Nos non concedemus de cetero alicui quod capiat auxilium de liberis hominibus ſuis niſi ad corpus ſuum redimendum et ad faciendum primogenitum filium ſuum militem et ad primogenitam filiam ſuam ſemel maritandam et ad hec non fiat niſi rationabile auxilium Nullus diſtringatur ad faciendum majus ſervitium de feodo militis nec de alio libero tenemento quam inde debetur Communia placita non ſequantur curiam noſtram ſet teneantur in aliquo loco certo Recognitiones de nova diſſaiſina de morte anteceſſoris et de ultima preſentatione non capiantur niſi in ſuis comitatibus et hoc modo Nos vel ſi extra regnum fuerimus capitalis juſticiarius noſter mittemus duos juſticiarios per unumquemque comitatum per quatuor vices in anno qui cum quatuor militibus cujuſlibet comitatus electis per comitatum capiant in comitatu et in die et loco comitatus aſſiſas predictas Et ſi in die comitatus aſſiſe predicte capi non poſſint tot milites et libere tenentes remaneant de illis qui interfuerint comitatui die illo per quos poſſint judicia ſufficienter fieri ſecundum quod negotium fuerit majus vel minus Liber homo non amercietur pro parvo delicto niſi ſecundum modum delicti et pro magno delicto amercietur ſecundum magnitudinem delicti ſalvo contenemento ſuo et mercator eodem modo ſalva mercandiſa ſua et villanus eodem modo amercietur ſalvo wainnagio ſuo ſi inciderint in miſericordiam noſtram et nulla predictarum miſericordiarum ponatur niſi per ſacramentum proborum hominum de viſneto Comites et barones non amercientur niſi per pares ſuos et non niſi ſecundum modum delicti Nullus clericus amercietur de laico tenemento ſuo niſi ſecundum modum aliorum predictorum et non ſecundum quantitatem beneficii ſui eccleſiaſtici Nec villa nec homo diſtringatur facere pontes ad riparias niſi qui ab antiquo et de jure facere debent Nullus vicecomes conſtabularius coronatores vel alii ballivi noſtri teneant placita corone noſtre Omnes comitatus hundredi wapentak' et trething' ſint ad antiquas firmas abſque ullo incremento exceptis dominicis maneriis noſtris Si aliquis tenens de nobis laicum feodum moriatur et vicecomes vel ballivus noſter oſtendat litteras noſtras patentes de ſummonitione noſtra de debito quod defunctus nobis debuit liceat vicecomiti vel ballivo noſtro attachiare et inbreviare catalla defuncti inventa in laico feodo ad valentiam illius debiti per viſum legalium hominum ita tamen quod nichil inde amoveatur donec perſolvatur nobis debitum quod clarum fuerit et reſiduum relinquatur executoribus ad faciendum teſtamentum defuncti et ſi nichil nobis debeatur ab ipſo omnia catalla cedant defuncto ſalvis uxori ipſius et pueris rationabilibus partibus ſuis Si aliquis liber homo inteſtatus deceſſerit catalla ſua per manus propinquorum parentum et amicorum ſuorum per viſum eccleſie diſtribuantur ſalvis unicuique debitis que defunctus ei debebat Nullus conſtabularius vel alius ballivus noſter capiat blada vel alia catalla alicujus niſi ſtatim inde reddat denarios aut reſpectum inde habere poſſit de voluntate venditoris Nullus conſtabularius diſtringat aliquem militem ad dandum denarios pro cuſtodia caſtri ſi facere voluerit cuſtodiam illam in propria perſona ſua vel per alium probum hominem ſi ipſe eam facere non poſſit propter rationabilem cauſam et ſi nos duxerimus vel miſerimus eum in exercitum erit quietus de cuſtodia ſecundum quantitatem temporis quo per nos fuerit in exercitu Nullus vicecomes vel ballivus noſter vel aliquis alius capiat equos vel caretas alicujus liberi hominis pro cariagio faciendo niſi de voluntate ipſius liberi hominis Nec nos nec ballivi noſtri capiemus alienum boſcum ad caſtra vel alia agenda noſtra niſi per voluntatem ipſius cujus boſcus ille fuerit Nos non tenebimus terras illorum qui convicti fuerint de felonia niſi per unum annum et unum diem et tunc reddantur terre dominis feodorum Omnes kydelli de cetero deponantur penitus de Thamiſia et de Medewaye et per totam Angliam niſi per coſteram maris Breve quod vocatur Precipe de cetero non fiat alicui de aliquo tenemento unde liber homo amittere poſſit curiam ſuam Una menſura vini ſit per totum regnum noſtrum et una menſura cerviſie et una menſura bladi ſcilicet quarterium London' et una latitudo pannorum tinctorum et ruſſettorum et halbergettorum ſcilicet due ulne infra liſtas de ponderibus autem ſit ut de menſuris Nichil detur vel capiatur de cetero pro brevi inquiſitionis de vita vel membris ſet gratis concedatur et non negetur Si aliquis teneat de nobis per feodifirmam vel per ſokagium vel per burgagium et de alio terram teneat per ſervitium militare nos non habebimus cuſtodiam heredis nec terre ſue que eſt de feodo alte-

I rius

rius occaſione illius feodifirme vel ſokagii vel burgagii nec habebimus cuſtodiam illius feodifirme vel ſokagii vel burgagii niſi ipſa feodifirma debeat ſervitium militare Nos non habebimus cuſtodiam heredis vel terre alicujus quam tenet de alio per ſervitium militare occaſione alicujus parve ſergenterie quam tenet de nobis per ſervitium reddendi nobis cultellos vel ſagittas vel hujuſmodi Nullus ballivus ponat de cetero aliquem ad legem ſimplici loquela ſua ſine teſtibus fidelibus ad hoc inductis Nullus liber homo capiatur vel impriſonetur aut diſſaiſiatur aut utlagetur aut exuletur aut aliquo modo deſtruatur nec ſuper eum ibimus nec ſuper eum mittemus niſi per legale judicium parium ſuorum vel per legem terre Nulli vendemus nulli negabimus aut differemus rectum aut juſticiam Omnes mercatores habeant ſalvum et ſecurum exire de Anglia et venire in Angliam et morari et ire per Angliam tam per terram quam per aquam ad emendum et vendendum ſine omnibus malis toltis per antiquas et rectas conſuetudines preterquam in tempore gwerre et ſi ſint de terra contra nos gwerrina et ſi tales inveniantur in terra noſtra in principio gwerre attachientur ſine dampno corporum et rerum donec ſciatur a nobis vel capitali juſticiario noſto quomodo mercatores terre noſtre tractentur qui tunc invenientur in terra contra nos gwerrina et ſi noſtri ſalvi ſint ibi alii ſalvi ſint in terra noſtra Liceat unicuique de cetero exire de regno noſtro et redire ſalvo et ſecure per terram et per aquam ſalva fide noſtra niſi tempore gwerre per aliquod breve tempus propter communem utilitatem regni exceptis impriſonatis et utlagatis ſecundum legem regni et gente de terra contra nos gwerrina et mercatoribus de quibus fiat ſicut predictum eſt Si quis tenuerit de aliqua eſcaeta ſicut de honore Walingeford Notingeham Bon' Lainkaſtr' vel de aliis eſkaetis que ſunt in manu noſtra et ſunt baronie et obierit heres ejus non det aliud relevium nec faciat nobis aliud ſervitium quam faceret baroni ſi baronia illa eſſet in manu baronis et nos eodem modo eam tenebimus quo baro eam tenuit Homines qui manent extra foreſtam non veniant de cetero coram juſticiariis noſtris de foreſta per communes ſummonitiones niſi ſint in placito vel pleggii alicujus vel aliquorum qui attachiati ſint pro foreſta Nos non faciemus juſticiarios conſtabularios vicecomites vel ballivos niſi de talibus qui ſciant legem regni et eam bene velint obſervare Omnes barones qui fundaverunt abbatias unde habent cartas regum Anglie vel antiquam tenuram habeant earum cuſtodiam cum vacaverint ſicut habere debent Omnes foreſte que aforeſtate ſunt tempore noſtro ſtatim deafforeſtentur et ita fiat de ripariis que per nos tempore noſtro poſite ſunt in defenſo Omnes male conſuetudines de foreſtis et warennis et de foreſtariis et warennariis vicecomitibus et eorum miniſtris ripariis et earum cuſtodibus ſtatim inquirantur in quolibet comitatu per duodecim milites juratos de eodem comitatu qui debent eligi per probos homines ejuſdem comitatus et infra quadraginta dies poſt inquiſitionem factam penitus ita quod numquam revocentur deleantur per eoſdem ita quod nos hoc ſciamus prius vel juſticiarius noſter ſi in Anglia non fuerimus Omnes obſides et cartas ſtatim reddemus que liberate fuerunt nobis ab Anglicis in ſecuritatem pacis vel fidelis ſervitii Nos amovebimus penitus de balliis parentes Gerardi de Athyes quod de cetero nullam habeant balliam in Anglia Engelardum de Cygony Andream Petrum et Gyonem de Cancell' Gyonem de Cygony Galfridum de Martyni et fratres ejus Philippum Mark et fratres ejus et Galfridum nepotem ejus et totam ſequelam eorundem Et ſtatim poſt pacis reformationem amovebimus de regno omnes alienigenas milites baliſtarios ſervientes ſtipendiarios qui venerint cum equis et armis ad nocumentum regni Si quis fuerit diſſeiſitus vel elongatus per nos ſine legali judicio parium ſuorum de terris caſtallis libertatibus vel jure ſuo ſtatim eo ei reſtituemus et ſi contentio ſuper hoc orta fuerit tunc inde fiat per judicium viginti quinque baronum de quibus fit mentio inferius in ſecuritate pacis de omnibus autem illis de quibus aliquis diſſeiſitus fuerit vel elongatus ſine legali judicio parium ſuorum per Henricum regem patrem noſtrum vel per Ricardum regem fratrem noſtrum que in manu noſtra habemus vel que alii tenent que nos oporteat warantizare reſpectum habebimus uſque ad communem terminum cruceſignatorum exceptis illis de quibus placitum motum fuit vel inquiſitio facta per preceptum noſtrum ante ſuſceptionem crucis noſtre cum autem redierimus de peregrinatione noſtra vel ſi forte remanſerimus a peregrinatione noſtra ſtatim inde plenam juſticiam exhibebimus Eundem autem reſpectum habebimus et eodem modo de juſticia exhibenda de foreſtis deafforeſtandis vel remanſuris foreſtis quas Henricus pater noſter vel Ricardus frater noſter afforeſtaverunt et de cuſtodiis terrarum que ſunt de alieno feodo cujuſmodi cuſtodias hucuſque habuimus occaſione feodi quod aliquis de nobis tenuit per ſervitium militare et de abbatiis que fundate fuerint in feodo alterius quam noſtro in quibus dominus feodi dixerit ſe jus habere et cum redierimus vel ſi remanſerimus a peregrinatione noſtra ſuper hiis conquerentibus plenam juſticiam ſtatim exhibebimus Nullus capiatur nec impriſonetur propter appellum femine de morte alterius quam viri ſui Omnes fines qui injuſte et contra legem terre facti ſunt nobiſcum et omnia amerciamenta facta injuſte et contra legem terre omnino condonentur vel fiat inde per judicium viginti quinque baronum de quibus fit mentio inferius in ſecuritate pacis vel per judicium majoris partis eorumdem una cum predicto Stephano Cant' archiepiſcopo ſi intereſſe poterit et aliis quos ſecum ad hoc vocare voluerit et ſi intereſſe non poterit nichilominus procedat negotium ſine eo ita quod ſi aliquis vel aliqui de predictis viginti quinque baronibus fuerint in ſimili querela amoveantur quantum ad hoc judicium et alii loco illorum per reſiduos de eiſdem viginti quinque tantum ad hoc faciendum electi et jurati ſubſtituantur Si nos diſſaiſivimus vel elongavimus Walenſes de terris vel libertatibus vel rebus aliis ſine legali judicio parium ſuorum in Anglia vel in Wallia eis ſtatim reddantur et ſi contentio ſuper hoc orta fuerit tunc inde fiat in marchia per judicium parium ſuorum de tenementis Anglie ſecundum legem Anglie de tenementis Wallie ſecundum legem Wallie

Wallie de tenementis marchie ſecundum legem marchie idem facient Walenſes nobis et noſtris De omnibus autem illis de quibus aliquis Walenſium diſſaiſitus fuerit vel elongatus ſine legali judicio parium ſuorum per Henricum regem patrem noſtrum vel Ricardum regem fratrem noſtrum que nos in manu noſtra habemus vel que alii tenent que nos oporteat warantizare reſpectum habebimus uſque ad communem terminum cruceſignatorum illis exceptis de quibus placitum motum fuit vel inquiſitio facta per preceptum noſtrum ante ſuſceptionem crucis noſtre cum autem redierimus vel ſi forte remanſerimus a peregrinatione noſtra ſtatim eis inde plenam juſticiam exhibebimus ſecundum leges Walenſium et partes predictas Nos reddemus filium Lewelini ſtatim et omnes obſides de Wallia et cartas que nobis liberate fuerunt in ſecuritatem pacis Nos faciemus Allexandro regi Scottorum de ſororibus ſuis et obſidibus reddendis et libertatibus ſuis et jure ſuo ſecundum formam in qua faciemus aliis baronibus noſtris Anglie niſi aliter eſſe debeat per cartas quas habemus de Willielmo patre ipſius quondam rege Scottorum et hoc erit per judicium parium ſuorum in curia noſtra Omnes autem iſtas conſuetudines predictas et libertates quas nos conceſſiſſimus in regno noſtro tenendas quantum ad nos pertinet erga noſtros omnes de regno noſtro tam clerici quam laici obſervent quantum ad ſe pertinet erga ſuos Cum autem pro Deo et ad emendationem regni noſtri et ad melius ſopiendum diſcordiam inter nos et barones noſtros ortam hec omnia predicta conceſſerimus volentes ea integra et firma ſtabilitate gaudere in perpetuum facimus et concedimus eis ſecuritatem ſubſcriptam videlicet quod barones eligant viginti quinque barones de regno quos voluerint qui debeant pro totis viribus ſuis obſervare tenere et facere obſervari pacem et libertates quas eis conceſſimus et hac preſenti carta noſtra confirmavimus ita ſcilicet quod ſi nos vel juſticiarius noſter vel ballivi noſtri vel aliquis de miniſtris noſtris in aliquo erga aliquem deliquerimus vel aliquem articulorum pacis aut ſecuritatis tranſgreſſi fuerimus et delictum oſtenſum fuerit quatuor baronibus de predictis viginti quinque baronibus illi quatuor barones accedant ad nos vel ad juſticiarium noſtrum ſi fuerimus extra regnum proponentes nobis exceſſum petent ut exceſſum illum ſine dilatione faciamus emendari et ſi nos exceſſum non emendaverimus vel ſi fuerimus extra regnum juſticiarius noſter non emendaverit infra tempus quadraginta dierum computandum a tempore quo monſtratum fuerit nobis vel juſticiario noſtro ſi extra regnum fuerimus predicti quatuor barones referant cauſam illam ad reſiduos de viginti quinque baronibus et illi viginti quinque barones cum communa totius terre diſtringent et gravabunt nos modis omnibus quibus poterunt ſcilicet per captionem caſtrorum terrarum poſſeſſionum et aliis modis quibus poterunt donec fuerit emendatum ſecundum arbitrium eorum ſalva perſona noſtra et regine noſtre et liberorum noſtrorum et cum fuerit emendatum intendent nobis ſicut prius fecerunt Et quicumque voluerit de terra juret quod ad predicta omnia exequenda parebit mandatis predictorum viginti quinque baronum et quod gravabit nos pro poſſe ſuo cum ipſis et nos publice et libere damus licentiam jurandi cuilibet qui jurare voluerit et nulli umquam jurare prohibebimus Omnes autem illos de terra qui per ſe et ſponte ſua noluerint jurare viginti quinque baronibus de diſtringendo et gravando nos cum eis faciemus jurare eoſdem de mandato noſtro ſicut predictum eſt Et ſi aliquis de viginti quinque baronibus deceſſerit vel a terra receſſerit vel aliquo alio modo impeditus fuerit quo minus iſta predicta poſſent exequi qui reſidui fuerint de predictis viginti quinque baronibus eligant alium loco ipſius pro arbitrio ſuo qui ſimili modo erit juratus quo et ceteri In omnibus autem que iſtis viginti quinque baronibus committuntur exequenda ſi forte ipſi viginti quinque preſentes fuerint et inter ſe ſuper re aliqua diſcordaverint vel aliqui ex eis ſummoniti nolint vel nequeant intereſſe ratum habeatur et firmum quod major pars eorum qui preſentes fuerint providerit vel preceperit ac ſi omnes viginti quinque in hoc conſenſiſſent et predicti viginti quinque jurent quod omnia antedicta fideliter obſervabunt et pro toto poſſe ſuo facient obſervari Et nos nichil impetrabimus ab aliquo per nos nec per alium per quod aliqua iſtarum conceſſionum et libertatum revocetur vel minuatur et ſi aliquid tale impetratum fuerit irritum ſit et inane et numquam eo utemur per nos nec per alium Et omnes malas voluntates indignationes et rancores ortos inter nos et homines noſtros clericos et laicos a tempore diſcordie plene omnibus remiſimus et condonavimus Preterea omnes tranſgreſſiones factas occaſione ejuſdem diſcordie a paſcha anno regni noſtri ſextodecimo uſque ad pacem reformatam plene remiſimus omnibus clericis et laicis et quantum ad nos pertinet plene condonavimus Et inſuper fecimus eis fieri litteras teſtimoniales patentes domini Stephani Cant' archiepiſcopi domini Henrici Dublin' archiepiſcopi et epiſcoporum predictorum et magiſtri Panduſſi ſuper ſecuritate iſta et conceſſionibus prefatis Quare volumus et firmiter precipimus quod Anglicana eccleſia libera ſit et quod homines in regno noſtro habeant et teneant omnes prefatas libertates jura et conceſſiones bene et in pace libere et quiete plene et integre ſibi et heredibus ſuis de nobis et heredibus noſtris in omnibus rebus et locis in perpetuum ſicut predictum eſt Juratum eſt autem tam ex parte noſtra quam ex parte baronum quod hec omnia ſupradicta bona fide et ſine malo ingenio obſervabuntur Teſtibus ſupradictis et multis aliis Data per manum noſtram in prato quod vocatur Runingmed' inter Windeleſorum et Stanes quinto decimo die Junii anno regni noſtri ſeptimo decimo.

ab. VI

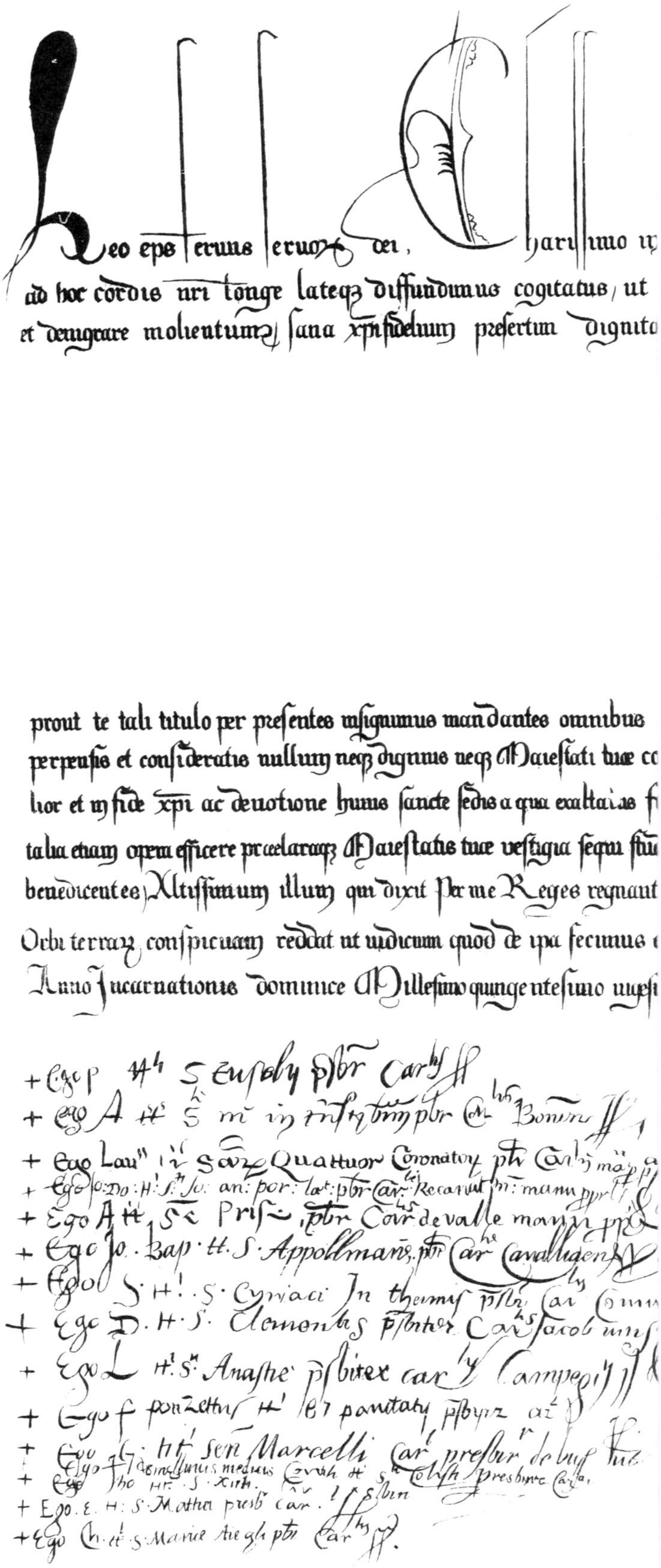

es Bauire.

EXPLANATIO TABULÆ VI.

Bulla Leonis X. Papæ pro Titulo Defensoris Fidei.

Rymer v. 13. Fo. 756. A. D. 1521. An. 15. H. 8. Ex. Origine.

LEO Epifcopus Servus Servorum Dei Chariffimo in Chrifto Filio, Henrico Angliæ Regi Fidei Defenfori Salutem, & Apoftolicam Benedictionem.

Ex fupernæ Difpofitionis arbitrio, licet imparibus meritis, Univerfalis Ecclefiæ Regimini præfidentes, ad hoc cordis noftri longè latèque diffundimus cogitatus, ut Fides Catholica, fine quâ nemo proficit ad Salutem, continuum fufcipiat Incrementum, & ut ea, quæ pro cohibendis conatibus illam deprimere aut pravis mendacibufque comentis pervertere & denigrare molentium, fanâ Chrifti Fidelium, præfertim Dignitate Regali fulgentium, doctrinâ funt difpofita, continuis proficiant Incrementis. Partes noftri Minifterii & Operam impendimus efficaces:

Et, ficut alii Romani Pontifices, Prædeceffores noftri, Catholicos Principes (prout Rerum & Temporum qualitas exigebat) fpecialibus Favoribus profequi confueverunt, illos præfertim, qui procellofis temporibus, & rabidâ Scifmaticorum & Hæreticorum fervente perfidia, non folum in Fidei ferenitate & devotione illibatâ Sacrofanctæ Romanæ Ecclefiæ immobiles perftiterunt, verum etium, tanquam ipfius Ecclefiæ legitimi Filii, ac fortiffimi Athletæ Scifmaticorum & Hereticorum, infanis Furofibus fpiritualiter & temporaliter fe oppofuerunt; ita etiam Nos Majeftatem tuam, propter Excelfa & Immortalia ejus erga Nos & hanc Sanctam Sedem, in quâ, permiffione Divinâ, fedemus, Opera & Gefta condignis & immortalibus Præconiis & Laudibus efferre defideramus, ac ea fibi concedere propter quæ invigilare debeat a Grege Dominico Lupos arcere, & Putida Membra, quæ Mifticum Chrifti Corpus inficiunt, Ferro & Materiali Gladio abfcindere, & nutantium Corda Fidelium in Fidei foliditate confirmare.

Sane cum nuper dilectus Filius Johannes Clerk, Majeftatis tuæ apud Nos Orator, in confiftorio noftro, coram Venerabilibus Fratribus noftris Sanctæ Romane Ecclefiæ Cardinalibus & compluribus aliis Romanæ Curiæ Prelatis, Librum, quam Majeftas tua, Charitate quæ omnia fedulo & nihil perperam agit, Fideique Catholicæ Zelo accenfa, ac Devotionis erga Nos & hanc Sanctam Sedem fervore inflamata, contra Errores diverforum Hæreticorum, fepius ab hac Sancta Sede damnatos, nuperque per Martinum Lutherum fufcitatos & innovatos, tanquam nobile ac falutare quoddam antidotum compofuit, Nobis examinandum, & deinde Auctoritate noftrâ approbandum, obtuliffet, ac luculentâ Oratione fuâ expofuiffet Majeftatem tuam partam & difpofitam effe ut, quemadmodum veris Rationibus ac irrifragabilibus Sacræ Scripturæ & Sanctorum Patrum Auctoritatibus notorios Errores ejufdem Martini confutaverat, ita etiam omnes eos fequi & defenfare præfumentes totius Regni fui Viribus & Armis perfequatur.

Nofque ejus Libri admirabilem quandam & Cæleftis Gratiæ rore confperfam Doctrinam diligenter accurateque; introfpeximus, Omnipotenti Deo, a quo omne Datum optimum & omne Donum perfectum eft, immenfas Gratias egimus, qui optimam & ad omne Bonum inclinatam mentem tuam infpirare; eique tantam Gratiam fupernè infundere dignatus fuit, ut ea fcriberes quibus Sanctam ejus Fidem contra novum Errorem Damnatorum hujufmodi Sufcitatorem defenderes, ac reliquos Reges & Principes Chriftianos tuo Exemplo invitares ut Ipfi etiam Orthodoxæ Fidei & Evangelicæ Veritati, in periculum & difcrimen adductæ, omni ope fua adeffe opportunèque favere vellent; æquum autem effe confentes Eos, qui pro Fidei Chrifti hujufmodi Defenfione pios Labores fufciperunt, omni Laude & Honore afficere; Volentefque non folum ea, quæ Majeftas tua contra eundem Martinum Lutherum abfolutiffimâ Doctrinâ nec minori Eloquentia fcripfit, condignis Laudibus extollere ac magnificare; Auctoritateque noftrâ approbare & confirmare, fed etiam, Majeftatem ipfam tali Honore & Titulo decorare, ut noftris ac perpetuis futuris temporibus Chrifti Fideles omnes intelligant quàm gratum acceptumque Nobis fuerint Majeftatis tuæ Munus, hoc præfertim tempore nobis oblatum.

Nos, qui Petri, quem Chriftus, in Cælum afcenfurus, Vicarium fuum in Terris reliquit, & cui Curam Gregis fui commifit, veri Succeffores fumus, & in hac Sanctâ Sede, a qua omnes Dignitates ac Tituli emanant, fedemus, habita fuper hiis cum eifdem Fratribus noftris maturâ Deliberatione, de eorum unanimi Confilio & Affenfu, Majeftati tuæ Titulum hunc (videlicet) Fidei Defenforem donare decrevimus,

prout Te tali Titulo per Præfentes infignimus; Mandantes omnibus Chrifti Fidelibus ut Majeftatem tuam hoc Titulo nominent, & cum ad eam fcribent, poft Dictionem Regi adjungant Fidei Defenfori.

Et profectò, hujus Tituli excellentia & dignitate ac ſingularibus Meritis tuis diligenter perpenſis & conſideratis nullum neque dignius neque Majeſtati tuæ convenientius Nomen excogitare potuiſſemus, quod quoties audies aut leges, totiens, propriæ Virtutis optimique Meriti tui accordaberis; nec hujuſmodi Titulo intumeſces vel in Superbiam elevaberis, ſed ſolitâ tuâ Prudentiâ humilior, & in Fide Chriſti ac Devotione hujus Sanctæ Sedis, a qua exaltatus fueris, fortior & conſtantior evades, ac in Domino Bonorum omnium Largitore lætaberis perpetuum hoc & immortale Gloriæ tuæ Monumentum Poſteris tuis relinquere, illiſque viam oſtendere ut, ſi tali Titulo ipſi quoque inſigniti optabunt talia etiam Opera efficere, præclaraque Majeſtatis tuæ Veſtigia ſequi ſtudeant; quam, prout de Nobis & dictâ Sede optimè merita eſt, unâ cum Uxore & Filiis ac omnibus qui a Te & ab illis naſcentur, Noſtrâ Benedictione, in Nomine illius, a quo illam concedendi Poteſtas Nobis data eſt, largâ & liberali Manu benedicentes, Altiſſimum illum, qui dixit, per Me Reges Regnant & Principes imperant, & in cujus Manu Corda ſunt Regum, rogamus & obſecramus ut eam in ſuo Sancto Propoſito confirmet, ejuſque Devotionem multiplicet, ac præclaris pro Sancta Fide Geſtis ita illuſtret, ac toti Orbi Terrarum conſpicuam reddat ut Judicium, quod de ipſa fecimus, eam tam inſigni Titulo decorantes, a Nemine falſum aut vanum judicari poſſit; demum, Mortalis hujus Vitæ finito Curriculo, Sempiternæ illius Gloriæ conſortem atque participem reddat.

Dat. Romæ, apud Sanctum Petrum, Anno Incarnationis Dominicæ Milleſimo, Quingenteſimo, Vigeſimo primo, Quinto Idus Octobris, Pontificatus noſtri Anno nono.

+ Ego Leo Decimus Catholicæ Eccleſiæ
Epiſcopus. Ss.
Locus Signi.

	Explicatio Nominum Titulorum & Familiarum.
	Epiſcopi Cardinales.
+ Ego. B. Epiſc. Oſtien. Card. S ſs.	*Bernardus Carvaial Hiſpanus Epiſcopus Oſtien Cardinalis Sanctæ Crucis.*
+ Ego N. Card. de Fliſco Epiſc. Albn. ſs.	*Nicholaus Cardinalis de Fliſco Epiſcopus Albn.*
+ Ego A. Epiſc. Tuſcul. de Farnetiis. ſs.	*Alexander Epiſcopus Tuſculanus de Farneſiis.*
+ Ego A. Epiſc. Alban. ſs.	*Antonius de Monte Sancti Sabini Epiſcopus Albanus.*
	Preſbyteri Cardinales.
+ Ego P. Tit. S. Euſebii Preſbyt. Card. ſs.	*Petrus de Accoltis Tituli Sancti Euſebii Preſbyter Cardinalis.*
+ Ego A. Tit. S. Mariæ Tranſtyberim Preſbyt. Card. Bonon. ſs.	*Achilles de Craſſis Tituli Sanctæ Mariæ trans Tyberim Preſbyter Cardinalis Bononiem.*
+ Ego Laur. Tit. Sanctorum quatuor Coronatorum Preſbyt. Card. manu propriâ ſs.	*Laurentius Puccius Tituli Sanctorum quatuor Coronatorum Preſbyter Cardinalis.*
+ Ego Jo. Do. Tit. S. Jo. an. Por. Lat. Preſbyt. Cardin. Recanaten. Manû propriâ ſs.	*Johannes Dominicus de Cupis Sancti Johannis ante Portam Latinam Preſbyter Cardinalis Recanaten.*
+ Ego A. Tit. S. Priſce Preſbyt. Card. de Valle manu propriâ ſs.	*Andreas de Valle Tituli Sancte Priſcæ Preſbyter Cardinalis de Valle.*
+ Ego Jo. Bap. Tit. S. Appolinaris Preſbyt. Card. Cavallicen ſs.	*Jo. Baptiſta Palavicinus Tituli Sancti Apollinaris Preſbyter Cardinalis Cavallicen.*
+ Ego S. Tit. S. Cyraici in Thermis Preſbyt. Car. Comen. ſs.	*Scarramuccia Trivultius Sancti Cyraici in Thermis Preſbyter Cardinalis Comenſis.*
+ Ego D. Tit. S. Clementis Preſbyt. Car. Jacobinus. ſs.	*Dominicus Jacobaticus Tituli Sancti Clementis Preſbyter Cardinalis Jacobinus.*
+ Ego L. Tit. S. Anaſtiæ Preſbyt. Car. Campegius, ſs.	*Laurentius Campegius Tituli Sanct. Anaſtaſiæ Preſbyter Cardinalis Campegius.*
+ Ego F. Ponzettus Tit. S. Pancratii Preſbyt. Car. ſs.	*Ferdinandus Ponzettus Tituli Sancti Pancratii Preſbyter Cardinalis.*
+ Ego G. Tit. S. Marcelli Car. Preſbyt. de Vei, ſs.	*Guillielmus Raymundus de Vieos Tituli Sancti Marcelli Cardinalis Preſbyter de Vei.*
+ Ego F. Armellinus Medices Tit. S. Caliſti Preſbyt. Car. ſs.	*Franciſcus Armellinus Medices Tituli Sancti Caliſti Peſbyter Cardinalis.*
+ Ego Tho. Tit. S. Xiſti Card. Preſbyt. ſs.	*Frater Thomas de Vio Tituli Sancti Xiſti Preſbyter Cardinalis.*
+ Ego E. Tit. S. Mathæi Preſbyt. Card. ſs.	*Frater Egidius Viterbenſis Tituli Sancti Mathæi Preſbyter Cardinalis.*

+ Ego Ch. Tit. Mariæ Aræ Cœli Presbyt. Car. ss.

Frater Christophorus Humalius Tituli Sanctæ Mariæ de Ara Cæli Presbyter Cardinalis.

Diaconi Cardinales.

+ Ego F. S. Mariæ in Cosmedin Diacon. Car. Ursinus manu prop. ss.

Franciottus Ursinus Sanctæ Mariæ in Cosmedin Diaconus Cardinalis Ursinus.

+ Ego P. S. Eustachii Diaconus Car. manu propriâ ss.

Paulus de Cæsis Sancti Eustachii Diaconus Cardinalis.

+ Ego Alex. S. Sergii & Bacchi Diacon. Car. Cæsarinus manu prop. ss.

Alexander Cæsarinus Sanctorum Sergii & Bacchi Diaconus Cardinalis Cæsarinus.

+ Ego Jo. S. S. Cosmæ & Dam. Diacon. Car. de Salviatis manu prop. ss.

Johannes Salviatus Sanctorum Cosmæ & Damiani Diaconus Cardinalis de Salviatis.

+ Ego N. S. Viti & Mod. Diacon. Car. Rodulphus manu prop. ss.

Nicholaus Rodulphus Sanctorum Viti & Modesti in Mecello Diaconus Cardinalis Rodulphus.

+ Ego Her. S. Agathæ Diaconus Car. de Rangon. manu prop. ss.

Hercules Comes de Rangonibus Sanctæ Agathæ Diaconus Cardinalis de Rangonibus.

+ Ego Aug. S. Hadriani Diaconus Car. Trivultius manu prop. ss.

Augustinus Trivultius Sancti Adriani Diaconus Cardinalis Trivultius.

+ Ego F. S. Mariæ in Porticu Car. Pisanus manu propriâ ss.

Franciscus de Pisanis Sanctæ Mariæ in Porticu Diaconus Cardinalis Pisanus.

Locus Sigilli

Subter Plicam.

H. de Comitibus.

Exemplar CHARTARUM ad res privatas spectantium in Officio Augment. remanentium.

27 Hen. 2.

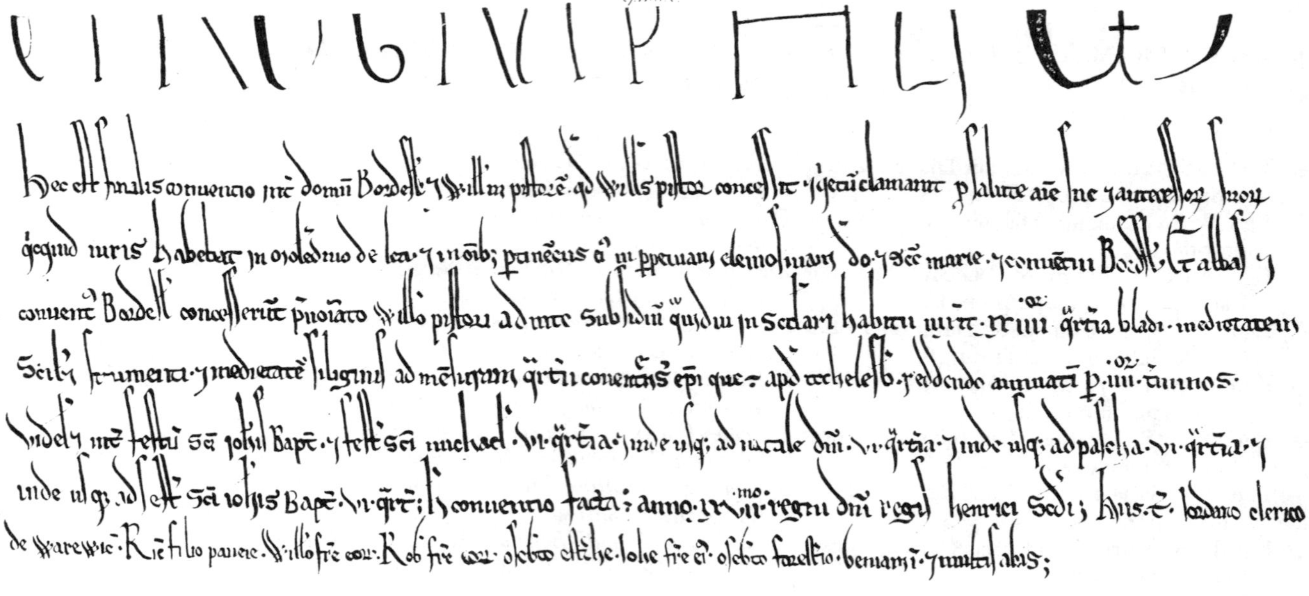

Hec est finalis conventio inter domum Bordesl' et Willelmum pistorem. quod Willelmus pistor concessit et quietum clamavit pro salute anime sue et antecessorum suorum quicquid iuris habebat in molendino de Lea et in omnibus pertinentiis eius in perpetuam elemosinam deo et sancte Marie et conventui Bordesl'. Et abbas et conventus Bordesl' concesserunt prenominato Willelmo pistori ad vite subsidium quamdiu in seculari habitu vixerit xxiiii^or quarteria bladi. medietatem scilicet frumenti et medietatem siliginis ad mensuram quarterii conventus episcopi que est apud Tachelesb. reddendo annuatim per iiii^or terminos. videlicet inter festum sancti Johannis Baptiste et festum sancti Michaelis vi quarteria. et inde usque ad natale domini vi quarteria. et inde usque ad pascha vi quarteria. et inde usque ad festum sancti Johannis Baptiste vi quarteria. Hec conventio facta est anno xxvii^mo regni domini regis Henrici Secundi. His testibus. Ledmano clerico de Warewic. Ricardo filio panetarii. Willelmo fratre eius. Roberto fratre eius. Osberto Eltche. Iohanne fratre eius. Osberto forestario. Beniamin et multis aliis.

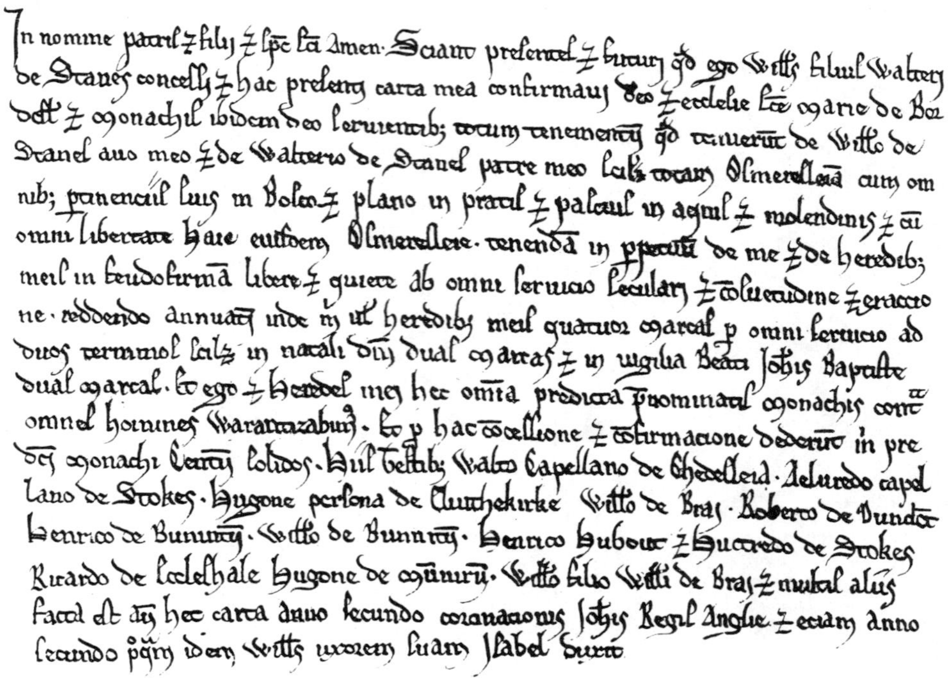

In nomine patris et filii et spiritus sancti amen. Sciant presentes et futuri quod ego Willelmus filius Walteri de Stanes concessi et hac presenti carta mea confirmavi deo et ecclesie sancte Marie de Bordesl' et monachis ibidem deo servientibus totum tenementum quod tenuerunt de Willelmo de Stanes avo meo et de Waltero de Stanes patre meo scilicet totam Olmeresleam cum omnibus pertinentiis suis in bosco et plano in pratis et pascuis in aquis et molendinis et cum omni libertate hactenus eiusdem Olmeresleie. tenenda in perpetuum de me et de heredibus meis in feudofirmam libere et quiete ab omni servicio seculari et consuetudine et exactione. reddendo annuatim inde mihi vel heredibus meis quatuor marcas pro omni servicio ad duos terminos scilicet in natali domini duas marcas et in vigilia beati Johannis Baptiste duas marcas. Et ego et heredes mei hec omnia predicta prenominatis monachis contra omnes homines warantizabimus. Et pro hac concessione et confirmatione dederunt mihi predicti monachi centum solidos. His testibus. Waltero capellano de Chedesleia. Aelurido capellano de Stokes. Hugone persona de Cluthekirke. Willelmo de Bras. Roberto de Dunclent. Henrico de Bunintun. Willelmo de Bunintun. Henrico Hubout et Hucredo de Stokes. Ricardo de Scelhale. Hugone de Muntun. Willelmo filio Willelmi de Bras et multis aliis. Facta est autem hec carta anno secundo coronationis Johannis Regis Anglie et etiam anno secundo postquam idem Willelmus uxorem suam Isabel duxit.

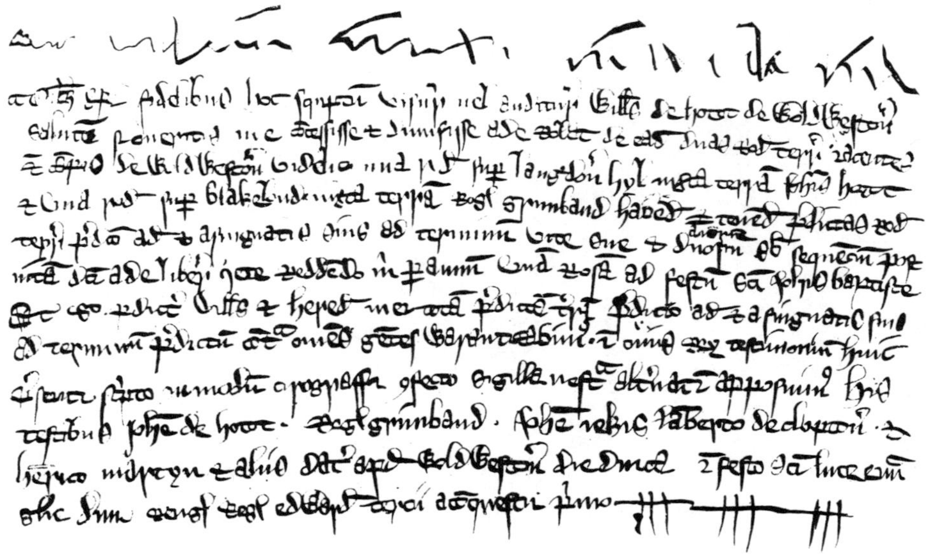

EXPLANATIO TABULÆ VII.

EXEMPLAR CHARTARUM AD RES PRIVATAS SPECTANTIUM IN OFFICIO AUGMENT' REMANENTIUM.

27 Hen. 2.

Cirographum.

Hæc eſt finalis Conventio inter Domum Bordeſle et Willelmum Piſtorem quod Willelmus Piſtor conceſſit et quictum clamavit pro Salute animæ ſuæ et anteceſſorum ſuorum quicquid juris habebat in Molendino de Lea et in omnibus pertinentijs ejus in perpetuam elemoſinam Deo et Sanctæ Mariæ et Conventui Bordeſle et Abbas et Conventus Bordeſle conceſſerunt prænominato Willelmo Piſtori ad vitæ ſubſidium quamdiu in ſæculari habitu vixerit 24 Quarteria Bladi medietatem ſcilicet Frumenti et medietatem Siliginis ad menſuram Quarterij Coventrienſis Epiſcopi quæ eſt apud Techeleſbroc reddendo annuatim per 4^or^ terminos Videlicet inter Feſtum Sancti Johannis Baptiſtæ & Feſtum Sancti Michaelis 6 Quarteria et inde uſque ad Natale Domini 6 Quarteria et inde uſque ad Paſcha 6 Quarteria et inde uſque ad Feſtum Sancti Johannis Baptiſtæ 6 Quarteria Hæc Conventio facta eſt Anno 27mo Regni Domini Regis Henrici Secundi. Hijs Teſtibus Jordano Clerico de Warewic Ricardo Filio Paveie Willelmo Fratre eorum. Roberto Fratre eorum Oſeberto Eſtreche Johanne Fratre ejus, Oſeberto Foreſtario, Benjamin et multis alijs.

2 Joh.

In Nomine Patris & Filij et Spiritûs Sancti Amen. Sciant præſentes et futuri quod ego Willelmus Filius Walteri de Stanes conceſſi et hac præſenti Carta mea confirmavi Deo et Eccleſiæ Sanctæ Mariæ de Bordeſle et Monachis ibidem Deo ſervientibus totum Tenementum quod tenuerunt de Willelmo de Stanes Avo meo et de Waltero de Stanes Patre meo ſcilicet totam Oſinereſleia cum omnibus Pertinentijs ſuis in Boſco et Plano in Pratis et Paſcuis in Aquis et Molendinis et cum omni Libertate Haiæ ejuſdem Oſinereſleiæ tenendam in perpetuam de me et de Hæredibus meis in Feudofirmam libere et quiete ab omni ſervitio ſæculari et conſuetudine et exactione reddendo annuatim inde mihi vel Hæredibus meis quatuor Marcas pro omni Servitio ad duos terminos ſcilicet in Natali Domini duas Marcas et in Vigilia Beati Johannis Baptiſtæ duas Marcas et ego et Hæredes mei hæc omnia prædicta prænominatis Monachis contra omnes Homines warantizabimus et pro hac conceſſione et confirmatione dederunt mihi prædicti Monachi Centum Solidos. Hijs Teſtibus Waltero Capellano de Chedeſleia, Aeluredo Capellano de Stokes, Hugone Perſona de Elvithekirke Willelmo de Brai, Roberto de Dundet', Henrico de Bunintun, Willelmo de Bunintun, Henrico Hubout & Huctredo de Stokes, Ricardo de Eccleſhale Hugone de Muniru' Willelmo Filio Willelmi de Brai et multis alijs. Facta eſt autem hæc Carta Anno ſecundo Coronationis Johannis Regis Angliæ et etiam Anno ſecundo poſtquam idem Willelmus uxorem ſuam Iſabellam duxit.

1 Edw. 3.

Omnibus Chriſti Fidelibus hoc Scriptum viſuris vel audituris Willelmus de Hotot de Woldweſton Salutem. Noveritis me conceſſiſſe & dimiſiſſe Adæ Robat de eadem duas Rodas Terræ jacentes in Campis de Woldweſton Videlicet una Roda ſuper Langdonhyl juxta Terram Johannis Hotot et una Roda ſuper Blakelond juxta Terram Rogeri Grumbaud habendum et tenendum prædictas Rodas Terræ prædicto Adæ et Aſſignatis ſuis ad Terminum Vitæ ſuæ et duorum Annorum ſubſequentium poſt vitam dictæ Adæ libere quiete reddendo mihi per Annum unam Roſam ad Feſtum Sancti Johannis Baptiſtæ et ego prædictus Willelmus et Hæredes mei totam prædictam Terram prædicto Adæ et Aſſignatis ſuis ad Terminum prædictum contra omnes Gentes warantizabimus. In cujus rei Teſtimonium huic præſenti ſcripto in modum Cirograffi confecto Sigilla noſtra alternatim appoſuimus His Teſtibus Johanne de Hotot Rogeri Grumbaud, Johanne Jekis, Lamberto de Clopton et Henrico Martyn et alijs Datum apud Woldweſton Die Dominica in Feſto Sancti Lucæ Evangeliſtæ Anno Regni Regis Edwardi Tertij a Conqueſtu primo.

Exemplar CHARTARUM *ad res privatas spectantium in Officio Augment' remanentium*

13 Ric. 2.

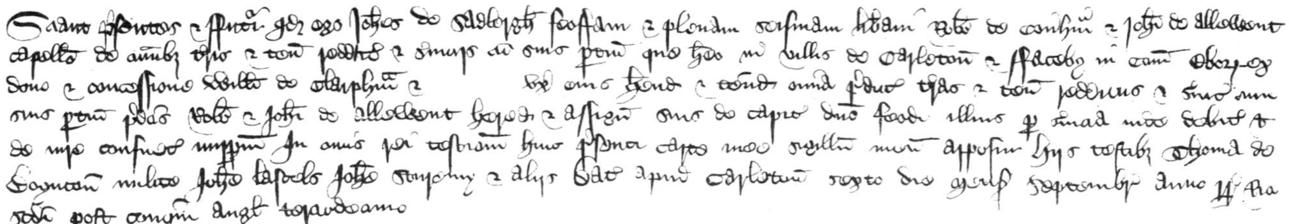

10 Hen. 4.

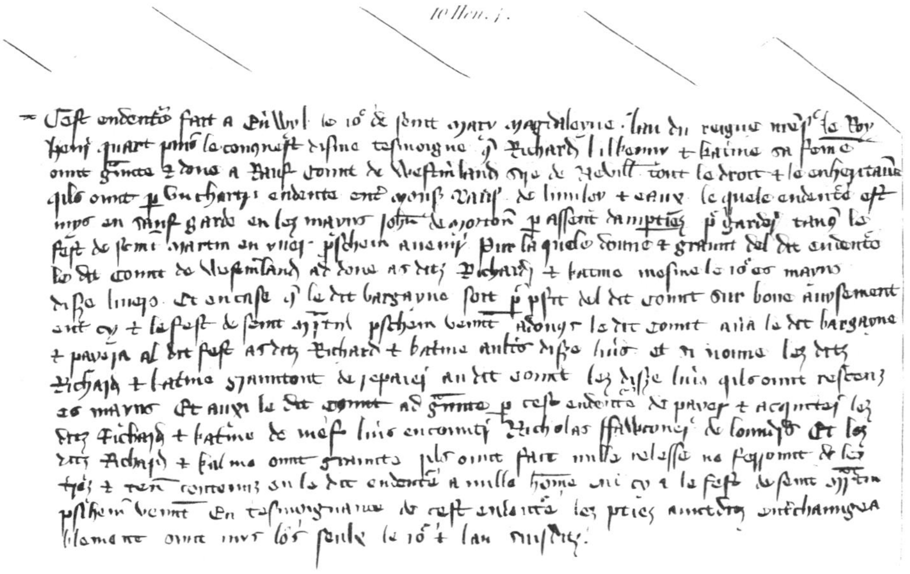

2 Ric. 3.

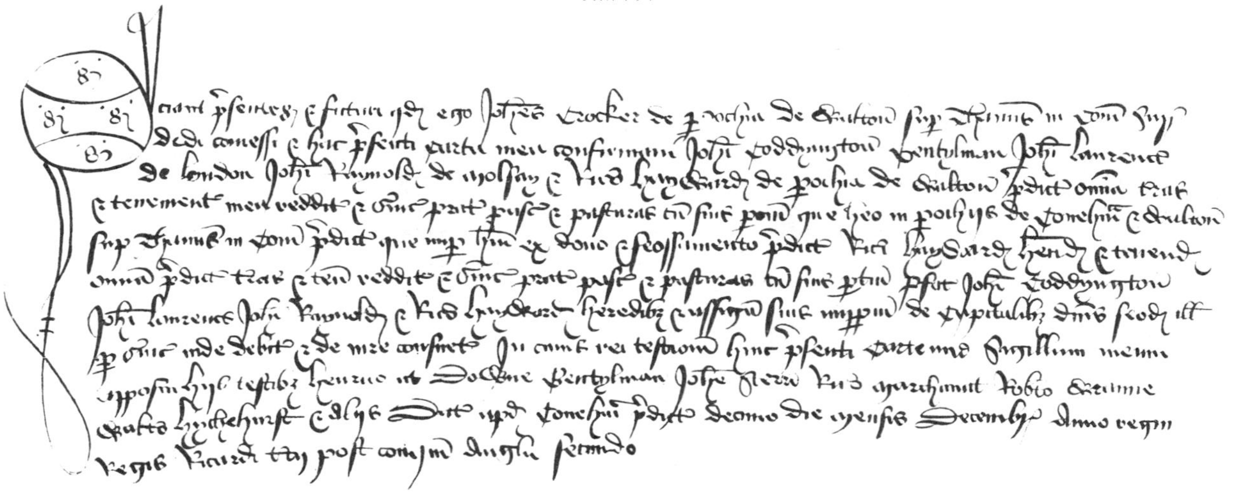

27 Hen. 8.

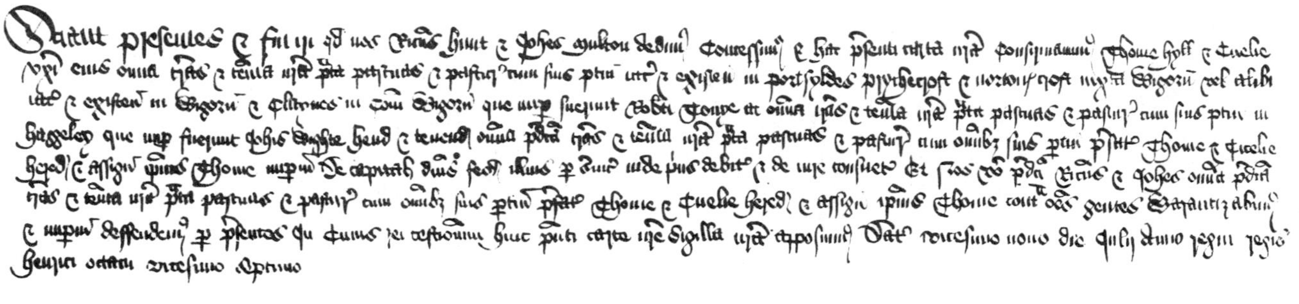

Engraved for the REPORT ON THE Public Records OF THE Kingdom, &c.

Ordered to be printed 1st July 1800.

Engraved by James Basire.

EXPLANATIO TABULÆ VIII.

EXEMPLAR CHARTARUM AD RES PRIVATAS SPECTANTIUM IN OFFICIO AUGMENT REMANENTIUM.

13 *Ric.* 2.

SCIANT præfentes et futuri quod ego Johannes de Sadbergh feoffavi et plenam Seifinam liberavi Roberto de Coverham et Johanni de Allewent Capellano de omnibus Terris et Tenementis Redditibus et Servitijs cum fuis pertinentijs quæ habeo in Villis de Carleton et Faceby in Comitatu Eborum ex dono et conceffione Willelmi de Claipham et . . . . Uxoris ejus habenda et tenenda omnia prædicta Terras et Tenementa redditus & fervitia cum fuis pertinentijs prædictis Roberto et Johanni de Allewent Hæredibus et Affignatis fuis de capitali Domino Feodi illius per fervitia inde debita et de jure confueta imperpetuum In cujus rei teftimonium huic præfenti Cartæ meæ figillum meum appofui. Hijs Teftibus Thoma de Boynton Milite Johanne Lafcels Johanne Sturemy et alijs. Datum apud Carleton fexto Die Menfis Septembris Anno Regni Regis Ricardi Secundi poft Conqueftum Angliæ tertio decimo.

10 *Hen.* 4.

Ceft Endenture fait a Everwyk le jour de Seint Mary Magdaleyne l'an du reigne noftre Seigneur le Roy Henry Quart puis le Conqueft difme tefmoigne que Richard Kilkenny & Katerine fa Femme ount graunte et done a Rauf Count de Weftmerland Sire de Nevill tout le droit et le enheritance qils ount per un Chartre endente entre Monsr Rauf de Lumley & eaux lequel Endenture eft mys en fauf garde en lez Mayns John de Morton par affent dampartiez pour garder tanque le Feft de Seint Martin en Yver profchein avenir pur la quele donne & graunt del dit Endenture le dit Count de Weftmerland ad done as ditz Richard & Katerine mefme le jour es mayns difze livers et en cafe que le dit bargayne foit pur profit del dit Count fur bone avyfement entre cy & le Feft de Seint Martin profchein venant adonque le dit Count avera le dit bargayne & payera al dit Feft as ditz Richard & Katerine aulters difze livers et fi nonne lez ditz Richard & Katerine grauntont de repaier au dit Count les difze livers qils ount refceuz es mayns et auxi le dit Count ad graunte par ceft Endenture de payer et acquitter lez ditz Richard & Katerine de nief livers encountre Nicholas Fawconer de Loundres et lez ditz Richard & Katerine ount graunte qils ount fait nulle releffe ne ferrount de lez Terres et Tenements contenuz en le dit Endenture a nulle Homme entre cy et le Feft de Seint Martin profchein venant en tefmoignance de ceft Endenture lez Partiez avantditz entrechaungeablement ount mys lours feulx le jour et l'an fuifditz.

2 *Ric.* 2.

Sciant præfentes et futuri quod ego Johannes Crocker de Parochia de Walton fuper Thamifin in Comitatu Surriæ dedi conceffi & hac præfenti Carta mea confirmavi Johanni Coddyngton Gentylman Johanni Laurence de London Johanni Raynold de Molfay & Ricardo Hayward de Parochia de Walton prædicta omnia Terras & Tenementa mea Redditus & Servitia Prata Pafcua et Pafturas cum fuis pertinentijs quæ habeo in Parochijs de Coveham & Walton fuper Thamifin in Comitatu prædicto quæ nuper habui ex dono & feoffamento prædicti Ricardi Hayward habenda & tenenda omnia prædicta Terras & Tenementa Redditus & Servitia Prata Pafcua & Pafturas cum fuis Pertinentijs præfatis Johanni Coddyngton Johanni Laurence Johanni Raynold et Ricardo Hayward Hæredibus et Affignatis fuis imperpetuum de capitalibus Dominis Feodi illius per Servitia inde debita & de jure confueta In cujus rei teftimonium huic præfenti Cartæ meæ Sigillum meum appofui Hijs Teftibus Henrico at Downe Gentylman Johanne Sterre Ricardo Marchaunt Roberto Wranne Waltero Hychhurft et alijs Datum apud Coveham prædictam decimo Die Menfis Decembris Anno Regni Regis Ricardi Tertij poft Conqueftum Angliæ fecundo.

27 *Hen.* 8.

Sciant præfentes et futuri quod nos Ricardus Hunt et Johannes Multon dedimus conceffimus et hac præfenti Carta noftra confirmavimus Thome Hyll & Ciceliæ Uxori ejus omnia Terras & Tenementa noftra Prata Pafcuas & Pafturas cum fuis pertinentijs jacentia et exiftentia in Portfyldes Prychecroft & Nortons Croft juxta Wigorniam vel alibi jacentia et exiftentia in Wigornia et Claynes in Comitatu Wigorniæ quæ nuper fuerunt Roberti Tonye ac omnia Terras et Tenementa noftra Prata Pafcuas & Pafturas cum fuis Pertinentijs in Haggeley quæ nuper fuerunt Johannis Wighte habenda & tenenda omnia prædicta Terras & Tenementa noftra Prata Pafcuas & Pafturas cum omnibus fuis pertinentijs præfatis Thomæ & Ciceliæ Hæredibus et Affignatis ipfius Thomæ imperpetuum de Capitalibus Dominis Feodi illius per Servitia inde prius debita & de jure confueta et Nos vero prædicti Ricardus & Johannes omnia prædicta Terras & Tenementa noftra Prata Pafcuas & Pafturas cum omnibus fuis pertinentijs præfatis Thomæ & Ciciliæ Hæredibus et Affignatis ipfius Thomæ contra omnes Gentes warantizabimus et imperpetuum deffendemus per præfentes In cujus rei teftimonium huic præfenti Cartæ noftræ Sigilla noftra appofuimus. Data vicefimo nono Die Julij Anno Regni Regis Henrici Octavo vicefimo feptimo.

EXEMPLARIA de Magnis Rotulis Pipæ extracta.

18 Hen: 1.

NOVA PLACITA, ET NOVI CONVENTIONES.

Vluric' bertebes r. redd Cōpot. de .ij. m. arg. p defect duelli. In thauro libauit. Et Quiet' est.
Telari de Huntedona redd Cōpot. de .xl. s. p Gilda sua. In thauro libauer. Et Quieti sunt.
Abbas de Torina redd Cōpot. de .j. m. auri. p mercato de Sachesleia. Ric de belcamp libauit .ix. m. arg. p .j. m. auri. p libert. Et Quiet' est.

Nova Placita et Novi Conventiones:

Ulvricus Bertebers reddit Compotum de 2 Marc Argenti per defectum duelli. In Thesauro liberavit. Et quietus est.
Telarii de Huntedona reddunt Compotum de 40.s pro Gilda sua. In Thesauro liberaverunt. Et quieti sunt.
Abbas de Torria reddit Compotum de una Marca Auri pro Mercato de Sacheslea Ric de Belcampo liberavit 9. M. Argenti per unam M. Auri pro libertate sua. Et quietus est.

2 Hen: 2.

HURTFORDSCIRA. Ric de luci redd Comp. de firma de Hurtfordscir. In th. lvi. li. 7. xvij. s. et
Et in Elem nouit const Militib. de templo .xiij. s. 7. iiij. d.

Hurtfordscira Ricardus de Luci reddit Compotum de firma de Hurtfordscira. In Thesauro £. 56. & 17.s et
Et in Elemosina noviter constituta Militibus de Templo. 13.s 4.d

2 Hen: 2

DORSETA. Idem Ric. redd Comp de firma de DORSETA.

Dorseta. Idem Ricardus reddit Compotum de firma de Dorseta.

3 Joh.

De oblatis.

[illegible]
Rad de bellocampo ccc. m. p hnda custod terr 7 hedis Rogii de pavilly cu maritag.

De Oblatis.

Sibilla de Plugenai & Hawisa de Dinat debent 60. Marcas pro habendo recto sicut continetur in Anno præcedente.
Radulfus de Bellocampo 300. Marcas pro habenda custod. Terræ & Hæredis Rogeri de Pavilly cum Maritagio.

Ordered to be printed 4th July 1800.

Engraved for the REPORT ON THE **Public Records** OF THE **Kingdom** &c.

Engraved by James Basire.

EXEMPLAR Rotuli Hundredi de Oxon.

7. Edw. 1.

Quarta Aldermannia in Burgo Oxon.

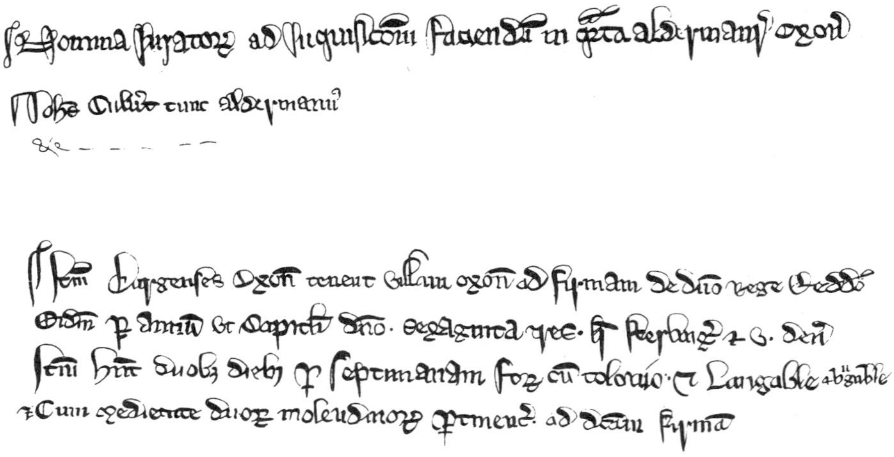
Forma Juratorum ad inquisicionem faciendam in quarta aldermannie Oxon

Johes Culiut tunc Aldermanni

&c.

Item Burgenses Oxon tenent villam Oxon ad firmam de dno Rege reddendo eidem p annum ad Scaccarium dno.

EXEMPLAR Perambulationis Forestæ de Exemore Com. Somerset.

7. Edw. 1.

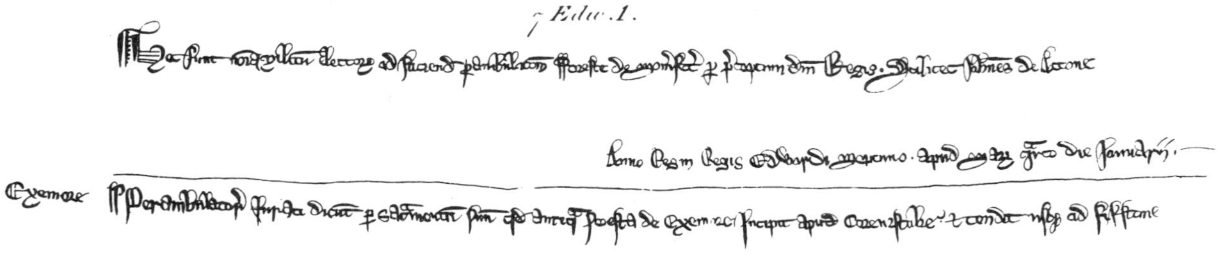
Exemore

EXEMPLAR Extentæ Manerij de Upton Com. Berk.

23 Edw. 1.

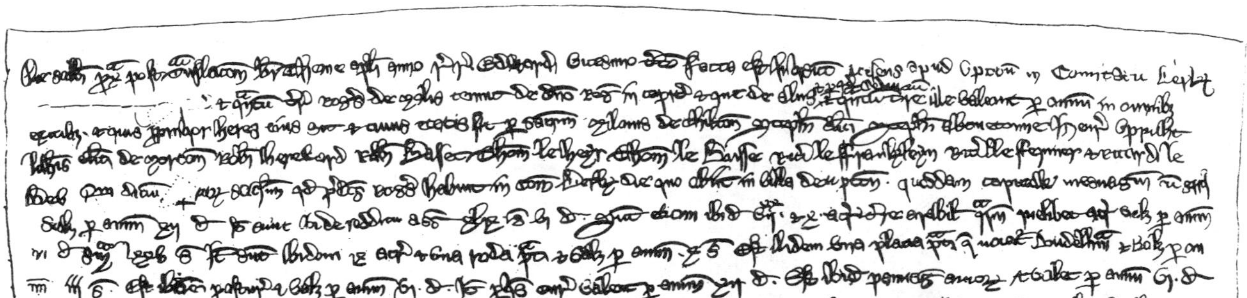

Ordered to be printed 4th July 1800. Engraved for the REPORT ON THE Public Records OF THE Kingdom &c. Engraved by James Basire.

EXPLANATIO TABULÆ X.

Exemplar Rotuli Hundredi de Oxon'.

7 Edw. 1.

ſ. Quarta Aldermanria in Burgo Oxon'.

ſ. Nomina Juratorum ad Inquiſitionem faciendam in Quarta Aldermanria Oxon'.

ſ. Johannes Culvert tunc Aldermannus, &c.

ſ. Item Burgenſes Oxoniæ tenent Villam Oxoniæ de Domino Rege reddendo eidem per Annum ut Capitali Domino ſexaginta tres Libras ſterlingorum & quinque Denarios.

Item habent duobus Diebus per ſeptimanam forum cum tolonio & Langable & Longable et cum medietate duorum Molendinorum pertinentium ad dictam firmam.

Exemplar Perambulationis Forestæ de Exemore Com' Somerset'.

7 Edw. 1.

Hec ſunt Nomina Militum electorum ad faciendam perambulationem Foreſtæ de Somerſet' per præceptum Domini Regis ſcilicet Johannes de Actone.

Anno Regni Regis Edwardi ſeptimo apud Sarum quarto die Januarij.

Exemore ſſ. Perambulatores jurati dicunt per Sacramentum ſuum quod antiqua Foreſta de Exemore incipit apud Coreneſtcombe & tendit uſque ad Fifstane.

Exemplar Extentæ Manerij de Upton' Com' Berk'.

23 Edw. 1.

Die Sabbati proxime poſt tranſlationem beati Thomæ Apoſtoli Anno Regni Regis Edwardi viceſimo tertio facta eſt Inquiſitio præſens apud Upton in Comitatu Berk'.... quid & quantum Terræ Rogerus de Molis tenuit de Domino Rege in Capite & quæ de aljis & per quod ſervitium & quantum terræ illæ valeant per Annum in omnibus exitibus & quis propinquior hæres ejus ſit et cujus ætatis ſit per Sacramentum Milonis de Chilton Stephani Clerici Stephani Ebonetonne Henrici Upricht Johannis Clerici de Morton Roberti Bereward Radulfi Baſſet Thomæ le Heyr Thomæ de Baiſſe Ricardi le Frankyleyn Ricardi le Fermer & Ricardi le Web Qui dicunt ſuper Sacramentum quod prædictus Rogerus habuit in Comitatu Berk' die quo obijt in Villa de Upton quoddam capitale Meſuagium cum gardino ſcilicet per Annum 12^{d} Item ſunt ibidem Redditus Aſſiſæ 49^{s} 6^{d} ſunt etiam ibidem $\overset{xx}{vii}$ & x Acræ Terræ arabilis quarum quælibet Acra valet per Annum 6^{d} Summa 75^{s} Item ſunt ibidem ix Acræ & una Roda Prati & valent per Annum 10^{s} Eſt ibidem una Placea Prati quæ vocatur Budelham et valet per Annum 3^{s} Eſt ibidem Paſtura et valet per Annum 6^{d} Item Perquiſitæ Curiarum valent per Annum 12^{d} Eſt ibidem Pannagium Averiorum & valet per Annum 6^{d} Sunt ibidem Opera Cuſtumariorum et valent per Annum 11^{s} 6^{d} Item Cuſtumarij dabunt Ova & valent per Annum 1^{d} Summa totalis 7^{l} 12^{s} 1^{d} Et quando Scutagium currit Galfridus de Frethorne de Celereye ſolvet Scutagium ſuum Hæredibus Rogeri de Molis et de eis habebit Wardam & Maritagium et dicunt quod iſtud Manerium de Upton tenetur de Domino Rege in Capite per Servitium militare Item dicunt quod Johannes filius dicti Rogeri eſt ejus Hæres et plene ætatis eſt videlicet de 26 Annis In cujus rei Teſtimonium præſentibus literis prædicti Juratores Sigilla ſua appoſuerunt.

ALPHABETS.

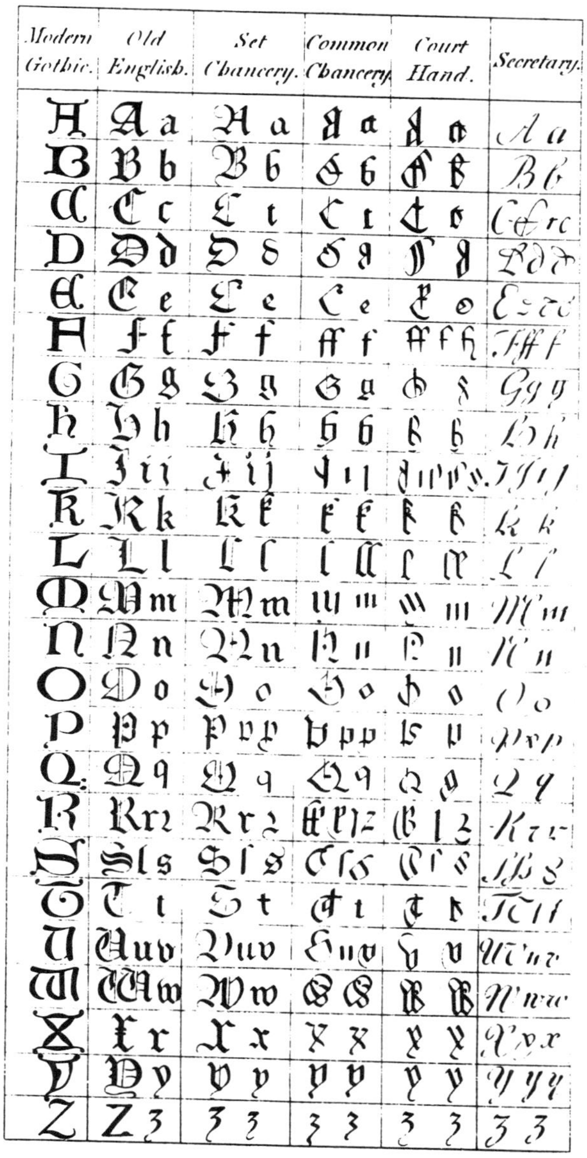

Engraved, for the REPORT ON THE Public Records OF THE Kingdom, *&c.*

Ordered to be printed 4th July 1800.

Engraved by James Basire.

Declaratio parliamenti ubi Johes primogenitus Roberti habet succedere in regnum

1371

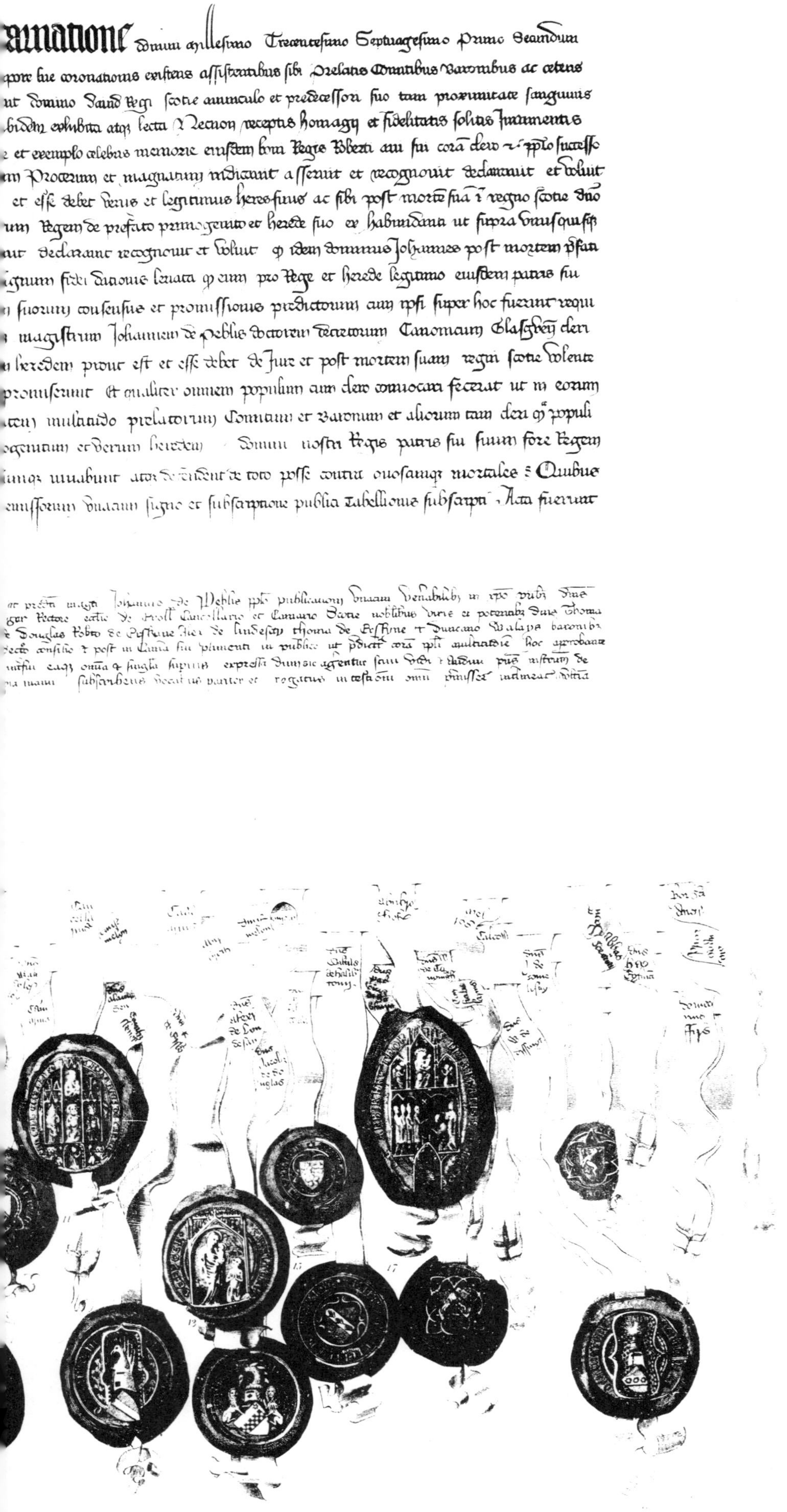
...rnatione Domini Millesimo Trecentesimo Septuagesimo Primo Secundum
...pore sue coronationis existens assistentibus sibi Prelatis Comitibus Baronibus ac ceteris
...ut domino David Regi Scotie avunculo et predecessori suo tam proximitate sanguinis
...bidem exhibita atque lecta Necnon receptis homagiis et fidelitatis solitis Juramentis
...e et exemplo celebris memorie eiusdem domini Regis Roberti avi sui coram clero et populo successo
...um Procerum et magnatum indicavit asseruit et recognovit declaravit et voluit
... et esse debet verus et legitimus heres suus ac sibi post mortem suam in regno Scotie ...
...um Regem de prefato primogenito et herede suo ex habundanti ut supra ...
...ut declaravit recognovit et voluit quod idem dominus Johannes post mortem prefati
...ignum fidei dationis levata quod eum pro Rege et herede legitimo eiusdem patris sui
...n suorum consensus et promissionis predictorum cum ipsi super hoc fuerunt requi
... magistrum Johannem de Peblis doctorem decretorum Canonicum Glasguensis clerici
...n heredem prout est et esse debet de Jure et post mortem suam regni Scotie volente
...promiserunt Et mulier omnem populum cum clero convocari fecerat ut in eorum
...tem multitudo prelatorum Comitum et Baronum et aliorum tam clerici quam populi
...ognitum et verum heredem ... domini nostri Regis patris sui suum fore Regem
...tamque vivabunt atque defendent de toto posse contra quoscumque mortales Quibus
...eiusdem huiusmodi signo et subscriptione publica tabellionis subscripti Acta fuerunt

...ac prefati magistri Johannis de Peblis ... publicacionem huiusmodi venerabilibus in christo patribus dominis
...ger Rectore ecclesie de ... Cancellario et Camerario Scotie nobilibus viris et potentibus dominis Thoma
...de Douglas Roberto de Erskine Alexandro de Lindesay Thoma de Erskine et Duncano Walays baronibus
...decto consilio et post in Camera sui parliamenti in publico ut predicitur coram populi multitudine hoc approbante
...interfui eaque omnia et singula supradicta expressa dum sic agerentur ... vidi et audivi ... instrumentum de
...ria manu subscribens ... rogatus in testimonium omnium premissorum ...

Drawn & Engraved by Jam...

EXPLANATIO TABULÆ XII.

Declaratio Parliamenti, ubi Johannes, Primogenitus Roberti, Habet Succedere in Regnum. 1371.

In Nomine ſanctæ et individuæ Trinitatis, Patris et Filii et Spiritus Sancti. Amen. Anno, ab Incarnatione Domini, milleſimo, trecenteſimo ſeptuageſimo primo, ſecundum morem et computationem eccleſiæ Scotticanæ, menſis Martii die viceſimo ſeptimo; Sereniſſimus Princeps Dominus Robertus, Dei gratia, Rex Scottorum illuſtris, apud Sconam, tempore ſuæ coronationis, exiſtens; aſſiſtentibus ſibi Prælatis, Comitibus, Baronibus, ac ceteris de clero et populo regni ſui; poſt ſacra unctionis et coronationis ſuæ peracta ſolennia, factâque declaratione juris, quo idem Sereniſſimus Princeps ſucceſſit, ac ſuccedere debuit, Domino David Regi Scotiæ, avunculo et prædeceſſori ſuo, tam proximitate ſanguinis, quam ex quadam declaratione, per quædam inſtrumenta confecta tempore inclitæ memoriæ Domini Roberti Regis Scotiæ, avi et prædeceſſoris ipſius Domini noſtri Regis, ibidem exhibita atque lecta; Nec non, receptis homagii et fidelitatis ſolitis juramentis ab ipſis Prælatis, Comitibus, Baronibus, et aliis de clero et populo ibidem exiſtentibus, in coronatione Regum Scotiæ ab olim præſtari conſuetis et debitis; Volens, more et exemplo celebris memoriæ ejuſdem boni Regis Roberti, avi ſui, coram clero et populo, ſucceſſorem et verum heredem ſuum declarare ibidem, licet de ipſo clare conſtitit atque conſtet; ex habundanti, et unanimi conſenſu et aſſenſu dictorum Prælatorum, Comitum, Procerum et Magnatum, indicavit, aſſeruit et recognovit, declaravit et voluit, Quòd cùm ipſum contigerit, pro diſpoſitione Divina, ab hac luce migrare, Dominus Johannes, filius ſuus primogenitus, Comes de Carrik et Seneſcallus Scotiæ, erit, et eſſe debet, verus et legitimus heres ſuus, ac ſibi, poſt mortem ſuam, in regno Scotiæ, Domino diſponente, ſuccedet, et ſuccedere debet, et poſt eum ſedebit, et ſedere debebit, ſuper ſolium regni ſui. Quâ declaratione, ſic factâ per ipſum Dominum noſtrum Regem, de præfato primogenito et herede ſuo, ex habundanti, ut ſuprâ, unuſquiſque Prælatorum, Comitum, Procerum, Magnatum, et aliorum ibidem exiſtentium, voce propriâ, ſingillatim, pro ſe, heredibus et ſucceſſoribus ſuis, aſſeruit, affirmavit, declaravit, recognovit et voluit, Quòd idem Dominus Johannes, poſt mortem præfati patris ſui ſuperſtes et vivus, ſit, Divina favente gratiâ, futurus Rex Scotiæ, tanquam heres legitimus ejuſdem patris ſui: Promittens quilibet, bonâ fide, et manu, in ſignum fidei dationis, levatâ, Quòd eum pro Rege et herede legitimo ejuſdem patris ſui habiturus erit; ipſumque juvabit atque defendet contra quoſcunque mortales: nec non ſigillum ſuum ſcripto, ſeu inſtrumento, ſuper hoc fiendo, apponet, in ſignum ſuorum conſenſûs et promiſſionis prædictorum, cùm ipſi ſuper hoc fuerint requiſiti. Quibus recognitione, promiſſo et fidei datione, in conſilio Domini noſtri Regis, ſic præmiſſis et actis, idem Dominus noſter Rex, per venerabilem virum magiſtrum Johannem de Peblis, doctorem Decretorum, canonicum Glaſguen. clericum ſuum, proponi fecit in publicum, Qualiter, ex habundanti, indicavit et declaravit, præfatum Dominum Johannem, filium ſuum primogenitum, verum ſuum heredem, prout eſt, et eſſe debet de jure, et poſt mortem ſuam, regni Scotiæ, volente Deo, Regem futurum; et qualiter præfati Comites, Proceres, et alii de conſilio, affirmaverunt, recognoverunt, conſenſerunt, et fide mediâ, ut præmittitur, promiſerunt; et qualiter omnem populum cum clero convocari fecerat, ut in eorum præſentia, et de eorum conſenſu unanimi, fieret et publicaretur, ne aliquis ſuper hoc ignorantiam prætendere poſſet aliqualiter in futurum. Tota autem multitudo Prælatorum, Comitum et Baronum, et aliorum tam cleri quàm populi, unanimi voluntate et clamore conſono, nullo penitus reclamante, affirmaverunt, recognoverunt et voluerunt, ipſum Dominum Johannem, tanquam primogenitum et verum heredem Domini noſtri Regis, patris ſui, ſuum fore Regem futurum; ac manu levata, in ſignum fidei dationis, promiſerunt, Quòd eum pro Rege ſuo futuro, volente Deo, habituri erunt poſt mortem patris ſui, ipſumque juvabunt atque defendent, de toto poſſe, contra quoſcunque mortales. Quibus ſic actis, præfati Prælati, Comites et Barones ibidem exiſtentes, ſigilla ſua huic ſcripto appoſuerunt, ad perpetuam et futuram memoriam, in teſtimonium omnium præmiſſorum, unà cum ſigno et ſubſcriptione publici tabellionis ſubſcripti. Acta fuerunt hæc apud Abbathiam de Scona, menſe, die et anno ſupra dictis.

Et ego Johannes Rollo Clericus, Moravienſis diœceſis, publicus Apoſtolicâ auctoritate notarius, prædictis indicationi, declarationi, affirmationi, nec non promiſſioni, manuum levationi, ac prædicti magiſtri Johannis de Peblis populo publicationi; unà cum venerabilibus in Chriſto patribus, Dominis Willelmo, Waltero, et Patricio Sancti Andreæ, Glaſguenſis et Brechinenſis eccleſiarum epiſcopis; ac diſcretis viris, Dominis Johanne de Carryc,

Carryc, Canonico Glasguensi, Waltero de Bygar, rectore ecclesiæ de Erol, Cancellario, et Camerario Scotiæ; nobilibus viris, et potentibus Dominis, Thoma de Mar, Willelmo de Douglas, et Roberto Senescal. Comitibus; Thoma de Haya, Willelmo de Keth, Constabulario et Marescallo Scotiæ; Archebaldo de Douglas, Jacobo de Douglas, Roberto de Erskyne, Alexandro de Lindesay, Thoma de Erskyne et Duncano Walays, Baronibus ac Militibus; magistro Johanne de Peblis supradicto; et multis aliis testibus, ad præmissa vocatis pariter et rogatis, primò in secreta camera prædicti Domini Regis in suo secreto consilio, et post in camera sui Parliamenti, in publico, ut prædicitur, coram populi multitudine hoc approbante, factum, anno, die, mense et locis supra dictis, indictione nonâ, pontificatûs sanctissimi in Christo patris et Domini nostri Domini Gregorii, divinâ providentiâ Papæ undecimi, anno primo; præsens interfui, eaque omnia et singula superiùs expressa, dum sic agerentur, scivi, vidi et audivi; præsens instrumentum, de manu alterius scriptum, signo meo consueto, ad instantiam prædicti Domini Johannis, ipsius Domini Regis primogeniti, Comitis de Carryk, Scotiæ Senescalli, signavi hîc me propriâ manu subscribens, vocatus pariter et rogatus, in testimonium omnium præmissorum; interlineationem in ultima linea meæ subscriptionis, *Johannis*, approbando.

SECOND REPORT.

SECOND REPORT.

THE COMMITTEE appointed to inquire into the State of the Public Records of this Kingdom, and of ſuch other Public Inſtruments, Rolls, Books, and Papers, as they ſhall think proper; and to report to the Houſe the Nature and Condition thereof; together with what they ſhall judge fit to be done for the better Arrangement, Preſervation, and more convenient Uſe of the ſame—Have proceeded further to inquire into the ſeveral Matters referred to them; and have agreed upon the following Report.

YOUR Committee, in their Firſt Report upon the Nature and State of the Public Records of the Realm, have laid before the Houſe, 1ſt. The Reſult of their Inquiries into the Proceedings of former Times upon this Subject; 2dly. The Courſe of their own Proceedings upon the preſent Occaſion; and, 3dly. An Examination of ſuch further Meaſures as in their Judgment it will be adviſeable to adopt for the future Preſervation and Arrangement of all the Manuſcripts comprehended within the Scope of their Examination, and for rendering the Uſe of them more acceſſible to the Public.

In that Report, they have alſo ſtated, that they had proceeded to ANALYSE the Contents of all the Returns tranſmitted to them, ſo far as to aſcertain all the various Sorts of Public Records, Rolls, Inſtruments, Books and Papers, preſerved in each Repoſitory; and that, under the Authority of the Houſe, they had employed certain learned and experienced Perſons to arrange theſe Articles in Two diſtinct TABLES; the One, exhibiting them SYSTEMATICALLY claſſed under the leading Heads of our Conſtitution, Government, and Juriſprudence; and the other, exhibiting them in ALPHABETICAL Order, with the Addition of explanatory Notes, and References to the moſt authentic Copies, Catalogues, and Indexes, relating to each of the principal Articles.

This Analyſis, and theſe Tables, Your Committee now proceed to lay before the Houſe; truſting that, in this Reſpect at leaſt, they have rendered a laſting Service to the Public, by making the Reſult of their Inquiries ſo far practically uſeful.

ANALYSIS

OF THE

CONTENTS OF ALL THE RETURNS TRANSMITTED;

Shewing the Principal Matters referred to

In the various Sorts of RECORDS, ROLLS, INSTRUMENTS, BOOKS, and PAPERS, preferved in the feveral

PUBLIC REPOSITORIES.

ANALYSIS.

ENGLAND.
SCOTLAND.
IRELAND.
ENGLISH DOMINIONS BEYOND SEA.

ENGLAND.

I. THE KING, ROYAL FAMILY, AND HOUSEHOLD:

1. THE KING:
2. THE QUEEN:
3. THE PRINCE OF WALES:
   .... Houfehold, Privy Seals, and Correfpondence;
   Principality of WALES;
   Duchy of CORNWALL.
4. CUSTOS REGNI .... LIEUTENANT .... PROTECTOR .... REGENT .... LORDS JUSTICES, &c.
5. HOUSEHOLD:
6. THE KING'S CHAMBER.

II. THE ROYAL COUNCILS:

1. PARLIAMENT:
   .... The Houfe of Lords;
   The Houfe of Commons.
2. PRIVY COUNCIL.

III.

ENGLAND . . . *continued.*

III. THE ROYAL PREROGATIVE.

1. IN ECCLESIASTICAL AFFAIRS:
   - During Popery;
   - Since the Reformation;
   - Commonwealth Proceedings.

2. IN CIVIL AFFAIRS:
   - General Adminiſtration of the Realm;
   - Honours and Offices;
   - Trade and Coin.

3. IN MILITARY AFFAIRS:

4. IN FOREIGN AFFAIRS:

IV. THE ROYAL REVENUES.

1. ORDINARY:
   - Land Revenues;
   - Caſual Revenues.

2. EXTRAORDINARY.

V. COURTS OF JUSTICE.

1. OF ABOLISHED OR OBSOLETE JURISDICTION:
   - Curia Regis;
   - Placita de Aſſiſis;
   - Placita Itineraria;
   - Placita Foreſtæ;
   - Placita Coronæ;
   - Placita Aulæ;
   - Placita de Quo Warranto;
   - Star Chamber Proceedings;
   - Court of Requeſts;
   - Court of Wards and Liveries;
   - Court of Augmentations;
   - Surveyor General's Court;
   - High Commiſſion Court.
   - Court of Chivalry; viz. Conſtable and Marſhal.

2. OF OCCASIONAL JURISDICTION:
   - Special Commiſſions;
   - Court of Judicature for determining Differences after the Fire of London;
   - High Court of Juſtice.

(continued)

V. COURTS OF JUSTICE: . . . . . . *continued.*

3. OF ESTABLISHED JURISDICTION:

- Chancery . .
  - In its Ordinary Jurifdiction;
  - In its Extraordinary Jurifdiction.
- King's Bench
  - Pleas of the Crown;
  - Pleas in Civil Suits.
- Common Pleas:
- Exchequer
  - Of Account
    - The King's Remembrancer's Office;
    - The Lord Treafurer's Remembrancer's Office.
  - Of Receipt
    - Tellers;
    - Tally Court;
    - Auditor or Tally Writer;
    - Pell Office;
    - Auditors of Impreft, or Commiffioners for Auditing the Public Accounts;
- Exchequer
  - Of Pleas;
  - Of Error.
- Marfhalfea and Palace Courts:
- Circuits of England;
- Seffion of Oyer and Terminer, and Gaol Delivery for London, and Gaol Delivery for Middlefex;
- Great Seffions of Wales;
- Duchy of Lancafter;
- Counties Palatine;
- Cinque Ports;
- Stannary Courts;
- Commiffions of Sewers;
- Quarter Seffions and Clerks of the Peace.
- Maritime Courts . . .
  - Admiralty Inftance Court;
  - Admiralty Prize Court;
  - Court of Appeal in Prize Caufes.
- Ecclefiaftical Jurifdiction
  - Epifcopal;
  - Archiepifcopal;
  - Appellate Jurifdiction;
  - Deans and Chapters.

Court for Offences in India.

VI. UNIVERSITIES AND COLLEGES, SCHOOLS, &c.

1. UNIVERSITIES AND COLLEGES:

2. ROYAL SCHOOLS ... CHAUNTRIES ... HOSPITALS ... COLLEGES ... FREE CHAPELS ... FRATERNITIES ... AND GUILDS.

VII. ALIENATION OF PRIVATE PROPERTY.

6 P SCOTLAND.

SCOTLAND.

1. THE KING:

- Title;
- Great Seal;
- Privy Seal;
- Signet;
- Chancery;
- Revenues and Expenfes;
- Acts of Civil Government;
- Ecclefiaftical Government.

2. PARLIAMENT:

3. PRIVY COUNCIL:

4. GENERAL REGISTERS:

5. COURTS OF JUSTICE:

- Court of Seffion;
- Jufticiary Court;
- Court of Exchequer;
- Admiralty Court;
- Commiffary Courts;
- Court of Teinds;
- Sheriff Court.

6. UNIVERSITIES.

IRELAND.

ENGLISH DOMINIONS BEYOND SEA.

1. IN FRANCE.
2. GUERNSEY AND JERSEY.
3. ISLE OF MAN.
4. GIBRALTAR, MINORCA, AND TANGIER.
5. PLANTATIONS:

&c. &c. &c.

I.

TABLE OF THE PUBLIC RECORDS,

&c.

SYSTEMATICALLY CLASSED

ACCORDING TO THE MATTERS TO WHICH THEY RELATE;

Diſtinguiſhing the Sorts of Records or other Inſtruments belonging to each Matter; the Periods of Time to which they refer; and the Places where they are kept reſpectively.

FAITHFULLY ABSTRACTED

FROM THE ORIGINAL RETURNS,

BY ME,

AL. LUDERS.

JULY 3, 1800.

TABLE I.

Syſtematical Arrangement of the Public Records.

I. THE KING, ROYAL FAMILY, AND HOUSEHOLD.

RECORDS and other INSTRUMENTS.	DATE.	WHERE KEPT.	Appendix to the Firſt Report.
1. THE KING.			
CORONATION:			
Coronation Rolls - - - - - - -	Ed. 2. Ric. 2. - / Hen. 4. & 5. -	Tower - - -	A. 2.
	1 Jac. 1. to Geo. 2.	Rolls Chapel - - -	D. 1.
Expenſes:			
Of James II. - - - - - - -	Jac. 2. - - -	Office of Board of Gr. Cloth	C. 5.
Of George III. - - - - - - -	1761 - - -	Great Wardrobe Office -	C. 5. b.
Claims, Ceremonies, &c. - - - - - -	1483 to 1660 -	Old State Paper Office - -	C. 1.
Accounts of, in the Heralds Books - - -	— —	Herald's Office - -	C. 8.
Claims at Coronation of Ric. II. - - -	Ric. 2. - - -	Lincoln's Inn Library -	Q. 3.
Commiſſion for Claims at Coronation of Geo. III. and the Oaths - - - - - - -	Geo. 3. - - -	Clerk of Crown in Chancery	D. 2.
Papers and Inſtruments relating to - - -	Ed. 6. to Geo. 1.	Dean & Chapter Weſtminſter	N. 12.
The like - - - - - - - -	Date wanting -	Inner Temple Library -	Q. 2. b.
Proceedings at the Coronation - - - -	Geo. 1. - - -	Inner Temple Library -	Q. 2. b.
ROYAL LETTERS:			
Inſtructions of Hen. VII. to negotiate his Marriage with the Queen of Naples - - -	Hen. 7. - - -	Chapter Houſe - - - -	A. 1.
To Foreign Princes - - - - - -	1527 to 1702 -	Old State Paper Office -	C. 1.
- - - from them to England - - - - -	1684 to 1777 -	New State Paper Office -	Ibid.
Entries and Copies of, to Lords Juſtices and Lieutenants of Ireland - - - - - -	1626 to 1800 -	Signet Office - - -	C. 4.
Letters of Kings and Queens to the Dean and Chapter of Exeter - - - - - -	Hen. 5. to Eliz. -	Dean and Chapter Exeter -	N. 6.
Of Charles I. to the Univerſity of Cambridge, commending their Choice of Buckingham for Chancellor - - - - - - - -	1626 - - -	Univerſity Library Camb. -	P. 1.
Mandatory and of Diſpenſation, of various Sovereigns upon Univerſity Affairs - - -	— —	Colleges of Univerſities -	O. & P.
Various - - - - - - - - -	Hen. 8. to Eliz. -	Inner Temple Library - -	Q. 2. b.
To the Biſhop of Oxford - - - - -	Car. 1. - - -	Regiſtry Biſhop of Oxford -	L. 28.
ROYAL VOYAGES - - - - - - - -	1 Hen. 4. - -	Tower - - - - -	A. 2.
ROYAL MARRIAGES:			
Books of - - - - - - - - -	Date wanting -	Herald's Office - -	C. 8.
Lettres de l'Ambaſſadeur de Louis XIII. en Angleterre, pour y negocier le Marriage d'Henriette Marie avec Charles I. - - - - - -	1624 - - -	Bodleian Library. *Carte* -	O. 1.
Articles of Marriage of Charles I. with Henrietta Maria of France - - - - - -	Car. 1. - - -	Univerſity Library Camb.	P. 1.
Commiſſion (Copy) for treating of a Marriage between Prince Charles and Chriſtiana, 2d Daughter of France - - - - - -	1616 - - -	Univerſity Library Camb.	P. 1.
Propoſitions for the Marriage with the Infanta -	Jac. 1. - - -	Univerſity Library Camb.	P. 1.
ROYAL WILLS:			
Of Hen. II. - - - - - - -	— —	King's Rememb. Exchequer	G. 6.
Ric. II. - - - - - - - -	— —	Chapter Houſe - -	A. 1.
Hen. V. - - - - - - - -	— —	Ibidem - - - - (See Copy in Caius Coll. Camb.)	A. 1.
Hen. VII. - - - - - - -	— —	Ibidem - - - -	A. 1.
Hen. VIII. - - - - - - -	— —	Ibidem - - -	A. 1.
ROYAL FUNERALS. (See Wardrobe D. of Cornwall.)			
Books of - - - - - - - - -	Dates wanting -	Herald's Office - -	C. 8.
Papers relating to - - - - - - -	Hen. 3. to Anne -	Dean & Chapter Weſtminſter	N. 12. b.

I. THE KING, ROYAL FAMILY, and HOUSEHOLD—*(continued.)*

RECORDS and other INSTRUMENTS.	DATE.	WHERE KEPT.	Appendix to the Firſt Report.
2. THE QUEEN.			
Jointures:			
Account of Revenue of Queen Philippa	18 Ed. 3.	Chapter Houſe	A. 1.
Treaſurers, &c. Accounts	Ed.6. Jac.1. Car.1.	Auditors Land Revenue	G. 15.
Inrolments of Treaſurers and Miniſters Accounts	Hen. 8.	Augmentation Office	G. 19.
State of the Honours, Manors, &c. in Jointure, which are demiſeable, with the Rent and Names of Steward, Bailiff, and Feodary	Date wanting	Univerſity Library Camb.	P. 1.
Accounts of Eſtates of the Queen Dowager of Henry VIII. Queen Conſort of James I. and Queen Dowagers of Charles I. and Charles II.	Hen. 8. to Car. 2.	— —	G. 15.
Declarations of Treaſurers and Receivers Accounts of Anne Queen of James I.	1603 to 1617		
The like of Henrietta Maria Queen of Charles I.	Car. 1 & 2.		
The like of Catharine Queen of Charles II.	1664 to 1701		
Grants to Queen Henrietta Maria	6 & 10 Car. 1.	Auditors Land Revenue	G. 15. d.
Fines for Leaſes of her Lands	1638, 1639 & 1640		
Account of Manors aſſigned to her	1630		
Decree in Exchequer relating to her Jointure	12 Car. 2.		
Leaſes of Fee Farms in Cambridgeſhire, Parcel of her Jointure	Car. 1.		
Receiver's Account for the ſame in Dorſet and Somerſet	16 Car. 1.		
Certificate of the Queen's Copyholds, whoſe Fines are uncertain, or Demeſne Lands not 30 Years in Leaſe, in the Auditor's Office	Car. 1.	Univerſity Library Camb.	P. 1.
Certificate in the ſame Office of all Honours, &c. in Jointure	1632		
Proceedings reſpecting Inglewood Honour	Car. 1. & 2.		
Sale of Knareſboro', &c. by Truſtees for Queen Henrietta Maria	1629		
Accounts of Receivers General for Wales of her Revenues there	7, 8, & 12 Car. 1.		
The like for England	1632	Auditors Land Revenue	G. 15. d.
Views of Accounts, Acquittances for Fees, Penſions, &c. Tradeſmens Bills and Warrants for the ſame Queen	Car. 1.		
Books of Eſtabliſhment of Officers of the ſame	Car. 1.		
Jointure Grant to Queen Catharine	15 Car. 2.		
Counterparts of Leaſes of the ſame	Car. 2.		
Grants to the ſame	17, 19, 21, 24 Car. 2. & 1 Jac. 2.		
Appointment of new Truſtees for the ſame	3 Jac. 2.	Auditors Land Revenue	G. 15. b. & d.
Commiſſion for Revenues of the ſame	2 Will. & Mary		
Survey of Norton in Worceſterſhire, in the ſame Jointure	4 Jac. 2.		
Certificate of Eſtates ſettled on the ſame	Car. 2.	Surveyor General's Office	G. 14.
Divorces:			
Proceedings in the Divorce of Queen Catharine	Hen. 8.	Chapter Houſe,	A. 1.
3. THE PRINCE OF WALES.			
Household:			
- - - of Prince Henry, Son of James I.	Jac. 1.	Office of Board of Gr. Cloth	C. 5.
Accounts of the Cofferer of the Houſehold of Prince Charles	Jac. 1.	Univerſity Library Camb.	P. 1.
Privy Seals and Correspondence:			
During the Expedition of Charles Prince of Wales in Spain, &c.	1622 to 1626	Duchy of Cornwall Office	C. 7.
Principality of Wales:			
Charter of Liberties to the Prince	14 Jac. 1.	Auditors Land Revenue	G. 15. d.
Welſh Rolls	4 to 23 Ed. 1.	Tower	A. 2.
- - - Copies of Ditto	6 to 10 Ed. 1.	Lincoln's Inn Library	Q. 3.

I. THE KING, ROYAL FAMILY, AND HOUSEHOLD—*(continued.)*

RECORDS and other INSTRUMENTS.	DATE.	WHERE KEPT.	Appendix to the First Report.
PRINCIPALITY OF WALES—*(continued.)*			
Accounts of Revenues	47 to 49 Ed. 3.	Tower	A. 2.
The like	Ed. 3. to Mar.	Augmentation Office	G. 19.
Extenta Maneriorum Edwardi Principis Walliæ	19 Ed. 3.	University Library Camb.	P. 1.
Papers relating to, —— Its Liberties, &c.	1550 to 1660	Old State Paper Office	C. 1.
Ministers Accounts	Dates wanting	King's Rememb. Exchequer	G. 6.
General Accounts of Receivers and Bailiffs, in divers Counties, to Prince Charles	Jac. 1.	Auditors Land Revenue	G. 15.
Nomina Maneriorum, &c. Caroli Principis Walliæ	Jac. 1.		
Names of Benefices in the Gift of the Prince of Wales	Jac. 1.		
Records delivered to the Commissioners of the Revenue of Charles Prince of Wales	Jac. 1.	University Library Camb.	P. 1.
Rental of Lands in North and South Wales, Parcel of the Principality or lately annexed	1642		
DUCHY OF CORNWALL:			
Council Proceedings	13 Jac. 1. to 1800	Duchy Office	C. 7.
CHARTERS and GRANTS:			
- - - - Various	Ed. 3.	Chapter House	A. 1.
- - - - To the Dukes of Cornwall	11 Ed. 3. to 20 Car. 1.		
- - - - To the Queen of James I.	Jac. 1.	Duchy Office	C. 7.
- - - - To Richard D. of Gloucester	Ed. 4.	British Museum	U.
COURT ROLLS and BOOKS:			
Of Duchy Lands, and of Manors not Parcel of the Duchy	1 Ed. 1. to 1800	Duchy Office	C. 7.
Books and Papers relating to the Duchy	Date wanting	British Museum	U.
ASSESSION ROLLS and BOOKS:			
Of the Manors for which Assessions were held every Seventh Year	7 Ed. 3. to 1800		
Articles and Answers relating to the same	15 Car. 2. to 1800		
INROLMENT OF PATENTS, &c.		Duchy Office	C. 7.
Commissions of Offices, Leases, Warrants, and Particulars	8 Jac. 1. to 1800		
ACCOUNTS OF MINISTERS AND RECEIVERS	Ed. 3. & seq.	King's Rememb. Exchequer	G. 6.
The like	30 Ed. 3.	Auditors Land Revenue	G. 15.
Both of Original Duchy Lands and others	19 Ed. 3. to 1800	Duchy Office	C. 7.
The like	Date wanting	Augmentation Office	G. 19.
Brief Certificate of all the Revenues belonging to the Duchy	18 Car. 1.	University Library Camb.	P. 1.
TIN ROLLS:			
Covenants for Tin Works	14 Hen. 8.	Chapter House	A. 1.
Rolls of Account of Tin coined	43 Eliz. to 1800		
TREASURERS ACCOUNTS	42 Ed. 3. to 11 Geo. 3.		
WARDROBE:			
Account, including Funeral of James I. and Coronation of King Charles	1625 and 1626	Duchy Office	C. 7.
STANNARIES:			
Act of Convocation of Tinners Parliament, assembled 25th August 1776, and continued to	11 Sept. 1777		
Appeals in Stannary Causes	1788 to 1794		
Cornish Stannary Returns	Date wanting	Auditors Land Revenue	G. 15.
SALES OF DUCHY ESTATES:			
Proceedings in	43 Eliz. to 1800	Duchy Office	C. 7.
SURVEYS:			
Of the whole Duchy, immediately after the Grant to the Black Prince	11 Ed. 3.	King's Rememb. Exchequer	G. 6.
- - - - Copy thereof	— —	Duchy Office	C. 7.
Surveys and Plans (including the Commonwealth Surveys) and antient Surveys of Knights Fees	11 Ed. 3. to 1800		

I. THE KING, ROYAL FAMILY, and HOUSEHOLD—(*continued.*)

RECORDS and other INSTRUMENTS.	DATE.	WHERE KEPT.	Appendix to the First Report.
4. CUSTOS REGNI, LIEUTENANT, PROTECTOR, REGENT.—(See Commons Report, 12 Dec. 1788.)			
PATENTS:			
In the Patent and Close Rolls - - - -	37 Hen. 3. to 36 Hen. 8. - - -	Tower and Rolls -	A. 2. & D. 1.
Commissions and Instructions - - - -	1695 to 1755 -	State Paper Office, and Secretary of State's Office -	C. 1.
PROCEEDINGS IN PARLIAMENT:			
In the Parliament Rolls - - - - -	4 Ed. 3. to 34 Hen. 6. - - -	Tower, and Chapter House -	A.1.& 2.
5. HOUSEHOLD:			
GENERAL ACCOUNTS:			
Proclamations, Accounts, Rules and Orders, Inventories, &c. - - - - - - -	1478 to 1706 -	Old State Paper Office -	C. 1.
The like - - - - - - - -	Car. 1. to Geo. 3.	Office of Board of Gr. Cloth	C. 5.
States and Draughts of Accounts - - -	1728 to 1797 -	Auditors Land Revenue -	G. 15.
Two Books of Accounts - - - -	20 Ed. 4. - -	Library of Antiq. Society	S.
A Book of all Compositions from each County, for the Yearly Expense of his Majesty's Household	14 Car. I. - -	Library of Antiq. Society	S.
Books and Papers - - - - - -	Date wanting -	British Museum - -	U.
Accounts - - - - - - - -	Ed. 3. to Jac. 1. -	Auditors Land Revenue -	G. 15.
The like - - - - - - - -	Eliz. to Car. 1. -	Ibidem - - - -	G. 15. d.
ORDERS for its Government - - - - -	Hen. 8. Mary, James 1. Cha. 1. and Geo. 3. - -	Office of Board of Gr. Cloth	C. 5.
Ordinances - - - - - - -	Jac. 1. - -	Library of Antiq. Society -	S.
Papers relating to - - - - - - -	1622 - -	Inner Temple Library -	Q. 2. b.
ESTABLISHMENT of the Household - - -	Car. 1. to Geo. 3.	Office of Board of Gr. Cloth	C. 5.
FEES allowed in the different Offices - - -	Hen. 8. to C. 2.	Office of Board of Gr. Cloth	C. 5.
DIETS for the different Tables, Services of Corn, Cattle, &c. and Prices - - - - -	Hen. 8. to C. 2. -	Office of Board of Gr. Cloth	C. 5.
EXPENDITURE - - - Various Articles of - -	Jac. 1. to Geo. 3. -	Office of Board of Gr. Cloth	C. 5.
COURT of VIRGE, Proceedings - - - -	1676 to 1791 -	Office of Board of Gr. Cloth	C. 5.
The like - - - - - - - - -	Date wanting -	Bodleian Library - -	O. 1.
SERVANTS Warrants and Certificates - - -	1626 to 1800 -	Office of Board of Gr. Cloth	C. 5.
ACCOUNTS of GREAT WARDROBE and BOARD of GREEN CLOTH:			
General Account - - - - - - -	10 Edw. 1. 18 Ed. 1. 17 Ed. 2. -	Tower - - - -	A. 2.
General Account by Lord Treasurer for One Year	12 Hen. 8. - -	Chapter House - -	A. 1.
Sundry Purveyors, Cofferers, and other Household Accounts - - - - - - - -	Before 1660 - -	Auditors Land Revenue -	G. 15.
Accounts - - - - - - chiefly	temp. Hen. 8.	Augmentation Office - -	G. 19.
The like - - - - - - - -	Ed. 1. Car. 2. -	King's Rememb. Exchequer	G. 6.
The like - - - - - - - -	Ed. 1. & Eliz. -	Auditors Land Revenue -	G. 15.
Inventories - - - - - - - -	Of various Dates.	British Museum - -	U.
Patents, Warrants, and Estimates - - - -	1749 to 1775 -	Great Wardrobe Office	C. 5. b.
Books of Salaries and Liveries - - -	1750 to 1779 -	Great Wardrobe Office	C. 5. b.
Quarterly and Yearly Accounts and Day Books -	1752 to 1777 -	Great Wardrobe Office	C. 5. b.
COMPTROLLERS ACCOUNTS:			
Of Receipts and Expenses - - - - -	28 Ed. 1. - -	Library of Antiq. Society	S.
The like - - - - - - - - -	10, 11, & 18 Ed. 2. - - - -	Library of Antiq. Society	S.
Bills - - - - - - - - -	1730 to 1792 -	Great Wardrobe Office -	C. 5. b.
COFFERERS:			
Accounts - - - - - - - -	Ed. 1. to Car. 2.	King's Rememb. Exchequer	G. 6.
The like - - - - - - - -	Eliz. to Car. 1. -	Auditors Land Revenue -	G. 15. d.

I. THE KING, ROYAL FAMILY, AND HOUSEHOLD—(*continued.*)

RECORDS and other INSTRUMENTS.	DATE.	WHERE KEPT.	Appendix to the First Report.
5. HOUSEHOLD—(*continued.*)			
CHIEF BUTLER:			
Accounts	Ed. 1. to Car. 2.	King's Rem. Exchequer	G. 6.
The like	15 & 17 Ed. 2.	Auditors Land Revenue	G. 15. d.
The like	Eliz. to Car. 1.		
PAYMASTER of the WORKS, and SURVEYOR:			
Accounts of Expenses for Repairs and building Castles and Palaces	Ed. 1. to Car. 2.	King's Rem. Exchequer	G. 6.
Accounts	Hen. 8. & antea	Chapter House	A. 1.
Accounts of Reparations	Hen. 8. to Car. 2.		
INVENTORIES:			
Of Wardrobe, Pictures, Statues, &c. of Cha. I. by Parliamentary Commission	In 1649	Auditors Land Revenue	G. 15.
Of Wardrobe of Queen Elizabeth	42 Eliz.		
Of Jewels, Plate, Stuff, &c.	Hen. 8.	Library of Antiq. Society	S.
Of Jewel Office and Wardrobe	Date wanting	British Museum	U.
6. THE KING'S CHAMBER:			
ACCOUNTS:			
Household Book	Hen. 7.	2d Secondy King's Rem.	G. 6. a.
LORD CHAMBERLAIN:			
His Account of Privy Purse	Ed. 6.	Auditors Land Revenue	G. 15.
TREASURERS of the CHAMBER:			
Payments by the Treasurer of the King's Chamber	29 to 33 Hen. 8.	Royal Society Library	R.
Accounts of Lord Harrington	11 & 15 Jac. 1.	Bodleian Library. *Rawl.*	O. 1.
Treasurer's Book of Debts to the King	Hen. 8. & Ed. 6.	Auditors Land Revenue	G. 15.
JEWEL OFFICE:			
Jewel Accounts	Hen. 8 & antea	Chapter House	A. 1.
The like	Car. 1.	Auditors Land Revenue	G. 15.
Jewels annexed to the Crown	Jac. 1.	Chapter House	A. 1.
Inventories of Jewels of Anne Queen of James I.	1605 to 1615	Auditors Land Revenue	G. 15.
Inventories	Of various Dates	British Museum	U.
Accounts of Jewels, Plate, &c.	Ed. 1. to Car. 2.	King's Rem. Exchequer	G. 6.
PRIVY PURSE:			
Lord Chamberlain's Accounts	Ed. 6.	Auditors Land Revenue	G. 15.
Orders for Government of the Bed Chamber	Will. 3.	Bodleian Library	O. 1.

II. THE ROYAL COUNCILS.

RECORDS and other INSTRUMENTS.	DATE.	WHERE KEPT.	Appendix to the First Report.
1. PARLIAMENT:			
ROLLS of PARLIAMENT and STATUTES:			
Books of Statutes	John to Hen. 8.	1 Second. King's Remem.	G. 6. a.
Statute Rolls	6 Ed. 1. to 8 Ed. 4.	Tower	A. 2.
The like, called Parliament Rolls	1 Ric. 3. to 39 Geo. 3.	Rolls	D. 1.
Statuta Walliæ	12 Ed. 1.		
Statute Roll	13 Ed. 1.	Chapter House	A. 1.
Rolls of Parliament	18 to 21 Ed. 1.		
The like—(Copies of D° to Ric. II. in Bodl. Lib.)	1311 to 1483	Tower	A. 2.
Roll	7 Hen. 5.	Chapter House	A. 1.
Original Statutes	12 Hen. 7. to 40 G. 3.	Parliament Office	B. 1.
Concordia inter Regem & Barones pro electione Vicecomitum	Hen. 3.	Chapter House	A. 1.
Ordinance of Parliament respecting Purveyance	Ed. 2.	Dean & Chapter Durham	N. 24.
Statutes exemplified under the Great Seal	6 Hen. 8. to Geo. 3.	Rolls	D. 1.
Placita Parliamentaria	Ed. 1. to Ed. 2.	Bodleian Library	O. 1.
Rotuli Parliamentorum	Ed. 2. to Hen. 6.	Middle Temple Library	Q. 1.
Collection of Statutes	From Mag. Charta	British Museum	U.
The like, Private Acts	Hen. 8. & Car. 1.		
The like	Hen. 8. to Car. 2.	Inner Temple Library	Q. 2. b.
The like, Antient Statutes	Date wanting	Corp. Christi Coll. Camb.	P. 5.
The like	Date wanting	Dean and Chapter Glouc.	N. 7.
The like, very extensive	Date wanting	Bodleian Library	O. 1.
The like	Mag. Ch. to Hen. 4.	Lincoln's Inn Library	Q. 3.
The like	Mag. Ch. to Hen. 6.	Inner Temple Library	Q. 2. b.
Copies of Parliament Rolls in the Tower, and Extracts of those at the Rolls	5 Ed. 2. to 19 Hen. 7.	Magd. College, Camb.	P. 14.

II. THE ROYAL COUNCILS—(continued.)

RECORDS and other INSTRUMENTS.	DATE.	WHERE KEPT.	Appendix to the First Report.
Rolls of Parliament, &c.—(*continued.*)			
Copies of Parliament Rolls	Ric. 2.	Bodleian Library	O. 1.
The like	Ed. 2. to Hen. 8.	Inner Temple Library	Q. 2. b.
The like	Ed. 1. to Ed. 4.	Lincoln's Inn Library	Q. 3.
Catalogue of Acts removed to the Rolls	1483 to 1625		
Calendars of Statutes in White Tower, Westminster	12 Hen. 7. to Eliz.	Bodleian Library	O. 1.
Petitions:			
Bundles of	Ed. 1. to 17 Ed. 4.	Tower	A. 2.
Copies of Petitions	Ed. 1. to Hen. 4.	Lincoln's Inn Library	Q. 3.
Writs:			
Of Summons and Returns	16 Ed. 1. to 17 E. 4.	Tower	A. 2.
	33 H. 8. to 12 Car. 2.	Rolls	D. 1.
Entries of Returns of, to House of Commons	1688. Convention	Clerk of Crown in Chan.	D. 2.
Precepts for the Convention Parliament	1688	Petty Bag Office	D. 5.
Summons to Parliament	49 Hen. 3. to 20 E. 2.	Ashmolean Museum	O. 2.
Copies of Summons	Ric. 2. to Ed. 4.	Lincoln's Inn Library	Q. 3.
Declarations, Speeches, Addresses, Messages, and Reports:			
Papers of	1527 to 1698	Old State Paper Office	C. 1.
The like	1706 to 1763	New State Paper Office	Ibid.
Journals of Lords and Commons	1660 to 1688		
Debates in Parliament	1628		
Speeches	1623		
Orders, &c. on Affairs of Ireland	1642 to 1644		
Perfect Copies of all the Votes, &c. in the Treaty at Newport, by Sir E. Walker	1648	Bodleian Library. *Rawl.*	O. [illegible]
Printed Act, with MS. Memorandums of the Committee, relating to the Goods of Charles I.	Car. 1.		
Journal	1620 to 1621 & 1640		
Journal of Interregnum, from withdrawing of King James, to Meeting of Convention	1688		
Transactions relating to Scotch Affairs	1649 to 1653		
Proceedings	1572 to 1663	Ibidem. *Tanner*	Ibid.
Solemn League and Covenant	1643	British Museum	U.
General Association of the Realm in Support of the King	Will. 3.	Tower	A. 2.
Transactions of Parliament (by Ashmole)	1673, 7, 8	Ashmolean Museum	O. 2.
Prynne's MS. of Cases argued in Parliament	Date wanting		
Miscellaneous Collection of Proceedings in Parliament, by Petyt	Various Dates	Inner Temple Library	Q. 2. b.
Passages in Parliament	1 to 13 Eliz.	Caius College, Cambridge	P. 7.
HOUSE OF LORDS:			
Account of Parliaments, from Ed. II. to Ed. IV. containing Names of the Peers	— —	University Library Camb.	P. 1.
Entries of Returns of Peers of Scotland	Since 1707	Clerk of Crown in Chan.	D. 2.
Parliament Pawns	21 Hen. 8. to 1800	Petty Bag Office	D. 5.
Journals of different Periods	Car. 1. to 1696		
Proceedings in the Case of Sir J. Fenwick	1696	Bodleian Library. *Rawl.*	O. 1.
Proceedings on the Claim of Lord Purbeck	Car. 1. & Car. 2.		
Lord Chancellor Bacon's Submission to the Lords	Jac. 1.	Ashmolean Museum	O. 2.
Original Journals	1 Hen. 8.		
Minute Books	1624		
Books of Committee of Privileges	1660		
Proceedings on Private Bills, and in other Committees	1621		
Proxy Books	1621		
Witness Books	1661		
Pedigrees of Peers	1767		
Commissions for passing Bills, Prorogations, Lord High Stewards, &c.	1539	to 1800 — Parliament Office	B. 1.
Test Rolls	1675		
Garter's Rolls of Peers	1660		
Appeals and Proceedings on them	1690		
Recognizances on the same	1738		
Writs of Error	1661		

II. THE ROYAL COUNCILS—(continued.)

RECORDS and other INSTRUMENTS.	DATE.	WHERE KEPT.	Appendix to the First Report.
HOUSE OF LORDS—(continued.)			
Paper Bills and Petitions, and Proceedings	1660 } to 1800	Parliament Office	B. 1.
Certificates of Returns of Peers for Scotland	1707 } to 1800	Parliament Office	B. 1.
Orders of Committees on Petitions, and Proceedings	1661 to 1663	Parliament Office	B. 1.
Books of Orders and Judgments	1642 to 1719	Parliament Office	B. 1.
Books of Cognizances on Appeals	1680 to 1735	Parliament Office	B. 1.
Books of Protections	1690 to 1696	Parliament Office	B. 1.
Books of Warrants for Witnesses	1640 to 1648	Parliament Office	B. 1.
Journal	1660 to 1671	Middle Temple Library	Q. 1.
The like	Hen. 8. to 32 Car. 2.	Inner Temple Library	Q. 2. b.
HOUSE OF COMMONS:			
Writs of Summons and Indentures of Return. Vid. sup. eundem Tit.:			
Entries of Returns	1688 to 1800	Clerk of Crown in Chan.	D. 2.
Indentures [Those of the Two last Parliaments, for the Time being, remain with the Clerk of the Crown.]	12 Car. 2. to 30 G. 3	Petty Bag Office	D. 5.
Writs	Eliz. Jac. 1. & Car. 1.	Bodleian Library. *Tanner.*	O. 1.
Writs of Summons to Council and Parliament	Date wanting	Dean and Chapter Westm.	N. 12. b.
RETURN BOOKS:			
From Office of Clerk of the Crown	1625 to 1800	Clerk of Journals	B. 2.
MEMBERS WAGES:			
Assessment upon a Hundred in Surrey, for Knights of the Shire	31 Hen. 6.	Dean and Chapter Westm.	N. 12. b.
TEST ROLLS	1698 to 1800	Clerk of Journals	B. 2.
QUALIFICATION ROLLS	1727 to 1800	Clerk of Journals	B. 2.
CERTIFICATES of QUALIFICATION	Anne to Geo. 3.	Petty Bag Office	D. 5.
PETITIONS, Public and Private	1607 to 1800	Clerk of Journals	B. 2.
IMPEACHMENT:			
Articles by the Commons against Simon de Burley	Ric. 2.	Dean and Chapter Westm.	N. 12. b.
ACCOUNTS and PAPERS presented	1607 to 1800	Clerk of Journals	B. 2.
Miscellaneous Papers of each Session	Date wanting	Clerk of Journals	B. 2.
Books and Papers of Commissioners of Public Accounts	1780 to 1787	Clerk of Journals	B. 2.
Various printed Books and Papers unarranged	1495 to 1737	Clerk of Journals	B. 2.
Books and Papers presented to Commissioners of Accounts	Will. 3.	Clerk of Journals	B. 2.
BILLS presented to the House	1607 to 1800	Clerk of Journals	B. 2.
REPORTS:			
Reports from Committees to the House	1607 to 1800	Clerk of Journals	B. 2.
—— from Commissioners for Survey of Courts of Justice	Geo. 2.	Clerk of Journals	B. 2.
Sir F. Bacon's Report on the Spanish Greivances	5 Jac. 1.	Bodleian Library	O. 1.
MINUTES:			
Minutes taken at the Table	1685 to 1800	Clerk of Journals	B. 2.
BOOKS of EVIDENCE:			
At the Bar of the House, and before Committees of the whole House, and Committees of Privileges	1736 to 1800	Clerk of Journals	B. 2.
Before Election Committees	10 Geo. 3. to 1800	Clerk Commit. of Elect.	Ibid.
JOURNALS and DEBATES:			
Original Journals of the House	1 Ed. 6. to 1800	Clerk of Journals	Ibid.
Rules and Orders out of Commons Journals	Ed. 6. to Jac. 1.	Bodleian Library. *Rawl.*	O. 1.
Journal	1572	Bodleian Library. *Rawl.*	O. 1.
The like	43 Eliz.	Bodleian Library. *Rawl.*	O. 1.
The like	1604 to 1707	Inner Temple Library	Q. 2. b.
The like	20 Jan. to 10 Mar. 4 Car. 1.	Bodleian Library. *Rawl.*	O. 1.
The like, under Richard Cromwell	1658 to 1659	Bodleian Library. *Rawl.*	O. 1.
The like	1661 to 1678	Middle Temple Library	Q. 1.
Proceedings in Convention	1688	Bodleian Library. *Rawl.*	O. 1.
Journal	1701	Bodleian Library. *Rawl.*	O. 1.
Minutes of Committees	1697, 8, & 1699	Bodleian Library. *Rawl.*	O. 1.

II. THE ROYAL COUNCILS—*(continued.)*

RECORDS and other INSTRUMENTS.	DATE.	WHERE KEPT.	Appendix to the Firſt Report.
JOURNALS AND DEBATES—*(continued.)*			
Speeches	1620 to 1628	Bodleian Library. *Tanner*	O. 1.
The like	1627 to 1628	Ibidem. *Rawlinſon*	O. 1.
Letters and Speeches by Sir J. Holland	Car. 2.	Ibidem. *Tanner*	O. 1.
Votes	1688 to 1690	Ibidem	O. 1.
SPEAKER:			
His Appointments of Members to iſſue Warrants of Election	Since 1784	Clerk of Crown in Chan.	D. 2.
2. PRIVY COUNCIL:			
PETITIONS:	Ed. 1, 2, & 3. & H. 5.	Tower	A. 2.
Petitions and Reports	1600 to 1683	Old State Paper Office	C. 1.
ORDINANCES	1 Hen. 6.	Tower	A. 2.
Orders of Privy Council	Eliz. to Car. 1.	Britiſh Muſeum	U.
COUNCIL BOOKS	31 H. 8. to 40 G. 3.	Council Office	C. 2.
Regiſter of Council Cauſes	1591 & ſeq.	Bodleian Library	O. 1.
Tranſactions of the Council of State	1650 to 1659	Bodleian Library	O. 1.
III. THE ROYAL PREROGATIVE.			
1. ECCLESIASTICAL AFFAIRS:			
PAPAL BULLS AND LETTERS:			
Bulls	1155 to 1534	Lambeth Library	T.
The like (*int. al.* that of Clem. VII. conferring upon Henry VIII. the Title of Defender of the Faith)	1194 to Hen 8.	Chapter Houſe and Britiſh Muſeum	A. 1. & U.
Of Innocent III. Gregory IX. &c.	Hen. 3.	Red Book, Exchequer	G. 6. a.
Bulls and Letters	John to Hen. 6.	Tower	A. 2.
The like	Of various Dates	Inner Temple Library	Q. 2. b.
Books of Inrolment of Bulls, Grants of Lands to Popes, Leagues, &c. *Theſe are the Books referred to by Rymer as Lib. A. & B.*	Dates wanting	Chapter Houſe	A. 1.
Bull of Paul V. to the Catholics of England	1606	Univerſity Lib. Camb.	P. 1.
Letter of Greg. XV. to Prince Charles (Car. I.)	1623	Univerſity Lib. Camb.	P. 1.
Proteſtatio Magnatum Angliæ ſuper Literas Bonifacii VIII. Papæ, tangentes jus Superioritatis Dom. Regis Angliæ in Regnum Scotiæ	28 Ed. 1.	Aſhmolean Muſeum	O. 2.
ROMAN ROLLS:	34 E. 1. to E. 4. 1483	Tower	A. 2.
Copies of	1 to 26 Ed. 3.	Lincoln's Inn Library	Q. 3.
TAXATIONS:			
Valor, or Liber Taxationis of Pope Nicholas	20 Ed. 1.	Tower, and King's Remembrancer Exch.	A. 2. & G. 6. a.
The like	20 Ed. 1.	Britiſh Muſeum	U.
The ſame, deſcribed as a Book of the Taxation of the Dioceſes of York and Durham, and of the Province of Canterbury	20 Ed. 1	1ſt Second. King's Rem.	G. 6. a.
Another Copy	— — —	Augmentation Office	G. 19.
Another	— — —	Dean and Chapter of Lichfield and Coventry	N. 9.
Another	— — —	Dean and Chapter Lincoln	N. 10.
Taxation of Tenths of the Clergy of Canterbury	20 Hen. 6.	1ſt Second. King's Rem.	G. 6. a.
Several Taxations of Benefices	Of various Dates	Britiſh Muſeum	U.
Taxations to the King and the Pope	Ed. 1	Dean and Chap. Weſtm.	N. 12. b.
Decimæ Collectæ in ſubſidium Terræ Sanctæ	Date wanting	Dean and Chap. Weſtm.	N. 12. b.
RELIGIOUS HOUSES:			
CHARTULARIES, LEDGERS, REGISTERS, &c.			
Many of every Deſcription	Of various Dates	Britiſh Muſ. (See the Liſts in their printed Catalogue.)	U.
Many Charters of Foundation	Of various Dates	Britiſh Muſ. (See the Liſts in their printed Catalogue.)	U.
Chartularies	Date wanting	Augmentation Office	G. 19.
Regiſtrum Chartarum Eccleſiæ Sarum	Date wanting	Inner Temple Library	Q. 2. b.
Book of Knights Templars	1185	1ſt Second. King's Rem.	G. 6. a.
Ledger Books, Rentals, and other Accounts of Monaſteries, Priories, &c.	Ed. 3. & ſeq.	1ſt Second. King's Rem.	G. 6. a.

III. THE ROYAL PREROGATIVE—(continued.)

RECORDS and other INSTRUMENTS.	DATE.	WHERE KEPT.	Appendix to the First Report.
CHARTULARIES, &c.—(continued.)			
Calendars of Abbey Leases - - - -	34, 35, & 37 Hen. 8.	2d Secondary King's Rem.	G. 6. a.
Entries of the like - - - - - -	Hen. 8. - - -	Ibidem - - - - -	G. 6. a.
Visitations of Monasteries - - - - -	Date wanting - -	Chapter House - - -	A. 1.
Charters, &c. of Abbies, &c. - - - -	Hen. 3. to Hen. 8.	Auditors Land Revenue -	G. 15.
- - - of Ely Monastery - - - -	Edgar to Ed. 3. -	Ely House - - - -	L. 9. a.
Accounts of Expenses of St. Paul's Cathedral	1382 to 1642 - -	Auditors Land Revenue -	G. 15.
Papers and Instruments relating to the Priory of St. John of Jerusalem - - - -	13th Century - -	Dean and Chapter Westm.	N. b. 12.
Original Deeds and Charters of the Possessions of the Knights Templars, and of St. John -	— —	Bodleian Library - -	O. 1.
Repertory of Foundations and Endowments in the Tower Records - - - - -	— —	British Museum - -	U.
Collection of Extracts from Registers of Religious Houses, by Hutton - - - -	— —	British Museum - -	U.
Ledgers, Registers, &c. - - - - -	Hen. 8. - - - -	Auditors Land Revenue -	G. 15.
REPORTS of VISITORS - - - - - - -	Hen. 8. - - - -	Chapter House - -	A. 1.
PAPERS and LETTERS relating to their STATE and DISSOLUTION:			
Letters to Lord Cromwell of their Enormities -	Hen. 8. - - - -	Chapter House - -	A. 1.
Various Documents - - - - - -	Hen. 8. - - - -	British Museum - - -	U.
Relating to the Knights Templars - -	Date wanting - -	Inner Temple Library -	Q. 2. b.
SURVEYS of ABBIES, &c.			
Abbies under £. 200. - - - - - -	28 Hen. 8. - - -	Chapter House - - -	A. 1.
Of several Abbies, Priories, Chauntries, &c. with Rentals and Accounts; a very extensive Collection - - - - - - - -	Hen. 7. to Car. 1. -	Auditors Land Revenue	G. 15.
Surveys and Extents of Alien Priories - -	Ed. 1. & seq. - -	King's Rememb. Excheq.	G. 6. a.
Liber Supervisus omnium Monast. Terrar. & Tenement. dom. Reg. Eliz. in Insulâ Vectis	25 Eliz. - - - -	University Library Camb.	P. 1.
INQUISITIONS:			
Of Abbies, &c. surrendered to Cardinal Wolsey	Hen. 8. - - - -	Rolls - - - - -	D. 1.
CONVENTUAL LEASES - - - - - - -	Ed. 4. to Hen. 8. -	Augmentation Office -	G. 19.
SURRENDERS:			
Abbies, &c. to the Crown and Cardinal Wolsey	Hen. 8. - - - -	Chapter House - -	A. 1.
Hospitals - - - - - - - -	Hen. 8. & Ed. 6. -	Augmentation Office -	G. 19.
Monasteries, &c. - - - - - - -	Hen. 8. - - - -	Augmentation Office -	G. 19.
LEASES of ABBEY LANDS - - - - - -	Hen. 8. & Ed. 6. -	2d Secondary King's Rem.	G. 6. a.
INVENTORIES:			
Of Church Goods, Chattels, Ornaments, Plate, &c. - - - - - - - - -	Hen. 8. to Mary -	Auditors Land Revenue	G. 15.
The like - - - - - - - - -	Ed. 6. - - - -	Augmentation Office -	G. 19.
PENSIONS granted to Abbots, &c. after the Dissolution	Hen. 8. - - - -	Augmentation Office -	G. 19.
TENURES:			
Of those held in Capite in Gloucestershire - -	18 Eliz. - - - -	Chapter House - - -	A. 1.
APPROPRIATIONS of CHURCHES, &c.			
Many among the Chartæ Antiquæ - - (See the Returns from the Universities and Bishops Courts.)	Will. 1. to Hen. 8. -	Augmentation Office -	G. 19.
INJUNCTIONS to the CLERGY:			
The original Articles signed by the King, Protector, and Council - - - - -	Ed. 6. - - - -	Corp. Christi Coll. Camb.	P. 5.
THE KING'S SUPREMACY:			
Instruments of Acknowledgment by the Bishops, &c. - - - - - - -	Hen. 8. - - - -	Chapter House - - -	A. 1.
Papers relating to - - - -	1532 to 1699 - -	Old State Paper Office -	C. 1.
Books for and against - - - -	1532 to 1699 - -	Chapter House - - -	A. 1.

III. THE ROYAL PREROGATIVE—(*continued.*)

RECORDS and other INSTRUMENTS.	DATE.	WHERE KEPT.	Appendix to the First Report.
1. ECCLESIASTICAL AFFAIRS—(*continued.*)			
SURVEYS, ACCOUNTS, and VALUATIONS of BENEFICES and CHURCH LANDS:			
Collection, intitled, Divers Diocefes - -	Date wanting - -	Chapter Houfe - -	A. 1.
Surveys, &c. - - - - - - -	1377 to 1679 - -	Old State Paper Office -	C. 1.
Of all Ecclefiaftical Benefices, Dignities, and Promotions Spiritual, purfuant to Stat. 26 Hen. VIII. - - - - - - -	26 & feq. Hen. 8. -	First Fruits Office - -	G. 18.
Surveys and Accounts of Bifhopricks, Sede Vacante - - - - - - -	Hen. 8. to Car. 1.	Augmentation Office -	G. 19.
Of Deaneries and Jurifdictions in Somerfet -	Ed. 6. - - - -	Auditors Land Revenue	G. 15.
Benefices of all Defcriptions in many Counties	Ph. & Mary - -	Auditors Land Revenue	G. 15.
Accounts of vacant Bifhopricks - - -	Hen. 8. to Car. 1. -	Auditors Land Revenue	G. 15.
Accounts of Farmers of Church Lands, in Devon, Somerfet, and Wilts - - -	3 & 4 Ph. and M.	Auditors Land Revenue	G. 15.
New Valuation of fome Bifhopricks and other Spiritual Promotions - - - - -	1 Mar. to 3 Geo. 1.	First Fruits Office - -	G. 18.
Notitia Parochialis, or Returns of the State and Condition of Churches - - -	In 1705 - - - -	Lambeth Library - -	T.
INSTITUTION and PATRONAGE:			
Bifhops Certificates of - - - -	1554 to 1800 - -	First Fruits Office -	G. 18.
FIRST FRUITS and TENTHS:			
Orders of Exchequer, relating to Benefices difcharged therefrom - - - - -	1 Mar. to 3 Geo. 1.	First Fruits Office -	G. 18.
Certificates of Benefices difcharged, purfuant to Stat. 6 Anne - - - - -	After 6 Anne - -	First Fruits Office -	G. 18.
Proceedings in the Exchequer, againft Receivers of Firft Fruits, and upon Sheriffs Accounts relating to them - - -	1 Mar. to 3 Geo. 1.	First Fruits Office -	G. 18.
ENDOWMENTS:			
Certificates and Anfwers from Parifh Minifters and Churchwardens, as to Foundations and Endowments: And from the Mafters, &c. of Crafts and Companies in London - -	Hen. 8. to Mar. -	Auditors Land Revenue -	G. 15.
Of Vicarages, many among the Chartæ Antiquæ	Will. 1. to Hen. 8.	Augmentation Office -	G. 19.
Charters of Endowments of Cathedrals -	Hen. 8. - - - -	Corp. Chrifti Coll. Camb.	P. 5.
Charters of Endowment - - - -	Of various Dates -	Britifh Mufeum - -	U.
References to Endowments of Vicarages, by Dr. Du Carel - - - - - -	— —	Lambeth Library - -	T.
DISPENSATIONS—from the Popes - - - -	1194 to Hen. 8. -	Britifh Mufeum - -	U.
ARTICLES of RELIGION, LITURGY, and SCRIPTURES:			
The Book of Common Prayer, with Great Seal appendant (according to Stat. 13, 14 Car. II. Cap. 4. Sec. 28.) - - - - -	Car. 2. - - - -	Tower - - -	A. 2.
Another - - - - - - - - -	— —	Dean & Chapter Hereford	N. 8.
Another - - - - - - - - -	— —	1ft Second King's Rem.	G. 6. a.
Another, the Great Seal torn from it - -	— —	Balliol College, Oxford -	O. 5.
Order for the Tranflation of the Bible - -	Date wanting - -	Univerfity Library Camb.	P. 1.
Two Originals of the 39 Articles, one Latin, one Englifh - - - - - - -	Eliz. - - - -	Corp. Chrifti Coll. Camb.	P. 5.
RECUSANTS:			
Accounts of, in London - - - -	1590 to 1708 - -	Old State Paper Office -	C. 1.
CONVOCATION:			
Writs of - - - - - - -	— —	Confiftory Courts - -	L.
COMMONWEALTH PROCEEDINGS:			
SURVEYS:			
Of Church Livings - - - - - -	Temp. Oliv. Crom.	Rolls - - - - -	D. 1.
Of Poffeffions of Bifhops, Deans and Chapters, &c. under Ordinances of Parliament -	1649 to 1660 - -	Lambeth Library - -	T.
INROLMENT of SALES:			
Of Dean and Chapter Lands, in the Clofe Rolls	— —	Rolls - - - - -	D. 1.
AUGMENTATIONS OF LIVINGS - - - -	1647 to 1658 - -	Lambeth Library - -	T.
PRESENTATIONS TO BENEFICES - - - -	1646 to 1660 - -	Lambeth Library - -	T.
COUNTERPARTS OF LEASES OF CHURCH LANDS -	1652 to 1658 - -	Lambeth Library - -	T.
PLUNDER'D MINISTERS, Books of Orders relating to	Date wanting - -	Auditors Land Revenue -	G. 15. d.

III. THE ROYAL PREROGATIVE—(continued.)

RECORDS and other INSTRUMENTS.	DATE.	WHERE KEPT.	Appendix to the First Report.
2. IN CIVIL AFFAIRS:			
GENERAL ADMINISTRATION OF THE REALM:			
See Entries of Writs and Records of various Descriptions upon the Close and Patent Rolls	John to Hen. 6. - Hen. 6. to 1800 -	Tower - - - Rolls - - - -	A. 2. D. 1.
SURVEYS, INQUISITIONS, AND BOOKS OF TENURES:			
Domesday, 2 Vols. - - - - - -	Will. 1. - -	Chapter House - -	A. 1.
Another Copy, 1 Vol. - - - -	— —	1st Second. King's Rem.	G. 6. a.
The like of Somerset, Dorset, Devon, and Cornwall - - - - - -	— —	Dean and Chapter Exeter	N. 6.
Imperfect Abstract of Domesday - - -	— —	Royal Society Library -	R.
Domesday for the City of Winchester - -	1148 - - - -	Antiq. Society Library -	S.
Dugdale's Extracts from Domesday and the Hundred Rolls - - - - - -	— —	Ashmolean Museum - -	O. 2.
Nomina Villarum, commonly called Testa de Neville - - - - - - -	Hen. 3. & Ed. 1. -	King's Rem. Exchequer	G. 6. a.
Another Copy - - - - - - -	— —	1st Second. King's Rem.	
The like - - - - - - - -	— —	Lord Treasurer's Rem. -	G. 7.
The like - - - - - - - -	— —	Chapter House - -	A. 1.
Hundred Rolls of Inquisitions - - -	2 Ed. 1. - -	Tower - - -	A. 2.
The like - - - - - - - -	3 & 4 Ed. 1. - -	Chapter House - -	A. 1.
The like - - - - - - - -	Ed. 2. - - - -	Tower - - -	A. 2.
Feoda in Capite - - - - - -	24 Ed. 1. - - -	Chapter House - -	A. 1.
Feoda Militum - - - - - -	Ed. 1. - - - -	Tower - - -	A. 2.
Feoda Militum in com. Norfolk and Suffolk -	31 Ed. 1. - -	University Library Camb.	P. 1.
Black Book of Knights Fees - - -	Date wanting - -	1st Second. King's Rem.	G. 6. a.
Nomina Villarum - - - - - -	1316 to 1559 -	British Museum - -	U.
Nomina Villarum com. Ebor. - - -	9 Ed. 2. - - -	Chapter House - -	A. 1.
Book of Knights Fees for Essex - - -	Hen. 3. to Car. 2. -	Lord Treasurer's Rem. -	G. 7.
Inquisitions of Fens in Nottinghamshire and Derby - - - - - - -	Ed. 3. - - - -	Chapter House - -	A. 1.
Tenuræ Terrarum com. Dorset and Bucks -	Date wanting - -	University Library Camb.	P. 1.
Brevia Regia - - - - - - -	1Ed.3. to 1422.H.5.	Tower - - -	A. 2.
Nomina Villarum.—Claims of Liberties allowed - - - - - - - -	1672 to 1800 - -	Foreign Apposer Exch. -	G. 11.
Inrolments of Grants of Bailiwicks - -	Jac 1. to Car. 1. -	Augmentation Office -	G. 19.
Extracts from Hundred Rolls in Oxfordshire -	7 Ed. 1. - - -	Lincoln's Inn Library -	Q. 3.
CHARTERS:			
Chartæ Antiquæ - - - - - -	Will. 1. to Hen. 3.	Tower - - -	A. 2.
The like - - - - - - - -	Will. 1. to Hen. 3.	1st Second. King's Rem. -	G. 6. a.
Copies of the above - - - - - -	— —	Lincoln's Inn Library	Q. 3.
Charters - - - - - - - -	Hen. 1. - - -	1st Second. King's Rem.	G. 6. a.
The like - - - - - - - -	Will. 1. to Hen. 8.	Augmentation Office -	G. 19.
The like - - - - - - - -	Heptarchy to Car. 1.	British Museum - -	U.
To the Priory and Church of Durham - -	Will. 1. to Jac. 1. -	Dean and Chap. Durham	N. 24.
Charter of Hen. 1. to Alexander I. of Scotland -	Hen. 1. - - -	Chapter House - -	A. 1.
Charters to Abbies - - - - - -	Steph. & Hen. 2. -	Bodleian Library - -	O. 1.
Book of Antient Charters - - - -	Date wanting - -		
Two Originals of Magna Charta - - -	John - - - -	British Museum - -	U.
Confirmation of it - - - - - -	25 Ed. 1. - - -		
Capitula Magnæ Chartæ - - - -	John - - - -		
Inspeximus of Magna Charta - - -	John - - - -	1st Second. King's Rem.	G. 6. a
Charta Johannis facta Papæ - - - -	John - - - -	Corp. Chris. Col. Camb.	P. 5.
Confirmatio Magnæ Chartæ - - - -	Hen. 3. - - - -		
Magna Charta - - - - - - -	In minor. Hen. 3. -	Bodleian Library - -	O. 1.
The like - - - - - - - -	In minor. Hen. 3. -	Dean and Chap. Durham	N. 24.
The like - - - - - - - -	In minor. Hen. 3. -	Ashmolean Library - -	O. 2.
Confirmation of the same - - - -	21 Hen. 3. - - -	Bodleian Library - -	O. 1.
Magna Charta (called an Original) - -	John - - - -	Dean and Chapter Lincoln	N. 10.
Chartæ & Leges - - - - - -	John, & Hen. 3. -	Corp. Chris. Coll. Camb.	P. 5.
Charters of London - - - - -	Ric. 1. John, & H. 3.		
Magna Charta Confirmata - - - -	9 Hen. 3. - - -		
Charters and Grants of Privileges and Lands -	Hen. 3. & Pr. Ed.	1st Second. King's Rem.	G. 6. a.
Charters of several Kings - - - -	Date wanting - -	Chapter House - -	A. 1.
The like - - - - - - - -	John to Eliz. - -	Corp. Christi Coll. Camb.	P. 5.
The like relating to Scotland - - -	To 1532. First Date wanting - - -	British Museum - -	U.
Charta de Forestis - - - - - -	Hen. 3. - - - -	Corpus Christi Coll. Camb.	P. 5.
The like - - - - - - - -	Hen. 3. - - - -	Dean and Chap. Durham	N. 24.
The like - - - - - - - -	Hen. 3. - - - -	Ashmolean Museum - -	O. 2.

III. THE ROYAL PREROGATIVE—*(continued.)*

RECORDS and other INSTRUMENTS.	DATE.	WHERE KEPT.	Appendix to the First Report.
CHARTERS—*(continued.)*			
Magna Charta	9 Ed. 1.	Corpus Christi Coll. Cam.	P. 5.
The like of Confirmation	28 Ed. 1.	Dean and Chap. Durham	N. 24.
Charters	Ed. 1.	1st Second. King's Rem.	G. 6. a.
Charta Libertatum Surriæ	Ed. 1.	Corpus Christi Coll. Cam.	P. 5.
Magna Charta of Confirmation	Ed. 1.	Dean and Chap. Norwich	N. 13.
The like of Charter of Hen. III.	Ed. 1.	Oriel College, Oxford	O. 8.
The like of Charta Forestæ	Ed. 1	Ibidem	
Confirmation Charter	Ed. 2.	Dean and Chap. Norwich	N. 13.
Exemplification of Charter of Ed. III. of Creation of Dukedom of Lancaster, and the County Palatine	Ed. 4.	Ashmolean Museum	O. 2.
Inspeximus of the same	Ric. 2.		
Confirmation of Privileges of Duchy of Lancaster	2 Hen. 5.	Bodleian Library	O. 1.
Transcripts and Extracts of Charters	Will. 1. & seq.	King's Rememb. Exch.	G. 6. a.
The like from the Patent and Close Rolls	6 Ed. 2. to 51 Ed. 3.	Ashmolean Museum	O. 2.
Charters relating to the See of Canterbury	chiefly of Hen. 8. Dates wanting before and after	Lambeth Library	T.
Charters to the Office of Arms	Ed. 6. Eliz. & Car. 2.	Ashmolean Museum	O. 2.
Patent to the Printers	Jac. 1.		
Charter to the University of Cambridge	Eliz.	Corpus Christi Coll. Cam.	P. 5.
CHARTER and CONFIRMATION ROLLS	1 John to Ed. 4.	Tower	A. 2.
Charter Rolls	1 Ric. 3. to 8 Hen. 8. After this, see Patent Rolls.	Rolls	D. 1.
Confirmation Rolls	1 Ric. 3. to 12 Jac. 1.		
Extracts from the Charter Rolls	John to Ed. 4.	Inner Temple Library	Q. 2. b.
SURRENDER and SPECIFICATION ROLLS	12 Car. 2. to 1800.	Rolls	D. 1.
FINE ROLLS, or LORD TREASURER'S:			
Fines for Alienation, &c.	6 John to Ed. 4.	Tower	A. 2.
Containing Grants of Offices in the Gift of the Lord Treasurer; also General Liveries, during the Court of Wards and Liveries	Ed. 5 to 17 Car. 1.	Rolls	D. 1.
BREVIA REGIA	9 Car. 1. to 1800.	Petty Bag Office	D. 5.
CLOSE ROLLS	6 John to E. 4. 1483.	Tower	A. 2.
Extracts from	Hen. 3.	Chapter House	A. 1.
The like	John to Ed. 4.	Inner Temple Library	Q. 2. b.
The like	Ed. 5. to 24 Geo. 3.	Rolls	D. 1.
The like	25 Geo. 3. to 1800.	Clerk Inrolments in Chan.	D. 13.
The like	Date wanting	British Museum	U.
Copies of	John to Ed. 3.	Lincoln's Inn Library	Q. 3.
Abstracts	13 H. 3. to 21 R. 2.		
(N. B. For the Contents of the Close Rolls, See their Description in the Return from the Keeper of the Records in the Tower, Appendix, A. 2. a.)			
PATENT ROLLS	3 John to E. 4. 1483.	Tower	A. 2.
	John, H. 3. E. 2. H. 6.	Chapter House	A. 1.
	Ed. 5. to 27 Geo. 3.	Rolls	D. 1.
Copies of	Hen. 3.	Lincoln's Inn Library	Q. 3.
Extracts of	Hen. 3. to Ric. 2.		
The like	John to Ed. 4.	Inner Temple Library	Q. 2. b.
Extracts by Madox	Date wanting	British Museum	U.
(N. B. For the Contents of the Patent Rolls, See their Description in the Return from the Keeper of the Records in the Tower, Appendix, A. 2. a.)			
LIBERATE ROLLS	2 John to 22 Ed. 4.	Tower	A. 2.
PRIVY SEALS:			
For Loans	Hen. 7 and 8.	Chapter House	A. 1.
Warrants	Ed. 1. to Ed. 4.	Tower	A. 2.
The like	1634 to 1712	British Museum	U.
Docket Books of all Grants and Appointments	1571 to 1799	Privy Seal Office	C. 1.
Privy Seals	1 to 18 Hen. 8.	Bodleian Library	O. 3.

III. THE ROYAL PREROGATIVE—(continued.)

RECORDS and other INSTRUMENTS.	DATE.	WHERE KEPT.	Appendix to the First Report.
PRIVY SEALS—(continued.)			
Privy Seals and Signed Bills	Hen. 7. to 27 Geo. 3.	Rolls	D. 1.
Warrants, Orders, &c.	Eliz. to Car. 1.	British Museum	U.
Privy Seal Bills and Warrants, inrolled	1725 to 1800	Petty Bag Office	D. 5.
Account of Monies paid thereon for a Loan	1604	University Library Camb.	P. 1.
Books and Papers of the Privy Seal Office	Of various Dates	British Museum	U.
Lord Treasurer Burleigh's Register of Grants passing the Privy Seal, Signet, or Sign Manual	Ed. 5. & Ric. 3.	British Museum	U.
Letters and Dockets of Duke of Newcastle	1709 to 1711	British Museum	U.
Dockets of what passed the Great Seal by Privy Seal, or by immediate Warrant	1710 to 1718	Middle Temple Libr.	Q. 1.
The like of what passed without Privy Seal	1710 to 1714	Middle Temple Libr.	Q. 1.
SIGNET BILLS	Ric. 2. to Car. 1.	Tower	A. 2.
Original Grants and Appointments	1661 to 1800	Signet Office	C. 4.
Dockets of the same	1584 to 1800	Signet Office	C. 4.
SIGNS MANUAL	Hen. 7. to Eliz.	Chapter House	A. 1.
WARRANT BOOKS:			
Containing Warrants, Pensions, Preferments, Passes, Licences, Pardons, &c.	1661 to 1711	New State Paper Office	C. 1.
Privy Seal Warrants	1634 to 1712	British Museum	U.
MEMORIALS:			
Petitions and Reports	1704 to 1761	New State Paper Office	C. 1.
COMMISSIONS, INSTRUCTIONS, PETITIONS, and REPORTS	1377 to 1676	Old State Paper Office	C. 1.
Collection of Commissions, &c.	Ed. 3. to Jac. 2.	British Museum	U.
Petitions to the King, and Reports	1600 to 1683	Old State Paper Office	C. 1.
Instructions to the Commissioners for Knighthood	6 Car. 1.	University Library Camb.	P. 1.
Commissions pursuant to Statutes for fortifying the Dock Yards, Coasts and Havens, and Powder Magazines, &c. and the Proceedings thereon	1714 to 1784	Clerk of Crown in Chan.	D. 2.
PROCLAMATIONS (See Patent Rolls.)	1532 to 1699	Old State Paper Office	C. 1.
For General Fast	1743	Clerk of the Crown	D. 2.
For executing the Laws against Papists	1743	Clerk of the Crown	D. 2.
Collection of	Of various Dates	Antiq. Society Library	S.
The like	Ed. 3. to Jac. 1.	British Museum	U.
Of Peace between Hen. VIII. and Spain	Hen. 8.	Ashmolean Museum	O. 2.
In Earl of Essex's Rebellion	1600	Ashmolean Museum	O. 2.
Concerning the Scots (Two Copies)	1639	Ashmolean Museum	O. 2.
DISPENSATIONS	1532 to 1699	Old State Paper Office	C. 1.
Dispensation Roll	37 Eliz. to 20 Geo. 2.	Rolls	D. 1.
LICENCES in MORTMAIN:			
To Cardinal Wolsey for his College	Hen. 8.	Chapter House	A. 1.
To the Colleges of the Universities	Of Various Dates	University Libraries	O. & P.
Rolls of Lands in Mortmain in London	7 to 30 Ed. 1.	Chapter House	A. 1.
PARDONS. (See Patent Rolls.)			
Roll of General and Particular	26 Ed. 1. to 22 Ed. 4.	Tower	A. 2.
- - - -	1532 to 1699	Old State Paper Office	C. 1.
Roll of	Ric. 3. to Jac. 1.	Rolls	D. 1.
PAPERS relating to COURTS of JUSTICE, and LAW MATTERS:			
Papers relating to Law Matters	Jac. 1. to Anne	Auditors Land Revenue	G. 15.
Cases, Reports, Speeches, Orders	1540 to 1648	Old State Paper Office	C. 1.
Law Papers, and Reports of Law Officers	1663 to 1768	New State Paper Office	C. 1.
Papers relating to Judicial Proceedings	1639 to 1640	Privy Seal Office	C. 3.
Papers on the Penal Law and Test	1687	Bodleian Library	O. 1.
Collectanea of Law Records by Sir S. Dewes	Jac. 1.	British Museum	U.
Antient Copies of the early Law Tracts; viz. Glanville, Bracton, Fleta, Horne, Liber Niger Admiralitatis, and the Year Books	Various Dates	Lincoln's Inn Library	Q. 3.
Reports and Year Books	Ed. 3. & Hen. 4.	Bodleian Library	O. 1.
The like	Ed. 2.	Middle Temple Library	Q. 1.

III. THE ROYAL PREROGATIVE—*(continued.)*

RECORDS and other INSTRUMENTS.	DATE.	WHERE KEPT.	Appendix to the First Report.
Papers relating to Courts, &c.—*(continued.)*			
Year Books	Ed. 3. & Hen. 6.	Inner Temple Library	Q. 2. b.
MS. Reports	Mar. to Car. 1. and 1750 to 1765		
Corporation Papers:	1540 to 1648	Old State Paper Office	C. 1.
- - - - - - - - -	Date wanting	New State Paper Office	
Relating to London	1687 to 1767		
Many Charters of Towns and Guilds	Various Dates	British Museum	U.
Papers relating to the City of Westminster	Eliz. & seq.	Dean and Chapt. Westm.	N. 12. b.
Charters, Privileges, &c. of London	Car. 2.	Inner Temple Library	Q. 2. b.
De Cartis Concessis Civibus & Burgis	Date wanting		
State Correspondence Domestic:			
To and from Secretaries of State, &c.	1665 to 1766		
Relating to Plots, Rebellion, Treason, &c.	1685 to 1767	New State Paper Office	C. 1.
- - - Criminal Affairs generally	1687 to 1765		
- - - Ecclesiastical Affairs	1684 to 1769		
Thurloe's State Papers not printed, as well as the printed Collection, 67 Volumes	1638 to 1660		
Letters on State Affairs	1683 to 1688, 1721 to 1729		
Letters to Secretary of State, and Board of Trade	1721 to 1729	Bodleian Library	
Letters of Charles II.	Car. 2.		
Miscellaneous Collections of State Papers	Hen. 8. to Will. 3.		
Letters and Papers of State	Eliz. Jac. 1. & Car. 1.	Ibidem. *Tanner*	
Lord Fitzwilliam's Papers	Eliz.		O. 1.
Thurloe's Letters	Oliver Cromwell	Ibidem. *Carte*	
Philip Lord Wharton's Papers	Date wanting		
Lord Huntingdon's Papers	Date wanting		
Letters, Memorials, Orders of Council, &c.	Date wanting	Ibidem. *Tanner*	
Articles propounded by the Earl of Essex, with Considerations by Lord Burleigh, &c.	1596		
Letters and Papers relating to Departments of Ordnance, Admiralty, Customs, and Excise	Of various Dates	British Museum	U.
HONOURS and OFFICES. (For Creations, See Patent Rolls.)			
De Creatione Nobilium in Parliamento, et extra	Date wanting	Inner Temple Library	Q. 2. b.
Instructions touching Knighthood	1630	University Library Camb.	P. 1.
Collection of all Offices, with their Fees	Eliz.	Bodleian Lib. *Tanner*	O. 1.
Discourses on Offices, by Sir Robert Cotton, &c.	Date wanting		
A Book of Fees and Offices	1 Mar. 1553	Antiq. Society Library	S.
Tables of Fees	Date wanting	Bodleian Library	O. 1.
Grants and Admissions:			
Inrolment of Admissions of Officers of Chancery, Serjeants at Law, &c.	40 Eliz. to 1800	Petty Bag Office	D. 5.
Estreats from Chancery, of all Grants whereon Rent or Service is due	Hen. 3. to 1800	Lord Treas. Rem. Exch.	G. 6. b.
Oaths of Office:			
Entries of those administered by the Clerk of the Crown	1639 to 1800	Clerk of the Crown	D. 2.
List of the several Officers, and their Oaths	— —		
Rolls of Nine different Oaths	— —	Petty Bag Office	D. 5.
Oaths of Exchequer Officers, in the Black Book	— —	Chapter House	A. 1.
The like in the Red Book	— —	1st Second. King's Remb.	G. 6. a.
Surrenders of Offices:			
In the Law	5 Geo. 2. & Geo. 3.	Clerk of the Crown	D. 2.
Inrolments of	8 Anne, to 1800	Petty Bag Office	D. 5.
Knighthood:			
Statutes of the Garter, and French Order of St. Michael	Hen. 8.	Chapter House	A. 1.
Statutes of the Garter	Hen. 8.	Ashmolean Museum	O. 2.
Certificates of Persons who compounded for not taking the Honour of Knighthood	6 & 7 Car. 2.	Auditors Land Revenue	G. 15. c.
Visitations:			
Books of	21 Hen. 8. to 2 Jac. 2.	Herald's Office	C. 8.
The like	21 Hen. 8. to 2 Jac. 2.		
The like	21 Hen. 8. to 2 Jac. 2.	British Museum	U.
The like	Of various Dates	Caius College, Camb.	P. 7.

III. THE ROYAL PREROGATIVE—(continued.)

RECORDS and other INSTRUMENTS.	DATE.	WHERE KEPT.	Appendix to the First Report.
HONOURS AND OFFICES—(continued.)			
ARMORIAL BEARINGS, LICENCES, PEDIGREES, MARRIAGES, FUNERALS:			
Papers of Genealogies and Heraldry, English and Foreign - - - -	1246 to 1604 - -	Old State Paper Office	
- - of Precedency, Pedigrees, &c. - -	1399 to 1625 -		C. 1.
The like - - - - - - -	1604 to 1761 - -	New State Paper Office -	
Books of Pedigrees and Arms during the Time of Visitations, and since - - -	— —		
The like of the Peers of the Realm - -	1767 to 1800 - -		
The like of Baronets - - - -	3 Dec. 1783 to 1800.		
Funeral Certificates during the Time of Visitations - - - - - -	21 Hen. 8. to 2 Jac. 2.	Herald's Office - -	C. 8.
Books of Arms of Knights of the Garter and Bath, from their Institutions to - -	1800 - - - -		
Books of Arms and Pedigrees - - -	Of various dates -	British Museum - - -	U.
Papers of Heraldry - - - - -	Of various Dates -	Inner Temple Library -	Q. 2. b.
TRADE AND COIN.			
BOARD of TRADE, and FOREIGN TRADE:			
Papers relating to Merchants Ships, and Foreign Trade - - - - -	1572 to 1608 - -	Old State Paper Office	
- - - to Domestic and Foreign Trade	1562 to 1690 - -		
Letters and Memorials to Board of Trade -	1668 to 1767 - -	New State Paper Office -	C. 1.
Papers upon Foreign Trade, with the Hanse Towns, Holland, America, East Indies, &c.	1474 to 1708 - -	Old State Paper Office	
Letters to Board of Trade - - -	1721 to 1729 - -	Bodleian Library - -	O. 1.
Decree relating to Hanse Towns - -	Ed. 6. - - - -		
TRADING COMPANIES:			
Indenture between Queen Anne and the Two East India Companies, for their Union -	July 1702 - - -	1st Second. King's Rem.	G. 6. a.
Letters and Papers relating to the East India Company - - - - - - -	1585 to 1763 - -	New State Paper Office	C. 1.
The like to the South Sea Company - -	1713 to 1763 - -		
Letters relating to the African Company -	1680 to 1686 - -		
Papers relating to the India Company - -	Car. 2. and Anne -	Bodleian Library - -	O. 1.
Copy of Charter to the Turkey Company -	— —		
QUARANTINE:			
Orders and Regulations in case of Plague -	1625 to 1631 - -		
FISHERIES:			
Papers relating to those of Greenland, Newfoundland, &c. - - - - - -	1583 to 1677 - -	Old State Paper Office	C. 1.
Miscellaneous Collection relating to - -	Date wanting - -	Inner Temple Library -	Q. 2. b.
PLANTATIONS:			
Orders of Council, Commissions, and Regulations - - - - - - - -	1663 to 1707 - -	Old State Paper Office -	C. 1.
State Correspondence with America and West Indies - - - - - -	1679 to 1770 -	New State Paper Office -	
Letters and other original Papers, Accounts, and Minutes of Council, from Bermudas, Georgia, Jamaica, and West Indies; New York, New Hampshire, and Surat - -	Car. 2. to Geo. 1. -		
Law Proceedings concerning Barbadoes -	1647 - - - -	Bodleian Library -	O. 1.
Proceedings at Sessions in Bermudas - -	1689 - - - -		
VOYAGES and DISCOVERIES:			
Instructions relating to - - - - -	1576 to 1676 - -	Old State Paper Office -	C. 1.
Sea Charts of India, by Baffin and Somerson -	Date wanting - -	Bodleian Library - -	O. 1.
NEW INVENTIONS. (See Surrender and Specification Rolls.)			
Petitions - - - - - - - -	1685 to 1767 - -	New State Paper Office	C. 1.
Inrolment of Specifications - - - -	8 Anne to 1800 -	Petty Bag Office - -	D. 5.
The like - - - - - - -	25 Geo. 3. to 1800	Inrolment Office - -	D. 13.
COIN:			
Standard Pieces - - - - - -	Ed. 4. & seq. -	Chamberlain's Exchequer	G. 2.
Proclamations relating to - - - - -	1528 to 1600 - -		
Extract of Council Books relating to - -	1660 to 1730. -	Antiq. Society Lib. -	S.
The like - - - - - -	Hen. 8. - - -		
Collection of Papers intitled *De Monetâ* - -	Date wanting - -	Inner Temple Library -	Q. 2. b.

III. THE ROYAL PREROGATIVE—(continued.)

RECORDS and other INSTRUMENTS.	DATE.	WHERE KEPT.	Appendix to the First Report.
TRADE AND COIN—(continued.)			
MINT:			
Indentures	Ed. 3. to Car. 1.	Chapter House	A. 1.
Accounts	Ed. 6. to Will. 3.	Auditors Land Revenue	G. 15.
The like	Anne	1st Second. King's Rem.	G. 6. a.
The like	Ed. 1. to Car. 2.	King's Rem. Exchequer	G. 6. a.
The like	6 Ric. 2. to 2 Hen. 4. and 3 Hen. 6.	Tower	A. 2.
Papers relating to	1560 to 1690	Old State Paper Office	C. 1.
Laws and Ordinances	Date wanting	British Museum	U.
Extracts from Records relating to	Date wanting	Lincoln's Inn Library	Q. 3.
ASSAY ROLLS	Ed. 1.	Chapter House	A. 1.
WEIGHTS and MEASURES:			
Standards	1582, &c.	Chamberlain's Excheq.	G. 2.
Counterparts of Indentures of	1700 to 1800	Chamberlain's Excheq.	G. 2.
A Collection of Weights and Measures deposited by Order of the House of Commons	20 May 1760	Clerk of Journals	B. 2.
Papers relating to Weights	Eliz.	Auditors Land Revenue	G. 15.
3. IN MILITARY AFFAIRS.			
NAVY:			
Commissions, Warrants, Estimates, and Surveys	1509 to 1716	Old State Paper Office	C. 1.
Admiralty Correspondence, Warrants, Commissions, &c.	1689 to 1761	New State Paper Office	C. 1.
Collection of Letters, Instructions, Orders, Reports, Accounts, Lists, Proceedings of Courts Martial, and various other Documents, relating to Naval Affairs and the Ordinance	1589 to 1711	Bodleian Library. *Rawl.*	O. 1.
Inventory of the King's Ships (Hen. VIII's) in charge of Officers of the Admiralty, with the Names, Tonnage, and Number of Men, and their Stations	1 Ed. 6.	Antiq. Society Library	S.
Accounts relating to	Ed 1. to Car. 2.	King's Rem. Exchequer	G. 6. a.
Miscellaneous Collection of Papers relating to	Date wanting	Inner Temple Library	Q. 2. b.
Books of Works, and Household Accounts of Greenwich Hospital	1716 to 1724	Auditors Land Revenue	G. 15. d.
ARMY:			
MUSTERS: Return of Men capable of bearing Arms in Hants	12 Hen. 8.	Chapter House	A. 1.
Of Men at Arms, &c. in divers Shires	Hen. 8.	Chapter House	A. 1.
Commissions, Instructions, Musters, Letters, and Articles of War	1586 to 1705	Old State Paper Office	C. 1.
Correspondence with Secretary at War, and others	1683 to 1762	New State Paper Office	C. 1.
Accounts of Disbursements	Ed. 6.	Auditors Land Revenue	G. 15.
Orders for raising a Regiment, by the Marquis of Hamilton, and the Officers Pay	Car. 1.	University Libr. Camb.	P. 1.
Instructions for General Musters in Norfolk	Eliz.	University Libr. Camb.	P. 1.
Forts in Essex, Captains and Soldiers there	1 Ed. 6.	Auditors Land Revenue	G. 15.
ACCOUNTS	Ed. 1. to Car. 2.	King's Remembr. Exch.	G. 6. a.
Relating to War with Scotland	Hen. 8.	Auditors Land Rev.	G. 15.
Treasurer at War's Acquittances	1651	Auditors Land Rev.	G. 15.
INDENTURES of WAR:			
Indenture between Henry IV. and the Prince of Wales, whereby the Prince engages to serve his Father with 600 Men at Arms, and 1,800 Archers	Hen. 4.	Dean and Chap. West.	N. 12. b.
EXPENSES:			
Roll of Henry VII.'s Expenses in the War to assist the Duchess of Brittany	Hen. 7.	Dean and Chap. West.	N. 12. b.
Works at Carlisle Castle	1584, 1604, & 1605	Auditors Land Revenue	G. 15. d.
ORDINANCE:			
Correspondence	1683 to 1762	New State Paper Office	C. 1.
Accounts of Deliveries	1568 to 1582	Auditors Land Revenue	G. 15.
Collection of various Papers relating to	1570 to 1693	Bodleian Library. *Rawl.*	O. 1.
Inventory of Ordinance and Munition in the King's Castles, on the Death of Henry VIII.	1 Ed. 6.	Antiq. Society Library	S.
Of Armories, in charge of Sir T. Darcy, Master of the same	1 Ed. 6.	Antiq. Society Library	S.

III. THE ROYAL PREROGATIVE—(*continued.*)

RECORDS and other INSTRUMENTS.	DATE.	WHERE KEPT.	Appendix to the First Report.
4. IN FOREIGN AFFAIRS.			
COMMISSIONS, CREDENTIALS, and INSTRUCTIONS to AMBASSADORS - - - - -	Edw. 3. to Geo. 1.	British Museum - - -	U.
Commissions to Ambassadors - - -	1509 to 1706 -	Old State Paper Office	C. 1.
- - - - to Ambassadors with Eastern Princes	1576 to 1669 - -		
Instructions to Ambassadors at French Court	Eliz. - - - -	University Lib. Camb	P. 1.
The like with the Emperor - - - -	Hen. 8 - - - -		
Papers relating to Privileges of Ambassadors	1672 to 1768 -	New State Paper Office	C. 1.
Original Letters and Instructions relating to Denmark and Sweden - - -	Jac. 1. Car. 1. & 2.	Bodleian Lib. *Rawl.*	O. 1.
Instructions, Commissions, and Credentials	1663 to 1686 - -		
- - - - to Ambassadors	Date wanting -	Inner Temple Library -	Q. 2. b.
Memorial for the Colloquy at Bruges -	1564 - - - -	University Lib. Camb.	P. 1.
Instructions to several Ambassadors to the different Courts of Europe - - - -	Eliz. - - - -		
CORRESPONDENCE with AMBASSADORS:			
Letters to Hen. VIII. and his Ministers -	Hen. 8. - - - -	Chapter House -	A. 1.
Letters to the Queen and Council, and Lord Burleigh, &c. - - - - - -	Eliz. - - - -	University Library, Camb.	P. 1.
Correspondence with Ambassadors in all Countries	1530 to 1678 -	Old State Paper Office -	C. 1.
The like - - - - - - -	1663 to 1780 -	New State Paper Office	
The like, with France chiefly - -	1560 to 1567 -	Bodleian Library. *Perrot*	O. 1.
Letters of Sir Amyas Pawlet, in France -	1577 - - -	Ibidem. *Rawlinson* - -	
Sir R. Southwell's Account of the Court of Portugal - - - - - - - - -	1667 - - - -	Ibidem - - -	
Expenses of Messengers, Ambassadors, &c.	Edw. 1. to Car. 2.	King's Rem. Exchequer	G. 6. a.
MEMORIALS and NEGOTIATIONS with FOREIGN STATES:			
Large Collection - - - - -	Edw. 3. to Jac. 1. -	British Museum -	U.
The like - - - - - - - -	1340 to 1708 - -	Old State Paper Office	C. 1.
Sir Francis Walsingham's Negotiations in France	1570 - - - -	Bodleian Lib. *Rawl.*	O. 1.
Negotiations in East Friesland - - -	1584 - - - -		
Journal of Conference between his Majesty's Commissioners and the King of Spain's, &c. -	1604 - - - -		
Lettres & Negociations de M. de Noailles	1553 - - - -	Ibidem. *Carte* -	
Negotiations of Sir T. Clifford, in Denmark	1664-5 - - - -	Ibidem. *Rawlinson*	
Papers relating to the Dutch War - - -	1666 - - - -	Ibidem. *Tanner* -	
Negotiations de M. la Boderie, en Angleterre	1606, &c. - - -	Ibidem. *Carte* -	
- - - - de M. Sebron, en Angleterre	1644 - - - -	Ibidem - - -	
Relatio Legationis Com. Leycestriæ ad Christ. 4. Dan. Reg. - - - - -	1632 - - - -	Ibidem. *Rawlinson* -	
Originals and Copies of Memorials between Spain and England - - - - -	1636 - - - -		
Thurloe's State Papers, the whole Collection, published and unpublished - - -	1638 to 1660 - -		
Books of Negotiations - - - -	1677-8. 1686-7-8		
Letters from the Protector to Foreign States	Oliver Cromwell -		
Letters and Original Papers of Bishop of Bristol, Earl of Strafford, Mr. Prior, &c. relating to the Treaty of Utrecht - - -	1711-12-13 - -		
Correspondence with Foreign Ministers - - -	1710 to 1756 -	New State Paper Office	C 1.
TREATIES and TRANSACTIONS:			
With Scotland and other European States	1161 to 1624 - -	Chapter House - -	A. 1.
Fœdus pactum inter Hen. II. & Lud. VII.	Hen. 2. - - -	Corp. Christi Coll. Camb.	P. 5.
Meslanges d'Actes, &c. entre les Rois de France et d'Angleterre - - - -	1190 to 1625 - -	Bodleian Library -	O. 1.
Traitez et Memoires de France et d'Angleterre	1193 to 1331 - -		
Collection of Treaties - - - -	Ed. 3 to Jac. 1.	British Museum -	U.
Copies of Treaties, Declarations, &c. with France - - - - -	Ed. 3. - - - -	Ashmolean Museum -	O. 2.
Treaties and Transactions of all Sorts -	1432 to 1712 - -	Old State Paper Office	C. 1.
Treaties - - - - - - -	Henry 7. & 8. & Jac. 1. - - -	Bodleian Library, *Rawl.*	O. 1.
The like - - - - - - -	Eliz. & Jac. 1. -	University Library Camb.	P. 1.
Treaty or Foreign Rolls - - - -	Ed. 5. to 19 Car. 2.	Rolls Chapel - -	D. 1.
Articuli Pacis inter SS. RR. Hispaniæ & Mag. Britanniæ & Arcid. Austriæ - -	1604 - - - -	Bodleian Library. *Rawl.*	O. 1.

III. THE ROYAL PREROGATIVE—(continued.)

Records and other Instruments.	Date.	Where Kept.	Appendix to the First Report.
Treaties, &c.—(continued.)			
The like in English - - - - - - -	— —	Bodleian Library. *Rawl.*	O. 1.
Treaties and Transactions with Eastern Princes -	1606 to 1762 - -	New State Paper Office	C. 1.
The like with European States - - - -	1712 to 1760 - -		
Articles of Peace with the Scots - - -	Car 1. 1639 - -	Ashmolean Museum -	O. 2.
Copies, Extracts, and Abstracts - - - -	1700 to 1763 - -	New State Paper Office -	C. 1.

IV. THE ROYAL REVENUES.

1. Ordinary:			
The Great Roll of the Exchequer - -	Stephen to 1800 -	Pipe Office, Exchequer -	G. 8.
Pipe Roll - - - - - - -	John - - -	Chapter House - - -	A. 1
Duplicates of those in the Exchequer - -	6 Ric. 1. to 7 John -	Tower - - - - -	A. 2.
Pipe Rolls - - - - - - -	Ed. 4. - - - -	Lincoln's Inn Library -	Q. 3.
The Controlment Roll - - - -	Ric. 1. to 1800 -	Controller of Pipe Exch.	G. 9.
Land Revenue:			
Surveys - - - - - - - - - - -	Of various Dates -	Augmentation Office -	G. 19.
Of Manors, &c. - - - - - -	1493 to 1715 - -	Auditors Land Revenue	G. 15. d.
Lands and Manors - - - - -	Edw. 6. to Jac. 1. -	Chapter House - -	A. 1.
Forfeited Estates - - - - - -	Hen. 8. - - - -		
—of Duke of Norfolk and Earl of Arundel -	Eliz. - - - - -	2d Second. King's Rem.	G. 6. a.
Concealed Lands - - - - - -	3 to 17 Eliz. - -		
Manors in Lincolnshire - - - - -	Eliz. - - - -	1st Second. King's Rem.	
Eltham, Kent - - - - - - -	Jac. 1. 1605 - -		
Greenwich, Kent - - - - - -	7 Will. 3. - - -	Petty Bag Office - - -	D. 5.
Surveys taken prior to the Death of Charles I. -	Before 1649 - -	Survey. Gen. Cr. Lands	G. 14.
The like, Parliamentary during the Commonwealth - - - - - -	1649 to 1660 - -		
The like - - - - - - -	— —	Augmentation Office -	G. 19.
Maps and Plans - - - - - - -	1608 to 1800 - -	Surveyor General, &c. -	G. 14.
Surveys in Wales - - - - - -	2 to 39 Eliz. - -	Auditor for Wales - -	G. 16.
Collection of Names of the King's Castles, Mansions, Parks, Forests, Chases, within the Survey of the Court of Exchequer, and Duchy of Lancaster - - - - -	Date wanting - -	University Lib. Cmab.	P. 1.
View and Survey of all Woods and Underwoods in Forests, Parks, &c. - - -	1575 - - - -		
Lands in Wales out of Lease - - -	Date wanting - -		
Estates in Wales, Worcestershire, Leicestershire, Lancashire, and Northamptonshire, not granted in Fee Farm - - - - - - -	1629 - - - -		
Of South Stoke, &c. in com. Somerset - -	Eliz. - - - -		
Extents of Manors - - - - - -	Ed. 1, 2, & 3. - -	King's Rem. Exch. among the Inq. Post Mortem -	G. 6. a.
Surveys under Special Commissions - -	Eliz. to Car. 2. - -	King's Remem. Exch.	
Extents of Possessions of Knights Templars -	Ed. 2. - - - -		
—of Manors, Farms, Woods, Rectories, &c. -	Ed. 3. to Anne - -	Auditors Land Reven.	G. 15.
Rentals - - - - - - - - - -	Ed. 3. to Anne - -		
Of Tenants paying Castleward to Dover Castle -	1 Ed. 4. - - - -	Library Antiq. Society -	S.
Of Fee Farm and other Rents in Wales -	1 Anne to 1800 -	Auditor for Wales -	G. 16.
Of Chief Rents of Denbigh - - - -	Date wanting - -		
Of Crown Lands in Somerset - - - -	1606 - - - -	University Lib. Camb.	P. 1.
Of Abbey Lands and Forfeited Estates in Essex, Herts, Middlesex, and London - -	1638 - - - -		
Several - - - - - - - - -	Various Dates - -	Augmentation Office -	G. 19.
Court Rolls: - - - - - - - -	Ed. 1. to Hen. 8. -	Augmentation Office -	G. 19
- - - - - - - - - -	Ed. 1. to Hen. 8. -	Chapter House - - -	A. 1.
- - - - - - - - - -	Ed. 2. to Car. 2. -	Auditors Land Revenue -	G. 15.
The like with Rentals - - - - -	John to Jac. 1. - -	Tower - - - - -	A. 2.
Antient and Modern - - - - -	Hen. 8. to 1800 -	Auditors Land Revenue	G. 15.
Of the Manor of Clerkenwell - - - -	Mar. & Eliz. - -	University Library Camb.	P. 1.
Inrolments:			
Of Indentures, Copies of Grants, Particulars, &c.	Hen. 8. to Car. 2. -	Auditors Land Reven.	G. 15.
Books of, containing Letters Patent under the Great Seal and Exchequer Seal, and a Variety of Miscellaneous Entries - - - -	Hen. 8. to 1800 -		
Books of Inrolment and Entry for Wales -	Hen. 7. to 1800 -	Auditor for Wales - -	G. 16.
Indentures of Bargain and Sale - - -	34 & 35 Hen. 8. -	2d Second. King's Rem.	G. 6. a.

IV. THE ROYAL REVENUES—(continued.)

RECORDS and other INSTRUMENTS.	DATE.	WHERE KEPT.	Appendix to the First Report.
LAND REVENUE—(continued.)			
COLLECTIONS and COMPILATIONS relative to the LAND REVENUE:			
Of various Particulars of Grants, Settlements, Schedules, Registers, and Surveys, at different Periods from - - - - - -	Ed. 1. to 1702. -	Surv. Gen. Crown Lands	G. 14.
General Report for Five Years, ending - -	43 Eliz. - - - -	University Library Camb.	P. 1.
COMMON ENTRY BOOKS - - - - - -	1698 to 1800 - -	Auditors Land Rev. - -	G. 15.
LEASES - - - - - - - - - -	Eliz. & Jac. 1. - -	Augmentation Office -	G. 19.
- - - - - - - - - -	Jac. 1 to 1800. -	Pipe Office - - - -	G. 8.
Particulars for - - - - -	Eliz. & Jac. 1. - -	Augmentation Office -	G. 19.
Leases under the Great Seal - - -	Eliz. - - - -	University Lib. Camb.	P. 1.
Liber Dimissionum - - - - - -	29 Eliz. to 5 Jac. 1.	University Lib. Camb.	P. 1.
Proceedings relating to Leases - - -	Car. 1. to 1800. -	Surv. Gen. Crown Lands	G. 14.
Leases of Mines in Gloucestershire & Somerset	After Rich. 2. - -	Chapter House - - -	A. 1.
Original Petitions for Leases—Reports, Warrants, &c. - - - - - - -	1730 to 1800. - -	Surv. Gen. Crown Lands	G. 14.
PARTICULARS of GRANTS - - - - - -	Hen. 8. to Eliz. -	Augmentation Office -	G. 19.
Of Lands and Parcels intended to be granted to the Prince - - - - - - -	1610 and 1624. -	University Lib. Camb.	P. 1.
Of Forests, Chases, and Parks, granted to the Prince - - - - - - -	Date wanting. - -	University Lib. Camb.	P. 1.
PARTICULARS and CONTRACTS for SALE, PURCHASE, and EXCHANGE:			
Deeds of Sale, Purchase, and Exchange -	Edw. 1. - - - -	Chapter House - - -	A. 1.
Deeds of Sale - - - - - - -	Hen. 8. & Ed. 6. -	Augmentation Office -	G. 19.
Parliamentary Sales during the Commonwealth	1649 to 1660 - -	Surv. Gen. Crown Lands	G. 14.
Particulars for Sale, and Deeds, of Fee-farm Rents - - - - - - - -	1649 to 1660 - -	Augmentation Office -	G. 19.
Particulars of Parliamentary Surveys - -	1649 to 1660 - -	Ibidem & K. Rem. Exch.	G. 19. & 6.
Books of Commissioners Proceedings on the Sales - - - - - - - -	1649 to 1660 - -	Augmentation Office -	G. 19.
Particulars, Prices, and Purchasers Names -	1649 to 1655 - -	University Library Camb.	P. 1.
Sales of Fee-farm Rents, &c. in Wales - -	Oliver Cromwell -	Auditor for Wales - -	G. 16.
Of Lands purchased, chiefly about Windsor -	Will. 3. to Geo. 2.	Surv. Gen. Cr. Lands	G. 14.
PARTICULARS and CONSTATS - - - -	1626 to 1686 - -	Surv. Gen. Cr. Lands	G. 14.
SALES under Stat. 34 Geo. 3. c. 75. and 38 Geo. 3. c. 60. Proceedings thereon - - - - -	— —	Surv. Gen. Cr. Lands	G. 14.
CERTIFICATES, and ACCOUNTS of SHERIFFS, MINISTERS, and RECEIVERS:			
Ministers Accounts - - - - - -	Hen. 3. to Eliz. -	King's Rememb. Exch. -	G. 6. a.
The like - - - - - - -	Ric. 2. to Eliz. -	Augmentation Office	G. 19.
The like of several Honours - - -	Hen. 8. & Ed. 6. -	Augmentation Office	G. 19.
The like of Estates acquired by Purchase, Exchange, &c. - - - - - -	Hen. 8. to Eliz. -	Augmentation Office	G. 19.
The like of the Dissolved Monasteries, &c. and of those acquired by Forfeiture or Escheat -	Hen. 8. to Car. 1. -	Auditors Land Revenue	G. 15.
The like of Alien Priories - - - -	Ed. 1. to Ric. 2. -	King's Rememb. Exch.	G. 6. a.
The like of Possessions of the Knights Templars	Ed. 1. to Ric. 2. -	King's Rememb. Exch.	G. 6. a.
The like of Estates acquired by Attainder or Forfeiture - - - - - - -	Hen. 6. to Ed. 6. -	Augmentation Office -	G. 19.
Ministers and Receivers Accounts - -	Ed. 1. to Car. 1. -	Auditors Land Reven.	G. 15.
Accounts and Views of Accounts - -	Hen. 5. to Car. 2. -	Auditors Land Reven.	G. 15.
Accounts of Wood Sales - - - -	Hen. 8. - - - -	Augmentation Office -	G. 19.
Ministers Accounts for Wales - - -	7 H. 7. to 15 Car. 2.	Auditors Land Reven.	G. 15.
The like - - - - - - -	Eliz. & Car. 1. to G. 1.	Auditors Land Reven.	G. 15.
The like of Lands in Wales of Sir J. Perrott and Owen Glynn, attainted - - - -	Eliz. - - - - -	Auditors Land Reven.	G. 15.
Receivers Accounts - - - - - -	Hen. 8. to Car. 2. -	Auditors Land Reven.	G. 15.
The like - - - - - - -	Hen. 8. to Eliz. -	Augmentation Office -	G. 19.
The like for Wales - - - - -	13 Car. 2. to 1800.	Auditor for Wales - -	G. 16.
Receivers Accounts - - - - -	1640 to 1647 - -	University Lib. Camb.	P. 1.
The like of Lincolnshire and Oxfordshire -	1649 - - - - -	University Lib. Camb.	P. 1.
The like of Estates sequestered - - -	1645 - - - - -	University Lib. Camb.	P. 1.
Certificate of Officers of Augmentation Office for Cambridgeshire - - - - -	30 Hen. 8. - - -	Auditors Land Revenue	G. 15.

IV. THE ROYAL REVENUES—(*continued.*)

RECORDS and other INSTRUMENTS.	DATE.	WHERE KEPT.	Appendix to the First Report.
Certificates, &c.—(*continued.*)			
Certificate of Manors, &c. in Northamptonshire, Warwick, Leicester, Stafford, Hereford, Worcester, Cumberland, Westmoreland, and Lancaster, not granted in Fee Farm - - - - - - - -	1629 - - - - -		
Certificate of the Honour of Bolingbroke in Lincoln, York, Stafford, and Derby - -	36 Eliz. & 16 Car 1.	University Lib. Camb.	P. 1.
Certificate of Estates of the King, Queen, and Prince, not granted in Fee Farm - -	1647 - - - - -		
Computus Constabularii Castri Regis Burdeg' -	8 Hen. 6. - - -	2d Second. King's Rem.	G. 6. a.
A Collector's Account - - - -	Ric. 2. - - - -	1st Secondary, ibidem -	
The like of the Constable of Windsor Castle -	19 Jac. 1. - - -	Auditors Land Reven.	G. 15.
Accounts of Stewards, Bailiffs, &c. - -	Various Dates to 1800		
Sheriffs Views for Wales - - - - -	13 Car. 2. to 38 Geo. 3.	Auditor for Wales -	G. 16.
Receivers D° - - - - - - -	1 Eliz. to 1 Ann. -		
Miscellaneous Accounts - - - - -	Ed. 1. to Car. 2. -	Auditors Land Revenue -	G. 15.
The like of Bailiffs - - - - - -	Ed. 1. to Car. 2. -	King's Rem. Exchequer -	G. 6. a.
Accounts, Rentals, &c. of Forfeited and Sequestered Estates - - - - -	Hen. 8. to Car. 1. -	Auditors Land Reven.	G. 15.
Declarations of Receivers and Ministers Accounts - - - - - - - -	1600 to 1700 - -		
Certificates and Accounts of Auditors General, Surveyors and Receivers General:			
Account of Surveyor of Works - - - -	Hen. 8. et antea -	Chapter House - - -	A. 1.
Receivers Accounts, and Office States thereof -	Hen 8. to 1800 -	Auditors Land Revenue -	G. 15.
Account of Forfeited Estates - - - -	1660 - - - -		
Of Estates granted to the Duke of Albemarle -	1660 - - - -	Surv. Gen. Cr. Lands	G. 14.
- - - undisposed of in - - - - -	1701 - - - - -		
Of Woods and Forests - - - - -	(No first date) to 1800	Auditors Land Revenue -	G. 15.
Of Auditors of the Land Revenue, of the State of the Revenue in their Charge - -	1660 to 1701 - -	Surv. Gen. Crown Lands	G. 14.
Entries of Receiver General of Money received	1645 - - - - -	University Library Camb.	P. 1.
Declared Accounts for Wales - - - -	Date wanting - -	Auditor for Wales - -	G. 16.
Fee Farm Rents:			
Rolls of, during the Commonwealth - -	Car. 1. & 2. - -	Augmentation Office -	G. 19.
State of Arrears of - - - - - -	1649 - - - - -	University Library Camb.	P. 1.
Books of, for Wales - - - - - -	Date wanting - -	Auditor for Wales - -	G. 16.
Casual Revenue:			
Prefines and Postfines:			
Fines in the Common Bench - - - -	25 & 26 Ed. 3. -	Auditors Land Reven.	G. 15. d.
Alienation-Office Books of Fines - -	Eliz. to Car. 2. - -		
Postfines of the Court of Common Pleas estreated - - - - - - - - -	Trin. 6 Geo. 3. to 1800	Clerk Foreign Estreats	G. 10.
Estreats of the like at the Exchequer - -	1681 to 1766 - -		
Accounts of Sheriffs - - - - - -	Ed. 1. to Car. 2. -	King's Rem. Exchequer -	G. 6. a.
States of - - - - - - - -	Hen. 3. to 1800 -	Comptroller of Pipe - -	G. 9.
Summonses and Returns of Sheriffs to the Exchequer, of Alienation Fines, and other Debts to the Crown - - - - - -	Car. 1. to Jac. 2. -	Auditors Land Revenue -	G. 15. d.
Annual Statements of Sheriffs Accounts -	1752 to 1800 - -	Foreign Apposer - - -	G. 11.
Estreat Rolls:			
Of Inquisitions - - - - - - -	3 Ed. 1. - - - -	Chapter House - - -	A. 1.
Estreats of Fines of Manor Courts - -	Ed. 2. to Car. 1. -		
Estreats for Wales - - - - - -	Car. 1. to Geo. 1. -		
Of Fines at the Sessions in Kent - - -	12 Hen. 7. - - -	Auditors Land Reven.	G. 15. d.
Amerciaments in the Common Pleas - -	22 Ed. 4. - - -		
The like in the Exchequer - - - -	2 Ric. 3. - - -		
Fines from the King's Bench, and Clerks of Peace, Assize, Sewers, and Corporations -	1681 to 1800 - -	Clerk Foreign Estreats	G. 10.
Affidavits of Claims of Fines by Bailiffs of Liberties - - - - - - - -	Date wanting - -		
Duplicates of Estreats in Process - - -	Date wanting - -	Foreign Apposer - - -	G. 11.
Escheats:			
Rolls of - - - - - - - - -	Ed. 1. & seq. - -	King's Rem. Exchequer -	G. 6. a.
The like, of various Dates, but chiefly - -	Hen. 4. - - - -	Augmentation Office - -	G. 19.
The like - - - - - - - - -	5 & 8 Ed. 2. - -	Chapter House - - -	A. 1.
The like in Essex and Herts - - -	Ed. 3. - - - -	Auditors Land Revenue -	G. 19.
The like of Alien Priories - - - -	Ed. 1. to Ric. 2. -	King's Rem. Exchequer	G. 6. a.

IV. THE ROYAL REVENUES—(continued.)

RECORDS and other INSTRUMENTS.	DATE.	WHERE KEPT.	Appendix to the First Report
ESCHEATS—(continued.)			
Terræ Normannorum - - - - -	Hen. 3. - - - -	Chapter House -	A. 1.
Escheators Accounts - - - - -	Eliz. - - - -	Auditors Land Revenue	G. 15.
Extracts of Records of Escheats, by Mr. Cole	— —	British Museum -	U.
Papers relating to Escheats - - -	1199 to 1666 - -	Old State Paper Office -	C. 1.
CONCEALED LANDS:			
Entries of Returns to Commissions of - -	3 to 17 Eliz. - -	2d Second. King's Rem. -	G. 6. a.
Particulars for Grants of - - - - -	Eliz. - - - -	Augmentation Office -	G. 19.
INQUISITIONS POST MORTEM - - - -	1 Hen. 3. to 3 Ric. 3.	Tower - - -	A. 2.
- - - - - - - -	1 Hen. 7. to 20 Car. 1.	Rolls - - - -	D. 1.
Transcript of those in the Tower, and Rolls, and some Originals - - - -	Ed. 1. to Car. 1. -	King's Rememb. Exch. -	G. 6. a.
Of Estates of Henry Earl of Huntingdon -	39 Eliz. - - -	Auditors Land Revenue	G. 15.
CORONERS ROLLS,			
Of Inquisitions - - - - - -	Ed. 1. to Hen. 4. -	Chapter House - -	A. 1.
OUTLAWS:			
Writs and Returns of their Estates - -	Oliver Cromwell -	Auditors Land Revenue	G. 15. d.
RECUSANTS:			
Roll of - - - - - - -	Eliz. - - - -	Augmentation Office -	G. 19.
Rentals of their Estates - - - - -	Eliz. - - - -	Auditors Land Revenue	G. 15.
Certificates of Papists Convict - - -	Anne, to Geo. 3. -	Petty Bag Office - -	D. 5.
INVENTORIES of ATTAINTED PERSONS:			
Jewels, Wardrobe, and Effects of Thomas Duke of Norfolk - - - - -	1524 - - - -	University Library Camb.	P. 1.
The like of the Duke of Norfolk, and Earl of Surrey - - - - - - -	38 Hen. 8. - - -	Auditors Land Revenue	G. 15.
The like of the Duke of Somerset - -	7 Ed. 6. - - -		
The like of the Duke of Northumberland, and others - - - - - -	1 Mar. - - - -		
Collection of Inventories - - - -	Mar. to Car. 1. -		
2. EXTRAORDINARY REVENUE:			
ROLL of FOREIGN ACCOUNTS - - - -	A few before 1688 -	Pipe Office, Exchequer	G. 8.
Books of Accounts and Treasury Warrants -	From 1684 - - -		
Taxation of Jews - - - - - -	19 Ed. I. - - -	Tower - - -	A. 2.
Rotuli de Cartis tangentibus Pecuniam Iudæorum	Hen. 3. to Ed. 1. -	Dean & Chap. Westm. -	N. 12. b.
AIDS and SUBSIDIES:			
Papers relating thereto, and to Loans - -	1199 to 1666 - -	Old State Paper Office -	C. 1.
Subsidy and Tax Rolls - - - - -	20 Ed. 1. & seq. -	King's Rememb. Exch. -	G. 6. a.
Nonæ Rolls of the Ninth and Fifteenth -	14 & 15 Ed. 3. -	Ibidem - - -	G. 6. c.
Accounts of Tenths and Subsidies - -	Ed. 3. to Hen. 4. -	Augmentation Office -	G. 19.
Aids, Scutages, and Subsidies - - -	31 Ed. 1. & 5 Hen. 4.	Tower - - -	A. 2.
Tax Accounts and Subsidies - - -	Ed. 3. to Geo. 3. -	Auditors Land Revenue	G. 15.
Book of Aid - - - - - -	20 Edw. 3. - - -	First Secondary King's Rememb. Exch. -	G. 6. a.
- - - Tenth and Fifteenth of Laity -	3 Hen. 5. - - -		
- - - Subsidies and Knights Fees - -	Hen. 6. - - - -		
Account of Tenths and Fifteenths -	Eliz. - - - -	Auditors Land Revenue	G. 15.
Collectors Acquittances of the Subsidy - -	21 Jac. 1. - - -		
Account of the Quarterly Poll - - -	9 & 10 Will. 3. -	First Secondary King's Remembrancer - -	G. 6. a.
- - - of the Subsidy - - - -	10 & 11 Will. 3. -		
OFFERINGS and FREE GIFTS - - - -	1, 2, 3 John, 3, 9 Ed. 2. 1. to 26 Ed. 3.	Tower - - -	A. 2.
Receivers Accounts of - - - -	13 Car. 2. - - -	Auditors Land Revenue	G. 15. d.
PERMANENT TAXES:			
CUSTOMS:			
Papers relating to Customs - - -	1199 to 1666 - -	Old State Paper Office -	C. 1.
Accounts of Receivers - - - -	Hen. 7. to Car. 1. -	Auditors Land Revenue	G. 15.
Official Correspondence - - - -	1689 to 1761 - -	New State Paper Office -	C. 1.
A Book relative to Wines of the Household, signed by Lord Burleigh - - -	1597 to 1598 - -	Auditors Land Revenue	G. 15.
Letters and Orders to Farmers of the Customs, and Officers of the Port of London - -	1605 to 1618 - -	Bodleian Lib. *Perrott* -	O. 1.
Custom Accounts - - - - - -	1655 to 1656 - -	Ibidem. *Rawlinson* -	
Surveyors Port Entries - - - - -	Date wanting - -	Auditors Land Revenue	G. 15

IV. THE ROYAL REVENUES—(continued.)

RECORDS and other INSTRUMENTS.	DATE.	WHERE KEPT.	Appendix to the First Report.
PERMANENT TAXES—(continued.)			
EXCISE:			
Official Correfpondence	1716 to 1748	New State Paper Office	C. 1.
Excife Book	1645 to 1652	Bodleian Library. *Rawl.*	O. 1.
Accounts	1672 to 1674	Bodleian Library. *Rawl.*	O. 1.
LAND and ASSESSED TAXES:			
Account of Land Tax	12, 13 Will. 3.	1ft Second. King's Rem.	G. 6. a.
Land and Poll Tax, and Hearth Money Duplicates	Car. 2. to Will. 3.	Auditors Land Revenue	G. 15.
Accounts of the feveral Taxes, from their Commencements	to 1800	Auditors Land Revenue	G. 15.
Declared Accounts of Receivers General for Wales	to 37 Geo. 3.	Auditor for Wales	G. 16.
POST OFFICE:			
Official Correfpondence	1698 to 1745	New State Paper Office	C. 1.

V. COURTS OF JUSTICE.

RECORDS and other INSTRUMENTS.	DATE.	WHERE KEPT.	Appendix to the First Report.
1. ABOLISHED OR OBSOLETE JURISDICTION:			
CURIA REGIS:			
Rolls of this Court	Ric. 1. John, & Hen. 3.	Chapter Houfe	A. 1.
Placita	Ed. 1. 2. & 3.	Inner Temple Library	Q. 2. b.
The like	Ed. 1.	Middle Temple Library	Q. 1.
PLACITA de ASSISIS:	6 Ric. 1. to Ed. 4.	Chapter Houfe	A. 1.
Affize Rolls	31 Ed. 1.	Tower	A. 2.
Placita	Ed. 1.	Inner Temple Library	Q. 2. b.
Placita apud Ebor'	1 to 19 Ed. 2.	Tower	A. 2.
- - apud Cant'	6 Ed. 2.	Bodleian Library	O. 1.
Placita	20 Ed. 3.	Dean and Chap. Durham	N. 24.
The like	Ed. 3. & Hen. 4.	Lincoln's-Inn Library	Q. 3.
PLACITA ITINERARIA:			
Itinera	Ed. 1. to Ed. 3.	Lincoln's-Inn Library	Q. 3.
Apud Northampton	3 Ed. 3.	Bodleian Library. *Rawl.*	O. 1.
Iter de Northampton	3 Ed. 3.	Ibidem. *Tanner*	O. 1.
Acquietantia pro Itinere Juftitiariorum	Ed. 3.	Dean and Chap. Durham	N. 24.
PLACITA FORESTÆ:			
Rolls of, Perambulations, &c.	1208 to 1377	Chapter Houfe	A. 1.
Perambulations	7, 28, 29 Ed. 1.	Tower	A. 2.
Placita in Ducat. Lancaftriæ	8 Ed. 3.	Chapter Houfe	A. 1.
Laws, Perambulations, Claims, &c.	1199 to 1660	Old State Paper Office	C. 1.
Accounts of Fines for Offences againft Foreft Laws	Ed. 1. to Car. 2.	King's Rememb. Excheq.	G. 6. a.
Proceedings North of Trent	30, 31 Hen. 8.	Chapter Houfe	A. 1.
Perambulations and other Proceedings	Car. 1. et antea	Univerfity Library Camb.	P. 1.
Claims	Car. 1.	Tower	A. 2.
Perambulations	17 Car. 1.	Petty Bag Office	D. 5.
Warrants of Difafforeftation	1637 to 1639	Univerfity Library Camb.	P. 1.
Proceedings South of Trent	Car. 2.	Chapter Houfe	A. 1.
Papers relating to Foreft Courts	Date wanting	Britifh Mufeum	U.
PLACITA CORONÆ	10 Hen. 3. to Edw. 3.	Chapter Houfe	A. 1.
PLACITA AULÆ, or Antient Marfhalfea	12 Ed. 1. 10, 11 Ed. 2. 15 to 32 Ed. 3.	Chapter Houfe	A. 1.
Accounts of Profits of this Court	Ed. 1. & feq.	King's Rememb. Excheq.	G. 6. a.
PLACITA de QUO WARRANTO:			
Rolls	Edw. 1, 2, 3.	Chapter Houfe	A. 1.
Placita	Ed. 1.	Bodleian Library. *Rawl.*	O. 1.
STAR CHAMBER:			
Hiftory of the Court and its Jurifdiction	Date wanting	Auditors Land Revenue	G. 15.
Proceedings	3 Hen. 7. to 16 Car. 1.	Chapter Houfe	A. 1.
Judgments exemplified under the Great Seal	from 6 Hen. 8.	Rolls Chapel	D. 1.
Information by Heath, Attorney General, againft the Earl of Bedford, Selden and others, for Sedition	Car. 1.	Univerfity Lib. Camb.	P. 1.
The like againft Elliot, Holles, and others, with the Decree	Car. 1.	Univerfity Lib. Camb.	P. 1.

V. COURTS OF JUSTICE—(continued.)

RECORDS and other INSTRUMENTS.	DATE.	WHERE KEPT.	Appendix to the First Report.
STAR CHAMBER—(continued.)			
Courfe of Proceeding and Reports - - -	4 Car. 1. - - -	Bodleian Library - -	O. 1.
Proceedings - - - - - - - -	1632 - - - -	Bodleian Library	O. 1.
Cafes in - - - - - - - -	Car. 1. - - - -	Bodleian Library	O. 1.
Fees - - - - - - - -	Date wanting - -	Bodleian Library	O. 1.
Papers relating to, and Tracts - - -	Hen. 8. to Car. 1.	Britifh Mufeum - -	U.
Proceedings - - - - - - -	12 Jac. 1. & 5, 14, 16 Car. 1. - -	Afhmolean Mufeum -	O. 2.
Decree for Orders in Printing - - -	28 Eliz. - - -	Afhmolean Mufeum	O. 2.
Act of Court on the Petitions of Baftwick and Prynne, with Judges Opinion and Certificate	Car. 1. - - - -	Inner Temple Library -	Q. 2. b.
Papers relating to the Court - - -	Date wanting - -	Inner Temple Library	Q. 2. b.
The like - - - - - - -	1558 to 1633 - -	Old State Paper Office -	C. 1.
COURT of REQUESTS:			
Proceedings of - - - - - -	9 H. 7. to 17 Car. 1.	Chapter Houfe - -	A. 1.
COURT of WARDS and LIVERIES:			
Valuation of Eftates of Earl of Northumberland and Lord Lifle, the King's Wards - -	Date wanting - -	Dean and Chap. Weftm.	N. 12. b.
Proceedings and Muniments of Eftates in Ward	32 H. 8. to 12 Car. 2.	Chapter Houfe - -	A. 1.
Inquifitions poft Mortem - - - -	32 H. 8. to 12 Car. 2.	Chapter Houfe	A. 1.
The like - - - - - - -	Hen. 8. & Eliz. -	Auditors Land Revenue	G. 15.
The like - - - - - - -	Hen. 8. - - -	Bodleian Library - -	O. 1.
Ordinance of Lords and Commons concerning its Revenues - - - - -	10 Nov. 1647 - -	2d Second. King's Rem.	G. 6. a.
Collection of Decrees in French, by John Hare	1581 - - - -	Univerfity Lib. Camb.	P. 1.
Other Papers concerning the Court - -	Of various Dates -	Univerfity Lib. Camb.	P. 1.
Fees - - - - - - - -	Date wanting - -	Bodleian Library - -	O. 1.
Extracts of Records, by Mr. T. Cole - -	— —	Britifh Mufeum - -	U.
Papers relating to the Court - - -	Date wanting - -	Inner Temple Library -	Q. 2. b.
The like - - - - - - -	1558 to 1633 - -	Old State Paper Office -	C. 1.
COURT of AUGMENTATIONS:			
Proceedings—Bills, Pleadings, and Depofitions	27 Hen. 8. to 1 Mar.	Augmentation Office -	G. 19.
The like - - - - - - -	27 Hen. 8. to 1 Mar.	Britifh Mufeum - -	U.
DECREES - - - - - - -	Ed. 6. - - - -	Augmentation Office -	G. 19.
DECREES	Hen. 8. & Edw. 6.	King's Remem. Exch. -	G. 6. a.
DECREES	Ed. 6. - - - -	Britifh Mufeum - -	U.
DECREES	1 to 7 Ed. 6. - -	2d Second[y] King's Rem.	G. 6. a.
Entries of - - - - - - -	Hen. 8. - - - -	2d Second[y] King's Rem.	G. 6. a.
Calendars of - - - - - - -	30 H. 8. to 7 Ed. 6.	2d Second[y] King's Rem.	G. 6. a.
LEASES by the Court, inrolled - - - -	27 Hen. 8. to 1 Mar.	Augmentation Office -	G. 19.
COURT of SURVEYOR GENERAL:			
Leafes and Decrees of, from its Inftitution to its Diffolution - - - - - - -	33 to 38 Hen. 8. -	Augmentation Office	G. 19.
COURT of HIGH COMMISSION:			
Regifter of Acts - - - - - -	1631 to 1633 - -	Univerfity Library Camb.	P. 1.
COURT of CHIVALRY:			
Placita Exercitûs Regis - - - -	24 Edw. 1. - - -	Chapter Houfe - -	A. 1.
Roll relating to the Marfhal - - -	8 Edw. 2. - - -	Tower - - - -	A. 2.
Proceedings of the Earl Marfhal's Court -	Eliz. to Car. 2. -	Herald's Office - -	C. 8.
Curia Militaris (Cafes of Duel) - - -	Hen. 6. - - - -	Lincoln's Inn Library -	Q. 3.
Proceedings in the Cafe of Ramfey and Lord Reay - - - - - - - -	1631 - - - -	Bodleian Library - -	O. 1.
2. OCCASIONAL JURISDICTION:			
SPECIAL COMMISSIONS for TREASONS and FELONIES, and GAOL DELIVERY:			
Gaol Deliveries - - - - - -	Edw. 1. to Edw. 4.	Chapter Houfe - -	A. 1.
Rebelliones in diverfis Comitatibus - -	12 Hen. 7. - - -	Chapter Houfe	A. 1.
Infurrections in Yorkfhire, &c. - - - -	Hen. 8. - - - -	Chapter Houfe	A. 1.
Roll of Criminal Affairs, Attainders, &c. -	15 Ed. 2. 1 Hen. 4.	Tower - - - -	A. 2.
Oyer and Terminer and Gaol Delivery at Briftol	July 1753 - - -	Clerk of Crown in Chan.	D. 2.
Attainders - - - - - - - -	— —	Baga de Secretis King's Bench Treafury - -	E. 1.
Proceedings in the North, in London, Suffex, and Kent - - - - - - -	1715, 1746, 1780, 1794, 1795, 1798	Cuftody of the Clerk of the Record Committee	[See 1ft Report, p. 6.]

V. COURTS OF JUSTICE—(continued.)

RECORDS and other INSTRUMENTS.	DATE.	WHERE KEPT.	Appendix to the First Report.
OCCASIONAL JURISDICTION—(continued.)			
Special Commissions and Inquisitions for forfeited Estates - - - -	Jac. 1. to 40 Geo. 3.	Petty Bag Office - -	D. 5.
Divers others - - - - - -	Dates unknown -	Baga de Secretis, K. B. -	E. 1.
Terræ Normannorum - - - -	Hen. 3. - - - -	Chapter House - -	A. 1.
Special Commissions in Matrimonial Causes:			
Totus Processus in Causâ Divortii propter Consanguinitatem, &c. inter Annam Plantagenet Filiam Ric. Ducis Ebor. & Henr. Holand Filium Joh. Ducis Excestriæ - - -	1470 to 1471 - -	Bodleian Library -	O. 1.
Court for determining Differences after the Fire of London, 1666:			
Proceedings of this Court at large - -	Car. 2. - - - -	British Museum - -	U.
High Court of Justice, for Trial of Charles I.			
The Journal of the Court - - - -	1648-9 - - - -	Bodleian Library - -	O. 1.
3. ESTABLISHED JURISDICTION:			
CHANCERY:			
Ordinary Jurisdiction:			
Petition or Monstrans de Droit:			
Pleadings and Judgments - - - -	Hen. 7. to 1800 -	Rolls - - - -	D. 1.
Original Writs:			
Roll or Register of - - - - -	1140 - - - -	Chapter House - -	A. 1.
Collectio Brevium - - - - -	Hen. 6. - - - -	Antiq. Society Library -	S.
By and against Officers of the Court:			
Judgments by Default - - - -	Eliz. to 1800 - -	Petty Bag Office - -	D. 5.
Scire Facias:			
Pleadings and Judgments - - - -	Hen. 7. to 1800 -	Rolls - - - -	D. 1.
- - - - - -	Eliz. to 1800 - -	Petty Bag Office - -	D. 5.
Audita Querela & Ex Gravi Querela:			
Pleadings and Judgments - - - -	Hen. 7. to 1800 -	Rolls - - -	D. 1.
Statutes Staple:			
Certificates of Extents and Liberate - -	Hen. 7. to 1800 -	Rolls - - -	D. 1.
Extents and other Proceedings - - -	Jac. 1. to 1800 -	Petty Bag Office - -	D. 5.
Inquisitions and Proceedings upon Charitable Uses:			
Commissions of - - - - - -	Hen 7. to 1800 -	Rolls - - - -	D. 1.
Inquisitions and Decrees, with Proceedings -	43 Eliz. to 1800 -	Petty Bag Office - -	D. 5.
Ideocy and Lunacy:			
Proceedings on the Writ De Lunatico Inquirendo	1 Hen. 7. to 1800 -	Rolls - - - -	D. 1.
Commissions, Inquisitions, &c. - - -	1 Car. 2. to 1800 -	Petty Bag Office - -	D. 5.
Orders, Reports, Accounts, &c. - - -	1689 to 1800 - -	Clk. of Cust. of Ideots, &c.	D. 18.
Bankruptcy:			
Proceedings inrolled - - - -	Jan. 1758 to Mar. 1799 - - -	Clerk Inrolments in Bankruptcy - - -	D. 14.
Dockets of Commissions and Petitions, and Orders for Renewals and Supersedeas -	1731 to 1800 - -	Patentee of Bankruptcy -	D. 15.
Patents—Dockets of - - - - - -	1595 to 1602. 1643 to 1800 - - -	Clerk of Crown in Chan.	D. 2.
Certificates of Papists, and Persons concealed -	Anne, to Geo. 3. -	Petty Bag Office - -	D. 5.
Inquisitions:			
Ad quod Damnum - - - - -	1 Ed. 2. to 38 Hen. 6.	Tower - - -	A. 2.
Among the Brevia Regia - - - -	9 Car. 1. to 1800 -	Petty Bag Office - -	D. 5.
Certificates of Excommunication:			
From Ecclesiastical Courts - - -	Hen. 7. to 1800 -	Rolls - - - -	D. 1.
Sheriffs Rolls:			
Of Names of Sheriffs - - - - - -	1720 to 1800 - -	Six Clerks Office - -	D. 12.
Commissions of the Peace:			
Dedimus to swear Justices, and Returns -	Date wanting - -	Clerk of Crown in Chan.	D. 2.
Inrolment of Patents and Warrants:			
Of Bishops, Customers, and Searchers - -	1725 to 1800 - -	Petty Bag Office - -	D. 5.
Of Patents for the last 10 Years, for the Time being - - - - - - -	— —	Petty Bag Office - -	D. 5.

V. COURTS OF JUSTICE—*(continued.)*

RECORDS and other INSTRUMENTS.	DATE.	WHERE KEPT.	Appendix to the Firſt Report.
CHANCERY — ORDINARY JURISDICTION *(continued.)*			
BARGAINS and SALES, &c.—Inrolled	25 Geo. 3. to 1800		
RECOGNIZANCES—Inrolled	22 Geo. 2. to 1800	Inrolment Office	D. 13.
ANNUITIES—Memorials of Securities for, regiſtered	17 Geo. 3. to 1800		
EXTENTS—Docket of Writs	1601 to 1800	Clerk of Crown in Chan.	D. 2.
DISPENSATIONS and FACULTIES—Regiſters of	1692 to 1800	Clerk of Diſpenſations	D. 17.
THE GREAT SEAL:			
Books of Entries of all Inſtruments paſſing the Great Seal	1600 to 1798	Hanaper Office	D. 4.
Dockets of Letters Patent	Jac. 1. to 1800	Clerk of Letters Patent	D. 16.
Dockets of what paſſed the Great Seal without Privy Seal	1710 to 1714	Middle Temple Library	Q. 1.
MISCELLANEOUS PAPERS relating to the Court	1558 to 1633	Old State Paper Office	C. 1.
EXTRAORDINARY JURISDICTION:			
PROCEEDINGS in EQUITY by BILL and ANSWER	Eliz. to 1714	Tower	A. 2.
- - - -	1714 to 1800	Six Clerks Office	D. 12.
Exemplification of a Grant to the Chancellor to give Relief in Equity, after Judgment in a Court of Law	Jac. 1.	Dean and Chap. Weſtm.	N. 12. b.
COMMISSIONS, INTERROGATORIES, and DEPOSITIONS:			
In Suits in Chancery	1500 to 1800	Examiner's Office	D. 11
Depoſitions by Commiſſion, and unpubliſhed	1600 to 1800	Six Clerks Office	D. 12.
COMMISSIONS of PARTITION and DOWER, with Proceedings	1714 to 1800		
ORDERS and DECREES of the Court	1547 to 1798	Report Office	D. 9.
REPORTS of Maſters in Chancery	1590 to 1800		
DECREES:			
Judgment or Decree Roll	25 Hen. 8. to 6 Geo. 3.	Rolls	D. 1.
Inrolments of	Eliz. to 1800	Six Clerks Office	D. 12.
CERTIFICATES of Accountant General of Suitors Property	From the Inſtitution of the Office, 12 George 1. to 1800	Report Office	D. 9.
ACCOUNTS of Property of Suitors in Chancery	12 George 1. to 1800		
AFFIDAVITS, with Indexes	1632 to 1800	Regiſter of Affidavits	D. 10.
KING'S BENCH.			
PLACITA	John to Hen. 4.	Lincoln's-Inn Library	Q. 3.
ROLLS OF	1 Edw. 1. to Hen. 5.	Chapter Houſe	A. 1.
WRITS OF, generally	14 Hen. 3. to 3 Ric. 3.	Tower	A. 2.
- - - Original and Special	Hen. 2. to Will. 3.	Chapter Houſe	A. 1.
PLEAS of the CROWN:			
Indictments, Preſentments, Informations, and Convictions	1 W. & M.	Crown Office	E. 1.
Pannels of Grand Juries	1760		
Inquiſitions on View of Priſoners dead	1771	Dep. Coroner Crown Office	E. 2.
Recognizances upon Writs of Certiorari, &c.	5 W. & M.		
Eſtreats of Recognizances forfeited	12 Car. 2.		
Writs and Returns	5 W. & M.		
Entries of Rules	31 Eliz.		
Affidavits (except thoſe at Judges Chambers)	12 Car. 2.		
Interrogatories and Anſwers on Attachments	12 Will. 3. — to 1800	Crown Office	E. 1.
Roll of Oaths of Allegiance	1688 to 1800		
Certificates of Sacrament and Subſcriptions	1 George 2.		
Returns of Convicts, purſuant to Stat. 16 George III. Chapter 43	16 George 3.		
Minutes of Appearances and Pleas	12 George 1.		
- - of Notices of Trial	10 Wm. 3.		
Dockets of Proceedings and Controlment Rolls, containing Minutes of Proceedings	3 Edw. 3.		
PLEAS in CIVIL SUITS:			
ROLLS of ATTORNIES	No Date, except to the Index from 1656	Maſter of King's Bench	E. 2.
WARRANTS to ſue and defend	Nov. 1785 to 1800	Filazer	E. 7.

V. COURTS OF JUSTICE—(continued.)

RECORDS and other INSTRUMENTS.	DATE.	WHERE KEPT.	Appendix to the Firſt Report.
KING'S BENCH—(continued.)			
Writs and Returns:			
Entries of all Writs of the Filazer's Office			
Special Capias, Exigents and Proclamations			
Recognizances of Bail.—Docket Books of	Date wanting	Filazer	E. 7.
Entries of Common Appearance			
Proceedings in Outlawry:			
Writs, Inquiſitions, and Judgments in Outlawry			
Rules:			
Of each Term	Hi. 1603 to Mic. 1799		
Original Minutes of the ſame	Hil. 1739 to Tr. 1800		
Receipts for Money paid into Court	1789 to 1800	Clerk of Rules	E. 3.
Affidavits:			
(Except thoſe before Judges at Chambers)	1733 to 1800		
Of Debt and Service in Suits by Original	Date wanting	Filazer	E. 7.
Priſoners:			
Petitions for Day Rules	1757 to 1800	Clerk of Rules	E. 3.
Papers	1763 to 1800		
Pleadings in Actions	1777 et ant.	Clerk of Papers	E. 4.
Collection of Paper Books	14 to 27 Geo. 2.	Inner Temple Library	Q. 2. b.
Bills of Exceptions	Date wanting	Maſter of King's Bench	E. 2.
Dockets			
Judgments and other Proceedings inrolled of Record	1 Hen. 6. to 1800	Cuſtos Brevium	E. 5.
Reports of Caſes adjudged	15, 16, & 20 Jac. 1.	Univerſity Library Camb.	P. 1.
Writs of Error and Allowances, pending the Cauſes in Error	Date wanting	Clerk of Errors	E. 6.
Fees:			
Of this Court	Date wanting	Bodleian Library.	O. 1.
Hanaper Account of Profits of the Seal of this Court	Eliz.	Auditors Land Revenue	G. 15.
COMMON PLEAS:			
Placita	John to Hen. 4.	Lincoln's-Inn Library	Q. 3.
Rolls of	Ed. 1. & Hen. 7.	Chapter Houſe	A. 1.
The like	Part of Hen. 7.	Treaſury Common Pleas	F. 4.
Rolls of Attornies and Register of Clerks:			
Inrolment of Attornies	1554 to 1800	Clerk of Warrants, Inrolments, and Eſtreats	F. 3.
Clerks Articles	Date wanting		
Filazer's Remembrance Rolls:			
Containing Præcipes for Writs	1780 to 1800	Filazer	F. 5.
Warrants to sue and defend:			
Purſuant to Stat. 25 Geo. III.	1780 to 1800		
Writs and Returns:			
Original and Special	Hen. 2. to Will. 3.	Chapter Houſe	A. 1.
The like	1688 to 1800	Cuſt. Brev. Com. Pleas	F. 4.
Bills of Privilege:			
Againſt Attornies and Officers	1688 to 1800		
Essoin Rolls	Anne to 1800	Clerk of Eſſoins	F. 2.
Affidavits:			
Of Debt and Service, Special Bail Books and Pieces, and Entries of Common Appearance	1780 to 1800	Filazer's Office	F. 5.
Proceedings in Outlawry:			
Proclamations	1680 to 1800	Cuſtos Brevium	F. 4.
Reverſals	10 Geo. 2. to 1800	Clerk of Reverſals	F. 9.
Rules:			
(See Entries of Rules and Orders in the Secondary's Remembrance Rolls.)			
Nisi Prius Records	20 Car. 2. to 1800	Prothonotary's Office	F. 1.
Posteas	1688 to 1800	Cuſtos Brevium	F. 4.
Elegits	1688 to 1800		
Writs of Inquiry	1688 to 1800		

V. COURTS OF JUSTICE—(continued.)

RECORDS and other INSTRUMENTS.	DATE.	WHERE KEPT.	Appendix to the First Report.
COMMON PLEAS—(continued.)			
PROTHONOTARY'S DOCKET ROLLS:			
Of Pleadings in Suits - - -	3 Ed. 6. to 1800 -	Prothonotaries Office -	F. 1.
SECONDARY'S Remembrance Rolls - - -			
JUDGMENTS:			
Common - - - - - - -	3 Car. 1. to 1800		
Special - - - - - - - -	14 Car. 2. to 1800		
Entries by Warrant of Attorney, of all Judgments - - - - - - -	Date wanting - -	Clerk of Warrants -	F. 3.
MITTIMUS and Transcript - - - - - -	1688 to 1800 - -	Custos Brevium - -	F. 4.
ENTRIES on Roll - - - - - -	Hilary 12. Anne, to 1800 - - -	Prothonotaries Office -	F. 1.
INROLMENT of Deeds, &c. - - - - - -	1554 to 1800 - -	Clerk of Warrants -	F. 3.
DOCKETS of FINAL JUDGMENT:			
Pursuant to Statutes 4 & 5 W. & M. c. 20.	4 & 5 W. & M. to 1800 - - - -	Clerk of Essoins - -	F. 2.
FINES:			
Records of - - - - - - -	Hen. 2. to Will. 3.	Chapter House - -	A. 1.
	6 John to 1483 -	Tower - - - -	A. 2.
The like of various Dates, chiefly - - -	Hen. 8. - - - - -	Augmentation Office -	G. 19.
Entries - - - - - - - -	1571 to 1800 - -	Alienation Office - -	G. 17.
Copies of Writs of Covenant - - -	1576 to 1800 - -		
Entries of Writs of Covenant - - -	1627 to 1800 - -	Clerk of Return Office -	F. 8.
Concords of Fines, Dedimus, Affidavits, and Feet of Fines - - - - - -	1688 to 1782 - -	Custos Brevium -	F. 4.
Books of Fines - - - - - -	Ed. 6. to 1800 - -	King's Silver Office -	F. 6.
Rolls of Fines - - - - - - -	Hen. 8. to 1800 -	Chirographers - -	F. 7.
Postfines - - - - - - - -	6 Geo. 3. to 1800 -	Clerk of Foreign Estreats, Exchequer - -	G. 10.
RECOVERIES:			
Warrants of Attorney - - - - -	— —	Cursitor's Office - -	D. 3.
Writs of Entry, &c. - - - - - -	1688 to 1800 - -	Custos Brevium - -	F. 4.
Entries of Ditto, and Returns, and Affidavits by Dedimus - - - - - - -	1627 to 1800 - -	Clerk of Return Office -	F. 8.
Redisseisin Rolls - - - - - -	Dates wanting - -	Tower - - - -	A. 2.
Remembrance Rolls - - - - - -	2 Ed. 6. to 1800 -	Prothonotaries Office -	F. 1.
Extracts from Recovery Rolls - - -	1507 to 1800 - -	Clerk of Warrants -	F. 3.
EXCHEQUER:			
EXCHEQUER OF ACCOUNT.			
THE KING'S REMEMBRANCER'S OFFICE:			
MEMORANDA: Containing,			
1. Matters inrolled; viz. Proceedings for Recovery of Debts to the Crown, upon Writs of Scire Facias, Extent, and Commissions of Inquiry: Commissions and Inquisitions in Cases of Attainder and Forfeiture: Informations and other Proceedings relating to the Customs: Personal Informations for Forfeitures or Penalties: Transcripts of Outlawries and Process thereon: Recognizances to the Crown: Profers of Sheriffs and Bailiffs: Patents and Grants, under Great and Privy Seals: Warrants and Constitutions under the Sign Manual: Conveyances of Estates by Subjects: Proceedings in Equity, by English Bill and Information.	From Hen. 3. -	King's Remembrancer's Office - - -	G. 6. a.
2. Records not inrolled; viz. Informations by the Attorney General, in Cases of Revenue, Charities, and Trusts: Proceedings by English Bill in Private Suits: Depositions: Orders and Decrees:	Few of these Records		

(continued)

V. COURTS OF JUSTICE—*(continued.)*

RECORDS and other INSTRUMENTS.	DATE.	WHERE KEPT.	Appendix to the First Report.
THE KING'S REMEMBRANCER—*(continued.)*			
Commissions, &c. on the Subsidy 14 Ed. III.:	cords are earlier than 1 Eliz.	King's Remembrancer's Office, Exchequer -	G. 6. a.
Perambulations, Extents, and Surveys of Alien Priories:			
Annual Port Books of the Customs, which have ceased since 14th March 1799:			
Forfeited Port Bonds:			
Process against Receivers of Taxes:			
Decrees of Commissioners under Statutes for the Dock Yards and Harbours, since 1758:			
States of Accounts of Receivers:			
Duplicates of Land Tax and Assessed Taxes:			
Bonds for due Execution of Offices - -	— —	Ibidem, Temple - -	
OATHS of OFFICERS of the COURT:			
In the Red Book - - - - - -	31 Hen. 3. - - -	1st Second[r] King's Rem.	
PRESENTATIONS of OFFICERS of the COURT:			
Entries of - - - - - - -	From Hen. 3. - -	Lord Treasurer's Remem.	G. 7. a.
COPIES of Exchequer Records; viz.			
Communia - - - - - -	23 to 46 Ed. 3. -	Lincoln's-Inn Library -	Q. 3.
Memoranda - - - - - -	1 to 22 Ed. 3. -		
ORIGINAL DECREES and Orders in Equity - -	Date wanting - -	King's Remembrancer -	G. 6. a.
EXTRACTS from Records of the Exchequer, by Madox - - - - - - -	Date wanting - -	British Museum - - -	U.
THE LORD TREASURER'S REMEMBRANCER'S OFFICE:			
1. MEMORANDA; containing,	From Hen. 3. -	Lord Treasurer's Remem. Office, Somerset Place	G. 7. a.
Pleadings at Common Law, inter alia, in			
Quo Titulo,			
Quare Maneria,			
Petitions of Right,			
Claims of Franchise,			
Estreats of Fines and Amerciaments.			
Commissions of Survey.			
Proceedings upon Sheriffs and Ministers Accounts:			
Charge and Discharge of Debtors;			
States and Views of Accounts.			
[See Writs from this Court for Debts to the Crown -	Ric. 2 to Eliz. - -	Auditors Land Revenue] - -	
Auditor's Memoranda of Debts and Arrears -	Eliz. to Car. 2. - -		
Orders of the Court concerning the Land and Casual Revenue. *(These begin in 35 Car. II.)*			
Entries of Presentations and Admissions of Officers			
Inrolments of Deeds acknowledged - - -			
2. ORIGINALIA; containing,			
Estreats from Chancery of Grants from the Crown	From Hen. 3. - -		
3. MISCELLANIES; containing, besides some original Rolls, the following Articles; viz.			
Petitions of Allowances:			
Commissions and Returns:			
Writs and Inquisitions:			
Pleadings, Affidavits, and other Proceedings in Suits - - - - - - - -	Of antient Dates -	Lord Treasurer's Rem.	
4. AGENDA BOOKS; containing,			
Entries of Awards, Judgments, and other Business signed by this Remembrancer - -	Date wanting - -		
Catalogues of Books in Custody of the King's and Treasurer's Remembrancer - -	Date wanting - -	Ashmolean Museum - -	O. 2.
EXCHEQUER OF RECEIPT:			
TELLERS CHARGE BOOKS, and DEBENTURES or VOUCHERS FOR PAYMENT - - - -	Date wanting - -	Exch. Off. Somerset Place	G. 3.
The Four Tellers Accounts - - -	1 to 2 Jac. 1. - -	Royal Society Library -	R.

V. COURTS OF JUSTICE—*(continued.)*

RECORDS and other INSTRUMENTS.	DATE.	WHERE KEPT.	Appendix to the Firſt Report.
Exchequer of Receipt—*(continued.)*			
Tally Court:			
Tallies of the ſeveral Perſons entitled to them -	— —	Chamberlains of Exch. -	G. 2.
Auditor and Tally Writer:			
Teller's Bills - - - - - - -	1681 - -		
Certificate and Regiſter Books - - -	1706 - -		
Iſſue Books by Debenture - - - -	1662 - -		
The like by Orders - - - - -	1688 - -		
Caſh Books - - - - - - -	1689 - -		
Patent Books - - - - - - -	1619 - - to 1800		
Privy Seal Books - - - - - -	1620 - -		
Letter Books - - - - - -	1689 - -		
Certificate Books - - - - - -	1688 - -		
Impreſt Roll Books - - - - -	1685 - -		
Books of Declarations - - - - -	1666 - -	Auditors Office Exch. -	G. 1.
Account Books - - - - - -	Date wanting - -		
Iſſue Books of Exchequer Bills, and Certificate Books - - - - - - -	1697 - -		
Iſſue, Regiſter, and Poſting Books of Annuities -	1693 - -		
The like - - - - - - - -	1704 - - to 1800		
Day, Out-caſh, and Certificate Books of the ſame - - - - - - - - -	1693 - -		
Computus Domini I. de Ockam de Scaccario -	4 Ed. 3. - - - -	Bodleian Library. *Rawl.* -	O. 1.
Chamberlains:			
Counterparts of Indentures of Weights and Meaſures - - - - - - -	1700 to 1800 - -	Exchequer Court - -	G. 2.
Pell Office:			
Record of Introitus - - - - - -	1715 - -		
Record of Exitus - - - - -	1725 - -		
Half-yearly Declarations of Receipts and Iſſues -	1698 - - to 1800	Pell Office, Exchequer -	G. 4.
Patents, Conſtitutions and Contracts - -	Eliz. - -		
Signs Manual and Privy Seals - - -	1612 - -		
Catalogue of Rolls and Privy Seals in Pell Office -	— —	Bodleian Library. *Carte* -	O. 1.
Auditors of Impreſt, or Commiſſioners for Auditing Public Accounts:			
Books of the late Auditors; viz.			
Entries of General Certificates of Accountants - -	1732 - -		
of Reports to the Treaſury - - - -	1622 - -		
of Patents, Signs Manual, Warrants, &c. - -	1568 - -		
of General Impreſt Rolls - - - -	1700 - -		
of Powers of Attorney, Wills, &c. - -	1682 - - to 1785		
of Conſtats of Church Preferments, ſubject to Tenths - - - - - - - -	1764 - -		
of Accounts, and Obſervations thereon - -	1702 - -		
of Inſtructions to Public Offices - - -	1685 - -	Account Office, Somerſet Place - -	G. 5.
Books eſtabliſhed by the Board for recording their Proceedings, deſcribed in the App. G. 5 b. -	1785 to 1800 - -		
Accounts and Vouchers of the late Auditors before 1785, and ſince received - - - - - -	to 1800 - - - -		
Proceedings of Commiſſioners of Public Accounts -	1690 to 1697 - -	Britiſh Muſeum - -	U.
The like - - - - - - - -	1702 & 1780 to 1787	Clerk of Journals - -	B. 2.
Exchequer of Pleas:			
Rolls of Attornies - - - - - - -	Date wanting - -		
Warrants to ſue and defend - - - -	32 Geo. 3.		
Writs and Returns - - - - - -	Ed. 3. -		
Appearances for Defendants - - - -	28 Eliz. -		
Recognizances of Bail - - - - - -	Jac. 1. -		
Books of Orders - - - - - - -	3 Ed. 6. -		
Bills, Bailpieces, and Affidavits - - - -	14 Ed. 4.		
Affidavits of Debt - - - - - - -	1791 - - to 1800	Clerk of the Pleas - -	G. 20.
Pleadings and Judgments - - - - -	Edw. 1. -		
Judgments upon Warrants of Attorney - -	Edw. 1. -		
Minute Books - - - - - - - -	Eliz. - -		
Docket Books of the Inrolments - - -	Jac. 1. -		
Remembrancer's Rolls of Writs - - - -	Eliz. - -		
Inrolments of Deeds - - - - - -	Ed. 1. -		
Proceedings in Error, Minutes of - - - -	Date wanting - -		

V. COURTS OF JUSTICE—(*continued.*)

Records and other Instruments.	Date.	Where kept.	Appendix to the First Report.
Exchequer—(*continued.*)			
Exchequer of Error, or the Exchequer Chamber:			
Transcripts of Judgments from the Court of King's Bench - - - - - -	1790 - - } to 1800	Clerk of Errors - - -	G. 20.
Books of Proceedings thereon - - -	1764 - - } to 1800	Clerk of Errors	G. 20.
Books of Entries of Remittitur	1764 - - } to 1800	Clerk of Errors	G. 20.
Miscellaneous Papers relating to the Court of Exchequer - - - - - - - -	1558 to 1633 - -	Old State Paper Office -	C. 1.
Marshalsea and Palace Court:			
Pleadings in Actions from the Creation of the Court - - - - - -	6 Car. 1. to 1800 -	Prothonotary of the Court	G. 22.
Circuits of England, and Sessions of Newgate:	- - -	- - - - -	H. 1. to 7.
The Clerks of the Assizes, and of the Crown for the Circuits of England, and the Clerk of Sessions of Newgate, and Oyer and Terminer of London, have the following Records; viz.:			
Rolls of Indictments, Inquisitions, and Presentments, and Proceedings thereon, Justices Names, Grand Jury Pannels and Precepts. Minute Books of Proceedings on Pleas of the Crown. Gaol Books, containing Names of Prisoners, and Abstracts of Proceedings respecting them. Order Books of Matters relating to Bridges, Highways, Settlements, Restitutions, &c. Transportation Books, and Bonds and Contracts respecting them. Process Books, containing Extracts of Indictments for Misdemeanors, and against Persons at large. Insolvent Debtors Papers. Files of Informations, Depositions, and Examinations, before Justices of Peace. Recognizances and Bail Books. Estreats of Fines and Forfeitures. Calendars of Judgments signed by the Judges. Pardons, and Secretaries of State's Letters and other Papers relating to them. Associates Minute Books of Proceedings on the Nisi Prius Side. Nisi Prius Records, which the Parties have neglected to take away. Lists of Sheriffs. The Commissions of Oyer and Terminer and Gaol Delivery, and Nomina Ministrorum.	A few of these Records have been regularly kept for about 40 or 50 Years; but in general for the last 20 or 30 only.—The most antient Date *specified* in the Returns, (though there may be some older) is of the Year 1610, in the Return of the Western Circuit; but there are not many of a Hundred Years old.	By the respective Clerks of the Assizes; excepting those for London, and the Northern Circuit; the former being deposited in the Sessions House of London, and the latter in an Office built for the Purpose in the Castle of York.	
Great Sessions of Wales:			
Records of each Circuit; viz.:			
Chester - - - - - - - - -	1 Ed. 6. } to 1800		
North Wales - - - - - - -	1700 } to 1800		
Caermarthen - - - - - - -	Jac. 2. } to 1800		
Brecon - - - - - - - -	35 Hen. 8. } to 1800		
The Prothonotaries of the Great Sessions have the following Records; viz.:			
Fines - - - - - - - - Recoveries - - - - - - - Files containing Writs of Summons, and Nomina Ministrorum - - - - - - Writs and Inquisitions - - - - - Plea Rolls - - - - - - Paper Files of Pleadings in Actions - - - Docket Books - - - - - - - Rolls of Judgments - - - - - - Rolls of Attornies - - - - - -	Of various Dates.	Castle of Chester, and Shire Halls of the other Counties - - - - -	H. 8. to H. 11.
The Records in Pleas of the Crown are similar to those of the Circuits of England, and kept by the respective Clerks of the Crown, whose Office is generally united with that of Prothonotary; the Registrars and Clerks of Chancery of the several Circuits, have the Records of the Proceedings in Chancery.			

V. COURTS OF JUSTICE—(continued.)

RECORDS and other INSTRUMENTS.	DATE.	WHERE KEPT.	Appendix to the First Report.
3. ESTABLISHED JURISDICTION—(continued)			
DUCHY of LANCASTER:			
CHARTERS and GRANTS:			
Under the Great Seal, of Duchy Lands -	Stephen to Eliz. -	Duchy Office - -	C. 6.
Grants in Fee Farm, some inrolled, others not	51 Ed. 3. to Anne -	Duchy Office - -	C. 6.
Confirmation of Privileges - - -	2 Hen. 5. - - -	Bodleian Library - -	O. 1.
Copies of Charters relating to the Duchy -	Hen. 4. to Ed. 4. -	Ashmolean Museum -	O. 2.
Exemplification of the Grant of Creation of the County Palatine - - - - -	1 Ed. 4. - - -	Ashmolean Museum -	O. 2.
Patents of Offices under the Duchy Seal -	1 Hen. 8. to 1800	Bodleian Library - -	O. 1.
Grants of Rents under Statutes - - -	1780 to 1800 - -	Duchy Office - -	C. 6.
INQUISITIONS POST MORTEM - - - - -	1 Hen. 5. to Car. 1.	Bodleian Library - -	O. 1.
Transcripts of, for Duchy Lands in Western Counties - - - - - - -	16 Car. 1. - - -	University Lib. Camb.	P. 1.
SEWERS—Special Commissions - - - -	23 Eliz. to 1800 -	University Lib. Camb.	P. 1.
SURVEYS:			
Of Woods and Underwoods - - - -	1575 - - - -	University Lib. Camb.	P. 1.
Feoda Militum Regis Caroli Ducis Lancastriæ - - - - - - -	Car. 1. - - - -	University Lib. Camb.	P. 1.
PRIVY SEALS and Bills - - - - - -	1 Jac. 1. to 1800 -	Duchy Office -	C. 6.
AWARDS for Inclosures - - - - -	1754 to 1800 - -	Duchy Office -	C. 6.
PRESENTATIONS to Livings under Duchy Seal -	1510 to 1800 - -	Duchy Office -	C. 6.
COURT ROLLS:			
Of Manors formerly of the Duchy, and of those now in Demise - - - -	1283 to 1800 - -	Duchy Office -	C. 6.
LEASES:			
Registers of, together with Warrants and other Documents under Sign Manual - -	51 Ed. 3. to 8 H. 6.	Duchy Office -	C. 6.
Drafts and Inrolments of - - - -	1 Hen. 8. to 1800	Duchy Office -	C. 6.
RENTALS and PARTICULARS:			
Of Duchy Lands, Alphabetically arranged -	51 Ed. 3. to 1800	Duchy Office -	C. 6.
Fee Farm Rent Rolls during the Commonwealth - - - - - - -	Car. 1 & 2. - -	Augmentation Office -	G. 19.
General Rental - - - - - -	1648 - - - -	University Lib. Camb.	P. 1.
The like for Dorset, Somerset, Wilts, and Hants - - - - - - -	1636 to 1640 - -	University Lib. Camb.	P. 1.
ACCOUNTS:			
Of Ministers and Receivers - - -	1135 to 1800 - -	Duchy Office - -	C. 6.
Of Money arising by Sales, under Statutes -	1780 to 1800 - -	Duchy Office - -	C. 6.
Of Receiver in the County of Lancaster, and annexed Lands of Clithero, Furness, and Haulton - - - - - - - -	Date wanting - -	University Library Camb.	P. 1.
PLEADINGS and DECREES—By Bill and Answer -	1 Hen. 7. to 1800 -	Duchy Office - -	C. 6.
REVENUE Proceedings - - - - -	1630 to 1800 - -	Duchy Office - -	C. 6.
COUNTY PALATINE of LANCASTER:			
CHANCERY:			
Bills, Pleadings, Depositions, Orders, and Decrees - - - - - - -	1740 to 1800. Dates wanting before 1740	Register of the County Palatine - - -	H. 13.
COMMON PLEAS:			
Fines and Recoveries, Writs, Minutes, Proceedings in Actions, and Inrolments of Deeds -	Geo. 3. - - -	Prothonotary's Office at Preston - - -	H. 13. b.
The Records before His present Majesty's Reign - - - - - - -	Dates wanting - -	Castle, Lancaster - -	H. 13.
PLEAS of the CROWN:			
Indictments and other Criminal Proceedings, and Books of Entries - - - -	About 50 Years before 1800 - - -	Castle, Lancaster - -	H. 13.

V. COURTS OF JUSTICE—(*continued.*)

RECORDS and other INSTRUMENTS.	DATE.	WHERE KEPT.	Appendix to the Firft Report.
3. ESTABLISHED JURISDICTION—(*continued.*)			
County Palatine of Durham:			
Chancery:			
Curfitors Office - - - - - -	— —	Exchequer, Durham -	H. 12.
Præcipes for Writs of the Chancery of Durham	Date wanting.		
Affidavits of Debt - - - - - -			
Writs of the King's Courts, on which the Bifhop's Mandate iffues - - - -			
Books of Entries of Writs - - - -	1780 to 1800.		
Clofe Rolls of the Latin Chancery - -	1333 to 1800.		
Copyhold Books - - - - - -	Hen. 5. to 17 Jac. 1.		
Inquifitions poft Mortem - - - -	1333 to 1628.		
Mandates and Returns of Writs for Parliament	1727 to 1800.		
Registers Office:			
Decrees and Orders - - - -	1613 to 1800 - -	Ibidem - - -	H. 12.
Awards upon Inclofures - - - -	Date wanting - -		
Common Pleas:			
Writs and Pleadings in Suits, Recognizances, &c.	Date wanting - -	Caftle, Durham - -	
Rolls of Fines and Recoveries - - -	Eliz. to 1800 - -		
Pleas of the Crown:			
Indictments, Informations, Writs and Returns, Recognizances, &c. - - - -	Dates wanting - -	Clerk of the Crown Dur.	
Cinque Ports:			
Chancery:—Books of Entry of Proceedings - -	1615 to 1717 - -	Regifter of the Cinque Ports - - -	H. 14.
Admiralty:			
Books of Entry of Proceedings - - -	1632 to 1800 - -		
Papers of Claims of Derelicts, Salvage, &c. -			
Court of Lode-manage:			
Books of Entry of Proceedings - - -	1496 to 1800 - -		
Miscellaneous Collection of Papers relating to the Cinque Ports - - - - - - - -	Date wanting - -	Britifh Mufeum - -	U.
Les Services que les Barons des Cinq. Ports Doivent au Roi par mer - - - - - -	14th Century - -	Corp. Chrifti Coll. Cam.	P. 5.
Stannary Courts:			
Suits in the Vice Warden's Court:			
Regifters and Entries of Suits and Proceedings	1760 to 1800 - -	Vice Warden of Stannaries	H. 16.
Appeals in Stannary Caufes - - - - -	1788 to 1794 - -	Duchy of Cornwall Office	C. 7.
Proceedings in the Four Law Courts:			
Books of Proceedings - - - -	1751 to 1800 -	Stewards of the Courts -	H. 17.
Plaint and Entry Papers - - - -			
Certificates of Tin fmelted - - - -			
Proclamations of Tin Bounds - - -			
Act of Convocation of the Stannaries - - -	26 Geo. 3. - - -	Duchy Office - -	C. 7.
Miscellaneous Collection relating to the Stannaries - - - - - - - -	Date wanting - -	Inner Temple Library -	Q. 2. b.
Commissions of Sewers:			
Laws and Adjudications - - - - - -	Hen. 7. & feq. - -	Rolls - - - -	D. 1.
- - - - - - - - - - -	Jac. 1. to Car. 2. -	Petty Bag Office - -	D. 5.

V. COURTS OF JUSTICE—*(continued.)*

RECORDS and other INSTRUMENTS.	DATE.	WHERE KEPT.	Appendix to the First Report.
3. ESTABLISHED JURISDICTION—*(continued.)*			
QUARTER SESSIONS AND CLERKS OF THE PEACE:			
THE CLERKS OF THE PEACE have the RECORDS following; viz.	— —	— — —	I. 1. to 52.
The Commissions of the Peace, and Lists of the Justices and Officers. Records of Sessions in Pleas of the Crown, entered upon the Sessions Rolls; comprizing Indictments, Informations, Presentments, Convictions, Inquisitions, Recognizances, &c. Minute Books of Orders and Proceedings in Sessions. Presentments and Returns of Constables. Treasurers Accounts. Books of Estreats. Insolvent Debtors Papers. Pardons. Freeholders Lists and Books, and Poll Books of contested County Elections. Inrolments of Deeds and Wills of Papists, of Awards upon Inclosures, and Annuity Memorials. Rolls of Oaths of Allegiance, Qualifications of Militia Officers, &c. Proceedings of Commissioners for raising Men for the Navy and Army. Books of Orders and Contracts for County Works, and Plans of the same, as Bridges, Gaols, &c. and Bonds for Performance thereof. Certificates of having received the Sacrament. Certificates of Men raised under the Navy and Army Acts. Annual Militia and Gaolers Certificates. Registers of Drovers and Higlers Licences, Game-Keepers Deputations, of Boats and Vessels upon Navigations, of Licences to kill Game, for Hair Powder, Victuallers, and Lunatic Houses. Registers of Places of Worship for Dissenters, and of Printing Presses. Claims of Bounties under particular Statutes. Land Tax Assessments. Duplicates of Rules of Friendly Societies. Lists of Names of Members of Free Masons Lodges.	There are few whose Date is earlier than the Reign of Cha. 2.; but the greater Part of those of English Counties have Records of Sessions for more than a Century; altho' very few complete or regular, until within a more modern Period. The earliest Date specified, is of the Year 1547, in the Records of Middlesex. Those of Wales do not go further back than the Reign of Geo. 1. excepting Denbigh and Brecon; the former extending to 1650, and the latter in a regular Series to 1686.	Chiefly in the Shire Halls, or in Public Buildings of the same Kind. The rest in the Private Houses of the Clerks.	
MARITIME COURTS:			
INQUISITIONS:—At Lynn, before the Lord H. Admiral	Hen. 8. - - - -	Lincoln's-Inn Library -	Q. 3.
ADMIRALTY INSTANCE COURT:			
BOOKS and Papers of Proceedings - - - -	1543 to 1800 - -	Doctors Commons.	K.
ADMIRALTY PRIZE COURT:			
PATENTS of Vice Admirals, Governors of Plantations, Judges, and other Officers - -	1660 to 1800 - -	Doctors Commons.	K.
PROCEEDINGS IN CAUSES; viz.			
Monitions, Attestations, Ships Papers, Depositions, &c. - - - - - -	1643 to 1800 - -	Doctors Commons.	K.
In Vice Admiralty Court, South Carolina -	1717 - - - -	Bodleian Library -	O. 1.
Of Commissioners for Prizes - - -	1664 to 1678 - -	British Museum - -	U.
Assignation or Act Books, containing Minutes of each Cause - - - - - -	1664 to 1678 - -	Doctors Commons -	K.
Books of original Sentences of Condemnation, and of Entries of Letters of Marque - -	1664 to 1678 - -	Doctors Commons -	K.
—— Of Registers of Letters of Attorney to Prize Agents - - - - - - - -	1760 to 1800 - -	Doctors Commons -	K.

V. COURTS OF JUSTICE—(continued.)

RECORDS and other INSTRUMENTS.	DATE.	WHERE KEPT.	Appendix to the First Report.
MARITIME COURTS—(continued.)			
ADMIRALTY COURT OF APPEAL IN PRIZE CAUSES:			
PROCEEDINGS in COURT:			
Inhibitions, Citations, &c. - - - - -	1689 to 1800 - -	Doctors Commons - -	K.
Processes or Copies of Proceedings of the Court appealed from - - - - - -			
Assignation Books, containing Minutes of each Appeal - - - - - - -			
COURT of OYER and TERMINER for PIRACY:			
Indictments and other Proceedings - -	1577 to 1800 - -		
ECCLESIASTICAL JURISDICTION:			
CONSISTORY COURTS have the following RECORDS; viz.			
Registers of Episcopal Acts, as Admissions to Holy Orders, Presentations, Institutions, Resignations, Nominations of Curates, Consecrations of Churches, Faculties, Patents of Offices, &c. Judicial Proceedings, Wills and Administration Bonds, Marriage Licence Bonds and Allegations, Appropriations, Endowments, &c. Writs for the Convocation, Visitation Books, Taxations, Compositions, Terriers of Rectories and Vicarages, Copies of Parish Registers.	The earliest Date of any Original Wills preserved in the Consistory Courts, is in that of Lincoln, of 1484; and the earliest Judicial Proceedings are of 1450, in the Courts of York, and of Litchfield and Coventry.		
The earliest Dates of their several Registries are as follow:			
Lincoln - - - - - - -	1209 - - - -	Registry, Lincoln, and Palace, Buckden - -	L. 16.
York - - - - - - - -	1217 - - - -	York Cathedral - -	L. 4.
Exeter - - - - - - - -	1257 - - - -	Exeter - - -	L. 25.
Worcester - - - - - - -	1268 - - - -	Register Office Worcester	L. 10.
Hereford - - - - - - -	1275 - - - -	Hereford Cathedral -	L. 11.
Winchester - - - - - - -	1280 - - - -	Winchester Cathedral -	L. 7.
Salisbury - - - - - - -	1298 - - - -	Palace, Salisbury - -	L. 17.
Litchfield and Coventry - - - - -	1298 - - - -	Register Office Lichfield -	L. 13.
Norwich - - - - - - - -	1299 - - - -	Register Office Norwich -	L. 22.
London - - - - - - - -	1306 - - - -	St. Paul's - - -	L. 5.
Bath and Wells - - - - - -	1316 - - - -	Bishop's Palace Wells -	L. 8.
Ely - - - - - - - -	1337 - - - -	St. Mary's Cambridge -	L. 9.
Chichester - - - - - - -	1396 - - - -	Register's House Chich.	L. 27.
Rochester - - - - - - -	1440 - - - -	Chap. House. Rochester -	N. 16.
Chester - - - - - - - -	1500 - - - -	Registry, Chester - -	L. 18.
Gloucester - - - - - - -	1541 - - - -	Registry, Gloucester -	L. 20.
Bangor - - - - - - - -	1542 - - - -	Record Room, Bangor -	L. 12.
Oxford - - - - - - - -	1543 - - - -	Registry, Oxford - -	L. 28.
St. Asaph - - - - - - -	1600 - - - -	Registry, St. Asaph - -	L. 14.
Bristol - - - - - - - -	1682 - - - -	— — —	L. 26.
		And in some of the Archidiaconal Registries of the several Dioceses.	
ARCHIEPISCOPAL COURTS:			
COURT of ARCHES of the ARCHBISHOP of CANTERBURY:			
Proceedings on Appeals from inferior Jurisdictions - - - - - - -	1666 to 1800 - -	Register's House - -	L. 2.
Original Wills in Cases of Appeal - -	1666 to 1800 - -		
Collection of Proceedings - - - -	Eliz. - - - -	University Library, Camb.	P. 1.
COURTS of AUDIENCE and FACULTIES, CANTERBURY:			
Registers of the See - - - - - -	1279 to 1800 - -	Lambeth Library, and Doctors Commons -	T. & K.
PREROGATIVE COURT of CANTERBURY:			
(See Charters relating to the See of Canterbury, in the Return from the Lambeth Library, Appendix T.)			

V. COURTS OF JUSTICE—(continued.)

RECORDS and other INSTRUMENTS.	DATE.	WHERE KEPT.	Appendix to the First Report.
ARCHIEPISCOPAL COURTS—(continued.)			
Original Wills - - - - - - -	1505 to 1800	Doctors Commons - -	K.
Transcripts of Wills - - - - -	1383 to 1800	Doctors Commons	K.
Proceedings Testamentary - - - -	1526 to 1800	Doctors Commons	K.
Registers of Canterbury - - - -	1279 to 1747 - -	Lambeth Library - -	T.
The like - - - - - - -	1747 to 1800 - -	Doctors Commons - -	K.
PREROGATIVE COURT of YORK: - - - -	- - - - - -	Cathedral, York - - -	L. 3.
Original Wills - - - - - - -	1590 to 1800.		
Transcripts - - - - - - -	1389 to 1800.		
Proceedings Testamentary - - - -	Date wanting.		
The Wills and Records, during the Vacancy of the See, are preserved by the Dean and Chapter - - - - - - -	1683, and 1686 to 1688 - - - -	Dean and Chapter, York	N. 2.
APPELLATE JURISDICTION:			
COURT of DELEGATES:			
Proceedings in Court - - - - - -	1660 to 1800 - -	Doctors Commons - -	K.
Inhibitions, Citations, Libels, &c. - -	1660 to 1800	Doctors Commons	K.
Commissions of Appeal - - - -	1660 to 1800	Doctors Commons	K.
Assignation or Act Books, containing Minutes of each Cause - - - - - -	1660 to 1800	Doctors Commons	K.
Muniment Books, containing Probates of Wills, &c. - - - - - - - - -	1660 to 1800	Doctors Commons	K.
COLLECTION relating to Ecclesiastical Jurisdiction	Date wanting - -	Inner Temple Library -	Q. 2. b.
DEANS and CHAPTERS:			
Their Records consist of,			
Royal Charters of general Administration, and of Grant and Confirmation of private Rights -	Of various Dates, from the Time of the Conquest.	Generally kept in the Cathedrals or Chapter Houses - - - -	N. 1. to 25.
Copies of Charters.	Of various Dates.	Generally kept in the Cathedrals or Chapter Houses	N. 1. to 25.
Statutes of their own Institutions.	Of various Dates.	Generally kept in the Cathedrals or Chapter Houses	N. 1. to 25.
Chartularies, Ledger Books, and Accounts.	Of various Dates.	Generally kept in the Cathedrals or Chapter Houses	N. 1. to 25.
Papal Constitutions.	Of various Dates.	Generally kept in the Cathedrals or Chapter Houses	N. 1. to 25.
Absolutions and Indulgences.	Of various Dates.	Generally kept in the Cathedrals or Chapter Houses	N. 1. to 25.
Proceedings in Election of Bishops.	Of various Dates.	Generally kept in the Cathedrals or Chapter Houses	N. 1. to 25.
Convocation Writs.	Of various Dates.	Generally kept in the Cathedrals or Chapter Houses	N. 1. to 25.
Register Books.	Of various Dates.	Generally kept in the Cathedrals or Chapter Houses	N. 1. to 25.
Court Rolls.	Of various Dates.	Generally kept in the Cathedrals or Chapter Houses	N. 1. to 25.
Grants in Fee Farm before 1 Eliz.	Of various Dates.	Generally kept in the Cathedrals or Chapter Houses	N. 1. to 25.
Taxations and Valuations.	Of various Dates.	Generally kept in the Cathedrals or Chapter Houses	N. 1. to 25.
Appropriations and Endowments.	Of various Dates.	Generally kept in the Cathedrals or Chapter Houses	N. 1. to 25.
Parliamentary and other Surveys of their Estates, and Parliamentary Deeds of Sale - -	1649 to 1656.	Generally kept in the Cathedrals or Chapter Houses	N. 1. to 25.
Wills and Consistorial Records of Peculiars -	Those of London are mostly subsequent to the Fire in 1666. None of the rest have Dates earlier than the latter Part of the Fifteenth Century specified.	Generally kept in the Cathedrals or Chapter Houses	N. 1. to 25.
COURT FOR OFFENCES COMMITTED IN INDIA:			
LISTS OF PEERS AND COMMONERS, severally named by each House of Parliament for Judges of the Court - - - - - - -	— —	Clerk of the Crown in Chancery - -	D. 2.

VI. UNIVERSITIES, COLLEGES, SCHOOLS, &c.

1. UNIVERSITIES AND COLLEGES:			
CHARTERS:			
Of Foundation, Grant, and Confirmation, and University Statutes. (See Returns of the several Colleges, and of the University Library, Cambridge.)			
Foundation of Magdalen College, Oxford -	Hen. 6. - - - -	Chapter House - - -	A. 1.
REVENUES of the Several Colleges - - - -	37 Hen. 8. - - -	Augmentation Office -	G. 19.
VISITATION by Thomas Lord Cromwell - - -	Hen. 8. - - - -	Peterhouse, Cambridge -	P. 2.
COMMISSION of James II. in the Affair of Magdalen College, Oxford, and Register of Proceedings thereon - - - - - - - - -	1687-8 - - - -	Magdalen Coll. Oxford -	O. 13.

VI. UNIVERSITIES, COLLEGES, SCHOOLS, &c.—(*continued.*)

RECORDS and other INSTRUMENTS.	DATE.	WHERE KEPT.	Appendix to the Firſt Report.
UNIVERSITIES AND COLLEGES—(*continued.*)			
GENERAL MATTERS:			
Letters, &c. relating to the Univerſities	1684 to 1769	New Sate Paper Office	C. 1.
Collections relating to them compiled by Thomas Baker	Date wanting	Britiſh Muſeum	U.
Collection of Statutes of Colleges	Date wanting	Britiſh Muſeum	U.
Indenture between Oxford Univerſity and the Stationer's Company; Confirmation thereof by the High Commiſſion	8 Jac. 1.	Aſhmolean Muſeum	O. 2.
2. ROYAL SCHOOLS, COLLEGES, HOSPITALS, CHAUNTRIES, FREE CHAPELS, FRATERNITIES, and GUILDS.			
PARTICULARS of FOUNDATIONS:			
Charters, &c. of Hoſpital in the Savoy	Hen. 8. to 1702	Surveyor General's Office	G. 14.
Books of the Foundation of Hen. VIIth's Chapel	Hen. 7.	Chapter Houſe	A. 1.
CERTIFICATES and PARTICULARS	Hen. 8. and Ed. 6.	Augmentation Office	G. 19.

VII. ALIENATIONS OF PRIVATE PROPERTY.

RECORDS and other INSTRUMENTS.	DATE.	WHERE KEPT.	Appendix to the Firſt Report.
INROLMENTS IN COUNTY REGISTERS:			
WEST RIDING of YORKSHIRE		Wakefield	M. 4.
Memorials of Deeds, Conveyances, Wills, and Deviſes concerning Lands	1704 to 1800.		
Books of Tranſcripts of ſuch Memorials	1704 to 1800.		
Inrolments of Bargains and Sales	1707 to 1800.		
Memorials of Judgments, Statutes, and Recognizances, and Books of Entry of ſuch Memorials	1707 to 1800.		
Certificates of the Diſcharge of Mortgages, Judgments, &c. and Entries thereof	1708 to 1800.		
Awards under Incloſure Acts; Matters relating to the Leeds Canal	Date wanting.		
EAST RIDING of YORKSHIRE		Beverley	M. 3.
Inrolments of Bargains and Sales, and other Deeds, Wills, and Incumbrances affecting Lands; Books of Memorials of ſuch Inrolments; Books of Memorials of Judgments	1708 to 1800.		
MIDDLESEX		Regiſter Office, Bell Yard	M. 1.
Memorials or Records of Deeds, &c.	1709 to 1800.		
Copies of ſuch Memorials	1709 to 1800.		
Certificates of Diſcharge of Mortgages, &c.	1709 to 1800.		
Inquiſitions under Acts for building Weſtminſter Bridge	Geo. 2.		
NORTH RIDING YORKSHIRE		North Allerton	M. 2.
Memorials of Deeds, Wills, &c. regiſtered	1736 to 1800.		
Inrolments of Bargains and Sales, Deeds, Wills, and Awards	1736 to 1800.		
Books of Entries of Memorials	1736 to 1800.		
FOR DEEDS, WILLS, and COURT ROLLS, of PRIVATE PROPERTY: See the Returns from The Chapter Houſe, Augmentation Office, Britiſh Muſeum, Bodleian Library, Univerſity Library Camb.			

SCOTLAND.

RECORDS and other INSTRUMENTS.	DATE.	WHERE KEPT.	Appendix to the First Report.
1. THE KING.			
ROYAL FAMILY:			
Letters of the Queen of James VI. and the young Princes	Jac. 6.	Advocate's Library	Z.
Charge exhibited by the Regent against Queen Mary	Mary	University Library Camb.	P. 1.
Proceedings against the Queen of Scots	Eliz.	Bodleian Library	O. 1.
TITLE:			
Scotch Rolls	19 Ed. 1. to 22 Ed. 4.		
HOMAGE to the KINGS of ENGLAND:		Tower	A. 2.
Homage Rolls	Ed. 1.		
Carta cujus tit: "Quomodo Edwardus Rex Angliæ receptus est in Superiorem Dominum totius Scotiæ"	19 Ed. 1.		
Mandatum ad Recipiendum Juramentum Regis Scotiæ	2 Hen. 5.	Dean and Chapt. Durh.	N. 24.
Proceeding between Bruce and Baliol, in an antient Roll in Latin	Of uncertain Date	Dean and Chapter Exeter	N. 6.
Renuntiatio Edwardi Regis Angliæ facta Roberto Regi Scotiæ	Ed. 1.	Dean and Chapter Durh.	N. 24.
Charters from Kings of Scotland	(First Date wanting) to 1532	British Museum	U.
GREAT SEAL:			
Record of the Great Seal	About 1318 to 1788	Register House	
Warrants for Writs	Date wanting	Deputy Keeper	
PRIVY SEAL:			V. a.
Record of Privy Seal	1499 to 1774	Register House	
Record of Grants, with the Warrants	1795 to 1800	Ibidem.	
SIGNET OFFICE:			
Minute Book of Writs, with the Warrants	1649 to 1800	Clerks of Signet	W. 3.
Signatures for Precepts	1607 to 1800		
LYON OFFICE:			
ARMORIAL BEARINGS:			
Record of Armorial Bearings of the Royal Family, Bishops, Nobility, Gentry, and Royal Burghs	Since 1678		
PRECEDENCY:			
Register of Processions, Precedency, &c.	Since 1681	Lyon Office	W. 4.
Birth Brief Register	Since 1728		
COURT PROCEEDINGS and Official Acts	1629 to 1800 (not regular)		
CHANCERY:			
Records of Crown Charters, and of Lands holding of the Prince or Stewart	1620 to 1788	Register House	V. a.
	For the current 10 Years	Chancery Office	X. 4.
Commissions, Pardons, and Patents	(First Date wanting) to 1766	Register House	V. a.
	1766 to 1800	Chancery Office	X. 4.
Retours of Services	1547 to 1800		
Precepts on Special Services or Retours	1750 to 1751	Register House	V. a.
Respondes	1588 to 1800		
Charters of Anne of Denmark, Q. of Ja. VI.	Jac. 6.	Advocate's Library	Z.
REVENUES and EXPENSES:			
General Account Books of Exchequer			
Household Accounts			
Expenses of Royal Works			
Treasurers, Comptrollers, &c. Accounts	Of different Periods: the most antient begin in 1449; the latest end in 1659.	Register House	V. a.
Rentals			
Accounts of Thirds of Benefices			
Books of Rates, of the Customs, and of Taxations			
Artillery and Army Accounts			
ACTS OF CIVIL GOVERNMENT:			
CHARTERS:			
Original Charters	Will. L. to 1550	Advocate's Library	Z.
The like, and Proclamations	Date wanting	Register House	V. a.

SCOTLAND—*(continued.)*

RECORDS and other INSTRUMENTS.	DATE.	WHERE KEPT.	Appendix to the First Report.
1. THE KING: Acts of Civil Government *(continued.)*			
State Letters and Dispatches:			
To and from different Princes and States	1505 to 1524		
From James V. and Earl of Arran, to England, France, &c.	1539 to 1542		
Correspondence with France relative to Scots in France	Jac. 6.		
Originals and Copies	Eliz. to Car. 1.	Advocate's Library	Z.
Negotiations with France	Jac. 6.		
The like, with Denmark and Norway	Jac. 6. to Car. 1.		
Earl of Stirling's Letters of Charles I.	1626–7		
Correspondence with Princes of Italy	Jac. 6. to Car. 1.		
The like with Germany, Sweden and Poland	1600 to 1626		
State Papers relating to Public Disturbances	Car. 1.		
State Papers and Treaties	1491 to 1669	Old State Paper Office	C. 1.
State Correspondence, Warrant Books, &c.	1670 to 1756	New State Paper Office	
Ecclesiastical Affairs:			
Bulls of Popes	1155 to 1555		
Chartularies and other Muniments of the Bishoprick of Aberdeen, and of several Religious Houses	11th to 16th Century	Advocate's Library	Z.
Transactions of Presbytery of Aberdeen	1593 to 1600		
The like of Synod of Lothian and Tweedale	1657 to 1661		
A few Records of Ecclesiastical Matters	Date wanting		
2. PARLIAMENT.			
Records of Parliament	1210 to 1707	Register House	V. a.
Peers of Great Britain:			
Warrants of the Elections of Peers to Parliament	1707 to 1798		
Records of the Elections	1761 to 1798		
Returns for the Two last Parliaments for the Time being	— —	Clerk of Crown in Chan.	D. 2.
The like before such Two last	from 1707	Petty Bag Office	D. 5.
Records of Conventions of Estates	Dates wanting	Register House	V.
Minutes of the Convention	March 1689 to 1690	Advocate's Library	Z.
Convention of Burghs:			
Setts of all the Royal Burghs	15th July 1708	City Clerks, Edinburgh	W. 5.
3. PRIVY COUNCIL.			
Acts and Decreets	1571 to 1705	Clerk of Justiciary, Register House	
State Record, or Proceedings in Matters of State	1661 to 1703		V. a.
Some Volumes of the Privy Council Record	1545 to 1644	Lord Clerk Register, Register House	
Writs or Deeds of James VI. by Advice of his Secret Council	1586 to 1588	Advocate's Library	Z.
Writs passing the Signet, with Advice of Privy Council	1630 to 1642		
4. GENERAL REGISTERS.			
Sasines:			
General Register	1617 to 1800		
Particular Register	1600 to 1800	Register House	
Tailzies:			
Record of Tailzies	1685 to 1800		
Record of Inventaries	1695 to 1800		
Interruption or Horning Office:			
Interruptions, Summonses, &c.	1602 to 1780	Ibidem, except for the Current Ten Years; for which Time they remain in the Interruption Office	
Inhibitions, Interdictions, and Petitions for Sequestration	1602 to 1780		
Letters of Hornings	1602 to 1780		
Particular Register of Hornings and Inhibitions	About 1580 to 1800		V. a.
Forfeitures—Registers of Forfeitures	Date wanting		
Cautions:			
Records of Cautionries in Confirmed Testaments	Date wanting	Ibidem	
The like in keeping Lawburrows	Date wanting		
The like for loosing Arrestments	Date wanting		
Allowances of Apprisings, and Abbreviates of Adjudications	1636 to 1785		

SCOTLAND—(*continued.*)

RECORDS and other INSTRUMENTS.	DATE.	WHERE KEPT.	Appendix to the First Report.
5. COURTS OF JUSTICE.			
COURT of SESSION:			
Books of Sederunt	1553	Court Room	X. 1. a.
Annual General Minute Book	Jac. 6. to 1800 *	Register House	X. 1. b.
Records of Deeds registered	1554 to 1800 *	Ibidem	V. a. & X. 1. a.
Extracted Decrees, with the Warrants	1478 to 1800 *	Ibidem	
	* Except for the Current Ten Years, while they remain with the Clerks.		
Books of Council and Session	Date wanting	Ibidem	
Record of Probative Writs	(First Date wanting) to 1800	Ibidem	
JUSTICIARY:			
Scroll or Minute Books	1536 to 1800	Ibidem	V. a.
Warrants of the Minute Books	Complete from 1672		
Books of Adjournal	1685 to 1800		
Records of the Three Circuit Courts	1707 to 1800		
Proceedings on a Commission of Oyer and Terminer	In 1746		
Proceedings of Itinerant Courts	Jac. 4.	Advocate's Library	Z.
COURT of EXCHEQUER:			
Collection of Documents relating to the Exchequer	1264 to 1750		
Antient Record Books of Exchequer, viz.			
Responde Books	1449 to 1659	Register House	V. a.
Signatures			
Decrees of Exchequer			
THE KING'S REMEMBRANCER:			
Exchequer Minutes and Orders	1660 to 1708	Court of Exchequer	X. 3.
Treasury Minutes and Orders	1660 to 1708		
Public Accounts	1688 to 1707		
Signatures	1660 to 1708		
Resignations	1636 to 1703		
Borough Rolls	1300 to 1707		
Rent Rolls of Bishopricks	In 1689 & 1690		
Accounts of Payments to the Army	1689 to 1707		
COURT of JUDICATURE	1707 to 1800.		
Minute Books	— —		
Book of Rules			
Rolls of Judicial Proceedings	— —	Register House	V. a.
Files of Writs	— —		
Register of Decrees and Orders			
Inrolments of Letters Patent		Court of Exchequer	X. 3.
The like of Commissions for Limits of the Ports, with the Returns			
BOARD OF TREASURY:			
Minute Books	— —		
Book of Orders			
Memorials, Petitions, Brieves, and Reports			
Record of Memorials, &c.			
Register of Signatures			
- - - Resignations			
Borough Roll	1708	Register House	V. a.
Record of Patents, Commissions, and Warrants	1707 to 1800	Court of Exchequer	X. 3.
BOARD OF REVENUE:			
Signed Particulars of Accountants	1707 to 1800	Register House	V. a.
Record of the same when declared			
Letter Book	1707 to 1800	Court of Exchequer	X. 3.
Record of Sums paid on Seizures	1707 to 1800	King's Remembrancer	
Controlment Roll of Seizures			
Duplicates of Surveys and Assessed Taxes	1707 to 1800	Register House	V. a.
Record of Appeal	20 Geo. 2. to 1800	Court of Exchequer	X. 3.
- - of Opinions of Crown Counsel	1708 to 1800		
- - of Bonds and Recognizances			
COMMISSION OF FORFEITED ESTATES:			
Books, Accounts, Rent Rolls, and Proceedings of Commissioners	1715		
The like of Estates forfeited in 1745–6, and under the Court of Exchequer	1746 to 1752		
The like of Commissioners	1752 to 1784		

SCOTLAND—(*continued.*)

RECORDS and other INSTRUMENTS.	DATE.	WHERE KEPT.	Appendix to the First Report.
5. COURTS OF JUSTICE: Court of Exchequer (*continued.*)			
Lord Treasurer's Remembrancer:			
Rolls of Sheriffs Accounts	1400 to 1799	Court of Exchequer	X. 3.
Rental of Petty, Feu, and Blanch Duties	1708 to 1800	Court of Exchequer	X. 3.
Orders of Allowances to Sheriffs, &c.	1708 to 1800	Court of Exchequer	X. 3.
Accounts of Payments to Receiver General by Sheriffs, &c.	1708 to 1800	Court of Exchequer	X. 3.
Roll of Crown Vassals and other Accountants	1708 to 1800	Court of Exchequer	X. 3.
Book of Fiars	1708 to 1800	Court of Exchequer	X. 3.
Petitions, Reports, and Orders	1708 to 1800	Court of Exchequer	X. 3.
Record of Public Accounts	1708 to 1800	Court of Exchequer	X. 3.
- - of Letters Patent, Commissions, and Imprest Warrants	1708 to 1800	Court of Exchequer	X. 3.
Inrolments of Letters Patent	1708 to 1800	Court of Exchequer	X. 3.
Roll of Valuation of Argyle	In 1750	Court of Exchequer	X. 3.
Auditor's Office:			
Chamberlains Rolls	1326 to 1549	Register House	V. a.
Property Roll	1709 to 1800	Court of Exchequer	X. 3.
Rentals of Bishopricks	1708 to 1800	Court of Exchequer	X. 3.
Record of Compositions on Signatures	1708 to 1800	Court of Exchequer	X. 3.
- - - - of Compositions on Leases of Bishops Teinds	1710 to 1800	Court of Exchequer	X. 3.
- - - - of Public Accounts	1707 to 1800	Court of Exchequer	X. 3.
- - - - of Civil List Establishment	1708 to 1800	Court of Exchequer	X. 3.
- - - - of Signs Manual, Patents, Grants, &c.	1709 to 1800	Court of Exchequer	X. 3.
- - - - of Commissions to all Officers on the Establishment	1709 to 1800	Court of Exchequer	X. 3.
Clerk of the Pipe:			
Great Roll of Public Accounts	1708 to 1800. There are likewise a few Accounts earlier	Register House	V. a.
Record Books of Quietuses	1708 to 1800. There are likewise a few Accounts earlier	Register House	V. a.
Admiralty:			
Commissions to the Judge Admirals, and by them to their Officers	1674 & 1702 to 1800	Register House	V. a.
Commissions of Vice Admiralty	1674 & 1702 to 1800	Register House	V. a.
Bonds of Caution in Causes	1674 & 1702 to 1800	Register House	V. a.
Indentures between Seamen	1674 & 1702 to 1800	Register House	V. a.
Diet Books of the Procedure in Actions	1702 to 1800	Register House	V. a.
Receipt Books	1702 to 1800	Register House	V. a.
Commissary Court:			
Register of Causes Consistorial, with the Warrants or Originals	1560 to 1799	Register House	V. a.
Edicts or Applications for Administration	1560 to 1799	Register House	V. a.
Tutorial and Curatorial Inventaries	1560 to 1799	Register House	V. a.
Suits against Executors	1560 to 1799	Register House	V. a.
Record for Testaments	1560 to 1799	Register House	V. a.
Record of Bonds granted by Executors	1560 to 1799	Register House	V. a.
Register of Deeds, Wills, and other Writings		Register House	V. a.
Teind Office, or Court of Commission:			
Reports of Sub-commissioners of sundry Presbyteries	1629 to 1631	Register House	V. a.
Procedure of the High Commission	1630 to 1633	Register House	V. a.
Procedure of the Court of Commission, with the Decreets and Warrants	1707 to 1800	Register House	V. a.
Various Papers relative to Teinds	Date wanting	Register House	V. a.
Sheriff Courts:			
Contain the Records following; viz. of			
Judicial Proceedings	Of Dates specified in the next Page, and in general regular, for the greater Part of the Period since the Union to the Year 1800.	Sometimes in the Town Halls of the Chief Burghs, but more frequently in the Houses of the Sheriff Clerks.	
Hornings, Inhibitions, &c. (which are regularly transmitted to the General Register at Edinburgh)			
Deeds registered			
Probative Writs			
Freeholders Courts, and Parliament Elections			
Services			
Tutorial and Curatorial Acts and Inventaries			
Annual Fiars, and Monthly Prices of Grain			
Improvement of Entailed Estates	1770 to 1800		
Commissions to Sheriffs			
Lists of Jurors			

SCOTLAND—(continued.)

RECORDS and other INSTRUMENTS.	DATE.	WHERE KEPT.	Appendix to the First Report.
5. COURTS OF JUSTICE: SHERIFF COURTS (continued.)			
The earliest Dates specified of the above Records are as following; viz. for		Sometimes in the Town Halls of the Chief Burghs, but more frequently in the Houses of the Sheriff Clerks.	See the Letter Y.—The Returns are placed in the Alphabetical Order of the Counties.
JUDICIAL PROCEEDINGS, in			
Perth	1543		
Orkney	1612		
Dumfries	1674		
Shetland	1687		
Aberdeen and Kincardine	1697		
Kirkudbright and Clackmannan	1698		
Elgin, Wigtown, and Forfar	1700		
Argyle and Edinburgh	1709		
Ayr	1717		
Inverness	1720		
Renfrew	1739		
Lanerk	1748		
DEEDS registered, in			
Perth	1570		
Orkney	1611		
Aberdeen	1630		
Elgin	1654		
Argyle, Lanerk, and Kirkudbright	1665–7		
Ayr	1682		
Wigtown	1690		
Forfar	1693		
Kincardine	1697		
Edinburgh, Fife, and Linlithgow	1700		
Clackmannan and Inverness	1707		
PROBATIVE WRITS, in			
Aberdeen	1630		
Kincardine	1715		
Dumfries	1716		
Ayr	1735		
Kirkudbright	1746		
FREEHOLDERS COURTS, and ELECTIONS, in			
Kincardine	1698		
Wigtown and Ayr	1702		
Argyle, Edinburgh, and Haddington	1707		
Perth	1724		
Aberdeen, Forfar, and Inverness	1727		
Dumfries, Fife, Linlithgow, and Orkney	1733–4		
[Record of Elections in Linlithgow]	1685		
Kirkudbright	1739		
SERVICES, in			
Perth	1596		
Aberdeen	1649		
Kincardine	1664		
Wigtown	1676		
Lanerk	1696		
Argyle	1700		
Ayr and Dumfries	1715		
Edinburgh	1750		
Lanerk	1754		
TUTORIAL, &c. ACTS in			
Perth	1597		
Aberdeen	1649		
Kincardine	1688		
Kirkudbright	1744		
ANNUAL FIARS, in			
Dumfries, Haddington, and Perth	1626–30		
Ayr	1658		
Linlithgow	1667		
Fife	1700		
Aberdeen	1705		
Forfar	1728		
Kincardine	1752		
6. UNIVERSITIES:			
Papers relative to Visitations of the Universities	Date wanting	Register House	V. a.

IRELAND.

RECORDS and other INSTRUMENTS.	DATE.	WHERE KEPT.	Appendix to the First Report.
PETITIONS - - - - - - - -	Ed. 1. & feq. - -	Tower - - - -	A. 2.
CHARTERS OF GRANT:			
Of Ireland, Gafcony, &c. to Prince Edward -	Hen. 3. - - - -	Chapter Houfe - -	A. 1.
To the Town of Waterford - -	Ed. 1. & 2. - - -	Corp. Chr. Coll. Camb.	P. 5.
Pro Emendatione Status Hiberniæ - -	Ed. 1. - - - - -		
- - - - - OF PARDON - - - - - -	Hen. 5. - - - -	Chapter Houfe - -	A. 1.
ANTIENT REVENUE of the CROWN:			
Collection of Grants, Leafes, &c. of the King's Lands - - - - - - - -	Dates wanting - -	Bodleian Library, Oxford	O. 1.
ORDERS and PROCEEDINGS of COUNCIL:			
For Cuftoms - - - - - - -	43 Ed. 3. - - -	Chapter Houfe - -	A. 1.
For Commiffions of Royal Affent to Statutes -	1703 to 1800 - -	Clerk of Crown in Chan.	D. 2.
Speeches in Council upon the Truce concluded by the Earl of Effex - - - - -	Eliz. - - - - -	University Lib. Camb.	P. 1.
Articles relating to the Settlement of Munfter -	Eliz. - - - - -		
Orders of Committee of Parliament for Ireland	1641 to 1644 - -	Bodleian Library - -	O. 1.
Account of Ships and Forces fent to Ireland -	1691 - - - -		
BILLS of PARLIAMENT of IRELAND, tranfmitted for the King's Approbation - - - - - -	Till 1782 - - -	Clerk of Crown in Chan.	D. 2.
ACTS PASSED:			
Rolls of - - - - - - - -	10 Car. 1. - - -	Rolls - - - - -	D. 1.
CORRESPONDENCE with LORDS JUSTICES, and LIEUTENANTS:			
Relating to Forfeited Eftates, Government, and Revenue - - - - - - -	1500 to 1676 - -	Old State Paper Office -	C. 1.
Collection of Correfpondence - - -	Date wanting - -	Chapter Houfe - -	A. 1.
Letters of Perrott, Lord Deputy - -	1584 to 1586 - -	Bodleian Library - -	O. 1.
Correfpondence - - - - - -	1684 to 1775 - -	New State Paper Office -	C. 1.
Entries and Copies of Royal Letters - -	1626 to 1800 - -	Signet Office - - -	C. 4.
Ormond Papers of Correfpondence - -	Car. 2. - - - -	Bodleian Library. *Carte* -	O. 1.
Reprefentation des Maires, Bailiffes, et Communautez des Cités, au Juftices et Confeil de l' Etat d' Irelande - - - - - -	Date wanting - -	Corp. Chrifti Coll. Camb.	P. 5.
ACCOUNTS and MISCELLANEOUS PAPERS:			
Collection of - - - - - - -	Date wanting - -	Chapter Houfe - -	A. 1.
Accounts of Treafurer and Chamberlain in Ireland - - - - - - - -	Ed. 1. & feq. - -	King's Rem. Excheq. -	G. 6. a.
Status Scaccarii Dublin' - - - -	Ed. 1. - - - -		
Aid from Ireland to Edward III. - -	Ed. 3. - - - -	Dean and Chapter Weftm.	N. 12. b.
Collection relating to the Revenue, Hiftory, Antiquities, and Municipal Laws of Ireland -	Dates wanting - -	Britifh Mufeum - -	U.
Accounts of Lord Deputy, Treafurer at War, and Victualling Accounts - - -	Mar. to Jac. 1. and 1649 to 1650 -	Auditors Land Revenue -	G. 15. a.

ENGLISH DOMINIONS BEYOND THE SEA.

RECORDS and other INSTRUMENTS.	DATE.	WHERE KEPT.	Appendix to the First Report.
1. ISLE OF MAN.			
Commission and Inquisition of Crown Lands there - - - - - - - -	24 Eliz. - - - -	King's Rememb. Excheq.	G. 6. a.
Instructions to Commissioners relative to the Rights of the Crown and Duke of Athol, and Report thereon - - - - - -	31 Geo. 3. - -	Secretary of State's Office, Home Departm nt.	
2. GUERNSEY, JERSEY, &c.			
Various Judicial and other Proceedings relating to these Islands - - - - -	Ed. 1, 2, & 3. - -	Chapter House - -	A. 1.
Papers relating to them, and Reports: Liberties, &c. - - - - - - - -	1498 to 1705 - -	Old State Paper Office -	C. 1.
The like - - - - - - - - -	1573 to 1756 - -	New State Paper Office -	C. 1.
Extent of Profits of Jersey - - -	5 Ed 3. - - -	King's Rememb. Excheq.	G. 6. a.
Affairs of Jersey - - - - - -	Date wanting - -	Bodleian Library - -	O. 1.
Commission and Return upon the State of the Laws relative to a Trial by Jury, &c. - -	31 & 33 Geo. 3. -	Council Office - -	C. 2.
3. IN FRANCE.			
Gascon Rolls - - - - - - - -	26 Hen. 3. to 39 H. 6.	Tower - - - -	A. 2.
Norman Rolls - - - - - - - -	2 John to 10 Hen. 5.	Tower - - - -	A. 2.
French Rolls - - - - - - - -	16 H. 3. to 22 Ed. 4.	Tower - - - -	A. 2.
Declaration of State of Revenue of France, in the Time of John Duke of Bedford, Regent	1427-8 - - - -	Antiq. Society Library -	S.
STAPLE of CALAIS:			
Accounts of - - - - - - - -	Hen. 8. - - -	Chapter House - -	A. 1.
The like, Calais and Guisnes - - -	Hen. 8 & Ed. 6. -	Auditors Land Revenue -	G. 15. a.
Patents of Offices in the Treaty or Foreign Rolls	- - - - - -	Rolls - - - -	D. 1.
Victualling Accounts of this and other Towns in France - - - - - - -	Hen. 8. & Ed. 6. -	Auditors Land Revenue -	G. 15. a.
4. GIBRALTAR AND MINORCA.			
Official Correspondence and Papers - -	1705 to 1767 - -	New State Paper Office -	C. 1.
TANGIER.			
Letters, Accounts, &c. relating to - -	Car. 2. - - - -	Bodleian Library - -	O. 1.
Papers relating to the Trade - - -	1661 to 1677 - -	Old State Paper Office -	C. 1.
5. OTHER FOREIGN DOMINIONS.			
See PLANTATIONS, &c. &c.			

II.

TABLE OF THE PUBLIC RECORDS,

&c.

ALPHABETICALLY ARRANGED;

WITH

Explanatory Notes and References to the moſt authentic Copies, Catalogues, and Indexes, relating thereto.

FAITHFULLY ABSTRACTED
FROM THE ORIGINAL RETURNS,

BY

J. PLANTA,
JOHN CALEY.

JULY 1800.

7 C 2

TABLE II.

Alphabetical Arrangement of the Public Records.

RECORDS and other INSTRUMENTS.	DATE.	WHERE KEPT.	Appendix to the First Report.
ABBEY LANDS:			
Many Records refpecting them	Various Dates	Augmentation Office	G. 19. a.
Leafes of fome of them	Hen. 8. Edw. 6.	King's Rememb. Office	G. 6. a.
Entries of Leafes	Hen. 8.	King's Rememb. Office	G. 6. a.
Calendars of Leafes	34, 35, 37 Hen. 8.	King's Rememb. Office	G. 6. a.
Rentals of, and of Forfeited Eftates in Effex, Herts, Middlefex, and London	1638	Univerfity Library, Camb.	P. 1.
Grants of, on the Patent Rolls. Vide Patent Rolls.			
ABBIES, &c.			
Chartularies of various	— —	Augmentation Office	G. 19. a.
Repertory of Foundations and Endowments of, preferved in the Tower	— —	Britifh Mufeum	U.
Minifters Accounts of	— —	Augmentation Office	G. 19. a.
Minifters Accounts of, feveral	Hen. 3. to Eliz.	King's Rememb. Office	G. 6. a.
Surveys of, previous and fubfequent to the Diffolution	Temp. Hen. 8.	Augmentation Office	G. 19. a.
Surveys and Valuations of	26 Hen. 8.	Firft Fruits Office	G. 18.
Surveys of feveral, under the Value of £. 200.	28 Hen. 8.	Receipt of the Exchequer	A. 1. a.
v. Endowments.—Ministers Accounts.			
ABBOTS:			
Charters, being Grants to them	1185 to 1640	Britifh Mufeum	U.
Penfions granted to Abbots after the Diffolution	Hen. 8.	Augmentation Office	G. 19. a.
v. Pensions.			
ACCOUNTS, Public:			
Refpecting the Victualling and Muftering of Forces, Ordnance, Cuftoms, Calais, Guifnes	Hen. 8. to Jac. 1.	Auditors Office Land Rev.	G. 15.
Office Books delivered over to the Commiffioners for Auditing the Public Accounts by the late Auditors of Impreft	1622 to 1785	Office for Auditing Pub. Acc.	G. 5. a.
Accounts	Jac. 2. & Will. 3.	Bodleian Library	O. 1.
Books and Papers belonging to the Commiffion for ftating the Public Accounts, in the Reign of King William III. &c.	Will. 3.	Paper Office, Houfe of Commons	B. 2.
Minutes of the Commiffioners of Public Accounts, who fat from 1690 to 1697	1690 to 1697	Britifh Mufeum	U.
Proceedings of the Commiffioners for ftating the Public Accounts of the Kingdom	1690 to 1697	Britifh Mufeum	U.
Books and Papers of the Commiffioners of Public Accounts, who fat from 1780 to 1787	1780 to 1787	Clerk of the Journals of the Houfe of Commons	B. 2.
Accounts both Ordinary and Extraordinary, with the Vouchers relating thereto, both before and fubfequent to the Inftitution of the Board	1785	Office of the Commiffioners for Auditing the Public Accounts	G. 5. a.
Office Books, being Entries of the Proceedings of the Commiffioners for Auditing the Public Accounts; viz. Minutes, Reports to the Treafury, Letters from and to the Treafury, Memorials of Accountants, Regifters of Accounts, Entries of Impreft Rolls, Inftructions to the Public Officers, &c.	1785 to the prefent Time	Office of the Commiffioners for Auditing the Public Accounts	G. 5. a.
Duplicates of the Declared Accounts	— —		
Commiffioners of, their Oaths	— —	Petty Bag Office	*Page* 229.
v. Customs.—Excise.—Imprest.			

ALPHABETICAL ARRANGEMENT OF THE PUBLIC RECORDS.

RECORDS and other INSTRUMENTS.	DATE.	WHERE KEPT.	Appendix to the First Report.
ADMIRALTY:			
Various Papers relating thereto - - -	— —	British Museum - - - -	U.
Liber Niger—Copy of - - - - - -	— —	Lincoln's Inn Library - -	Q. 3.
Instructions, Committee Books, &c. of the Admiralty - - - - - - -	— —	Bodleian Library - - -	O. 1.
Commissions, Warrants, Estimates, Surveys, &c. -	1509 to 1716 - -	State Paper Office - - -	C. 1. a.
Inventory of the Ships of King Hen. VIII. in Charge of Officers of the Admiralty; with the Names, Tonnage, and Number of Men, and their Stations - - - - - - - -	1 Edw. 6. - -	Library of Society of Antiquaries - - - - - -	S.
Letters from Admirals and Commanders, to the Lords of the Admiralty, Lists of Ships and Vessels, Warrants, Commissions, &c. - -	1689 to 1761 - -	State Paper Office - - -	C. 1. a.
v. Claus Rolls.			
Court of:			
Piracy—Trials, &c. for - - - - - -	1577		
Patents of Vice Admirals of Counties, &c. - - } Patents of Governors of Islands and Plantations - } Patents of Judges and other Officers of that Court }	1660		
Prize Court:			
Assignation or Act Books - - - - - } Sentences of Condemnation - - - - } Letters of Marque - - - - - - }	1643		
Registers of Letters of Attorney to Agents for Prizes - - - - - - - -	1760 } to the present Time	Admiralty Court, Doctors Commons - - - -	K.
v. Prizes.			
Court of Appeal for Prizes:			
Assignation Books - - - - - -	1689		
Instance Court:			
Proceedings of - - - - - - -	1543		
Court of Delegates:			
Assignation or Act Books - - - - } Muniment Books - - - - - - }	1660		
ADVOWSONS. *v.* Claus Rolls.			
AFFIDAVITS:			
To Copies of Precipes and Warrants of Attorney for suffering Recoveries, acknowledged by Tenants or Vouchees - - - - - -	14 Geo. 3. to the present Time.	Clerk of Returns Prothonotary's Office - - -	F. 8.
Register of Affidavits in Chancery, his Oath - -	— —	Clerk of the Crown - - -	*Page* 221.
v. Exchequer of Account.			
AFRICAN COMPANY:			
Letters relating thereto - - - - - -	1680 to 1686 -	Bodleian Library - - -	O. 1.
AIDS and SUBSIDIES:			
Papers relating thereto - - - - - -	1199 to 1666 -	State Paper Office - -	C. 1. a.
Subsidy and Tax Rolls - - - - - -	20 Edw. 1. et seq.	King's Rememb. Office -	G. 6. a.
Scutages and Subsidies - - - - - -	38 Edw. 1. - -	Tower - - - - - -	A. 2. a.
Aids from Ireland - - - - - -	Edw. 3. - -	Dean & Chapter Westminster	N. 12. b.
Accounts of Tenths and Subsidies - - -	Edw. 3. to Hen. 4.	Augmentation Office - -	G. 19. a.
Nonæ Rolls - - - - - - -	14 Edw. 3. - -	} King's Rememb. Office	G. 6. a.
Commission on Subsidy granted - - -	20 Edw. 3. - -	}	
Book of - - - - - - - -	14 Edw. 3. - -	}	
Records concerning Scutages and Subsidies - -	5 Hen. 4. - -	Tower - - - - - -	A. 2. a.
Books of Tenths and Fifteenths of the Laity -	3 Hen. 5. - -	} King's Rememb. Office -	G. 6. a.
Books of Subsidies and Knights Fees - -	Hen. 6. - - -	}	
Account of Tenths and Fifteenths - - -	Eliz. - - - -	} Auditors Office Land Rev.	G. 15.
Collectors Acquittances of the Subsidy - -	21 Jac. 1. - -	}	
Account of Quarterly Poll and Subsidy - -	Will. 3. - - -	King's Rememb. Office - -	G. 6. a.
v. Claus Rolls.—Revenue Royal.—Tenths.			
ALBAN'S, St. Abbey:			
Register of, &c. - - - - - - - -	— —	University Library, Cambridge - - - - - -	P. 1.
v. Chartularies.—Henry VII.			

ALPHABETICAL ARRANGEMENT OF THE PUBLIC RECORDS.

RECORDS and other INSTRUMENTS.	DATE.	WHERE KEPT.	Appendix to the First Report.
ALBEMARLE, DUKE OF:			
Lands granted to him	— —	Office of Surv. Gen. Crown Lands	G. 14.
ALDERNEY. *v.* GUERNSEY.—JERSEY.			
ALGIERS AND TRIPOLY:			
Abstracts of Accounts concerning them	1675	Bodleian Library	O. 1.
ALIENATION:			
Writs of Covenant, Entries of	1571 to the present Time	Alienation Office	G. 17.
Writs of Covenant on which Fines have been paid	1576 to the present Time	Alienation Office	G. 17.
Collections respecting the Alienation Office	— —	Inner Temple Library	Q. 2 b.
Books of the Commissioners of	Eliz. to Car. 2.	Audit. Office Land Rev.	G. 15.
Summonses and Returns of Sheriffs of Alienation Fines	Car. to Jac.	Audit. Office Land Rev.	G. 15.
Licences and Pardons for. *v.* PATENT ROLLS.			
ALIEN PRIORIES:			
Extents or Surveys of them	— —	King's Rememb. Office	G. 6. a.
Valuations and Ministers Accounts of	— —	King's Rememb. Office	G. 6. a.
Escheat, Rolls of	Edw. 1. to Ric. 2.	King's Rememb. Office	G. 6. a.
Perambulations, Surveys and Extents of	Eliz.	King's Rememb. Office	G. 6. a.
ALLEGIANCE, AND SUPREMACY AND ABJURATION:			
Oaths to be taken by Persons requiring them to be administered	— —	Petty Bag Office	*Page* 228.
ALNAGERS:			
Accounts of	— —	King's Rememb. Office	G. 6. a.
AMBASSADORS:			
Papers relating to	— —	Dean and Chapter Westm.	N. 12. b.
Instructions to, Copies of	— —	Inner Temple Library	Q. 2. b.
Messengers, &c. Account of their Expenses	— —	King's Rememb. Office	G. 6. a.
Commissions, Credentials, and Instructions to	Edw. 3. to Geo. 1.	British Museum	U
Instructions to them at the Emperor's Court	Hen. 8.	University Library, Camb.	P. 1.
Commissions, Instructions, Credentials, Letters to, their Correspondences, &c.	1509 to 1706	State Paper Office	C. 1. a.
Instructions to them at the French Court	Eliz.	University Library Camb.	P. 1.
Instructions to several of them at the different Courts of Europe	Eliz.	University Library Camb.	P. 1.
Correspondence with, chiefly in France	Eliz.	Bodleian Library	O. 1.
Memorial for the Colloquy at Bruges	1564	University Library, Camb.	P. 1.
Commissions to, with Eastern Princes	1576 to 1669	State Paper Office	C. 1. a.
Original Letters and Instructions relative to Sweden	Jac. 1. Car. 1. & 2.	Bodleian Library	O. 1.
Instructions, Commissions, and Credentials for	1663 to 1672	Bodleian Library	O. 1.
Papers relating to Ambassadors Privileges	1672 to 1768	State Paper Office	C. 1. a.
Letters from Foreign Ministers	1710 to 1756	State Paper Office	C. 1. a.
v. CLAUS ROLLS.—STATE PAPERS.			
AMERCIAMENTS:			
Many Rolls of	Edw. 4. and Ric. 3.	Auditors Office Land Rev.	G. 15.
AMERICA AND WEST INDIES:			
Letters from Governors of Provinces, Instructions, Orders in Council, &c.	1679 to 1770	State Paper Office	C. 1. a.
v. PLANTATIONS.—TRADE FOREIGN.			
AMERICAN CLAIMS:			
Issue Books, Assignments, Letters of Attorney, &c. of the American Payments and Tontine	— —	Office for American Payments and Tontine, Auditors Office, Exchequer	G. 1.
v. EXCHEQUER OF RECEIPT.			
ANNE OF DENMARK, QUEEN OF JAMES I.			
Accounts of her Receiver General	— —	Audit. Office Land Rev.	G. 15.
Inventories of her Jewels	1605 to 1615	Audit. Office Land Rev.	G. 15.
Account of her Estates	1605 to 1615	Audit. Office Land Rev.	G. 15.
v. LAND REVENUE.			
ANNUITIES:			
Register of Grants of Annuities pursuant to Stat.	3 Geo. 3.	Clerks of the Peace	
Memorials for Securities of, and Inrolments of	17 Geo. 3. to the present Time	Inrolment Office	D. 13.
APPROPRIATIONS:			
Of Churches, Chapels, &c.	— —	Augmentation Office	G. 19. a.

ALPHABETICAL ARRANGEMENT OF THE PUBLIC RECORDS.

RECORDS and other INSTRUMENTS.	DATE.	WHERE KEPT.	Appendix to the Firſt Report.
ARCHBISHOPRICKS:			
Eccleſiaſtical Charters, being Grants thereto and to others	1185 to 1640	Britiſh Muſeum	U.
Surveys and Valuations of	26 Hen. 8.	Firſt Fruits Office	G. 18.
v. Canterbury and York.—Chartæ Antiquæ.			
ARCHDEACONRIES:			
Surveys and Valuations of	26 Hen. 8.		
ARCHES, Court of:			
A Collection of Libels, Sentences, Depoſitions, Inhibitions, &c. in this and other Eccleſiaſtical Courts	Temp. Eliz.	Univerſity Library, Camb.	P. 1.
Proceedings in Cauſes appealed, Office Copies of	1666 to the preſent Time	Regiſtry of the Court of Arches	L. 2.
Wills Original, coming before the ſaid Court of Appeal			
ARMORIAL BEARINGS:			
Books of Arms of Knights of the Garter and Bath	— —	College of Arms	C. 8.
Books of Arms and Pedigrees during the Viſitations	— —		
Dockets and Copies of all Grants of Arms	— —		
Books of Arms and Pedigrees	Various Dates	Britiſh Muſeum	U.
Papers of Heraldry	Various Dates	Inner Temple Library	Q. 2. b.
Books of the Earl Marſhal reſpecting the Arms of the Blood Royal	Temp. Eliz.	College of Arms	C. 8.
Arms and Pedigrees of the Peers of the Realm	1767 to preſent Time		
The like of Baronets	1783 to preſent Time		
v. Baronets.—Bath.—Garter.—Heraldry.—Marshal, Earl.—Pedigrees.—Peers.—Visitations.			
ARMS, College of:			
Charter of Privileges with Confirmations	Edw. 6.	Aſhmolean Muſeum	C. 2.
ARMY:			
Accounts of	— —	King's Rememb. Office	G. 6.
An Indenture of War between Henry IV. and the Prince of Wales, whereby the Prince engages to ſerve his Father with 600 Men at Arms and 1,800 Archers	Hen. 4.	Dean & Chapter Weſtm.	N. 12. b.
Roll of Expenſes of the War of Henry VII. to aſſiſt theDucheſs of Britanny	Hen. 7.		
Accounts relating to the War with Scotland	Hen. 8.	Audit. Office Land Rev.	G. 15.
Accounts of Diſburſements	Edw. 6.		
Commiſſions, Inſtructions, Muſters, Letters, &c.	1586 to 1705	State Paper Office	C. 1. a.
Orders for raiſing a Regiment by the Marquis of Hamilton, and the Officers Pay	Car. 1.	Univerſity Library, Camb.	P. 1.
Treaſurer at War's Acquittances	1651	Auditors Office Land Rev.	G. 15.
Papers relating to the Dutch War	1666	Bodleian Library	O. 1.
Letters of the Secretary at War, Office of Ordnance, Military Commiſſions, &c.	1683 to 1762	State Paper Office	C. 1. a.
v. Accounts Public.—Musters.			
ARRAGON:			
Treaties and Tranſactions with	1289 to 1515	Receipt of the Exchequer	A. 1. a.
ARTICLES, Thirty-nine:			
v. Church of England.			
ASAPH, St. Diocese:			
Eccleſiaſtical Survey	26 Hen. 8.	Firſt Fruits Office	C. 18.
Consistory Court:			
Copies of Wills	1565 to 1700	Regiſtry at St. Aſaph	L. 14. a.
Proceedings of	From 1600, and ſome previous		
Terriers of Glebe Lands	1660 to the preſent Time		
Marriages, Births, and Burials, Rolls of			
Original Wills	A few in 1638, and from 1660 to the preſent Time		

ALPHABETICAL ARRANGEMENT OF THE PUBLIC RECORDS.

RECORDS and other INSTRUMENTS.	DATE.	WHERE KEPT.	Appendix to the Firſt Report.
ASSIZE:			
Rolls	6 Ric. 1. to the End of Hen. 6. and a few of Edw. 4.	Receipt of the Exchequer	A. 1. a.
Placita	Edw. 1.	Inner Temple Library	Q. 2. b.
Account of	31 Edw. 1.	Tower	A. 2. a.
Placita apud Ebor'	1 to 19 Edw. 2.	Tower	A. 2. a.
Placita apud Cant'	6 Edw. 2.	Bodleian Library	O. 1.
Copies and Abſtracts of Aſſize Rolls	20 Edw. 3. to 8 Hen. 4.	Lincoln's Inn Library	Q. 3.
Placita	20 Edw. 3.	Dean and Chapter Durham	N. 24.
The like	Edw. 3. & 4.	Lincoln's Inn Library	Q. 3.
ASSOCIATIONS of COUNTIES, CITIES, &c.			
Rolls of	Wm. 3.	Tower	A. 2. a.
ATTAINDERS:			
Baga de Secretis, containing Records of Attainders	— —	Cuſtos Brevium K. B.	E. 5.
Commiſſions on Attainders, Forfeitures for Treaſons, Felony, &c.	— —	King's Rememb. Office	G. 6. a.
Accounts of, and of Forfeitures and Criminal Affairs	15 Edw. 2. to 1 Hen. 4.	Tower	A. 2. a.
Miniſters Accounts of Perſons attainted	Hen. 6. to Edw. 6.	Augmentation Office	G. 19. a.
Inventories of Goods and Records of Attainted Perſons	Hen. 7. & 8.	Receipt of the Exchequer	A. 1. a.
Inventories of Jewels, Wardrobe, and Effects of the Duke of Norfolk, attainted	1524	Univerſity Library, Camb.	P. 1.
The like of the Duke of Norfolk and Earl of Surrey	38 Hen. 8.	Audit. Office Land Rev.	G. 15. a.
The like of the Duke of Somerſet	7 Edw. 6.	Audit. Office Land Rev.	G. 15. a.
The like of the Duke of Northumberland, and others	1 Mar.	Audit. Office Land Rev.	G. 15. a.
Collection of Inventories of Attainted Perſons	Mar. to Car. 1.	Audit. Office Land Rev.	G. 15. a.
Miniſters Accounts of Eſtates of Sir J. Perrott and Owen Glynn, attainted	Eliz.	Audit. Office Land Rev.	G. 15. a.
v. CLAUS ROLLS.—EXCHEQUER OF ACCOUNT.—KING'S BENCH.—INVENTORIES.			
ATTORNEY GENERAL:			
His Oath	— —	Clerk of the Crown in Chan.	*Page* 218.
ATTORNIES and PRIVILEGED PERSONS:			
Bills againſt	1180 to 1688	Receipt of the Exchequer	A. 1. a.
Oath of Attornies of the Exchequer of Pleas	— —	King's Rememb. Office	*Page* 234.
ATTORNEY:			
Warrants of, in every Recovery ſuffered by virtue of the Writ of Dedimus Poteſtatem	— —	Curſitors Office	D. 3.
AUDITORS:			
State of the Revenue in their Charge	1660 to 1708	Surveyor General's Office	G. 14.
Office Books delivered by the late Auditors to the Commiſſioners for Auditing the Public Accounts	1662 to 1785	Office for Auditing Pub. Acc.	G. 5.
Oath of the Auditors of the Exchequer	— —	King's Rememb. Office	*Page* 233.
v. ACCOUNTS PUBLIC.—CLAUS ROLLS.—LAND REVENUE.			
AUGMENTATION:			
OFFICE: *			
Miniſters or Bailiffs and Receivers Accounts	Ric. 2. to Eliz. and ſome ſince	Augmentation Office	G. 19. a.
Certificate of the Officers of this Office for Cambridge	Hen. 8.	Auditors Office Land Rev.	G. 15. a.
COURT OF:			
The Proceedings of; viz. Bills, Anſwers, Depoſitions, Decrees, and Leaſes	27 Hen. 8. to 1 Mary	Augmentation Office	G. 19. a.
Decrees and ſome Leaſes of	Hen. 8. & Edw. 6.	King's Rememb. Office	G. 6. a.
Proceedings of the Court of Augmentation	1535 to 1558	Britiſh Muſeum	U.
AUGUSTIN, ST. (KENT):			
Leidger Book of the Monaſtery	— —	King's Rememb. Office	G. 6. a.
AULA DOMINI REGIS:			
Account of the Profits of	Edw. 1.	King's Rememb. Office	G. 6. a.
Antient Placita	Edw. 2. and 3.	Receipt of the Exchequer	A. 1. a.
v. MARSHALSEA.			
AURUM REGINÆ. *v.* CLAUS ROLLS.			

* To this Office have been lately transferred the Miniſters Accounts, which were in the Auditors Office of the Land Revenue.

ALPHABETICAL ARRANGEMENT OF THE PUBLIC RECORDS.

RECORDS and other INSTRUMENTS.	DATE.	WHERE KEPT.	Appendix to the Firſt Report.
BACON (NICHOLAS) Lord Keeper:			
Speeches on Political Subjects - - - -	1559 to 1569 - -	Univerſity Lib. Camb.	P. 1.
BACON (FRANCIS) Viſcount St. Alban's:			
Proceedings againſt him in Parliament, together with his Confeſſion and humble Submiſſion -	— —	Univerſity Lib. Camb.	P. 1.
His Report on the Spaniſh Grievances - -	5 Jac. 1. - - -	Bodleian Library - -	O. 1.
BAGA DE SECRETIS. *v.* King's Bench.			
BAILIFFS:			
Some Accounts of - - - - - - *v.* Augmentation Office.	— —	King's Rememb. Office -	G. 6.
BAILIFFS OF LIBERTIES:			
Affidavits of Claims of Fines - - - - -	1681 to the preſent Time - - -	Foreign Eſtreats Office -	G. 10.
Proffers, being Money paid Half-yearly by Bailiffs of Liberties - - - - - - *v.* Estreats.—Exchequer of Account.	— —	King's Remem. Office -	G. 6.
BAILIWICKS:			
Inrolments of Grants of them - - - -	Jac. 1. and Car. 1. -	Augmentation Office -	G. 19. a.
BAKER, Thomas:			
Collectanea reſpecting the Univerſity of Cambridge, by him - - - - - - *v.* Cambridge University.	— —	Britiſh Muſeum - - -	U.
BANGOR DIOCESE:			
Eccleſiaſtical Survey - - - - - -	26 Hen. 8. - -	Firſt Fruits Office - -	G. 18.
Mandates of various Kinds - - - -	— —	Regiſter's Office, Bangor - - - -	L. 12. a.
Petitions for regiſtering Diſſenting Chapels -	— —	Regiſter's Office, Bangor	L. 12. a.
Adminiſtrations, Bonds given on granting them, and Inventories on obtaining them - -	— —	Regiſter's Office, Bangor	L. 12. a.
Letters Teſtimonial and Credential previous to Ordination - - - - - - -	— —	Regiſter's Office, Bangor	L. 12. a.
Preſentations to Livings - - - - - -	— —	Regiſter's Office, Bangor	L. 12. a.
Reſignations of Livings - - - - - -	— —	Regiſter's Office, Bangor	L. 12. a.
Inſtitutions, Commiſſions for - - - -	— —	Regiſter's Office, Bangor	L. 12. a.
Inſtitutions and Collations to Benefices - -	1542 to 1783 - -	Regiſter's Office, Bangor	L. 12. a.
Wills - - - - - - - - - -	1635 to the preſent Time	Regiſter's Office, Bangor	L. 12. a.
Terriers of Glebe Lands - - - - -	1719 to the preſent Time	Regiſter's Office, Bangor	L. 12. a.
Conſiſtory Court, Acts of - - - - -	1730 to the preſent Time	Regiſter's Office, Bangor	L. 12. a.
Marriage Licences - - - - - -	1762 to the preſent Time -	Regiſter's Office, Bangor	L. 12. a.
BANISHMENTS. *v.* Claus Rolls.			
BANKRUPTS:			
Dockets or ſhort Particulars for each Commiſſion, Procedendo, and Superſedeas - - - -	1731 to the preſent Time - -	Patentee Office, Bankruptcy - - -	D. 15.
Petitions and Orders from the Court of Chancery, for renewing Commiſſions, Superſedeas, &c. -	— —	Patentee Office, Bankruptcy - - -	D. 15.
Inrolments of Proceedings in Bankruptcy - -	1758 to the preſent Time - - -	Clerk of the Inrolment Office - - -	D. 14.
Oaths of the Clerk of the Bankrupt Office - - *v.* Chancery.—Claus Rolls.	— —	Petty Bag Office - -	*Page* 231.
BARBADOES:			
Law Proceedings concerning it - - -	1647 - - -	Bodleian Library - -	O. 1.
BARBARY STATES:			
Treaties with England - - - - - -	1669 to 1760 - -	State Paper Office - -	C. 1. a.
BARGAINS AND SALES:			
Indentures of - - - - - -	34 & 35 Hen. 8. -	King's Remem. Office -	G. 6. a.
Inrolments of - - - - - - *v.* Chartæ Antiquæ.—Claus Rolls.	25 Geo. 3. to the preſent Time -	Inrolment Office - -	D. 13.
BARKING:			
Account of the Monaſtery of - - - - *v.* Land Revenue.	— —	Auditors Office Land Rev.	G. 15. a.
BARONETS:			
Pedigrees and Arms of, under a Royal Warrant of 3d December 1783 - - - - - -	— —	College of Arms - - -	C. 8.

ALPHABETICAL ARRANGEMENT OF THE PUBLIC RECORDS.

RECORDS and other INSTRUMENTS.	DATE.	WHERE KEPT.	Appendix to the Firſt Report.
BARONS OF THE CINQUE PORTS:			
Services due by them to the King - - - - v. CINQUE PORTS.	— —	Corp. Chriſti Coll. Camb.	P. 5.
BARONS OF THE EXCHEQUER:			
Their Oath - - - - - - - - -	— —	King's Rememb. Office -	*Page* 233.
BATH, ORDER OF THE:			
Books of Arms of the Knights of the Bath, from their Inſtitution - - - - - - v. ARMORIAL BEARINGS.	— —	College of Arms - - -	C. 8.
BATH, SOMERSET:			
Regiſter of the Abbey of - - - - -	— —	Corp. Chriſti Coll. Camb.	P. 5.
Another Regiſter Book of that Abbey - -	— —	Lincoln's Inn Library -	Q. 3.
Grant of Grammar School - - - -	Temp. Edw. 6. - -	Biſhop's Regiſtry Wells -	L. 8.
BATH AND WELLS DIOCESE:			
Extracts from Regiſters by Dr. Hutton - -	— —	Britiſh Muſeum - - -	U.
Proceedings reſpecting Churches and Chapelries of Queen Elizabeth, Copies of - - -	— —		
Epiſcopal Regiſters, containing Judicial Acts of the Biſhops, Endowments of Vicarages, &c. -	1316 to the preſent Time -	Biſhop's Regiſt. Wells	L. 8.
Terriers and Preſentations to Livings - -	1660 to the preſent Time -	Biſhop's Regiſt. Wells	L. 8.
Wills and Bonds on granting Letters of Adminiſtration - - - - - - - - - v. CHARTULARIES.	1666 to the preſent Time -	Biſhop's Regiſt. Wells	L. 8.
BATTLE, SUSSEX:			
Regiſter Book of the Abbey - - - - -	— —	Lincoln's Inn Library -	Q. 3.
BEDFORD, COUNTY:			
Antient Deeds, &c. relative to Eſtates therein -	— —	Dean and Chapter Weſtm.	N. 12. b.
Nomina Villarum - - - - - - -	— —	Lord Treaſ. Rem. Office	G. 7. a.
Iters, Copies of - - - - - - -	3 & 4 Edw. 3. - -	Lincoln's Inn Library -	Q. 3.
Nona Roll - - - - - - - -	15 Edw. 3. - - -	King's Rememb. Office -	G. 6. b.
LEVEL:			
Awards, &c. - - - - - - -	— —	Petty Bag Office - - -	D. 5.
Proceedings relating thereto - - - - -	— —	Auditors Office Land Rev.	G. 15.
BEDFORD (FRANCIS) EARL OF:			
Information againſt him in the Star Chamber - v. STAR CHAMBER.	Car. 1. - - - -	Univerſity Library Camb.	P. 1.
BENEFICES, ECCLESIASTICAL:			
Taxations of ſeveral - - - - - -	— —	Britiſh Muſeum - - -	U.
Certificates of Inſtitutions and Patronages - -	— —	Firſt Fruits Office -	G. 18.
Surveys of all Eccleſiaſtical Benefices, Dignities, and Promotions Spiritual - - - - -	26 Hen. 8. - - -	Firſt Fruits Office -	G. 18.
Orders of the Exchequer relating to Benefices diſcharged from Firſt Fruits and Tenths - -	1 Mary to 3 Geo. 1.	Firſt Fruits Office -	G. 18.
Surveys - - - - - - - - -	Philip and Mary -	Auditors Office Land Rev.	G. 15.
Names of, in the Gift of the Prince of Wales -	Jac. 1. - - - -	Univerſity Library Camb.	P. 1.
Certificates of all, not exceeding £. 50. per Ann. - v. CHURCH LIVINGS.	6 Anne to the preſent Time - -	Firſt Fruits Office - -	G. 18.
BERKS COUNTY:			
Antient Deeds, &c. relative to Eſtates therein -	— —	Dean and Chapter Weſtm.	N. 12. b.
Nona Roll - - - - - - - -	15 Edw. 3. - - -	King's Rememb. Office -	G. 6. b.
Oath of the Sheriff of - - - - - -	— —	Clerk of Crown in Chan.	*Page* 233.
BERMUDAS:			
Minutes of Council, Original Papers relating thereto, &c. - - - - - - - v. PLANTATIONS.	— —	Bodleian Library - - -	O. 1.
BIBLE:			
An Order concerning the Tranſlation thereof -	— —	Univerſity Library Camb.	P. 1.
BISHOPS:			
Inrolment of their Patents - - - - - v. ARCHBISHOPS.—PATENTS.	1725 to the preſent Time - - -	Petty Bag Office - - -	D. 5.
BISHOPRICKS:			
Surveys and Valuations of - - - - -	— —	Firſt Fruits Office - -	G. 18.
Various Records reſpecting them - - - -	— —	Auditors Office Land Rev.	G. 15. a.
Charters, being Grants to Biſhops, &c. - -	1185 to 1640 -	Britiſh Muſeum - - -	U.
Miniſters Accounts of - - - - - -	Hen. 3. to Eliz. -	King's Rememb. Office -	G. 6.

ALPHABETICAL ARRANGEMENT OF THE PUBLIC RECORDS.

RECORDS and other INSTRUMENTS.	DATE.	WHERE KEPT.	Appendix to the First Report.
BISHOPRICKS—(*continued.*)			
Accounts of Receivers and others (fede vacante)	Hen. 8. to Car. 1.	Auditors Office Land Rev.	G. 15. a.
Surveys and Minifters Accounts	Hen. 8. to Car. 1.	Augmentation Office	G. 19. a.
v. The feveral DIOCESES.—CHARTÆ ANTIQUÆ.—MINISTERS ACCOUNTS.			
BOHEMIA and the PALATINATE:			
Proceedings relative thereto	1620 to 1623	State Paper Office	C. 1. a.
BOLINGBROKE:			
Certificate of the Honour of, in the Counties of Lincoln, York, Stafford, and Derby	36 Eliz. & 16 Car. 1.	Univerfity Library Camb.	P. 1.
BONDS:			
Bonds and other obligatory Writings	— —	Augmentation Office	G. 19. a.
BRANDENBURG:			
Treaties and Ratifications with England	1661 to 1700	State Paper Office	C. 1. a.
BRECON, COUNTY:			
Survey of	19 Eliz.	Auditors Off. Land Rev. Wales	G. 16. a.
CIRCUIT AND CHANCERY there			
Recoveries, Fines, Judgments, Paper Files, Gaol Files, and Docket Books	35 H. 8. to pres^t Time	Prothon. Brecon Circuit	H. 10. a.
Affidavits, Subpœnas, Proceffes of Contempt, &c. Books of Entry, wherein the Proceedings are entered; Bills, Anfwers, Exceptions, &c.; Depofitions of Witneffes, Interrogatoties, &c.	Various Dates.	Chancery Clerks, Brecon	H. 10. b.
Interrogatories and Depofitions; Minutes and Orders; Decrees	1706 / 1711 to the prefent Time	Regifter Brecon	H. 10. c.
ARCHDEACONRY OF ST. DAVID'S:			
Proceedings in Caufes in the Confiftory Court, and the Original Wills	1600 to the prefent Time	Archdeaconry of St. David's, Brecon	L. 24. d.
BRETAGNE:			
Treaties and Tranfactions with	1213 to 1491	Receipt of the Exchequer	A. 1. a.
BREVIA REGIA:			
Brevia Regia	1327 to 1422	Tower	A. 2. a.
Writs of Ad Quod Damnum, Dedimuffes to fwear Mafters Extraordinary in Chancery, &c. Inquiry of Damages, Certiorari to remove Records, calling Serjeants at Law, Returns of Writs for electing Coroners, Verdurers, and Regarders of Forefts	9 Car. 1. to the prefent Time	Petty Bag Office	D. 5.
BRISTOL, CITY:			
Conftitutions of	— —	Corp. Chrifti Coll. Camb.	P. 5.
A fpecial Commiffion of Oyer and Terminer and Gaol Delivery	1753	Clerk of the Crown in Chancery	D. 2. a.
v. OYER and TERMINER.			
DIOCESE:			
Wills, Adminiftration Bonds, Licenfe Bonds, Tranfcripts of Parifh Regifters, Prefentations, and other Ecclefiaftical Papers	— —	Bifhop's Regiftry, Briftol	L. 26.
Wills and Adminiftrations; Terriers; Copies of Regifters exhibited Annually; Licenfe Bonds and Allegations	1683 / 1731 to the prefent Time	Bifhop's Reg. Blandford	L. 26.
BRITISH MUSEUM:			
The Number of Originals, Tranfcripts, Collections, and Repertories of Records in this Repofitory, being too great to be fpecified in a Return, mention is here made of the Catalogues now extant, from which further Intelligence may be derived when required.			
Catalogue of the Harleian Library, by Humphry Wanley and David Cafley, 2 Vols. Fol.			
- - - - - of the King's Library, by David Cafley, 1 Vol. 4to.			

ALPHABETICAL ARRANGEMENT OF THE PUBLIC RECORDS.

RECORDS and other INSTRUMENTS.	DATE.	WHERE KEPT.	Appendix to the Firſt Report.
BRITISH MUSEUM—*(continued.)*			
Catalogue of the Cottonian Library, by Dr. Smith, 1 Vol. Fol.			
- - - - - of the Cottonian Library, publiſhed by Hooper, 1 Vol. 8vo.			
- - - - - more copious, of the Cottonian Library, by Mr. Planta; as yet in MS.			
- - - - - of the Sloanian Library, and the Additions to the Muſeum to the Year 1782, by the Rev. Samuel Ayſcough, 2 Vols. 4to.	— —	Britiſh Muſeum - -	U.
- - - - - of the Additions to the Muſeum ſince the Year 1782; as yet in MS.			
- - of the Original Charters, Rolls, and other Deeds in the Muſeum, by the Rev. Samuel Ayſcough; as yet in MS.			
BUCKS, COUNTY:			
Antient Records relative to Eſtates therein -	— —	Dean & Chapter Weſtm.	N. 12. b.
Tenuræ Terrarum - - - - - -	— —	Univerſity Library Camb	P. 1.
Nomina Villarum - - - - - -	— —	Lord Treaſ. Rem. Exch.	G. 7. a.
Nona Roll - - - - - - -	15 Edw. 3. - - -	King's Rememb. Office -	G. 6. b.
Perambulation of Royal Forests - - - *v.* FORESTS.	26 Hen. 8. - - -	Univerſity Library Camb.	P. 1.
BULLS OF POPES. *v.* LIBER RUBEUS.—POPES.			
BURGUNDY:			
Treaties and Tranſactions with - - -	1419 to 1484 - -	Receipt of the Exchequer	A. 1. a.
BURLEY (SIMON):			
His Impeachment by the Commons - -	Ric. 2. - - - -	Dean & Chapter Weſtm.	N. 12. b.
BURRELL, SIR WILLIAM:			
His Collections reſpecting the Hiſtory and Antiquities of Suſſex - - - - - -	— —	Britiſh Muſeum - -	U.
BURY ST. EDMUND'S ABBEY, SUFFOLK:			
Chartularies, &c. belonging thereto - - - *v.* CHARTULARIES.—LAND REV.	— —	Univerſity Library Camb.	P. 1.
BUTLER, ROYAL:			
Accounts of - - - - - - -	— —	King's Rememb. Office -	G. 6.
The like - - - - - - - -	15 and 17 Edw. 2. -	Audit. Office Land Rev.	G. 15.
The like - - - - - - - -	Eliz. to Car. 1. - -	Audit. Office Land Rev.	G. 15.
CALAIS:			
Patents of Offices, in the Treaty or Foreign Rolls -	— —	Rolls Chapel - - - -	D. 1.
Declarations and Proceedings concerning the Failure of an Expedition thereto, under Viſcount Wimbledon and Colonel Cecil - - -	— —	Univerſity Library Camb.	P. 1.
Accounts relating to Calais and Guiſnes - -	Hen. 6. to Edw. 6.	Auditors Office Land Rev.	G. 15. a.
Victualling and other Accounts of this and other Towns in France - - - - - -	Hen. 6. to Edw. 6.	Auditors Office Land Rev.	G. 15. a.
Accounts relating to the Staple - - - *v.* ACCOUNTS PUBLIC.	Temp. Henry 8. and previous - - -	Receipt of the Exchequer	A. 1. a.
CAMBRIDGE, COUNTY:			
Antient Deeds, &c. relative to Eſtates therein -	— —	Dean & Chapter Weſtm.	N. 12. b.
Hundred Roll - - - - - - -	Temp. Edw. 1. - -	Tower - - - - - -	A. 2. a.
Placita apud Cant' - - - - - -	6 Edw. 2. - - -	Bodleian Library - -	O. 1.
Certificates of Officers of the Augmentation Office for Cambridge - - - - - - -	30 Hen. 8. - - -	Auditors Office Land Rev.	G. 15.
Leaſes of Fee Farms in Jointure to Henrietta Maria, Queen of Charles I. - - - - *v.* TESTA DE NEVILL.	Car. 1. - - - -	Univerſity Library Camb.	P. 1.

ALPHABETICAL ARRANGEMENT OF THE PUBLIC RECORDS.

RECORDS and other INSTRUMENTS.	DATE.	WHERE KEPT.	Appendix to the First Report.
CAMBRIDGE—*(continued.)*			
UNIVERSITY:			
Collectanea respecting the University, by Thomas Baker	— —	British Museum	U.
Mandate of Henry VIII. for the Reformation of the University, at a Visitation, by Thomas Cromwell (Copy)	Hen. 8.	Peter House Coll. Camb.	P. 2.
Charter of its Privileges	Eliz.	Corp. Christi Coll. Camb.	P. 5.
Letter of King James I. in Behalf of the University against the Corporation (Copy)	Jac. 1.	Peter House Coll. Camb.	P 2.
King James I.'s Letter to the University, commending the Election of the Duke of Buckingham for their Chancellor	Jac. 1.	University Library Camb.	P. 1.
Oath of the Sheriff	— —	Clerk of Crown in Chan.	*Page* 223.
v. HENRY VIII.—UNIVERSITIES.—The several COLLEGES.			
CANTERBURY DIOCESE:			
Registers of the Archbishops, consisting of all Kinds of Judicial Acts and Instruments passing under the Cognizance of the Archbishop	1279 to 1747	Lambeth Library	T.
N. B. The Registers since 1747 are in the Vicar General's Office, Doctors Commons.			
Taxation of Tenths of the Clergy of Canterbury	20 Hen. 6.	King's Rememb. Office	G. 6. a.
Charters relative to the Estates of the See	chiefly temp. Hen. 8.	Lambeth Library	T.
Surveys of the Possessions of the Diocese, and of the Peculiars thereunto belonging	1646 to 1654	Lambeth Library	T.
v. ARCHES COURT OF.—CHANCERY.—NICHOLAS IV.—PARLIAMENTARY SURVEYS.			
PREROGATIVE COURT OF:			
Wills, Transcripts of	1383 to the present Time	Registers Prerogative Court, Canterbury	L. 1.
Wills, Original	1505 to the present Time	Registers Prerogative Court, Canterbury	L. 1.
Probate Acts	1526 to the present Time	Registers Prerogative Court, Canterbury	L. 1.
Acts of Court, Transcripts of	1539 to the present Time	Registers Prerogative Court, Canterbury	L. 1.
Administration Acts	1572 to the present Time	Registers Prerogative Court, Canterbury	L. 1.
Depositions in Causes	1656 to the present Time	Registers Prerogative Court, Canterbury	L. 1.
Allegations in Causes	1665 to the present Time	Registers Prerogative Court, Canterbury	L. 1.
Answers in Causes	1672 to the present Time	Registers Prerogative Court, Canterbury	L. 1.
Administration Bonds	1718 to the present Time	Registers Prerogative Court, Canterbury	L. 1.
Inventories	1727 to the present Time	Registers Prerogative Court, Canterbury	L. 1.
Exhibits in Causes	1731 to the present Time	Registers Prerogative Court, Canterbury	L. 1.
Proceedings in the Court of Delegates	1660 to present Time	Doctors Commons	K.
v. ARCHES COURT OF.			
DEAN AND CHAPTER OF:			
Various antient Registers and Instruments respecting Tythes, &c. in Places with which this Cathedral has at present no Concern	— —	Canterbury Cathedral	N. 1.
v. TODD's Catalogue of Canterbury Library.			
CHRIST CHURCH:			
Register of Charters	1285 to 1327	University Lib. Camb.	P. 1.
ST. GREGORY:			
Register thereof	Temp. Henry 3.	University Lib. Camb.	P. 1.
ST. AUGUSTIN. v. CHARTULARIES.			
CARDIGAN, COUNTY:			
Survey of	19 Eliz.	Aud. Land Rev. Wales	G. 16. a.
v. CAERMARTHEN.			
ARCHDEACONRY:			
Wills, Original	1746 to present Time	Register's Office, Haverfordwest	L. 24. a.
CARLISLE, DIOCESE:			
Ecclesiastical Survey	26 Henry 8.	First Fruits Office	G. 18.
Parliamentary Survey, and other private Writings of the See	— —	Bishop's Palace, Rose Castle	L. 21.

ALPHABETICAL ARRANGEMENT OF THE PUBLIC RECORDS.

RECORDS and other INSTRUMENTS.	DATE.	WHERE KEPT.	Appendix to the First Report.
CAERMARTHEN, County:			
Surveys of	19 & 39 Eliz.	Auditors Land Revenue, Wales	G. 16. a.
Town:			
Survey of the	2 Eliz.	Auditors Land Revenue, Wales	G. 16. a.
Circuit, containing the Counties of Caermarthen, Pembroke, and Cardigan; Caermarthen and Haverfordwest Towns:			
Precipe Book, containing Entries of Actions	Jac. 1. to the present Time	Prothonotary, Caermarthen, &c.	H. 11. b.
Imparlance or Continuance Book	Jac. 1. to the present Time	Prothonotary, Caermarthen, &c.	H. 11. b.
Pleadings	Jac. 1. to the present Time	Prothonotary, Caermarthen, &c.	H. 11. b.
Remembrance Rolls of Recoveries	Jac. 1. to the present Time	Prothonotary, Caermarthen, &c.	H. 11. b.
Fines	Jac. 1. to the present Time	Prothonotary, Caermarthen, &c.	H. 11. b.
Declarations and other Pleadings	Jac. 1. to the present Time	Prothonotary, Caermarthen, &c.	H. 11. b.
Writs	Jac. 1. to the present Time	Prothonotary, Caermarthen, &c.	H. 11. b.
Gaol Bundles, Books of Rules, Affidavits, Writs for summoning Great Sessions and Returns	None older than 35 Years	Secondary and Deputy Clerk of the Crown, Caermarthen Circuit	H. 11. a.
Oath of the First Justice of this Circuit	— —	Clk. of Crown in Chan.	Page 219.
Oath of the Second Justice	— —	Clk. of Crown in Chan.	Page 219.
Archdeaconry:			
Consistory Court, Proceedings of	— —	Registry at Caermarthen	L. 24. b.
Wills and Administrations	For nearly 200 Years back	Registry at Caermarthen	L. 24. b.
CAERNARVON Circuit. v. Wales North Circuit:			
Oath of the First Justice of this Circuit	— —	Clk. of Crown in Chan.	Page 219.
Oath of the Second Justice	— —	Clk. of Crown in Chan.	Page 219.
CAROLINA (South):			
Proceedings in the Vice Admiralty Court in	1717	Bodleian Library	O. 1.
CASTILE:			
Treaties and Transactions with	1254 to 1481	Receipt of the Exchequer	A. 1. a.
CATHEDRALS:			
Charters of Endowments	Henry 8.	Corp. Christi Coll. Camb.	P. 5.
v. Chartularies.—Henry 8.—Statutes.			
CATHARINE, Queen Consort of Charles II.:			
Many Books and Papers relating to her Estates, and Counterparts of Leases, &c.	— —	Auditors Office Land Rev.	G. 15.
Lands, &c. settled on her	— —	Aud. Off. Land Rev. and	G. 15.
v. Queens.		Office of Surveyor General of Crown Lands	G. 14.
CERTIFICATES:			
To discharge Mortgages	1709 to present Time	Register Office for Middlesex	M. 1.
CERTIORARI:			
Bundles, consisting of Acts of Parliament removed by Certiorari	6 Hen. 8 to the present Time	Rolls Chapel	D. 1.
v. King's Bench.—Star Chamber.			
CHACES. v. Forests.—Special Commissions.			
CHANCELLOR, Lord High:			
His Oaths	— —	Clerk of Crown in Chan. & Petty Bag	Page 216. — 229.
CHANCERY:			
Bills, Answers, Depositions, and other Proceedings	Eliz. to 1714	Tower	A. 2. a.
Papers relative thereto	1558 to 1633	State Paper Office	C. 1. a.
Judgment or Decree Roll	25 Henry 8. to 6 Geo. 3.	Rolls Chapel	D. 1. a.
Surrender and Specification Rolls	Restoration to the present Time	Rolls Chapel	D. 1. a.
Exemplification of a Grant to a Chancellor to give Relief in Equity after Judgment in a Court of Law	Jac. 1.	Dean & Chapter Westm.	N. 12. b.
Bills, Answers, and Replications	1714 to the present Time	Six Clerks Office	D. 12.
Depositions of Witnesses taken by Commission in the Country	1714 to the present Time	Six Clerks Office	D. 12.
Commissions of Partition	1714 to the present Time	Six Clerks Office	D. 12.
Commissions for assigning Dower	1714 to the present Time	Six Clerks Office	D. 12.
Examinations of Parties	1714 to the present Time	Six Clerks Office	D. 12.
Inrolments of some Decrees	1714 to the present Time	Six Clerks Office	D. 12.
Dockets or Warrants for Inrolments	1714 to the present Time	Six Clerks Office	D. 12.

ALPHABETICAL ARRANGEMENT OF THE PUBLIC RECORDS.

RECORDS and other INSTRUMENTS.	DATE.	WHERE KEPT.	Appendix to the First Report.
CHANCERY—(continued.)			
Depositions sealed up and never published - -	1600 to present Time	Six Clerks Office - -	D. 12.
Some Inrolments of Decrees not transmitted to the Rolls - - - - - - -	2 Eliz. to the present Time - - - -		
Interrogatories, Depositions, and Examinations of Witnesses - - - - - - - -	1500 } to the present Time -	Examiners Office - { J. Morgan, Esq. - -	D. 11. b.
The like - - - - - - - - -	1658 }	H. Flitcroft, Esq. - -	D. 11. a.
Causes depending in this Court referred to the Masters	— —	Office of Masters in Chan.	D. 7.
Entries of Decrees and Orders - - -	38 Hen. 8 to 1793 -	Report Office - - -	D. 9.
Masters Reports - - - - - - -	1590 to present Time		
Certificates and Journals of the Accountant General, touching the Property of the Suitors of the Court - - - - - - -	— —		
Manuscript Books of Accounts kept with the Bank, and certified to the Report Office - - -	— —	Accompt. General's Office	D. 8.
Affidavits - - - - - - - - -	— —	Register of Affidavits -	D. 10.
Memorials of Deeds and other Securities for Annuities and Inrolments - - - - -	1777 to present Time	Clerk of Inrolments - -	D. 13.
Warrants, Fiats, and other Authorities for Business transacted - - - - - - -	— —	Clerk of the Crown in Chancery - - -	D. 2. a.
Dockets of Commissions - - - - -	1595 to 1602, and from 1643 to the present Time -		
Dockets of Writs - - - - - - -			
Dockets of Writs of Extent - - - -	1601 to present Time		
Admissions of Officers - - - - - -	40 Eliz. to the present Time- - -	Petty Bag Office - -	D. 5.
Judgments by Default; on Scire Facias; to revoke Letters Patent; to put Recognizances in Suit; and Judgments by and against Officers of the Court - - - - - - - -	A few temp. Eliz. and Jac. 1. and from 1 Car. 1. to the present Time -		
Special Commissions to inquire of Estates forfeited to the Crown, with the Inquisitions and Traverses thereon - - - - - - -	A few temp. Jac. 1. and from 31 Car. 1. to the present Time - - -		
Inrolments of Patents and the Estreats thereof, with the Warrants or Privy Seal Bills - -	For the last 10 Years		
Docket Books of Letters Patent - - - -	Jac. 1. to the present Time - - -	Clerk of the Letters Patent	D. 16.
Commendams, Dispensations, Degrees, and Notarial Faculties granted by the Archbishops of Canterbury for the Time being - - -	1692 to present Time	Clerk of the Dispensations and Faculties - - -	D. 17.
Dockets for Commissions of Bankrupts, Procedendo, and Supersedeas - - - - - -	1731 to the present Time -	Patentee of the Bankrupt Office - - -	D. 15.
Petitions and Orders of the Court of Chancery relating to Bankruptcy - - - - - -			
Inrolments of Proceedings in Bankruptcy - -	1758 to the present Time - - - -	Clerk of Inrolment Office	D. 14.
Oaths of several of the Officers of this Court; viz.			
Of the Masters in Chancery - - - -	— —	Clerk of Crown in Chan. and Petty Bag - -	Page 218. — 223.
Of the Clerk of the Crown - - - -	— —	Clerk of Crown in Chan.	— 221.
Of the Register - - - - -	— —	Petty Bag - - -	— 230.
Of the Deputy Registers - - - -	— —	Clerk of Crown in Chan.	— 221.
Of the Six Clerks - - - - -	— —	Petty Bag - -	— 230.
Of the Under Clerks - - - - -	— —		
Of the Examiners - - - - - -	— —	Clerk of Crown in Chan. and Petty Bag - -	— 224. — 230.
Of the Prothonotaries - - - - -	— —	Petty Bag - - -	— 231.
Of the Porter - - - - - -	— —		
Of the Masters Extraordinary - - - -	— —		

ALPHABETICAL ARRANGEMENT OF THE PUBLIC RECORDS.

RECORDS and other INSTRUMENTS.	DATE.	WHERE KEPT.	Appendix to the First Report.
CHANTRIES:			
Surveys and Valuations - - - - -	— —	Augmentation Office, First Fruits Office, and Aud. Office Land Rev.	G. 19 a. G. 18. G. 15.
Book of their Valuations in several Counties -	Temp. Eliz. - -	King's Rememb. Office -	G. 6. a.
v. COLLEGES.—LANCASTER DUCHY.—LAND REV.			
CHAPELS:			
Surveys and Valuations of - - - - -	— —	First Fruits Office - -	G. 18.
v. COLLEGES.			
CHARITABLE USES:			
Commissions of - - - - - - - -	— —	Rolls Chapel - - - -	D. 1. a.
Inquisitions and Decrees of Commissioners - -	43 Eliz. to the present Time -	Petty Bag Office - - -	D. 5.
Inrolments of Confirmations or Dismissions of Decrees and Appeals - - - -			
v. EXCHEQUER OF ACCOUNT.			
CHARLES PRINCE (afterwards Charles I.):			
Accounts of his Revenues - - - -	— —	Auditors Land Rev. Eng.	G. 15. a.
Accounts of the Cofferer of his Household - -	Jac. 1. - - -	University Lib. Camb.	P. 1.
Records delivered to the Commissioners of his Revenue - - - - - - - -			
Names of Manors, Honors, Castles, &c. belonging to him, and Names of Livings in his Gift -			
Commission (Copy of) for treating of a Marriage between him and Christina, second Daughter of France - - - - - - - -	1616 - - - -		
Privy Seals and Correspondence during his Expedition in Spain - - - - - -	1622 to 1626 - -	Duchy Cornwall Office -	C. 7.
Pope Gregory the XVth's Letter to him - -	1623 - - - -	University Library Camb.	P. 1.
CHARLES the FIRST:			
Account of his Coronation - - - - -	1625 - - - -	Duchy of Cornwall - -	C. 7.
Act of Parliament, with MS. Memorandums of the Committee relating to the Goods of Cha. I.	Car. 1. - - - -	Bodleian Library - -	O. 1.
The Marquis D'Effiat's Letters concerning his Marriage with Henrietta Maria of France - -	Car. 1. - - - -		
Articles of Marriage of Charles I. with Henrietta Maria - - - - - - - -	— —	University Library Camb.	P. 1.
Inventories of Wardrobe, Pictures, Statues, &c. belonging to him, taken by Parliamentary Commissioners - - - - - -	Temp. Interregni -	Auditors Office Land Rev.	G. 15.
Some Particulars of his Possessions, and Contracts for the Sale of them, and a few Surveys - -	Temp. Interregni -	King's Rememb. Office -	G. 6.
v. CORNWALL.—INVENTORIES.—JEWELS.—LANCASTER DUCHY.			
CHARLES the SECOND:			
Receivers Accounts of Contributions to him -	13 Car. 2. - - -	Auditors Office Land Rev.	G. 15.
v. STATE PAPERS.			
CHARTÆ ANTIQUÆ:			
Chartæ Antiquæ - - - - - - - -	Will. 1. to Hen. 3.	Tower - - - - -	A. 2. a.
Chartæ Antiquæ - - - - - - -	Will. 1. to Hen. 8.	Augmentation Office -	G. 19. a
Authentic Transcripts of antient Charters - -	From the Saxon Kings downwards	King's Rememb. Office -	G. 6.
Royal Charters, mostly Foundations and Endowments of Religious Houses - - - -	From about 800 to 1640 - - -	British Museum - - -	U.
Chartæ Antiquæ - - - - - - - -	Hen. 1. - - - -	King's Rememb. Office -	G. 6.
Charter of Henry I. to Alexander I. of Scotland -	Hen. 1. - - - -	Receipt of the Exchequer	A. 1. a.
Ecclesiastical Charters, being Grants of Archbishops, Bishops, Deans, Abbots, &c. - - -	1185 to 1640 - -	British Museum - - -	U.
Chartæ & Leges - - - - - - -	Joh. and Hen. 3. -	Corpus Christi Coll. Cam.	P. 5.
Various private Deeds, consisting of Feoffments, Deeds of Bargain and Sale, of Lease and Release, Exchange, and all Manner of Contracts, Agreements, and Covenants, between private Individuals - - - - - - - -	From Ric. 2. to Car. 1.	British Museum - - -	U.
Royal Charters and Grants to Religious Houses -	— —	Bodleian Library - -	O. 1.
Book of antient Charters - - - - -	— —		

ALPHABETICAL ARRANGEMENT OF THE PUBLIC RECORDS.

RECORDS and other INSTRUMENTS.	DATE.	WHERE KEPT.	Appendix to the First Report.
CHARTÆ ANTIQUÆ—*(continued.)*			
Copies of ſome antient Charters at the Tower -	— —	Lincoln's Inn Library -	Q. 3.
v. CONFIRMATIONS.—HEN. VIII.—LANCASTER DUCHY.			
CHARTER ROLLS - - - - - -	1199 to 1483 - -	Tower - - - - -	A. 2. a.
The like - - - - - - -	1 Ric. 3. to 8 Hen. 8.	Rolls Chapel - - - -	D. 1. a.
Copies and Extracts of Charter Rolls - -	Joh. to Edw. 4. -	Inner Temple Library -	Q. 2. b.
Examen Cartarum - - - - -	Temp. Edw. 2. - -	Bodleian Library - -	O. 1.
v. LIBER RUBEUS.			
CHARTERS:			
Of ſeveral Kings - - - - - - -	— —	Receipt of the Exchequer	A. 1. a.
Tranſcripts and Extracts of - - - - -	Will. et ſeq. - -	King's Rememb. Office -	G. 6.
Charters of London - - - - - -	Ric. 1. Joh. and Hen. 3. - - -		
Charta Johannis facta Papæ - - - -	Joh. - - - - -	Corp. Chr. Coll. Cam.	P. 5.
Charters - - - - - - -	Joh. to Eliz. - -		
Charters and Grants of Privileges and Lands -	Hen. 3. - - - -	King's Rememb. Office	G. 6.
Charters - - - - - - -	Edw. 1. - - - -		
Charta Libertatum Surriæ - - - - -	Edw. 1. - - - -	Corp. Chriſti Coll. Camb.	P. 5.
Tranſcripts and Extracts of Charters from Claus Rolls - - - - - - - -	6 Edw. 2. to 51 Edw. 3. - - -	Aſhmolean Muſeum - -	O. 2.
Various Charters and Grants to the Dukes of Cornwall - - - - - - -	Edw. 3. - - - -	Receipt of the Exchequer	A. 1. a.
Charters and Grants to the ſame - - -	11 Edw. 3. to 20 Car. 1. - - -	Duchy of Cornwall - -	C. 7.
Charters relating to the See of Canterbury - -	Chiefly Hen. 8. - -	Lambeth Library - -	T.
Charters relating to Scotland - - - -	1572 - - - -	Britiſh Muſeum - - -	U.
Catalogue of Charters throughout England and Wales - - - - - - - -	— —	Aſhmolean Muſeum - -	O. 2.
v. CONFIRMATIONS.—HEN. VIII.—KING'S BENCH.—LANCASTER DUCHY.—PATENT ROLLS.			
CHARTULARIES:			
Of Monaſteries - - - - - - -	— —	Augmentation Office -	G. 19. a.
Regiſters and Leidger Books of moſt of the Cathedrals, Monaſteries, and Religious Houſes in the Kingdom - - - - - - -	— —	Britiſh Muſeum - -	U.
Of the Military Orders of the Temple, and St. John of Jeruſalem - - - - -	— —		
Of divers Hoſpitals and Guilds - - -	— —		
Extracts from various Regiſters of Religious Houſes, chiefly in the Dioceſe of Bath and Wells, by Mr. Hutton - - - -	— —		
Of St. Edmund's Bury, Glaſtonbury, Nyneham in Manerio de Axminſter, St. Alban's, Dartford, St. John Colcheſter, Sybeton, St. Auguſtin Canterbury, and Tyntern - - -	— —	Royal Society Library -	R.
A Liſt of about 150 Chartularies, in the Cottonian Library, is contained in the 8vo Edition of the Catalogue of that Library, p. 42—48; thoſe in other Parts of the Britiſh Muſeum, may amount to nearly 100 more.—See alſo Tanner's Notitia Monaſtica.			
CHATHAM. *v.* HARBOURS.			
CHERTSEY, SURREY:			
Leidger Book of the Monaſtery - - - -	— —	King's Rememb. Office	G. 6. a.
CHESTER, COUNTY:			
A large Collection of Materials relating to the Hiſtory and Antiquities of the County and City of Cheſter, made by the Three Holmes - -	— —	Britiſh Muſeum - - -	U.
Eccleſiaſtical Survey - - - - - -	26 Hen. 8. - - -	Firſt Fruits Office - -	G. 18.
CIRCUIT, Counties of Denbigh and Montgomery -			
The Calendar containing Nomina Miniſtrorum, Inquiſitions, Pannels, Recognizances, Examinations, Indictments, Preſentments, &c. on the Crown Side - - - - - - -	From the Firſt Inſtitution of the Court, to the preſent Time -	Prothonotary of Great Seſſions for Denbigh and Montgomery -	H. 8. a.

ALPHABETICAL ARRANGEMENT OF THE PUBLIC RECORDS.

RECORDS and other INSTRUMENTS.	DATE.	WHERE KEPT.	Appendix to the First Report.
CHESTER, CIRCUIT—(*continued.*)			
Writs of Covenant, Precipes and Concords, Writs of Entry, Originals in Ejectment, Writs of Inquiry, Inquisitions, &c. - - - -			
Declarations, Pleas, and Pleadings, on the Civil Side - - - - - - - -			
Plea Roll, containing Inrolments of Fines and Recoveries, Pleadings in Actions which proceed to Issue and Trial, Patents of Judges, &c. - -	From the First Institution of the Court, to the present Time -	Prothonotary of Great Sessions for Denbigh and Montgomery -	H. 8. a.
Judgments and Imparlances, Dockets of all Judgments of every Session, and Files of Affidavits			
COURT OF SESSION, Counties of Chester and Flint:			
Rolls of Attornies admitted, &c. - - - -	— —		
List of Commissioners for swearing Affidavits -	— —		
Affidavits, Warrants, Bail Pieces, &c. - - -	— —		
Mainprize Files, containing Inquisitions, Indictments, and other Proceedings on the Crown Side	From a very early Period - -		
Files of Declarations, Pleas, and other Pleadings			
Docket Books of Fines and Recoveries - -	For Chester, from 1 Edw. 6. and for Flint, from Eliz. - - - (to the present Time.)		
Inrolments of Fines, Recoveries, Pleadings, and Deeds - - - - - - - - - -		Prothonotary and Clerk of the Crown, Chester - - - - -	H. 8. b.
Writs of Entry, Dedimus Potestatem, Original Writs, &c. - - - - - - - -	Eliz. - - (to the present Time.)		
Rule Books - - - - - - -	From Jac. 1 - (to the present Time.)		
Crown Books - - - - - - - -	1 Anne - - - (to the present Time.)		
Register of Contracts, and Indentures of Clerkship directed by Stat. of - - - - - -	34 Geo. 3. - - -		
Oath of the Chief Justice - - - -	— —	Clerk of the Crown in Chancery - - -	*Page* 219.
- - - of the Second Justice - - - -	— —		— 220.
DIOCESE:			
Installations of Bishops, Patents of Officers, &c. -	— —		
Terriers and Parish and Chapel Registers - -	— —		
Presentations to Benefices, Nominations to Curacies and Schools - - - -	— —		
Appropriations, Endowments, Compositions, Grants, Agreements, Leases, Orders, &c. -	— —		
Licences of Marriage, Probates of Wills, and Letters of Administration - - -	— —	Bishop's Registry, Chester - - - -	L. 18. a.
Proceedings in Causes, and Books of Acts of the Consistory Court - - - - - -	— —		
Presentations and Institutions to Ecclesiastical Benefices - - - - - - - -	Commencing 1500		
Consecrations of Churches, Chapels, &c. and Faculties for rebuilding Churches - - -	1525 to the present Time -		
Original Wills or Copies of - - - -	1590 to the present Time -		
Population of Parishes, Account of - -	1714 - - - -		
RICHMOND ARCHDEACONRY, CONSISTORY COURT:			
Wills, Original - - - - - - -	— —		
Bonds on granting Letters of Administration, &c.	— —		
Marriage Licences, and Affidavits thereon - -	— —		
Parochial Registers, Copies of - - -	— —	Consistory Registry, Richmond - -	
Act Books, containing Entries of Probates -	— —		L. 18. b.
Proceedings in Suits - - - - - -	— —		
Inrolments of Faculties for Pews, &c. - -	— —		
Terriers - - - - - - - - -	— —		
Duplicates of Parish Registers - - - -	— —		
Wills, Original - - - - - - -	1748 to the present Time - -		
Administration, Curation, and Tuition Bonds -		Commissary Registry, Lancaster - - -	
Act Books, containing Entries of Probates - -			L. 18. c.
CHICHESTER DIOCESE:			
An antient Copy of the Register of Bishop Read	— —	Dean & Chap. Chichester	N. 4.
Inventories, and many Miscellaneous Papers of Proceedings in the Bishop's Registry and Consistory Court - - - - - - - -	— —		
Books, containing Entries of Charters, Grants, Confirmations, &c. - - - -	Before and since the Conquest - - -	Bishop's Registry, Chester - - -	L. 27.

ALPHABETICAL ARRANGEMENT OF THE PUBLIC RECORDS.

RECORDS and other INSTRUMENTS.	DATE.	WHERE KEPT.	Appendix to the First Report.
CHICHESTER – *(continued.)*			
Act Books of the Consistory Court	From an early Period to present Time		
Book of Visitations	— —		
Episcopal Registers	1396 to 1722		
Register Books of Wills	1518 to present Time, with a few Chasms		
Original Wills	1600 to present Time, excepting the Usurpation	Bishop's Registry, Chichester	L. 27.
Terriers of Parishes within the Archdeaconry	Exhibited principally in 1615, 1635, 1663		
CHIVALRY:			
Placita Exercitus Regis	24 Edw. 1.	Receipt of the Exchequer	A. 1. a.
Roll relating to the Earl Marshal	8 Edw. 2.	Tower	A. 2. a.
Curia Militaris (Cases of Duels)	Hen. 6.	Lincoln's Inn Library	Q. 3.
Proceedings of the Earl Marshal's Court	Eliz. to Car. 2.	College of Arms	C. 8.
Proceedings in the Cause of Ramsay and Lord Reay	1631	Bodleian Library	O. 1.
v. CLAUS ROLLS.			
CHRIST CHURCH, LONDON. *v.* LAND REV.—LONDON.			
CHURCH OF ENGLAND:			
Various Records respecting Church Livings	— —	Auditors Office Land Rev.	G. 15. a.
The 39 Articles, Latin and English	Temp. Eliz.	Corpus Christi Coll. Cam.	P. 5.
Valuations of Rectories and other Church Possessions in various Counties	1553 to 1557	Auditors Office Land Rev.	G. 15. a.
Notitia Parochialis, or Returns of Churches in different Parts of England	1606		
Augmentations of Livings, Salaries, and Pensions, made by Order of Parliament	1647 to 1658	Lambeth Library	T.
Leases of Lands during the Time of the Commonwealth	Temp. Interregni		
Presentations to Livings			
Surveys of Church Livings	Temp. Interregni	Rolls Chapel	D. 1. a.
Orders relating to plundered Ministers	1652	Auditors Office Land Rev.	G. 15. a.
v. CLAUS ROLLS.—CHARLES, PRINCE.—INVENTORIES.—PARLIAMENTARY SURVEYS.			
CINQUE PORTS:			
Collections concerning their Laws, Customs, and Privileges	— —	British Museum	U.
Collections about the Cinque Ports	— —	Inner Temple Library	Q. 2. b.
Services due by the Barons to the King	— —	Corp. Christi. Coll. Camb.	P. 5.
Proceedings of the Court of Loadmanage, for the Regulation and Government of Pilots of the Cinque Ports	1496 to present Time		
Proceedings of the Court of Chancery thereof, together with Bills, Answers, Replications, &c. relating thereto	1615 to 1717, with a Chasm	Register of the Cinque Ports	H. 14.
Proceedings of the Court of Admiralty thereof, together with Papers relating to Claims of Derelicts, Salvage, &c.	1632 to present Time, with some Chasms		
v. CLAUS ROLLS.			
CIRCUITS. *v.* HOME, MIDLAND, NORFOLK, NORTHERN, OXFORD, WESTERN, and for WALES.			
CITIES AND BOROUGHS:			
Many Charters	— —	British Museum	U.
Copies of Charters of	— —	Inner Temple Library	Q. 2. b.
Oath of the Mayors and Bailiffs of	— —	King's Rememb. Office	*Page* 236.
v. CONFIRMATIONS.—CORPORATIONS.			
CLAIMS. *v.* EXCHEQUER OF ACCOUNT.—FORESTS.—NOMINA VILLARUM.			
CLAIMS, COURT OF:			
Commission for, at the Coronation of Geo. III.	— —	Clerk of the Crown in Chancery	D. 2. a.
v. CORONATIONS.			
CLAIMS OF FINES. *v.* BAILIFFS.—ESTREATS FOREIGN.			

ALPHABETICAL ARRANGEMENT OF THE PUBLIC RECORDS.

RECORDS and other INSTRUMENTS.	DATE.	WHERE KEPT.	Appendix to the First Report.
CLAUS ROLLS:			
Claus Rolls - - - - - - -	1204 to 1483 - -	Tower - - - - - -	A. 2. a.

Among the Variety of Matters contained in the CLAUS ROLLS, in the Tower, the following Heads ought to be particularly noticed:

Admiralty, Advowsons, Aids and Taxes, Alien Priories, Ambassadors, Attainders, Auditors, Aurum Reginæ, Banishment, Chancery, Chivalry, Church, Cinque Ports, Coinage, Coronations, Coroners, Credentials, Crusades,

Customs, Custos Regni, Demesnes Antient, Divorces Royal, Dower, Ecclesiastical Affairs, Error, Escheat, Exchequer, Exemptions, Fines, Fisheries, Forests, Forfeitures, Gascony,

Gavelkind, Grain, Habeas Corpus, Heralds, Heretics, Homage, Horses Royal, Household Royal, Ideots, Jewels Crown, Jews, Inquisitions, Invasions, Ireland, King's Bench, Knights Hospitallers,

Letters Royal, London, Marriages Royal, Marshal, Mortmain, Navy, Nobility, Oaths, Ordnance, Outlawries, Pardons, Parliament, Piracy, Plague, Poll Tax, Poor, Pope's Bulls,

Pre-emption, Privy Seal, Proclamations, Prohibitions, Protections, Purveyance, Reprisals, Revenue, Scotland, Scutage, Seal Great, Serjeants at Law, Stannaries, Tallage, Tallies, Taxes, Thames,

Treaties, Truces, Tythes, Verdurers, Universities, Voyages Royal, Wales, Wardrobe, Warrens, Weights and Measures, Wills, Wool, Works Royal, Writs ne exeant Regn' York.

Some Account of the ROLLS in the Tower, digested in their Chronological Order, is contained in Powell's Repertory, p. 145. 215.

RECORDS and other INSTRUMENTS.	DATE.	WHERE KEPT.	Appendix to the First Report.
Claus Rolls, Copies of - - - - - -	— —	British Museum - -	U.
Copies of - - - - - - -	6 ad finem Joh.—Hen. 3.—3 ad 13 Ed. 1.—1 ad 20 Ed. 2.—Ed. 3. -	Lincoln's Inn Library -	Q. 3.
Copies and Extracts of - - - - -	Joh. to Edw. 4. -	Inner Temple Library -	Q. 2. b.
A Roll containing Extracts from - - -	Temp. Hen. 3. - -	Receipt of the Exchequer	A. 1. a.
Abstracts of - - - - - - -	13 Hen. 3. to 21 Ric. 2. - - -	Lincoln's Inn Library -	Q. 3.
Transcripts and Extracts of Charters from the Claus and Patent Rolls - - - -	Temp. Edw. 2. & 3.	Ashmolean Museum -	O. 2.
Claus Rolls - - - - - - -	Edw. 5. to 24 Geo. 3.	Rolls Chapel - - -	D. 1. a.
Claus Rolls, containing Inrolments of Bargains and Sales, Settlements and Wills of Roman Catholics, Conveyances of Bankrupts Estates, Recognizances, Memorials of Deeds, Register Books of Deeds, &c. - - - - - - -	1785 to the present Time - - - -	Clerks of the Inrolments	D. 13.
CLAXBY, LINCOLNSHIRE:			
Book of Survey - - - - - - -	24 Eliz. - - - -	King's Rememb. Office	G. 6. a.
CLERGY:			
A Collection of Papers as to their Jurisdiction, &c.	— —	Inner Temple Library	Q. 2. b.
Their Procuratorial Letters, &c. - - - -	— —		
Articuli Cleri in Parl. Lincoln - - -	9 Edw. 2. - - -	Corp. Christi Coll. Camb.	P. 5.
Injunctions to them by Edw. VI. - - -	Edw. 6. - - -		
CLERKENWELL:			
Court Rolls of the Manor - - - -	Mar. & Eliz. - -	University Lib. Camb'	P. 1.
CLERKS OF THE PEACE. *v.* PEACE.			
CLITHERO:			
Rental of Lands belonging to the Duchy of Lancaster there - - - - - - -	— —		
COFFERERS:			
Accounts of - - - - - - - -	— —	King's Rememb. Office	G. 6. a.
Accounts of - - - - - - - -	1626 - - - -	Auditors Office Land Rev.	G. 15. a.
v. HOUSEHOLD.			
COGNIZANCES, on Appeals to the House of Lords. *v.* LORDS, HOUSE OF.			

ALPHABETICAL ARRANGEMENT OF THE PUBLIC RECORDS.

RECORDS and other INSTRUMENTS.	DATE.	WHERE KEPT.	Appendix to the First Report.
COIN:			
Collections of Papers, entitled "De Moneta"	— —	Inner Temple Library	Q. 2. b.
Assay Rolls	Edw. 1.	Receipt of the Exchequer	A. 1. a.
Standard Pieces	Edw. 4. & seq.	Chamberlain's Off. Exc.	G. 2.
Copies of Proclamations, and Extracts from the Council Books, concerning Money and Coinage. *v.* CLAUS ROLLS.—EXCHEQUER RECEIPT.—MINT.—MONEY.	Temp. Hen. 8. 1568 to 1600, and from Car. 2. to 1730	Antiq. Society Library	S. a.
COLCHESTER, ST. JOHN. *v.* CHARTULARIES.			
COLE, THOMAS. *v.* ESCHEATS—WARDS and LIVERIES.			
COLLEGES, CHANTRIES, and FREE CHAPELS.			
Certificates and Particulars	Hen. 8.—Edw. 6.	Augmentation Office	G. 19. a.
v. CHANTRIES.—CHARTULARIES.—STATUTES.			
COMMENDAMS:			
Commendams, Dispensations, Degrees, and Faculties granted by the Archbishops of Canterbury. *v.* CHANCERY.	1692 to present Time	Clerk of the Dispensations and Faculties	D. 17.
COMMISSIONS. *v.* CHANCERY.—LAND REVENUE.—LORDS, HOUSE OF.—STATE PAPERS.			
On Attainders or Forfeitures / Of Inquiry } *v.* EXCHEQUER OF ACCOUNT.			
COMMONS, HOUSE OF:			
Articles of Impeachment against Simon de Burley	Ric. 2.	} Dean & Chap. Westm.	N. 12. b.
Assessment upon a Hundred in Surrey, for Wages for Knights of the Shire	31 Hen. 6.		
Various printed Books and Papers unarranged	1495 to 1737	} Clerk of the Journals and Papers	B. 2.
Journals of the House of Commons	1547 to the present Time		
Rules and Orders	Edw. 6. to Jac.	} Bodleian Library	O. 1.
Journal	1572		
The like	43 Eliz.		
Writs	Eliz. Jac. 1. & Car. 1.		
Copies of Journals	1604 to 1707	Inner Temple Library	Q. 2. b.
Report of Sir F. Bacon, on the Spanish Grievances	5 Jac. 1.	Bodleian Library	O. 1.
Accounts and Papers presented to the House	} 1607 to present Time	} Clerk of the Journals	B. 2.
Petitions to the House, both Public and Private			
Bills and Reports made from the Committees of the House of Commons			
Speeches	1620 to 1628	} Bodleian Library	O. 1.
Journal	4 Car. 1.		
Return Books from the Office of Clerk of the Crown to the House of Commons	1625 to present Time	Clerk of the Journals	B. 2.
The like under Richard Cromwell	1658 to 1659	} Bodleian Library	O. 1.
Letters and Speeches of Sir J. Holland	Car. 2.		
Copies of Journals	1660 to 1671	Middle Temple Library	Q. 1.
Journals	1660 to 1688	Bodleian Library	O. 1.
Minutes taken at the House of Commons, and before Committees of the whole House	1685 to present Time	Clerk of the Journals	B. 2.
Proceedings in Convention	1688	} Bodleian Library	O. 1.
Votes therein	1688 to 1690		
Minutes of Committees	1697 to 1699		
Test Rolls	1698 to the present Time		
Journal	1701		
Certificates of Qualification	Anne to Geo. 3.	Petty Bag Office	D. 5.
Qualification Rolls	1727 to present Time	} Clerk of the Journals	B. 2.
Reports from Commissioners for Survey of Courts of Justice	Geo. 2.		
Evidence taken at the House of Commons, and before Committees of the whole House, and of Privileges and Elections	1737 to the present Time		

ALPHABETICAL ARRANGEMENT OF THE PUBLIC RECORDS.

RECORDS and other INSTRUMENTS.	DATE.	WHERE KEPT.	Appendix to the First Report.
COMMONS, HOUSE OF—(*continued.*)			
Evidence respecting controverted Elections - -	1771 to the present Time - - - -	Clerk of the Committees of Privileges & Elections	D. 5.
Books and Papers of Commissioners of Public Accounts - - - - - - - -	1780 to 1787 - -	Clerk of the Journals -	B. 2.
Returns of Members - - - - - -	1689 to the present Time - - - -	Clerk of the Crown in Chancery - -	D. 2. a.
Instruments of the Speaker appointing Members to issue Warrants to the Clerk of the Crown, in Cases specified by Stat. 24 Geo. III. c. 26. -	24 Geo. 3. et seq. -		
Oath of the Clerk of the House of Commons -	— —	Clerk of Cown in Chan.	*Page* 221.
v. CONVENTION.—DURHAM.—EAST INDIA COMPANY. — ESTREATS, FOREIGN. — PARLIAMENT.—PEACE, CLERKS OF.			
COMMON PLEAS, COURT OF:			
Placita - - - - - - -	Joh. to Hen. 4. -	Lincoln's Inn Library -	Q. 3.
Writs, Original and Special - - - - -	Hen. 2. to Will. 3. -	Receipt of Exchequer	A. 1. a.
Rolls - - - - - - - - -	Edw. 1. and Hen. 7.		
The like - - - - - - - -	Hen. 7. - - -	Treasury Custos Brevium - - - -	F. 4.
Writs, Original and Special - - - - -	1688 to the present Time - -		
Attornies, Bills against - - - - - -			
Writs of Inquiry - - - - - - -			
Posteas - - - - - - - -			
Venire Facias - - - - - - -			
Outlawries, Proclamations, &c. - - - -			
Elegits - - - - - - - -			
Writs of Entry, Summons, and Seisin - -			
Mittimus and Transcript - - - -			
Dedimus and Affidavits - - - - - -	1788 to 1782 - -		
Fines, Concords, and Feet of Fines - - -			
Reversals of Outlawries - - - - -	Geo. 2. to the present Time - -	Clerk of the Reversals -	F. 9.
Affidavits of Debt to hold to Bail, and Affidavits of Service, &c. - - - - - - -	— —	Filacer's Office - -	F. 5. a.
Special Bail Books and Pieces - - - -	— —		
Process Books, containing Entries of Common Appearances - - - - - - - -	— —		
Remembrance Rolls - - - - - -	— —		
Warrants to sue and defend, filed pursuant to Stat. 25 Geo III. - - - - - - -	— —		
Declarations and other Pleadings - - -	— —	Prothonotaries Office -	F. 1.
Secondaries Remembrance Rolls - - -	— —		
Docket Rolls - - - - - - - -	1 Hen. 8. - to the present Time		
Recovery Remembrance Rolls - - -	26 Hen. 8. -		
Common Judgments - - - - - -	3 Car. 1. -		
Nisi Prius Records - - - - - -	20 Car. 1. -		
Special Judgments - - - - - -	14 Car. 2. -		
Entries on the Roll - - - - - -	12 Anne - -		
Posteas and Inquiries - - - - - -	A few Years back -	Clerk of the Judgments -	F. 1.
Essoign Rolls - - - - - - -	For nearly 100 Years back - - - -	Clerk of the Essoigns -	F. 2.
Final Judgments: Dockets of them all - -	Since Stat. 4 & 5 Will. & Mary, c. 20.		
Attornies, Inrolment of Admissions of, and Lists of their Certificates - - - - - -	— —	Clerk of the Warrants, Inrolments, and Estreats - - -	F. 3.
Attornies, Articles of Clerks to - - -	— —		
Termages, Entries of - - - - -	— —		
Estreat Rolls - - - - - - -	— —		
Rolls of Fines - - - - - - -	— —		
Entries of all Judgments signed in the Court, and on all Fines - - - - - - -	— —		
Recovery Book - - - - - - -	Commencing 1507		
Inrolments of Deeds, Books of - - -	Commencing 1554		
Oath of the Chief Justice - - - -	— —	Clerk of Crown in Chan.	*Page* 217.
- - of the other Judges - - - - -	— —	Ibidem - - -	— 218.
v. COURTS OF JUSTICE. — ESTREATS. — LAW CASES.—KING'S BENCH.—PLACITA.			

ALPHABETICAL ARRANGEMENT OF THE PUBLIC RECORDS.

RECORDS and other INSTRUMENTS.	DATE.	WHERE KEPT.	Appendix to the Firſt Report.
COMMON PRAYER:			
Book of, delivered into the Exchequer, purſuant to Act of Uniformity - - - - - -	13 & 14 Car. 1. -	King's Rememb. Office -	G. 6. a.
Book of, with the Great Seal appendant - -	}	{ Tower - - -	A. 2. a.
Another - - - - - - - - -	} 1662 - - -	{ Dean & Chap. Hereford	N. 8.
Another, with the Great Seal torn from it - -	}	{ Balliol College, Oxford	O. 5.
v. Exchequer.—King's Rememb. Office.			
COMPOSITIONS:			
Real - - - - - - - - - -	— —	Augmentation Office -	G. 19. a.
COMPTROLLERS. v. Pipe.—Wardrobe.			
CONCEALMENTS:			
A Book containing the Entries of the Return of the Commiſſioners for concealed Lands - -	Eliz. - - -	King's Rememb. Office -	G. 6. a.
Particulars for Grants of concealed Lands - -	Eliz. - - -	Augmentation Office -	G. 19. a.
v. Lands.—Special Commissions.			
CONCILIA:			
Acta Synodorum Conciliorum, &c. ad calcem Chronicæ Regum Angliæ, Manu Dugdalii -	W. 1. to Hen. 3. -	Aſhmolean Muſeum - -	O. 2.
CONFIRMATION:			
Deeds of - - - - - - - - -	— —	Augmentation Office - -	G. 19. a.
Rolls, containing Confirmations of Charters to Cities, Boroughs, &c. - - - - - -	Ric. 3. to 12 Jac. 1.	Rolls Chapel - - -	D. 1. a.
v. Charters.			
CONSTATS:			
Books of - - - - - - - - -	Jac. 1. & Car. 1. -	Auditors Office Land Rev.	G. 15. a.
CONSTITUTIONS. v. Lancaster Duchy.—Sign Manual.			
CONTRACTS:			
For Sale of the Poſſeſſions of Charles I. - -	Temp Interregni -	King's Rememb. Office -	G. 6.
v. Exchequer of Receipt.			
CONVENTION Parliament:			
Returns to - - - - - - - -	1688 - - - -	Clerk of the Crown in Chancery - - - -	D. 2. a.
CONVICTIONS. v. King's Bench.			
CONVOCATION:			
Writs of - - - - - - - - -	— —	Conſiſtory Courts - -	L.
Writs, Appointment of Proxies, &c. - -	None older than 17th Century - - -		
COOKHAM, BERKS:		Dean & Chapter Weſtm.	N. 12. b.
Accounts of - - - - - - -	Temp. Ric. 2. -	King's Rememb. Office -	G. 6. a.
CORNWALL, County:			
Domeſday Book for - - - - - -	— —	Dean & Chapter Exeter	N. 6.
Iter, Copy of - - - - - - -	30 Edw. 1. - - -	Lincoln's Inn Library -	Q. 3.
Nona Roll - - - - - - -	15 Edw. 3. - - -	King's Rememb. Office -	G. 6. b.
Covenants with the Commoners for Tin Works -	1522 - - - -	Receipt of the Exchequer	A. 1. a.
v. Domesday Book.—Mines.			
Duchy of:			
Divers Papers relating to the Duchy Court -	— —	Britiſh Muſeum - - -	U.
*Miniſters Accounts, and other Records - -	— —	Augmentation Office - -	G. 19. a.
A few Records concerning it - - - - -	— —	{ Auditors Office Land	
Summary Returns - - - - - -	— —	{ Revenue - -	G. 15. a.
Tranſcripts of Charters, Letters relating thereto; Letters and Warrants of the Prince of Wales, Duke of Cornwall, and Earl of Cheſter, containing Preſentations to Churches, Fines, Grants, &c. - - - - - - - -	Edw. 3. - - - -	Receipt of the Exchequer	A. 1. a.
Survey of Manors, Boroughs, &c. immediately after the Grant to Edward the Black Prince -	11 Edw. 3. - - -	} King's Rememb. Office	G. 6. a.
Other Surveys and Miniſters Accounts - -	Temp. Edw. 3. &c.	}	
Court Rolls and Court Books - - -	1273 } to the preſent Time.	}	
Affeſſion Rolls and Affeſſion Books, with Articles, Anſwers, or Returns made by Jurors - -	1333 }	}	
Charters and Grants to the Dukes of Cornwall, and to Queen Anne, Wife of James I. - -	1337 to 1644 - -	} Duchy of Cornwall -	C. 7.
Surveys and Plans - - - - -	1337 } to the preſent Time.	}	
Miniſters and Receivers Accounts - - -	1345 }	}	
Treaſurers Accounts - - - - -	1368 to 1771 - -	}	

* Theſe have lately been transferred to the Office of the Duchy of Cornwall.

ALPHABETICAL ARRANGEMENT OF THE PUBLIC RECORDS.

RECORDS and other INSTRUMENTS.	DATE.	WHERE KEPT.	Appendix to the First Report.
CORNWALL, DUCHY OF—*(continued.)*			
Charters and Grants to Richard Duke of Gloucester	Edw. 4. - - - -	British Museum - - -	U.
Covenants for Tin Works - - - - -	14 Hen. 8. - - -	Receipt of the Exchequer	A. 1. a.
Green Wax, &c. Account of - - - -	Jac. 1. to Car. 2. -	Duchy of Cornwall -	C. 7.
Tin Rolls, or Account of Tin coined - -	1601 to present Time	Duchy of Cornwall -	C. 7.
Proceedings on Sale of Duchy Manors and Estates	1601 to 1654 - -	Duchy of Cornwall -	C. 7.
Inrolments of Patents of Offices, Commissions, Leases, &c. - - - - - - -	1610 to the present Time.	Duchy of Cornwall -	C. 7.
Proceedings in Council - - - - - -	13 Jac. 1. to the present Time.	Duchy of Cornwall -	C. 7.
Minutes, Orders, Letters, and Proceedings of the Council - - - - - - - -	1615 to the present Time.	Duchy of Cornwall -	C. 7.
Book of Privy Seals, and a Book of King Charles I. containing his Correspondence with his Council whilst in Spain - - - - - -	1622 to 1626 - -	Duchy of Cornwall -	C. 7.
Wardrobe Accounts, including Funeral of James I. and Coronation of Car. I. - - - -	1625 to 1626 - -	Duchy of Cornwall -	C. 7.
Brief Certificate of the Revenues belonging to the Duchy - - - - - - - - -	18 Car 1. - - -	University Library Camb.	P. 1.
Act of Convocation of the Stannators, or Parliament of Tinners - - - - - -	1752 and 1753 -	Duchy of Cornwall -	C. 7.
The like, assembled 25th August 1776, and continued to 1777 - - - - - -	1777 - - - -	Duchy of Cornwall -	C. 7.
Appeals in Stannary Causes - - - -	1788 to 1794 - -	Duchy of Cornwall -	C. 7.
Proceedings under the Act for the Redemption of the Land Tax - - - - - -	1798 to the present Time - - -	Duchy of Cornwall -	C. 7.
v. STANNARIES.			
CORONATIONS:			
Collections about them - - - - -	— —	Inner Temple Library -	Q. 2. b.
Oaths with His Majesty's Signature - - -	— —	Clerk of the Crown Chan.	D. 2. a.
Claims at - - - - - - - -	Edw. 2. Ric. 2. Hen. 4. & 5. - - -	Tower - - - - -	A. 2. a.
Copies of Claims - - - - - -	Temp. Ric. 2. - -	Lincoln's Inn Library -	Q. 3.
Claims, Ceremonies, &c. - - - - -	1483 to 1660 - -	State Paper Office - -	C. 1. a.
Accounts of - - - - - - -	21 Hen. 8. to 2 Jac. 2. - - - -	College of Arms - - -	C. 8.
Papers and Instruments - - - - -	Ed. 6. to Geo. 1. -	Dean and Chap. Westm.	N. 12. a.
Coronation Rolls - - - - - - -	Jac. 1. to Geo. 2. -	Rolls Chapel - - -	D. 1. a.
Account of the Coronation of Cha. I. - -	1625 - - - -	Duchy of Cornwall Office	C. 7.
Expenses of the Coronation of James II. - -	Jac. 2. - - - -	Board of Green Cloth -	C. 5. a.
Proceedings at the Coronation of Geo. I. - -	Geo. 1. - - - -	Inner Temple Library -	Q. 2. b.
Commission for Claims at the Coronation of Geo. III. and the Oaths - - - - - -	Geo. 3. - - - -	Clerk of the Crown Chan.	D. 2.
Expenses of - - - - - - - - -	Geo. 3 - - - -	Great Wardrobe Office -	C. 5. b.
v. CLAUS ROLLS.—COURT OF CLAIMS.—OATHS.			
CORONERS:			
Rolls or Inquisitions - - - - - -	Ed. 1. to Hen. 4. -	Receipt of the Exchequer	A. 1. a.
v. CLAUS ROLLS.—BREVIA REGIA.—WRITS.			
CORPORATIONS:			
Papers relative to them - - - - - -	— —	State Paper Office - -	C. 1. a.
Many Charters of Towns and Guilds, (Copies) -	Various Dates - -	British Museum - - -	U.
De Chartis concessis Civibus & Burgis (a Copy)	— —	Inner Temple Library -	Q. 2. b.
Papers relating to the City of Westminster -	Eliz. - - - -	Dean and Chap. Westm.	N. 12. b.
Copies of Charters and Privileges of London -	Car. 2. - - - -	Inner Temple Library -	Q. 2. b.
Papers relating to London - - - - -	1687 to 1767 - -	State Paper Office - -	C. 1. a.
v. CITIES AND BOROUGHS.—LONDON.—WESTMINSTER.			
CORPUS CHRISTI COLLEGE, CAMBRIDGE:			
v. NASMITH's Catalogue of the MSS. there.—UNIVERSITIES.			
CORRESPONDENCE, DOMESTIC:			
Letters, Memorials, and Orders of Council -	— —	Bodleian Library - -	O. 1.
Letters and Papers relating to the Departments of Ordnance, Admiralty, Customs, and Excise -	Various Dates - -	British Museum - - -	U.

ALPHABETICAL ARRANGEMENT OF THE PUBLIC RECORDS.

RECORDS and other INSTRUMENTS.	DATE.	WHERE KEPT.	Appendix to the First Report.
CORRESPONDENCE, DOMESTIC:—(continued.)			
Letters and Papers of State - - - -	Eliz. Jac. 1. & Car. 1.	Bodleian Library - -	O. 1.
- - - - - - to and from Secretaries of State, &c. - - - - - - -	1665 to 1766 - -	State Paper Office - -	C. 1. a.
Letters, Orders, &c. of His Majesty's Principal Secretaries of State - - - - - -	1674 to 1724 - -	State Paper Office - -	C. 1. a.
Letters on State Affairs - - - - -	1683 to 1688 - 1721 to 1729 -	Bodleian Library - -	O. 1.
Papers, &c. relating to Ecclesiastical Affairs -	1684 to 1769 - -	State Paper Office -	C. 1. a.
- - - - relating to Plots, Rebellion, and Treason	1685 to 1767 - -	State Paper Office -	C. 1. a.
- - - - relating to Criminal Affairs, generally	1687 to 1765 - -	State Paper Office -	C. 1. a.
Letters to Secretaries of State and Board of Trade	1721 to 1729 - -	Bodleian Library - -	O. 1.
CORRESPONDENCE WITH AMBASSADORS:			
Letters of Hen. VIII. and his Ministers - -	Hen. 8. - - - -	Receipt of the Exchequer	A. 1. a.
Correspondence with, in all Countries - -	1530 to 1780 - -	State Paper Office - -	C. 1. a.
Letters to the Queen and Council, Lord Burleigh, &c. - - - - - - - - - -	Eliz. - - - -	University Library Camb.	P. 1.
Correspondence with France, chiefly - -	1560 to 1567 - -	Bodleian Library - -	O. 1.
Letters of Sir Amyas Pawlet, while in France -	1577 - - - -	Bodleian Library - -	O. 1.
Sir S. Southwell's Account of the Court of Portugal - - - - - - - -	1677 - - - -	Bodleian Library - -	O. 1.
COTTONIAN LIBRARY:			
Oath of the Keeper of - - - - - -	— —	Petty Bag Office - -	Page 231.
COVENTRY, WARWICK:			
Book of Rental of the Priory - - - - -	Temp. Hen. 4. - -	King's Rememb. Office	G. 6. a.
v. LICHFIELD.			
COUNCIL:			
Orders of, for preparing Commissions for the Royal Assent to Bills - - - - -	1703 to the present Time - - - -	Clerk of Crown in Chan.	D. 2. a.
v. LORDS, HOUSE OF.—PRIVY COUNCIL.			
COURTS OF JUSTICE:			
Return of Commissioners and Sub Commissioners for Survey of the Courts of Justice, in the Year 1732, &c.			
v. Vol. 21. Com. Journ. p. 660—892.			
Vol. 27. - - - - - - p. 740—756.			
COURT OFFICES:			
Proclamations, Accounts, Rules, Orders, Inventories, &c. - - - - - - -	1478 to 1706 - -	State Paper Office - -	C. 1. a.
COURT ROLLS,			
Court Rolls and Rentals, some - - - -	— —	King's Rememb. Office -	G. 6. a.
Of divers Manors - - - - - -	— —	British Museum - - -	U.
Of Manors, some - - - - - -	Different Reigns -	Tower - - - - -	A. 2. a.
Of Manors formerly in the Possession of the Crown	Edw. 1. to Hen. 8.	Receipt of the Exchequer	A. 1. a.
Of Manors, &c. - - - - - - -	Edw. 1. to Hen. 8.	Augmentation Office -	G. 19. a.
Court Rolls - - - - - - -	Edw. 2. to the present Time - -	Auditors Office Land Rev.	G. 15.
Of the Manor of Clerkenwell - - - -	Mar. & Eliz. - -	University Library Camb.	P. 1.
CREDENTIALS. v. CLAUS ROLLS.			
CRIMES:			
Collections respecting Criminal Prosecutions, chiefly on State Affairs - - - - -	— —	Inner Temple Library -	Q. 2. b.
Rolls of Criminal Affairs, Attainders, &c. - -	15 Ed. 2. to 1 Hen. 4.	Tower - - - - -	A. 2. a.
Examinations, Certificates relative to Felons convicted, and Reports thereon - - -	1687 to 1765 - -	State Paper Office - -	C. 1. a.
v. ATTAINDERS.			
CROMWELL, THOMAS LORD.			
v. HENRY VIII.—MONASTERIES.—UNIVERSITIES.			
CROWN LANDS:			
Various Accounts, Rentals, Statements, and Papers relating thereto, together with Grants thereof to Queens, Princes, &c. - - - - -	— —	University Library Camb.	P. 1.
Calendars and Indexes of Surveys, and Records relative thereto - - - - - -	— —	Office of Surveyor General of Crown Lands	G. 14.
Grants in Fee Tail, Accounts of - - -	1 Edw. 1. to 26 Eliz.	Office of Surveyor General of Crown Lands	G. 14.
Surveys of Lands and Manors - - -	Edw. 6. Ph. & Mar. Eliz. & Jac. 1. -	Receipt of the Exchequer	A. 1. a.

ALPHABETICAL ARRANGEMENT OF THE PUBLIC RECORDS.

RECORDS and other INSTRUMENTS.	DATE.	WHERE KEPT.	Appendix to the First Report.
CROWN LANDS—(continued.)			
Leases of Crown Lands	Eliz & Jac. 1.	Augmentation Office	G. 19. a.
Maps and Plans	1603 to present Time	Pipe Office	G. 8.
Contracts for Sale of Lands of the Crown	1603 to present Time		
Surveys, Antient and Parliamentary, of Estates belonging to the Crown	Prior to Car. 1. and to the present Time		
Particulars of Estates belonging to the Crown			
Grants for long Terms	1660 to 1702	Office of Surveyor General of Crown Lands	
Lands undisposed of	1660 to 1701		G. 14.
Lands purchased for the Use of the Crown at and near Windsor	W. 3. Anne. & Geo. 2.		
Surveys of Crown Lands	1730 to present Time		
Commissions to survey them (some)	— —		
Oath of the Surveyor General	— —	Clerk of the Crown in Chancery, and Petty Bag Office	*Pages* 224, & 234.
v. EXCHEQUER OF ACCOUNT.—KING'S BENCH.—LAND REVENUE.—MINISTERS ACCOUNTS.—REVENUE, ROYAL.—SPECIAL COMMISSIONS.			
CRUSADES. v. CLAUS ROLLS.			
CUMBERLAND:			
Certificate of Manors, &c. therein, not granted in Fee Farm	1629		
v. TESTA DE NEVIL.			
CUMBWELL, PRIORY:		University Lib. Camb.	P. 1.
Register thereof	— —		
CURIA REGIS: (so called to the Reign of Edw. III.)			
Rolls of this Court	Ric. 1. Joh. & Hen. 3.	Receipt of the Exchequer	A. 1. a.
v. KING'S BENCH.			
CUSTOMS:			
Various Papers relating thereto	— —	British Museum	U.
Accounts of Receivers for various Ports	— —	Auditors Office Land Rev.	G. 15.
Papers relating to Customs	1199 to 1666	State Paper Office	C. 1. a.
Accounts of Receivers	Hen. 7. to Car. 1.	Auditors Office Land Revenue	
A Book relative to Wines of the Household, signed by Lord Burleigh	1597 to 1598		G. 15. a.
Letters and Orders to Farmers of the Customs and Officers of the Port of London	1605 to 1618	Bodleian Library	O. 1.
Accounts	1655 to 1656		
Letters and Papers between the Commissioners of the Customs and the Lords of the Treasury, &c.	1689 to 1761	State Paper Office	C. 1. a.
Inrolment of Patents, and Warrants of Customers and Searchers of Accounts	1725 to the present Time	Petty Bag Office	D. 5.
v. ACCOUNTS PUBLIC.—CLAUS ROLLS.—EXCHEQUER OF ACCOUNT.—PATENTS.—REVENUE, ROYAL.			
CUSTOS ANGLIÆ. v. CUSTOS REGNI.			
CUSTOS REGNI—CUSTOS ANGLIÆ—LOCUM TENENS ANGLIÆ—PROTECTOR ET DEFENSOR REGNI—REGENT—LORDS JUSTICES:			
Patents	37 Hen. 3. to 36 Hen. 8.	Tower and Rolls Chapel	A. 2. a. D. 1. a.
Commissions and Instructions	1695 to 1755	State Paper Office	C. 1. a.
Proceedings in Parliament relating to them. v. ROLLS OF PARLIAMENT, from 4 Edw. III. to 24 Hen. VI. printed; and the JOURNALS subsequently.—STATUTES, from 25 Hen. VIII. to 5 Geo. III.; some not printed.			
v. CLAUS ROLLS.—PATENT ROLLS.			

ALPHABETICAL ARRANGEMENT OF THE PUBLIC RECORDS.

RECORDS and other INSTRUMENTS.	DATE.	WHERE KEPT.	Appendix to the First Report.
DARTFORD, Kent : Monastery of. *v.* Chartularies.			
DAVID'S, St. Diocese :			
Ecclefiaftical Survey (a Copy) - - -	26 Hen. 8. - - -	Firft Fruits Office - -	G. 18.
Archdeaconry :			
Wills, Original - - - - - - -	1746 to prefentTime	Regifter Office, Haverfordweft - - -	L. 24. a.
DEANE, Gloucestershire :			
Proceedings in the Foreft Courts of Waltham and Deane - - - - - - - - *v.* Forests.	Temp. Car. 1. - -	Univerfity Library Camb.	P. 1.
DEANERIES :			
Surveys and Valuations of - - - - - *v.* Chartularies.	26 Hen. 8. - - -	Firft Fruits Office - -	G. 18.
DEANS and CHAPTERS : - - - - -	— —	— —	N.
Inrolments of Sales of their Lands - - -	— —	Rolls Chapel - -	D. 1.
The Deans and Chapters have in general in their Poffeffion the following Muniments and Records refpecting their Foundations, Endowments, and Government, and the Management of their Eftates:			
1. Charters, Grants, Deeds, Leidger Books, or Regifters.			
2. Statutes.			
3. Leafes, Patents, Prefentations, Appropriations, Compofitions, Inftallations.			
4. Proceedings at the different Courts belonging to the Chapters.			
For Catalogues of the Libraries, *v.* Catalogi Manufcriptorum Angliæ et Hiberniæ, Oxon. 1697.			
DEBENTURES. *v.* Exchequer of Receipt.			
DECREES and ORDERS :			
Original - - - - - - - - - *v.* Exchequer of Account.—Surveyor General's Court.	— —	King's Rememb. Office -	G. 6. a.
DEEDS :			
Inrolments of, acknowledged before the Barons of the Exchequer - - - - - - -	Hen. 3. to the prefent Time - -	Lord Treaf. Rem. Office	G. 7. a.
Regiftered Deeds, Records of - - -	1709 to prefentTime	Regifters Office for Middlefex - - -	M. 1.
Oath of the Regifter for Middlefex - - - *v.* Claus Rolls.—Common Pleas.—Exchequer of Account.	— —	Petty Bag Office - - -	*Page* 231.
DEMESNES, antient. *v.* Claus Rolls.			
DENIZATIONS. *v.* Patent Rolls.			
DENIZENS :			
A Lift of them figned by the King - - -	36 Hen. 8. - - -	Dean & Chapter Weftm.	N. 12. b.
DENBIGH :			
Rent Roll of the Lordfhip - - - -	— —	Auditors of Land Revenue, Wales - -	G. 16. a.
Circuit :			
Oath of the Chief Juftice of - - - -	— —	Clerk of the Crown in Chancery - - - -	*Page* 219.
Oath of the Second Juftice of - - - -	— —	Ibidem - - - - - -	— 221.

ALPHABETICAL ARRANGEMENT OF THE PUBLIC RECORDS.

RECORDS and other INSTRUMENTS.	DATE.	WHERE KEPT.	Appendix to the First Report.
DENMARK:			
Treaties and Ratifications with England	1432 to 1780	State Paper Office	C. 1. a.
Tranfactions with England	1485 to 1613	Britifh Mufeum	U.
Negotiations and Treaties with	Chiefly temp. Eliz.	Univerfity Library Camb.	P. 1.
Original Letters and Inftructions relating to Ambaffadors there	Jac. 1. Car. 1 & 2.	Bodleian Library	O. 1.
Negotiations in	1664 & 1665	Bodleian Library	O. 1.
DEPOPULATIONS:			
Commiffions of	5 Jac. 1.	Petty Bag Office	D. 5.
DERBY, COUNTY:			
Perambulation of Forefts	— —	King's Rememb. Office	G. 6. a.
Inquifitions concerning Fens	Temp. Edw. 3.	Receipt of the Exchequer	A. 1. a.
Iters, Copies of	4 & 8 Edw. 3.	Lincoln's Inn Library	Q. 3.
Ecclefiaftical Survey	26 Hen. 8.	Firft Fruits Office	G. 18.
Certificate of the Honour of Bolingbroke, partly within this County	Eliz. and Car. 1.	Univerfity Library Camb.	P. 1.
v. BOLINGBROKE.—FORESTS.			
DEVON, COUNTY:			
Domefday Book for this and fome other Counties	— —	Dean and Chapter Exeter	N. 6.
Nomina Villarum	— —	Lord Treaf. Rem. Office	G. 7. a.
Accounts of Farmers of Church Lands	3 & 4 Phil. & Mary	Auditors Land Revenue	G. 15.
COURTS OF STANNARIES:			
Covenants with Commoners for Tin Works	1522	Receipt of Exchequer	A. 1. a.
v. DOMESDAY BOOK.—MINES.—STANNARIES.—TESTA DE NEVIL.			
DIEM CLAUSIT EXTREMUM. *v.* FINE ROLLS.—WRITS.		Receipt of Exchequer	A. 1. a.
DIOCESES:			
Collections, intituled, "Divers Diocefes"	— —	Receipt of Exchequer	A. 1. a.
Collections about them	— —	Inner Temple Library	Q. 2. b.
DISPENSATIONS:			
From the Popes	1194 to Hen. 8.	Britifh Mufeum	U.
Difpenfations	1532 to 1699	State Paper Office	C. 1. a.
Rolls	37 Eliz. to 20 Geo. 2.	Rolls Chapel	D. 1. 2.
Regifters of	1692 to prefent Time	Clerk of the Difpenfations	D. 17.
v. CHANCERY. — POPES. — PREROGATIVE ROYAL.			
DISSENTERS. *v.* BANGOR DIOCESE.—PEACE, CLERKS OF.			
DISTRINGAS. *v.* WRITS.			
DIVORCES:			
Collections about them	— —	Inner Temple Library	Q. 2. b.
Proceedings on the Divorce between Henry Holland, Son of John Duke of Exeter, and Anne Plantagenet, Daughter of Richard Duke of York	1470 and 1471	Bodleian Library	O. 1.
v. CLAUS ROLLS.—HENRY VIII.			
DOCKS. *v.* HARBOURS.			
DOCK YARDS:			
Commiffions purfuant to Statutes for fortifying Dock Yards, Coafts and Havens, Powder Magazines, &c. and Proceedings thereon	1714 to 1784	Clerk of Crown Chancery	D. 2.
v. EXCHEQUER OF ACCOUNT.			
DOMESDAY BOOK:			
Domefday Book, 2 Vols.	Temp. Will. 1.	Receipt of the Exchequer	A. 1. a.
A Copy thereof, with more Abbreviations, and omitting the Enumeration of Villains, Borderers, and Stock	— —	King's Rememb. Office	G. 6. a.

ALPHABETICAL ARRANGEMENT OF THE PUBLIC RECORDS.

RECORDS and other INSTRUMENTS.	DATE.	WHERE KEPT.	Appendix to the Firſt Report.
DOMESDAY BOOK—*(continued.)*			
Abſtract of	— —	Royal Society Library	R.
An antient Abſtract of (imperfect)	— —		
Domeſday Book for the Counties of Somerſet, Dorſet, Devon, and Cornwall;—Either an antient Tranſcript, or the Original Documents from which the Account of thoſe Counties was taken	— —	Dean and Chapter Exeter	N. 6.
Domeſday Book for Wincheſter, made in the Reign of Hen. I.	1148	Antiq. Society Library	S. a.
Dugdale's Extracts from Domeſday and the Hundred Rolls	— —	Aſhmolean Muſeum	O. 2.
DORSET, County:			
Domeſday Book for this, and ſome other Counties	— —	Dean and Chapter Exeter	N. 6.
Tenuræ Terrarum	— —	Univerſity Library Camb.	P. 1.
Inquiſitiones de Miniſtris	4 Edw. 1.	Receipt of the Exchequer	A. 1. a.
Nona Roll	15 Edw. 3.	King's Rememb. Office	G. 6. b.
Eccleſiaſtical Survey	26 Hen. 8.	Firſt Fruits Office	G. 18.
Receivers Accounts of Leaſes of Fee Farms belonging to Queen Henrietta Maria	16 Car. 1.	Univerſity Library Camb.	P. 1.
v. Domesday Book.			
DOVER:			
The Names of the Tenants who pay Caſtle Ward Rent to Dover Caſtle	1 Ed. 4.	Antiq. Society Library	S. a.
Account of Money for Repairs of the Pier	1614	Auditors Office Land Rev.	G. 15.
DOWERS. *v.* Chancery.—Claus Rolls.			
DROGHEDA, Ireland:			
Two Charters relating thereto	— —	Corp. Chriſti Coll. Camb.	P. 5.
DUGDALE, Sir William:			
His Extracts from Domeſday Book and Hundred Rolls *	— —	Aſhmolean Muſeum	O. 2.
v. Concilia.—Parliament Records.			
DURHAM, County Palatine:			
Crown Court:			
Indictments and Preſentments, Informations and Recognizances, Traverſes of Indictments, Writs and Returns, Calendars of Priſoners, Minute and Order Books	— —	Clerk of the Crown, Durham	H. 12. a.
Court of Pleas:			
Writs, Original	For more than 100 Years back	Prothonotary of Durham	H. 12. b.
Bail Recognizances			
Affidavits and Petitions			
Declarations and other Pleadings in Cauſes depending			
Declarations for Judgments by Warrant of Attorney			
Bills of Coſts taxed			
Rolls of all Judgments, Common Recoveries, &c.			
The Inſtruments neceſſary for ſuffering Common Recoveries			
Writs of Covenant, and Dedimus Poteſtatem, and Precipes or Concords neceſſary for levying Fines			
Feet of Fines			
Remembrance Books			
Court of Chancery:			
Original Orders and Decrees	1613 to the preſent Time, with Chaſms	Regiſter Court of Chancery, Durham	H. 12. c.
Awards on Incloſures, &c.	— —		

* Great Collections of Dugdale and Dodſworth upon Monaſtic Affairs, &c. are in the Bodleian Library.

ALPHABETICAL ARRANGEMENT OF THE PUBLIC RECORDS.

RECORDS and other INSTRUMENTS.	DATE.	WHERE KEPT.	Appendix to the Firſt Report.
DURHAM—*(continued.)*			
CURSITORS:			
Precipes for Writs iſſued out of the Court of Chancery, at Durham - - - -	— —		
Affidavits for Debts - - - - - -	— —		
Writs iſſued out of the Courts at Weſtminſter, on which the Biſhop's Mandate is neceſſary -	— —		
Books, in which are entered all Writs iſſued -	Regular from 1764		
Cloſe Rolls of the Latin Chancery - - -	1333 to preſent Time		
Copyhold Books - - - - - - -	From 17th Year of Biſhop Hatfield to 17th Jac. 1. - -	Curſitor, Durham - -	H. 12. d.
Inquiſitiones Poſt Mortem - - - - -	1333 to 1628 - -		
Mandates and Returns of Writs for electing Members to ſerve in Parliament for the County and City - - - - - - -	1727 to the preſent Time - - - -		
DURHAM, COUNTY:			
Nona Roll - - - - - - - -	15 Ed. 3. - - -	King's Rememb. Office -	G. 6. b.
Eccleſiaſtical Survey - - - - - -	26 Hen. 8. - - -	Firſt Fruits Office - -	G. 18.
DIOCESE, CONSISTORY COURT:			
Terriers of Glebe Lands, &c. - - -	— —		
Regiſter Book, in which Wills and Faculties are entered - - - - - - - - -	— —	Conſiſtory Court, Durham - - -	L. 6. d.
Bonds on Adminiſtrations granted - - -	— —		
Marriage Licences - - - - -	— —		
Proceedings in Suits - - - - -	— —		
Wills and Copies of Regiſters - - -	— —	Biſhop's Regiſtry, Durham	L. 6. b.
v. An Account of the Records of this See, in Gutch's Collectanea Curioſa, Vol. 2.			
DEAN AND CHAPTER:			
A Series of Royal Charters, chiefly relating to the Poſſeſſions of the Priory and Church of Durham	Will. 1. to Jac. 1. -	Dean & Chap. Durham	N. 24. b.
Endowments, &c. of Livings in the Counties of Durham, York, &c. - - - -	— —		
EARL MARSHAL. *v.* MARSHAL.			
EAST INDIA COMPANY:			
Papers relating thereto - - - - -	— —	Bodleian Library - -	O. 1.
Letters and Papers relating thereto - - -	1585 to 1763 - -	State Paper Office - -	C. 1. a.
An Indenture between Queen Anne and the Two Companies for their Union - - - -	1702 - - - -	King's Rememb. Office	G. 6. a.
Liſts of Peers and Members of the Houſe of Commons, nominated purſuant to Stat. 24 Geo. III. c. 25. for Trial of Offences committed in India - - - - - - - - -	— —	Clerk of the Crown in Chancery - - -	D. 2. a.
v. TRADE, FOREIGN.			
EASTERN PRINCES. *v.* TURKEY.			
ECCLESIASTICAL AFFAIRS:			
Writs of Convocation - - - - -	— —	Conſiſtory Courts - -	L.
Collections, intituled, "Divers Dioceſes" - -	— —	Receipt of the Exchequer	A. 1. a.
An Order concerning the Tranſlation of the Bible	— —	Univerſity Library Camb.	P. 1.
Surveys, Benefices, Church Diſcipline, Commiſſions, &c. - - - - - - -	1377 to 1679 - -	State Paper Office - -	C. 1. a
Accounts of Farmers of Church Lands in Devon, Somerſet, and Wilts - - - - -	3 & 4 Phil. & Mary	Auditors Office Land Rev.	G. 15.
The Thirty-nine Articles - - - - -	temp. Eliz. - - -	Corpus Chriſti Coll. Camb.	P. 5.
Book of Common Prayer delivered into the Exchequer, purſuant to Act of Uniformity - -	13 & 14 Car. 1. -	King's Rememb. Office	G. 6. a.
Another with the Great Seal appendant - -	1622 - - - -	Tower - - - - -	A. 1. a.
Letters and Papers relative to the Univerſities Petitions, Reports, &c. - - - -	1684 to 1769 - -	State Paper Office -	C. 1. a.
v. CLAUS ROLLS.—CHARLES, PRINCE.—The ſeveral DIOCESES, UNIVERSITIES, COLLEGES, &c.			
COURTS:			
A Collection of antient Inſtruments, and Proceedings therein, 2 Vols. - - - -	— —	Inner Temple Library -	Q. 2. b.

ALPHABETICAL ARRANGEMENT OF THE PUBLIC RECORDS.

RECORDS and other INSTRUMENTS.	DATE.	WHERE KEPT.	Appendix to the Firſt Report.
EDWARD VI.			
His Inſtructions to the Clergy - - - - -	Edw. 6. - - - -	Corp. Chriſti Coll. Camb.	P. 5.
v. Clergy.			
EDWARD, Prince of Wales (the Black Prince):			
Survey of Manors and Boroughs granted to him -	11 Ed. 3. - - -	King's Rememb. Office -	G. 6. a.
Extents of Manors belonging to him - -	19 Ed. 3. - - -	Univerſity Lib. Camb.	P. 1.
v. Cornwall Duchy.			
ELENS, St. Bishopsgate. *v.* Land Revenue.			
ELLIOT, Sir John:			
Proceedings againſt him and others in the Star Chamber - - - - - - - - -	— —	Univerſity Lib. Camb.	P. 1.
v. Star Chamber.			
ELSING SPITTLE, Cripplegate.			
v. Land Revenue.			
ELTHAM, Kent:			
Survey of the Manor - - - - - - -	1605 - - - -	King's Rememb. Office -	G. 6. a.
ELY, Diocese:			
Charters, many curious and antient - - -	King Edgar to Ed. 3.	Ely Houſe, Dover St.	L. 9. a.
Bulls of Popes concerning the Foundation - -	— —	Ely Houſe, Dover St.	L. 9. a.
Repertory to the Records, by Biſhop Wren -	— —	Ely Houſe, Dover St.	L. 9. a.
Surveys of the Manors of the See - - -	— —	Ely Houſe, Dover St.	L. 9. a.
Terriers of Livings - - - - -	— —	Saint Mary's Church, Cambridge - -	L. 9. a.
Endowments of Livings - - - - - -	— —	Saint Mary's Church, Cambridge - -	L. 9. a.
Wills - - - - - - - - - -	— —	Saint Mary's Church, Cambridge - -	L. 9. a.
Epiſcopal Regiſter Books, containing Appropriations and Endowments - - - - -	1337 to 1540 - -	Regiſter of Ely, Camb.	L. 9. b.
EMPEROR and AUSTRIA:			
Negotiations and Treaties with - - -	— —	Univerſity Library Camb.	P. 1.
ENDOWMENTS:			
A Repertory of the Foundations and Endowments of Abbies, &c. preſerved in the Tower - - - - - - - - -	— —	Britiſh Muſeum - -	U.
Certificates and Anſwers from Pariſh Miniſters and Churchwardens, as to Foundations and Endowments, and from the Maſters, &c. of Crafts and Companies in London - - - - -	Hen. 8. to Mar. -	Auditors Office Land Rev.	G. 15.
Charters of Endowments - - - - -	Various Dates - -	Britiſh Muſeum - -	U.
v. The ſeveral Dioceses.—Chartæ Antiquæ.—Land Revenue.—Vicarages.			
ENGLISH Bills and Informations.			
v. Exchequer of Account.			
ERROR. *v.* Claus Rolls.—King's Bench.—Lords, House of.—Writs.			
ESCHEAT:			
Rolls - - - - - - - - - -	— —	Augmentation Office -	G. 19. a.
Papers relating to Eſcheats - - - - -	— —	State Paper Office - -	C. 1. a.
Extracts of Records of Eſcheats by Mr. Cole -	— —	Britiſh Muſeum - -	U.
Terræ Normannorum - - - - - -	Hen. 3. - - - -	Receipt of the Exchequer	A. 1. 2.
Rolls, being Accounts of Lands, &c. eſcheated to the Crown - - - - - - -	Edw. 1. & ſeq. - -	King's Rememb. Office -	G. 6.
The like - - - - - - - -	5 & 6 Edw. 2 - -	Receipt of the Exchequer	A. 1. a.
The like in Eſſex and Herts - - - - -	Edw. 3. - - - -	Auditors Office Land Rev.	G. 15.
Bundles of - - - - - - - -	1 Hen. 7. to 20 Car. 1.	Rolls Chapel - - - -	D. 1. a.
Miniſters Accounts of Lands acquired by Eſcheat	Hen. 8. to Car. 1. -	Auditors Office Land Revenue - - -	G. 15.
v. Claus Rolls. — Inquisitiones post Mortem. — Leicester County.—Revenue Royal.			
ESCHEATORS:			
Accounts of - - - - - - - - -	Hen. 6. - - - -	Auditors Office Land Revenue - - -	G. 15.
Rolls, called Lord Treaſurer's Rolls, containing Inrolments of Patents to them - - -	Ed. 5. to 17 Car. 1.	Rolls Chapel - - -	D. 1. a.
Their Oath - - - - - - - -	— —	King's Rememb. Office	Page 234.
v. Fine Rolls.			

ALPHABETICAL ARRANGEMENT OF THE PUBLIC RECORDS.

RECORDS and other INSTRUMENTS.	DATE.	WHERE KEPT.	Appendix to the First Report.
ESSEX, COUNTY:			
Antient Deeds, &c. relative to Eſtates therein -	— —	Dean and Chap. Weſtm.	N. 12. b.
Book of Knights Fees - - - - - -	Hen 3. to the Abolition of Military Tenures - - -	Lord Treaf. Rem. Office	G. 7. a.
Perambulatio facta in Com. Eſſex - - -	9 Hen. 3. - - -	Bodleian Library -	O. 1.
Inquiſitiones de Miniſtris - - - -	4 Edw. 1. - - -	Receipt of the Exchequer	A. 1. a.
Nona Roll - - - - - - - -	15 Edw. 3. - - -	King's Rememb. Office -	G. 6. b.
Rolls, being Accounts of Lands eſcheated to the Crown - - - - - -	Edw. 3. - - - -	Auditors Office Land Revenue -	G. 15. a.
Account of Forts in Eſſex - - - -	1 Edw. 6. - - -	(Auditors Office Land Revenue)	G. 15. a.
Rentals of Abbey Lands, and Forfeited Eſtates in Eſſex, &c. - - - - - - -	1638 - - - - -	Univerſity Library Camb.	P. 1.
ESTREATS:			
Great Numbers of them, in various Reigns -	— —	Auditors Office Land Rev.	G. 15. a.
Duplicates of, entered into Proceſs - - -	— —	Foreign Appoſer - -	G. 11.
Rolls of Inquiſitions - - - - -	3 Edw. 1. - - -	Receipt of the Exchequer	A. 1. a.
Of Fines at the Seſſions in Kent - - -	12 Hen. 7. - - -	Auditors Office Land Rev.	G. 15. a.
FOREIGN:			
Rolls of Fines and Recognizances—King's Bench	— —	Foreign Eſtreats Office	G. 10.
Poſt Fine Rolls—Common Pleas - - -	— —	Foreign Eſtreats Office	G. 10.
Recognizances returned from the Houſe of Commons - - - - - - -	— —	Foreign Eſtreats Office	G. 10.
Eſtreats from Chancery of all Grants whereon Rent or Service is due - - - - -	— —	Lord Treaf. Rem. Office	G. 7. b.
Eſtreats returned by Clerks of Aſſize and Sewers	1631 to the preſent Time - -	Foreign Eſtreats Office -	G. 10.
- - - - by the Clerks of the Peace and Town Clerks - - - - - -	1631 to the preſent Time - -	Foreign Eſtreats Office -	G. 10.
Affidavits of Claims of Fines by Bailiffs of Liberties - - - - - - -	1631 to the preſent Time - -	Foreign Eſtreats Office -	G. 10.
v. CHANCERY.—COMMON PLEAS.—EXCHEQUER OF ACCOUNT.—KING'S BENCH.—PEACE, CLERKS OF THE.			
ETON, BUCKS:			
A Collection reſpecting Eton College, by the Rev. Mr. Huggett - - - - - -	— —	Britiſh Muſeum - -	U.
EXCHANGE AND PURCHASE:			
Deeds of - - - - - - - -	Hen. 8. & Edw. 6.	Augmentation Office -	G. 19. a.
EXCHEQUER OF ACCOUNT:			
Collectanea, or Extracts from the Records in the Exchequer, Patent, and Cloſe Rolls, &c. by Thomas Madox, Eſq; - - - -	— —	Britiſh Muſeum - -	U.
Miſcellanies, Bundles, and Files, conſiſting chiefly of Petitions of Allowances, Commiſſions with their Returns, Writs with their Returns, Inquiſitions, Pleadings, Affidavits, &c. - -	From very antient Times to the preſent	Lord Treaſurer's Remembrancer's Office -	G. 7. a.
Memoranda, conſiſting of Pleadings in Suits, and Judgments thereon; particularly upon Writs of "Quo Titulo Clamat" and "Quare Maneria," &c. Pleadings on Petitions of Right, on Claims of Franchiſes and Privileges, and on Eſtreats; Commiſſions to ſurvey Crown Lands, &c. Proceedings concerning Sheriff's Accompts, Orders of the Court concerning the Land and Caſual Revenue, Entries of Admiſſions of Officers, and Inrolments of Deeds, &c. acknowledged before the Barons - - - - -	Hen. 3. to the preſent Time - -	Lord Treaſurer's Remembrancer's Office -	G. 7. a.
Originalia, containing Eſtreats of all Grants from the Crown, whereon Rents are reſerved, Salaries payable, or Services performed - -	Hen. 3. to the preſent Time - -	Lord Treaſurer's Remembrancer's Office -	G. 7. a.
Catalogue of Books in Cuſtody of the King's and Lord Treaſurer's Remembrancer - -	— —	Aſhmolean Muſeum -	O. 2.
Index or Repertory of Decrees, Orders, Inrolments, &c. - - - - - - -	Edw. 1. to Geo. 3.	Inner Temple Library -	Q. 2. b.

ALPHABETICAL ARRANGEMENT OF THE PUBLIC RECORDS.

RECORDS and other INSTRUMENTS.	DATE.	WHERE KEPT.	Appendix to the First Report.
EXCHEQUER OF ACCOUNT—*(continued.)*			
Memoranda, Copies of - - - - - -	1 to 22 Edw. 3. -	Lincoln's Inn Library -	Q. 3.
Computus Dñi Johis de Okham de Scaccario -	4 Edw. 3. - - -	Bodleian Library - -	O. 1.
Communia, Copies of - - - - - -	23 to 46 Edw. 3. -	Lincoln's Inn Library -	Q. 3.
Commissions, Repertory to - - - -	Ric. 3. to 3 Car. 1.		
Papers relative to the Court of Exchequer -	1558 to 1633 - -	State Paper Office - -	C. 1. a.
Several Grants and Patents under the Great and Privy Seal - - - - - - -	— —		
Perambulations - - - - - - -	— —		
Bonds for due Execution of Offices and Trusts -	— —		
Proffers, being Money paid Half-yearly by Sheriffs of Counties, and Bailiffs of Liberties - -	— —		
Accounts of Receivers of Taxes, Inrolments of -	— —		
Process against Receivers and Collectors of Assessments and Taxes - - - - - -	— —		
Commissions, &c. on Subsidy, 14 Edward III. -	— —		
Decrees of Commissioners for purchasing Lands, &c. for Security of Dockyards at Portsmouth, Plymouth, &c. - - - - - -	— —		
Commissions of Inquiry, and Proceedings thereon, whereby the Estates of Debtors and Accomptants of the Crown, and Estates forfeited to the Crown, are seized into the King's Hands -	— —		
Commissions on Attainders, or Forfeitures for Treason or Felony - - - - - - -	— —		
Informations on Seizures of Goods forfeited -	— —		
Affidavits for Goods on which Custom hath been paid, but which have been lost at Sea or taken by Enemies - - - - - - -	— —	King's Remembrancer's Office - - -	G. 6. a.
Recognizances taken in Court - - -	— —		
Personal Informations, and Proceedings thereon, for Forfeitures arising to the Crown, and Informers, for Offences committed against Penal Laws - - - - - - - - -	— —		
Proceedings by English Information in the Name of the Attorney General, on Behalf of the Revenue, and on Account of Charities, Trusts, &c.	Commencing 1 Eliz.		
Writs of Scire Facias, and Proceedings thereon for Recovery of Debts due to the Crown - -	— —		
Writs of Extent, and Proceedings thereon - -	— —		
Proceedings in Equity by English Bill, and Information, and Decrees - - - - - -	— —		
English Bills and Answers between Party and Party - - - - - - - -	— —		
Special Commissions and Inquisitions - -	— —		
Depositions taken by virtue of Commissions for Examination of Witnesses - - -	— —		
Depositions taken before Barons of the Court who have resigned or are dead - - - -	— —		
Orders and Decrees of the Court - - -	— —		
A Book of Orders and Decrees - - -	28 and 31 Eliz. -		
Agenda Rolls, containing short Entries of Awards, Judgments, &c. - - - - - -	— —		
Orders, Books of Minutes, and Books of Entries	From Jac. 2. - -	Lord Treasurer's Remembrancer's Office	G. 7. a.
v. Claus Rolls.—Courts of Justice.—Law Cases.—Lib. Nig.—Lib. Rub.			
Oath of the Chancellor of the Exchequer - -	— —		
Oath of the Chamberlain - - - -	— —		
Oath of his Deputy - - - - - -	— —		
Oath of the Examiner - - - - - -	— —		
Oath of the Marshal - - - - - -	— —	King's Remem. Office	*Pages* 233 to 235.
Oath of the Messengers - - - - -	— —		
Oath of the Remembrancers - - - -	— —		
Oath of the Chief Usher	— —		
Of the Under Usher - - - - - -	— —		
Oath of the Barons. *v.* Barons.			

ALPHABETICAL ARRANGEMENT OF THE PUBLIC RECORDS.

RECORDS and other INSTRUMENTS.	DATE.	WHERE KEPT.	Appendix to the First Report.
Of Receipt:			
Waste or Charge Book, for Entries of Payments into the Exchequer - - - - - -	— —	Tellers Office - -	G. 3.
Debentures and Vouchers for Payments into the Exchequer - - - - - - -	— —		
Accounts of the Four Tellers - - - -	1 & 2 Jac. 1. - -	Library of the Royal Soc.	R.
Tallies to be delivered to the several Persons entitled to them - - - - - - -	— —	Chamberlain's Office -	G. 2.
Standard Pieces of Gold and Silver - - -	Temp. Edw. 4. - Hen. 8. Eliz. - Jac. 1. Car. 2. Anne and Geo. 2.		
Standard Pieces of Silver for Ireland - -	Temp. Hen. 8. and Eliz. - - - -		
Certificates of their being according to the Old Standard - - - - - - -	Edw. 4. - - -		
Standard Weights - - - - - -	1582 and 1588 -		
Standard Measures of Length - - -	Hen. 7. - - - -		
Standard Measures of Capacity - - -	Hen. 7. Eliz. Anne, and Geo. 2. - -		
Counterparts of Indentures of Weights and Measures	1700 to present Time		
Books of Accounts - - - - - -	— —	Auditors First Office -	G. 1.
Patent Books - - - - - - -	1619 to the present Time - -		
Privy Seal Books - - - - - -	1620		
Books of Issues by Debentures - - -	1662		
Books of Declarations - - - - - -	1666		
Tellers Bills - - - - - - -	1681 to present Time	Tally Writers Office -	
Imprest Roll Books - - - - - -	1685 - to the present Time		
Book of Issues by Orders - - - - -			
Certificate Books - - - - - -	1688	Auditors First Office -	
Cash Books - - - - - - -			
Letter Books - - - - - - -	1689		
Certificates & Register Books - - - -	1706 to present Time	Tally Writers Office -	
Transcripts of Patents, Constitutions, Contracts, Signs Manual, Privy Seals, Treasurers Warrants, and other Instruments connected with the Receipt or Issues of the Exchequer - - -	1612 to the present Time -	Pell Office - - - -	G. 4.
Transcripts of the Declarations of the Receipts and Issues made up at Easter and Michaelmas, and transmitted to the Treasury - - -	1693		
The Introitus, or Record of Monies received into the Exchequer - - - - - -	1715		
The Exitus, or Record of Monies issued out of the Exchequer - - - - - - - -	1725		
Catalogue of Rolls and Privy Seals in the Pell Office - - - - - - - - -	— —	Bodleian Library - -	O. 1.
Issue and Certificate Books of Exchequer Bills -	1697 to present Time	Exchequer Bill Office in the Auditors Office -	G. 1.
Books of Issues, with the Registers and Posting Books for the First Annuities	1693 to present Time	First Annuity Office at the Auditors Office -	
Books of Issues, with the Registers and Posting Books for the Second Annuities - - -	1704 to present Time	Second Annuity Office at the Auditors Office -	
Day Books, Out Cash Books, and Certificate Books of the Payments of the several Exchequer Annuities - - - - - - -	From Commencement of each Annuity, to the present Time - -	Examiners of Tellers Vouchers at the Auditors Office - -	
Issue Books, Assignments, Letters of Attorney, &c. of the American Payments and Tontine Annuities - - - - - - -	— —	Office for American Payments and Tontine Annuities, at the Auditors Office -	
v. Claus Rolls.—Measures.—Liber Rubeus.—Pells.—Tallies.—Weights.			
Oath of the Deputy Chamberlain - - -	— —	Receipt of the Exchequer - -	*Page* 232.
Oath of the Messengers - - - - -	— —		
Oath of the Usher of - - - - -	— —		
Oath of the Usher to the Lord Treasurer - -	— —		

ALPHABETICAL ARRANGEMENT OF THE PUBLIC RECORDS.

RECORDS and other INSTRUMENTS.	DATE.	WHERE KEPT.	Appendix to the First Report.
EXCHEQUER—*(continued.)*			
Of Pleas:			
Certificates of Attornies, Entries of - - -	— —		
Proceedings in Error, Minutes of - - -	— —		
Rolls, containing Pleadings and Judgments, Copies of Deeds inrolled, and other Proceedings - -	Ed. 1. - - -		
Writs, Files of - - - - - - -	Ed. 3. - - -		
Files of Bills or Declarations, of Bail Pieces, and Affidavits, and Rules or Orders made Rules of Court - - - - - - -	14 Ed. 4. -		
Books of Orders, containing Rules of Court, Judgments, Notices of Trial, and Execution of Writs of Inquiry - - - - -	3 Ed. 6. - -		
Remembrancers Rolls, and Rolls of Writs -	Temp. Eliz. & from 1690 - (to the present Time.)	Clerk of the Pleas -	G. 20.
Appearances for Defendants, &c. Books of, -	28 Eliz. - -		
Minute Books - - - - - - -	One Temp. Eliz and from 1722 - -		
Docket Books - - - - - - -	Jac. 1. - -		
Writs of Subpœna, Books of Entries of - -	1785 - - -		
Files of Affidavits of Debt - - - -	1791 - - -		
Warrants of Retainer to prosecute and defend -	1792 - - -		
EXCISE:			
Various Papers relating thereto - - -	— —	British Museum - - -	U.
Excise Books and Accounts - - - -	1645 to 1647, with Chasms - - -	Bodleian Library - - -	O. 1.
Matters relative thereto - - - -	1716 to 1748 - -	State Paper Office - -	C. 1. a.
EXCOMMUNICATIONS:			
Certificates of, from the Ecclesiastical Courts - - *v.* King's Bench.—Liber Rubeus.—Significavits.—Writs.	— —	Rolls Chapel - -	D. 1. a.
EXEMPLIFICATIONS:			
Of Statutes under the Great Seal - - - *v.* Land Revenue.	6 Hen. 8. to 10 Geo. 3.		
EXEMPTIONS. *v.* Claus Rolls.			
EXERCITUS REGIS. *v.* Chivalry.			
EXETER, Diocese:			
Ecclesiastical Survey - - - - - -	26 Hen. 8. - - -	First Fruits Office - -	G. 18.
Episcopal Registers - - - - - -	1257 to present Time		
Wills and Administrations - - - -	1592 to 1653 inclusive, and from 1660 to prt Time		
Consistorial Court:			
Wills and Administrations - - - -	1591 to 1650 inclusive, and from 1660 to prt Time	Bishop's Registry, Exeter - -	L. 25. a.
Causes, Judicial Proceedings in - - -	1604 to present Time		
Dean and Chapter:			
Letters of Kings and Queens to the Dean and Chapter - - - - - - -	Hen. 5. to Eliz. -	Dean and Chapter Exeter	N. 6.
EXTENTS:			
Of Manors - - - - - - - -	Temp. Ed. 1. 2. 3. &c.	King's Remembrancer's Office - - -	
Of Possessions of Knights Templars - -	Edw. 2. - - - -		G. 6.
Of Manors, Farms, Woods, Rectories, &c. -	Edw. 3. to Anne -	Auditors Office Land Rev.	G. 15. a.
Dockets of Writs of - - - - - -	1601 to present Time	Clerk of Crown in Chan.	D. 2.
v. Chancery.—Exchequer of Account.—Knights Templars.—Land Revenue.—Manors.—Statutes Staple.			
EYRE:			
Proceedings in. *v.* Forests.			

ALPHABETICAL ARRANGEMENT OF THE PUBLIC RECORDS.

RECORDS and other INSTRUMENTS.	DATE.	WHERE KEPT.	Appendix to the First Report
FARNHAM, SURREY:			
Placita Concilii (Copy) - - - - -	1569 - - - -	University Library Camb.	P. 1.
FASTS:			
Proclamations for - - - - - -	1743 - - - -	Clerk of Crown in Chan.	D. 2. a.
FEE FARM RENTS:			
Accounts of Fee Farm Rents belonging to Queen Henrietta Maria, Queen of Charles I. - -	}		
Particulars for Sale of Fee Farm Rents - -	} 16 Car. 1. - -	University Library Cam.	P. 1.
Sales of Fee Farm Rents in Wales - - -	16 Car. 1. - - -	Auditor for Wales - -	G. 16.
State of Arrears of - - - - -	1649 - - - -	University Library Camb.	P. 1.
Rolls for each County - - - - - -	}		
Particulars for Sale of them - - - -	} Temp. Interregni.	Augmentation Office -	G. 19. a.
Deeds of Sale of them - - - - -	}		
Rentals of in Wales - - - - -	1 Anne to the present Time - - -	Auditor for Wales - -	G. 16.
v. LAND REVENUE.—SURVEYOR GENERAL.			
FELONS. *v.* CRIMES.—EXCHEQUER OF ACCOUNT.—FORFEITURES.—TRANSPORTATION.			
FENS:			
Inquisitions concerning Fens - - - -	Temp. Edw. 3. -	Receipt of the Exchequer	A. 1. a.
v. NOTTINGHAM and DERBY.			
FENWICK, SIR JOHN:			
Proceedings against him in the House of Lords -	1696 - - - -	Bodleian Library - -	O. 1.
FEOFFMENTS:			
Feoffments - - - - - - - - -	— —	Augmentation Office -	G. 19. a.
v. CHARTÆ ANTIQUÆ.			
FEVERSHAM. *v.* GUNPOWDER MAGAZINES.			
FIFTEENTHS. *v.* TENTHS.			
FINES:			
Proclamations, Writs of Entry, Exigents, Writs of Covenant, Concords, Summons, Mittimus, Seisin, &c. - - - - - - -	1180 to 1688 - -	Receipt of the Exchequer	A. 1. a.
Rolls - - - - - - - - -	1204 to 1483 - -	Tower - - - - -	A. 2. a.
Indentures of - - - - - - -	Ric. 2 to Car. 1. -	British Museum - - -	U.
Fine Rolls, otherwise called the Lord Treasurer's Rolls, containing Inrolments of Patents to Escheators, &c. General Liveries, and Entries of Writs of Diem Clausit Extremum - -	Edw. 5. to 17 Car. 1.	Rolls Chapel - - - -	D. 1. a.
Fines - - - - - - - - -	Hen. 8. &c. - -	Augmentation Office -	G. 19. a.
Records of - - - - - - - -	Beginning of Hen. 8. to the present Time	Chirographer's Office -	F. 7.
Books of, containing a Description of the Estates, &c. on which Fines are levied in all Counties in England, except the Counties Palatine - -	Edw. 6. to the present Time - - -	King's Silver Office - -	F. 6.
Writs of Covenant for passing Fines - -	1627 to the present Time - - - -	Clerk of the Returns, Prothonotaries Office -	F. 8.
v. CLAUS ROLLS.—COMMON PLEAS.—ESTREATS.			
FIRST FRUITS:			
Pleas and Proceedings respecting them - -	}		
Proceedings in the Exchequer against Receivers of First Fruits and Tenths, and upon Sheriffs Accounts respecting them - - - -	} 1 Mary to the present Time - -	First Fruits Office - -	G. 18.
FISHERIES:			
Collections about them - - - - - -	— —	Inner Temple Library -	Q. 2. b.
Of Greenland, Newfoundland, &c. - - - -	1583 to 1677 - -	State Paper Office - -	C. 1. a.
v. CLAUS ROLLS.			
FITZWILLIAM, LORD:			
His Papers - - - - - - - -	Temp. Eliz. - -	Bodleian Library - -	O. 1.
FLANDERS:			
Treaties and Transactions with - - - -	1161 to 1408 - -	Receipt of the Exchequer	A. 1. a.
Negotiations, Instructions, Correspondences, &c. -	1340 to 1677 - -	State Paper Office - -	C. 1. a.

ALPHABETICAL ARRANGEMENT OF THE PUBLIC RECORDS.

RECORDS and other INSTRUMENTS.	DATE.	WHERE KEPT.	Appendix to the First Report.
FLORIDA:			
Oath of the Commiſſioners appointed by Statute 26 George III. for aſcertaining Loſſes of Perſons in conſequence of the Ceſſion of the Province to Spain	— —	Petty Bag Office	*Page* 229.
FOREIGN APPOSER:			
His Oath	— —	King's Rememb. Office	— 234.
FOREIGN ACCOUNTS. *v.* Pipe Rolls.			
FOREIGN ESTREATS. *v.* Estreats.			
FOREIGN PRINCES. *v.* Princes.			
FOREIGNERS, in London, &c.:			
Papers concerning them	1571 to 1635	State Paper Office	C. 1. a.
FORESTS:			
A Variety of Materials reſpecting Foreſt Juriſdictions	— —	Britiſh Muſeum	U.
Collections reſpecting them	— —	Inner Temple Library	Q. 2. b.
Extracts of Surveys and other Records	— —	Office of Surveyor General Crown Lands	G. 14.
Account of Woods and Foreſts	— —	Auditors Office Land Rev.	G. 15. a.
Accounts of Fines for Offences committed againſt the Foreſt Laws	— —	King's Rememb. Office	G 6. a.
Laws, Perambulations, Claims, &c.	1199 to 1666	State Paper Office	C. 1. a.
Placita Foreſtæ, Perambulations, and other Proceedings	10 John to the End of Edw. 3.	Receipt of the Exchequer	A. 1. a.
Perambulations	Temp. Hen. 3. & 7. 28 & 29 Edw. 1.	Tower	A. 2. a.
Charta Generalis de Foreſtis	2 Hen. 3.	Dean and Chap. Durham	N. 24. b.
Charta de Foreſtis	Hen. 3.	Corp. Chriſti Coll. Camb.	P. 5.
The like	Hen. 3.	Aſhmolean Muſeum	O. 2.
Charta de Foreſta of Henry III. Confirmation thereof by Edward	28 Edw. 1.	Oriel College, Oxford	O. 8.
Claims	Temp. Edw. 1. and Car. 1.	Tower	A. 2. a.
Perambulations	17 Car. 1.	Petty Bag Office	D. 5.
Perambulation of Foreſts in Derbyſhire	— —	} King's Rememb. Office	
Placita Foreſtæ in Ducat' Lancaſtriæ	8 Edw. 3.		G. 6. a.
Perambulation of Royal Foreſts in Bucks	26 Hen. 8.	Univerſity Library Camb.	P. 1.
Survey of Inglewood Foreſt in Cumberland	1619	King's Rememb. Office	G. 6. a.
Proceedings in the Foreſt Courts of Waltham and Deane	Temp. Car. 1.	} Univerſity Library Cambridge	
Proceedings in Eyre of the Foreſts North of Trent	30 and 31 Hen. 8.		P. 1.
Claims, Perambulations, and various Proceedings in Eyre, of the Foreſts South of Trent	Car. 2.	Receipt of the Exchequer	A. 1. a.
Warrants of Diſafforeſtation	1637 to 1639	Univerſity Library Camb.	P. 1.
v. Brevia Regia.—Claus Rolls.—Inglewood.—Lancaster, County Palatine and Duchy.—Land Revenue.—Parliament.—Special Commissions.			
FORFEITED ESTATES:			
Commiſſions on Attainders and Forfeited Eſtates for Treaſon, Felonies, &c.	— —	} King's Remembrancer's Office, Exchequer	
Commiſſions of Inquiry, and Proceedings thereon, when Eſtates forfeited to the Crown are ſeized into the King's Hands	— —		G. 6. a.
Accounts of Forfeited Eſtates, as alſo of Sequeſtrations	— —	Auditors Office Land Rev.	G. 15.
Miniſters Accounts of	— —	Augmentation Office	G. 19. a.
Some Surveys and Accounts of	Temp. Hen. 8.	Receipt of the Exchequer	A. 1. a.
Survey of Eſtates of Duke of Norfolk and Earl of Arundel	Eliz.	King's Rememb. Office	G. 6. a.
Special Commiſſions for Survey of Forfeited Eſtates	Jac. 1. to preſt Time	Petty Bag Office	D. 5.
Rentals of Forfeited Eſtates in Eſſex, Herts, Middleſex, and London	1638	Univerſity Library Camb.	P. 1.
Accounts of	1660	Office of Surveyor General Crown Lands	G. 14.
v. Attainders.—Chancery.—Claus Rolls.—Exchequer of Account.—Felons.—King's Bench.—Ireland.—Treasons.			

ALPHABETICAL ARRANGEMENT OF THE PUBLIC REPORTS.

RECORDS and other INSTRUMENTS.	DATE.	WHERE KEPT.	Appendix to the Firft Report.
FORTRESSES:			
Collections about them - - - - -	— —	Inner Temple Library -	Q. 2. b.
Forts in Effex, Accounts of, and of Captains and Soldiers there - - - - - - -	Edw. 6. - - - -	Auditors Office Land Revenue - - - -	G. 15. a.
Accounts of, and of Expenfes of Works at Carlifle Caftle - - - - - - -	1584, 1604, 1605 -	Auditors Office Land Revenue - - - -	G. 15. a.
Commiffion relative to Forts for the Defence of the Coafts - - - - - - - -	1762 - - - -	Clerk of Crown in Chan.	D. 2. a.
FRANCE:			
Divers Negotiations between France and England	— —	Bodleian Library - -	O. 1.
Treaty between Henry II. and Lewis VII. King of France - - - - - - -	Hen. 2. - - - -	Corpus ChriftiColl. Cam.	P. 5.
Treaties and Tranfactions with - - -	Ric. 1. and Joh. and 1254 to 1612 - -	Receipt of the Exchequer	A. 1. a.
French Rolls - - - - - - - -	1232 to 1483 - -	Tower - - - - -	A. 2. a.
Copies of Declarations, Treaties, &c. refpecting France - - - - - - - -	Edw. 3. - - - -	Afhmolean Mufeum - -	O. 2.
King of England's Dominions in France. A Declaration of the Revenues of France, Normandy, and the Counties of Mayne, Harecourt, and Dreux, in the Time of John Duke of Bedford, Regent in France (a Copy) - -	1427 and 1428 - -	Antiq. Society Library -	S. a.
Tranfactions between England and France - -	1485 to 1613 - -	Britifh Mufeum - - -	U.
Roll of Henry VIIth's Expenfes to affift the Duchefs of Britanny - - - - -	Temp. Hen. 7. - -	Dean & Chapter Weftm.	N. 12. b.
Treaties and Ratifications with England - -	1528 to 1776 - -	State Paper Office - -	C. 1. a.
Negotiations and Treaties with, and various Inftructions to Ambaffadors - - - - -	Chiefly Temp. Eliz.	Univerfity Library Camb.	P. 1.
Letters and Inftructions to Ambaffadors, &c. -	Temp. Eliz. - -	Bodleian Library - -	O. 1.
Sir Francis Walfingham's Negotiations in France *v.* STATE PAPERS.	1570 - - - -	Bodleian Library - -	O. 1.
FRANCHISES:			
Pleadings on Claims of Franchifes and Privileges *v.* CLAIMS.—EXCHEQUER OF ACCOUNT.—NOMINA VILLARUM.	— —	Lord Treaf. Rem. Office	G. 7. a.
FRANKALMOIGNE:			
Deeds of - - - - - - - - -	— —	Augmentation Office -	G. 19. a.
FRIEZELAND, EAST:			
Negotiations in - - - - - - - -	1584 - - - -	Bodleian Library - - -	O. 1.
FUNERALS:			
Papers relative to Royal Funerals - - -	Hen. 3. to Anne -	Dean & Chapter Weftm.	N. 12. b.
Books of Entries of Funeral Certificates, &c. -	21 Hen. 8. to 2 Jac. 2.	College of Arms - - -	C. 8.
Account of the Funeral of James I. - -	1625 - - - -	Duchy of Cornwall - -	C. 7.
FURNESS, LANCASTER:			
Receivers Accounts of Lands belonging to Duchy of Lancafter there - - - - - -	— —	Univerfity Library Camb.	P. 1.
GAOL:			
Deliveries, Special Commiffions for - - -	1272 to 1460, and a few of Edw. 4. -	Receipt of the Exchequer	A. 1. a.
The like for Briftol - - - - - -	1753 - - - -	Clerk of Crown in Chan.	D. 2. a.
GARTER, ORDER OF:			
Statutes of - - - - - - - - -	— —	Receipt of the Exchequer	A. 1. a.
The like - - - - - - - - -	— —	Afhmolean Mufeum - -	O. 2.
Books of Arms of the Knights of the Garter, from their Inftitution - - - - - - -	— —	College of Arms - -	C. 8.
Inftructions for the Manner of delivering the Infignia thereof, to Ferdinand Archduke of Auftria - - - - - - - - - *v.* ARMORIAL BEARINGS.	Temp. Hen. 8. - -	Univerfity Library Camb.	P. 1.
GARTER, KING AT ARMS. *v.* LORDS, HOUSE OF.			
GASCONY:			
Gafcon Rolls - - - - - - - - *v.* CLAUS ROLLS.	1242 to 1460 - -	Tower - - - - -	A. 2. a.
GAVELKIND. *v.* CLAUS ROLLS.			

ALPHABETICAL ARRANGEMENT OF THE PUBLIC RECORDS.

RECORDS and other INSTRUMENTS.	DATE.	WHERE KEPT.	Appendix to the Firſt Report.
GENEALOGY:			
Engliſh and Foreign Heraldry and Genealogy -	1246 to 1761 - -	State Paper Office - -	C. 1. a.
GENERAL LIVERIES:			
Fine Rolls, called Lord Treaſurer's Rolls, containing Inrolments of Patents, General Liveries, &c. - - - - - - -	Ed. 5. to 17 Car. 1.	Rolls Chapel - - -	D. 1. a.
v. Fine Rolls.			
GENOA:			
Tranſactions with England - - - -	1684 to 1775 - -	State Paper Office - -	C. 1. a.
GEORGE I.			
Proceedings at his Coronation - - -	Geo. 1. - - - -	Inner Temple Library -	Q. 2. b.
GEORGE III.			
Commiſſion for Claims at his Coronation - -	— —	Clerk of Crown in Chan.	D. 2.
Expenſes at his Coronation - - - -	1761 - - - -	Inner Temp. Library, and Office of Great Wardrobe	Q. 2. b.
GEORGIA, America:			
Papers relating thereto - - - - - -	— —	Bodleian Library - -	O. 1.
GERMANY:			
Treaties and Tranſactions with - - -	1278 to 1582 - -	Receipt of the Exchequer	A. 1. a
Tranſactions with England - - - -	1485 to 1613 - -	Britiſh Muſeum - - -	U.
Emperor of:			
Treaties and Ratifications with England - -	1509 to 1753 - -	State Paper Office - -	C. 1. a.
Inſtructions to Ambaſſadors at his Court - -	Hen. 8. - - - -	Univerſity Library Camb.	P. 1.
Princes of:			
Treaties and Ratifications with England - -	1559 to 1776 - -		
Towns of:			
Treaties with England - - - -	1663 to 1718 - -	State Paper Office -	C. 1. a.
GIBRALTAR:			
Letters from Governors of Gibraltar to the Secretaries of State - - - - - - -	1705 to 1767 - -		
GLAMORGAN, County:			
Survey of - - - - - - - -	3 and 19 Eliz. - -	Aud.Off.LandRev.Wales	G. 16. a.
GLAMORGAN, BRECON, and RADNOR:			
Oath of the Firſt Juſtice - - - - - -	— —	Clerk of the Crown in Chancery - - -	*Page* 220.
Oath of the Second Juſtice - - - - -	— —		
GLASTONBURY ABBEY. *v.* Chartularies.—Land Revenue.			
GLOUCESTER, County:			
Antient Deeds, &c. relative to Eſtates therein -	— —	Dean and Chap. Weſtm.	N. 12. b.
Repertory of Eſcheats, Inquiſitions, &c. in the Tower - - - - - - - -	— —	Lincoln's Inn Library -	Q. 3.
Leaſes of Mines of Gold and Silver - - -	Temp. Ric. 2. - -	Receipt of the Exchequer	A. 1. a.
Eccleſiaſtical Survey - - - - -	26 Hen. 8. - - -	Firſt Fruits Office - -	G. 18.
Tenures of all the Monaſteries, Priories, Caſtles, Manors, &c. held of the Queen in Capite -	18 Eliz. - - - -	Receipt of the Exchequer	A. 1. a.
v. Testa de Nevil.			
Diocese, Consistory Court:			
Court Book of Eccleſiaſtical Cauſes - -	— —		
Proceſſes in Cauſes for Subtraction of Tythes, Teſtamentary Cauſes, &c. - - - -	— —		
Excommunications, Abſolutions, Penances, Nominations of Pariſh Clerks, &c. Bundles and Files of	— —		
Terriers of Glebe Lands, &c. - - -	— —		
Wills, original - - - - - - -	1541 to preſent Time		
Inſtitutions to Benefices and Subſcriptions by Clergymen - - - - - - -	1551 to 1797 - -	Regiſtry of Conſiſtory Court, Glouceſter -	L. 20.
Baptiſms, Marriages, and Burials, Tranſcripts of	1571 } to the preſent Time - -		
Adminiſtration Acts and Bonds - - -	1604 }		
Marriage Acts and Bonds - - - -	1637 }		
Ordinations of Clergymen - - - -	1683 to 1769. N.B. Thoſe ſubſequent with the Biſhop -		
Copies of Deeds of Exchange, and other Matters of Eccleſiaſtical Cognizance - - -	1771 to 1797 - -		

ALPHABETICAL ARRANGEMENT OF THE PUBLIC RECORDS.

RECORDS and other INSTRUMENTS.	DATE.	WHERE KEPT.	Appendix to the First Report.
GLOUCESTER—(*continued.*)			
Faculties and Confirmations of Seats in Churches Sequestrations of Benefices - - - - Certificates for Places of Divine Worship, &c. -	1731 to the present Time - - -	Registry of Consistory Court, Gloucester - -	L. 20.
RICHARD, DUKE OF:			
Grant to him - - - - - - -	Edw. 4. - - -	British Museum - - -	U.
GODSTON, OXON:			
Leidger Book of its Charters, &c. - - -	— —	King's Rememb. Office -	G. 6. a.
GOLD AND SILVER. *v.* EXCHEQUER RECEIPT.—MINT.—MINES.			
GRAIN. *v.* CLAUS ROLLS.			
GRANTS:			
From the Crown, Particulars of - - - *v.* EXCHEQUER OF ACCOUNT.—INROLMENTS.	Hen. 8. Edw. 6. Phil. and Mary, & Eliz.	Augmentation Office -	G. 19. a.
In Fee or Perpetuity, and Of Escheat Lands - - } *v.* PATENT ROLLS.			
GREAT SEAL. *v.* SEAL.			
GREEN CLOTH, BOARD OF:			
Proceedings in the Court of Verge - - -	— —	Bodleian Library - -	O. 1.
Orders for the Government of the King's Household - - - - - - - -	H. 8. Mary, Jac. 1. Car. 1. & Geo. 3.	Office of the Board of Green Cloth - --	C. 5.
Fees allowed in different Offices - - - Diets for different Tables, Accounts of Cattle and Corn to be served by the several Counties, and Prices of Provisions - - - -	Hen. 8. to Car. 2.		
Expenditures of divers Princes - - - -	Jac. 1. to 1782, with Chasms - - -		
Establishments of the Household - - -	Car. 1. to Geo. 3. -		
Servants Warrants and Certificates - - -	1626 to present Time		
Proceedings in the Court of Verge - - -	1676 to 1791 - -		
GREENLAND AND NEWFOUNDLAND. *v.* FISHERIES.			
GREENWICH, EAST, KENT:			
Survey of the Manor of - - - - - -	7 Will. 3. - - -	Petty Bag Office - - -	D. 5.
HOSPITAL and PARK:			
Books of the Works and Household Accounts - *v.* GUNPOWDER MAGAZINES.	1716 to 1729 - -	Auditors Office Land Rev.	G. 15. a.
GREEN WAX *v.* CORNWALL.			
GREGORY XV. POPE:			
Brief to Charles Prince of Wales - - -	1623 - - - -	University Library Camb.	P. 1.
GUERNSEY, &c.:			
Placita Varia - - - - - - -	Edw. 1. 2. and 3. -	Receipt of the Exchequer	A. 1. a.
State of Liberties and Privileges - - - Matters relating to the Affairs of - - - *v.* JERSEY.	1498 to 1756 - - 1570 to 1756 - -	State Paper Office - -	C. 1. a.
GUISNES. *v.* ACCOUNTS, PUBLIC.—CALAIS.			
GUNPOWDER MAGAZINES:			
Commission for removing them from Greenwich to Purfleet, and Return thereto - - - Commission and Return respecting them at Feversham - - - - - - - -	1760 - - - - 1784 - - - -	Clerk of the Crown in Chancery - - - -	D. 2. a.

ALPHABETICAL ARRANGEMENT OF THE PUBLIC RECORDS.

RECORDS and other INSTRUMENTS.	DATE.	WHERE KEPT.	Appendix to the First Report.
HABEAS CORPUS, Writs of. *v.* Claus Rolls.—King's Bench.—Writs.			
HALES, Gloucester:			
Survey of the Monastery - - - - -	Temp. Hen. 8. - -	King's Rememb. Office -	G. 6. a.
HAMBURGH:			
Treaties and Ratifications with England - -	1672 to 1780, with Chasms - - -	State Paper Office - -	C. 1. a.
HANAPER:			
Account of the Keeper of the - - - - -	Temp. Eliz. - -	AuditorsOffice Land Rev.	G. 15. a.
Books of Entry of the several Instruments which pass the Great Seal, relating to Bankruptcy -	1600 to present Time	Secretary of Bankrupts -	D. 4.
HANOVER:			
Treaties and Negotiations with England - -	1689 to 1755 - -	State Paper Office - -	C. 1. a.
HANS TOWNS:			
Treaties with England - - - -	1473 to 1673 - -	(State Paper Office, as above)	(C. 1. a.)
Transactions with England - - - - -	1485 to 1613 - -	British Museum - - -	U.
Process and Decree relating to the Merchants thereof - - - - - - - -	6 Edw. 6. - - -	Bodleian Library - -	O. 1.
v. Trade, Foreign.			
HANTS, County:			
Nomina Villarum - - - - - -	— —	Lord Treas. Rem. Office	G. 7. a.
Nona Roll - - - - - - - - -	15 Edw. 3. - - -	King's Rememb. Office	G. 6. a.
Return of the Commissioners of the Number of Men in each Parish of the County capable of bearing Arms - - - - - - -	12 Hen. 8. - - -	Receipt of the Exchequer	A. 1. a.
Ecclesiastical Survey - - - - - -	26 Hen. 8. - - -	First Fruits Office - -	G. 18.
Rental of Lands belonging to the Duchy of Lancaster - - - - - - - -	1636 to 1640 - -	University Library Camb.	P. 1.
v. Testa de Nevil.			
HARBOURS and DOCKS:			
Commissions respecting them at Portsmouth, Plymouth, Sheerness, Chatham, Harwich, and Milford Haven - - - - - -	— —	Clerk of Crown in Chan.	D. 2. a.
Decrees of Commissioners for purchasing Lands, &c. for Security of the Dock Yards at Portsmouth, Plymouth, &c. - - - - -	— —	King's Rememb. Office	G. 6. a.
HARWICH. *v.* Harbours.			
HAULTON:			
Receivers Accounts of Lands belonging to the Duchy of Lancaster there - - - - -	— —	University Library Camb.	P. 1.
HEARTH TAX:			
Records of - - - - - - - - -	— —	King's Rememb. Office -	G. 6. a.
Returns of - - - - - - - - -	— —	Auditors Office Land Rev.	G. 15. a.
HENRIETTA MARIA, Queen of Charles I.			
The Marquis D'Effiat's Letters concerning her Marriage - - - - - - -	— —	Bodleian Library - -	O. 1.
Articles of her Marriage - - - - -	— —	University Libr. Camb.	P. 1.
Accounts of Fee Farm Rents belonging to her -	— —	(University Libr. Camb.)	(P. 1.)
Various Accounts and Deeds relating to her Estates	— —	Auditors Off. LandRev.	G. 15. a.
Sale of Lands by her Trustees at Knaresboro' -	1629 - - - -	(Auditors Off. LandRev.)	(G. 15. a.)
v. Dorset. — Charles I. — Fee Farm Rents.—Queens.—Cambridge.			
HENRY II.:			
His Will - - - - - - - - -	— —	King's Rememb. Office -	G. 6. a.
HENRY V.:			
His Will - - - - - - - - -	— —	Receipt of Exchequer	A. 1. a.
HENRY VII.:			
Instructions to negotiate his Marriage with the Queen of Naples - - - - - -	Hen. 7. - - - -	(Receipt of Exchequer)	(A. 1. a.)

ALPHABETICAL ARRANGEMENT OF THE PUBLIC RECORDS.

RECORDS and other INSTRUMENTS.	DATE.	WHERE KEPT.	Appendix to the First Report.
HENRY VII.—*(continued.)*			
Several Books respecting the Foundation of his Chapel	Hen. 7.	Receipt of the Exchequer	A. 1. a.
Indentures between him and the Abbies of Westminster and St. Alban's	1504 and 1505	British Museum	U.
Books respecting an Anniversary for him	Hen. 7.	Dean and Chap. Westm.	N. 12. a.
His Will	— —	Receipt of the Exchequer	A. 1. a.
HENRY VIII.:			
Charters of Endowments of Cathedrals by him	— —	Corpus Christi Coll. Cam.	P. 5.
Letters and Cyphers of Ambassadors to him, to Cardinal Wolsey, and to Lord Cromwell	— —	Receipt of Exchequer	A. 1. a.
Proceedings respecting his Divorce from Queen Catharine	— —	Receipt of Exchequer	A. 1. a.
Instruments of several Bishops, and of the University of Cambridge, acknowledging his Supremacy	— —	Receipt of Exchequer	A. 1. a.
Oath as to the Succession of the Children by Queen Anne	— —	Clerk of Crown Chancery	*Page* 224.
His Will	— —	Receipt of the Exchequer	A. 1. a.
Inventory of Jewels, Plate, Stuff, Ordnance, Ships, Ammunition, &c. belonging to him	1 Edw. 6.	Antiq. Society Library	S. a.
v. CAMBRIDGE. — JEWELS, &c. — POLE, CARDINAL.—POPES.			
HENRY PRINCE OF WALES, SON OF JAMES I.:			
Account of his Household	Jac. 1.	Office of Board of Green Cloth	C. 5.
HERALDRY:			
Collections respecting it	— —	Inner Temple Library	Q. 2. b.
Various Collections of Coats of Arms and Crests, both tricked and blazoned	— —	College of Arms British Museum	C. 8. U.
English and Foreign Heraldry and Genealogy	1246 to 1761	State Paper Office	C. 1. a.
Precedency, Pedigrees, Certificates, &c.	1399 to 1625, and 1604 to 1761	State Paper Office	C. 1. a.
HERALDS:			
v. CLAUS ROLLS.			
HEREFORD, COUNTY:			
Ecclesiastical Survey	26 Hen. 8.	First Fruits Office	G. 18.
Certificate of Manors and Estates therein, not granted in Fee Farm	1629	University Lib. Camb.	P. 1.
v. TESTA DE NEVIL.			
DIOCESE:			
Rental of Lands in Preston, &c. belonging to this Church	— —	University Lib. Camb.	P. 1.
Register Books, containing Institutions, Ordinations, Faculties, &c.	1275 to present Time, except Bishop Westfaling's Time	Bishop's Registry, Hereford	L. 11.
Wills and Administrations	1517 to present Time, with Chasms between 1517 & 1663	Bishop's Registry, Hereford	L. 11.
Act Books and Proceedings in Testamentary and other Ecclesiastical Causes	1660 to present Time	Bishop's Registry, Hereford	L. 11.
Births, Burials, and Marriages, Transcripts of	1660 to present Time	Bishop's Registry, Hereford	L. 11.
Marriage Licences, Indexes thereto	1686 to present Time	Bishop's Registry, Hereford	L. 11.
Presentations to Benefices	1663 to present Time	Bishop's Registry, Hereford	L. 11.
HERETICS. *v.* CLAUS ROLLS.			
HERTS, COUNTY:			
Antient Deeds, &c. relative to Estates therein	— —	Dean and Chap. Westm.	N. 12. b.
Inquisitiones de Ministris	4 Edw. 1.	Receipt of the Exchequer	A. 1. a.
Escheat Rolls of Lands escheated to the Crown	Edw. 3.	Auditors Office Land Rev.	G. 15. a.
Rentals of Abbey Lands and Forfeited Estates	1638	University Lib. Camb.	P. 1.
HIGH COMMISSION COURT:			
Register of the Acts thereof	1631 to 1638	University Lib. Camb.	P. 1.

ALPHABETICAL ARRANGEMENT OF THE PUBLIC RECORDS.

RECORDS and other INSTRUMENTS.	DATE.	WHERE KEPT.	Appendix to the Firſt Report.
HIGH COURT OF JUSTICE for Trial of Charles I.			
Journal of the Court - - - - - -	1648–9 - - - -	Bodleian Library - - -	O. 1.
HOLLAND:			
Treaties and Tranſactions with - - - -	1440 to 1624 - -	Receipt of the Exchequer	A. 1. a.
Inſtructions, Correſpondence, Negotiations, &c. -	1547 to 1686 - -	State Paper Office - -	C. 1. a.
v. Trade, Foreign.—United Provinces.			
HOLLAND, Sir John:			
His Letters and Speeches - - - - -	Car. 2. - - - -	Bodleian Library - -	O. 1.
HOLLES DENZEL:			
Information againſt him and others in the Star Chamber - - - - - - - - -	— —	Univerſity Library Camb.	P. 1.
v. Star Chamber.			
HOLMES:			
Collectanea reſpecting the Counties Palatine of Cheſter and Lancaſter - - - - -	— —	Britiſh Muſeum - -	U.
v. Chester.—Lancaster.			
HOLY TRINITY, Priory of, London:			
Rental of the Lands of - - - - - -	35 Edw. 3. - - -	King's Rememb. Office -	G. 6. a.
v. London.			
HOMAGE:			
Rolls reſpecting the Kings of Scotland to the Kings of England - - - - - -	Temp. Edw. 1. - -	Tower - - - - - -	A. 2. a.
v. Claus Rolls.—Scotland.			
HOME CIRCUIT:			
Files of Proceedings, conſiſting of Precepts and Proceſs, Rolls of Names, Gaol Calendars, Pannels, Indictments, Coroners Inquiſitions, &c. -	From Phil. & Mary to the preſent Time	Clerk of Aſſize, and Clerk of the Crown, Home Circuit - -	H. 1.
Proceſs Books - - - - - - -	1650 to the preſent Time		
Grand Jury Preſentments - - - - -	1674 to the preſent Time		
Calendars of Gaol Delivery - - - -	1689 to the preſent Time		
Pardons under Sign Manual - - - - -	1706 to the preſent Time		
Tranſportation, Secretaries of State's Letters relative thereto - - - - - - -	1718 to the preſent Time		
Bonds and Contracts for Tranſportation of Offenders - - - - - - - -	1718 to 1789 - -		
Eſtreat Papers - - - - - - - -	1732 to preſent Time		
Records of Convictions and Acquittals, Rolls of	7 Geo. 2. and ſome Time before, to the preſent Time - -		
Commiſſions, Bundles of - - - - -	1740 to preſent Time		
Informations, Confeſſions, Affidavits, &c. - -	1750 to preſent Time		
Recognizances, Bundles and Books of - -	1750 to preſent Time		
Niſi Prius Records, with Poſteas indorſed - -	— —		
Niſi Prius Books - - - - - - -	1672 to preſent Time		
Agenda, or Entry Books - - - - -	Complete from 1747, ſome prior - - -		
HONOURS:			
Miniſters Accounts of - - - - - -	Hen. 8. and Edw. 6.	Augmentation Office - -	G. 19. a.
Certificate of the Honour of Bolingbroke, in the Counties of Lincoln, York, Stafford, and Derby	Eliz. and Car. 1. -	Univerſity Lib. Camb.	P. 1.
State of Honours and Manors in Jointure to ſeveral Queens - - - - - -	1647 - - - - -	Univerſity Lib. Camb.	P. 1.
Proceedings reſpecting Inglewood Honour - -	Car. 1. and 2. - -	Univerſity Lib. Camb.	P. 1.
Creations of.—v. Patent Rolls.			
v. Surveys and Rentals.			
HORSES, Royal:			
Accounts of - - - - - - -	— —	King's Rememb. Office -	G. 6. a.
v. Claus Rolls.			

ALPHABETICAL ARRANGEMENT OF THE PUBLIC RECORDS.

RECORDS and other INSTRUMENTS.	DATE.	WHERE KEPT.	Appendix to the First Report.
HOSPITALS:			
Surveys and Valuations of - - - - -	26 Hen. 8. - - -	First Fruits Office - -	G. 18.
Surrenders of - - - - - -	Hen. 8. and Edw. 6.	Augmentation Office - -	G. 19. a.
v. CHARTULARIES.			
HOUSEHOLD, ROYAL:			
Various Papers relating thereto - - -	— —	British Museum - - -	U.
Accounts of Treasurers of His Majesty's Chamber	— —	Bodleian Library - - -	O. 1.
Accounts of the Royal Household - - -	18 Edw. 1. - - -	Tower - - - - - -	A. 2. a.
Accounts - - - - - - - -	Edw. 3. to Jac. 1. -	Auditors Office Land Rev.	G. 15. a.
Two Books of Accounts - - - - - -	20 Edw. 4. - - -	Antiq. Society Library -	S. a.
Proclamations, Accounts, Rules and Orders, Inventories, &c. - - - - - - -	1478 to 1706 - -	State Paper Office - -	C. 1. a.
Book of Receipts - - - - - -	Temp. Hen. 7. - -	King's Rememb. Office -	G 6. a.
Treasurers of the Chamber's Account of Debt due to the Kings - - - - - - -	Hen. 8. and Edw. 6.	Auditors Office Land Rev.	G. 15. a.
Orders for its Government - - - -	Hen. 8. Mary, Jac. 1. Car. 1. & Geo. 3. -	Off. Board Green Cloth	C. 5.
Diets for different Tables, &c. - - -	Hen. 8. to Car. 2. -	Off. Board Green Cloth	C. 5.
Treasurers Books of Debts due to the King	Hen. 8. to Edw. 6.	Auditors Office Land Rev.	G. 15. a.
Lords Treasurers Accounts of Money received and paid - - - - - - -	12 Hen. 8. - - -	Receipt of the Exchequer	A. 1. a.
Payments by the Treasurers of the King's Chamber - - - - - - - - - -	29 to 33 Hen. 8. -	Royal Society Library -	R.
Books of Fees and Offices in the Royal Establishment - - - - - - - -	1 Mary - - - -	Antiq. Society Library -	S. a.
Accounts - - - - - - - -	Eliz. to Car. 2. - -	Auditors Office Land Rev.	G. 15. a.
Collections respecting the Royal Household -	Previous to 1622 -	Inner Temple Library -	Q. 2. b.
Ordinances for the Government and Ordering of the Household of King James I. (published.) -	Jac. 1. - - - -	Antiq. Society Library -	S. a.
Various Articles of Expenditure - - -	Jac. 1. to Geo. 3. -	Office Board Green Cloth	C. 5.
Accounts of Lord Harrington, Treasurer of the Chamber - - - - - - - -	11 and 15 Jac. 1. -	Bodleian Library - -	O. 1.
Proclamations, Accounts, &c. - - - -	Car. 1. to Geo. 3.	Office Board Green Cloth	C. 5.
Establishment of the Household	Car. 1. to Geo. 3.	Office Board Green Cloth	C. 5.
A Book of all Compositions from every County, for the Yearly Expense of his Majesty's Household (a Copy) - - - - -	14 Car. 1. - - -	Antiq. Society Library -	S. a.
Several Purveyors, Cofferers, and other Household Accounts - - - - - - -	Before 1660 - -	Auditors Office Land Rev.	G. 15. a.
Orders for the Government of the King's Bedchamber and Privy Lodgings - - -	Temp. Will. 3. -	Bodleian Library - - -	O. 1.
States, &c. of Accounts - - - -	1728 to 1797 - -	Auditors Office Land Rev.	G. 15. a.
v. BUTLER ROYAL. — CLAUS ROLLS. — GREEN CLOTH.—LAND REVENUE.			
HUGGETT. *v.* ETON.—WINDSOR.			
HUNDREDS:			
Rolls of Inquisitions - - - - - -	2 Edw. 1. - - -	Tower - - - - - -	A. 2. a.
Hundred Rolls - - - - - - -	2, 3, and 4 Edw 1. -	Receipt of the Exchequer	A. 1. a.
Hundred Rolls	Temp. Edw. 2. - -	Tower - - - - - -	A. 2. a.
Dugdale's Extracts - - - - - -	— —	Ashmolean Museum - -	O. 2.
v. CAMBRIDGE. — HUNTINGDON.—INQUISITIONS.—LINCOLN.—OXFORD.			
HUNTINGDON, COUNTY:			
Hundred Roll - - - - - - -	Temp. Edw. 1. - -	Tower - - - - - -	A. 2. a.
Oath of the Sheriff of - - - -	— —	Clerk of Crown in Chan.	*Page* 223.
HUNTINGDON, LORD:			
His Papers - - - - - - - -	— —	Bodleian Library - -	O. 1.
Inquisitiones Post Mortem of the Estates of Henry Earl of - - - - - - -	39 Eliz. - - - -	Auditors Office Land Rev.	G. 15. a.
HURLEY PRIORY, BUCKS:			
Antient Deeds - - - - - - -	— —	Dean and Chap. Westm.	N. 12. b.
HUTTON:			
Extracts by him from various Registers of Religious Houses, chiefly in the Diocese of Bath and Wells - - - - - - - -	— —	British Museum - -	U.
v. BATH and WELLS DIOCESE.—CHARTULARIES.			

ALPHABETICAL ARRANGEMENT OF THE PUBLIC RECORDS.

RECORDS and other INSTRUMENTS.	DATE.	WHERE KEPT.	Appendix to the First Report.
JAMAICA:			
Papers relating thereto	1689 to 1715	Bodleian Library	O. 1.
v. Plantations.			
JAMES I.			
His Letter on Behalf of the Univerfity of Cambridge	Jac. 1.	Peter Houfe Coll. Camb.	P. 2.
Account of his Funeral	1625	Duchy Cornwall Office	C. 7.
v. Cambridge.—Cornwall Duchy.			
JAMES II.:			
Expenfes at his Coronation	Jac. 2.	Office of Board Gr. Cloth	C. 5.
Journal during the Conventional Parliament	1688	Bodleian Library	O. 1.
v. Convention.—Parliament.			
IDIOTS. v. Chancery.—Claus Rolls.—Lunacy and Ideocy.			
JERSEY:			
Affairs relating thereto	— —		
Placita Varia refpecting Jerfey, Guernfey, Alderney, and Sark	Edw. 1, 2, & 3.	Receipt of the Exchequer	A. 1. a.
Extract of the Profits of the Ifland of Jerfey	5 Edw. 3.	King's Rememb. Office	G. 6.
State of Reports, Liberties, and Privileges, &c.	1498 to 1756	State Paper Office	C. 1. a.
Commiffion and Return upon the State of the Laws relative to a Trial by Jury, &c.	31 & 33 Geo. 3.	Council Office	C. 2.
v. Guernsey, &c.			
JEWELS, PLATE, &c.:			
Accounts of	— —	King's Rememb. Office	G. 6.
Inftruments and Papers concerning them	Hen. 3. to Eliz.	Dean and Chapter Weftm.	N. 12. b.
Indentures and Inventories	Temp Hen. 8. and previous thereto, and temp. Jac. 1.	Receipt of the Exchequer	A. 1. a.
Accounts	Hen. 8. & antea	Receipt of the Exchequer	A. 1. a.
Inventory of the Jewels, Plate, Stuff, Ordnance, Ships, Ammunition, &c. belonging to Hen. VIII. (a Copy)	1 Edw. 6.	Antiq. Society Library	S. a.
Jewels annexed to the Crown	Jac. 1.	Receipt of the Exchequer	A. 1. a.
Inventory of Jewels of Anne Queen of James I.	1605 to 1615	Auditors Off. Land Rev.	G. 15. a.
Accounts of the Jewels of Charles I. pawned in the Low Countries	Car. 1.	Auditors Off. Land Rev.	G. 15. a.
Jewel Accounts	Car. 1.	Auditors Off. Land Rev.	G. 15. a.
Various Papers relating to the Jewel Office	— —	Britifh Mufeum	U.
v. Claus Rolls.			
JEWS:			
Deeds refpecting them	Hen. 3. to Edw. 1. &c.	Dean and Chapter Weftm.	N. 12. b.
Taxations of their Houfes and Property	19 Edw. 1.	Tower	A. 1. a.
v. Claus Rolls.			
IMPEACHMENTS:			
Articles of, againft Simon de Burley, by the Houfe of Commons	Ric. 1.	Dean and Chapter Weftm.	N. 12. b.
IMPREST. v. Accounts, Public.—Exchequer of Receipt.—Money.			
INCENDIARIES. v. Rebellion.			
INDENTURES. v. Inrolments.			
INDIA COMPANY:			
Papers relating thereto	Car. 2. & Anne	Bodleian Library	O. 1.
INFORMATIONS. v. Exchequer of Account.			
INGLEWOOD, Cumberland:			
Survey of the Foreft	1619	King's Rememb. Office	G. 6. a.
Proceedings refpecting Inglewood Honor	Car. 1. & 2.	Univerfity Library Camb.	P. 1.
INGROSSER of the Great Roll of the Exchequer:			
His Oath	— —	King's Rememb. Office	*Page* 234.
INQUISITIONS:			
Of various Sorts	— —	Britifh Mufeum	U.
Concerning Hundreds	10 Edw. 2.	Tower	A. 2. a.

ALPHABETICAL ARRANGEMENT OF THE PUBLIC RECORDS.

RECORDS and other INSTRUMENTS.	DATE.	WHERE KEPT.	Appendix to the First Report.
INQUISITIONS—*(continued.)*			
Under several Acts of Parliament, temp. Geo. II. for building Westminster Bridge - - -	Geo. 2. - - - -	Register Office Middlesex	M. 1.
v. SPECIAL COMMISSIONS.			
INQUISITIONES AD QUOD DAMNUM - - -	1307 to 1460 - -	Tower - - -	A. 2. a.
The like - - - - - - - -	9 Car 1. to the present Time - -	Petty Bag Office -	D. 5.
v. BREVIA REGIA.			
INQUISITIONES DE MINISTRIS in Com. Norf. Suff. Essex, Hertf. Dorset, and Northumb. - -	4 Edw. 1. - - -	Receipt of the Exchequer	A. 1. a.
INQUISITIONES POST MORTEM:			
Collectanea diversa in Bundellis Inquisitionum intra Turrim Londinensem existentibus—Manu Dugdalii - - - - - - -	— —	Ashmolean Museum -	O. 2.
Inquisitiones post Mortem, called also Escheats -	1216 to 1488 - -	Tower - - -	A. 2.
The like - - - - - - - -	Hen. 7. to Car. 1. -	Rolls Chapel - -	D. 1. a.
Transcripts of some of those in the Tower and at the Rolls - - - - - -	Edw. 1. to Car. 1. -	King's Rememb. Office -	G. 6.
Inquisitiones post Mortem - - - -	Temp. Hen. 8. - -	Bodleian Library -	O. 1.
Authentic Transcripts or Duplicates, from the Erection of the Court of Wards to its Abolition -	1540 to 1636 - -	Receipt of the Exchequer	A. 1. a.
Of the Estates of Henry Earl of Huntingdon.	39 Eliz. - - -	Auditors Office Land Rev.	G. 15.
v. CLAUS ROLLS.—ESCHEATS.—EXCHEQUER OF ACCOUNT.—LANCASTER DUCHY.—LAND REVENUE.—WARDS AND LIVERIES.			
INROLMENTS:			
Books of Inrolment and Entries for Sales - -	Hen. 7. to pres^t Time	Auditor for Wales - -	G. 16.
Books, containing Entries of Grants, Particulars, Leases, &c. - - - - - - -	Hen. 8. to Car. 2. -	Auditors Office Land Rev.	G 15. a.
Oath of the Deputy Clerk of - - - -	— —	Petty Bag Office - -	*Page* 231.
v. COMMON PLEAS.			
INSTALLATIONS:			
Collections about them - - - -	— —	Inner Temple Library -	Q. 2. b.
INVASIONS. v. CLAUS ROLLS.			
INVENTIONS:			
Petitions on - - - - - - -	1685 to 1761 - -	State Paper Office - -	C. 1. a.
Inrolments of Patents, and Specifications of - -	8 Anne to pres^t Time	Petty Bag Office - -	D. 5.
The like - - - - - - - -	25 Geo. 3. to the present Time - -	Inrolment Office -	D. 13.
v. CLAUS ROLLS.—PATENT ROLLS.—SPECIFICATIONS.			
INVENTORIES:			
Of Goods, Chattels, Ornaments, Plate, and Moveables of Churches - - - -	Hen. 8. and Mary -	Auditors Office Land Rev.	G. 15. a.
The like - - - - - - -	Edw. 6. - - - -	Augmentation Office -	G. 19. a.
Containing Accounts of Pictures, Busts, &c. belonging to Charles I. - - - -	Car. 1. - - - -	Auditors Office Land Rev.	G. 15. a.
v. JEWELS.—LANCASTER DUCHY.			
JOHN OF GAUNT, DUKE OF LANCASTER. v. LANCASTER.			
JOHN, ST. OF JERUSALEM:			
Original Deeds and Charters respecting the Knights of	— —	Bodleian Library - -	O. 2.
Papers and Instruments respecting the Priory of	Chiefly in the 13th Century - - -	Dean and Chap. Westm.	N. 12. b.
v. CHARTULARIES.—LAND REVENUE.			
JOHN, ST. CLERKENWELL, MONASTERY OF.			
v. CHARTULARIES.—LAND REVENUE.			
JOINTURES OF QUEENS.			
Inrolments and Ministers Accounts - - -	Hen. 8. &c. - -	Augmentation Office -	G. 19. a
v. QUEENS.			
IPSWICH, SUFFOLK:			
Surrenders of Monasteries to Cardinal Wolsey, for the Endowment of his College there -	Hen. 8. - - - -	Receipt of the Exchequer	A. 1. a.
v. WOLSEY.			

ALPHABETICAL ARRANGEMENT OF THE PUBLIC RECORDS.

RECORDS and other INSTRUMENTS.	DATE.	WHERE KEPT.	Appendix. to the Firſt Report.
IRELAND:			
Papers relating to the Affairs of Ireland, among which are Letters, Accounts of Treaſurers and Auditors.—A Great Roll of Pardons and Grants made by Henry V. &c. &c. - -	— —	Receipt of the Exchequer.	A. 1. a.
Petitions concerning Ireland - - -	Divers Periods - -	Tower - - -	A. 2. a.
Miſcellaneous Collection relating to the Public Accounts of - - - - - -	— —	Auditors Office Land Rev.	G. 15. a.
A Collection of Materials relating to Revenue, Hiſtory, Antiquities, and Municipal Laws -	— —	Britiſh Muſeum - -	U.
A Collection of the King's Leaſes, Grants of Lands, &c. in Ireland - - - - - -	— —	Bodleian Library - -	O. 1.
Literæ Patentes pro Emendatione Status Terræ Hiberniæ - - - - - - -	— —	} Corp. Chriſti Coll. Cam.	} P. 5.
Repreſentation des Maires and des Cites au Conſeil d'Irlande - - - - - -	— —		
Two Charters relating to Drogheda - -	— —		
Speeches of the Lord Treaſurer, Lord Keeper, &c. in Council, upon the Affairs of Ireland, after the Truce with the Earl of Tyrone -	— —	Univerſity Library Camb.	P. 1.
Accounts of the Treaſurer and Chamberlain of the Exchequer of Dublin	Temp Edw. 1. &c. -	King's Rememb. Office -	G. 6.
Charters of Grants to the Town of Waterford -	Edw. 1. & 2. - -	Corp. Chriſti Col. Camb.	P. 5.
Counter Roll of the Aid to Edward III. - -	9 Edw. 3. - - -	Dean and Chapter Weſtm.	N. 12. b.
Orders of Council reſpecting the Cuſtoms -	43 Edw. 3. - - -	Receipt of the Exchequer	A. 1. a.
Letters and Correſpondence, Forfeited Eſtates, Government, Revenue, &c. - - -	1500 to 1676 - -	State Paper Office - -	C. 1. a.
Standard Pieces of Silver for Ireland -	Temp. Hen. 8. & Eliz.	Chamberlain's Office Exc.	G. 2.
Articles relating to the Settlement of Munſter -	Eliz. - - - -	Univerſity Library Camb.	P. 1.
Letters from Sir John Perrot, Lord Deputy, to Queen Eliz. &c. - - - - -	1584 to 1586 - -	Bodleian Library - -	O. 1.
Entries or Copies of Royal Letters to the Lord Lieutenants and other Chief Governors in Ireland - - - - - - - -	1626 to preſent Time, with a Chaſm - -	Signet Office - - -	C. 4.
Acts of Parliament paſſed there, Rolls of - -	10 Car. 1. - - -	Rolls Chapel - - -	D. 1. a.
Act of the Council concerning an Oath to be taken by the Scots profeſſing their Abhorrence of Diſturbances in Ireland - - -	15 Car. 1. - -	Univerſity Library Camb.	P. 1.
Bills tranſmitted from Ireland for his Majeſty's Approbation - - - - - - -	From . . . . to 1782	Clerk of Crown Chancery	D. 2. a.
Orders, &c. of Parliament, on Affairs of Ireland -	1642 to 1644 - -	Bodleian Library - -	O. 1.
Letters and Papers from the Lord Juſtices of Ireland to the Secretaries of State, &c. -	1684 to 1775 - -	State Paper Office - -	C. 1. a.
Account of Ships and Forces ſent to Ireland - -	1691 - - - -	} Bodleian Library - -	} O. 1.
Duke of Ormond's Papers relating to Ireland -	— —		
Oath of Perſons qualifying for Offices in - -	— —	Petty Bag Office - -	*Page* 226.
v. CLAUS ROLLS.—EXCHEQUER OF RECEIPT.—ROMAN CATHOLICS.			
ITALY:			
Treaties and Tranſactions with - - -	1351 to 1527 - -	Receipt of the Exchequer	A. 1. a.
Inſtructions, Correſpondence, Negotiations, &c. -	1527 to 1668 - -	} State Paper Office - -	} C. 1. a.
Treaties between England and Italian States and Towns - - - - - - - - -	1634 to 1779 - -		
ITERS:			
Itinera - - - - - - - - -	Edw. 1. to Edw. 3.	Lincoln's Inn Library -	Q. 3.
Acquietancia Mille Marcarum pro Itinere Juſticiariorum Domini Regis Edw. III. - - -	Edw. 3. - - -	Dean and Chap. Durham	N. 24. b.
Iter apud Northampton - - - - -	} 3 Edw. 3. - -	} Bodleian Library - -	} O. 1.
Iter de Northampton - - - - - -			
v. NORTHAMPTON, NOTTINGHAM, &c.			

ALPHABETICAL ARRANGEMENT OF THE PUBLIC RECORDS.

RECORDS and other INSTRUMENTS.	DATE.	WHERE KEPT.	Appendix to the First Report.
KENT, COUNTY:			
Antient Deeds, &c. relative to Estates therein	— —	Dean and Chapter Westm.	N. 12. b.
Knights Fees	— —	Antiq. Society Library	S. a.
Iters, Copies of	Edw. 1. & 6 Edw. 2.	Lincoln's Inn Library	Q. 3.
Nona Roll	15 Edw. 3.	King's Rememb. Office	G. 6. b.
Ecclesiastical Survey	26 Hen. 8.	First Fruits Office	G. 18.
Survey of the Manor of Eltham	Jac. 1.	King's Rememb. Office.	G. 6. a.
———— of Greenwich	7 Will. 3.	Petty Bag Office	D. 5.
KINGS:			
Offerings and Free Gifts to them	Joh. Edw. 2. & 3.	Tower	A. 2. a.
Receivers Accounts of Offerings and Free Gifts	13 Car. 2.	Auditors Office Land Rev.	G. 15. a.
KING'S BENCH:			
Baga de Secretis; containing Records of Attainders, Convictions, and other Matters, chiefly relating to the Crown's Title to Lands	— —	Custos Brevium Office	E. 5.
Fees of this Court, Account of	— —	Bodleian Library	O. 1.
Rolls of the Curia Regis	Ric. 1. Joh. & H. 3.	Receipt of the Exchequer	A. 1. a.
Placita	John to Hen. 4.	Lincoln's Inn Library	Q. 3.
Writs, Original and Special	Hen. 2. to Will. 3.	Receipt of the Exchequer	A. 1. a.
Writs of Habeas Corpus, Distress, and other Proceedings	14 H. 3. to 3 Ric. 3.	Tower	A. 2. a.
Hanaper Account of Profits of the Seal of this Court	Eliz.	Auditors Office Land Rev.	G. 15. a.
Oath of the Chief Justice Oath of the other Judges	} — —	Clerk of Crown in Chan.	*Page* 127.
CROWN SIDE:			
Rules, Entries of	31 Eliz. to the present Time		
Affidavits filed Recognizances forfeited in Court, Estreats of	} From Restoration to present Time		
Informations exhibited			
Indictments and Presentments found by the Grand Jury			
Indictments, Presentments, and Convictions removed by Certiorari, or Writ of Error	1 W. & Mary to the present Time		
Recognizances taken upon Writs of Certiorari, &c.			
Rolls, containing Names of Persons who have taken the Oaths of Allegiance and Supremacy in Court			
Writs of Certiorari, and other Writs issued from the Crown Side of the Court, with their Returns, and Writs issued out of the Court of Chancery, and returned in the King's Bench, where the King is a Party	5 W. & M.	Crown Office	E. 1.
Notices of Trial	10 W. 3		
Interrogatories filed on Attachments, for Contempts against the Court, and Answers sworn thereto	12 W. 3. } to the present Time		
Appearances and Pleas, Minutes of	12 Geo. 1.		
Certificates of Sacrament and Subscriptions	1 Geo. 2.		
Pannels of Grand Juries	Beginning of Geo. 3. to the present Time		
Inquisitions taken on View of Bodies of Prisoners who have died in the King's Bench Prison, or within the Rules	1771 to present Time		
Convicts, Returns of, pursuant to Stat. 16 Geo. III.	1775		
PLEA SIDE:			
Affidavits of Debt, and Service of Process			
Writs of Special Capias, Alias, Pluries, Exigents, and Proclamations			
Writs of Special Capias Utlagatum, and Inquisitions thereon			
Writs of Re. fa. lo. and Returns thereto	1760 to the present Time		
Book of all Writs that are issued from the Office			
Common Appearances to Original Writs		Filacer, Exigenter, and Clerk of the Outlawries	E. 7.
Bail, Recognizances of, to Special Capias's—Files and Dockets of			
Judgments of Outlawries, Dockets of			
Warrants to prosecute and defend	1785 to present Time		
Paper Books and Pleadings	14 to 27 Geo. 2.	Inner Temple Library	Q. 2. b.

7 P

ALPHABETICAL ARRANGEMENT OF THE PUBLIC RECORDS.

RECORDS and other INSTRUMENTS.	DATE.	WHERE KEPT.	Appendix to the First Report.
KING'S BENCH, Plea Side—*(continued.)*			
Special Pleadings in Actions brought in this Court	From 1777, and fome earlier - -	Clerk of the Papers - -	E. 4.
Rules, Book of Entries of - - - - -	1603 to the prefent Time, with Chafms		
Rules, Original Minutes of - - - - -	1739 to prefent Time		
Mifcellaneous Bundles of Judges Orders, Orders of Affize and Nifi Prius, Agreements, Admiffions of Guardians, &c. - - - - -	From 1720 - - -		
Affidavits of various Sorts - - - - -	The earlieft in 1733	Clerk of the Rules -	E. 3.
Prifoners Papers - - - - - - -	From 1763, with fome Chafms -		
Petitions from Prifoners for Day Rules - -	From 1787 - - -		
Receipts by the Signer of the Writs, for Money paid into Court - - - - -	Beginning 1789 -		
Attornies Names, Inrolments of - - -	— —		
Writs of Habeas Corpus, and Returns thereto -	— —		
Writs of Certiorari, and Returns thereto - -	— —	Mafter of King's Bench Office - - -	
Bills of Exceptions - - - - - -	— —		E. 2.
Dockets of Judgments, and other Entries - -	1656 to prefent Time		
Judgments and other Proceedings inrolled -	1 H. 6. to pres^t Time	Cuftos Brevium Office -	E. 5.
Writs of Error and Allowances thereof, and Memorandums of Recognizances of Bail - -	— —	Clerk of the Errors, King's Bench - - -	E. 6.
Books, in which are entered Proceedings on Writs of Error, until affirmed or reverfed - -	1764 to prefent Time		
Judgments in Writs of Error, Tranfcripts of -	— —	Clerk of the Errors, Exchequer - -	G. 21.
Books of Remittitur - - - - - -	— —		
v. Claus Rolls.—Courts of Justice.—Law Cases.—Placita.			
KING'S Counsel:			
Their Oath - - - - - - -	— —		
Serjeants:		Clerk of Crown Chanc.	*Pages* 218 and 219.
Their Oath - - - - - - -	— —		
KINGSTON-UPON-HULL.			
All that relates to the Regifters Office for the Eaft Riding of York, is applicable to this Place. *v.* York, East Riding.			
KNARESBOROUGH, Worcestershire:			
Sale of Lands there by Truftees for Queen Henrietta Maria - - - - - - -	1629 - - - -	Auditors Office Land Rev.	G. 15. a.
v. Henrietta Maria.			
KNIGHTS FEES.			
Rolls of Knights Fees and Efcuages - -	— —	King's Rem. Office -	G. 6. a.
Books of - - - - - - - -	— —		
Some Inquifitions concerning them - -	— —	Lord Treaf. Rem. Office	G. 7.
Copies of - - - - - - - -	Temp. Hen. 3. -	Afhmolean Mufeum -	O. 2.
Knights Fees - - - - - - -	Edw. 1. - - - -	Tower - - -	A. 2. a.
Feoda in Capite, fecundum Inquifitionem Adami Kirkby (a Copy) - - - - - -	24 Edw. 1. - - -	Receipt of the Exchequer	A. 1. a.
v. Aids and Subsidies.—Liber Niger.—Liber Rubeus.—Lancaster Duchy.—Essex.—Kent.—Norfolk.—Suffolk.			
KNIGHTS Hospitallers: *v.* Claus Rolls.			
Of St. John of Jerusalem. *v.* John St. of Jerusalem.			
Templars:			
Original Deeds and Charters refpecting them -	— —	Bodleian Library - -	O. 1.
Collections refpecting them - - - -	— —	Inner Temple Library -	Q. 2. b.
Extents and Minifters Accounts of - - -	— —	King's Rem. Office -	G. 6. a.
Books of fome of their Poffeffions - - -	About 1185 - -		
v. Chartularies.			
Of the Garter. *v.* Garter.			
Of the Bath. *v.* Bath.			
KNIGHTHOOD:			
Inftructions concerning - - - - -	1630 - - - -	Univerfity Library Camb.	P. 1.
Certificates of Perfons who compounded for not taking the Honour of Knighthood - -	6 & 7 Car. 2. - -	Auditors Office Land Rev.	G. 15. a.

ALPHABETICAL ARRANGEMENT OF THE PUBLIC RECORDS.

RECORDS and other INSTRUMENTS.	DATE.	WHERE KEPT.	Appendix to the First Report.
LACOCK, WILTS:			
Leidger Book of Lands formerly belonging to that Monastery	Temp. Eliz.	King's Rememb. Office	G. 6. a.
LANCASTER, COUNTY PALATINE:			
Collectanea relating to the History and Antiquities thereof, made by the Three Holmes	— —	British Museum	U.
Collection of Names of the King's Castles, Mansions, Parks, Forests, Chaces, &c. within the Survey of the Duchy of Lancaster	— —	University Library Camb.	P. 1.
Iter Forestæ	8 Ed. 3.	Lincoln's Inn Library	Q. 3.
Nona Roll	15 Ed. 3.	King's Rememb. Office	G. 6. b.
Exemplification of a Grant to John of Gaunt, creating him Duke of Lancaster, and making the County a County Palatine, and some subsequent Acts and Deeds relating to the said County	51 Ed. 3.	Ashmolean Museum	O. 2.
Inspeximus of the same	Ric. 2.		
Ecclesiastical Survey (a Copy)	26 Hen. 8.	First Fruits Office	G. 18.
Survey of Estates therein not granted in Fee Farm	1629	University Library Camb.	P. 1.
COURTS OF:			
Indictments and other Proceedings in the Criminal Court	— —	Clerk of the Crown for Lancaster	H. 13. c.
Fines and Recoveries, Writs, Minutes, Papers, and Proceedings in Real, Personal, and mixed Actions in the Civil Court	— —	Prothonotary Common Pleas for Lancaster	H. 13. b.
Inrolments of Deeds, a few	— —		
Bills, Answers, and other Proceedings, Depositions, Order Books, Decrees, and Decree Books in the Court of Chancery	— —	Register's Office, Preston	H. 13. a.
DUCHY OF:			
Confirmation of its Privileges	— —	Bodleian Library	O. 1.
A few Records concerning it	— —	Auditors Office Land Rev.	G. 15. a.
Receivers Accounts in the County of Lancaster, and annexed Lands of Clithero, Furness, and Haulton	— —	University Library Camb.	P. 1.
Ministers and Receivers Accounts of the Rents and Revenues	1135 to present Time	Duchy of Lancaster	C. 6.
Charters and Grants of various Kings	1135 to 1558		
Court Rolls	1283 to present Time		
Forests, Pleas of	8 Ed. 3.	King's Rememb. Office	G. 6. a.
Rentals and Particulars of Lands belonging to the Duchy	1377 to present Time	Duchy of Lancaster	C. 6.
Registers of Grants, Leases, Warrants, and Commissions	1377 to 1430		
Charters and Grants in Fee Farm	1377 to 1702		
Inquisitiones Post Mortem	1 Hen. 5. to 18 Car. 1.		
Bills, Answers, and Depositions	1487 to the present Time		
Books of Decrees and Orders			
Leases	1510 to the present Time		
Presentations to Ecclesiastical Benefices			
Patents of Offices			
Surveys of Woods and Underwoods	1575	University Library Camb.	P. 1.
Special Commissions of Sewers and Surveys of Lands	23 Eliz. to the present Time	Duchy of Lancaster	C. 6.
Privy Seals and Bills	1 Jac. 1. to the present Time		
Revenue, Proceedings of the Court relating thereto	1630 to the present Time		
Rental for Dorset, Somerset, Wilts, and Hants	1636 to 1640	University Lib. Camb.	P. 1.
Knights Fees therein belonging to Charles I.	Temp. Interregni		
General Rental			
*Fee Farm, Rolls of	Temp. Interregni	Augmentation Office	G. 19. a.
Awards for Inclosures	1754 to the present Time	Duchy of Lancaster	C. 6.
Grants of Rents under the several Acts	1780 to the present Time		
Accounts of Purchase Money arising from the Sale of Rents			
LANDS, CONCEALED:			
Deeds of Sale, Gift, Purchase, and Exchange	Beginning with Ed. 1.	Receipt of the Exchequer	A. 1. a.
Commissions of concealed Lands, a Book containing Entries of their Returns	3 to 17 Eliz.	King's Rememb. Office	G. 6. a.
v. CONCEALMENTS.—SPECIAL COMMISSIONS.			

* These Records, and a few others of the Duchy of Lancaster, which were in the Augmentation Office, have been lately transferred to the Duchy Office.

ALPHABETICAL ARRANGEMENT OF THE PUBLIC RECORDS.

RECORDS and other INSTRUMENTS.	DATE.	WHERE KEPT.	Appendix to the First Report.
LAND REVENUE, ENGLAND:			
Accounts of Monasteries, Priories, &c. viz. Sion, Barking, Glastonbury, Wyndham, St. Edmund's Bury, St. Osyth, St John's near Colchester, St. Mary Clerkenwell, St. John of Jerusalem at Clerkenwell, Christ Church London, St. Elens Bishopsgate, St. Mary Spittle Bishopsgate, Elsing Spittle Cripplegate, &c. - - -	— —		
Inventories of the Jewels of Queen Anne of Denmark; of the Wardrobe of Queen Elizabeth; of the Jewels, Wardrobe, &c. of Thomas Duke of Norfolk and Henry Earl of Surrey, attainted 38 Hen. VIII.; of the Wardrobe, &c. of the Lord Protector Somerset, of John Duke of Northumberland, and others of the Nobility; also of Church Goods, Foundations and Endowments of Chantries, Reparations of Houses, Parks, &c. - - - - - - -	— —	Auditors Office Land Revenue, England -	G. 15. a.
Royal Inventories of the Wardrobe, Pictures, Statutes, Jewels, Cabinets and Effects of Charles I. taken by Commissioners under the Act passed in 1649 for the Sale thereof - - -	— —		
Accounts of Woods and Forests from Stewards, Bailiffs, &c. - - - - - - -	From various Periods to the present Time - -		
Various Particulars of Grants, Settlements, Schedules, Registers and Surveys - - -	Ed. 1. to 1702 - -	Surv. Gen. Crown Lands	G. 14.
*Ministers and Receivers Accounts - - -	Ed. 1. to Car. 2. -		
Surveys of the Crown Lands - - -	1493 to 1715 - -		
Inrolment Books, containing Letters Patent, Surveys, Inquisitions, Charters, Manumissions, Exemplifications of Pleadings, Judgments, and Decrees, Particulars of Estates, Privy Seals, Commissions, Constitutions, Wills, Probates, Treasury Warrants and Letters, Auditors Reports, &c. - - - - - - - - -	Hen. 8. to the present Time -	Auditors Office Land Revenue - - -	G. 15. a.
Court Rolls - - - - - - - - -			
General Report for Five Years, ending - -	43 Eliz. - - - -	University Library Camb.	P. 1.
Accounts of the State of the Revenues in Charge of the Auditors - - - - - - -	1660 to 1701 - -	Surv. Gen. Crown Lands	G. 14.
Common Entry Books, containing Commissions of Receivers General of Taxes, Constitutions, Warrants, Orders, Letters, Reports, &c. -	1698 to present Time		
The King's Household Accounts - - -	1728 to 1797 - -	Auditors Office Land Revenue - - -	G. 15. a.
Tax Accounts, viz. Land Tax and various Assessed Taxes - - - - - - -	From the Commencement of each Tax to the present Time - - - -		
WALES:			
† Ministers Accounts - - - - - -	7 Hen. 7. to 15 Car. 2. - - -		
Receivers Views, being Abstracts of Rentals -	1 Eliz. to 1 Ann -		
Account of Fee Farm Rents granted away in Oliver Cromwell's Time - - - -	Temp Interregni -	Auditors Office Land Revenue, Wales -	G. 16. a.
Receivers Accounts - - - - - -	13 Car. 2. to 38 Geo. 3. - -		
Sheriffs Views, or Annual Accounts - - -			
Rentals of Fee Farms and Leasehold Rents -	1 Ann to present Time - - - -		
v. EXCHEQUER OF ACCOUNT.—PARLIAMENT.—RADNOR COUNTY.			
LAND TAX:			
Records of - - - - - - - -	— —	King's Remem. Office	G. 6. a.
Duplicates of Assessments of - - - - -	— —		

* These Ministers Accounts have been lately transferred to the Augmentation Office.

† Lately removed to the Augmentation Office.

ALPHABETICAL ARRANGEMENT OF THE PUBLIC RECORDS.

RECORDS and other INSTRUMENTS.	DATE.	WHERE KEPT.	Appendix to the First Report.
LAND TAX—*(continued.)*			
Duplicates of Land and Poll Tax and Hearth Money	— —		
Accounts from the Commencement of the Tax - } Declared Accounts of Receiver General for Wales }	Car. 1. to the present Time - - - -	} Aud. Office Land Rev.	G. 15. & 16.
v. LAND REV.—PEACE, CLERKS OF.—RADNOR COUNTY.—SURVEYOR GENERAL.			
LANGDON ABBEY, KENT:			
Leidger Book of its Charters, &c. - -	— —	King's Rememb. Office -	G. 6. a.
LAW PAPERS:			
Antient Copies of the early Law Treatises, viz. Glanville, Bracton, Fleta, Horne, Lib. Niger. Admiralitatis, and the Year Books - -	Various Dates - -	Lincoln's Inn Library -	Q. 3.
Reports and Year Books - - - - -	Ed. 2. - - - - -	Middle Temple Library -	Q. 1.
The like - - - - - - - -	Ed. 3. and Hen. 4. -	Bodleian Library - -	O. 1.
Year Books - - - - - - - -	Ed. 3. and Hen. 6. -	} Inner Temple Library	Q. 2. b.
Reports, a Volume of, containing some Cases -	Some in Ed. 3. and Hen. 6. but chiefly Phil. and Mary, & Eliz. - - -		
MS. Reports - - - - - -	Mary to Car. 1. and 1750 to 1765 -		
Cases, Reports, Speeches, Orders, Rules - } Charters of Corporations, &c. - - - - }	1540 to 1648 - -	State Paper Office - -	C. 1. a.
Reports not Official - - - - - -	Temp. Eliz. Jac. 1.		
Cases in King's Bench, Common Pleas, and Exchequer - - - - - - - -	& Car. 1. - - - -	Lincoln's Inn Library -	Q. 3.
	Idem - - - -	Inner Temple Library -	Q. 2. b.
Papers relative to Law Matters - - -	Jac. 1. to Anne -	Auditors Office Land Rev.	G. 15.
Collectanea of Law Records by Sir S. D'Ewes -	Jac. 1. - - - -	British Museum - - -	U.
Papers relating to Judicial Proceedings - -	1639 to 1640 - -	Privy Seal Office - - -	C. 3.
Cases, Memorials, and Petitions, with Reports of His Majesty's Law Officers thereupon - -	1663 to 1768 - -	State Paper Office - -	C. 1. a.
Papers on the Penal Law and Test - - -	1687 - - - -	Bodleian Library - - -	O. 1.
Cases in Law and Equity - - - -	1750 to 1765 - -	Inner Temple Library -	Q. 2. b.
LEAGUES:			
The Original solemn League and Covenant -	1643 - - - - -	British Museum - - -	U.
v. POPES.			
LEASES:			
Conventual - - - - - - - -	Ed. 4. to Hen. 8. -	} Augmentation Office -	G. 19. a.
Particulars of - - - - - - -	Eliz. & Jac. 1. - -		
Leases under the Great Seal - - - -	Eliz. - - - - -	} University Lib. Camb. -	P. 1.
Liber Dimissionum - - - - -	29 Eliz. to 5 Jac. 1.		
Leases - - - - - - - - -	Jac. 1. to the present Time - - - -	Pipe Office - - -	G. 8.
Proceedings relating to - - - - - -	Car. 1. } to the present Time		
Original Petitions for Leases, Reports, Warrants, &c. - - - - - - - -	1730 - }	Surveyor General Crown Lands - - - - -	G. 14.
v. AUGMENTATION, COURT OF.—CROWN LANDS.—INROLMENTS.—LAND REVENUE.—PATENT ROLLS.—REVENUE ROYAL.—SURVEYOR GENERAL.—TREASURY WARRANTS.			
LEICESTER, COUNTY:			
Repertory of Escheats, Inquisitions, &c. in the Tower relating to this County - - -	— —	Lincoln's Inn Library -	Q. 3.
Ecclesiastical Survey - - - - - -	26 Hen. 8. - - -	First Fruits Office - -	G. 18.
Survey of Estates therein not granted in Fee Farm	1629 - - - - -	University Library Camb.	P. 1.
LEIDGER BOOKS, OR REGISTERS OF MONASTERIES, ABBEYS, &c.			
Of St. Augustin, Kent;—Godston; Osney, Oxon; —Lacock; Langdon; Malmsbury, Wilts;—Newsted, Nottinghamshire;—Ramsey, Huntingdon;—Torre, Devon;—Winchcombe; Hales, Gloucester - - - - - -	— —	King's Rememb. Office -	G. 6. a.

ALPHABETICAL ARRANGEMENT OF THE PUBLIC RECORDS.

RECORDS and other INSTRUMENTS.	DATE.	WHERE KEPT.	Appendix to the First Report.
LETTERS PATENT. *v.* Inventions.—Patents.—Specifications.			
LETTERS, Royal:			
Mandatory and of Dispenſation of various Sovereigns upon Univerſity Affairs - - -	— —	Colleges of Univerſities -	O. & P.
Letters from Kings and Queens of England to the Dean and Chapter of Exeter - - -	Hen. 5. to Eliz. -	Chapter of Exeter - -	N. 6.
Letters from Kings and Queens of England to Foreign Princes and Nobility, Tranſcripts, &c.	1527 to 1702 - -	State Paper Office - -	C. 1. a.
Original Letters with Signs Manual, &c. - -	chiefly Hen. 8. to Eliz.	Inner Temple Library -	Q. 2. b.
Sylloge Epiſtolarum CCCVI. a Ser. Regina Elizabetha ad Principes et alios ſcriptarum -	Eliz. - - - - - -	University Lib. Camb.	P. 1.
Of Charles I. to the Univerſity of Cambridge, commending their Choice of the Duke of Buckingham for Chancellor - - - - -	1626 - - - - -	University Lib. Camb.	P. 1.
To the Biſhop of Oxford - - - -	Car. 1. - - - - -	Regiſtry, Oxford - - -	L. 28.
Letters from King Charles II. to the Dean and Chapter of Wells - - - - - -	Car. 2. - - - -	Dean and Chapter Wells	N. 18.
Letters of Charles II. - - - - - - -	Car. 2. - - - -	Bodleian Library - -	O. 1.
Letters from Foreign Princes and States to the Kings and Queens of England - - -	1684 to 1777 - -	State Paper Office - -	C. 1. a.
Political:			
Original Letters from the Earl of Northampton relating to the Divorce of the Earl of Eſſex, &c.	— —	Univerſity Library Camb.	P. 1.
Letters from Perſons reſiding in Foreign Parts, Cyphers, and Communications - - -	1657 to 1706 - -	State Paper Office -	C. 1. a.
Letters to the Secretaries of State and others, on various Points of Buſineſs - - - - -	1665 to 1766 - -	State Paper Office -	C. 1. a.
v. Claus Rolls.—Correspondence.—Popes.—State Papers.			
LEVANT COMPANY:			
Foundation Charter - - - - - -	1671 - - - -	Hertford College Library	O. 22.
LIBELS. *v.* Rebellion.			
LIBERATE:			
Rolls - - - - - - - -	1200 to 1483 - -	Tower - - - - - -	A. 2. a.
LIBER NIGER; or,			
Black Book of the Exchequer, containing Knights Fees in ſeveral Counties, the Will of Hen. II. and other Wills and Charters - - -	Temp. Hen. 2. -	King's Rememb. Office	G. 6. a.
Copy of - - - - - - - -	— —	Receipt of the Exchequer	A. 1. a.
LIBER RUBEUS; or,			
Red Book of the Exchequer, containing amongſt other Things - - - - - - -	Temp. Hen. 3. -	King's Rememb. Office	G. 6. a.
1. Oath of the Officers of the Court.			
2. Dialogus de Scaccario (printed).			
3. Magna Charta, 9 Hen. III.			
4. Sentence of Excommunication againſt Tranſgreſſors of the Charters, 37 Hen. III.			
5. Divers Charters of Will. I. Hen. I. & Ed. I.			
6. Divers Bulls of Popes.			
7. Serjeanties.			
8. Knights Fees.			
9. Prima Scutagia, Hen. II. &c.			
LICENCES passing the Great Seal. *v.* Mortmain.—Patent Rolls.—Warrant Book.			
LICHFIELD and COVENTRY, Dioceſe:			
Eccleſiaſtical Survey - - - - - -	26 Hen. 8. - - -	Firſt Fruits Office - -	G. 18.
Terriers of Rectories and Vicarages - -	— —	Biſhop's Regiſtry, Lichfield - - -	L. 13.
Regiſters, containing Inſtitutions of Rectors and Vicars, Appropriations of Rectories, and Endowments of Vicarages - - - -	1298 to the preſent Time, with Chaſms	Biſhop's Regiſtry, Lichfield - - -	L. 13.
Judicial Proceedings in Cauſes - - -	1450 to preſ^t Time	Biſhop's Regiſtry, Lichfield - - -	L. 13.
Wills and Grants - - - - -	1526 to preſ^t Time	Biſhop's Regiſtry, Lichfield - - -	L. 13.
Adminiſtration, Letters of - - - -	1526 to preſ^t Time	Biſhop's Regiſtry, Lichfield - - -	L. 13.
Licences - - - - - - -	1660 to preſ^t Time	Biſhop's Regiſtry, Lichfield - - -	L. 13.
Regiſters of Pariſhes - - - - -	1660 to preſ^t Time	Biſhop's Regiſtry, Lichfield - - -	L. 13.

ALPHABETICAL ARRANGEMENT OF THE PUBLIC RECORDS.

RECORDS and other INSTRUMENTS.	DATE.	WHERE KEPT.	Appendix to the First Report.
LICHFIELD, DEAN AND CHAPTER:			
Regiſtrum Album, containing Grants, Appropriations, Endowments, &c.	— —	Dean & Chap. Lichfield	N. 9. a.
LINCOLN, COUNTY:			
Antient Deeds, &c. relative to Eſtates therein	— —	Dean & Chap. Weſtm.	N. 12. b.
Nomina Villarum	— —	Lord Treaſ. Rem. Office	G. 7. a.
Hundred Roll	Temp. Ed. 1.	Tower	A. 2. a.
Nona Roll	15 Ed. 3.	King's Rememb. Office	G. 6. a.
Surveys of Manors	Eliz.	King's Rememb. Office	G. 6. a.
Certificate of the Honour of Bolingbroke, partly therein	36 Eliz. & 16 Car. 1.	University Library, Cambridge	P. 1.
Receivers Accounts	1649	University Library, Cambridge	P. 1.
CITY:			
Charter granted by Charles I.	Car. 1.	University Library, Cambridge	P. 1.
DIOCESE:			
Regiſter Book of Biſhop Remigius, ſaid to be the Founder of the See of Lincoln in the 11th Century, containing Entries of various Charters, Grants of Lands to the Dean and Chapter of Lincoln, and of the Endowments of ſeveral Livings in their Patronage	— —	Dean and Chapter of Lincoln	N. 10.
Taxation Book, in which the Names of all the Religious Houſes, Eccleſiaſtical Dignities and Benefices, together with their Valuations, are entered	— —	Dean and Chapter of Lincoln	N. 10.
The Wills of Perſons dying within the Juriſdiction of the Dean and Chapter of Lincoln, and a Regiſter of Adminiſtrations of ſuch Perſons as die inteſtate therein	— —	Dean and Chapter of Lincoln	N. 10.
Eccleſiaſtical Survey	26 Hen. 8.	Firſt Fruits Office	G. 18.
Admiſſions to Holy Orders	1209 to 1641, ſince that Time at Buckden	Biſhop's Regiſtry, Lincoln	L. 16.
Appropriations of Churches	1209 to 1641, ſince that Time at Buckden	Biſhop's Regiſtry, Lincoln	L. 16.
Endowments of Vicarages	1209 to 1641, ſince that Time at Buckden	Biſhop's Regiſtry, Lincoln	L. 16.
Benefices, Collations to	1209 to 1641, ſince that Time at Buckden	Biſhop's Regiſtry, Lincoln	L. 16.
Inſtitutions	1209 to 1641, ſince that Time at Buckden	Biſhop's Regiſtry, Lincoln	L. 16.
Taxation of Religious Houſes and Benefices	26 Hen. 8.	Biſhop's Regiſtry, Lincoln	L. 16.
Acts and Proceedings relative to the Diſtricts made Part of the Sees of Oxford and Peterborough	Previous to 1542	Biſhop's Regiſtry, Lincoln	L. 16.
Terriers of Livings	Beginning 1577	Biſhop's Regiſtry, Lincoln	L. 16.
Pariſh Regiſters	1587 but with Chaſms	Biſhop's Regiſtry, Lincoln	L. 16.
Wills of Perſons dying within the County of Lincoln	1531 to the preſent Time, but 8 Years Chaſm temp. Uſurpationis	Biſhop's Regiſtry, Lincoln	L. 16.
Adminiſtration Bonds and Inventories	For nearly the laſt 100 Years	Biſhop's Regiſtry, Lincoln	L. 16.
Adminiſtrators Accounts of	— —	Biſhop's Regiſtry, Lincoln	L. 16.
Cauſes Eccleſiaſtical, Proceedings in	— —	Biſhop's Regiſtry, Lincoln	L. 16.
LISLE, LORD:			
Valuation of his Eſtates in Ward to the King *v.* WARDS and LIVERIES.	— —	Dean and Chap. Weſtm.	N. 12. b.
LIVINGS:			
Augmentation of	1647 to 1658	Lambeth Library	T.
Surveys of *v.* CHURCH OF ENGLAND.	Temp. Interregni	Rolls Chapel	D. 1.
LLANDAFF, DIOCESE:			
Eccleſiaſtical Survey	26 Hen. 8.	Firſt Fruits Office	G. 18.
Preſentations to Benefices	— —	Regiſtry at Llandaff	L. 15. a.
Inſtitution and Ordination Acts	— —	Regiſtry at Llandaff	L. 15. a.
Pariſh Regiſters, Tranſcripts of	— —	Regiſtry at Llandaff	L. 15. a.
Leaſes, Regiſters of, and old Leaſes	— —	Regiſtry at Llandaff	L. 15. a.
Acts of the Conſiſtory Court	— —	Regiſtry at Llandaff	L. 15. a.
Wills proved	— —	Regiſtry at Llandaff	L. 15. a.
Adminiſtrations granted	— —	Regiſtry at Llandaff	L. 15. a.

ALPHABETICAL ARRANGEMENT OF THE PUBLIC RECORDS.

RECORDS and other INSTRUMENTS.	DATE.	WHERE KEPT.	Appendix to the First Report.
LOADMANAGE, Court of. *v.* Cinque Ports.			
LOANS. *v.* Aids.—Revenue Royal.			
LOCUM TENENS ANGLIÆ. *v.* Custos Regni.			
LONDON, City:			
Charters of - - - - - - - -	Ric. 1. Joh. & Hen. 3.	Corp. Chrifti Coll. Camb.	P. 5.
Rolls of Lands given in Mortmain - - -	7 & 30 Edw. 1. -	Receipt of the Exchequer	A. 1. a.
Regifter Book of St. Martin's-le-Grand - -	— —	Dean and Chapter Weftm.	N. 12. b.
Iter, Copy of - - - - - - - -	14 Edw. 2. - - -	Lincoln's Inn Library -	Q. 3.
Rental of the Lands of the Priory of the Holy Trinity - - - - - - -	35 Edw. 3. - - -	King's Rememb. Office -	G. 6. a.
Reports, Accounts, and Vouchers, concerning the Repairs of St. Paul's Cathedral - - -	1282 to 1642 - -	AuditorsOfficeLand Rev.	G. 15. a.
Ecclefiaftical Survey, a Copy - - - -	26 Hen. 8. - - -	Firft Fruits Office - -	G. 18.
Survey of Eftates of the Duke of Norfolk and his Son on their Attainder - - - - -	31 & 32 Eliz. - -	King's Rememb. Office -	G. 6. a.
Letters and Orders concerning the Cuftoms of the Port of London - - - - -	1605 to 1618 - -	Bodleian Library - -	O. 1.
Rentals of Abbey Lands and Forfeited Eftates -	1638 - - - -	Univerfity Library Camb.	P. 1.
Copies of the Charters, &c. of London - -	Previous to Car. 2. -	Inner Temple Library -	Q. 2. b.
Proceedings of the Commiffioners for fettling the Claims after the Fire of London - - -	Car. 2. - - - -	Britifh Mufeum - -	U.
Matters relative to London - - - -	1687 to 1767 - -	State Paper Office -	C. 1. a.
Oath of the Lord Mayor of - - - -	— —	King's Rememb. Office	Page 236. & 235.
Oath of the Appraifers of the Port of - -	— —		
Oyer and Terminer and Gaol Delivery for London:			
Names of Perfons profecuted at Commiffions of Oyer and Terminer and Gaol Delivery - -	1665 } to the prefent Time - -		
Contractors Bonds to tranfport Felons - - -	1739 }		
Minutes of Proceedings - - - - -	1775 to the prefent Time; fome as early as 1750 - - -		
Commiffions of Oyer and Terminer and Gaol Delivery - - - - - - - -	1775		
For London and Middlesex:			
Warrants of the Attorney General on Indictments Nolle Profequi, &c. - - - - -	1685 } to the prefent Time - -		
Gaol Calendars - - - - - - -	1736		
Files of the refpective Seffions, containing Precepts, Jury Pannels, Indictments, Verdicts, and Judgments, Special Pleas, Records of Acquittal and Conviction, Coroners Inquifitions, and Recognizances of Profecutors and Witneffes - -	1743	Clerk of the Seffions, Old Bailey - - -	H. 7.
N. B. Previous to 1703, believed to be depofited in the Record Room, Guildhall.			
Books of Eftreats, Fines, and Amerciaments -	For London from 1747, and for Middlefex from 1773, to the prefent Time		
Letters from the Secretaries of State, fignifying His Majefty's Mercy to Capital Convicts on Condition of Tranfportation - - -	1782 } to the prefent Time - -		
Minutes of Recognizances - - - -	1784		
Judgment Papers of Names of Convicts, and their Sentences - - - - - -	1786		
Informations and Examinations of Profecutors, Witneffes, and Prifoners, taken by Juftices of Peace - - - - - - - -	1790		
N. B. From 1785 to 1789, depofited in the Record Room, Guildhall.			
Informations of Profecutors and Witneffes - -	1790		
N. B. Previous to 1790, depofited in the Record Room, Guildhall.			
London and Westminster Sessions:			
Accounts of Expenfes of repairing Highways and Sewers - - - - - - - -	— —	King's Rememb. Office -	G. 6. a.

ALPHABETICAL ARRANGEMENT OF THE PUBLIC RECORDS.

RECORDS and other INSTRUMENTS.	DATE.	WHERE KEPT.	Appendix to the Firſt Report.
LONDON—(*continued.*)			
Diocese:			
Terriers of Glebe Lands, &c. - - - - -	— —		
Ordinations and Inſtitutions to Livings and Faculties under the Biſhop's Seal - - -	1306		
Original Wills and Adminiſtration Acts - -	1373		
Proceedings in Cauſes in the Conſiſtory Court -	1467	Conſiſtory Court of London - - - -	L. 5. a.
Faculties and other Inſtruments under the Vicar General's Seal - - - - -	1520 } to the preſent Time - -		
Viſitation Books - - - - - - -	1554		
Preſentations to Livings - - - - -	1633		
Marriage Licences, Warrants and Bonds for them	1660		
LORDS JUSTICES. *v.* Custos Regni.			
LORDS, House of:			
Journals - - - - - - - -	1 Hen. 8. to the preſent Time - -	Parliament Office - -	B. 1.
Journals - - - - - - - -	Car. 1. to 1696 - -	Bodleian Library - - -	O. 1.
Copies of - - - - - - - -	Hen. 8. to 32 Car. 2.	Inner Temple Library -	Q. 2. b.
The like - - - - - - - -	1660 to 1671 - -	Middle Temple Library	Q. 1.
Commiſſions for paſſing Bills, proroguing the Parliament, and appointing Lords High Stewards and Lords Speakers - - - -	1539 to preſent Time	Parliament Office - -	B. 1.
Lord Chancellor Bacon's Submiſſion - -	Jac. 1. - - - -	Aſhmolean Muſeum -	O. 2.
Books containing the Proceedings of Committees on Private Bills and other Matters - -	1621 } to preſent Time -		
Proxy Books - - - - - - -	1624 -		
Minute Books - - - - - - -		Parliament Office - -	B. 1.
Books of Warrants for Witneſſes - - -	1640 to 1648 - -		
Books of Orders and Judgments - - -	1642 to 1719 - -		
Proceedings on the Claim of Lord Purbeck -	Car. 1. and 2. - -	Bodleian Library - - -	O. 1.
Books of the Committee of Privileges - -	1660 to the preſent Time - -		
Garter King of Arms, Rolls of the Peers - -			
Paper Bills and Petitions, and the Proceedings on them - - - - - - - -			
Witneſs Books - - - - - - -	1661 to 1733, and 1753 to the preſent Time -		
Writs of Error, and Proceedings thereon - -	1661 to preſent Time	Parliament Office - -	B. 1.
Orders of Committees on Petitions and Proceedings - - - - - - - -	1661 to 1663 - -		
Teſt Rolls - - - - - - - -	1675 to preſent Time		
Books of Cognizances on Appeals - - -	1680 to 1735 - -		
Appeals and Proceedings thereon - - -	1690 to preſent Time		
Books of Protections - - - - -	1690 to 1696 - -		
Proceedings on the Caſe of Sir J. Fenwick -	1696 - - - -	Bodleian Library - - -	*Page* 223.
Certificates of the Returns of the 16 Peers elected for Scotland - - - - - - -	1707 to preſent Time	Parliament Office, and Clerk of Crown Chan.	B. 1. D. 2. a.
Recognizances on Appeals - - - - -	1738 } to the preſent Time - -		
Books of Pedigrees of Peers, and Pedigrees -	1767	Parliament Office - -	B. 1.
Oath of the Clerk of - - - - -	— —	Clerk of the Crown in Chancery - - - -	D. 2. a.
v. Council.—Pedigrees.—Peers.—Scotland.			
LUFFIELD, Northamptonshire:			
Regiſter Book of - - - - - - -	— —	Dean and Chapter Weſtm.	N. 12. b.
LUNACY and IDEOCY:			
Commiſſions and Inquiſitions, and Traverſes thereon - - - - - - -	Laſt Year of Car. 1. to the preſent Time	Petty Bag Office - - -	D. 5.
Orders reſpecting - - - - -	1689 to the preſent Time - -		
Maſters Reports and Committees Accounts -			
Inrolments of Grants and Revocations - -		Clerk of the Cuſtodies of Ideots and Lunatics -	
Superſedeas of Commiſſions - - - -			D. 18.
LYNN, Norfolk:			
Inquiſitions taken before the High Admiral (Copies of) - - - - - - -	Temp. Hen. 8. - -	Lincoln's Inn Library -	Q. 3.

ALPHABETICAL ARRANGEMENT OF THE PUBLIC RECORDS.

RECORDS and other INSTRUMENTS.	DATE.	WHERE KEPT.	Appendix to the Firſt Report.
MADOX, Thomas:			
Collectanea, or Extracts from the Records in the Exchequer by him - - - - - -	— —	Britiſh Muſeum - -	U.
v. Exchequer of Account.			
MAGDALEN COLLEGE, Oxford:			
Foundation of - - - - - - -	Temp. Hen. 6. - -	Receipt of the Exchequer	A. 1. a.
MAGNA CHARTA:			
Capitula Magnæ Chartæ - - - - -	} 1215 - - - -	Britiſh Muſeum - - -	U.
Two Originals of - - - - - - -			
An Original - - - - - - - -	— —	Dean & Chapter Lincoln	N. 10.
An Original, and ſeveral Confirmations - -	— —	Dean & Chapter Durham	N. 24. b.
A Tranſcript of - - - - - - -	— —	Aſhmolean Muſeum -	O. 2.
Inſpeximus of - - - - - - -	John - - - - -	King's Rememb. Office -	G. 6. a.
Magna Charta Confirmata - - - -	9 Hen. 3. - - -	Corp. Chriſti Coll. Camb.	P. 5.
Of Hen. III. and Confirmation thereof by the ſame King - - - - - -	2 & 21 Hen. 3. -	Bodleian Library - -	O. 1.
Confirmation of the Great Charter - - -	1297 - - - -	Britiſh Muſeum - -	U.
Magna Charta - - - - - - -	9 Ed. 1. - - - -	Corp. Chriſti Coll. Camb.	P. 5.
Confirmation of Henry the Third's Charter by Edw. I. - - - - - - - -	28 Ed. 1. - - -	Oriel College Oxford -	O. 8.
Confirmations thereof by Edw. I. and II. - -	Ed. 1. & 2. - - -	Dean and Chapt. Norwich	N. 13.
Confirmation of - - - - - - -	1 Ed. 3. - - - -	Dean and Chapter Wells	N. 18.
v. Liber Rubeus.			
MALMSBURY Monastery, Wilts:			
Leidger Book of its Charters, &c. - - -	— —	} King's Rememb. Office	G. 6. a.
MAN, Isle of:			
Commiſſion and Inquiſition relative thereto -	34 Eliz. - - - -		
Inſtructions to Commiſſioners relative to the Rights of the Crown and of the Duke of Athol, and Report thereon - - - - - -	31 Geo. 3. - - -	Secretary of State's Office, Home Department.	
MANCA and MISA:			
Records concerning them - - - -	Joh. & Hen. 3. -	Tower - - -	A. 2. a.
MANORS:			
Surveys of - - - - - - - -	Various Dates - -	Augmentation Office -	G. 19. a.
State of, in Jointure to ſeveral Queens - -	— —	Univerſity Library Camb.	P. 1.
Extents of Manors - - - - - -	Ed. 1. 2. & 3. - -	King's Rememb. Office -	G. 6. a.
Extents of Manors, Farms, Woods, Rectories, &c.	Ed. 3. to Anne - -	} Auditors Office Land Revenue - - - -	G. 15. a.
Surveys of Manors and Lands - - -	1493 to 1725 - -		
- - - of Manors in Lincolnſhire - - -	3 to 17 Eliz. - -		
- - - of South Stoke, Somerſet - - -	Eliz. - - - - -	Univerſity Library Camb.	P. 1.
- - - of Eltham, Kent - - - -	Jac. 1. - - - -	King's Rememb. Office	G. 6. a.
- - - of Greenwich, Kent - - - -	7 Will. 3. - - -	Petty Bag Office - -	D. 5.
v. Court Rolls.—Extents.—Norfolk.—Rentals.			
MANUMISSIONS. *v.* Land Revenue.			
MARITIME COURTS:			
Inquiſitions at Lynn before the Lord High Admiral (Copies) - - - - - - -	Hen. 8. - - - -	Lincoln's Inn Library -	Q. 3.
Proceedings in the Admiralty Court of the Cinque Ports - - - - - - -	1632 to the preſent Time, with Chaſms	Reg. of the Cinque Ports	H. 14.*
Proceedings in the Vice Admiralty Court, South Carolina - - - - - - -	1717 - - - -	Bodleian Library - -	O. 1.
v. Admiralty.			
MARRIAGES, Royal:			
Accounts of - - - - - - -	21 Hen. 8. to 2 Jac. 2.	College of Arms - -	C. 8.
Treaties of - - - - - - - -	1553 to 1709, & 1732 to 1743 - -	State Paper Office - -	C. 1. a.
Treaties of, between Henry Prince of Wales and the Infanta Catharine, and between the Prince of Wales and Henrietta Maria of France -	— —	} Univerſity Lib. Cambr.	P. 1.
A Commiſſion to Lord Hayes, &c. to treat of a Marriage between Prince Charles and Chriſtiana, Second Daughter of France - -	1616 - - - -		

ALPHABETICAL ARRANGEMENT OF THE PUBLIC RECORDS.

RECORDS and other INSTRUMENTS.	DATE.	WHERE KEPT.	Appendix to the Firſt Report.
MARRIAGES Royal—*(continued.)*			
Letters to the Ambaſſador of Louis XIII. of France, to negotiate the Marriage of Henrietta Maria with Charles I. - - - - -	1624 - - - -	Bodleian Library - -	O. 1.
Articles of Marriage of Charles I. with Henrietta Maria - - - - - - - -	— —	Univerſity Library Camb.	P. 1.
v. Claus Rolls.			
MARSHAL EARL:			
Accounts relative to him and his Juriſdiction -	8 Edw. 2. - - -	Tower - - -	A. 2. a.
Curia Militaris (Caſes of Duel) - - -	Hen. 6. - - - -	Lincoln's Inn Library -	Q. 3.
Books of the Earl Marſhal, being Entries reſpecting the Arms of the Blood Royal; Licences for Change of Surnames and Arms; and various Proceedings in his Court - - -	Temp. Eliz. - -	College of Arms - -	C. 8.
v. Claus Rolls.			
MARSHALSEA COURT, or Palace Court:			
Profits of, Accounts of - - - -	— —	King's Rememb. Office -	G. 6. a.
Placita Aulæ Domini Regis - - - -	Edw. 1. & 2. - -	Receipt of the Exchequer	A. 1. a.
Pleadings in Actions at Law in the Marſhalſea and Palace Courts - - - - - -	Temp. Car. 2. to the preſent Time - -	Marſhalſea and Palace Court - - - -	G. 22.
v. Aula Domini Regis.			
MARY QUEEN OF SCOTS:			
Proceedings againſt her - - - -	— —	Bodleian Library - -	O. 1.
Inventory of Letters and State Papers relating to her, &c. - - - - - - -	— —	Univerſity Library Camb.	P. 1.
MARY, St. Clerkenwell, Monaſtery of. } v. Land Revenue.			
MARY, St Spittle, Biſhopsgate. }			
MEASURES of length:			
Standards being an Ell and a Yard, marked E with a Crown - - - - - - - - -	— —		
- - - - - a Yard, being a Rod of Braſs - -	Hen. 7. - - - -	Chamberlain's Office, Exchequer - - -	G. 2.
of capacity:			
Several Standard Meaſures - - - -	Hen. 7. Eliz. Anne, Geo. 2. - - -		
v. Exchequer of Receipt.			
MEMORANDA. v. Exchequer of Account.			
MEMORIALS:			
Memorials, with Reports thereupon - - -	1704 to 1761 - -	State Paper Office - -	C. 1. a.
Of Deeds regiſtered - - - - -	1709 to preſent Time	Regiſter Office for Middleſex - - -	M. 1.
v. Claus Rolls.—Law Papers.			
MICHAEL, St. Knights of:			
Order and Statutes of, ſent by Francis I. to Hen. VIII. - - - - - - -	— —	Receipt of the Exchequer	A. 1. a.
MIDDLESEX, County:			
Antient Deeds, &c. relative to Eſtates therein -	— —	Dean and Chapt. Weſtm.	N. 12. b.
Nona Roll - - - - - - - -	15 Edw. 3. - - -	King's Rememb. Office -	G. 6. b.
Eccleſiaſtical Survey - - - - - -	26 Hen. 8. - - -	Firſt Fruits Office - -	G 18.
Rental of Abbey Lands and Forfeited Eſtates -	1638 - - - -	Univerſity Library Camb.	P. 1.
Gaol Delivery:			
Minutes of Proceedings - - - - -	1754 to the preſent Time - - -	Clerk of the Seſſions, Old Bailey - - -	H. 7.
Names of Perſons proſecuted - - - -			
Contractors Bonds to tranſport Felons - -			
Files of the Seſſions - - - - - -			
N. B. Previous to 1756 they are with the Clerk of the Peace for the County.			
MIDLAND CIRCUIT:			
Circuit Commiſſions and Nomina Miniſtrorum -	— —	Clerk of Aſſize and Clerk of the Crown, Midland Circuit - - - - -	H. 2.
Minute Books - - - - - - -	— —		
Niſi Prius Records and Poſteas - - - -	— —		
Aſſociates Minute Books - - - - -	— —		
Liſts of Sheriffs - - - - - - -	1 Jac. 1. to the preſent Time		
Proceſs Books - - - - - - -	31 Geo. 2.		
Gaol Books - - - - - - - - -	1761 - -		
Informations and Depoſitions taken by Juſtices of the Peace - - - - - - -	1766 - -		

ALPHABETICAL ARRANGEMENT OF THE PUBLIC RECORDS.

RECORDS and other INSTRUMENTS.	DATE.	WHERE KEPT.	Appendix to the Firſt Report.
MIDLAND CIRCUIT—*(continued.)*			
Rolls, containing Coroners Inquiſitions, Indictments, &c. and Verdicts and Judgments thereon	1766 to the preſent Time	Clerk of Aſſize and Clerk of the Crown, Midland Circuit	H. 2.
Recognizances			
MILFORD HAVEN. *v.* Harbours.			
MINES:			
Accounts of, in Devon and Cornwall	— —	King's Rememb. Office	G. 6. a.
Leaſes of Mines of Gold and Silver in Glouceſter and Somerſet	Temp. Hen. 8.	Receipt of the Exch.	A. 1. a.
Bundles of Letters relative thereto	Temp. Eliz.		
Accounts of Iron Mines	Ric. 2.	Auditors Office Land Rev.	G. 15. a.
v. Cornwall—Devon—Glouceſter—Somerſet.			
MINISTERS, Foreign:			
Letters from Foreign Miniſters to the Secretaries of State	1710 to 1756	State Paper Office	C. 1. a.
MINISTERS ACCOUNTS:			
Several Miniſters Accounts of Crown Lands, vacant Biſhopricks, Abbies, &c.	Hen. 3. to Eliz.	King's Rememb. Office	G. 6. a.
The like of Alien Priories	Edw. 1. to Ric. 2.		
The like of the Poſſeſſions of the Knights Templars			
* Miniſters and Receivers Accounts	Edw. 1. to Car. 1.	Auditors Office Land Rev.	G. 15. a.
Miniſters Accounts	Ric. 2. to Eliz.	Augmentation Office	G. 19. a.
Accounts and Views of Accounts	Hen. 5. to Car. 2.	Auditors Office Land Rev.	G. 15. a.
Miniſters Accounts of Eſtates acquired by Attainder or Forfeiture	Hen. 6. to Edw. 6.	Augmentation Office	G. 19. a.
The like of ſeveral Honours	Hen. 8. & Edw. 6.		
The like of Eſtates acquired by Purchaſe, Exchange, &c.	Hen. 8. to Eliz.		
The like of Wood Sales			
† The like of Diſſolved Monaſteries, &c. and of thoſe acquired by Forfeiture or Eſcheat	Hen. 8. to Car. 1.	Auditors Office Land Revenue	G. 15. & 16. a.
The like for Wales	Eliz. Car. 1. & G. 1.		
The like of Lands in Wales of Sir J. Perrot and Owen Glynn, attainted	Eliz.		
Declarations of	1600 to 1700		
v. Augmentation Office.—Cornwall Duchy.—Lancaster Duchy.—Land Revenue.			
MINORCA:			
Papers relative thereto	1714 to 1756	State Paper Office	C. 1. a.
MINT:			
Various Papers relating thereto	— —	Britiſh Muſeum	U.
Extracts from Records relating thereto	— —	Lincoln's Inn Library	Q. 3.
Accounts of	— —	King's Rememb. Office	G. 6. a.
Old Aſſays, &c. of Gold and Silver in ſeveral Reigns	— —	Receipt of the Exchequer	A. 1. a.
Aſſay Rolls	Temp. Edw. 1.		
Indentures between the Crown and the Maſters of the Mint, and other Papers relative thereto	Edw. 3. to Car. 1.		
Accounts of	6 Ric. 2. 2 Hen. 4. 1 & 3 Hen. 6.	Tower	A. 2. a.
Accounts of	Edw. 6. to Will. 3.	Auditors Office Land Rev	G. 15. a.
Papers and Collections relative thereto	1566 to 1690	State Paper Office	C. 1 a.
An Indenture concerning it	1702	King's Rememb. Office	G. 6. a.
Oath of the Maſters and Workers	— —	Clerk of the Crown in Chancery	*Page* 224.
v. Claus Rolls.—Coin.—Exchequer of Receipt.—Money.			
MISA. *v.* Manca.			
MODENA:			
Treaties and Ratifications with England	1747 to 1753	State Paper Office	C. 1. a.

* Theſe Miniſters Accounts have been lately transferred to the Augmentation Office.

† Theſe have alſo, in like Manner, been lately transferred to the Augmentation Office.

ALPHABETICAL ARRANGEMENT OF THE PUBLIC RECORDS.

RECORDS and other INSTRUMENTS.	DATE.	WHERE KEPT.	Appendix to the First Report.
MONASTERIES:			
Collections respecting them	— —	British Museum, and Inner Temple Library	U. Q. 2. b.
Various Surveys, Rentals, Leidgers, Registers, &c. respecting several Monasteries, Priories, Chantries, &c.	— —	Auditors Office Land Rev.	G. 15. a.
Surveys of; Visitations of; Papers and Letters relating to their State and Dissolution	— —	Receipt of the Exchequer	A. 1. a.
Charters, &c.	Hen. 3. to Hen. 8.	Auditors Office Land Rev.	G. 15. a.
Leidger Books, Rentals, and other Accounts	Edw. 3.	King's Rememb. Office	G. 6. a.
Reports relative to several of them by Visitors; Statements of Enormities committed in several of them, in Letters to Lord Cromwell; Surrenders of several	Temp. Hen. 8.	Receipt of the Exchequer	A. 1. a.
Surrenders of	Temp. Hen. 8.	Augmentation Office	G. 19. a.
Monasteries surrendered to Cardinal Wolsey, Inquisitions thereon	Temp. Hen. 8.	Rolls Chapel	D. 1. a.
Surveys of	26 Hen. 8.	First Fruits Office	G. 18.
Liber Supervisus omnium Monast. Terrar. & Tenement. Dom. Reg. Eliz. in Insula Vectis	25 Eliz.	University Library Camb.	P. 1.
v. CHARTÆ ANTIQUÆ.—CHARTULARIES.—GLOUCESTER COUNTY.—LAND REVENUE.—LEIDGER BOOKS.			
MONEY:			
Collections respecting it	— —	Inner Temple Library	Q. 2. b
Accounts of Money imprested	12. John	Tower	A. 2. a.
v. COIN.—EXCHEQUER OF RECEIPT.—MINT.			
MONMOUTH, COUNTY:			
Survey of	3 Eliz.	Auditors Office Land Rev. Wales	G. 16. a.
MONSTRANS DE DROIT:			
Pleadings and Judgments therein	Hen. 7. to the present Time	Rolls Chapel	D. 1. a.
MOROCCO AND FEZ:			
Instructions to Edmund Higgins, sent to the King of	1577	University Library Camb.	P. 1.
MORTGAGES. *v.* CERTIFICATES.			
MORTMAIN:			
Licences to the Colleges of the Universities	Various Dates	University Library Camb.	P. 1.
Rolls of Lands given in Mortmain, in London; Licence to Cardinal Wolsey for his College	7 to 30 Edw. 1.; Hen. 8.	Receipt of the Exchequer	A. 1. a.
v. CLAUS ROLLS.—UNIVERSITIES.			
MUNSTER, IRELAND:			
Projects concerning the Lands and Peopling of Munster	— —	University Library Camb.	P. 1.
v. IRELAND.			
MUSCOVY:			
Transactions with England	1485 to 1613	British Museum	U.
MUSTERS:			
Of Men at Arms, Hobilers, and Buttmen, in divers Shires; Return of Commissioners of the Number of Men capable of bearing Arms in Com. Hants	Temp. Hen. 8.; 12 Hen. 8.	Receipt of the Exchequer	A. 1. a.
Instructions for General Musters in Norfolk	Eliz.	University Library Camb.	P. 1.
Commissions, Musters, &c.	1586 to 1705	State Paper Office	C. 1. a.
v. ARMY.			
NAVARRE:			
Treaties and Transactions with	1378 to 1512	Receipt of the Exhcequer	A. 1. a.
NAVIGATIONS AND CANALS:			
v. PEACE, CLERKS OF.			
NAVY:			
Various Papers relating thereto	— —	British Museum	U.

ALPHABETICAL ARRANGEMENT OF THE PUBLIC RECORDS.

RECORDS and other INSTRUMENTS.	DATE.	WHERE KEPT.	Appendix to the First Report.
NAVY—*(continued.)*			
Collections about it	— —	Inner Temple Library	Q. 2. b.
Several Accounts of it	— —	King's Rememb. Office	G. 6. a.
Commissions, Warrants, Estimates, Surveys, &c.	1509 to 1716	State Paper Office	C. 1. a.
Instructions relative to Voyages and Discoveries	1576 to 1676		
Various Manuscripts (by Mr. Pepys) relating to Naval Affairs	1589 to 1695, with many Chasms	Bodleian Library	O. 1.
v. Admiralty.—Claus Rolls.—Jewels, &c.—Peace, Clerks of.			
NEGOTIATIONS with Foreign States:			
Large Collections of	Edw. 3. to Jac. 1.	British Museum	U.
The like	1340 to 1798	State Paper Office	C. 1. a.
With Foreign States and Powers, Alliances, &c.	1550 to 1699		
Letters and Negotiations of M. Noailles	1553		
Sir Francis Walsingham's Negotiations in France	1570		
Negotiations in East Friezland	1584		
Journal of Conferences between His Majesty's Commissioners the King of Spain's, &c.	1604		
Negotiations de M. la Boderie en Angleterre	1606, &c.		
Relatio Legationis Com. Leycestriæ ad Christ. 4 Dan. Reg.	1632	Bodleian Library	O. 1.
Originals and Copies of Memorials between Spain and England	1636		
Negotiations de M. Sebron en Angleterre	1644		
Negotiations of Sir T. Clifford, in Denmark	1664		
Letters from the Protector to Foreign States	Oliver Cromwell		
Books of Negotiations	1677 to 1688		
Correspondence with Foreign Ministers	1710 to 1756	State Paper Office	C. 1. a.
v. State Papers.			
NETHERLANDS:			
Transactions between England and the Low Countries	1485 to 1613	British Museum	U.
Negotiations with	Chiefly Temp. Eliz.	University Library Camb.	P. 1.
State of Revenues, Forces, &c.	1657 to 1676	State Paper Office	C. 1. a.
Treaties with England	1674 to 1763		
NEWENTON LONGVILLE Priory:			
Chartulary of	— —	New College Oxford	O. 10.
NEWFOUNDLAND, *v.* Fisheries.			
NEW-HAMPSHIRE and NEW-YORK, America:			
Papers relating thereto	— —		
v. Plantations.		Bodleian Library	O. 1.
NEWPORT:			
Copies of the Votes in Parliament, respecting the Treaty of	1648		
v. Parliament.			
NEWSTED, Notts:			
Leidger Book of its Charters, &c.	Temp. Hen. 6.	King's Rememb. Office	G. 6. a.
NICHOLAS IV. Pope:			
His Valor, being a Taxation of the Spiritualties and Temporalities of the Clergy in the Provinces of Canterbury and Dioceses of York and Durham	circa 1291	King's Rememb. Office and Parts of it in many of the Chapter Houses	G. 6. a. N.
Transcripts of his Taxation in several Counties	— —	Augmentation Office	G. 19. a.
Liber Taxationis	— —	British Museum	U.
Transcript of the Spiritualties thereof	— —	Tower	A. 2. a.
NICHOLLS, Sir Augustin:			
His Oath as one of the Justices of the Common Pleas	— —	Clerk of the Crown Chan.	*Page* 225.
NOBILITY:			
Collections respecting them	— —	Inner Temple Library	Q. 2. b.
Collections respecting their Creations	— —		
v. Claus Rolls.			

ALPHABETICAL ARRANGEMENT OF THE PUBLIC RECORDS.

RECORDS and other INSTRUMENTS.	DATE.	WHERE KEPT.	Appendix to the Firſt Report.
NOMINA VILLARUM:			
Rolls ſo called - - - - - - -	— —	Lord Treaſ. Rem. Office	G. 7. a.
Books ſo called, containing, amongſt other Things, "Teſta de Neville" - - - - - -	Temp. Hen. 3. & Edw. 1. - - -	King's Rememb. Office -	G. 6. a.
Nomina Villarum - - - - -	1316 to 1559 - -	Britiſh Muſeum - - -	U.
A Book, called Nomina Villarum, containing Claims of Lords of Liberties allowed by the Court of Exchequer - - - - -	1672 - - - -	Foreign Appoſer's Office	G. 11.
v. The ſeveral COUNTIES.			
NONÆ ROLLS. *v.* The ſeveral COUNTIES.			
NORFOLK, COUNTY:			
Antient Deeds, &c. relative to Eſtates therein -	— —	Dean and Chap. Weſtm.	N. 12. b.
Inquiſitiones de Miniſtris - - - - -	4 Edw. 1. - - -	Receipt of the Exchequer	A. 1. a.
Knights Fees in this County - - - -	31 Edw. 1. - - -	Univerſity Library Camb.	P. 1.
Eccleſiaſtical Survey - - - - - -	26 Hen. 8. - - -	Firſt Fruits Office - -	G. 18.
Inſtructions for a General Muſter of Men in this County - - - - - - -	Eliz. - - - -	Univerſity Library Camb.	P. 1.
Surveys of Manors, &c. on the Attainder of Thomas Duke of Norfolk and Philip his Son, in Norfolk, Suffolk, Suſſex, London and Middleſex - - - - - - - - -	31 & 32 Eliz. - -	King's Rememb. Office	G. 6. a.
CIRCUIT:			
Commiſſions of Aſſize and Niſi Prius, Oyer, Terminer, and Gaol Delivery - - - -			
Writs of Aſſociations and "Si non Omnes" - -			
Precepts for ſummoning Jurors, &c. - -			
Rolls of Names of Grand and Petty Jurors - -			
Niſi Prius, Records of - - - - - -			
Proceſſes for the Apprehenſion of Perſons charged with Offences, and Returns thereon - - - -	1689 to the preſent Time - - -		
Rolls of Names and Offences of Priſoners -			
Indictments, Bills of - - - - - -			
Coroners Inquiſitions - - - - - -			
Recognizances - - - - - - -			
Affidavits and Certificates - - - - -			
Depoſitions, Informations, Examinations, and Confeſſions - - - - - - -		Clerk of Aſſize and of the Crown, Norfolk Circuit - - -	H. 3.
Gaol Delivery Books - - - - - -	8 Geo. 2. to the preſent Time - -		
Preſentments by Grand Jurors - - -			
Eſtreats of Fines, &c. - - - - - -			
Memorials and Draughts of Memorials for Pardons and Reprieves, and Letters, &c. relative thereto - - - - - - - - -	1768 to the preſent Time - - -		
Contracts for Tranſportation - - - -			
Books of Names of Parties in Civil Actions, Indictments, or Informations - - - -	1774 to preſent Time		
NORFOLK, DUKE OF:			
Inventories of Jewels, Wardrobe, and Effects of Thomas Duke of Norfolk, attainted - -	1524 - - - -	Univerſity Library Camb.	P. 1.
The like of the Duke of Norfolk and Earl of Surrey - - - - - - - -	38 Hen. 8. - - -	Auditors Office Land Rev.	G. 15.
NORMANDY:			
Norman Rolls - - - - - - -	1200 to 1422 - -	Tower - - - -	A. 2. a.
v. FRANCE.			
NORTHAMPTON, COUNTY:			
Iters - - - - - - - - -	3 Edw. 3. - - -	Bodleian Library - - -	O. 1.
Copy thereof - - - - - - -	— —	Lincoln's Inn Library -	Q. 3.
Nona Rolls - - - - - - -	15 Edw. 3. - - -	King's Rememb. Office -	G. 6. b.
Eccleſiaſtical Survey - - - - - -	26 Hen. 8. - - -	Firſt Fruits Office - -	G. 18.
Survey of Eſtates therein not granted in Fee Farm	1629 - - - -	Univerſity Library Camb.	P. 1.

ALPHABETICAL ARRANGEMENT OF THE PUBLIC RECORDS.

RECORDS and other INSTRUMENTS.	DATE.	WHERE KEPT.	Appendix to the First Report.
NORTHERN CIRCUIT:			
The Ended Roll, containing the Judges Precepts, Names of Justices, Prisoners in Gaol, and their Commitments, &c. as also all Indictments, Informations, Records, and Presentments, Affidavits, Coroners Inquests, &c. - - - -	Jac. 1. to the present Time - -	Clerk of Assize and of the Crown, Castle of York - - -	H. 4.
The Extra or Presentment Roll, containing such Indictments, Informations, and Presentments, as have not been tried, or on which no Judgment has been given, which, when the Parties appear and Judgment is given, make Part of the Ended Roll - - - - - -	Jac. 1. to the present Time - -	Clerk of Assize and of the Crown, Castle of York - - -	H. 4.
Gaol Judgment or Order Books - - -	1657 to pres[t] Time; but with Chasms prior to 1736 -	Clerk of Assize and of the Crown, Castle of York - - -	H. 4.
Minute Books - - - - - - -	12 Anne to the present Time, with some Chasms -	Clerk of Assize and of the Crown, Castle of York - - -	H. 4.
NORTHUMBERLAND, County:			
Inquisitiones de Ministris - - - -	4 Edw. 1. - - -	Receipt of the Exchequer	A. 1. a.
Duke of:			
Inventory of his Jewels, Wardrobe, Effects, &c. when attainted - - - - - - - *v.* Attainders.	1 Mary - - - -	Auditors Office Land Rev.	G. 15. a.
Earl of:			
Valuations of his Estates in Ward to the King - *v.* Wards and Liveries.	— —	Dean & Chapter Westm.	N. 12. b.
NORTON, Worcestershire:			
Survey of Lands in Jointure to Queen Catharine, Consort of Charles II. - - - -	4 Jac. 2. - - -	Auditors Office Land Rev.	G. 15. a.
NORWICH Diocese:			
Ecclesiastical Survey - - - - - -	26 Hen. 8. - - -	First Fruits Office - -	G. 18.
Faculty Books - - - - - - - -	— —	Bishop's Registry, Norwich - - -	L. 22. a.
Institutions, Unions, Appropriations, and other similar Documents - - - - - -	1299 to the present Time, except during the Usurpation	Bishop's Registry, Norwich - - -	L. 22. a.
Register Book, containing Depositions in the Consistory Court - - - - - -	1490 to present Time, but not regular -	Bishop's Registry, Norwich - - -	L. 22. a.
Registers of the Acts of the Consistory Court -	1509 to present Time	Bishop's Registry, Norwich - - -	L. 22. a.
Wills, Original, and Registrations of, in Books -	1521 to the present Time, except during the Usurpation	Bishop's Registry, Norwich - - -	L. 22. a.
Original Terriers of Glebe Lands - - - -	1633 to 1794 - -	Bishop's Registry, Norwich - - -	L. 22. a.
Deeds of Exchange of Glebe Lands and Faculties	1636 to present Time	Bishop's Registry, Norwich - - -	L. 22. a.
Original Presentations to Benefices - - - -	1660 to present Time, except a few Years	Bishop's Registry, Norwich - - -	L. 22. a.
NOTARIAL FACULTIES. *v.* Chancery.			
NOTITIA PAROCHIALIS.			
Returns of Churches in different Parts of England - - - - - - - - *v.* Church of England.	1606 - - - -	Lambeth Library - -	T.
NOTTINGHAM, County:			
Antient Deeds, &c. relative to Estates therein -	— —	Dean & Chapter Westm.	N. 12. b.
Inquisitions concerning Fens - - - -	Temp. Edw. 3. -	Receipt of the Exchequer	A. 1. a.
Iters, Copies of - - - - - - -	3, 4, & 8 Edw. 3. -	Lincoln's Inn Library -	Q. 3.
Nona Roll - - - - - - - -	15 Edw. 3. - - -	King's Rememb. Office -	G. 6. b.
Ecclesiastical Survey (a Copy) - - -	26 Hen. 8. - - -	First Fruits Office - -	G. 18.
NOVUM CASTRUM super Tynam. *v.* Placita.			
NYNEHAM. *v.* Chartularies.			

ALPHABETICAL ARRANGEMENT OF THE PUBLIC RECORDS.

RECORDS and other INSTRUMENTS.	DATE.	WHERE KEPT.	Appendix to the First Report.
OATHS:			
Collections respecting Oaths Royal - -	— —	Inner Temple Library -	Q. 2. b.
Oaths of Exchequer Officers in the Black Book	— —	Receipt of the Exchequer	A. 1. a.
The like in the Red Book - - - - -	— —	King's Rememb. Office -	G. 6. a.
Nine Rolls of Oaths to be taken by various Persons	— —	Petty Bag Office - - -	D. 5.
List of several Officers, and their Oaths - - } Entries of Oaths to various Officers on being sworn into Office - - - - - -	1639 to pres^t Time	Clerk of Crown in Chan.	D. 2.
v. CLAUS ROLLS.—EXCHEQUER OF ACCOUNT AND RECEIPT.—KING'S BENCH.—LIBER NIGER.—LIBER RUBEUS.—PETTY BAG.—CROWN OFFICE—and the several Offices under their respective Names.			
OFFERINGS:			
Offerings and Free Gifts to Kings - - -	Joh. Edw. 2. and 3.	Tower - - - - -	A. 2. a.
Receivers Accounts of - - - -	13 Car. 2. - - -	AuditorsOfficeLand Rev.	G. 15. a.
v. KINGS.			
OFFICES:			
Discourses on Offices, by Sir R. Cotton - -	— —	} Bodleian Library - -	O. 1.
Table of Fees - - - - - - -	— —		
A Book of Fees and Offices - - - -	1 Mary - - - -	Antiq. Society Library -	S. a.
Collections respecting Offices, with their Fees -	Eliz. - - - - -	Bodleian Library - - -	O. 1.
Inrolments of Admissions of Officers in Chancery, Serjeants at Law, &c. - - - - -	40 Eliz. to the present Time - - -	Petty Bag Office - -	D. 5.
v. EXCHEQUER OF ACCOUNT.—PATENT ROLLS.			
ORANGE, PRINCE OF:			
Negotiations and Treaties with him, and also with the United States. Instructions to Ambassadors, &c. - - - - - - - -	Chiefly Temp. Eliz.	UniversityLibrary Camb.	P. 1.
ORDNANCE:			
Various Papers relating thereto - - -	— —	British Museum - - -	U.
Inventory of Ordnance and Munition in the King's Castles, on the death of Henry VIII. - } Inventory of Armories in Charge to Sir T. Darcy, Master of the Ordnance - - - - -	Edw. 6. - - -	Antiq. Society Library -	S. a.
Accounts of Deliveries - - - - -	1568 to 1582 - -	AuditorsOfficeLand Rev.	G. 15.
Collections concerning Affairs of the - -	1589 to 1633 - -	Bodleian Library - -	O. 1.
Correspondence relative thereto - - -	1683 to 1762 - -	State Paper Office - -	C. 1. a.
v. ACCOUNTS PUBLIC.—ARMY.—CLAUS ROLLS.—JEWELS.—INVENTORIES.			
OSNEY ABBEY, OXON:			
Leidger Book of - - - - - - -	— —	} King's Rememb. Office	G. 6. a.
OSYTH, ST. MONASTERY:			
v. LAND REVENUE.			
OUTLAWRIES:			
Transcripts of, certified into the Court of Exchequer, and Proceedings thereon - - -	— —		
Inquisitions upon - - - - - -	1180 to 1688 - -	Receipt of the Exchequer	A. 1. a.
Writs and Returns of Estates of Outlawed Persons - - - - - - - -	Temp. Interregni -	AuditorsOfficeLandRev.	G. 15. a.
Reversals of - - - - - - - -	10 Geo. 2. to the present Time - -	Clerk of the Reversals and Outlawries - -	F. 9.
v. CLAUS ROLLS.—COMMON PLEAS.—EXCHEQUER OF ACCOUNT.—KING'S BENCH.—USURPATION.			
OXFORD, COUNTY:			
Antient Deeds, &c. relative to Estates therein -	— —	Dean and Chap.Westmin.	N. 12. b.
Hundred Roll - - - - - - -	Temp. Edw. 1. - -	Tower - - - - - -	A. 2. a.
Hundred Roll of Bampton and Poughley, (Copy of)	7 Edw. 1. - -	Lincoln's Inn Library -	Q. 3.
Nona Roll - - - - - - - -	15 Edw. 3. - -	King's Rememb. Office -	G. 6. b.
Ecclesiastical Survey - - - - - -	26 Hen. 8. - -	First Fruits Office - -	G. 18.
Receivers Accounts - - - - - -	— —	University Library Camb.	P. 1.
Oath of the Sheriff - - - - - -	— —	Clerk of Crown in Chan.	*Page* 223.
Oath of the Mayor of the City of Oxford - -	— —	King's Rememb. Office	— 236.
v. TESTA DE NEVIL.			

7 T

279*

ALPHABETICAL ARRANGEMENT OF THE PUBLIC RECORDS.

RECORDS and other INSTRUMENTS.	DATE.	WHERE KEPT.	Appendix to the Firſt Report.
OXFORD University:			
Indenture between the Univerſity and the Company of Stationers, London, and Confirmation of the Stationers Gift to the Univerſity - - -	8 Jac. 1. - - -	Aſhmolean Muſeum -	O. 2.
v. The ſeveral Colleges.—Universities.—Wolsey.			
Diocese:			
Conſecrations of Churches, Patents of Officers, Deeds relative to Exchanges of Lands belonging to Benefices, Forms on building Parſonage Houſes, and other Inſtruments - - -	— —	Biſhop's Regiſtry Oxford	L. 28.
Acts and Proceedings relative to the Diſtricts made Part of this See - - - - - -	1542 - - - -	Biſhop's Regiſtry Lincoln	L. 16.
Inſtitutions to Benefices - - - - -	1543 to the preſent Time, with Chaſms		
Aſſignation or Minute Books of Cauſes in the Conſiſtory Court - - - - - -	1573 to 1687, and 1729 to the preſent Time - - - -		
Wills, Original - - - - - - -	1579 to preſent Time	Biſhop's Regiſtry Oxford	L. 28.
Compoſitions with Incumbents - - -	1579 to 1638 - -		
Adminiſtrations - - - - - - -	1604 to preſent Time		
Marriage Bonds - - - - - - -	For more than a Century paſt - -		
Faculties - - - - - - - -	1737 to preſent Time		
v. Lincoln Diocese.			
Circuit:			
Commiſſions (under the Great Seal) of Oyer and Terminer for the ſeveral Counties and Cities in this Circuit - - - - - - -	— —	Clerk of the Aſſize and Clerk of the Crown, Oxford Circuit - -	H. 6.
Proceſs Books - - - - - - -	— —		
Poſtea Books, Books of Orders at Niſi Prius, and Poſteas not taken away - - - -	— —		
Informations and Preſentments - - -	— —		
Indictments for Felonies and Miſdemeanours -	— —		
Special Pleas, Replications, Rejoinders, and Demurrers - - - - - - - -	— —		
Recognizances to Proſecute, &c. - - -	— —		
Gaol Books - - - - - - -	— —		
Judgment Rolls - - - - - - -	— —		
Eſtreats of Fines, &c. - - - - -	— —		
Calendars ſigned by the Judges - - -	— —		
OYER and TERMINER:			
A Special Commiſſion of, and of Gaol Delivery for Briſtol - - - - - - -	1753 - - -	Clerk of the Crown in Chancery - - -	D. 2. a.
v. The ſeveral Circuits.—London and Middlesex.			
PALACES, CASTLES, &c.:			
Accounts of Expenſes of - - - - -	— —	King's Rememb. Office -	G. 6. a.
Books of Works at Greenwich - - - -	1716 to 1729 - -	Auditors Office Land Rev.	G. 15. a.
PALATINE ELECTORS:			
Various Negotiations with and concerning them *v.* Bohemia.	— —	Univerſity Library Camb.	P. 1.
PAPISTS:			
Oath on their conforming to the Proteſtant Religion	— —	Petty Bag Office - - -	*Page* 227.
PARDONS:			
Collections reſpecting them - - - -	— —	Inner Temple Library -	Q. 2. b.
Records relative to General and Particular Pardons	Divers Reigns - -	Tower - - - - - -	A. 2. a.
Pardon Rolls - - - - - - - -	Ric. 3. to Jac. 1. -	Rolls Chapel - - -	D. 1. a.
v. Claus Rolls.—Patent Rolls.—Prerogative Royal.—Warrant Books.			
PARISHES. *v.* Church of England.—Notitia Parochialis.			

ALPHABETICAL ARRANGEMENT OF THE PUBLIC RECORDS.

RECORDS and other INSTRUMENTS.	DATES.	WHERE KEPT.	Appendix to the First Report.
PARLIAMENT:			
Collections respecting the Power, Antiquity, and Privileges of	— —	Inner Temple Library	Q. 2. b.
Cases in, by Prynne	— —		
Journals and Proceedings, (Copies of many of them)	— —	Bodleian Library	O. 1.
Writs of Summons to Council, and Parliament Papers	— —	Dean and Chapter Westm.	N. 12. b.
Concordia inter Regem et Barones pro Electione Vicecomitum	Hen. 3.	Receipt of the Exchequer	A. 1. a.
Summons to Parliament, in Dugdale's Hand-Writing	49 Hen. 3. to 20 Edw. 2.	Ashmolean Museum	O. 2.
Returns to	1288 to 1477	Tower	A. 2. a.
Petitions in	Ed. 1. to 17 Ed. 4.		
Copies of Petitions in	Edw. 1. 2. and 3. and Hen. 4.	Lincoln's Inn Library	Q. 3.
Rolls, Copies of	Edw. 1. to Edw. 4.		
Rolls	18 to 21 Edw. 1.	Receipt of the Exchequer	A. 1. a.
Placita Parliamentaria	Edw. 1. to Edw. 2.	Bodleian Library	O. 1.
Ordinatio Parliamenti quod Servientes Regis Edwardi II. non capiant aliqua bona pro Rege nisi solverint pro eisdem	Edw. 2.	Dean and Chap. Durham	N. 24. b.
Account of Parliaments holden	From 1 Edw. 2. to the End of Edw. 4.	University Lib. Camb.	P. 1.
Rolls	Edw. 2. to Hen. 6.	Middle Temple Library	Q. 1.
Copies of Rolls	Edw. 2. to Hen. 8.	Inner Temple Library	Q. 2. b.
Rolls	1311 to 1483	Tower	A. 2. a.
Copies of Rolls in the Tower, with Extracts of what further thereof is to be found in the Chapel of the Rolls, arranged in the order of Time	5 Edw. 2. to 19 Hen. 7.	Pepysian Library, Magdalen College Camb.	P. 14.
Summons to, Copies of	Ric. 2. Hen. 4. 5. 6. Edw. 4.	Lincoln's Inn Library	Q. 3.
Rolls, Copies of	Ric. 2.	Bodleian Library	O. 1.
A Roll	7 Hen. 5.	Receipt of the Exchequer	A. 1. a.
Rolls	1 Ric. 3. to the present Time	Rolls Chapel	D. 1. a.
Calendar of Public and Private Acts	1487 to 1685	Bodleian Library	O. 1.
Original Acts of	12 Hen. 7. to the present Time	Parliament Office	B. 1.
Calendar of Acts in the Clerk of Parliament's Office	12 Hen. 7. to 32 Car. 2.	Inner Temple Library	Q. 2. b.
Private Acts	Hen. 8. to Car. 2.		
The like	Hen. 8. to Car. 2.	British Museum	U.
Declarations, Reports, Speeches, Addresses, Votes, Acts, &c. in Parliamentary Affairs	1527 to 1698	State Paper Office	C. 1. a.
Parliament Pawns	21 Hen. 8. to the present Time	Petty Bag Office	D. 5.
Parliament Returns, Bundles of	33 Hen. 8. to the Restoration	Rolls Chapel	D. 1. a.
Passages in Parliament	1 to 13 Eliz.	Caius College Cambridge	P. 7.
Writs for electing Members	Temp. Eliz. Jac. 1. & Car. 1.	Bodleian Library	O. 1.
Proceedings	1572 to 1663		
Journal of	1597		
Names of Knights, &c. summoned	1620	University Lib. Cam.	P. 1.
Speeches in Parliament	1623	Bodleian Library	O. 1.
Acts (with MS. Memorandums) of the Committee relative to the Goods of Charles I.	Car. 1.		
Debates in Parliament	1628		
Orders, &c. on Affairs of Ireland	1642 to 1644		
Perfect Copies of the Votes, &c. in the Treaty of Newport, by Sir E. Walker	1648		
Transactions relative to Scottish Affairs	1649 to 1653		
Transactions in Parliament, collected by Ashmole	1673 to 1718	Ashmolean Museum	O. 2.
Indentures or Returns of Members	12 Car. 2. to 30 G. 3.	Petty Bag Office	D. 5.
Journals of Lords and Commons	1660 to 1688	Bodleian Library	O. 1.
Journal during the Interregnum, from the withdrawing of James II. to the Meeting of the Conventional Parliament	1688		

ALPHABETICAL ARRANGEMENT OF THE PUBLIC RECORDS.

RECORDS and other INSTRUMENTS.	DATE.	WHERE KEPT.	Appendix to the First Report.
PARLIAMENT—*(continued.)*			
Precepts for the Convention Parliament - -	1688 - - - -	Petty Bag Office - - -	D. 5.
Returns to the Convention Parliament - -	1688 - - -	Clerk of Crown in Chan.	D. 2. a.
Certificates of Qualifications of Members - -	From Anne to the present Time - -	Petty Bag Office - - -	D. 5.
Votes, Speeches, Addreſſes, Proteſts, &c. in Parliamentary Affairs - - - - - -	1706 to 1763 - -	State Paper Office - -	C. 1. a.
Reports to Parliament from Commiſſioners to inquire of Woods, Foreſts, and Land Revenues of the Crown, (ſince printed) - - -	26 & 30 Geo. 3. -	Survey.Gen.CrownLands	G. 14.
Oath of the Clerk of Parliament - - -	— —	Clerk of Crown in Chan.	*Page* 223.
v. BACON, VISCOUNT ST. ALBAN'S.—CLAUS ROLLS.—COMMONS, HOUSE OF.—LORDS, HOUSE OF—PEACE, CLERKS OF.—PIPE.—PLACITA.—STAR CHAMBER.—STATUTES.			
PARLIAMENTARY SURVEYS:			
Surveys - - - - - - - -	Temp. Interregni	Augmentation Office -	G. 19. a.
The like - - - - - - - -	Temp. Interregni	Surv. Gen. Crown Lands	G. 14.
Surveys, commonly called Oliverian Surveys -	Temp. Interregni	With ſeveral Deans and Chapters - - - -	N.
Surveys of Canterbury and various other Dioceſes	Temp. Interregni	Lambeth Library - -	T.
v. CROWN LANDS.			
PARSONAGES:			
Surveys and Valuations of - - - -	26 Hen. 8. - - -	Firſt Fruits Office - -	G. 18.
PARTICULARS:			
For Grants and Leaſes - - - - - -	— —	Augmentation Office -	G. 19. a.
Of Foreſts, Chaces, and Parks granted to the Prince - - - - - - -	— —	Univerſity Lib. Cam. -	P. 1.
Of Lands, &c. intended to be granted to the Prince - - - - - -	— —	Univerſity Lib. Cam. -	P. 1.
Particulars, &c. for Sale of Fee Farm Rents - -	1649 to 1660 - -	Augmentation Office - -	G. 19. a.
v. AUGMENTATION OFFICE. — CROWN LANDS.—GRANTS.—LAND REV.			
PARTITION. *v.* CHANCERY.			
PASSPORTS. *v.* CLAUS ROLLS.—WARRANT BOOKS.			
PATENT ROLLS:			
Rolls - - - - - - - -	Joh.Ed.2.&Hen.6.	Receipt of the Exchequer	A. 1. a.
Copies and Extracts of - - - - -	Joh. to Edw. 4. -	Inner Temple Library -	Q. 2. b.
Rolls - - - - - - - - -	1201 to 1483 - -	Tower - - - - - - -	A. 2. a.
A Roll containing Extracts from - - -	Temp. Hen. 3. - -	Receipt of the Exchequer	A. 1. a.
Copies and Abſtracts of - - - -	Temp. Hen. 3. - -	Lincoln's-Inn Library -	Q. 3.
Rolls - - - - - - - - -	Ed. 5. to 27 Geo. 3.	Rolls Chapel - - - -	D. 1. a.
PATENTS:			
Dockets of - - - - - - - -	Hen. 8. to Eliz. -	Bodleian Library - -	O. 1.
The like - - - - - - - -	1595 to 1602, and from 1643 to the preſent Time - -	Clerk of Crown in Chan:	D. 2. a.
Patents to Printers - - - - - -	Jac. 1. - - - -	Aſhmolean Muſeum - -	O. 2.
Inrolments of Biſhops, Cuſtomers, or Collectors, King's Waiters and Searchers, with the Privy Seal Bills, and Warrants for the ſame - -	1725 to preſent Time	Petty Bag Office - -	D. 5.
Oath of the Clerk of Letters Patent - -	— —	Clerk of Crown in Chan.	*Page* 221. & 222.
Oath of the Examiner of Letters Patent - -	— —	Clerk of Crown in Chan.	*Page* 221. & 222.
v. CHANCERY.—EXCHEQUER OF ACCOUNT.—EXCHEQUER OF RECEIPT.—INVENTIONS.—LAND REV.—SPECIFICATIONS.—WARDROBE.			
PAUL V. POPE:			
Bull to the Roman Catholics of England, concerning their Oath of Allegiance - - -	1606 - - - - -	Univerſity Library Camb.	P. 1.
PAUL'S, ST. DEAN AND CHAPTER:			
Acts, Collations, and Inſtitutions to Livings - -	1660 to preſent Time	Dean and Chap. St. Paul's	N. 11.
Faculties - - - - - - - -	1660 to preſent Time	Dean and Chap. St. Paul's	N. 11.

ALPHABETICAL ARRANGEMENT OF THE PUBLIC RECORDS.

RECORDS and other INSTRUMENTS.	DATE.	WHERE KEPT.	Appendix to the First Report.
PAUL'S, ST. DEAN AND CHAPTER—(continued.)			
Visitations - - - - - - - -			
Warrants and Bonds for Marriages - - -	1660 to present Time	Dean and Chapter of St. Paul's - - - -	N. 11.
Wills and Administration Acts - - -			
CATHEDRAL:			
Reports, Accounts, and Vouchers concerning the Repairs of St. Paul's Cathedral - - - v. LONDON.	1382 to 1642 - -	Auditors Office Land Rev.	G. 15. a.
PEACE, JUSTICES OF:			
Commissions of the Peace - - - -	— —	Clerk of the Crown in Chancery - - -	D. 2. a.
Dedimusses to swear them, and Returns of the Execution thereof - - - - - -	Delivered Yearly to the Petty Bag - -		
Their Oath - - - - - - - - -	— —	Clerk of Crown in Chan. King's Rememb. Office	Page 222. — 236.
PEACE, CLERKS OF:			
Their Oath - - - - - - - - -	— —	King's Rememb. Office -	— 234.

The Clerks of the Peace of the 52 Counties of England and Wales, have in general in their Custody the following Records:

1. Commissions of the Peace.
2. Order Books, containing all Orders, Resolutions, and Proceedings of the Court of Quarter and Petty Sessions, including Orders concerning Paupers, Bastards, &c.—Also Adjudications, &c.
3. Process Books, containing the Names of Persons presented at the Quarter Sessions, their Indictments and Offences, the Proceedings thereon, Verdicts, and Sentences.
4. Session Books or Files, consisting of Lists of Chairmen and Justices present at every Session; Processes and Sheriffs Returns; Minutes of Fines paid to the Sheriffs; Gaolers Annual Certificates; Calendars of Prisoners presented; Informations and Recognizances; Traverses of Indictments; Bench Warrants issued; Writs of Ad Quod Damnum, &c.
5. Books of Estreats, containing Extracts of all Issues, Fines, Amerciaments, and Recognizances assessed and forfeited to His Majesty, and Annually returned into the Exchequer.
6. Inrolments of Deeds, Inquisitions, &c.
7. Indictments, Presentments, and other Proceedings concerning Highways, Bridges, and Public Buildings.
8. Accounts of County Treasurers, with their Vouchers.
9. Books of County Rates.
10. Awards of Commissioners on Inclosures, and Proceedings on diverting Roads.
11. Returns of Poll Books for Members to serve in Parliament.
12. Registers of Freeholders Names liable to serve on Juries, and Returns of Chief Constables.
13. Qualification Rolls of Justices, Militia Officers, Deputy Lieutenants, with their Sacrament Certificates and Registers of Oaths; Qualifications of Dissenting Ministers, as prescribed by Law, and of Roman Catholics, under Stat. 31 Geo. III. with Registers of the Estates of Roman Catholics, and their Bargains and Sales, and of their Priests, and the Houses of Worship of Dissenters and Roman Catholics.
14. Proceedings and Accounts of Commissioners respecting Navigations and Canals, Registers of Boats, Barges, &c.
15. Registers of Grants of Annuities made pursuant to Stat. 3 Geo. III.
16. Duplicates of Land Tax Assessments.
17. Schedules of Debtors discharged under the Insolvent Act.
18. Inrolments of Men under the Navy Act, 35 Geo. III. and under the Army and Navy Act, 37 Geo. III.
19. Registers of Shooting Licences, and of Game Keepers Deputations.
20. Registers of Licences for keeping Ale Houses and Houses for the Reception of Lunatics.
21. Rules and Orders of Friendly and Beneficial Societies allowed by Stat. 33 Geo. III.
22. Free Masons Registers, and Printing Press Certificates, under Stat. 39 Geo. III.
23. Files of Vagrant Passes, and Bonds for transporting Felons.
24. Coroners Inquisitions.
25. Registers of Badgers, Drovers, and Higlers Licences.
26. Returns of Overseers of the Poor.
27. Distempered Cattle, Examinations and Orders respecting them.
28. Certificates for regulating Buildings and Party Walls, pursuant to Stat. 14 Geo. III.

*** N. B. Some Articles, such as those relating to Canals, particular Buildings, &c. are merely local, and therefore to be found only among the Records of some of the Counties.

ALPHABETICAL ARRANGEMENT OF THE PUBLIC RECORDS.

RECORDS and other INSTRUMENTS.	DATE.	WHERE KEPT.	Appendix to the First Report.

The earlieft Dates fpecified of the moft Important of the above Records, are as follow; viz.

Proceedings of the Court of Seffions for

Berks	1703
Bucks	1678
Cambridge	1660
- - - - Ifle of Ely	1778
Chefter	1569
Cornwall	1758
Derby	1649
Devon	1600
Dorfet	1663
Effex	1651
Gloucefter	1681
Hertford	1620
Kent	1625
Lancafter	1606
Leicefter	1665
Lincoln, Holland	1650
Middlefex	1547
Monmouth	1796
Norfolk	1700
Northampton	1630
Northumberland	1680
Nottingham	1606
Oxford	1690
Rutland	1756
Salop	1676
Somerfet	1646
Southampton	1690
Suffolk	1700
Surrey	1659
Suffex	1642
Weftmorland	1559
Wilts	1597
York, Eaft Riding	1711
York, North Riding	1600
York, Weft Riding	1687
Wales:	
Anglefey	1776
Brecnock	1686
Cardigan	1748

Wales (*continued*)

Caermarthen	1729
Denbigh	1650
Flint	1748
Glamorgan	1727
Merioneth	1733
Montgomery	1719
Pembroke	1783
Radnor	1770

Commiffions of the Peace for

Hertford	1705
Middlefex	1690
Northampton	1778
Wales:	
Cardigan	1747
Glamorgan	1760

Accounts of the Treafurers of Counties for

Bucks	1700
Cambridge	1779
Effex	1744
Hertford	1740
Northampton	1699
Northumberland	1693
York North Riding	1770
Wales:	
Anglefey	1785
Glamorga	1787

Freeholders Lifts and Poll Books for

Hertford	1761
Leicefter	1762
Northampton	1669
Northumberland	1767
Salop	1713
York, Eaft Riding	1763
York, North Riding	1780
Anglefey, in Wales	1784

Inrolments and Regifters of Deeds, &c. and Awards upon Inclofures in

Cambridge	1762
Chefter	1731
Derby	1731
Durham	1717
Effex	1774
Gloucefter	1717
Lancafter	1717
Leicefter	1775
Middlefex	1779
Northampton	1587
Northumberland	1713
Nottingham	1761
Oxford	1717
Warwick	1722
York, Eaft Riding	1717
York, North Riding	1723
Wales:	
Anglefey	1768
Denbigh	1777
Glamorgan	1767
Montgomery	1723

Land Tax Affeffments for

Bucks	1746
Cambridge	1779
Derby	1777
Hertford	1705
Lancafter	1780
Leicefter	1773
Monmouth	1799
Northampton	1783
Northumberland	1751
Nottingham	1782
Oxford	1787
Suffex	1780
York, Eaft Riding	1780
York, North Riding	1780
Wales:	
Anglefey	1783
Glamorgan	1782

RECORDS and other INSTRUMENTS.	DATE.	WHERE KEPT.	Appendix to the First Report.
PEDIGREES AND ARMS:			
Of the Nobility and Gentry, being Entries made in the Heralds Office, as well during the Time when Vifitations were in Ufe, as fince that Period	— —	College of Arms	C. 8.
v. Armorial Bearings.—Heraldry.—Visitations.			
PEERS:			
Pedigrees and Arms of, purfuant to a Standing Order of the Houfe of Lords of 11th May, 1767 *v.* Lords, House of.	— —	College of Arms	C. 8.
PELL OFFICE:			
Catalogue of Rolls and Privy Seals in	— —	Bodleian Library	O. 1.
Oath of the Clerk of	— —	Receipt of the Exchequer	*Page* 233.
PEMBROKE, County:			
Survey of *v.* Caermarthen.	19 Eliz.	AuditorsLandRev.Wales	G. 16. a.
PENRITH, Cumberland:			
Survey of the Honour	1619	King's Rememb. Office	G. 6. a.
PENSIONS:			
Granted to Abbots, &c. after the Diffolution *v.* Warrant Books.	Hen. 8.	Augmentation Office	G. 19. a.

ALPHABETICAL ARRANGEMENT OF THE PUBLIC RECORDS.

RECORDS and other INSTRUMENTS.	DATE.	WHERE KEPT.	Appendix to the First Report.
PEPYS. *v.* STATE PAPERS.—TANGIERS.			
PETERBOROUGH, DIOCESE:			
Terriers	— —	Bishop's Registry at Peterborough and Northampton	L. 23.
Presentations	— —		
Institution, Acts of	— —		
Registers of Parishes, or Copies of them	— —		
Acts and Proceedings relative to the Districts made Part of this See	1542	Bishop's Registry Lincoln	L. 16.
v. LINCOLN.			
ABBEY:			
Register of	— —	Antiq. Society Library	S. a.
PETITIONS:			
To the King and Council	Edw. 1. 2. and 3.	Tower	A. 2. a.
To the King, &c. and Reports thereupon	1600 to 1683	State Paper Office	C. 1. a.
Upon Inventions	1685 to 1767		
Petitions, with Reports thereupon	1704 to 1761		
v. SURVEYOR GENERAL'S OFFICE.			
PETITIONS OF RIGHT:			
Pleadings on	— —	Rolls Chapel	D. 1. a.
v. EXCHEQUER, COURT OF.—LAW PAPERS.			
PETTY BAG:			
Rolls of Oaths of Officers on being sworn into Office	— —	Petty Bag Office	*Page* 230.
Oath of the Clerk of	— —		
PHILIPPA, QUEEN:			
Account of her Revenues	18 Edw. 3.	Receipt of the Exchequer	A. 1. a.
v. QUEEN.			
PHYSICIANS, COLLEGE OF:			
Statutes thereof	— —	University Library Camb.	P. 1.
PIPE ROLLS:			
The Great Roll, containing an Account of the Revenue of the Crown	Temp. Steph. to 13 Geo. 3.	Pipe Office	G. 8.
Great Roll, Copy of, called the Comptroller or Chancellor's Roll	Ric. 1. to the present Time	Comptroller of the Pipe	G. 9.
Two Rolls	6 Ric. 1. & 7 Joh.	Tower	A. 2. a.
A Roll	Temp. Joh.	Receipt of the Exchequer	A. 1. a.
Copy of Pipe Roll	Temp. Edw. 4.	Lincoln's Inn Library	Q. 3.
Rolls of Foreign Accounts, being the Supplies, and the Part of the Revenue granted by Parliament	A few before 1688, from 1688 to the present Time	Pipe Office	G. 8.
States of Accounts, and Entries of Treasury Warrants respecting the Pipe	1684 to present Time		
OFFICE:			
Papers therefrom	— —	Bodleian Library	O. 1.
Sheriffs Accounts. States of, delivered in by the Attornies of the Pipe Office	— —	Comptroller of the Pipe	G. 9.
Clerks of, Certificates of the State of the Revenue in charge before them	1660 to 1701	Surv. Gen. of Cr. Lands	G. 14.
Accounts, in Folio Books	1685 to present Time	Comptroller of the Pipe	G. 9.
Oath of the Comptroller of the Pipe	— —	King's Rememb. Office	*Page* 234.
v. REVENUE ROYAL.			
PIRACY:			
Indictments and other Proceedings on Commissions of Oyer and Terminer	1577 to present Time	Doctors Commons	K.
v. ADMIRALTY.—CLAUS ROLLS.			
PIX:			
Trials of	— —	Receipt of the Exchequer	A. 1. a.
v. MINT.			
PLACES. *v.* WARRANT BOOKS.			

ALPHABETICAL ARRANGEMENT OF THE PUBLIC RECORDS.

RECORDS and other INSTRUMENTS.	DATE.	WHERE KEPT.	Appendix to the First Report.
PLACITA:			
Placita	In divers Reigns	Tower	A. 2. a.
Placita de Quo Warranto et Rageman (an Index to thofe Records in the Chapter Houfe)	— —	Lincoln's Inn Library	Q. 3.
Placita, Tranfcripts of	— —	Univerfity Library Camb.	P. 1.
Placita de Affifis	6 Ric. 1. to Edw. 4.	Receipt of the Excheq.	A. 1. a.
Copies and Abftracts of, in Banco Regis et de Communi Banco, &c.	1 Joh. to 14 Hen. 4.	Receipt of the Excheq.	A. 1. a.
Placita coram Rege (Copies of)	Joh. Edw. 1. 2. 3. &c.	Inner Temple Library	Q. 2. b.
Placita Coronæ	10 Hen. 3. to the End of Edw. 3.	Receipt of the Exchequer	A. 1. a.
Placita coram Rege	Edw. 1.	Middle Temple Library	Q. 1.
Placita de Juratis et Affifis apud Wigorn. Salop. Novum Caftrum fuper Tynam, &c. (Copies of)	Edw. 1.	Inner Temple Library	Q. 2. b.
Placita de Quo Warranto	Edw. 1.	Bodleian Library	O. 1.
Placita Parliamentaria	29 Ed. 1. 14 Ed. 2. &c.	Bodleian Library	O. 1.
Placita apud Ebor'	1 to 19 Edw. 2.	Tower	A. 2. a.
——— apud Cant'	6 Edw. 2.	Bodleian Library	O. 1.
Placita	20 Edw. 3.	Dean and Chap. Durham	N. 24.
v. COMMON PLEAS.—KING'S BENCH.			
PLAGUE:			
Orders and Regulations relative thereto, and to Quarantine	1625 to 1631	State Paper Office	C. 1. a.
v. CLAUS ROLLS.			
PLANTATIONS:			
Letters and other Original Papers, Accounts, Minutes of Council, &c. from Bermudas, Georgia, Jamaica, and the Weft Indies, New York, New Hampfhire, and Surat	Car. 2. to Geo. 1.	Bodleian Library	O. 1.
Orders of Council, Commiffions, Regulations, Acts, &c.	1663 to 1707	State Paper Office	C. 1. a.
State Correfpondence with America and Weft Indies	1679 to 1700	State Paper Office	C. 1. a.
v. AMERICA.—WEST INDIES.			
PLEADINGS:			
On Claims of Franchifes and Privileges	— —	Lord Treaf. Rememb. Off.	G. 7. a.
On Eftreats	— —	Lord Treaf. Rememb. Off.	G. 7. a.
On Petitions of Right	— —	Rolls Chapel	D. 1. a.
v. CLAIMS.—COMMON PLEAS.—EXCHEQUER OF ACCOUNT.—KING'S BENCH.—LAND REVENUE.			
PLOTS. *v.* REBELLION.			
PLYMOUTH. *v.* HARBOURS.			
POLAND:			
Negotiations and Treaties with	Chiefly Temp. Eliz.	Univerfity Library Camb.	P. 1.
Treaties and Ratifications with England	1595 to 1777	State Paper Office	C. 1. a.
POLE, CARDINAL:			
Letters from him to Hen. VIII. and the Council	Hen. 8.	Receipt of the Exchequer	A. 1. a.
POLITICAL SUBJECTS. *v.* BACON, NICHOLAS.—LETTERS.—PROJECTS.—STATE PAPERS.—TREATIES.			
POLL TAX, &c.			
Duplicates of	— —	Auditors Office Land Rev.	G. 15. a
States of Accounts of Receivers, Inrolments of	Temp. W. 3.	King's Rememb. Office	G. 6. a.
v. CLAUS ROLLS.—LAND-TAX.			
POOR. *v.* CLAUS ROLLS.—PEACE, CLERKS OF.			
POPES:			
Bulls of feveral, in various Times, particularly one of Clement VII. confirming the Title of Fidei Defenfor to Hen. VIII. with a Seal of folid Gold	— —	Receipt of the Exchequer	A. 1. a.

ALPHABETICAL ARRANGEMENT OF THE PUBLIC RECORDS.

RECORDS and other INSTRUMENTS.	DATE.	WHERE KEPT.	Appendix to the First Report.
POPES—(*continued.*)			
Books, containing Inrolments of Bulls, Leagues, Deeds of Lands conveyed to them by Kings, &c. Also Books for and against the King's Supremacy - - - - - - - -	— —	Receipt of the Exchequer	A. 1. a.
These are referred to by Rymer as Lib. A. and B.			
Papal Letters - - - - - - -	— —	Magdalen Coll. Oxford and Lambeth Library -	O. 13. T.
Papal Bulls and Letters - - - - - -	— —		
Collections about Papal Provisions in England -	— —	Inner Temple Library -	Q. 2. b.
Bulls 122 in Number - - - - - -	1155 to 1534 with Chasms - - - -	Lambeth Library - -	T.
Bulls, consisting of Indulgences, Dispensations, Grants, Mandates, &c. - - - -	1194 to 1467 - -	British Museum - - -	U.
Papal Bulls and Letters - - - -	Joh. to Hen. 6. -	Tower - - - - -	A. 2. a.
Bulls of Innocent III. Gregory IX. &c. -	Hen. 3. - - - -	King's Rememb. Office -	G. 6. a.
Protestatio Magnatum Angliæ super Literas Bonifacii VIII. Papæ tangentes jus Superioritatis Dom. Regis Angliæ in Regnum Scotiæ -	28 Edw. 1. - - -	Ashmolean Museum -	O. 1.
Bull of Paul V. to the Catholics of England concerning their Allegiance - - - -	1606 - - - - -	University Lib. Camb.	P. 1.
Letter of Gregory XV. to Prince Charles -	1623 - - - - -		
v. CLAUS ROLLS.—ELY DIOCESE.—GREGORY V.—KING'S BENCH.—NICHOLAS IV.—SCOTLAND.—TAXATIONS.—WOLSEY.			
POPE NICHOLAS'S VALOR. v. NICHOLAS.			
PORT:			
Bonds forfeited - - - - - - -	— —	King's Rememb. Office	G. 6. a.
Port Books (some) - - - - - -	— —	Augmentation Office -	G. 19. a.
PORTSMOUTH. v. HARBOURS.			
PORTUGAL:			
Treaties and Transactions with - - - -	1372 to 1489 - -	Receipt of the Exchequer	A. 1. a.
Treaties and Ratifications with England -	1442 to 1774 - -	State Paper Office - -	C. 1. a.
Transactions with England, &c. - -	1485 to 1613 - -	British Museum - - -	U.
Sir S. Southwell's Account of the Court of Portugal - - - - - - - -	1667 - - - - -	Bodleian Library - -	O 1.
POSTEAS:			
Posteas and Venires - - - - - -	1180 to 1688 - -	Receipt of the Exchequer	A. 1. a.
POST MORTEM & DIEM CLAUSIT EXTREMUM:			
Oath of the Clerk of the Writs of - -	— —	Clerk of Crown in Chan.	*Page* 225.
POST OFFICE:			
Letters and Advices to Secretaries of State, and Letters from Agents and Postmasters - -	1698 to 1745 - -	State Paper Office - -	C. 1. a.
POST FINES. v. ESTREATS, FOREIGN.			
POUGHLEY PRIORY, BERKS:			
Antient Deeds - - - - - - -	— —	Dean and Chap. Westm.	N. 12. b.
PRE-EMPTION. v. CLAUS ROLLS.			
PREFERMENTS. v. WARRANT BOOKS.			
PREROGATIVE ROYAL:			
Prerogative, Supremacy, Proclamations, Pardons, Dispensations, &c. - - - - - -	1532 to 1699 - -	State Paper Office - -	C. 1. a.
v. POPES.—STATE PAPERS.—SUPREMACY.			

ALPHABETICAL ARRANGEMENT OF THE PUBLIC RECORDS.

RECORDS and other INSTRUMENTS.	DATE.	WHERE KEPT.	Appendix to the First Report.
PRESENTATIONS:			
To Benefices - - - - - - - -	Temp. Ufurpationis	Lambeth Library - -	T.
v. Patent Rolls.			
PRESTON, Lancashire. *v.* Hereford Diocese.			
PRINCES, Foreign:			
Inftructions to Ambaffadors to Eaftern Princes -	1576 to 1669 - -	State Paper Office - -	C. 1. a.
Styles and Titles of Precedency, Subfcriptions, &c.	1580 to 1630 - -		
v. Rymer.—State Papers.			
PRIORIES:			
Surveys and Extents of Alien Priories - -	Edw. 1. - - - -	King's Rememb. Office -	G. 6. a.
Surveys and Valuations of - - - -	26 Hen. 8. - - -	Firft Fruits Office - -	G. 18.
v. Alien Priories.			
PRIVILEGED PERSONS:			
Proceedings againft - - - - -	1180 to 1608 - -	Receipt of the Exchequer	A. 1. a.
PRIVY COUNCIL:			
Various Papers relating thereto - - - - -	— —	Britifh Mufeum - - -	U.
Petitions to - - - - - - -	Ed. 1. 2. 3. & Hen. 5.	Tower - - - - -	A. 2. a.
Ordinances concerning - - - - -	1 Hen. 6. - - -		
Books, containing the Proceedings of - -	1540 to the prefent Time, with Chafms	Office of Privy Council -	C. 2.
A Regifter Book of Council Caufes - - -	1591 - - - - -	Bodleian Library - -	O. 1.
Petitions and Reports - - - - -	1600 to 1685,	State Paper Office - -	C. 1. a.
Tranfactions of the Privy Council of State - -	1650, 1651, 1659 -	Bodleian Library - -	O. 1.
Oaths of the Members of - - - - -	— —	Clerk of Crown in Chan. and King's Rem. Office	Page 222. — 235.
v. Parliament.—State Papers.			
PRIVY SEALS:			
Catalogue of, in the Pell Office - - -	— —	Bodleian Library - -	O. 1.
Warrants of - - - - - - - -	Edw. 1. to Edw. 4. and many Temp. Ric. 2. - - - -	Tower - - - - -	A. 2. a.
Regifters of Privy Seals - - - - - -	Edw. 5. and Ric. 3.	Britifh Mufeum - -	U.
Books and Papers of the Privy Seal Office - -	Various Dates - -		
Privy Seal Bundles - - - - - -	Hen. 7. to 27 Geo. 3.	Rolls Chapel - - -	D. 1. a.
Privy Seals for Loans of Money - - -	Temp. Hen. 7. & 8.	Receipt of the Exchequer	A. 1. a.
Privy Seals - - - - - - - -	1 to 18 Hen. 8. - -	Bodleian Library - -	O. 1.
Docket Books, containing Abftracts of all the Grants and Appointments which have paffed the Privy Seal - - - - - - - - -	1571 to the prefent Time, with Chafms	Office of Privy Seal - -	C. 3.
Account of Monies paid thereon for a Loan -	1604 - - - - -	Univerfity Library Camb.	P. 1.
Privy Seals during the Expedition of Charles Prince of Wales into Spain - - - - -	1622 to 1626 - -	Duchy Cornwall Office	C. 7.
Warrants - - - - - - - -	1634 to 1712 - -	Britifh Mufeum - -	U.
Letters and Dockets - - - - - -	1709 to 1711 - -		
Dockets - - - - - - - -	1710 to 1718 - -	Middle Temple Library	Q. 1.
Privy Seal Bills and Warrants inrolled - -	1725 to prefent Time	Petty Bag Office - -	D. 5.
Privy Seals or figned Bills - - - -	38 and 39 Geo. 3.	Six Clerks Office - -	D 12.
Bills and Kings Warrants for Patents and Commiffions, and Original Proclamations for the Current Year - - - - - - -	Delivered Yearly to Riding Six Clerk to be inrolled - -	Clerk of Crown in Chan.	D. 2. a.
Oath of the Keeper of the Privy Seal - -	— —	Clerk of Cro. in Chan.	Page 222.
Oath of the Commiffioners for executing the Office of Privy Seal - - - - - -			— 225.
v. Chancery.—Cornwall.—Exchequer of Receipt.—Lancaster Duchy.—Land Rev.—Patents.—Pell Office.			

ALPHABETICAL ARRANGEMENT OF THE PUBLIC RECORDS.

RECORDS and other INSTRUMENTS.	DATE.	WHERE KEPT.	Appendix to the Firſt Report.
PRIVY PURSE:			
Accounts of Lords Chamberlain, &c. -	Temp. Edw. 6. - -	AuditorsOfficeLand Rev.	G. 15. a.
v. HOUSEHOLD.			
PRIZES:			
Proceedings of the Commiſſioners for - -	1664 to 1678 - -	Britiſh Muſeum - - -	U.
v. ADMIRALTY.			
PROCESS. v. EXCHEQUER OF ACCOUNT.			
PROCLAMATIONS:			
Collections of - - - - -	Various Dates - -	Antiq. Society Library	S. a.
The like - - - - - - - -	Edw. 3 to Jac. 1.	Britiſh Muſeum - - -	U.
Of Peace between Hen. VIII. and Spain - -	Hen. 8. - - - -	Aſhmolean Muſeum - -	O. 2.
Proclamations - - - - - - -	1532 to 1699 - -	State Paper Office - -	C. 1. a.
In the Earl of Eſſex's Rebellion - .. -	1600 - - - - -	Aſhmolean Muſeum -	O. 2.
Concerning the Scots - - - - -	1639 - - - - -		
For a General Faſt - - - - -	1743 - - - -	Clerk of Crown in Chan.	D. 2.
For executing Laws againſt Papiſts - - -			
v. CLAUS ROLLS.—PATENT ROLLS.—PREROGATIVE, ROYAL.			
PROFFERS. v. BAILIFFS.—EXCHEQUER OF ACCOUNT.			
PROHIBITIONS. v. CLAUS ROLLS.			
PROJECTS:			
Counter Projects, Copies, Abſtracts, and Extracts of Treaties - - - - - - -	1700 to 1763 - -	State Paper Office - -	C. 1. a.
v. STATE PAPERS.			
PROTECTIONS. v. CLAUS ROLLS.			
PROTECTOR ET DEFENSOR REGNI. v. CUSTOS REGNI.			
PROVOSTSHIPS:			
Surveys and Valuations of - - - - -	26 Hen. 8. - - -	Firſt Fruits Office - -	G. 18.
PRUSSIA:			
Treaties and Ratifications with England - -	1700 to 1779 - -	State Paper Office - -	C. 1. a.
PRYNNE:			
His MS. Caſes argued in Parliament - -	— —	Inner Temple Library -	Q. 2. b.
PURBECK, LORD:			
Proceedings in the Houſe of Lords on his Claim -	Car. 1. and 2. - -	Bodleian Library - -	O. 1.
PURCHASE. v. EXCHANGE.			
PURFLEET. v. GUNPOWDER MAGAZINES.			
PURVEYANCE:			
Orders of Parliament reſpecting - - -	Edw. 2. - - - -	Dean and Chap. Durham	N. 24.
v. CLAUS ROLLS.—PARLIAMENT.			
PURVEYORS:			
Oath of the King's Purveyors - - - - -	— —	Clerk of Crown in Chan.	*Page* 223.
v. HOUSEHOLD.			

ALPHABETICAL ARRANGEMENT OF THE PUBLIC RECORDS.

RECORDS and other INSTRUMENTS.	DATE.	WHERE KEPT.	Appendix to the First Report.
QUAKERS:			
Their Affirmation	— —	Petty Bag Office	*Page* 229.
QUALIFICATIONS:			
Certificates of, in the King's Bench	— —	Crown Office	E. 1.
Oath of Persons qualifying for Offices	— —	Petty Bag Office	*Page* 226.
v. Commons, House of.—King's Bench.—Parliament.—Peace, Clerks of.			
QUARANTINE:			
Orders and Regulations in Cases of Plague, &c.	1625 to 1631	State Paper Office	C. 1. a.
v. Plague.			
QUARE MANERIA:			
Pleadings thereon	— —	Lord Treas. Rem. Office	G. 7. a.
v. Exchequer of Account.			
QUEENS:			
State of the Honours, Manors, &c. in Jointure, which are demisable, with the Rents and Names of Stewards, Bailiffs, and Feodaries	— —	University Library Camb.	P. 1.
Accounts of the Revenues of Queen Philippa	18 Edw. 3.	Receipt of the Exchequer	A. 1. a.
Treasurers, Receivers, and Ministers Accounts of various Queens	Hen. 8. to Car. 1.		
Accounts of Estates of the Queen Dowager of Henry VIII. Queen Consort of James I. and Queen Dowagers of Charles I. and II.	Hen. 8. to Car. 2.	Auditors Office Land Revenue	G. 15. a.
Declarations of Treasurers and Receivers Accounts of Anne Queen of James I.	1603 to 1617		
Inventories of the Jewels of Anne Queen of James I.	1605 to 1615		
Leases of Fee Farms in Cambridgeshire, Parcel of the Jointure of Henrietta Maria Queen of Charles I.			
Certificate of the same Queen's Copyholds, whose Fines are uncertain, or Lands not Thirty Years in Lease	Car. 1.	University Library Camb.	P. 1.
Views of Accounts, Acquittances for Fees, Pensions, &c. Tradesmens Bills, and Warrants of the same Queen	Car. 1.		
Books of Establishment of Officers of the same Queen			
Declarations of Treasurers and Receivers Accounts of the same Queen	Car. 1. & 2.		
Proceedings respecting Inglewood Honour			
Sale of Knaresborough, &c. by Trustees for Queen Henrietta Maria	1629	Auditors Office Land Revenue	G. 15. d.
Grants to the same Queen	6 & 10 Car. 1.		
Account of Manors assigned to the same Queen	1630		
Accounts of Receivers General for Wales, of the Revenues of the same Queen there	7, 8, & 12 Car. 1		
The like for England	1632		
Certificates of all Honours, &c. in Jointure to the same Queen	1632	University Lib. Camb.	P. 1.
Receivers Accounts of Leases of Fee Farms in Dorset and Somerset	16 Car. 1.		
Fines for Leases of the Lands of the same Queen	1638, 1639, 1640	Auditors Office Land Rev.	G. 15. d.
Certificates of Estates settled on Queen Catharine	Car. 2.	Surveyor General's Office	G. 14.
Counterparts of Leases of Lands in Jointure to the same Queen	Car. 2.		
Jointure Grant to the same Queen	15 Car. 2.		
Declarations of Treasurers and Receivers Accounts of the same Queen	1664 to 1701		
Grants to the same Queen	17, 19, 21 Car. 2. & 1 Jac. 2.	Aud. Office Land Rev.	G. 15. d.
Appointment of New Trustees for the same Queen	3 Jac. 2.		
Survey of Norton in Worcestershire, in Jointure to the same Queen	4 Jac. 2.		
Commission concerning the Revenues of the same Queen	2 Will. & Mar.		
v. Crown Lands.—Jointure.			

ALPHABETICAL ARRANGEMENT OF THE PUBLIC RECORDS.

RECORDS and other INSTRUMENTS.	DATE.	WHERE KEPT.	Appendix to the Firft Report.
QUO TITULO CLAMAT:			
Pleadings thereon - - - - - -	— —	Lord Treaf. Rem. Off. -	G. 7. a.
v. EXCHEQUER OF ACCOUNT.			
QUO WARRANTO:			
Rolls - - - - - - - -	Edw. 1, 2, & 3. -	Receipt of the Exchequer	A. 1. a.
Placita - - - - - - - -	Edw. 1. & feq. -	Bodleian Library - -	O. 1.
The like, being an Index thereto - - -	— —	Lincoln's Inn Library -	Q. 3.
v. EXCHEQUER OF ACCOUNT.			
RADNOR, COUNTY:			
Books of Inrolment and Entries - - -	1 H. 7. to prefent Time	Auditors Office Land Revenue, Wales - -	G. 16. a.
Survey of - - - - - - -	19 Eliz. - - - -		
States and Draughts of Declared Accounts of Receivers General of Land Tax, and other Parliamentary Taxes for this Country - - -	From Commencement of each Tax to 37 Geo. 3. - -		
RAMSEY, HUNTINGDON:			
Ledger Book of the Monaftery - - -	— —	King's Rememb. Office -	G. 6. a.
READ, BISHOP. *v.* CHICHESTER DIOCESE.			
REBELLION:			
Special Commiffion on Rebellion in divers Counties - - - - - - - -	12 Hen. 7. - -	Receipt of the Exchequer	A. 1. a.
Proclamation in the Earl of Effex's Rebellion -	1600 - - - -	Afhmolean Mufeum -	O. 2.
Rebellion, Sedition, Treafon, Plots, Libels, Incendiaries, &c. Examinations and Correfpondence relating thereto - - - - -	1685 to 1758 - -	State Paper Office - -	C. 1. a.
RECEIVERS ACCOUNTS - - - - - -	Edw. 1. to Car. 1. -	Auditors Office Land Rev.	G. 15. a.
The like - - - - - - -	Hen. 8. to Eliz. -	Augmentation Office -	G. 19. a.
The like for Wales - - - - - -	13 Eliz. to prs^t Time	Auditor for Wales - -	G. 16. a.
Accounts - - - - - - -	1640 to 1647 - -	Univ. Library Camb. -	P. 1.
The like of Eftates fequeftered - - -	1645 - - - -		
The like, Com' Lincoln' and Oxon' - -	1649 - - - -		
Declarations of Receivers and Minifters Accounts - - - - - - - -	1600 to 1700 - -	Auditors Office Land Rev.	G. 15. a.
v. AUGMENTATION OFFICE.—LAND REV.			
RECOGNIZANCES:			
Bundles of - - - - - - -	1782 to prefent Time	Clerk of Inrolments Chan.	D. 13.
v. CLAUS ROLLS.—ESTREATS, FOREIGN.—EXCHEQUER OF ACCOUNT.—KING'S BENCH.—LORDS, HOUSE OF.			
RECORDER OF LONDON:			
His Oath when a Serjeant - - - - -	— —	Clerk of Crown in Chan.	*Page* 224.
RECORDS:			
Many Tranfcripts, Repertories, and Collections -	— —	Britifh Mufeum - -	U.
References to, Tranfcripts of, Indexes to, and Extracts from, &c. - - - - -	1135 to 1544 - -	State Paper Office -	C. 1. a.

*** Tranfcripts and Copies of almoft every Species of PUBLIC RECORDS and INSTRUMENTS, are to be found in Dugdale's Collections at the Afhmolean Mufeum, Oxford; Dodfworth's MSS. Bodleian Library, Oxford; Madox and Holme's, Britifh Mufeum; Petyt's, Inner Temple; and Hale's, Lincoln's Inn.——N. B. Several Books have been publifhed, containing References to Records, and Directions for fearching them; viz. Powell's Repertorie, 1631, 4to.; Strachey's Index to the Records, 1739, 8vo. &c. For a complete Lift whereof, *v.* Worrall's Bibliotheca Legum Angliæ, 1788, 12mo. in the Second Part of which the "Index to the Records" is reprinted, with fome Additions.

ALPHABETICAL ARRANGEMENT OF THE PUBLIC RECORDS.

RECORDS and other INSTRUMENTS.	DATE.	WHERE KEPT.	Appendix to the First Report.
RECOVERIES:			
Rediffeifin Rolls	— —	Tower	A. 2. a.
Warrants of Attorney in every Recovery fuffered by virtue of the Writ of Dedimus Poteftatem	— —	Curfitor's Office	D. 3.
Remembrance Rolls	2 Edw. 6. to the prefent Time	Prothon. Office Com. Pl.	F. 1.
Extracts from Recovery Rolls	1507 to prefent Time	Clk. of Warrants, Co. Pl.	F. 3.
Writs of Entry, Summons, and Seifin	1627 to the prefent Time	Clerk of Returns, Prothonotary's Office	F. 8.
Affidavits to Copies of Precipes and Warrants of Attorney for fuffering Recoveries acknowledged by Tenants or Vouchees	14 Geo. 3. to the prefent Time	Clerk of Returns, Prothonotary's Office	F. 8.
v. Common Pleas.			
RECUSANTS:			
Sequeftered Eftates of	— —	Auditors Office Land Rev.	G. 15. a.
A Roll of	Eliz.	Augmentation Office	G. 19. a.
v. Roman Catholics			
REDISSEISIN:			
Rolls	— —	Tower	A. 2. a.
REFERENCES. *v.* Surveyor General.			
REGENT. *v.* Custos Regni.			
REGISTERS of Monasteries. *v.* Chartularies.—Leidger Books.			
REMIGIUS, Bishop. *v.* Lincoln Diocese.			
RENTALS:			
Of Lands	— —	Receipt of the Exchequer	A. 1. a.
Of Chief Rents in Denbigh	— —	Auditors Office for Wales	G. 16. a.
Of Manors (fome)	— —	Tower	A. 2. a.
Many	Of various Dates	Augmentation Office	G. 19. a.
Various Rentals	Edw. 3. to Anne	Auditors Office Land Rev.	G. 15. a.
Of Crown Lands, Com. Somerfet	1606	Univerfity Lib. Camb.	P. 1.
Of Abbey Lands and Forfeited Eftates in Effex, Herts, Middlefex, and London	1638	Univerfity Lib. Camb.	P. 1.
Of Fee Farms and other Rents in Wales	1 Anne to the prefent Time	Auditors Office for Wales	G. 16. a.
v. Surveys.			
REPORTS:			
v. Land Revenue.—Surveyor General.			
REPRIEVES. *v.* Warrant Books.			
REPRISALS. *v.* Claus Rolls.			
REQUESTS, Court of:			
Proceedings therein	9 Hen. 7. to 17 Car. 1.	Receipt of the Exchequer	A. 1. a.
Two Books of Judicial Proceedings before the King and Council, or, more properly, before the Lord Privy Seal and Mafter of Requefts	1639 to 1640	Office of Privy Seal	C. 3.
RESUMPTION:			
An Act of	20 Hen. 6.	Receipt of the Exchequer	A. 1. a.
REVENUE ROYAL:			
Several Statements, Affeffments, and other Accounts relating thereto	— —	Univerfity Library Camb.	P. 1.
Papers relating to Aids, Loans, Cuftoms, Subfidies, Leafes, Crown Lands, Efcheats, &c.	1199 to 1666	State Paper Office	C. 1. a.
Rolls of Accounts of the Part of the Revenues granted by Parliament	1688 to prefent Time	Pipe Office	G. 8.
v. Aids.—Claus Rolls.—Exchequer of Account.—Pipe Rolls.			

ALPHABETICAL ARRANGEMENT OF THE PUBLIC RECORDS.

RECORDS and other INSTRUMENTS.	DATE	WHERE KEPT.	Appendix to the First Report.
RICHARD II.			
His Will	— —	Receipt of the Exchequer	A. 1. a.
RICHMOND, MARGARET, COUNTESS OF:			
Papers relating to her Estates	Temp. Hen. 7. &c.	Dean & Chapter Westm.	N. 12. b
ARCHDEACONRY. v. CHESTER DIOCESE.			
ROCHESTER, DIOCESE:			
Two Books, entitled, Registrum Spirit. Ep. Roff. & Registrum Temp. Ep. Roff.	— —	Bishop's Registry, Rochester	L. 19. a.
Administrations	— —		
Marriage Licences	— —		
Acts of Court	— —		
Register of Wills	From 1440		
Wills, Original	1508 to the present Time		
ROLLS, MASTER OF THE:			
His Oath	— —	Clerk of Crown in Chan. and Petty Bag Office	Page 217. —— 230.
ROMAN CATHOLICS:			
Priests, Recusants, &c. in London, Accounts of	1590 to 1708	State Paper Office	C. 1. a.
Certificates of Popish Convicts and Persons concealed	From Anne to the present Time	Petty Bag Office	D. 5.
Proclamations against	1743	Clerk of Crown in Chan.	D. 2. a.
Protestation of the Roman Catholics in England, by which they express their Abhorrence of certain Doctrines imputed to them	1791	British Museum	U.
v. CLAUS ROLLS. — PAPISTS. — PEACE, CLERKS OF. — RECUSANTS. — SEQUESTRATION.			
ROME:			
Roman Rolls	1305 to 1488	Tower	A. 2. a.
Copies of Roman Rolls	1 to 26 Edw. 3.	Lincoln's Inn Library	Q. 3.
Treaties and Ratifications with England	1528	State Paper Office	C. 1. a.
RUSSIA:			
Instructions to an Ambassador sent thither, and Answer thereto	1571	University Library Camb.	P. 1.
Treaties and Ratifications with England	1679 to 1779	State Paper Office	C. 1. a.
RUTLAND, COUNTY:			
Nona Roll	15 Edw. 3.	King's Rememb. Office	G. 6. b.
RYMER, THOMAS:			
MS. Collection of State Papers	1115 to 1698	British Museum	U.
Various Instruments of Foreign Princes	1216 to 1448		
v. STATE PAPERS.			
SALE, PURCHASE, AND EXCHANGE OF LANDS:			
Deeds of	Edw. 1.	Receipt of the Exchequer	A. 1. a.
The like	Hen. 8. & Edw. 6.	Augmentation Office	G. 19. a.
Ministers Accounts of Estates acquired by Purchase or Exchange	Hen. 8. to Eliz.		
Particulars of Parliamentary Surveys	Temp. Interregni		
Particulars for Sale, and Deeds of Fee Farm Rents			
Books of Commissioners Proceedings on Sales			
Particulars of Prices, and Purchasers Names		University Library Camb.	P. 1.
Sales of Fee Farm Rents, &c. in Wales		Auditors Office for Wales	G. 16. a.
Lands purchased, chiefly about Windsor	Will. 3. to Geo. 2.	Surveyor General Crown Lands	G. 14.
Proceedings on Sales under Stat. 34 Geo. III. c. 75. and 38 Geo. III. c. 60.	Geo. 3.		

ALPHABETICAL ARRANGEMENT OF THE PUBLIC RECORDS.

RECORDS and other INSTRUMENTS.	DATE.	WHERE KEPT.	Appendix to the First Report.
SAINT MARTIN'S LE GRAND:			
Register Book of - - - - - - - -	— —	Dean & Chapter Westm.	N. 12. b.
v. LONDON.			
SALISBURY, DIOCESE:			
Registrum Chartarum Ecclesiæ Sarum - -	— —	Inner Temple Library -	Q. 2.
Writs for electing Proctors of the Clergy in Convocation - - - - - - -	— —	Bishop's Registry, Salisbury - - - - -	L. 17
Baptisms, Marriages, and Burials, Copies of Registers of - - - - - - -			
Episcopal Registers - - - - - -	1298 to present Time		
SALOP, COUNTY:			
Testimonium Donationum fact. Eccles. et Convent. Sti Pet. & Paul' - - - - -	— —	Corpus Christi Coll. Cam.	P. 5.
Nomina Villarum - - - - - -	— —	Lord Treas. Rem. Office	G. 7. a.
Nona Roll - - - - - - - - -	15 Edw. 3. - -	King's Rememb. Office -	G. 6. b.
Ecclesiastical Survey (a Copy) - - -	26 Hen. 8. - -	First Fruits Office - -	G. 18.
Laws and Customs of the Town of Shrewsbury -	— —	University Library Camb.	P. 1.
v. PLACITA.—TESTA DE NEVIL.			
SANDWICH, EARL OF:			
Letters to him - - - - - - -	— —	Bodleian Library - -	O. 1.
SARDINIA:			
Treaties and Ratifications with England - -	1669 to 1775 -	State Paper Office - -	C. 1. a.
SAVOY, HOSPITAL OF:			
Original Charters of Foundation, and other Writings concerning it - - - - - -	Hen. 8. to 1702 -	Office of Surveyor General of Crown Lands - -	G. 14.
Papers relating thereto - - - - - -	Temp. Eliz. - -	Dean & Chapter Westm.	N. 12. b.
SCHOOLS:			
Particulars of the Estates of - - - -	Edw. 6. - -	Augmentation Office -	G. 19. a.
v. The several DIOCESES.			
SCIRE FACIAS, WRITS OF:			
v. CHANCERY.—EXCHEQUER OF ACCOUNT.—WRITS.			
SCOTLAND:			
Many Papers relative thereto, and to the Monasteries there - - - - - - - -	— —	Dean & Chapter Durham	N. 24. b.
Collections respecting its Subordination to England	— —	Inner Temple Library -	Q. 2. b.
Miscellaneous Accounts relating thereto - -	— —	Auditors Office Land Rev.	G. 15. a.
Charters relating thereto - - - - -	From Alex. 1. or 2. to 1532 - -	British Museum - -	U.
Treaties and Transactions with - - - -	1189 to 1586 -	Receipt of the Exchequer	A. 1. a.
Homage Rolls - - - - - - - -	Edw. 1. - -	Tower - - - -	A. 2. a.
Charta quo modo Edwardus Primus Rex Angliæ receptus est in Superiorem Dominum totius Scotiæ - - - - - - - -	19 Edw. 1. - -	Dean and Chap. Durham	N. 24.
Renunciation of Edw. I. to his Claim over Scotland - - - - - - - - -	Edw. 1. - -		
Scotch Rolls - - - - - - - -	1291 to 1482 -	Tower - - - -	A. 2. a.
Proceedings in the Dispute between Bruce and Balliol for the Crown of Scotland - - - -	1291 - -	Dean & Chapter Exeter	N. 6.
Protestatio Magnatum Angliæ super Literas Bonif. VIII. Papæ tangentibus jus Superioritatis Regis Angliæ in Regnum Scotiæ - - - - -	28 Edw. 1. - -	Ashmolean Museum -	O. 2.
Mandatum Hen. V. Regis Priori et Conventui Dunelmensis ad recipiendum Juramentum Regis Scotiæ - - - - - - - - -	2 Hen. 5. - -	Dean and Chapt. Durham	N. 24. b.
Transactions between England and Scotland -	1485 to 1613 -	British Museum - -	U.
Instructions, Declarations, Letters, Treaties, and other Papers relative to the Kingdom of Scotland - - - - - - - - -	1491 to 1669 - -	State Paper Office - -	C. 1. a.
A Remonstrance of the Nobility, &c. of Scotland, vindicating themselves from the Crimes imputed to them by a late Proclamation in England -	1638 - - -	University Library Camb.	P. 1.

ALPHABETICAL ARRANGEMENT OF THE PUBLIC RECORDS.

RECORDS and other INSTRUMENTS.	DATE.	WHERE KEPT.	Appendix to the First Report.
SCOTLAND—*(continued.)*			
Treaties, Proclamations, &c. refpecting Scotland	1639 - - - -	Afhmolean Mufeum -	O. 2.
Tranfactions in Parliament relative to Scottifh Affairs - - - - - - -	1649 to 1653 - -	Bodleian Library - -	O. 1.
Letters and Papers, Warrant Books, Correfpondence, &c. relative to Scotland - - -	1670 to 1756 - -	State Paper Office -	C. 1. a.
Returns of the 16 Peers of, &c. - - -	From the Union to prefent Time - -	Clerk of Crown in Chancery, and Petty Bag Office	D. 2. a.
Oath of Peers qualifying to vote for the 16 Peers	— —	Petty Bag Office -	*Page* 228.
Oath of Perfons qualifying for Offices in Scotland	— —	Petty Bag Office -	& 226.
v. CLAUS ROLLS.—LORDS, HOUSE OF.			
SCUTAGES. *v.* AIDS. — CLAUS ROLLS. — LIBER RUBEUS.			
SEAL, GREAT:			
Exemplification of Statutes - - - -	6 Hen. 8. to G. 3. -	Rolls Chapel - -	D. 1. a.
Entries of all Inftruments paffing the Great Seal -	1600 to prefent Time	Hanaper Office - -	D. 4.
Dockets of Letters Patent - - - -	Jac. 1. to prefent Time	Clerk of the Patents -	D. 16.
Dockets of Inftruments which paffed the Great Seal without Privy Seal - - - - -	1710 to 1718 - -	Middle Temple Library	Q. 1.
Oath of the Lords Commiffioners of - -	— —	Clerk of Crown in Chancery - -	*Page* 217.
Oath of the Lord Keeper of - - - -	— —	Clerk of Crown in Chancery - -	— 216.
Oath of the Engraver of - - - -	— —	Clerk of Crown in Chancery - -	— 225.
v. CLAUS ROLLS.—HANAPER.—LEASES.—PATENTS.—PROCLAMATIONS.			
SEDITION. *v.* REBELLION.			
SEIZURES:			
Old Books of - - - - - - -	— —	Auditors Office Land Revenue, Wales - -	G. 16.
v. EXCHEQUER, OF ACCOUNT.			
SERJEANTS AT LAW:			
Inrolments of their Admiffions - - -	40 Eliz. to pres^t Time	Petty Bag Office - -	D. 5.
Their Oath - - - - - - -	— —	Clerk of Crown in Chanc.	*Page* 219.
v. CLAUS ROLLS.			
SERJEANTIES:			
A Roll of - - - - - - - -	— —	Lord Treaf. Rem. Office	G. 7. a.
v. LIBER RUBEUS.			
SEQUESTRATIONS:			
Receivers Accounts of Sequeftered Eftates -	1645 - -	Univerfity Library Cam.	P. 1.
Some Accounts of Eftates fequeftered - -	Temp. Interregni -	King's Rememb. Office -	G. 6. a.
v. FORFEITED ESTATES.—RECUSANTS.—ROMAN CATHOLICS.			
SERK. *v.* GUERNSEY.—JERSEY.			
SEWERS:			
Commiffioners and Adjudications, (a few) - -	— —	Rolls Chapel - -	D. 1. a.
Laws and Adjudications of - - - -	A few in Jac. 1. & Car. I. & feveral temp. Car. 2. - -	Petty Bag Office - -	D. 5.
Oath of the Commiffioners of - - - -	— —	Clerk of Crown in Chan.	*Page* 222.
v. ESTREATS, FOREIGN. —LONDON and WESTMINSTER.			
SHEEP:			
Oath of the Commiffioners concerning the Statute of Sheep and Tillage - - - - -	— —	Clerk of Crown in Chanc.	— 224.
SHEERNESS. *v.* HARBOURS.			
SHERFIELD, HENRY:			
Proceedings againft him and others for defacing Images, &c. at Salifbury - - - -	— —	Univerfity Library Camb.	P. 1.
v. STAR CHAMBER.			

ALPHABETICAL ARRANGEMENT OF THE PUBLIC RECORDS.

RECORDS and other INSTRUMENTS.	DATE.	WHERE KEPT.	Appendix to the First Report.
SHERIFFS:			
Accounts of	— —	King's Rememb. Office	G. 6. a.
States of Account	Hen. 3. to pre^t Time	Comptroller of the Pipe	G. 9.
Writs and Returns to and from them to the Court of Exchequer	Hen. 8. downwards	Auditors Office Land Revenue	G. 15. a.
Summonses of Green Wax to them to return to the Court of Exchequer Fines, Amerciaments, &c.	Car. 1. to Jac. 2.	(Auditors Office Land Revenue)	(G. 15. a.)
Rolls of their Names	1720 to present Time	Six Clerks Office	D. 12.
Annual Statements of their Accounts	1752 to present Time	Foreign Apposer's Office	G. 11.
Their Oaths	— —	Clerk of Crown in Chanc. and King's Rem. Office	*Page* 223. — 236.
v. Exchequer of Account.—Land Revenue.—Peace, Clerks of.—Pipe.			
SHIP MONEY:			
Orders concerning the levying thereof	— —	University Library Camb.	P. 1.
SHREWSBURY. *v.* Salop.			
SIGNED BILLS:			
Bundles of	Hen. 7. to 27 G. 3.	Rolls Chapel	D. 1. a.
SIGNET:			
Various Papers relating thereto	— —	British Museum	U.
Bills which remain in the Possession of the Lord Privy Seal	— — / Ric. 2. to Car. 1.	Privy Seal / Tower	C. 4. / A. 2. a.
Dockets or short Abstracts of Grants and Appointments which have passed the Signet	1584 to pres^t Time, with a few Chasms	Signet Office	C. 4.
Grants and Appointments which have passed through the Signet	1661 to present Time	(Signet Office)	(C. 4.)
SIGNIFICAVITS:			
From the Ecclesiastical Courts, upon which Writs de Excommunicato Capiendo issue	— —	Cursitors Office	D. 3.
v. Excommunication.—King's Bench.			
SIGNS MANUAL:			
Warrants and Constitutions under them	— —	King's Rememb. Office	G. 6. a.
Signs Manual	Hen. 7. to Eliz.	Receipt of the Exchequer	A. 1. a.
v. Exchequer of Receipt.			
SION Monastery. *v.* Land Revenue.			
SOLEMN LEAGUE and COVENANT. *v.* Leagues.			
SOLICITOR GENERAL:			
His Oath	— —	Clerk of Crown in Chan.	*Page* 218.
SOLICITORS:			
Oath on their Admission in the Court of Chancery,	— —	Petty Bag Office	— 228.
- - - - - - - if Roman Catholics	— —	(Petty Bag Office)	— 229.
SOMERSET, County:			
Domesday Book for	— —	Dean and Chapter Exeter	N. 6.
Leases of Mines of Gold and Silver	Temp. Ric. 2.	Receipt of the Exchequer	A. 1. a.
Ecclesiastical Survey	26 Hen. 8.	First Fruits Office	G. 18.
Survey and Valuation of Church Lands and Possessions	Temp. Edw. 6.	Auditors Office Land Revenue	G. 15. a.
Accounts of Farmers of Church Lands therein	3 & 4 Philip & Mary	(Auditors Office Land Revenue)	(G. 15. a.)
Survey of the Manor of South Stoke	Eliz.	University Library Cambridge	P. 1.
Rental of Crown Rents	1606	(University Library Cambridge)	(P. 1.)
Receivers Accounts of Leases of Fee Farms belonging to Queen Henrietta Maria	16 Car. 1.	(University Library Cambridge)	(P. 1.)
v. Domesday Book.			
Duke of:			
Inventory of his Effects when attainted	7 Edw. 6.	Auditors Office Land Rev.	G. 15. a.

ALPHABETICAL ARRANGEMENT OF THE PUBLIC RECORDS.

RECORDS and other INSTRUMENTS.	DATE.	WHERE KEPT.	Appendix to the First Report.
SOUTH SEA COMPANY:			
Matters relative thereto - - - -	1713 to 1763 - -	State Paper Office - -	C. 1. a.
SOUTH STOKE, SOMERSET:			
Survey of the Manor - - - - -	Eliz. - - -	University Library Camb.	P. 1.
SPAIN:			
Treaties and Ratifications with England - -	1442 to 1774 - -	State Paper Office - -	C. 1. a.
Transactions with England - - - -	1485 to 1613 - -	British Museum - -	U.
Treaties and Transactions with - - -	1492 to 1605 - -	Receipt of the Exchequer	A. 1. a.
Negotiations and Treaties with, also Instructions to Ambassadors, and Original Letters from them - - - - - - - - -	Chiefly temp. Eliz. -	University Library Camb.	P. 1.
Articles of Peace and Alliance between England and Spain on one Part, and Austria on the other - - - - - - - -	} 1604 - - -	} Bodleian Library -	O. 1.
Treaty of Peace between Spain and England -			
Negotiations between Spain and England - -	1636 - - - -		
SPECIAL COMMISSIONS:			
With Inquisitions, containing Surveys of Manors, Lands, Forests, Chaces, Tythes, &c. - -	Chiefly from Eliz. to Car. 2. inclusive -	King's Rememb. Office -	G. 6. a.
For Forfeited Estates - - - - - -	Jac. 1. to pres^t Time	Petty Bag Office - -	D. 5.
Commission relative to the Rights of the Crown and of the Duke of Athol in the Isle of Man -	31 Geo. 3. - -	Secretary of State's Office Home Department.	
Roll of, on Criminal Affairs, Attainders, &c. -	15 Edw. 2. to 1 H.4.	Tower - - - -	A. 2. a.
Rebelliones in diversis Comitatibus - - -	12 Hen. 7. - -	} Receipt of the Excheq.	A. 1. a.
Insurrections in Yorkshire, &c. - - -	Hen. 8. - -		
Proceedings under, in the North, London, Sussex, Kent - - - - - - - - -	1715 to 1798 -	Custody of the Clerk of Record Committee.	
v. BAGA DE SECRETIS.—CHANCERY.—EXCHEQUER OF ACCOUNT.			
SPECIAL LIVERIES. *v.* PATENT ROLLS.			
SPECIFICATIONS OF PATENTS. *v.* CHANCERY.—CLAUS ROLLS.—INVENTIONS.—PATENTS.			
SPIRITUAL POSSESSIONS:			
Oath of the King's Commissioners for ascertaining their Value - - - - - - -	— —	Clerk of Crown in Chan.	*Page* 224.
STAFFORD, COUNTY:			
Nomina Villarum - - - - - -	— —	Lord Treas. Rem. Office	G. 7. a.
Nona Roll - - - - - - -	15 Edw. 3. - -	King's Rememb. Office -	G. 6. b.
Ecclesiastical Survey - - - - -	26 Hen. 8. - -	First Fruits Office - -	G. 18.
Certificate of the Honour of Bolingbroke, partly within this County - - - - - -	Eliz. and Car. - -	} University Libr. Camb.	P. 1.
Certificate of Manors therein not in Fee Farm	1629 - - -		
v. TESTA DE NEVIL.			
STANNARIES:			
Collections about them - - - - -	— —	Inner Temple Library -	Q. 2. b.
CORNWALL:			
Plaisit and Entry Papers, and Books in which the Proceedings are entered - - -	— —	} Vice Warden of the Stannaries, Cornwall	H. 17.
Certificates of Blocks of Tin smelted, and Proclamations of Tin Bounds - - - -	— —		
Returns concerning Stannaries - - -	— —	Auditors Office Land Rev.	G. 15. a.
Act of Convocation of the Stannators or Tinners Parliament - - - - - -	1752 and 1753 -	} Duchy Cornwall Office	C. 7.
The like, assembled in 1776 - - - -	1776 - - -		
Appeals in Stannary Causes - - -	1778 to 1784 -		
DEVON:			
Proceedings and Minutes of Decrees in the Court of the Vice Warden thereof - - -	1784 to present Time	Vice Warden of the Stannaries, Devon -	H. 16.
v. CLAUS ROLLS.—CORNWALL.—DEVON.			

ALPHABETICAL ARRANGEMENT OF THE PUBLIC RECORDS.

RECORDS and other INSTRUMENTS.	DATE.	WHERE KEPT.	Appendix to the First Report.
STAR CHAMBER: (Erected by Act of Parliament 3 Hen. VII. diſſolved by Act 17 Car. I.)			
Hiſtory of the Court and its Juriſdiction - -	— —	Auditors Office Land Rev.	G 15. a.
Divers Tracts and Papers relating thereto - -	— —	Britiſh Muſeum - -	U.
Fees in this Court - - - - -	— —	Bodleian Library - -	O. 1.
Collections reſpecting it - - - - -	— —	Inner Temple Library -	Q. 2. b.
A few Judgments and other Proceedings removed by Certiorari - - - - - - - -	— —	Rolls Chapel - -	D. 1.
Information therein againſt Sir John Elliot, Denzil Holles, &c. for their Behaviour in Parliament, with the Order in the Star Chamber and Council in the ſaid Cauſe - - - - - -	— —	} Univerſity Libr. Camb.	P. 1.
Proceedings therein againſt Henry Sherfield, &c. for defacing Images, &c. at Saliſbury - -	— —		
Bills, Anſwers, Depoſitions, and other Proceedings	3 Hen. 7. to 16 Car. 1. with Chaſms -	* Receipt of the Excheq	A. 1. a.
Papers relative to the Star Chamber - - -	1558 to 1633 - -	State Paper Office - -	C. 1. a.
A Copy of a Decree therein for Orders in Printing	28 Eliz. - -	} Aſhmolean Muſeum -	O. 2.
Proceedings in - - - - - - - -	12 Jac. 1. to 16 C. 1.		
Courſe of Proceedings and Reports - - -	4 Car. 1. - -		
Caſes therein - - - - - -	Temp. Car. 1. -	} Bodleian Library - -	O. 1.
Proceedings therein - - - - - -	1632 - - -		
Act of Court on the Petitions of Baſtwick and Prynne, with Judges Opinion and Certificate -	Car. 1. - -	} Inner Temple Library	Q. 2. b.
Reports and Proceedings of the Star Chamber -	1629 to 1632 - -		
Information therein againſt a ſeditious Diſcourſe of Francis Earl of Bedford, &c. - - - -	1629 - - -	Univerſity Library Camb.	P. 1.
STATE PAPERS:			
Treaties, Commiſſions, Proclamations, Credentials, Inſtructions to Ambaſſadors and Agents, and Letters of Sovereigns, Miniſters, and other eminent Characters, relating to various Tranſactions between England and moſt of the Sovereigns and States of Europe. Some of ſo antient a Date as Edw. III.; but the greateſt Part relating to the Reigns of the Tudors, and down to 10th James I.; ſome alſo down to the laſt Reign - - - - - - -	Edw. 3. to Geo. 2.	Britiſh Muſeum - -	U.
The like - - - - - - - - -	1340 to 1708 - -		
Commiſſions, Inſtructions, Petitions, and Reports -	1377 to 1676 -		
State Tracts, Treaties, Diſcourſes on different Governments, &c. - - - - - -	1501 to 1673 - -	} State Paper Office -	C. 1. a.
Diſpenſations - - - - - - -	1532 to 1699		
Miſcellaneous Collections of - - - - -	Hen. 8. to Will. 3.	Bodleian Library - -	O. 1.
Letters from Cardinal Pole to Henry VIII. and the Council - - - - - - - -	Hen. 8. - - - -	Receipt of the Exchequer	A. 1. a.
Memorial for the Colloquy at Burges - -	1564 - - -	Univerſity Library Camb.	P. 1.
Papers, Letters, Memorials and Orders of Council	1570 to 1700 -		
Lord Fitzwilliam's Papers - - - - -	Eliz. - - -		
Book of Sir Amyas Powlett's Letters during his Embaſſy in France - - - - -	1577 - - -	} Bodleian Library - -	O. 1.
Articles propounded by the Earl of Eſſex, with Conſiderations by Lord Burleigh, &c. - -	1596 - - -		
Petitions to the King and Reports - - -	1600 to 1683 - -	} State Paper Office - -	C. 1. a.
Proceedings relative to Bohemia and the Palatinate - - - - - - - - -	1620 to 1623 -		
Secretary Thurloe's State Papers - - -	1638 to 1660 -		
Philip Lord Wharton's Papers - - -	— —		
Lord Huntingdon's Papers - - - - -	— —		
Letters from the Protector to Foreign States - -	Oliver Cromwell -	} Bodleian Library - -	O. 1.
Letters of Charles II. &c. on State Affairs - -	Car. 2. - -		
Negotiations - - - - - - - -	1677 to 1688 - -		
Letters of Mr. Secretary Pepys, Precepts, and other State Papers, 26 Vols. - - - -	1679 to 1683 -		
Memorials, Petitions, and Reports - - -	1704 to 1761 -	State Paper Office - -	C. 1. a.
v. AMBASSADORS.—CORRESPONDENCE—RYMER.			

* The Decrees of this Court (STAR CHAMBER) which ought to be in this Office, have been miſſing for many Years, and are not any where to be found.

ALPHABETICAL ARRANGEMENT OF THE PUBLIC RECORDS.

RECORDS and other INSTRUMENTS.	DATE.	WHERE KEPT.	Appendix to the First Report.
STATUTES:			
Collection of antient Statutes	— —	Dean & Chapt. Gloucester	N. 7.
Several antient Transcripts of the "Statuta Antiqua"	— —	British Museum	U.
Of many Cathedrals, Collegiate Churches, and Colleges	— —		
Antient Statutes	Magna Charta to Hen. 6.	Inner Temple Library	Q. 2. b.
Divers antient	From Magna Charta downwards	Corp. Christi Coll. Camb.	P. 5.
Several antient Copies of	Magna Charta to Hen. 4.	Lincoln's Inn Library	Q. 3.
Books of	Joh. to Hen. 8.	King's Rememb. Office	G. 6. a.
Several Volumes of Transcripts of antient Statutes	1215, &c.	Bodleian Library	O. 1.
A Roll, containing the Statutes made at Winchester	13 Edw. 1.	Receipt of the Exchequer	A. 1. a.
Rolls of	1277 to 1468	Tower	A. 2. a.
A Catalogue of Public and Private Acts of Parliament removed to the Chapel of the Rolls	1483 to 1625	British Museum	U.
A Collection of Private Acts passed in the Reigns of Hen. VIII. and Car. I.	Hen. 8. and Car. 1.		
Exemplifications of, under the Great Seal	6 Hen. 8. to Geo. 3.	Rolls Chapel	D. 1. a.
STATUTES STAPLE:			
Certificates, Extents, and Liberates	— —		
Extents, Re-extents, and other Proceedings in Bundles, under the Title of Writs of Execution	A few temp. Jac. 1. and from Beginning of Car. 1. to present Time	Petty Bag Office	D. 5.
STATIONERS, LONDON:			
An Indenture between the University of Oxford and the Company of Stationers, and Confirmation thereof	8 Jac. 1.	Ashmolean Museum	O. 2.
v. OXFORD.			
STEWARDSHIPS:			
Inrolments of Grants of them	Jac. 1. to Car. 1.	Augmentation Office	G. 19. a.
SUBSCRIPTIONS:			
Voluntary	13 Car. 2.	Auditors Office Land Rev.	G. 15. a.
SUBSIDIES. *v.* AIDS.—REVENUE ROYAL.—TAXES.—TENTHS.			
SUFFOLK, COUNTY:			
Antient Deeds, &c. relative to Estates therein	— —	Dean and Chapt. Westm.	N. 12. b.
Inquisitiones de Ministris	4 Edw. 1.	Receipt of the Exchequer	A. 1. a.
Knights Fees therein	31 Edw. 1.	University Library Camb.	P. 1.
Nona Roll	15 Edw. 3.	King's Rememb. Office	G. 6. b.
Ecclesiastical Survey	26 Hen. 8.	First Fruits Office	G. 18.
v. NORFOLK.			
SUMMONS:			
Writs of	1288 to 1477	Tower	A. 2. a.
SUPREMACY:			
Instruments of Acknowledgment of the King's Supremacy by the Bishops, &c.	Hen. 8.	Receipt of Exchequer	A. 1. a.
Books for and against	1532 to 1699		
Papers relating to			
v. HEN. VIII.—POPES.—PREROGATIVE ROYAL.			
SURRENDERS:			
Of Offices in the Law	— —	Clerk of Crown Chancery	D. 2. a.
Rolls of	12 Car. 1. to the present Time	Rolls Chapel	D. 1.
Inrolments of Surrenders of Offices	8 Anne to pres^t Time	Petty Bag Office	D. 5.
v. CHANCERY.—MONASTERIES.			
SURREY, COUNTY:			
Antient Deeds, &c. relative to Estates therein	— —	Dean & Chapter Westm.	N. 12. b.
Collections from Public Records relating thereto	Temp. Joh. to the End of Edw. 3.	University Library Camb.	P. 1.

ALPHABETICAL ARRANGEMENT OF THE PUBLIC RECORDS.

RECORDS and other INSTRUMENTS.	DATE.	WHERE KEPT.	Appendix to the First Report.
SURREY, COUNTY—*(continued.)*			
Charta Libertatum Surriæ - - - - -	Edw. 1. - -	Corp. Chrifti Coll. Camb.	P. 5.
Ecclefiaftical Survey - - - - - -	26 Hen. 8. - -	Firft Fruits Office - -	G. 18.
Affeffment for Wages for a Knight of the Shire -	31 Hen. 6. - -	Dean & Chapter Weftm.	N. 12. b.
v. TESTA DE NEVIL.		-	
SURVEYOR GENERAL:			
Leafes and Decrees of the Court of - -	Hen. 8. - -	Augmentation Office -	G. 19. a.
Proceedings in the Office of - - -	Temp. Car. 1. and from 1660 } to the prefent Time	} Office of Surveyor General of Crown Lands	G. 14.
Account of Eftates undifpofed of - - -	1701 - - } to the prefent Time	} Office of Surveyor General of Crown Lands	G. 14.
Original Petitions, References, and Reports -	1730 - - } to the prefent Time	} Office of Surveyor General of Crown Lands	G. 14.
Proceedings on Sales of Fee Farm Rents -	34 Geo. 3. - } to the prefent Time	} Office of Surveyor General of Crown Lands	G. 14.
Proceedings on Sales for Redemption of Land Tax - - - - - - - -	38 Geo. 3. - - -	} Office of Surveyor General of Crown Lands	G. 14.
Oath of the Surveyor General - - -	— —	Clerk of Crown in Chanc.	*Page* 222.
SURVEYS:			
Of Lands, Manors, &c. - - - - -	— —	Britifh Mufeum - -	U.
Collections of Names of the King's Caftles, Manfions, Parks, Forefts, Chaces, &c. within the Survey of the Court of Exchequer and Duchy of Lancafter - - - - - - -	— —	} Univerfity Library Cambridge - -	P. 1.
Of Lands in Wales out on Leafe - - -	— —	} Univerfity Library Cambridge - -	P. 1.
Of Honours, Manors, &c. - - - -	Various Dates - -	Augmentation Office -	G. 19. a.
Of Manors, &c. - - - - - - -	1493 to 1715 - -	Auditors Office Land Rev.	G. 15. a.
Of Forfeited Eftates - - - - -	Hen. 8. - - -	} Receipt of the Exchequer - - -	A. 1. a.
Of Lands and Manors - - - -	Edw. 6. to Jac. 1.	} Receipt of the Exchequer - - -	A. 1. a.
Of the Forfeited Eftates of the Duke of Norfolk and Earl of Arundel - - - -	} Eliz. - - - -	} King's Rememb. Office	G. 6. a.
Of Manors in Lincolnfhire - - - - -	} Eliz. - - - -	} King's Rememb. Office	G. 6. a.
Surveys under Special Commiffions - -	Eliz. to Car. 2. -	} King's Rememb. Office	G. 6. a.
Of South Stoke, Somerfet - - - -	Eliz. - - -	Univerfity Library Camb.	P. 1.
Surveys in Wales - - - - - -	2 to 39 Eliz. - -	Auditors Office for Wales	G. 16. a.
Of Concealed Lands - - - - - -	3 to 17 Eliz. - -	King's Rememb. Office -	G. 6. a.
Views and Surveys of all Woods and Underwoods in Forefts and Parks - - - -	1575 - - -	Univerfity Library Camb.	P. 1.
Survey of Eltham in Kent - - - - -	Jac. 1. - -	King's Rememb. Office -	G. 6. a.
Of Eftates in Wales, Worcefter, Leicefter, Lancafhire, and Northamptonfhire, not granted in Fee Farm - - - - - - -	1629 - - -	Univerfity Library Camb.	P. 1.
Surveys taken prior to the Death of Charles I. -	Before 1649 - -	Surveyor General Crown Lands - - -	G. 14.
Of Greenwich, Kent - - - - - -	7 Will. 3. - -	Petty Bag Office - -	D. 5.
v. PARLIAMENTARY SURVEYS.			
SUSSEX, COUNTY:			
Antient Deeds, &c. relative to Eftates therein -	— —	Dean and Chapt. Weftm.	N. 12. b.
A Collection refpecting the Hiftory and Antiquities of Suffex, by Sir William Burrell - -	— —	Britifh Mufeum - -	U.
Nona Roll - - - - - -	15 Edw. 3. - -	King's Rememb. Office	G. 6. b.
Ecclefiaftical Survey - - - - - -	26 Hen. 8. - -	Firft Fruits Office - -	G. 18.
v. NORFOLK.—TESTA DE NEVIL.			
SWEDEN:			
Tranfactions with England - - - -	1485 to 1613 - -	Britifh Mufeum - -	U.
Treaties and Ratifications with England - -	1568 to 1777 - -	State Paper Office - -	C. 1. a.
Original Letters and Inftructions relating thereto -	Jac. 1. Car. 1 & 2.	Bodleian Library - -	O. 1.
SWISSERLAND:			
Treaties and Ratifications with England - -	1672 to 1776 -	State Paper Office - -	C. 1. a.
SYBETON. *v.* CHARTULARIES.			

ALPHABETICAL ARRANGEMENT OF THE PUBLIC RECORDS.

RECORDS and other INSTRUMENTS.	DATE.	WHERE KEPT.	Appendix to the First Report.
TALLAGE. v. CLAUS ROLLS.			
TALLIES: Delivered out from Time to Time to the Perfons entitled to them Alfo the Foils of Tallies - v. CLAUS ROLLS.	— —	Chamberlain's Office Ex. -	G. 2.
TALLY WRITERS (NOW AUDITORS.) Their Oath - - - - - -	— —	Receipt of the Exchequer	*Page* 232.
TANGIERS: Papers relating thereto - - - - - -	1661 to 1677 - -	State Paper Office -	C. 1. a.
Reports of Mr. Pepys, concerning - - -	1683 - - - -	Bodleian Library - -	O. 1.
TAX ACCOUNTS. v. LAND REVENUE.			
TAXATIONS: To the King and the Pope - - - - - v. JEWS.—NICHOLAS IV.—POPES.	Chieflytemp. Edw. 1.	Dean and Chapter Weftm.	N. 12. b.
TAXES. v. AIDS.—CLAUS ROLLS.—EXCHEQUER OF ACCOUNT.—HEARTH TAX.—LAND REVENUE.—LAND TAX.—POLL TAX.—RADNOR COUNTY.—SUBSIDIES.—TENTHS.			
TELLERS OF THE EXCHEQUER: Their Oath - - - - - - - - -	— —	Receipt of the Exchequer	*Page* 232.
TEMPLARS. v. KNIGHTS.			
TENTHS OR SUBSIDIES: Rolls of Tenths and Fifteenths - - - -	— —	King's Rememb. Office	G. 6. a.
Tenths or Subfidies - - - - - -	Edw. 3. Hen. 4. &c.	Augmentation Office -	G. 19. a.
A Book of Tenths and Fifteenths - - -	3 Hen. 5. - - -	King's Rem. Office -	G. 6. a.
Taxation of Tenths - - - - - -	20 Hen. 6. - - -	King's Rem. Office -	G. 6. a.
Collectors Accounts of Tenths and Fifteenths - v. AIDS.	Temp. Eliz. - -	Auditors Office Land Rev.	G. 15. a.
TERRIERS: Of Church Lands (feveral) - - - - - v. The feveral DIOCESES.	— —	Britifh Mufeum - -	U.
TEST ROLLS. v. LORDS, HOUSE OF.			
TESTA DE NEVIL: For the Counties of Hereford, Devon, Salop, Hants, Oxon, Cambridge, Staff. Surry, Glouc. Suffex - - - - - - - - - v. NOMINA VILLARUM.	— —	Receipt of the Exchequer	A. 1. a.
THAMES. v. CLAUS ROLLS.			
THESAURARIUS ANGLIÆ: Forma Conftitutionis Thefaurarii Angliæ - -	— —	Clerk of Crown in Chan.	*Page* 222.
THURLOE: His State Papers (not printed) - - - - v. STATE PAPERS.	1638 to 1660 - -	Bodleian Library - -	O. 1.
TIN ROLLS. v. CORNWALL.			
TORRE, DEVON: Leidger Book of its Charters, &c. - -	— —	King's Rememb. Office -	G. 6. a.
TOWN CLERKS. v. ESTREATS, FOREIGN.			
TOWER: Oath of the Keeper of the Records there - -	— —	Petty Bag Office - -	*Page* 231.
TRADE, BOARD OF: Letters, Memorials, &c. and Reports thereupon -	1668 to 1767 - -	State Paper Office - -	C. 1. a.
Letters to the Board - - - - - -	1721 to 1729 - -	Bodleian Library - -	O. 1.
DOMESTIC AND FOREIGN - - - - -	1562 to 1690 - -	State Paper Office - -	C. 1. a.
FOREIGN: Papers relative to the Hans Towns, Holland, America, Eaft Indies, &c. - - - -	1474 to 1708 - -	State Paper Office -	C. 1. a
Papers relative to Merchant Ships, and Foreign Trade - - - - - - -	1572 to 1608 - -	State Paper Office -	C. 1. a

ALPHABETICAL ARRANGEMENT OF THE PUBLIC RECORDS.

RECORDS and other INSTRUMENTS.	DATE.	WHERE KEPT.	Appendix to the First Report.
TRADING COMPANIES:			
v. African—East India—Levant—South Sea, and Turkey Companies.			
TRANSCRIPTS:			
Of Placita, &c. - - - - - -	— —	University Library Camb.	P. 1.
TRANSPORTATION of Convicts:			
v. The feveral Circuits.—London and Middlesex Sessions.—Crimes.			
TREASONS:			
A Bag fo called, containing Papers relating to Infurrections in Yorkfhire, Lincolnfhire, &c. -	Temp. Hen. 8. -	Receipt of the Exchequer	A. 1. a.
v. Exchequer of Account.—Rebellion.			
TREASURER of the Chamber } *v.* Household.			
TREASURER, Lord - - } *v.* Household.			
Lord High:			
His Oath - - - - - - -	— —	Receipt of the Exchequer	*Page* 232.
of the King's Exchequer:			
His Oath - - - - - - -	— —	} King's Rememb. Office	—233.
Oath of the Under Treafurer - - -	— —	} King's Rememb. Office	—233.
TREASURY:			
Warrants for Leafes - - - - - -	1730 to prefent Time	Survey. Gen. Cr. Lands	G. 14.
v. Accounts, Public.—Exchequer of Receipt.—Land Revenue.—Pells.—Revenue, Royal.			
TREATIES:			
Catalogue of fome Treaties and Negotiations in the State Paper Office, by Carte - -	— —	Bodleian Library - -	O. 1.
Fœdus factum inter Hen. II. and Lud. VII. -	Hen. 2. - - - -	Corpus Chrifti Coll. Cam.	P. 5.
With Scotland and other European States - -	1161 to 1624 - -	Receipt of the Exchequer	A. 1. a.
Melanges d'Actes, &c. entre les Rois de France et Angleterre - - - - - - -	1190 to 1625 - -	} Bodleian Library - -	O. 1.
Traitez et Memoires de France et d'Angleterre -	1193 to 1331 - -	} Bodleian Library - -	O. 1.
Treaties and Tranfactions with Bretagne - -	1213 to 1491 - -	} Receipt of the Excheq.	A. 1. a.
Treaties and Tranfactions with Arragon - -	1289 to 1515 - -	} Receipt of the Excheq.	A. 1. a.
Collection of Treaties - - - - -	Edw. 3. to Jac. 1. -	Britifh Mufeum - -	U.
Copies of Treaties, Declarations, &c. with France -	Edw. 3. - - - -	Afhmolean Mufeum -	O. 1.
Treaties and Tranfactions with Burgundy - -	1419 to 1484 - -	Receipt of the Exchequer	A. 1. a.
Treaties and Tranfactions of all Sorts - -	1432 to 1712 - -	State Paper Office -	C. 1. a.
Treaty or Foreign Rolls - - - -	Edw. 5. to 19 Car.	Rolls Chapel - -	D. 1. a.
Treaties and Tranfactions with Denmark - -	1485 to 1613 - -	} Britifh Mufeum -	U.
Treaties between England and various Foreign Nations - - - - - - - - -	Chiefly from Hen. 7. to Jac. 1. - - -	} Britifh Mufeum -	U.
Treaties - - - - - - - - -	H. 7. & 8. & Jac. 2.	Bodleian Library -	O. 1.
The like - - - - - - - - -	Eliz. & Jac. 1. -	Univerfity Library Camb.	P. 1.
Articuli Pacis inter SS. RR. Hifpaniæ & Mag. Britanniæ & Archid. Auftriæ - - - -	} 1604 - - - -	Bodleian Library -	O. 1.
The like in Englifh - - - - -	} 1604 - - - -	Bodleian Library -	O. 1.
Treaties and Tranfactions with Eaftern Princes -	1606 to 1762 - -	State Paper Office -	C. 1. a.
Articles of Peace with the Scots - - -	Car. 1. to 1639 - -	Afhmolean Mufeum -	O. 2.
Treaties and Ratifications with Brandenburg -	1661 to 1700 - -	} State Paper Office -	C. 1. a.
Copies, Extracts, and Abftracts - - -	1700 to 1713 - -	} State Paper Office -	C. 1. a.
Treaties and Tranfactions with European States -	1712 to 1760 - -	} State Paper Office -	C. 1. a.
v. Claus Rolls.—Projects.—State Papers.			
TRUCES. *v.* Claus Rolls.			
TURKEY:			
Treaties and Ratifications between England and Turkey, and other Eaftern Princes - -	1579 to 1779 - -	} State Paper Office -	C. 1. a.
Company:			
Copies of Letters Patent for the Foundation of the Company - - - - - - -	— —	Bodleian Library - -	O. 1.

ALPHABETICAL ARRANGEMENT OF THE PUBLIC RECORDS.

RECORDS and other INSTRUMENTS.	DATE.	WHERE KEPT.	Appendix to the First Report.
TUSCANY:			
Tranfactions with England	1485 to 1613	Britifh Mufeum	U.
Treaties and Ratifications with England	1731	State Paper Office	C. 1. a.
TYNTERN, MONMOUTH. *v.* CHARTULARIES.			
TYTHES:			
A Variety of Deeds, fuch as Donations, Grants, Agreements, Refignations, Compofitions, Inquifitions, and Judgments, chiefly concerning Tythes, contained in a Bag, intituled, "Divers Diocefes"	— —	Receipt of the Exchequer	A. 1. a.
Decimæ collectæ in Subfidium Terræ Sanctæ	— —	Dean & Chapter Weftm.	N. 12. b.
v. CLAUS ROLLS.—The feveral DIOCESES.			
VENICE:			
Tranfactions with England	1485 to 1613	Britifh Mufeum	U.
Treaties with England	1625 to 1771	State Paper Office	C. 1. a.
VERDURERS. *v.* CLAUS ROLLS.—SEAL, GREAT.			
VERGE:			
Proceedings of the Court of Verge at St. James's	— —	Bodleian Library	O. 1.
The like	1676 to 1791	Board of Green Cloth	C. 5.
Oath of the Deputy Steward of the Court of, and Palace Court	— —	Clerk of Crown in Chan.	*Page* 225.
v. GREEN CLOTH.			
VICARAGES:			
Endowments and Ordinations of	— —	Augmentation Office	G. 19. a.
References to Endowments of Vicarages in different Diocefes, by Andrew Coltee Du Carel, LL. D.	— —	Lambeth Library	T.
Surveys and Valuations of	26 Hen. 8.	Firft Fruits Office	G. 18.
v. The feveral DIOCESES.			
VIEWS OF ACCOUNTS:			
Views of Accounts	Hen. 5. to Car. 2.	Auditors Office Land Rev.	G. 15. a.
Views of Sheriffs Accounts for Wales	13 Car. 2. to 38 G. 3.	Auditors Office for Wales	G. 16. a.
VISITATIONS:			
Books of Vifitations	Various Dates	Caius College Cambridge.	P. 7.
Books of, containing the Pedigrees and Arms of the Nobility and Gentry of the Kingdom }	21 H. 8. to 2 Jac. 2.	College of Arms	C. 8.
Funeral Certificates during the Time of the Vifitations }			
Of the Kings at Arms through all the Counties of England	1528 to 1636	Britifh Mufeum	U.
	1666	Bodleian Library	O. 1.
v. An ample Catalogue of them in GUTCH's COLLECTANEA CURIOSA, Vol. II. p. 210.—256.			
UNITED PROVINCES:			
Treaties and Ratifications with England }	1545 to 1779	State Paper Office	C. 1. a.
Papers relating to the Dutch War }			
v. HOLLAND.—ORANGE, PRINCE OF.			
UNIVERSITIES AND COLLEGES:			
Collections relating to them, by Thomas Baker	— —	British Mufeum }	U.
Collections of Statutes of Colleges	— —		
Foundation of Magdalen College, Oxford	Hen. 6.	Receipt of the Exchequer	A. 1. a.
Accounts of Univerfities, &c.	Hen. 8.	Augmentation Office	G. 19. a.
Vifitation of, by Thomas Lord Cromwell	Hen. 8.	Peterhoufe College Camb.	P. 2.
Act of Parliament for incorporating them	13 Eliz.	Afhmolean Mufeum	O. 2.
Letters, &c. relating to the Univerfities	1684 to 1769	State Paper Office	C. 1. a.

ALPHABETICAL ARRANGEMENT OF THE PUBLIC RECORDS.

RECORDS and other INSTRUMENTS.	DATE.	WHERE KEPT.	Appendix to the Firſt Report.
UNIVERSITIES and COLLEGES—*(continued.)*			
The Colleges in the Two Univerſities have in general in their Poſſeſſion:			
1. The Charters and Deeds relative to their Foundation, Endowment, and ſubſequent Improvements.			
2. Their Statutes uſually confirmed by the Sovereign.			
3. Exemplifications of Acts of Parliament, confirming their Poſſeſſions.			
4. Journals, Regiſters, and Entries of the Proceedings of the Colleges.			
5. Licences of Mortmain and Appropriations.			
6. Viſitations, temp. Hen. 8.			
7. Surveys.			
8. Accounts of their Revenues.			
For an Account of the Libraries of the Univerſities and Colleges, *v.* Catalogi Manuscriptorum Angliæ et Hiberniæ, Oxon. 1697.—*v.* Alſo the ſeveral Colleges, Cambridge.—Claus Rolls.—Ecclesiastical Affairs.—Oxford.—Hen. 8.—Wolsey.			
VOYAGES:			
Accounts of Royal Voyages - - - -	1 Hen. 4. - - -	Tower - - - -	A. 2. a.
Inſtructions for Voyages of Diſcovery - - *v.* Claus Rolls.	1576 to 1676 - -	State Paper Office - -	C. 1. a.
USURPATION:			
Journals of the Proceedings of the Truſtees for Sale of Crown Lands - - - - -	Temp. Interregni -	Augmentation Office - -	G. 19. a.
Writs and Returns of Eſtates of Perſons outlawed *v.* Charles I.—Land Revenue.	Temp. Interregni -	Auditors Office Land Rev.	G. 15. a.
UTRECHT:			
Peace of, Letters and Papers relating thereto -	1712 to 1713 - -	Bodleian Library - -	O. 1.
Treaty of - - - - - - - -	1748 - - - -	State Paper Office - -	C. 1. a.
WALES:			
Some Miniſters Accounts - - - - -	— —	King's Rememb. Office -	G. 6. a.
Lands out on Leaſe - - - - - -	— —	Univerſity Library Camb.	P. 1.
Welch Rolls - - - - - - -	1276 to 1295 - -	Tower - - - - -	A. 2. a.
Copies of Welch Rolls - - - - -	6 to 10 Edw. 1. -	Lincoln's Inn Library -	Q. 3.
Statuta Walliæ - - - - - - -	12 Edw. 1. - - -	Receipt of the Exchequer	A. 1. a.
Rolls concerning the Revenues of the Principality of - - - - - - - - - -	Temp. Edw. 3. -	Tower - - - - -	A. 2. a.
Miniſters and other Accounts - - - -	Edw. 3. to Ph. & M.	Augmentation Office -	G. 19. a.
Extenta Maneriorum Edwardi Principis Walliæ -	19 Edw. 3. - -	Univerſity Library Camb.	P. 1.
Indenture between Hen. IV. and his Son the Prince, touching the Welch Wars - -	Temp. Hen. 4. -	Dean and Chapter Weſtm.	N. 12. b.
Books of Inrolment and Entry for Wales - -	H. 7. to preſent Time	Auditors Office for Wales	G. 16. a.
* Miniſters Accounts - - - - - -	H. 8. Eliz. & Jac. 1.	Auditors Office Land Rev.	G. 15. a.
- - - - - - of Lands of Sir J. Perrot and Owen Glynn - - - - - - -	} Eliz. - - - -	Auditors Office for Wales	G. 16. a.
Surveys - - - - - - - - -			
Revenues, Accounts, Liberties, Privileges, &c. -	1550 to 1660 - -	State Paper Office - -	C. 1. a.
Charters and Liberties to the Prince - -	14 Jac. 1. - - -	{ Auditors Office Land Revenue - - -	G. 15. a.
General Accounts of Receivers and Bailiffs to Prince Charles - - - - -	Jac. 1. - - - -		
Nomina Maneriorum, &c. Caroli Princpis Walliæ	{ Jac. 1. - - -	{ Univerſity Library Cambridge - -	P. 1.
Names of Benefices in the Gift of the Prince -			
Records delivered to the Commiſſioners of the Revenue of Charles Prince of Wales - -			
Rental of Lands in North and South Wales, Parcel of the Principality lately annexed - -	1642 - - - -		

* Theſe have been lately removed to the Augmentation Office.

ALPHABETICAL ARRANGEMENT OF THE PUBLIC RECORDS.

RECORDS and other INSTRUMENTS.	DATE.	WHERE KEPT.	Appendix to the First Report.
WALES—(*continued.*)			
Account of Receivers General of the Revenues of Queen Henrietta Maria	7, 8, and 12 Car. 1.	Auditors Office Land Rev.	G. 15. a.
Sales of Fee Farm Rents, &c.	Temp. Interregni	Auditors Off. for Wales	G. 16. a.
Rentals of Fee Farm and other Rents in Wales	Anne to pres^t Time	Auditors Off. for Wales	G. 16. a.
v. CLAUS ROLLS.—LAND REVENUE.			
NORTH CIRCUIT:			
Attornies Certificates, Regifters, &c.	— —	Prothonotary and Clerk of the Crown, North Wales	H. 9.
Files, containing Minutes to profecute and defend	— —	Prothonotary and Clerk of the Crown, North Wales	H. 9.
Attornies Oaths and Subfcriptions	— —	Prothonotary and Clerk of the Crown, North Wales	H. 9.
Rolls of Memorandums, containing Writs of Summons, &c.	From 1700 to the prefent Time	Prothonotary and Clerk of the Crown, North Wales	H. 9.
Paper Files, containing Pleadings in Actions, &c.	From 1700 to the prefent Time	Prothonotary and Clerk of the Crown, North Wales	H. 9.
Books of Imparlance	From 1700 to the prefent Time	Prothonotary and Clerk of the Crown, North Wales	H. 9.
Books of Rules	From 1700 to the prefent Time	Prothonotary and Clerk of the Crown, North Wales	H. 9.
Plea Rolls	From 1700 to the prefent Time	Prothonotary and Clerk of the Crown, North Wales	H. 9.
Dockets of Judgments	From 1700 to the prefent Time	Prothonotary and Clerk of the Crown, North Wales	H. 9.
Chirographs of Fines	From 1700 to the prefent Time	Prothonotary and Clerk of the Crown, North Wales	H. 9.
Calendars, containing Indictments, &c.	From 1700 to the prefent Time	Prothonotary and Clerk of the Crown, North Wales	H. 9.
WALKER, SIR E.:			
His Account of the Votes in Parliament, on the Treaty of Newport	1648	Bodleian Library	O. 1.
WALTHAM, ESSEX. v. FORESTS.			
WARDEN AND VICE WARDEN OF THE STANNARIES. v. STANNARIES.			
WARDROBE:			
Various Papers relating thereto	— —	Britifh Mufeum	U.
Accounts of	— —	King's Rememb. Office	G. 6. a.
Accounts of, in feveral Reigns	— —	Auditors Office Land Rev.	G. 15. a.
General Accounts of the Great Wardrobe	10 Edw. 1. & feq.	Tower	A. 2. a.
Liber Cotidianus Contrarotulatoris de Recepta et Expenfis Garderobæ (publifhed)	28 Edw. 1.	Antiq. Society Library	S. a.
Accounts	10, 11 & 18 Edw. 2.	Antiq. Society Library	S. a.
Accounts	Hen. 8. &c.	Augmentation Office	G. 19. a.
General Accounts of the Great Wardrobe, for One Year	12 Hen. 8.	Receipt of the Exchequer	A. 1. a.
Inventory of the Wardrobe of Queen Elizabeth	42 Eliz.	Auditors Office Land Rev.	G. 15. a.
Comptrollers Bills of the Great Wardrobe	1730 to 1792	Office of Great Wardrobe	C. 5. b.
Patents, Warrants, Eftimates, &c. Books of	1749 to 17[illegible]5	Office of Great Wardrobe	C. 5. b.
Salaries and Liveries, Books of	1750 to 1779	Office of Great Wardrobe	C. 5. b.
Quarterly and Yearly Accounts and Day Books	1752 to 1777	Office of Great Wardrobe	C. 5. b.
v. CLAUS ROLLS.—CORNWALL.—JEWELS.—INVENTORIES.—LAND REVENUE.			
WARDS AND LIVERIES, COURT OF: erected 32 Hen. VIII. abolifhed 12 Car. I.			
Collections about the Court of	— —	Inner Temple Library	Q. 2. b.
Several Proceedings and Decrees in the Court of	— —	Univerfity Library Camb.	P. 1.
Valuation of the Eftates of Earl of Northumberland and Lord Lifle, the King's Wards	— —	Dean and Chapter Weftm.	N. 12. b.
Extracts from the Records of Efcheats therein, by Mr. Thomas Cole	— —	Britifh Mufeum	U.
General Liveries, during the Court of	Edw. 5. to 17 Car. 1.	Rolls Chapel	D. 1.
Proceedings, confifting of Bills, Anfwers, Decrees, Inquifitions Poft Mortem, &c.	32 H. 8. to 12 Car. 2.	Receipt of the Exchequer	A. 1. a.
Papers relative to Wards and Liveries	1558 to 1633	State Paper Office	C. 1. a.
Collection of Decrees in French, by John Hare	1581	Univerfity Library Camb.	P. 1.
An Ordinance concerning the Court of	1647	King's Rememb. Office	G. 6. a.
v. INQUISITIONES POST MORTEM.			
WARDSHIPS, GRANTS OF. v. PATENT ROLLS.			
WARRANT BOOKS:			
Containing Copies of Warrants, Grants of Penfions, Places, Preferments, Paffes, Licences, Pardons, Reprieves, &c.	1661 to 1711	State Paper Office	C. 1. a.
v CHANCERY.—LAND REVENUE.—PATENTS.—SIGNS MANUAL.			
WARRENS. v. CLAUS ROLLS.—EXCHEQUER OF ACCOUNT.			

ALPHABETICAL ARRANGEMENT OF THE PUBLIC RECORDS.

RECORDS and other INSTRUMENTS.	DATE.	WHERE KEPT.	Appendix to the First Report.
WARWICK, County:			
Antient Deeds, &c. relating to Estates therein	— —	Dean and Chapter Westm.	N. 12. b.
Book, containing an Account of the Church Lands	7 Edw. 1.	King's Rememb. Office	G. 6. a.
Ecclesiastical Survey	26 Hen. 8.	First Fruits Office	G. 18.
Certificate of Manors, &c. therein, not in Fee Farm	1629	University Library Camb.	P. 1.
Town:			
Leidger Book of St. Mary's College and the Priory	— —	King's Rememb. Office	G. 6. a.
WATERFORD, Ireland:			
Charters and Laws of the City of	Edw. 2. &c.	Corpus Christi Coll. Cam.	P. 5.
WEIGHTS and MEASURES, of Length and Capacity:			
Standards deposited by Order of Parliament	— —	Clerk of the Journals of the House of Commons	B. 2.
An Ell and a Yard marked E. and another Yard marked H. supposed to be of the Time of Hen. VII.	— —	Chamberlain's Office Exchequer	G. 2.
A Bushel temp. Hen. VII. Two Bushels of 1601, another of 40 Geo. II. &c.	— —		
Standard Weights, Avoirdupois, Bell Fashion	1582 & 1588		
- - - - - - Troy, both Flat and Nest	1588		
Papers relating to Weights	Eliz.	Auditors Office Land Rev.	G. 15. a.
Counterpart of Indentures of Weights and Measures sized by the Standards	1700 to present Time	Chamberlain's Office Ex.	G. 2.
Oath of the Justices of the Labourers of	— —	Ibidem	*Page* 223.
v. Claus Rolls.			
WELLS, Dean and Chapter:			
Three large Books of Endowments, &c.	— —	Dean & Chapter Wells	N. 18.
Wills, Original	— —		
Bonds on granting Administrations	— —		
Affidavits on granting Marriage Licences	— —		
v. Letters Royal.			
WESTERN Circuit:			
Nisi Prius Records and Posteas	— —	Clerk of Affize and Clerk of the Crown, Western Circuit	H. 5.
Insolvent Debtors, Papers of	— —		
Associates Minutes, and Postea Books	1610 to present Time		
Rolls for the several Counties, containing Coroners Inquisitions, Informations, Indictments, &c.	1610, but with many Chasms, to present Time		
Old Order Books about Restitution, Parochial Settlements, Highways, &c.	1629 to 1686		
Bail Books	1633		
Gaol Books	1670		
Process Books	1685 & 1686, & from 1717		
Minute Books, containing Entries of Proceedings on the Crown Side	1691		
Recognizances	1700		
Orders, Books and Bundles of	1704		
Informations, Depositions, Examinations, and Confessions	1720		
Transportation Order Books	1726		
Bundles of Papers of Interlocutory and Transitory Matters	1743		
Commissions and Nomina Ministrorum	1750, or longer, to the present Time.		
WEST INDIES:			
Papers relating thereto	— —	Bodleian Library	O. 1.
v. America.—Barbadoes.—Bermudas.—Jamaica.—Plantations.			
WESTMINSTER, City:			
Papers respecting the Government thereof	Temp. Eliz. &c.	Dean & Chapter Westm.	N. 12. a.
Papers concerning Charities and Almshouses therein	1593 to 1672		
Abbey:			
Extents of Manors belonging thereto	— —	University Library Camb.	P. 1.
Books of the Foundation of Henry VIIth's. Chapel	— —	Receipt of the Exchequer	A. 1. a.
v. Henry the VIIth.			

ALPHABETICAL ARRANGEMENT OF THE PUBLIC RECORDS.

RECORDS and other INSTRUMENTS.	DATE.	WHERE KEPT.	Appendix to the Firſt Report.
WESTMINSTER—*(continued.)*			
BRIDGE:			
Inquiſitions under ſeveral Acts of Parliament, for building of Weſtminſter Bridge - - -	Geo. 2. - - - -	Regiſter Office for Middleſex - - -	M. 1.
v. INQUISITIONS.			
WESTMORELAND, COUNTY:			
Eccleſiaſtical Survey - - - - - -	26 Hen. 8. - - -	Firſt Fruits Office -	G. 18.
Certificate of Manors, &c. therein not in Fee Farm	1629 - - - -	Univerſity Library Camb.	P. 1.
WETHERALL, CUMBERLAND:			
Chartulary of - - - - - - -	— —	Dean and Chap. Carliſle	N. 23.
WHARTON, PHILIP LORD:			
His Papers - - - - - - -	— —	Bodleian Library - -	O. 1.
WIGORNIA. *v.* PLACITA.			
WILLS, ROYAL:			
Of Henry II. - - - - - - -	Hen. 2. - - - -	King's Rememb. Office	G. 6. a.
Wills, Letters of Adminiſtration, &c. - -	1310 to 1674 - -	Dean & Chap. Weſtm. -	N. 12. b.
Of Richard II. - - - - - - -	— —	Receipt of the Excheq.	A. 1. a.
Henry V. - - - - - - - -	— —	Receipt of the Excheq.	A. 1. a.
Henry VII. - - - - - - -	— —	Receipt of the Excheq.	A. 1. a.
Henry VIII. - - - - - - -	— —	Receipt of the Excheq.	A. 1. a.
A Copy of the Will of Henry V. - - -	— —	Caius College Cambridge	P. 7.
WILTS, COUNTY:			
Nona Roll - - - - - - - -	15 Edw. 3. - -	King's Rememb. Office -	G. 6. b.
Eccleſiaſtical Survey - - - - - -	26 Hen. 8. - -	Firſt Fruits Office - -	G. 18.
Accounts of Farmers of Church Lands there -	3 & 4 Ph. & Mary	Auditors Office Land Rev.	G. 15. a.
WINCHCOMBE, GLOUCESTER:			
Survey of the Monaſtery - - - -	Temp. Hen. 8. -	King's Rememb. Office -	G 6. a.
WINCHESTER, CITY. *v.* DOMESDAY BOOK.—STATUTES.			
DIOCESE:			
Proceedings of Conſiſtory Court - - -	— —	Regiſters Office, Wincheſter - - - -	L. 7. a.
Eccleſiaſtical Records of the reſpective Biſhops - N. B. One or Two Regiſters wanting.	1280 to 1600 -	Regiſters Office, Wincheſter - - - -	L. 7. a.
Original Wills for Hants - - - -	1660 to preſent Time	Regiſters Office, Wincheſter - - - -	L. 7. a.
WINDSOR CASTLE:			
Account of the Conſtable of - - - -	19 Jac. 1. - -	Auditors Office Land Revenue - - -	G. 15. a.
Account of the Caſtle of - - - -	1622 to 1694 -	Auditors Office Land Revenue - - -	G. 15. a.
Account of Lands purchaſed about Windſor	Will. 3. to Geo. 2.	Survey. Gen. Crown Lands	G. 14.
v. CROWN LANDS.			
DEAN AND CHAPTER:			
A Collection reſpecting the Collegiate Church of Windſor, by the Rev. Mr. Huggett - -	— —	Britiſh Muſeum - -	U.
Charters and Statutes of the (Tranſcripts) - -	Edw. 3. - -	Aſhmolean Muſeum - -	O. 2.
WOLSEY, CARDINAL:			
Collections reſpecting him - - - -	— —	Inner Temple Library -	Q. 2. b.
Some of his Letters and Inſtructions, and Papers concerning him - - - - - -	— —	Univerſity Library Camb.	P. 1.
Penſions from him to the Pope - - -	— —	Receipt of the Exchequer - - - -	A. 1. a.
Surrenders of Monaſteries for the Endowment of his Colleges at Oxford and Ipſwich - -	— —	Receipt of the Exchequer - - - -	A. 1. a.
Licence of Mortmain for his College - -	— —	Receipt of the Exchequer - - - -	A. 1. a.
Enormities reſpecting him - - - -	Hen. 8. - -	Receipt of the Exchequer - - - -	A. 1. a.
Inquiſitions after his Death - - - -	Temp. Hen. 8. -	Rolls Chapel - -	D. 1. a.
v. COLLEGES:—HENRY VIII.—IPSWICH.—MONASTERIES.			

ALPHABETICAL ARRANGEMENT OF THE PUBLIC RECORDS.

RECORDS and other INSTRUMENTS.	DATE.	WHERE KEPT.	Appendix to the First Report.
WOOD LANDS:			
Accounts of Woods and Forests - - - -	— —	Auditors Office Land. Revenue - - -	G. 15. a.
Extents of Woods, &c. - - - - - -	Edw. 3 to Anne -		
View and Survey of all Woods and Underwoods in Forests, Parks, &c. - - - - -	1575 - - -	University Library Camb.	P. 1.
WOOD SALES:			
Ministers Accounts of - - - - - -	Hen. 8. - -	Augmentation Office -	G. 19. a.
WOOL. *v.* CLAUS ROLLS.			
WORCESTER, COUNTY:			
Antient Deeds, &c. relative to Estates therein -	— —	Dean and Chapt. Westm.	N. 12. b.
Ecclesiastical Survey - - - - - -	26 Hen. 8. - -	First Fruits Office - -	G. 18.
Survey of Estates therein not granted in Fee Farm	1629 - - - -	University Library Camb.	P. 1.
DIOCESE:			
Endowments, Institutions, and other Ecclesiastical Matters, in the Register Books of the several Bishops - - - - - - - -	1268 to present Time	Bishop's Registry Worcest.	L. 10. a.
WORKS:			
Accounts of Expenses for Repairs and building Castles and Palaces - - - - - -	Edw. 1. to Car. 2. -	King's Rememb. Office -	G. 6. a.
Accounts of Surveyors of - - - - -	Temp. Hen. 8. and previous thereto -	Receipt of the Exchequer	A. 1. a.
Accounts of Regulations - - - - -	Hen. 8. to Car. 2. -	Auditors Office Land Revenue - - - -	G. 15. a.
Books of Works at Greenwich - - - -	1716 to 1729 - -		
v. CLAUS ROLLS.—GREENWICH HOSPITAL.—LAND REVENUE.			
WRITS:			
Rolls or Registers of - - - - - -	— —	Bodleian Library - -	O. 1.
A Roll or Register - - - - - -	1240 - - -	Receipt of the Exchequer	A. 1. a.
Of "Audita Querela" and "Ex gravi Querela" -	— —	Rolls Chapel - -	D. 1. a.
Of "Scire Facias," and Judgments thereon -	— —		
Of Inquiry, Elegits, "ad eligend' Coronatores," &c. - - - - - - - - -	1180 to 1688 -	Receipt of the Exchequer	A. 1. a.
Of Distringas - - - - - - -	Temp. Eliz. - -	Auditors Office Land Rev.	G. 15. a.
Of Entry, Summons and Seisin, Returns of -	1627 to present Time	Clerks of Returns Prothonotaries Office -	F. 8.
v. ALIENATIONS.—BREVIA REGIA.—CHANCERY.—CIRCUITS.—CLAUS ROLLS.—COMMONS, HOUSE OF.—COMMON PLEAS.—ERROR.—EXCHEQUER.—FINES.—KING'S BENCH.—LAND REVENUE.—LORDS, HOUSE OF.—PARLIAMENT.—PEACE, CLERKS OF AND JUSTICES OF.—PLACITA.—RECOVERIES.—SIGNIFICAVITS.—STATE PAPERS.—STATUTES, STAPLE.—SUMMONS.			
YEAR BOOKS:			
Mostly in the Reigns of - - - - -	Edw. 1 & 2. - -	British Museum - -	U.
Year Books - - - - - - -	17 Edw. 1. to 10 Ed. 4. with Chasms -	Lincoln's Inn Library -	Q. 3.
Year Books - - - - - - -	1 Edw. 2. to the last Year of his Reign	Bodleian Library - -	O. 1.
Year Books - - - - - - -	1 Edw. 3. - - -		
Year Books - - - - - - -	10 to 16 Edw. 3. -	Inner Temple Library -	Q. 2. b.
Year Books - - - - - - -	38, 40, 41, 42 Ed. 3. & 3 Hen. 6. - -		

ALPHABETICAL ARRANGEMENT OF THE PUBLIC RECORDS.

RECORDS and other INSTRUMENTS.	DATE.	WHERE KEPT.	Appendix to the Firſt Report.
YORK, COUNTY:			
Antient Deeds, &c. relative to Eſtates therein	— —	Dean and Chapt. Weſtm.	N. 12. b.
Placita apud Ebor'	1 to 19 Edw. 2.	Tower	A. 2. a.
Nomina Villarum	9 Edw. 2.	Receipt of the Excheq.	A. 1. a.
Inquiſitiones coram Johe de Kirkby	24 Edw. 2.		
Eccleſiaſtical Survey	26 Hen. 8.	Firſt Fruits Office	G. 18.
Certificate of the Honour of Bolingbroke	Eliz. & Car.	Univerſity Library Camb.	P. 1.
v. BOLINGBROKE.—CLAUS ROLLS.—DURHAM, DEAN AND CHAPTER.—PLACITA.—TREASONS.			
NORTH RIDING:			
Nona Roll	15 Edw. 3.	King's Rememb. Office	G. 6. b.
Memorials of Deeds, Conveyances, Wills, Judgments, Statutes, and Recognizances	1730 to the preſent Time	Regiſter's Office for the North Riding, North Allerton	M. 2.
Bargains and Sales inrolled			
Awards of Incloſures			
EAST RIDING:			
Nona Roll	15 Edw. 3.	King's Rememb. Office	G. 6. b.
Memorials of Deeds, Conveyances, Wills, &c.	6 Anne to preſent Time	Regiſter's Office for Eaſt Riding, Beverley	M. 3. a.
Memorials of Judgments			
Deeds, Wills, Bargains and Sales, Awards of Incloſures } inrolled			
Certificates of Inrolments			
Incumbrances affecting Lands, &c.			
WEST RIDING:			
Nona Roll	15 Edw. 3.	King's Rememb. Office	G. 6. b.
Awards of Incloſures inrolled	— —		
Matters relating to Leeds Canal	— —		
Memorials of Deeds, Conveyances, and Wills	1704 to preſent Time	Regiſter's Office for Weſt Riding, Wakefield	M. 4.
Memorials of Judgments, Statutes, and Recognizances	1707		
Bargains and Sales inrolled	1707		
Certificates of Monies due upon Mortgages, Judgments, Statutes, and Recognizances, and Marginal Entries of Satisfaction	6 Anne		
DIOCESE, CONSISTORY COURT:			
Books, containing Acts on Inſtitutions, Faculties, Sentences of Conſecration, Pariſh Clerks and Schoolmaſters Licences, Sequeſtrations, Relaxations, and Subſcriptions	— —	Archbiſhop's Regiſtry, York	L. 3. & 4. a.
Viſitations, Books and Papers relating thereto, and to Conſecrations	— —		
Archiepiſcopal Regiſters, containing Appropriations, Endowments, Inſtitutions, Licences, and Faculties	1217 to preſ^t Time, Archbiſhops Powell & Ludlam excepted,		
Proceedings in Cauſes	1450		
Wills of Beneficed Clergymen	1542		
Wills of Lay Perſons (they are but few in Number)	1560		
Preſentations to Benefices	1560		
Nominations to Curacies, Schools, and to the Office of Pariſh Clerk	1581		
Pariſh Regiſters, Tranſcripts of, containing Marriages, Baptiſms, and Burials	1600 to the preſent Time		
Marriage Licences, Bonds thereon	1662		
Terriers of Pariſhes	1716		
—— PREROGATIVE COURT:			
Act Books, containing Acts and Proceedings of	— — —		
Bonds on Letters of Adminiſtration, &c.	— — —		
Regiſter Books, wherein Wills are entered at length	1389		
Wills, Original	1590		

ALPHABETICAL ARRANGEMENT OF THE PUBLIC RECORDS.

RECORDS and other INSTRUMENTS.	DATE.	WHERE KEPT.	Appendix to the Firſt Report.
YORK—(*continued.*)			
DIOCESE, CONSISTORY AND PREROGATIVE COURT:			
Endowments of Schools and Hoſpitals (Copies)	— —	Conſiſtory and Prerogative Regiſtry, York	L. 4. b.
Parliamentary Survey of the See, Copy of - -	1647 - - -	Conſiſtory and Prerogative Regiſtry, York -	L. 4. b.
Endowments, &c. *v.* DURHAM.			
DEAN AND CHAPTER:			
Regiſters of Charters, Grants, Endowments, &c. -	1258 to 1507 - -	Chapter Houſe, York -	N. 2.
Wills of Perſons dying within their Juriſdiction, with Bonds on granting Adminiſtrations, Curations, &c. - - - - - - -	Copies from 1321 to 1650. — Originals from 1650 to preſent Time - -	Chapter Houſe, York -	N. 2.
Regiſters of Births, Marriages, and Burials, of all the Pariſhes within the Juriſdiction; atteſted Copies - - - - - - - -	1663 to the preſent Time - -	Chapter Houſe, York -	N. 2.
Bonds and Affidavits on granting Marriage Licences - - - - - - - -	1678 to the preſent Time - -	Chapter Houſe, York -	N. 2.
ZEALAND:			
Account of Ships and Forces ſent thither - -	1691 - - -	Bodleian Library - -	O. 1.

SCOTLAND.

SCOTLAND.

ALPHABETICAL ARRANGEMENT OF THE PUBLIC RECORDS.

RECORDS and other INSTRUMENTS.	DATE.	WHERE KEPT.	Appendix to the Firſt Report.
ABBIES:			
Chartularies of divers - - - - - -	— —	Advocates Library -	Z.
v. CHARTULARIES.			
ABERDEEN:			
Tranſactions of the Preſbytery of - - -	1598 to 1600 - -		
v. CHARTULARIES.			
ACCOUNTS, PUBLIC:			
Of the Army, Militia, Mint, &c. - - - -	1688 to 1707 - -	King's Remembrancer -	X. 3.
Records of, made out by the Auditor of the Exchequer - - - - - -	1700 to preſent Time	Auditors of Exchequer -	X. 3.
Great Roll thereof, delivered and examined in the Pipe Office - - - - - -			
Record Books of the Quietus's or Diſcharges granted to Public Accountants, by the Clerk of the Pipe - - - - - - -	A few before the Union, but a regular Series from 1708 to preſent Time -	Joint Clerks of the Pipe - - -	X. 3.
Records of, kept by the Lord Treaſurer's Remembrancer - - - - - - -	1708 to preſent Time	Treaſurer's Remembran.	X. 3.
v. EXCHEQUER.			
ADJUDICATIONS:			
Abbreviates of - - - - - - -	Regular for 60 Years back, ſome earlier -	Office of Keepers of Abbreviates, Edinburgh.	
v. APPRISINGS.			
ADMIRALTY COURT:			
Bonds of Caution or Surety in Maritime Cauſes, Indentures between Seamen, &c. - -	— —		
The Diet Books or Rolls, containing the Procedures of the Court in all Cauſes relative to Maritime and Mercantile Tranſactions, and Condemnation of Prizes - - - -	— —		
Receipt Books, containing the Receipts of Procurators, for the Steps of Procedure in every Action - - - - - - -	— —	Court of Admiralty -	X. 6.
Record of the Commiſſions to the Judge Admirals and Vice Admirals of Scotland, and their Deputies, Clerks, &c. - - - -	1674 to preſent Time, with a Chaſm -		
ANNE OF DENMARK, QUEEN OF JAMES VI. OF SCOTLAND:			
Charters and other Deeds granted by her relating to the Lordſhip of Dunfermline - - -	1505 to 1626 -	Advocates Library -	Z.
Letters relating to her - - - -	— —		
v. CHANCERY.—DUNFERMLINE.—STATE PAPERS.			
APPRISINGS:			
Allowances of, and Abbreviates of Adjudications -	1636 to 1785 - -	General Regiſter Office -	V. a.
ARCHBISHOPS AND BISHOPS:			
Rent Rolls of their Eſtates annexed to the Crown -	1689 to 1690 - -	King's Remembrancer -	X. 3.
Rentals of their Eſtates annexed to the Crown -	1689 to 1690 - -	Auditors of Exchequer	X. 3.
Record of Compoſitions on Leaſes of their Teinds - - - - - - -	1710 to preſent Time		
v. CHARTULARIES.—TEINDS.			
ARGYLE:			
Roll of Valuation of that Shire - - -	1750 - - - -	Treaſurer's Remembran.	X. 3.
ARMORIAL BEARINGS. *v.* LYON OFFICE.			
ARMY:			
Accounts of - - - - - - -	1449 to 1659 -	General Regiſter Office	V. 2.
v. ACCOUNTS, PUBLIC.			
ARRESTMENTS:			
Cautionries for looſing them - - -	— —		
AUDITOR. *v.* ACCOUNTS, PUBLIC.			

ALPHABETICAL ARRANGEMENT OF THE PUBLIC RECORDS.

RECORDS and other INSTRUMENTS.	DATE.	WHERE KEPT.	Appendix to the First Report.
BISHOPS. *v.* Archbishops.			
BOROUGHS:			
Records of a few - - - - - -	— —	General Regifter Office -	V. a.
Setts of, being the Corporate Conftitutions of their Government - - - - -	— —	Auditors of Exchequer -	X. 3.
v. Exchequer, Court of.—Setts.—Treasury.			
CHAMBERLAINS ROLLS:			
Being the Inrolments of the Feu and Blanch Duties, and other Crown Rents and Revenues received Annually by the Chamberlain - -	1326 to 1549 -	General Regifter Office -	V. a.
CHANCERY:			
Royal Warrants, authorizing the Deputy Keeper of the Great Seal, to affix the faid Seal to Charters, Patents, Appointments, Pardons, &c. -	— —	In the Cuftody of the Deputy Keeper of Great Seal	W. 1.
Refpondes of the Sums payable by the Vaffals of Lands holding of the Crown or Prince and Stewart - - - - - -	— —	Chancery Office - -	X. 4.
Records of, being Charters of Lands and other Heretages held of the Crown - - -	1318 to 1788 - -	General Regifter Office -	V. a.
Retours of Services of Heirs to their Anceftors, and of other Services upon Brieves iffued from Chancery - - - - - - -	1547 to prefent Time with a Chafm - -	Chancery Office - -	X. 4.
Charters of Anne II. of Denmark, Confort of James VI. - - - - - -	Jac. - - - - -	Advocates Library -	Z.
Precepts upon Special Services, or Retours of Lands and other Heretages - - -	1750 to 1751 - -	Advocates Library -	Z.
Commiffions under the Great Seal, Remiffions or Pardons, Patents for Inventions, &c. - - -	1766 to prefent Time	Advocates Library -	Z.
v. Charters.—Seal, Great.			
CHARLES THE FIRST. *v.* State Papers.			
CHARTERS:			
Original detached Charters, Royal Proclamations, &c. relating thereto - - - - -	— —	General Regifter Office -	V. a.
Original Charters - - - - -	Will. 1. to 1550 -	Advocates Library - -	Z.
Records of - - - - - - - -	1318 to 1788 - -	General Regifter Office -	V. a.
Charters of Queen Anne, Confort of Jac. VI. -	Jac. - - - - -	Advocates Library - -	Z.
Of Lands and other Heretages held of the Crown	1788 to prefent Time	Chancery Office - -	X. 4.
v. Chancery.			
CHARTULARIES:			
Of the Archbifhoprick of Aberdeen, the Abbies of Arbroathe, Cambufkenneth, Dunfermline, Scone, Kelfo, Balmerinoch, Melrofs, Dryburgh, Newbottle, Lundoris, the Commendator of St. Andrew, the Prior and Abbey of Pitteneweem, the Hofpital of Sotra, and the Maifon Dieu near Elgin - - - - - - -	— —	Advocates Library - -	Z.
CIVIL LIST:			
Records of the Eftablifhment thereof, and of Inftruments, Warrants, Precepts, Certificates, &c. relating thereunto - - - - - -	1708 to prefent Time	Auditors of Exchequer -	X. 3.
CIRCUITS:			
Proceedings of the Three Courts - - -	1707 to prefent Time	Clerk of Jufticiary - -	X. 2.
v. Justiciary, High Court of.			
CLERGY. *v.* Teinds.			
COMMISSARY COURT:			
In this Court are preferved the following Records, from the Inftitution of the Office in 1560 to the prefent Time—Some are Extra Officially in the Cuftody of the Sheriff Clerks - - -	1560 to the prefent Time -	Commiffary Court Edinburgh; and alfo in the Commiffary Courts of the different Diocefes -	X. 5.

ALPHABETICAL ARRANGEMENT OF THE PUBLIC RECORDS.

INSTRUMENTS and other RECORDS.	DATE.	WHERE KEPT.	Appendix to the First Report.
COMMISSARY COURT—(*continued.*)			
1. A Regifter of all Caufes properly Confiftorial, confifting of the original Rolls, Writs, or Summonfes, the Vouchers produced, the Evidence of Witneffes, the Pleadings, the Interlocutory as well as Definitive Sentences, and the Decrees of the Court.			
2. A Record for regiftering Edicts or Applications, praying for Letters of Adminiftration, Tutorial and Curatorial Inventories, and Actions for Debts due by Perfons deceafed, againft their Executors.			
3. A Record for Teftaments, that is, for Letters of Adminiftration, including the Wills and Inventories on which the faid Letters are granted.			
4. A Record of the Bonds given in by Executors, and of their Sureties.			
5. A Regifter of Deeds of Conveyance, Wills, Bonds, Obligations, Contracts, and other Writings, brought in by the Owners, and recorded for Prefervation or Execution.			
COMMISSIONS:			
Records of Commiffions granted by His Majefty to the Lord Prefident, Lords of Seffion, and all other Officers on the Eftablifhment in Scotland - - - - - - - - -	— —	King's Rememb. Office	X. 3.
v. EXCHEQUER.—PATENT LETTERS.			
COMPOSITIONS. *v.* SIGNATURES.			
CONVENTIONS:			
Of Eftates, i.e. Meetings of the Three Eftates -	— —	General Regifter Office -	V. 2.
Of Eftates, Minutes thereof - - - -	1689 to 1690 - -	Advocates Library - -	Z.
Of Royal Burghs. *v.* SETTS.			
COUNCIL. *v.* SESSIONS, COURT OF.			
CROWN LANDS, RENTS, AND REVENUES:			
Roll of Crown Vaffals and others who are bound to account to the Exchequer for Crown Rents, &c. - - - - - - - - - - Petitions of Crown Vaffals, and Orders of the Court of Exchequer therein - - - - -	1708 to the prefent Time - -	Treafurer's Rememb. -	X. 3.
v. ARCHBISHOPS.—CHAMBERLAINS ROLLS.—CHANCERY.—CHARTERS.—EXCHEQUER.—SHERIFFS.			
CUSTOMS:			
Books of Rates - - - - - - -	1449 to 1659 - -	General Regifter Office -	V. 2.
v. EXCHEQUER.—PATENT LETTERS.			
DEEDS, REGISTERED. *v.* SESSIONS COURT OF.—SHERIFF CLERKS.			
DISTRESSES. *v.* HORNINGS.			
DUNFERMLINE:			
Charters and other Deeds granted by Queen Anne of Denmark, to different Vaffals in that Lordfhip - - - - - - - - -	— —	Advocates Library - -	Z.
DUTIES:			
Rental of Petty, Feu, or Blanch Duties, payable by the Vaffals of the Crown - - -	1708 to the prefent Time - - -	Treafurer's Rememb. -	X. 3.
v. CHAMBERLAINS ROLLS.—PROPERTY ROLLS.			

ALPHABETICAL ARRANGEMENT OF THE PUBLIC RECORDS.

RECORDS and other INSTRUMENTS.	DATE.	WHERE KEPT.	Appendix to the First Report.
ECCLESIASTICAL AFFAIRS:			
Some Records relative thereto	— —	General Regifter Office	V. a.
v. COMMISSARY COURT OF.—TEINDS.			
EXCHEQUER:			
Documents relating thereto	1264 to 1650	Advocates Library	Z.
Record Books, containing Refponde Books, Signatures, and Decrees			
Houfehold Accounts			
Expenfes of Royal Works			
Treafurers and Comptrollers Accounts			
Rentals	1449 to 1659	General Regifter Office	V. a.
Accounts of Thirds of Benefices			
Books of Rates of the Cuftoms and Taxations			
Artillery and Army Accounts			
COURT OF:			
Borough Rolls	1300 to 1707		
Refignations of Fiefs, towards the Renewal of the Infeoffments	1636 to 1703		
Signatures of Lords Paramount, authorizing Infeoffments and Grants	Prior to 1661		
Minutes of the Court	1661 to the prefent Time		
Orders and Rules of the Court			
Rolls of Judicial Proceedings therein			
Writs (Files of) iffued out of the Court	1708 to 1791	King's Remembrancer	X. 3.
Regifters of the Decrees, and Orders of the Court			
COURT OF JUDICATURE:			
Minute Books	— —		
Books of Rules	— —		
Files of Writs	— —		
Regifter of Decrees and Orders	— —		
Inrolments of Letters Patent	— —		
The like of Commiffioners for Limits of the Ports, with the Returns	— —		
Rolls of Judicial Proceedings	— —	General Regifter Office	V. a.
BOARD OF REVENUE:			
Record of Opinions of the Crown Lawyers on Public Matters			
Record of Bonds of Recognizances, from Accountants of the Crown			
Signed Particulars of Accounts of the Public Revenues, with the Vouchers, and the Record of the faid Accounts, after they have been declared	1780		
Letter Books or Correfpondence of the Board			
Record of Monies paid to the Receiver General of the Cuftoms, on Account of Seizures or Condemnations of prohibited Goods, and the Comptrolment Roll of Seizures			
Duplicates of Surveys, and Affeffments of Duties			
Record of Appeals from the Commiffioners of Affeffed Taxes, and Proceedings thereon	20 Geo. 2.	King's Remembrancer	X. 3.
v. ACCOUNTS, PUBLIC.			
BOARD OF TREASURY:	to the prefent Time		
Minute Book			
Book of Orders			
Petitions, Memorials, &c. to the Barons of the Exchequer, with the Records and Reports thereon	1708		
Signatures, Regifters of			
Borough Rolls			
Patent Letters, Commiffions, and Warrants recorded in the Court of Exchequer			
Refignations, Regifters of	1726		
v. SIGNET OFFICE.			
EXCISE. *v.* PATENT LETTERS.			

ALPHABETICAL ARRANGEMENT OF THE PUBLIC RECORDS.

RECORDS and other INSTRUMENTS.	DATE.	WHERE KEPT.	Appendix to the First Report.
FEU AND BLANCH DUTIES. *v.* CHAMBERLAINS ROLLS.—DUTIES.—PROPERTY ROLLS.			
FIARS:			
Books respecting the Annual Growth and Price of Grain - - - - - - - - *v.* SHERIFF CLERKS.	1708 to present Time	Treasurer's Remembran.	X. 3.
FORFEITED ESTATES:			
Books, Accounts, Rent Rolls and Procedures of the Commissioners for the Management of Estates forfeited for the Rebellions in 1715 and 1745 - - - - - - - -	— —	King's Remembrancer -	X. 3.
FORFEITURES:			
Registers of - - - - - - -	— —	General Register Office -	V. a.
GRAIN. *v.* FIARS.—SHERIFF CLERKS.			
HERALDS, &c. *v.* LYON OFFICE.			
HERETAGES. *v.* CHANCERY.—CHARTERS.			
HIGH COMMISSION COURT. *v.* TEINDS.			
HORNINGS:			
In this Office are kept Records of Interruptions, Summonses and other Instruments for preventing the Prescription of real Rights - -	1790 to the present Time - -	Horning Office - - -	X. 9.
Inhibitions, Interdictions, and Petitions for Sequestrations - - - - - - -			
Letters of Hornings - - - - - -			
All which are sent from Time to Time to the General Registry Office.			
General and Particular Register of Hornings, Inhibitions, Distresses, and Outlawries - - *v.* SHERIFF CLERKS.	1580 to 1730 - -	General Register Office -	V. a.
HOSPITALS. *v.* CHARTULARIES.			
JAMES THE FOURTH AND FIFTH. *v.* STATE PAPERS.			
JAMES THE SIXTH:			
Writs or Deeds by him, with Advice of his Secret Council - - - - - - - *v.* STATE PAPERS.	1586 to 1588 - -	Advocates Library - -	Z.
IMPREST. *v.* PATENT LETTERS.			
INFEOFFMENTS. *v.* EXCHEQUER COURT.—SASINES.			
INHIBITIONS. *v.* HORNINGS.—SHERIFF CLERKS.			
INVENTIONS, PATENTS FOR. *v.* CHANCERY.			
INVENTORIES:			
Record of the Register thereof - - - - N. B. Two Volumes, containing the Inventories from 1695 to 1721, are in this Return said to be in the General Register Office.	1721 to present Time	Register of Tailzies - -	X. 8.

ALPHABETICAL ARRANGEMENT OF THE PUBLIC RECORDS.

RECORDS and other INSTRUMENTS.	DATE.	WHERE KEPT.	Appendix to the Firſt Report.
JUSTICIARY, HIGH COURT OF:			
Records thereof - - - - - - -	1536 to the preſent Time, with ſome Chaſms - - -	Clerk of Juſticiary - -	X. 2.
Proceedings of Itinerant Courts of - - -	Temp. Jac. 4. - -	Advocates Library - -	Z.
Books of Adjournal - - - - - -	1685 - - - -	Clerk of Juſticiary - -	X. 2.
Records of the Three Circuit Courts of - -	1707 to preſent Time	Clerk of Juſticiary -	X. 2.
Proceedings on a Commiſſion of Oyer and Terminer - - - - - - - -	1746 - - - -	Clerk of Juſticiary -	X. 2.
LAWBURROWS, BINDING TO THE PEACE:			
Cautionries for keeping them - - - - - *v.* SHERIFF CLERKS.	— —	General Regiſtry Office -	V. a.
LETTERS PATENT. *v.* PATENT.			
LOTHIAN AND TWEEDALE:			
Proceedings of the Synod thereof - - -	1657 to 1661 - -	Advocates Library - -	Z.
LYON OFFICE:			
Old Proceſſes, and Old Current Bonds of Cautionry for Meſſengers in the Lyon Office -	— —	Lyon Office - - -	W. 4.
Record of Meſſengers Admiſſions - - -	1630 to preſent Time	Lyon Office - - -	W. 4.
Proceedings of the Lyon Court - - -	1650 to preſent Time	Lyon Office - - -	W. 4.
Record of Admiſſions of Heralds and Purſuivants	1660 to 1726 - -	Lyon Office - - -	W. 4.
Matriculations of Armorial Bearings of the Kings, Nobility, and Gentry - - - - -	1678 to preſent Time	Lyon Office - - -	W. 4.
Regiſter of Proceſſions, Letters of Precedency, Teſtificates, and Forefaulters - -	Commencing 1681 -	Lyon Office - - -	W. 4.
Decrees of the Lyon Court againſt Meſſengers -	1700 to 1703 - -	Lyon Office - - -	W. 4.
Birth Brief Regiſters - - - - -	Commencing 1728 -	Lyon Office - - -	W. 4.
Regiſter of Commiſſions to Heralds and Purſuivants - - - - - - - - -	1729 to 1796 - -	Lyon Office - - -	W. 4.
Reſponde Book of the Lyon Office - - -	1754 to 1770 - -	Lyon Office - - -	W. 4.
Minutes and Proceedings of the Office - -	1770 to 1775 - -	Lyon Office - - -	W. 4.
MARITIME AFFAIRS. *v.* ADMIRALTY.			
MERCANTILE AFFAIRS. *v.* ADMIRALTY.—CROWN RENTS AND REVENUES.			
MILITIA. *v.* ACCOUNTS, PUBLIC.—SHERIFF CLERKS.			
MINT. *v.* ACCOUNTS, PUBLIC.			
MORAY BISHOPRICK:			
Rental thereof - - - - - - -	1565 to 1569 - -	Advocates Library - -	Z.
NOBILITY. *v.* LYON OFFICE.			
NOTARIES:			
Protocol Books of Notaries - - - -	1537 to 1629, with ſome Chaſms - -	General Regiſtry Office Advocates Library -	V. a. Z.
OFFICERS. *v.* COMMISSIONS.—PATENT LETTERS.			
OUTLAWRIES. *v.* HORNINGS.			
OYER AND TERMINER:			
Commiſſion of, for trying Rebels in Scotland -	1746 - - - - -	Clerk of Juſticiary - -	X. 2.
PARAMOUNT, LORDS. *v.* EXCHEQUER.			
PARLIAMENT:			
Records of - - - - - - - - *v.* PEERS.	1210 to 1707 - -	General Regiſter Office -	V. a.
PARDONS. *v.* CHANCERY.			

ALPHABETICAL ARRANGEMENT OF THE PUBLIC RECORDS.

Records and other Instruments.	Date.	Where kept.	Appendix to the First Report.
PATENT LETTERS:			
Record thereof, and of Commiffions and Impreft Warrants for Surplufages - - - - -	1708 to the prefent Time - -	Treafurer's Rememb. -	X. 3.
Inrolments of Letters Patent to the Commiffioners of the Cuftoms and Excife, and other Officers of the Revenue who hold Patent Offices -			
Inrolments of Letters Patent - - - - -	1708 to 1791 - -	King's Remembrancer -	
v. Exchequer.—Treasury.			
PEERS:			
Warrants for their Elections to fit in the Houfe of Lords of the Britifh Parliament, with Records of thofe Elections from 1761 - - -	1707 to 1798 - -	General Regifter Office	V. a.
PENSIONS. v. Signs Manual.			
PIPE OFFICE. v. Accounts Public.			
POPES:			
Bulls from Pope Adrian IV. to Paul IV. - -	1155 to 1555 - -	Advocates Library - -	Z.
PORTS:			
Commiffions for fetting out their Limits - -	1708 to 1791 - -	King's Remembrancer -	X. 3.
PRECEDENCY. v. Lyon Office.			
PRESBYTERIES. v. Aberdeen.—Teinds.			
PRESCRIPTIONS. v. Hornings.			
PRINCE, or Stewart of Scotland.			
Charters of Lands and other Heretages held of him - - - - - - - - -	1620 to prefent Time	Chancery Office - - -	X. 4.
v. Chancery.			
PRIVY COUNCIL:			
One Volume of Records - - - - -	— —	Clerk of the Lyon Court	X. 2.
Records of - - - - - - -	1545 to 1644 - -	General Regifter Office -	V. a.
Records, being Acts and Decreets thereof, and Proceedings relating to the State - - -	1571 to 1705 - -	Jufticiary Office - -	X. 2.
Writs or Deeds of James VI. by Advice of his Secret Council - - - - - -	1586 to 1588 - -	Advocates Library -	Z.
Writs paffing the Signet with the Advice of Privy Council - - - - - - - - -	1630 to 1642 - -		
State, Record or Proceedings in Matters of State -	1661 to 1703 - -	General Regifter Office	V. a.
v. James VI.—Signet.			
PRIVY SEAL:			
Records of - - - - - - - - -	1499 to 1774 - -		
A Record of all Grants which have paffed the faid Office - - - - - - - - -	1795 to the prefent Time - - - -	Privy Seal Office - -	W. 2.
v. Signs Manual.			
PRIZES. v. Admiralty.			
PROHIBITIONS. v. Teinds.			
PROPERTY ROLL:			
Being the Record of all Feu and Blanch Duties exceeding £. 10. Scots Money - - -	1709 to the prefent Time - - - -	Auditors of Exchequer -	X. 3.
v. Duties.			
QUALIFICATIONS. v. Sheriff Clerks.			

ALPHABETICAL ARRANGEMENT OF THE PUBLIC RECORDS.

RECORDS and other INSTRUMENTS.	DATE.	WHERE KEPT.	Appendix to the First Report.
REBELLION. *v.* Forfeited Estates.—Oyer and Terminer.			
RECOGNIZANCES. *v.* Exchequer.			
REMISSIONS. *v.* Chancery.			
RESIGNATIONS. *v.* Exchequer.—Treasury.			
REVENUE. *v.* Exchequer.—Patent Letters.			
SASINES:			
Registers of Sasines of Infeoffments, being the Record of the actual Delivery of Lands, Tenements, or Moveables - - - - -	— —	Several in the Custody of the Sheriff Clerks - -	Y.
N. B. These are also from Time to Time sent to the General Register Office at Edinburgh.			
General and Particular Registers of - - -	1617 to present Time	General Register Office -	V. a.
SEAL, Great:			
Royal Warrants, authorizing the Deputy Keeper to affix the Great Seal to Charters, Patents, Appointments, Pardons, Writs, &c. - -	— —	Deputy Keeper - -	W. 1.
Records of the Great Seal - - - - -	1318 to 1788 - -	General Register Office	V. a.
v. Chancery.—Signs Manual.			
SEQUESTRATIONS. *v.* Hornings.			
SESSIONS, Court of:			
Extracted Decrees of the Old Session and Lords of the Council, and Warrants thereof - -	1478 to 1789 - -		
Books of Sederunt, being the Proceedings of the Court respecting itself and its subordinate Officers - - - - - - - - -	1553 to the present Time, with some Chasms - - -	Court of Sessions - -	X. 1.
Deeds registered in the Books thereof - -	1554 to 1789 - -	General Register Office -	V. a.
General Minute Books of the - - -	End of the 16th Century to the present Time - - - -	General Register House -	V. a. b.
Books of Council and Session, being Registers of all Kinds of Deeds, Obligations, &c. and Records of Probative Writs, and of Decrees pronounced by the Court - - - - -	1790 to the present Time - - - -	Clerk of Session Office -	X. 1.
v. Commissions.—Signet.			
SETTS OF ROYAL BURGHS:			
Delivered in by an Order of the Convocation of Royal Burghs - - - - - - - -	1708 - - - -	City Clerks, Edinburgh -	W. 5.
SHERIFF CLERKS in the 33 Counties of Scotland -	— —	Sheriffs Clerks of the different Counties - -	Y. 1.—33.

The following Records and Registers appear in general to be in the Custody of these respective Officers:

1. Judicial Proceedings, both Civil and Criminal, held before the Sheriffs, comprehending Actions for Debt, Injury, and Trespass, with Receipt Books for the Security of Steps of Process: To these may be added the Sederunt Court Books, and also the Diet Books, which appear to be Registers of Court Proceedings.

2. Freeholders Record, or Minutes of the Meetings of Freeholders, both Annually at Michaelmas, and for the Purpose of Elections.

3. Services of Heirs, being the Claims of Persons to the Inheritance of their Predecessors.

4. Tutorial and Curatorial Inventories.

5. Proceedings for the Improvement of Entailed Estates, by virtue of the Statute 10 Geo. III. c. 51.

6. Registers of Deeds for Preservation, Publication, and Diligence of the Law, being all Manner of Bonds, Testaments, Settlements, Contracts, Dispositions, Tacks (Leases), and other Instruments, containing Clauses of Registration, and Proceedings respecting Mortgages and Heretable Bonds, where the Original Deeds are retained in the Office; also Registers of Probative Wills, which, after being entered and certified, are returned to the Ingivers or Exhibitors; likewise Protests upon Bills of Exchange and Promissory Notes.

7. Records of Hornings, Inhibitions, Interdictions, and Lawburrows.

N. B. These are only for a few Years, being from Time to Time transmitted to the General Register Office at Edinburgh.

8. Records of Fiars or Medium Prices of Victuals Annually

ALPHABETICAL ARRANGEMENT OF THE PUBLIC RECORDS.

RECORDS and other INSTRUMENTS.	DATE.	WHERE KEPT.	Appendix to the Firft Report.

SHERIFF CLERKS—*(continued.)*

Records and Regifters which appear in general to be in the Cuftody of thefe refpective Officers—*(continued.)*

Annually ftruck by a Jury; alfo of the Monthly Return of the Victual Prices.

9. Records of the Commiffions of Sheriffs, Principal and Subftitute; and of the Admiffion of Clerks, Procurators, and Officers.

10. Records of Certificates for killing Game.

11. Qualification Rolls.

12. Proceedings of the Court of Lieutenancy upon the Militia.

The earlieft Dates fpecified of the moft important of the above Records are as follow; viz.

JUDICIAL PROCEEDINGS in

Aberdeen and Kincardine	1697.
Argyle and Edinburgh	1709.
Ayr	1717.
Dumfries	1674.
Elgin, Wigtoun, and Forfar	1700.
Invernefs	1720.
Kirkudbright and Clackmannan	1698.
Lanerk	1748.
Orkney	1612.
Perth	1543.
Renfrew	1739.
Shetland	1687.

DEEDS Regiftered in

Aberdeen	1630.
Argyle, Lanerk, and Kirkudbright	1665–7.
Ayr	1682.
Clackmannan and Invernefs	1707.
Edinburgh, Fife, and Linlithgow	1700.
Elgin	1654.
Forfar	1693.
Kincardine	1697.
Orkney	1611.
Perth	1570.
Wigtoun	1690.

PROBATIVE WRITS in

Aberdeen	1630.
Ayr	1735.
Dumfries	1716.
Kincardine	1715.
Kirkudbright	1746.

FREEHOLDERS COURTS and ELECTIONS in

Aberdeen, Forfar, and Invernefs	1727.
Argyle, Edinburgh, and Haddington	1797.
Dumfries, Fife, Linlithgow, and Orkney	1733–4.
Kincardine	1698.
Kirkudbright	1739.
Perth	1724.
Wigtoun and Ayr	1702.

SERVICES in

Aberdeen	1649.
Argyle	1700.
Ayr and Dumfries	1715.
Edinburgh	1750.
Kincardine	1664.
Lanerk	1696.
Lanerk	1754.
Perth	1596.
Wigtoun	1676.

TUTORIAL, &c. ACTS in

Aberdeen	1649.
Kincardine	1683.
Kirkudbright	1744.
Perth	1597.

ANNUAL FIARS in

Aberdeen	1705.
Ayr	1658.
Dumfries, Haddington, and Perth	1626–30.
Fife	1700.
Forfar	1728.
Kincardine	1752.
Linlithgow	1667.

RECORDS and other INSTRUMENTS.	DATE.	WHERE KEPT.	Appendix to the Firft Report.
SHERIFFS:			
Records of feveral Sheriffs Courts	— —	General Regifter Office	V. a.
Rolls of Sheriffs Accounts	About 1400 to 1799	Treafurer's Rememb.	X. 3.
Orders of the Court of Exchequer for allowing Sheriffs and Stewarts Depute Sums difburfed by them in the Public Service	1708 to the prefent Time	Treafurer's Rememb.	X. 3.
Accounts of their Payments to the Receiver General of the Crown Revenue	1708 to the prefent Time	Treafurer's Rememb.	X. 3.
v. EXCHEQUER.—FIARS.—SHERIFF CLERKS.			
SIGNATURES:			
Record of Compofitions thereon	1708 to the prefent Time	Auditors of Exchequer	X. 3.
v. EXCHEQUER COURT.—TREASURY.			

ALPHABETICAL ARRANGEMENT OF THE PUBLIC RECORDS.

RECORDS and other INSTRUMENTS.	DATE.	WHERE KEPT.	Appendix to the First Report.
SIGNET OFFICE:			
Summonses to Defendants in Suits before the Court of Session	— —	Signet Office	W. 3.
Writs issued by the Court of Session	— —	Signet Office	W. 3.
Writs for attaching Persons and Effects of Debtors by Authority of the Court of Session	— —	Signet Office	W. 3.
Precepts on Warrants issued by the Court of Exchequer	— —	Signet Office	W. 3.
Minute Book or Register of Writs	— —	Signet Office	W. 3.
Writs passing the Signet Office	1630 to 1642	Advocates Library	Z.
SIGNS MANUAL:			
Records of Royal Signs Manual, Patents and Grants under the Great and Privy Seals, Treasury Warrants for Pensions, &c.	1709 to the present Time	Auditors of the Exchequer	X. 3.
STATE PAPERS:			
Papers and Letters from and to James IV. V. and VI. Queen Anne of Denmark, Charles I. of England, &c.	1505 to 1626	Advocates Library	Z.
Letters from James V. and the Earl of Arran, to England, France, &c.	1539 to 1542	Advocates Library	Z.
Correspondence relative to the Scots in France	Jac. 6.	Advocates Library	Z.
Originals and Copies	Eliz. to Car. 1.	Advocates Library	Z.
Negotiations with France	Jac. 6.	Advocates Library	Z.
The like with Denmark and Norway	Jac. 6. to Car. 1.	Advocates Library	Z.
Correspondence with Princes of Italy	Jac. 6. to Car. 1.	Advocates Library	Z.
The like with Germany, Sweden, and Poland	1600 to 1626	Advocates Library	Z.
Papers relating to the Disturbances in Great Britain and Ireland, during the Reign of Charles I.	Car. 1.	Advocates Library	Z.
The Earl of Stirling's Letter to Charles I.	1626	Advocates Library	Z.
State Records, or Proceedings in Matters of State	1661 to 1703	General Register Office	V. a.
TAILZIES:			
Record of the Register thereof	1685 to present Time	Register of Tailzies	X. 8.
TAXES:			
Books of Taxations v. Exchequer.	1449 to 1659	General Register Office	V. a.
TEINDS OFFICE:			
Certain Records concerning the Valuation of Tythes, the Establishment of Churches, and the Stipends of the Clergy; viz.			
Registers and Extracts from authentic Records belonging to this Office, the Originals of which were burnt in 1700	— —	Teinds Office	X. 7.
Records of the Sub-commissioners of divers Presbyteries	1629 to 1630	Teinds Office	X. 7.
Procedure of the High Commission	1630 to 1633	Teinds Office	X. 7.
Registers of the Procedures of the Court of Commissioners, and the Warrants of their Decreets	1707 to present Time	Teinds Office	X. 7.
TESTAMENTS:			
Cautionries in confirmed Testaments v. Commissary Court.—Sheriff Clerks.	— —	General Register Office	V. a.
TREASURY:			
Minutes and Orders v. Exchequer.—Signs Manual.	1661 to 1708	King's Remembrancer	X. 3.
TYTHES. v. Teinds.			

ALPHABETICAL ARRANGEMENT OF THE PUBLIC RECORDS.

RECORDS and other INSTRUMENTS.	DATE.	WHERE KEPT.	Appendix to the First Report.
UNIVERSITIES:			
Visitations of - - - - - - -	— —	General Register Office -	V. a.
VASSALS OF THE CROWN. *v.* CROWN LANDS. DUNFERMLINE.—DUTIES.			
WARRANTS. *v.* EXCHEQUER.—SIGNS MANUAL.			
WILLS. *v.* TESTAMENTS.			
WRITS. *v.* EXCHEQUER.—SESSIONS, COURT OF.—SIGNET OFFICE.			

F I N I S.